Third Edition

Internet Marketing

Strategy, Implementation and Practice

Dave Chaffey

Fiona Ellis-Chadwick

Richard Mayer

Kevin Johnston

FT Prentice Hall
FINANCIAL TIMES

An imprint of Pearson Education

Harlow, England • London • New York • Boston • San Francisco • Toronto
Sydney • Tokyo • Singapore • Hong Kong • Seoul • Taipei • New Delhi
Cape Town • Madrid • Mexico City • Amsterdam • Munich • Paris • Milan

Pearson Education Limited

Edinburgh Gate
Harlow
Essex CM20 2JE
England

and Associated Companies throughout the world

Visit us on the World Wide Web at:
www.pearsoned.co.uk

First published 2000
Second edition published 2003
Third edition published 2006

ISBN 978-0-273-69405-2

British Library Cataloguing-in-Publication Data
A catalogue record for this book is available from the British Library

Library of Congress Cataloging-in-Publication Data
A catalogue record for this book is available from the Library of Congress

10 9 8 7 6 5 4 3
10 09 08 07

Typeset in 9/12.5pt Stone Serif by 30
Printed and bound by Mateu Cromo Artes Graficas, Spain

The publisher's policy is to use paper manufactured from sustainable forests.

Brief contents

Contents

Supporting resources

Visit **www.pearsoned.co.uk/chaffey** to find valuable online resources.

Companion Website for students
- Web links to case study materials, academic articles and examples of best practice
- A comprehensive online glossary

For instructors
- Complete, downloadable Instructor's Manual
- PowerPoint slides that can be downloaded and used as OHTs

For more information please contact your local Pearson Education sales representative or visit **www.pearsoned.co.uk/chaffey**.

Preface

Introduction

The Internet – opportunity and threat

The Internet represents a tremendous opportunity. For customers, it gives a much wider choice of products, services and prices from different suppliers and the means to select and purchase items more readily. For organisations marketing these products and services it gives the opportunity to expand into new markets, offer new services and compete on a more equal footing with larger businesses. For those working within these organisations it gives the opportunity to develop new skills and to use the Internet to improve the competitiveness of the company.

At the same time, the Internet gives rise to many threats to organisations. For example, start-up companies such as Amazon (books) (**www.amazon.com**), Expedia (travel) (**www.expedia.com**), AutoByTel (cars) (**www.autobytel.com**) and CDWOW (CDs) (**www.cdwow.com**) have captured a significant part of their market and struck fear into the existing players. Indeed the phrase 'amazoning a market sector' has become an often-used expression among marketers.

The Internet – management issues

With the success stories of companies capturing market share together with the rapidly increasing adoption of the Internet by consumers and business buyers has come a fast-growing realisation that all organisations must have an effective Internet presence to prosper, or possibly even survive! Michael Porter has said:

> *The key question is not whether to deploy Internet technology – companies have no choice if they want to stay competitive – but how to deploy it.*

What are these challenges of deploying Internet and digital technology? Figure 1 gives an indication of the marketing activities that need to be managed effectively which are covered in this book.

The figure shows the range of different marketing activities or operating processes needed to support acquiring new customers through communicating with them on third-party web sites, attracting them to a company web site, converting them to sale and then using online media to encourage further sales. Applying the Internet as part of multi-channel marketing to support customer journeys through different media is also a major theme throughout this text. Management processes related to Internet marketing include planning how Internet marketing can be best resourced to contribute to the organisation and integrate with other marketing activities. The increased adoption of Internet marketing also implies a significant programme of change that needs to be managed. New forms of objectives need to be set, new communications strategies developed and staff developed through new responsibilities and skills.

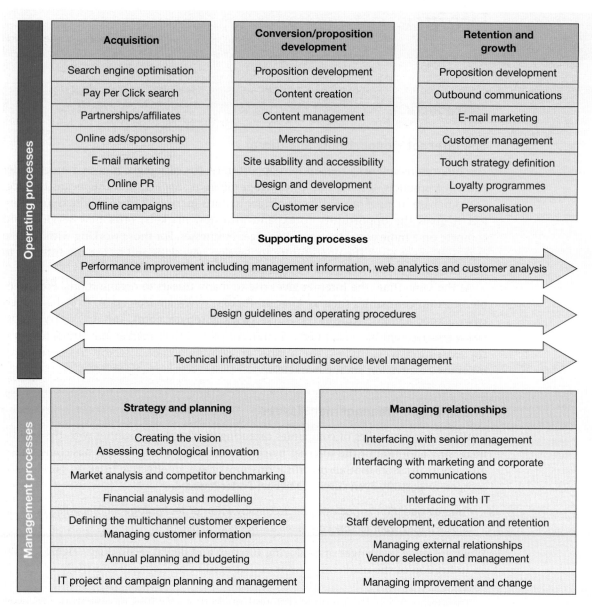

Figure 1 Key organisational processes for Internet marketing
Source: E-consultancy (2005), author Dave Chaffey

The Internet – new skills required?

The aim of this text is to provide you with a comprehensive guide to the concepts, techniques and best practice to support all the digital marketing processes shown in Figure 1. This book is based on emerging academic models together with best practice from leading adopters of digital media. The practical knowledge developed through reviewing these concepts and best practice is intended to enable graduates entering employment and marketing professionals to exploit the opportunities of marketing using the Internet while minimising the risks.

Specifically, this book addresses the following needs:

- There is a need to know to what extent the Internet changes existing marketing models and whether new models and strategies can be applied to exploit the medium effectively.
- Marketing practitioners need practical Internet marketing skills to market their products effectively. Knowledge of the new jargon – terms such as 'portal', 'clickthrough', 'cookie', 'hits', 'page impressions', 'digital certificate' – and of effective methods of site design and promotion such as search engine marketing will be necessary, either for direct 'hands-on' development of a site or to enable communication with other staff or agencies that are implementing and maintaining the site.
- Given the rapidly changing market characteristics and best practices of Internet marketing, web-based information sources are needed to update knowledge regularly. This text and the supporting companion web site contain extensive links to web sites to achieve this.

The content of this book assumes some existing knowledge of marketing in the reader, perhaps developed through experience or by students studying introductory modules in marketing fundamentals, marketing communications or buyer behaviour. However, the text outlines basic concepts of marketing, communications theory, buyer behaviour and the marketing mix.

Changes for the third edition of *Internet Marketing*

The acclaimed structure of the second edition has been retained since this provides a clear sequence to the stages of strategy development and implementation which are required to plan successfully for Internet marketing in existing and start-up companies. The third edition is a significant update with many revisions, new subsections and nearly 100 new figures to better explain Internet marketing concepts. The main changes are:

- In-depth cases written specifically for this book, illustrating best practices and the challenges of online marketing from well-known global e-businesses such as Amazon and eBay to European and Asian examples such as Tesco.com, dabs.com and start-ups such as Zopa.com. A full listing of cases is given in Table 1. Mini case studies and examples within each chapter have also been updated to include the full range of Internet marketing applications from transactional sites, lead-generation relationship-building sites, brand sites and media-owned sites;
- Updated to reference the full range of digital media that support Internet marketing including blogging, Really Simple Syndication (RSS), instant messaging, podcasting, digital TV and mobile marketing;
- More detail on understanding online buyer behaviour and the need to deliver effective online customer experiences consistent with this (Chapter 2);
- Updates on the legal constraints from data protection and privacy laws and accessibility legislation (Chapter 3);
- Additional coverage on the opportunities provided by technological developments in wireless and mobile media and broadband adoption (Chapter 3);
- Content on strategy updated to reflect the latest thinking on customer-centric online marketing using customer personas and journeys as part of multi-channel marketing (Chapters 4 and 5);
- Chapter 6 on relationship marketing now has an approach oriented to electronic customer relationship management (e-CRM) and includes more detail on techniques used by e-retailers and e-mail marketers such as lifetime value and recency-frequency-monetary (RFM) value analysis;
- Greater depth on online marketing communications techniques including affiliate marketing, search engine marketing, online PR and viral marketing (Chapter 8);

- Coverage on the latest approaches to using web analytics to measure and improve Internet marketing (Chapter 9).
- Chapter 10 provides more detailed insight into online consumers and their behaviour and examines how retailers are responding to the challenges created by raised customer expectations.
- Expanded discussion of B2B trading, trading partnerships and digital marketing strategies.

Table 1 In-depth case studies in *Internet Marketing*, 3rd edition

Chapter	Case study	Themes
1 Introduction	eBay thrives in the global marketplace	Business and revenue model, proposition, competition, objectives and strategies, risk management
2 Micro-environment	Zopa launches a new lending model	Assessing a consumer market, business models, marketing communications
3 Macro-environment	Boo hoo – learning from the largest European dot-com failure	Companion vision, branding, target market, communicating the proposition, challenges and reasons for failure
4 Internet marketing strategy	Tesco.com uses the Internet to support its diversification strategy	Business models, proposition and online product range, target market strategy
5 Internet marketing mix	The re-launched Napster changes the music marketing mix	Peer-to-peer services, revenue models, proposition design, strategy, competition, risk factors
6 Relationship marketing	Boots mine diamonds in their customer data	Influence of web site design on conversion, retention marketing, personalisation, e-CRM, RFM analysis
7 Online customer experience	Refining the online customer experience at dabs.com	Strategy, proposition, site design, on-site search capabilities
8 Interactive marketing communications	Making FMCG brands sizzle online	Communications mix, characteristics of digital media, applying online communications tools to support brands such as Birds Eye, Pepperami, Lynx and Persil.
9 Maintaining and monitoring the online presence	Learning from Amazon's culture of metrics	Strategy, measurement, online marketing communications, personalisation approach
10 Business-to-consumer marketing	lastminute.com: establishing and maintaining a competitive position	Online consumer profiles, purchasing behaviour and expectations and e-retailing
11 Business-to-business marketing	Growth, volume and dispersion of electronic markets	B2B trading environment, business markets, trading partnerships and digital marketing strategies

The structure and contents of this book

The book is divided into three parts, each covering a different aspect of how organisations use the Internet for marketing to help them achieve competitive advantage. Table 2 indicates how the book is related to established marketing topics.

Part 1 Internet marketing fundamentals (Chapters 1–3)

Part 1 relates the use of the Internet to traditional marketing theories and concepts, and questions the validity of existing models given the differences between the Internet and other media.

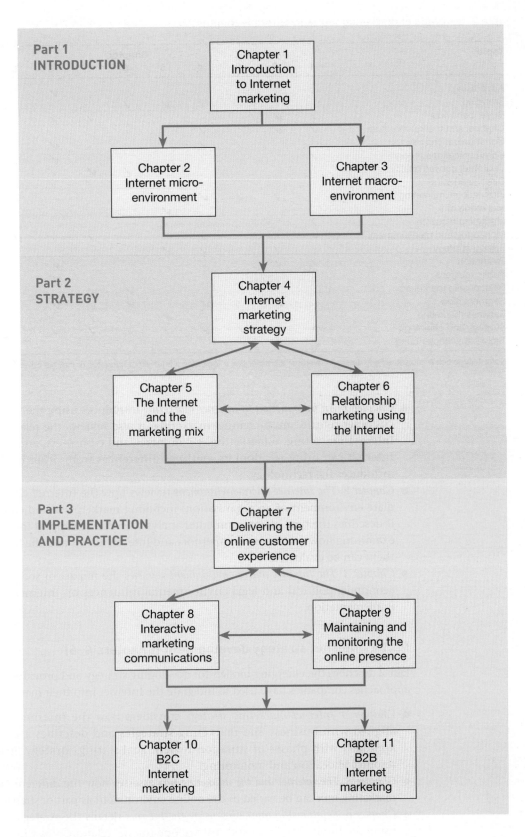

Figure 2 Structure of the book

Table 2 Coverage of marketing topics in different chapters

Topic	Chapter										
	1	2	3	4	5	6	7	8	9	10	11
Advertising								✔			
Branding				✓	✔	✓				✓	
Buyer behaviour	✓	✔					✓	✓		✓	✓
Channel and market structure	✓	✔		✓						✓	✓
Communications mix				✓				✔			
Communications theory	✓							✔			
Customer service quality						✓	✔	✓		✓	✓
Direct marketing						✔		✓			
International marketing		✓	✓	✔						✓	✓
Marketing mix					✔						
Marketing research	✓								✔		
Monitoring and measurement	✓			✓			✓	✓	✔		
Pricing strategy		✓		✓	✔						
Promotion	✓	✓		✓				✔			
Public relations								✔			
Relationship marketing						✔	✓				
Segmentation		✔		✔		✔		✔			
Services marketing					✔		✓				
Strategy and planning	✓	✓	✓	✔	✓	✓	✓	✓		✓	✓
Technology background	✓										

Note: A large tick ✔ indicates fairly detailed coverage; a smaller tick ✓ indicates a brief direct reference or indirect coverage.

- *Chapter 1 An introduction to Internet marketing* introduces using the Internet as part of customer-centric, multi-channel marketing; it also reviews the relationship between Internet marketing, e-marketing, e-commerce and e-business, and the benefits the Internet can bring to adopters, outlines differences from other media and briefly introduces the technology.

- *Chapter 2 The Internet micro-environment* reviews how the Internet changes the immediate environment of an organisation, including marketplace and channel structure. It describes the type of environmental analysis needed to support Internet strategy by examining how customers, competitors and intermediaries and the interplay between them can be evaluated.

- *Chapter 3 The Internet macro-environment* reviews the impact of social, technological, economic, political and legal environmental influences on Internet strategy and its implementation.

Part 2 Internet strategy development (Chapters 4–6)

Part 2 describes the emerging models for developing strategy and provides examples of the approaches companies have used to integrate the Internet into their marketing strategy.

- *Chapter 4 Internet marketing strategy* considers how the Internet strategy can be aligned with business and marketing strategies and describes a generic strategic approach with phases of situation review, goal setting, strategy formulation and resource allocation and monitoring.

- *Chapter 5 The Internet and the marketing mix* assesses how the different elements of the marketing mix can be varied in the online environment as part of strategy formulation.

- *Chapter 6 Relationship marketing using the Internet* details the strategies and tactics for using the Internet to build and sustain 'one-to-one' relationships with customers.

Part 3 Internet marketing: implementation and practice (Chapters 7–11)

Part 3 of the book explains practical approaches to implementing an Internet marketing strategy. Techniques for communicating with customers, building relationships and facilitating electronic commerce are all reviewed in some detail. Knowledge of these practical techniques is essential for undergraduates on work placements involving a web site and for marketing managers who are dealing with suppliers such as design agencies.

- *Chapter 7 Delivering the online customer experience* explains how an online presence is developed to support branding and customer service quality objectives. The stages, including analysis of customer needs, design of the site structure and layout, and creating the site, are covered together with key techniques such as user-centred design, usability and accessibility design.
- *Chapter 8 Interactive marketing communications* describes the novel characteristics of new media, and then goes on to review different online and offline promotion techniques necessary to build traffic to a web site and for other promotion objectives. Among the techniques covered are banner advertising, affiliate networks, promotion in search engines and directories, co-branding and sponsorship, e-mail, loyalty techniques and PR.
- *Chapter 9 Maintaining and monitoring the online presence* defines a process for successful updating of a site and online and offline methods for assessing the effectiveness of the site in delivering business and marketing benefits.
- *Chapter 10 Business-to-consumer Internet marketing* examines models of marketing to consumers, and provides case studies of how retail businesses are tackling such marketing.
- *Chapter 11 Business-to-business Internet marketing* examines the different area of marketing to other businesses, and provides many examples of how companies are achieving this to support international marketing. It also discusses the different stages of the buying decision such as supplier search, product evaluation and selection, purchase, post-purchase customer service, and evaluation and feedback.

Who should use this book?

Students

This book has been created primarily as the main student text for undergraduate and postgraduate students taking specialist marketing courses or modules which cover e-marketing, Internet and digital marketing, electronic commerce and e-business. The book is relevant to students who are:

- *undergraduates on business programmes* which include modules on the use of the Internet and e-commerce. This includes specialist degrees such as Internet marketing, electronic commerce, marketing, tourism and accounting or general business degrees such as business studies, business administration and business management;
- *undergraduate project students* who select this topic for final-year projects or dissertations – this book is an excellent supporting text for these students;
- *undergraduates completing a work placement* in a company using the Internet to promote its products;
- *students at college aiming for vocational qualifications* such as the HNC or HND in Business Management or Computer Studies;
- *postgraduate students* taking specialist masters degrees in electronic commerce or Internet marketing, generic MBAs and courses leading to qualifications such as Certificate in Management or Diploma in Management Studies which involve modules on electronic commerce and digital marketing.

Practitioners

There is also much of relevance in this book for marketing practitioners, including:

- *marketing managers or specialists such as e-commerce managers or e-marketing managers* responsible for defining an Internet marketing strategy and implementing and maintaining the company web site;
- *senior managers and directors* wishing to understand the potential of Internet marketing for a company and who need practical guidelines on how to exploit this potential;
- *technical project managers or webmasters* who may understand the technical details of building a site, but have a limited knowledge of marketing fundamentals and how to develop an Internet marketing strategy.

What does the book offer to lecturers teaching these courses?

The book is intended to be a comprehensive guide to all aspects of using the Internet and other digital media to support marketing. The book builds on existing marketing theories and concepts, and questions the validity of models in the light of the differences between the Internet and other media. The book references the emerging body of literature specific to Internet marketing. It can therefore be used across several modules. Lecturers will find the book has a good range of case studies, activities and exercises to support their teaching. Web site references are given in the text and at the end of each chapter to provide important information sources for particular topics.

Student learning features

A range of features have been incorporated into this book to help the reader get the most out of it. They have been designed to assist understanding, reinforce learning and help readers find information easily. The features are described in the order in which you will encounter them.

At the start of each chapter

The 'chapter at a glance' page provides easy navigation for each chapter. It contains:

- *main topics*: the main topics and their page numbers;
- *case studies*: the main cases and their page numbers;
- *learning objectives*: a list describing what readers can learn through reading the chapter and completing the exercises;
- *questions for marketers*: explaining the relevance of the chapter for practitioners;
- *links to other chapters*: a summary of related information in other chapters.

In each chapter

- *Definitions*: when significant terms are first introduced the main text contains succinct definitions in the margin for easy reference.
- *Web references*: where appropriate, web addresses are given to enable readers to obtain further information. They are provided in the main text where they are directly relevant as well as at the end of the chapter.
- *Case studies*: real-world examples of how companies are using the Internet for marketing. Questions at the end of the case study are intended to highlight the main learning points from the example.

- *Mini case studies*: short features which give a more detailed example, or explanation, than is practical in the main text. They do not contain supplementary questions.
- *Activities*: exercises in the main text which give readers the opportunity to practise and apply the techniques described in the text.
- *Chapter summaries*: intended as revision aids to summarise the main learning points from the chapter.

At the end of each chapter

- *Self-assessment exercises*: short questions which will test understanding of terms and concepts described in the chapter.
- *Essay questions*: conventional essay questions.
- *Discussion questions*: these require longer essay-style answers discussing themes from the chapter. They can be used either as topics for individual essays or as the basis for seminar discussion.
- *Examination questions*: typical short-answer questions of the type that are encountered in exams. These can also be used for revision.
- *References*: these are references to books, articles or papers referred to within the chapter.
- *Further reading*: supplementary texts or papers on the main themes of the chapter. Where appropriate a brief commentary is provided on recommended supplementary reading on the main themes of the chapters.
- *Web links*: these are significant sites that provide further information on the concepts and topics of the chapter. This list does not repeat all the web site references given within the chapter, for example company sites. For clarity, the web site address prefix 'http://' is generally omitted.

At the end of the book

- *Glossary*: definitions of all key terms and phrases used within the main text, cross-referenced for ease of use.
- *Index*: all key words and abbreviations referred to in the main text.

Support material

Free supplementary materials are available via the Pearson Education companion books web site at **www.pearsoned.co.uk/chaffey** and Dave Chaffey's web site at **www.davechaffey.com** to support all users of the book. This regularly updated web site contains advice, comment, support materials and hyperlinks to reference sites relevant to the text. There is a password-protected area for lecturers only to discuss issues arising from using the text; additional examination-type questions and answers; a multiple-choice question bank with answers; additional cases with suggestions for discussion; and a downloadable version of the Lecturer's Guide and OHP Masters.

Reference

E-consultancy (2005) Managing an e-commerce team. Integrating digital marketing into your organisation. 60-page report. Author: Dave Chaffey. Available from **www.e-consultancy.com**.

Guided tour

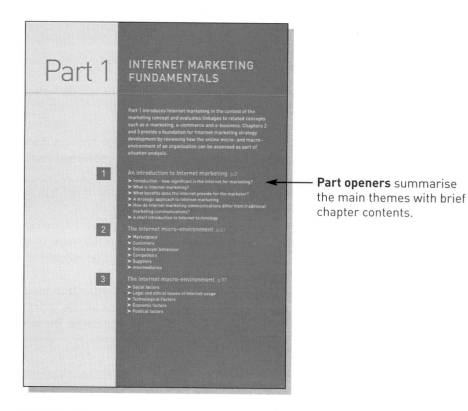

Part openers summarise the main themes with brief chapter contents.

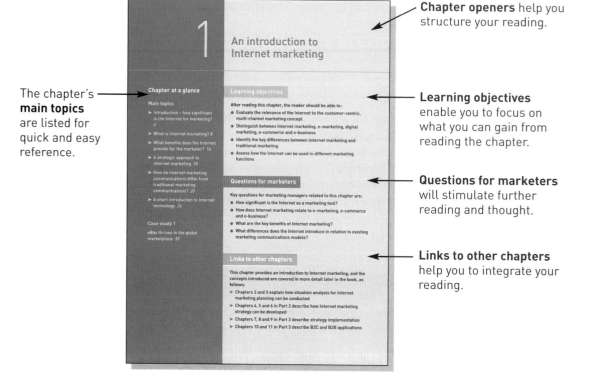

Chapter openers help you structure your reading.

The chapter's **main topics** are listed for quick and easy reference.

Learning objectives enable you to focus on what you can gain from reading the chapter.

Questions for marketers will stimulate further reading and thought.

Links to other chapters help you to integrate your reading.

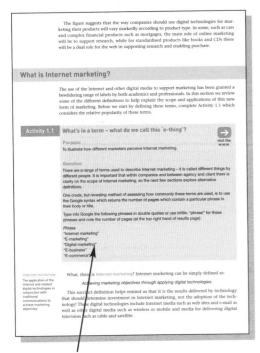

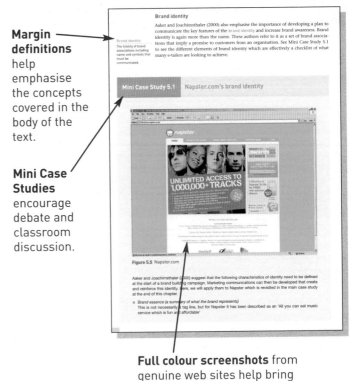

Margin definitions help emphasise the concepts covered in the body of the text.

Mini Case Studies encourage debate and classroom discussion.

Activities give readers the opportunity to practise and apply the techniques described in the text.

Full colour screenshots from genuine web sites help bring theory to life.

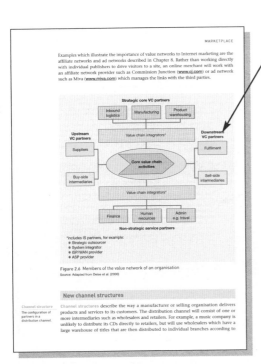

Figures and **tables** illustrate key concepts and processes, visually reinforcing your learning.

Case Studies are positioned at the end of each section, showcasing relevant theories and themes.

Summary

1 This chapter has focused on online consumers and e-retailers and in doing so has introduced some of the key issues that might eventually affect the overall success of e-retail markets.

2 Online customer expectations are being raised as they become more familiar with Internet and other digital technologies and as a result companies are being forced to adopt a more planned approach towards e-retailing. Additionally, in doing e-retail managers are considering who their customers are, how and where they access the Internet and the benefits they are seeking.

3 Web sites that do not deliver value to the online customer are unlikely to succeed. E-retailers need to develop a sound understanding of who their customers are and how best to deliver satisfaction via the Internet. Over time, retailers may begin to develop more strategically focused web sites.

4 Given current levels of growth in adoption from both consumers and retailers it is reasonable to suggest the Internet is now a well-established retail channel that provides an innovative and interactive medium for communications and transactions between e-retail businesses and online consumers.

5 The web presents opportunities for companies to adopt different retail formats to satisfy their customer needs which may include a mix of Internet and physical-world offerings. Furthermore, bricks-and-mortar retailers and pureplay retailers use the Internet in various ways and combinations including sales, ordering and payment, information provision and market research.

6 Web sites focusing on the consumer vary in their function. Some offer a whole suite of interactive services whereas others just provide information. The logistical problems associated with trading online are limiting the product assortment some retailers offer.

7 Trading via the Internet challenges e-retailers to pay close attention to the online markets they are wishing to serve and to understand there are differences between the on- and offline customer experiences.

8 The virtual environment created by the Internet and associated technologies is a growing trading platform for retailing. This arena is increasing both in terms of the number of retail businesses that are online and the extent to which the Internet is being integrated into almost every aspect of retailing. As a result retailers must choose how they can best employ the Internet in order to serve their customers rather than whether to adopt the Internet at all.

Summaries clinch the important concepts that have been presented in each section.

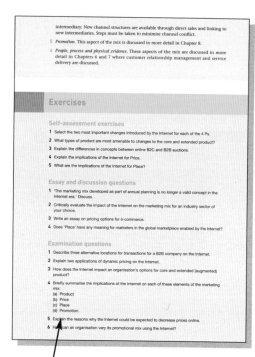

intermediary. New channel structures are available through direct sales and linking to new intermediaries. Steps must be taken to minimise channel conflict.

5 *Promotion.* This aspect of the mix is discussed in more detail in Chapter 8.

6 *People, process and physical evidence.* These aspects of the mix are discussed in more detail in Chapters 6 and 7 where customer relationship management and service delivery are discussed.

Exercises

Self-assessment exercises

1 Select the two most important changes introduced by the Internet for each of the 4 Ps.

2 What types of product are most amenable to changes to the core and extended product?

3 Explain the differences in concepts between online B2C and B2B auctions.

4 Explain the implications of the Internet for Price.

5 What are the implications of the Internet for Place?

Essay and discussion questions

1 'The marketing mix developed as part of annual planning is no longer a valid concept in the Internet era.' Discuss.

2 Critically evaluate the impact of the Internet on the marketing mix for an industry sector of your choice.

3 Write an essay on pricing options for e-commerce.

4 Does 'Place' have any meaning for marketers in the global marketplace enabled by the Internet?

Examination questions

1 Describe three alternative locations for transactions for a B2B company on the Internet.

2 Explain two applications of dynamic pricing on the Internet.

3 How does the Internet impact an organisation's options for core and extended (augmented) product?

4 Briefly summarise the implications of the Internet on each of these elements of the marketing mix:
(a) Product
(b) Price
(c) Place
(d) Promotion.

5 Explain the reasons why the Internet could be expected to decrease prices online.

6 How can an organisation vary its promotional mix using the Internet?

Each chapter ends with a number of **Exercises**, designed for use in class, as essay titles, and in exams.

At the end of each chapter you will also find a full list of **References**.

References

Aaker, D. and Joachimsthaler, E. (2000) *Brand Leadership.* Free Press, New York.
Allen, E. and Fjermestad, J. (2001) E-commerce marketing strategies: a framework and case analysis, *Logistics Information Management*, 14(1/2), 14–23.
Anderson, C. (2004) The Long Tail. *Wired*. 12.10. October. www.wired.com/wired/archive/12.10/tail.html.
Baker, W., Marn, M. and Zawada, C. (2000) Price smarter on the Net, *Harvard Business Review*, February, 2–7.
BBC (2005) Napster boss on life after piracy. *BBC*. By Derren Waters, 22 August. http://news.bbc.co.uk/1/hi/entertainment/music/4165868.stm.
Benjamin, R. and Wigand, R. (1995) Electronic markets and virtual value-chains on the information superhighway, *Sloan Management Review*, Winter, 62–72.
Berryman, K., Harrington, L., Layton-Rodin, D. and Rerolle, V. (1998) Electronic commerce: three emerging strategies, *McKinsey Quarterly*, No. 1, 152–9.
Bickerton, P., Bickerton, M. and Pardesi, U. (2000) *CyberMarketing*, 2nd edn. Butterworth Heinemann, Oxford.
Bicknell, D. (2002) Banking on customer service, *e.Businessreview*, January, 21–2.
Booms, B.H. and Bitner, M.J. (1981) Marketing strategies and organisational structures for service firms. In *Marketing of Services*, J. Donnelly and W. George, pp. 451–77. American Marketing Association, Chicago.
BrandNewWorld (2004) AOL research published at www.brandnewworld.co.uk.
Brynjolfsson, E., Smith, D. and Hu, Y. (2003) Consumer surplus in the digital economy: estimating the value of increased product variety at online booksellers, *Management Science*, 49(11), 1580–96. http://ebusiness.mit.edu/research/papers/176_ErkB_OnlineBooksellers2.pdf.
Burnett, J. (1993) *Promotional Management.* Houghton Mifflin, Boston.
Christodoulides, G. and de Chernatony, L. (2004) Dimensionalising on- and offline brands' composite equity, *Journal of Product and Brand Management*, 13(3), 168–79.
Davidow, W.H. and Malone, M.S. (1992) *The Virtual Corporation. Structuring and Revitalizing the Corporation for the 21st Century.* HarperCollins, New York.
Dayal, S., Landesberg, H. and Zeissberg, M. (2000) Building digital brands, *McKinsey Quarterly*, No. 2.
de Chernatony, L. (2001) Succeeding with brands on the Internet, *Journal of Brand Management*, 8(3), 186–95.
de Chernatony, L. and McDonald, M. (1992) *Creating Powerful Brands.* Butterworth Heinemann, Oxford.
Diamantopoulos, A. and Matthews, B. (1993) *Making Pricing Decisions. A Study of Managerial Practice.* Chapman & Hall, London.
Emiliani, V. (2001) Business-to-business online auctions: key issues for purchasing process improvement, *Supply Chain Management: An International Journal*, 5(4), 176–86.
Evans, P. and Wurster, T. S. (1999) Getting real about virtual commerce, *Harvard Business Review*, November, 84–94.
Fill, C. (2000) *Marketing Communications – Contexts, Contents and Strategies*, 3rd edn. Financial Times/Prentice Hall, Harlow.
Frazier, G. (1999) Organising and managing channels of distribution, *Journal of the Academy of Marketing Science*, 27(2), 222–40.
Ghosh, S. (1998) Making business sense of the Internet, *Harvard Business Review*, March–April, 127–35.
Gladwell, M. (2000) *The Tipping Point: How Little Things Can Make a Big Difference.* Little, Brown, New York.
Harridge-March, S. (2004) Electronic marketing, the new kid on the block. *Marketing Intelligence and Planning*, 22(3), 297–309.
Introna, L. (2001) Defining the virtual organisation. In S. Barnes and B. Hunt (eds). *E-Commerce and V-Business. Business Models for Global Success.* Butterworth Heinemann, Oxford.
Jevons, C. and Gabbott, M. (2000) Trust, brand equity and brand reality in Internet business relationships: an interdisciplinary approach, *Journal of Marketing Management*, 16, 619–34.

Suggested articles and texts for your **Further Reading** are listed, as are a number of useful **Web links**.

Further reading

Allen, E. and Fjermestad, J. (2001) E-commerce marketing strategies: a framework and case analysis, *Logistics Information Management*, 14(1/2), 14–23. Includes an analysis of how the 4 Ps are impacted by the Internet.
Baker, W., Marn, M. and Zawada, C. (2000) Price smarter on the Net, *Harvard Business Review*, February, 2–7. This gives a clear summary of the challenges and opportunities of Internet pricing.
Ghosh, S. (1998) Making business sense of the Internet, *Harvard Business Review*, March–April, 127–35. This paper gives many examples of how US companies have adapted their products to the Internet and asks key questions that should govern the strategy adopted.
Harridge-March, S. (2004) Electronic marketing, the new kid on the block. *Marketing Intelligence and Planning*, 22(3), 297–309. Like the Allen and Fjermestad (2001) paper, this gives a review of the impact of the Internet on different aspects of the marketing mix.
Kumar, N. (1999) Internet distribution strategies: dilemmas for the incumbent, *Financial Times*, Special Issue on Mastering Information Management, no. 7. Electronic Commerce (www.ftmastering.com). This article assesses the impact of the Internet on manufacturers and their distribution channels. The other articles in this special issue are also interesting.
Smith, P.R. and Chaffey, D. (2005) *E-Marketing Excellence: at the Heart of EBusiness*, 2nd edn. Butterworth Heinemann, Oxford. Chapter 2 is devoted to applying the marketing mix to Internet marketing.

Web links

• Chris Anderson has a blog site (www.thelongtail.com), the Long Tail, to support his book on the topic published in 2006 by Hyperion, New York.
• ClickZ (www.clickz.com). An excellent collection of articles on online marketing communications, US-focused. Relevant section for this chapter: Brand marketing.
• Gladwell.com (www.gladwell.com). Author's site with extracts from *The Tipping Point* and other books.
• Marketing on the internet (MOTI) by Greg Rich and colleagues from OhioLink educational establishments (http://iws.ohiolink.edu/moti/). This site provides a succinct summary, with examples, of how each of the 4 Ps of the Internet can be applied online.
• Paul Marsden's Viral Culture site (www.viralculture.com). Articles related to the tipping point and connected marketing.

About the authors

Dave Chaffey BSc, PhD, MCIM, MIDM

Dave Chaffey (www.davechaffey.com) is an Internet marketing trainer and consultant for Marketing Insights Limited. He is a lecturer on e-marketing courses at Cranfield and Warwick Universities and the Institute of Direct Marketing. Dave has been recognised by the CIM as one of 50 marketing 'gurus' worldwide who have shaped the future of marketing. He is also proud to have been recognised by the Department of Trade and Industry as one of the leading individuals who have provided input and influence on the development and growth of E-commerce and the Internet in the UK over the last 10 years.

Fiona Ellis-Chadwick PhD, BSc, Dip Sys Prac, PGCCE

Fiona Ellis-Chadwick is a lecturer in Marketing at the Business School at Loughborough University and is a member of the Marketing and Retailing Research Group. Fiona had a successful commercial career in retail management and development before joining the Business School in 2000 following completion of her PhD thesis titled 'An Empirical Study of Internet Adoption Among Leading United Kingdom Retailers'. Currently, her research interests are in the area of e-marketing and e-strategy and she has published and presented widely in the areas of retail Internet adoption and Internet marketing. Her work on these topics has been published in *Journal of Business Research, International Journal of Retail Distribution and Management, European Journal of Marketing, Internet Research, Journal of Retailing and Consumer Services* plus additional texts and practitioner journals.

Richard Mayer MA, DipM, MCIM

Richard Mayer is a Senior Lecturer in Marketing at the University of Derby and Director of his own Marketing Training Company specialising in Strategic Marketing, Business to Business Marketing and Marketing Communications. He is programme manager for the Chartered Institute of Marketing qualifications at the University of Derby. He has co-authored and contributed chapters to several marketing publications, including *Marketing – An Active Learning Approach* and *The Practice of Advertising*.

Kevin Johnston BSc, MBA

Kevin Johnston is a Senior Lecturer at Liverpool John Moores University, specialising in marketing, strategy and e-commerce. He previously lectured at the University of Derby, where he created one of the UK's first e-commerce degree programmes. He has been published in a number of marketing, management and e-commerce journals, and several times in the *International Journal of Internet Research*.

Acknowledgements

I am fortunate to have shared my journey of understanding how the Internet can be harnessed for marketing with thousands of students and marketing professionals and I thank you for sharing your experiences with me. I have also been fortunate to work with many e-marketing and e-commerce specialists to support them and their organisations on their journeys. These have been important in highlighting the success factors for digital marketing. So, thanks to Pip Chesters and David Grant at 3M, Piers Dickinson at BP, Julian Brewer at Barclays, Sonia Davidson at Bank of Scotland Corporate, Matt Dooley at HSBC, Eileen Pevreall and David Hedges at CIPD, Martyn Etherington and Mike Rizzo at Tektronix, and fellow 'e-consultants', Ashley Friedlein, Jim Sterne, Neil Mason, Danyl Bosomworth and Richard Coombes.

The authors would like to thank the team at Pearson Education in Harlow for their help in the creation of this book, especially Rhian McKay who managed the book through the production process.

As always, especial thanks go to my family for supporting me in the many hours, days and weeks of writing.

Dave Chaffey

The publishers are grateful to the following for permission to reproduce copyright material: Figures 1, 4.3, 4.22, 4.24 and 4.25 from Managing an E-commerce team. Integrating digital marketing into your organization, author: Dave Chaffey, reprinted by permission of E-consultancy.com Ltd. (E-consultancy 2005); Figure 1.1 screenshot from www.easyjet.com reprinted by permission of easyJet Airline Company Ltd.; Figures 1.1, 1.2, 1.7, 1.8, 1.15, 2.3, 2.8, 2.24, 2.25, 2.26, 4.11, 4.13, 4.17, 4.18, 5.2, 5.3, 5.5, 5.6, 5.9, 6.14, 6.15, 7.5, 7.9, 7.11, 7.12, 8.15a, 8.15b, 8.21, 10.1a, 10.1c, 10.1d, 10.2, 10.4, 10.6, 10.7, 11.1, 11.2d, 11.3 and 11.4 screenshot frames reprinted with permission from Microsoft Corporation; Table 1.1 reprinted from *EMarketing Excellence – at the Heart of EBusiness, 2nd Edition* by P. R. Smith and D. Chaffey, Copyright 2005, with permission from Elsevier (Smith, P. R. and Chaffey, D. 2005); Figure 1.2 screenshot from www.castrol.com reprinted by permission of Castrol Limited; Figure 1.7 screenshot from www.dubit.co.uk, © Dubit Limited 2006, reprinted by permission of Dubit Limited; Figure 1.8 screenshot from www.northwestsupplies.co.uk reprinted by permission of North West Supplies Ltd.; Figure 2.1 compiled from ABC Electronic, www.abce.org.uk, reprinted by permission of ABC Electronic; Figure 2.2 reprinted by permission of Interactive Media in Retail Group (IMRG); Table 2.4 from M. de Kare-Silver, *EShock 2000. The Electronic Shopping Revolution: Strategies for Retailers and Manufacturers*, pub 2000, Macmillan, reproduced with permission of Palgrave Macmillan (de Kare-Silver, M. 2000); Table 2.5 from *Omnibus Survey*, Office for National Statistics, reproduced under the terms of the Click-Use Licence (ONS 2005); Figure 2.6 from Deise *et al.* (2000) *Executive's Guide to E-business. From Tactics to Strategy.* Copyright © John Wiley & Sons, Inc. 2000. This material is used by permission of John Wiley & Sons, Inc.; Table 2.6 from H. Menteth *et al.*, Multi-channel experience consistency: evidence from Lexus in *Interactive Marketing*, Vol. 6, Issue 4, 2005, reproduced with permission of Palgrave Macmillan (Menteth, H. *et al.* 2005); Figure 2.8 screenshot from www.screentrade.co.uk reprinted by permission of Lloyds TSB Group plc; Figure 2.15 data from http://www.itu.int/ITU-D/ict/statistics/at_glance/Internet04.pdf reproduced with the kind permission of ITU; Figure 2.16 from Mori Technology Tracker, January 1997 – September 2005, reprinted by permission of Market and Opinion Research (MORI); Figures 2.17, 5.7, 5.8 and 8.13 from *Brand New World*: AOL UK/Anne Molen (Cranfield School of Management)/Henley Centre, 2004, reprinted by permission of AOL UK; Figure 2.18 from Hitwise (www.hitwise.co.uk) reprinted by permission of Hitwise UK Ltd.; Figures 2.19 and 2.20 from e MORI Technology Tracker, reprinted by permission of Market and Opinion Research (MORI); Figure 2.21, Table 11.2, Figures 11.6, 11.7, 11.8, and 11.9 from *Business in the Information Age – International Benchmarking Study 2004*, reproduced under the terms of the Click-Use Licence (DTI 2004); Figures 2.24, 8.15a, 8.15b and 11.2d screenshots reprinted by permission of Google, Inc.; Figure 2.25 screenshot from www.comet.co.uk reprinted by permission of Comet Group plc; Figure 2.26 screenshot from www.kelkoo.co.uk reprinted by permission of Kelkoo.com (UK) Ltd.; Figure 3.7 reprinted by permission of Mobile Data Association; Figure 3.9 from M. Svennevig, The Interactive Viewer: Reality or Myth? in *Interactive Marketing*, Vol. 6, Issue 2, Oct./Dec. 2004, reprinted by permission of Palgrave Macmillan (Svennevig, M. 2004); Figure 3.12 adapted from www.eiu.com, Economist Intelligence Unit and Pyramid Research e-readiness ranking, used with permission from Pyramid Research; Table 4.7 reprinted by permission of Neil Mason, Applied Insights; Figure 4.11 screenshot from www.smile.co.uk reprinted by permission of The Co-operative Bank; Figure 4.18 screenshot from www.britishairways.com reprinted by permission of British Airways plc; Figure 5.2 screenshot from www.osselect.co.uk reprinted by permission of Ordnance Survey on behalf of HMSO; Figure 5.3 screenshot from http://www.fisher-price.com/uk/myfp/age.asp?age=2month courtesy of Fisher-Price UK, www.fisher-price.com/uk; Figure 5.5 screenshot from www.napster.co.uk reprinted by permission of Napster UK Limited; Figure 5.9 screenshot from www.pricerunner.co.uk reprinted by permission of Pricerunner AB; Figure 6.6 screenshot of Thomson opt-in customer profiling form reprinted by permission of Thomson (TUI UK); Figure 6.13 from M. Patron, Case Study: Applying RFM segmentation to the SilverMinds catalogue in *Interactive Marketing*, Vol. 5, Issue 3, 9 January 2004, reproduced with permission of Palgrave Macmillan (Patron, M. 2004); Figure 6.14 screenshot from www.firebox.com reprinted by permission of Firebox.com Limited; Figure 6.15 screenshot from www.cipd.co.uk/communities reprinted by permission of Chartered Institute of Personnel and Development (CIPD); Figure 7.1 based on a diagram in L. de Chernatony, Succeeding with brands on the internet in *Journal of Brand Management*, 8 (3), 2001, reproduced with permission of Palgrave Macmillan and the author (de Chernatony, L. 2001); Table 7.2 adapted from Benchmarks – UK 100 Report, week starting 6 October 2005, reprinted by permission of Site Confidence, UK's leading website monitoring company; Table 7.4 reprinted by permission of OneStat.com; Figure 7.5 screenshot from www.hsbc.com reprinted by permission of HSBC Holdings Limited; Table 7.8 from D. Chaffey and M. Edgar, Measuring online service quality in *Journal of Targeting, Analysis and Measurement for Marketing*, 8 (4), May 2000, reproduced by permission of Palgrave Macmillan (Chaffey, D. and Edgar, M. 2000); Figure 7.9 screenshot from www.egg.com used with permission from Egg plc; Figure 7.11 screenshot from http://www.sainsburystoyou.com/webconnect/index.jsp reprinted by permission of J. Sainsbury plc; Table 8.1 from Janal, D. (1998) *Online Marketing Handbook. How to Promote, Advertise and Sell Your Products and Services on the Internet.* Copyright © John Wiley & Sons, Inc. 1998. This material is used by permission of John Wiley & Sons, Inc.; Figure 8.4 used with permission from Millward Brown UK Ltd.; Table 8.4 reprinted by permission of the Interactive Advertising Bureau; Figure 8.9 Norwich Union Rescue email reprinted by permission of Norwich Union Insurance; Figure 8.14 from http://www.atlassolutions.com/pdf/RankReport.pdf reprinted by permission of aQuantive, Inc. (Atlas 2004); Figure 8.20 reprinted by permission of Epsilon Interactive, http://www.epsiloninteractive.com; Table 9.1 from ABCe, www.abce.org.uk, reprinted by permission of ABC Electronic; Figure 9.8 screenshot reprinted by permission of IndexTools.com; Figure 10.1a screenshot from www.penguin.co.uk reprinted by permission of Penguin Books; Figure 10.2 screenshot from www.simplyvital.com reprinted by permission of Janice Wilson; Figure 10.4 screenshot from http://www.benjerry.co.uk/cinemaadverts/ reprinted by permission of Ben and Jerry's Homemade Ltd.; Tables 10.5 and 10.6 reprinted by permission of Allegra Strategies Ltd. (Allegra 2005); Figure 10.6 reprinted by permission of McArthurGlen Designer Outlets, Fox Kalomaski Ltd. – Destination Marketing and Adam B. Colour Services Ltd. – Photography; Figure 10.7 screenshot from www.sainsburys.co.uk reprinted by permission of J. Sainsbury plc; Figure 10.8 from *IAB Internet Advertising Revenue Report* (US Report), September 2005, reprinted by permission of Interactive Advertising Bureau (PricewaterhouseCoopers 2005); Figure 11.1 screenshot from http://www.ips.tv/ reprinted by permission of IPS (Intelligent Print Solutions); Figure 11.2a Microsoft product screenshot reprinted with permission from Microsoft Corporation; Figure 11.3 screenshot from http://mysolar.cat.com/cda/layout?m=6637&x=7 reprinted by permission of Solar Turbines; Table 11.3 adapted from T. S. H. Teo and Y. Pian, A contingency perspective on Internet adoption and competitive advantage in *European Journal of Information Systems*, Vol. 12, Issue 2, 2003, reproduced by permission of Palgrave Macmillan and the authors (Teo, T. S. H. and Pian, Y. 2003); Figure 11.4 screenshot from http://www.direct.gov.uk/Homepage/fs/en reproduced under the terms of the Click-Use Licence; Figure 11.5 from Implementing e-value strategies in UK retailing in *International Journal of Retail Distribution and Management*, 33 (6), republished with permission of Emerald Group Publishing Ltd. (Nicholls, A. and Watson, A. 2005).

Mini Case Study 1.1 written by Peter Davies, eCommerce Adviser at Menter Môn (www.menter.mon) for the Opportunity Wales project (www.opportunitywales.co.uk) reprinted by permission of the author; Mini Case Study 3.3 adapted from case study Comet: The Price is Right Promotion from http://www.virginradio.co.uk/sales/case_studies/25.html reprinted by permission of Virgin Radio; Chapter 3 extracts from Data Protection Act 1984, 1998 (DPA) and extracts from Privacy and Electronic Communications Regulations (PECR) Act 2003, Crown copyright material is reproduced with the permission of the Controller of HMSO and the Queen's Printer for Scotland; Mini Case Study 4.2 reprinted by permission of Euroffice Ltd.; Chapter 4, p. 188, extract adapted from Customer Promise from http://www.virginwines.com reprinted by permission of Virgin Wines; Mini Case Study 4.3 print ad copy for Have you clicked yet? campaign reprinted by permission of British Airways plc; Case Study 4 reprinted by permission of Tesco Stores Limited; Chapter 5, p. 219, definition of prosumer from http://www.wordspy.com/words/prosumer.asp, Copyright © 1995-2006 Paul McFedries and Logophilia Limited, reprinted by permission of Paul McFedries; Case Study 6 from article Interactive Being in *Computer Weekly*, 2nd May, reprinted by permission of Computer Weekly (Nicolle, L. 2001); Mini Case Study 8.1 extract from article The medium is part of the message, published in the proceedings of the ARF/ESOMAR Conference, Rio de Janiero, 12-14 November 2000, published in *ESOMAR Publications Series*, Vol. 241, reprinted by permission of the author (Branthwaite, A. 2000); Mini Case Study 8.2 from DEC Tsunami 2004/5, www.dec.org.uk, reprinted by permission of Disasters Emergency Committee; Case Study 8 reprinted by permission of Unilever; Mini Case Study 10.4 adapted from Internet stores expect a merry Christmas as online sales soar in *The Times*, 16 November 2005, http://www.timesonline.co.uk/article/0,,2-1874371,00.html, © Sarah Butler. NI Syndication Limited, 16.11.05, reprinted by permission of NI Syndication Ltd. (Butler, S. 2005); Case Study 10 reprinted by permission of lastminute.com; Mini Case Study 11.2 extract from JupiterResearch Internet Advertising Model, 7/05 (US only) and extract adapted from JupiterResearch's European Marketing & Advertising April 2005 report Online Video Advertising: Tune Content and Placements to Web Constraints reprinted by permission of JupiterResearch; Mini Case Study 11.4 adapted from NHS Purchasing and Supply Agency *E-Commerce Strategy for the NHS*, reproduced under the terms of the Click-Use Licence.

In some instances we have been unable to trace the owners of copyright material, and we would appreciate any information that would enable us to do so.

Part 1

INTERNET MARKETING FUNDAMENTALS

Part 1 introduces Internet marketing in the context of the marketing concept and evaluates linkages to related concepts such as e-marketing, e-commerce and e-business. Chapters 2 and 3 provide a foundation for Internet marketing strategy development by reviewing how the online micro- and macro-environment of an organisation can be assessed as part of situation analysis.

1

An introduction to Internet marketing

Chapter at a glance

Learning objectives

After reading this chapter, the reader should be able to:

● Evaluate the relevance of the Internet to the customer-centric, multi-channel marketing concept

● Distinguish between Internet marketing, e-marketing, digital marketing, e-commerce and e-business

● Identify the key differences between Internet marketing and traditional marketing

● Assess how the Internet can be used in different marketing functions

Questions for marketers

Key questions for marketing managers related to this chapter are:

● How significant is the Internet as a marketing tool?

● How does Internet marketing relate to e-marketing, e-commerce and e-business?

● What are the key benefits of Internet marketing?

● What differences does the Internet introduce in relation to existing marketing communications models?

Links to other chapters

This chapter provides an introduction to Internet marketing, and the concepts introduced are covered in more detail later in the book, as follows:

➤ Chapters 2 and 3 explain how situation analysis for Internet marketing planning can be conducted

➤ Chapters 4, 5 and 6 in Part 2 describe how Internet marketing strategy can be developed

➤ Chapters 7, 8 and 9 in Part 3 describe strategy implementation

➤ Chapters 10 and 11 in Part 3 describe B2C and B2B applications

Introduction – how significant is the Internet for marketing?

Customer journey

A description of modern multi-channel buyer behaviour as consumers use different media to select suppliers, make purchases and gain customer support.

How significant is Internet marketing to businesses today? The answer as always, is 'it depends'. The relative importance of the Internet for marketing for an organisation still largely depends on the nature of its products and services and the buyer behaviour of its target audience. For companies such as easyJet (**www.easyjet.com**), the low-cost European airline, the Internet is very significant for marketing its products – the Internet is now a vital part of the customer journey as consumers select the best supplier and make their purchase. EasyJet now achieves over 95% of its ticket sales online and aims to fulfil the majority of its customer service requests via the Internet (Figure 1.1). The figure shows how it has used the Internet to support its growth into many new markets. When returning to the site on subsequent visits, the relevant home page for that country is automatically displayed. For organisations whose products are not generally appropriate for sale online, such as energy company BP (**www.bp.com**) or consumer brands such as Unilever (**www.unilever.com**), the Internet is less significant, but is still rapidly growing in importance. We will see that a dramatic change in media consumption over the last 10 years towards digital media means that the Internet is becoming important for all product categories. Although the Internet is less commonly used for sale of products by such organisations, it is still important in increasing awareness of their products and brand values through online advertising on third-party sites. Once awareness is raised amongst different customer types, content and offers such as those in Figure 1.2 can be used to encourage them to start an online dialogue. The cover theme of this new edition of *Internet Marketing* alludes to customer journeys as we go about our daily lives. It also suggests the potential the web has for collaboration in communities and the sharing of information and experiences.

Figure 1.1 easyJet web site (www.easyjet.com)

This book explains how organisations can develop plans to manage all the different ways in which the Internet can be applied to support the marketing process. We take a customer-centric approach to Internet marketing (although many would regard this as a tautology since the modern-marketing concept places the customer at the heart of all marketing activity). By 'customer-centric' we mean the capability digital media give marketers to better understand and tailor propositions to individual customers, which is one of its greatest appeals and a common theme in each chapter.

As customers follow their journeys as they select products and interact with brands, they do not use the Internet in isolation – they consume other media such as print, TV, direct mail and outdoor. These media are still very important for marketers to communicate with customers who still spend the majority of their waking hours in the real world rather than the virtual world. It follows that an effective approach to using the Internet is as part of a multi-channel marketing strategy. This defines how different marketing channels should integrate and support each other in terms of their proposition development and communications based on their relative merits for the customer and the company. The multi-channel approach is also a common theme throughout this book.

In this introductory chapter we review different applications of Internet marketing and consider the impact of the Internet on marketing. We also explain the basic concepts of Internet marketing, placing it in the context of e-commerce and e-business and the technologies involved.

Customer-centric marketing
An approach to marketing based on detailed knowledge of customer behaviour within the target audience which seeks to fulfil the individual needs and wants of customers.

Multi-channel marketing strategy
Defines how different marketing channels should integrate and support each other in terms of their proposition development and communications based on their relative merits for the customer and the company.

Marketing applications of Internet marketing

Internet-based media offer a range of opportunities for marketing products and services across the purchase cycle. Companies such as easyJet and BP illustrate the applications of Internet marketing since they show how organisations can use online communications such as their web site, third-party web sites and e-mail marketing as:

- An *advertising medium*. For example, BP plc and its subsidiary companies, such as Castrol Limited, uses large-format display or interactive ads on media sites to create awareness of brands and products such as fuels and lubricants.
- A *direct-response medium*. For example, easyJet uses sponsored links when a user is researching a flight using a search engine to prompt them to directly visit the easyJet site by clicking through to it. Similarly the easyJet e-mail newsletter sent to customers can encourage them to click through to a web site to generate sales.
- A *platform for sales transactions*. For example, easyJet sells flights online to both consumers and business travellers.
- A *lead-generation method*. For example, when BP offers content to business car managers about selecting the best fuel for company cars in order to identify interest from a car fleet manager.
- A *distribution channel*. For example, for distributing digital products. This is often specific to companies with digital products to sell such as online music resellers such as Napster (**www.napster.com**) and Apple iTunes (**www.itunes.com**) or publishers of written or video content.
- A *customer service mechanism*. For example, customers serve themselves on easyJet.com by reviewing frequently asked questions.
- A *relationship-building medium* where a company can interact with its customers to better understand their needs and offer them relevant products and offers. For example, easyJet uses its e-mail newsletter and tailored alerts about special deals to help keep its customers and engage them in a dialogue to understand their needs through completing surveys and polls.

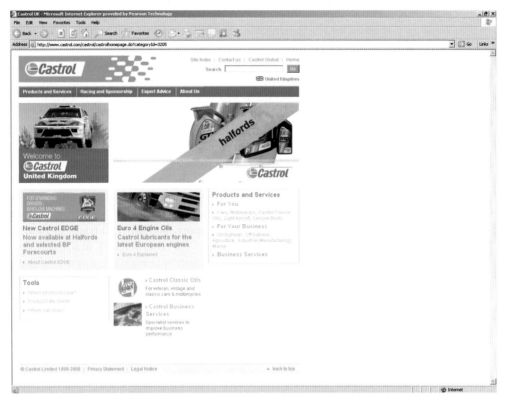

Figure 1.2 An extract from the Castrol.com web site, reproduced by permission of Castrol Limited. Any unauthorised reproduction is strictly prohibited

Our changing media consumption

Although the importance of the Internet varies for different organisations, what all share is changing behaviour in their stakeholder audiences whether they be prospects, customers, media, shareholders or other partners. Each of these audiences is increasing its consumption of Internet media (Figure 1.3) and there is a corresponding change in buyer behaviour. Figure 1.3 shows that in the UK, the Internet is the third most consumed medium following TV and radio (this figure excludes e-mail usage). During the business day, the web is the most frequently consumed medium.

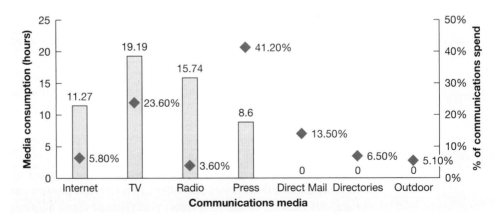

Figure 1.3 Variation in UK media consumption in hours (bars) compared to percentage media expenditure (diamonds)

Source: Compiled from EIAA (2005) and IAB (2005)

But has this change in media consumption been reflected in changes in advertising expenditure using different media? Figure 1.3 also shows that advertising expenditure for the Internet medium lags a long way behind expenditure on TV and press advertising (newspapers and magazines) although it has now overtaken radio and outdoor ad spend. This disconnect or mismatch between medium consumption and TV/press advertising expenditure illustrates the core challenge of Internet marketing – it is how organisations reallocate their resources to best maximise their returns from the Internet.

Our changing buyer behaviour

Figure 1.4 shows there is a dramatic difference in online consumer behaviour in different markets. For the majority of products such as travel and cinema and theatre tickets, people are researching and then buying online, while for some bigger purchases such as cars and properties, people use the internet mainly as a research tool.

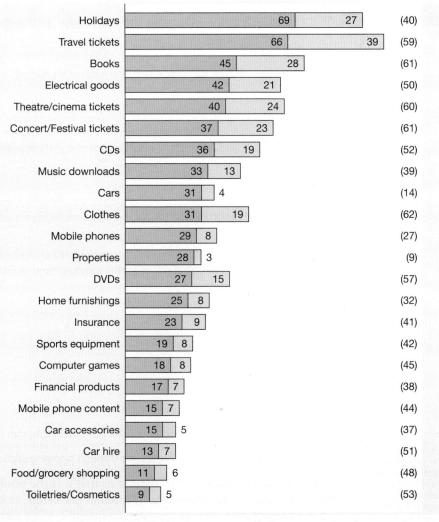

Figure 1.4 Percentage of Internet users in the EU and Norway browsing (dark bar) and buying (light bar). Conversion percentages (shown in brackets) are the proportions of all who research the product online who buy online

Source: EIAA (2005)

The figure suggests that the way companies should use digital technologies for marketing their products will vary markedly according to product type. In some, such as cars and complex financial products such as mortgages, the main role of online marketing will be to support research, while for standardised products like books and CDs there will be a dual role for the web in supporting research and enabling purchase.

What is Internet marketing?

The use of the Internet and other digital media to support marketing has been granted a bewildering range of labels by both academics and professionals. In this section we review some of the different definitions to help explain the scope and applications of this new form of marketing. Before we start by defining these terms, complete Activity 1.1 which considers the relative popularity of these terms.

Activity 1.1	What's in a term – what do we call this 'e-thing'?

Purpose

To illustrate how different marketers perceive Internet marketing.

visit the
w.w.w.

Question

There are a range of terms used to describe Internet marketing – it is called different things by different people. It is important that within companies and between agency and client there is clarity on the scope of Internet marketing, so the next few sections explore alternative definitions.

One crude, but revealing method of assessing how commonly these terms are used, is to use the Google syntax which returns the number of pages which contain a particular phrase in their body or title.

Type into Google the following phrases in double quotes or use intitle: "phrase" for these phrases and note the number of pages (at the top right hand of results page):

Phrase
"Internet marketing"
"E-marketing"
"Digital marketing"
"E-business"
"E-commerce"

Internet marketing

The application of the Internet and related digital technologies in conjunction with traditional communications to achieve marketing objectives.

What, then, is Internet marketing? Internet marketing can be simply defined as:

Achieving marketing objectives through applying digital technologies.

This succinct definition helps remind us that it is the results delivered by technology that should determine investment in Internet marketing, not the adoption of the technology! These digital technologies include Internet media such as web sites and e-mail as well as other digital media such as wireless or mobile and media for delivering digital television such as cable and satellite.

In practice, Internet marketing will include the use of a company web site in conjunction with online promotional techniques described in Chapter 8 such as search engine marketing, interactive advertising, e-mail marketing and partnership arrangements with other web sites. These techniques are used to support objectives of acquiring new customers and providing services to existing customers that help develop the customer relationship. However, for Internet marketing to be successful there is still a necessity for integration of these techniques with traditional media such as print, TV and direct mail.

E-marketing defined

The term 'Internet marketing' tends to refer to an external perspective of how the Internet can be used in conjunction with traditional media to acquire and deliver services to customers. An alternative term is e-marketing or electronic marketing (*see* for example McDonald and Wilson, 1999 and Smith and Chaffey, 2005) which can be considered to have a broader scope since it refers to digital media such as web, e-mail and wireless media, but also includes management of digital customer data and electronic customer relationship management systems (e-CRM systems).

E-marketing
Achieving marketing objectives through use of electronic communications technology.

The role of e-marketing in supporting marketing is suggested by applying the definition of marketing by the Chartered Institute of Marketing (**www.cim.co.uk**):

Marketing is the management process responsible for identifying, anticipating and satisfying customer requirements profitably.

This definition emphasises the focus of marketing on the customer, while at the same time implying a need to link to other business operations to achieve this profitability. Smith and Chaffey (2005) note that e-marketing can be used to support these aims as follows:

● *Identifying* – the Internet can be used for marketing research to find out customers' needs and wants (Chapters 7 and 9).
● *Anticipating* – the Internet provides an additional channel by which customers can access information and make purchases – understanding this demand is key to governing resource allocation to e-marketing as explained in Chapters 2 and 4.
● *Satisfying* – a key success factor in e-marketing is achieving customer satisfaction through the electronic channel, which raises issues such as: is the site easy to use, does it perform adequately, what is the standard of associated customer service and how are physical products dispatched? These issues of customer relationship management are discussed further in Chapters 6 and 7.

A broader definition of marketing has been developed by Dibb, Simkin, Pride and Ferrell (Dibb et al., 2001):

Marketing consists of individual and organisational activities that facilitate and expedite satisfying exchange relationships in a dynamic environment through the creation, distribution, promotion and pricing of goods, services and ideas.

This definition is useful since it highlights different marketing activities necessary to achieve the '*exchange relationship*', namely product development, pricing, promotion and distribution. We will review the way in which the Internet affects these elements of the marketing mix in Chapter 5.

Digital marketing defined

Digital marketing
This has a similar meaning to 'electronic marketing' – both describe the management and execution of marketing using electronic media such as the web, e-mail, interactive TV and wireless media in conjunction with digital data about customers' characterstics and behaviour.

Digital marketing is yet another term similar to Internet marketing. We use it here, because it is a term increasingly used by specialist e-marketing agencies and the new media trade publications such as *New Media Age* (**www.nma.co.uk**) and *Revolution* (**www.revolutionmagazine.com**). The Institute of Direct Marketing (IDM) has also adopted the term to refer to its specialist professional qualifications.

To help explain the scope and approaches used for digital marketing the IDM has developed a more detailed explanation of digital marketing:

Digital marketing involves:

Applying these technologies which form online channels to market:
– Web, e-mail, databases, plus mobile/wireless and digital TV.

To achieve these objectives:
– Support marketing activities aimed at achieving profitable acquisition and retention of customers ... within a multi-channel buying process and customer lifecycle.

Through using these marketing tactics:
– Recognising the strategic importance of digital technologies and developing a planned approach to reach and migrate customers to online services through e-communications and traditional communications. Retention is achieved through improving our customer knowledge (of their profiles, behaviour, value and loyalty drivers), then delivering integrated, targeted communications and online services that match their individual needs.

Let's now look at each part of this description in more detail. The first part of the description illustrates the range of access platforms and communications tools that form the online channels which e-marketers use to build and develop relationships with customers. The access platforms or hardware include PCs, PDAs, mobile phones and interactive digital TV and these deliver content and enable interaction through different online communication tools such as organisation web sites, portals, search engines, blogs (see Chapter 8), e-mail, instant messaging and text messaging. Some also include traditional voice telephony as part of digital marketing.

Blogs
Personal online diary, journal or news source compiled by one person or several people.

For example, an online bank uses many of these technologies to communicate with its customers according to the customers' preferences – some prefer to use the web, others wireless or interactive TV and others traditional channels. Svennevig (2004) summarises the growth in the usage of these digital technologies.

The second part of the description shows that it should not be the technology that drives digital marketing, but the business returns from gaining new customers and maintaining relationships with existing customers. It also emphasises how digital marketing does not occur in isolation, but is most effective when it is integrated with other communications channels such as phone, direct mail or face-to-face. As we have said, the role of the Internet in supporting multi-channel marketing is another recurring theme in this book and Chapters 5 and 6 in particular explain its role in supporting different customer communications channels and distribution channels. Online channels should also be used to support the whole buying process from pre-sale to sale to post-sale and further development of customer relationships.

Multi-channel marketing
Customer communications and product distribution are supported by a combination of digital and traditional channels at different points in the buying cycle.

The final part of the description summarises approaches to customer-centric e-marketing. It shows how success online requires a planned approach to migrate existing customers to online channels and acquire new customers by selecting the appropriate mix of e-communications and traditional communications. Retention of online customers needs to be based on developing customer insight by researching their characteristics, behaviour, what they value and what keeps them loyal, and then delivering tailored, relevant web and e-mail communications.

E-commerce and e-business defined

Customer insight
Knowledge about customers' needs, characteristics, preferences and behaviours based on analysis of qualitative and quantitative data. Specific insights can be used to inform marketing tactics directed at groups of customers with shared characteristics.

Electronic commerce (e-commerce)
All financial and informational electronically mediated exchanges between an organisation and its external stakeholders.

The terms 'e-commerce' and 'e-business' are often used in a similar context to 'Internet marketing' but their scope is different. It is important for those managing digital technologies within any organisations to achieve clarity on the meaning of e-marketing, e-commerce and e-business to help define the scope of what they are trying to achieve! Electronic commerce (e-commerce) is often thought to simply refer to buying and selling using the Internet; people immediately think of consumer retail purchases from companies such as Amazon. However, e-commerce refers to *both financial and informational* electronically mediated transactions between an organisation and any third party it deals with (Chaffey, 2006). It follows that non-financial transactions such as inbound customer e-mail enquiries and outbound e-mail broadcasts to prospects and customers are also aspects of e-commerce that need management.

Sell-side e-commerce
E-commerce transactions between a supplier organisation and its customers.

Buy-side e-commerce
E-commerce transactions between a purchasing organisation and its suppliers.

When evaluating the impact of e-commerce on an organisation's marketing, it is instructive to identify the role of buy-side and sell-side e-commerce transactions as depicted in Figure 1.5. Sell-side e-commerce refers to transactions involved with selling products to an organisation's customers. Internet marketing is used directly to support sell-side e-commerce. Buy-side e-commerce refers to business-to-business transactions to procure resources needed by an organisation from its suppliers. This is typically the responsibility of those in the operational and procurement functions of an organisation. Remember, though, that each e-commerce transaction can be considered from two perspectives: sell-side from the perspective of the selling organisation and buy-side from the perspective of the buying organisation. So in organisational marketing we need to understand the drivers and barriers to buy-side e-commerce in order to accommodate the needs of organisational buyers. For example, marketers from RS Components (**www.rswww.com**) promote its sell-side e-commerce service by hosting seminars for buyers within the purchasing department of its customers that explain the cost savings available through e-commerce.

E-business defined

Electronic business (e-business)
All electronically mediated information exchanges, both within an organisation and with external stakeholders, supporting the range of business processes.

Given that Figure 1.5 depicts different types of e-commerce, how does this relate to e-business? IBM (**www.ibm.com/e-business**), one of the first suppliers to coin the term explains it as follows:

> **e-business (e' biz' nis):** *The transformation of key business processes through the use of Internet technologies.*

Referring back to Figure 1.5, the key business processes in the IBM definition are the organisational processes or units in the centre of the figure. They include research and development, marketing, manufacturing and inbound and outbound logistics. The buy-side e-commerce processes with suppliers and the sell-side e-commerce processes involving exchanges with distributors and customers can also be considered to be key business processes. So e-commerce can best be conceived of as a subset of e-business, and this is the perspective we will use in this book.

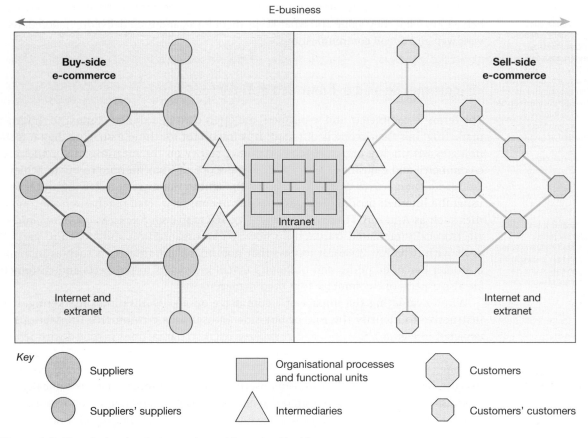

Figure 1.5 The distinction between buy-side and sell-side e-commerce

Business or consumer model?

Business-to-consumer (B2C)

Commercial transactions between an organisation and consumers.

Business-to-business (B2B)

Commercial transactions between an organisation and other organisations (inter-organisational marketing).

Consumer-to-consumer (C2C)

Informational or financial transactions between consumers, but usually mediated through a business site.

Consumer-to-business (C2B)

Consumers approach the business with an offer.

It is now commonplace to describe Internet marketing opportunities in terms of whether an organisation is transacting with consumers (business-to-consumer – B2C) or other businesses (business-to-business – B2B).

Figure 1.6 gives examples of different companies operating in the business-to-consumer (B2C) and business-to-business (B2B) spheres. Often companies such as easyJet and BP will have products that appeal to both consumers and businesses, so will have different parts of their site to appeal to these audiences. Figure 1.6 also presents two additional types of transaction, those where consumers transact directly with other consumers (C2C) and where they initiate trading with companies (C2B). Note that the C2C and C2B monikers are less widely used (e.g. *Economist*, 2000), but they do highlight significant differences between Internet-based commerce and earlier forms of commerce. Consumer-to-consumer interactions were relatively rare, but are now very common in the form of the community components such as discussion groups or forums on B2C or B2B sites. These interactions are also found on sites focusing on C2C interactions such as eBay (**www.ebay.com**) which are still run on a business basis and some blogs which are not run by companies, but individuals. Figure 1.7 is another example of a C2C site: the youth network Dubit (**www.dubit.co.uk**) which is also used by FMCG brands to research youth market trends and engage opinion formers. Hoffman and Novak (1996) suggest that C2C interactions are a key characteristic of the Internet that is important for companies to take into account, as is shown by Activity 1.2.

	From: Supplier of content/service		
To: Consumer of content/service	**Consumer or citizen**	**Business (organisation)**	**Government**
Consumer or citizen	**Consumer-to-Consumer (C2C)** • eBay • Peer-to-Peer (Skype) • Blogs and communities • Product recommendations	**Business-to-Consumer (B2C)** • Transactional: Amazon • Relationship-building: BP • Brand-building: Unilever • Media owner – News Corp • Comparison intermediary: Kelkoo, Pricerunner	**Government-to-Consumer (G2C)** • National government transactional: Tax – inland revenue • National government information • Local government services
Business (organisation)	**Consumer-to-Business (C2B)** • Priceline • Consumer-feedback, communities or campaigns	**Business-to-Business (B2B)** • Transactional: Euroffice • Relationship-building: BP • Media Owned: Emap business publications • B2B marketplaces: EC21	**Government-to-Business (G2B)** • Government services and transactions: tax • Legal regulations
Government	**Consumer-to-Government (C2G)** • Feedback to government through pressure group or individual sites	**Business-to-Government (B2G)** • Feedback to government businesses and non-governmental organisations	**Government-to-Government (G2G)** • Inter-government services • Exchange of information

Figure 1.6 Summary and examples of transaction alternatives between businesses, consumers and governmental organisations

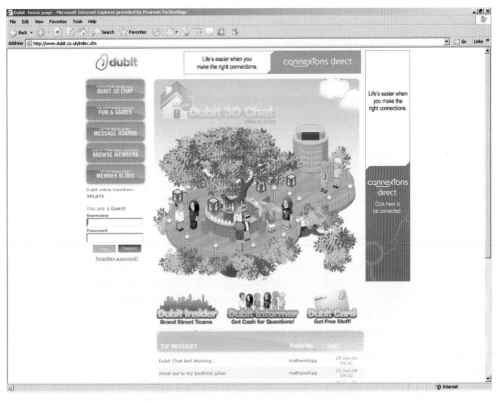

Figure 1.7 Dubit C2C site for a youth audience (www.dubit.co.uk)

E-government

The use of Internet technologies to provide government services to citizens.

The diagram also includes government and public services organisations which deliver online or e-government services. As well as the models shown in Figure 1.7, it has also been suggested that employees should be considered as a separate type of consumer through the use of intranets, which is referred to as employee-to-employee or E2E.

Activity 1.2 | **Why are C2C interactions important?**

Purpose

To highlight the relevance of C2C transactions to B2C companies.

Activity

Consult with fellow students and share experience of C2C interactions online. Think of C2C on both independent sites and organisational sites. How can C2C communications assist these organisations?

What benefits does the Internet provide for the marketer?

At the start of this chapter we described some of the applications of Internet marketing to support communications with customers across the purchase cycle from generating awareness, achieving direct response for lead generation or sale and supporting customer service and relationship marketing. Smith and Chaffey (2005) have defined the 5 Ss of e-marketing which suggest five broad benefits or reasons for adopting e-marketing which marketers can use to set objectives for e-marketing (Table 1.1).

Different types of online presence

The relative importance of the marketing benefits of the Internet shown in Table 1.1 depend upon the type of product and its market. Chaffey (2006) identifies four main types of online presence which each have different objectives and are appropriate for different markets. Note that these are not clear-cut categories of web sites since any company may combine these types, but with a change in emphasis according to the market they serve. As you review web sites, note how organisations have different parts of the site focusing on these functions of sales transactions, services, relationship-building, brand-building and providing news and entertainment. The four main types of site are:

1 Transactional e-commerce site

These enable purchase of products online. The main business contribution of the site is through sale of these products. The sites also support the business by providing information for consumers that prefer to purchase products offline.

Visit these examples: an end-product manufacturer such as Vauxhall (**www.vauxhall.co.uk**) or an online retailer such as Amazon (**www.amazon.com**).

Table 1.1 The 5 Ss of Internet marketing

Benefit of e-marketing	How benefit is delivered	Typical objectives
Sell – Grow sales	Achieved through wider distribution to customers you can't readily service offline or perhaps through a wider product range than in-store, or lower prices compared to other channels	• Achieve 10% of sales online in market • Increase online sales for product by 20% in year
Serve – Add value	Achieved through giving customers extra benefits online or inform product development through online dialogue and feedback	• Increase interaction with different content on site • Increase dwell-time duration on site by 10% (sometimes known as 'stickiness') • Increasing number of customers actively using online services (at least once per month) to 30%
Speak – Get closer to customers	This is creating a two-way dialogue through web and e-mail forms and polls and conducting online market research through formal surveys and informally monitoring chat rooms to learn about them. Also speak through reaching them online through PR	• Grow e-mail coverage to 50% of current customer database • Survey 1000 customers online each month • Increase visitors to community site section by 5%
Save – Save costs	Achieved through online e-mail communications, sales and service transactions to reduce staff, print and postage costs	• Generate 10% more sales for same communications budget • Reduce cost of direct marketing by 15% through e-mail • Increase web self-service to 40% of all service enquiries and reduce overall cost-to-serve by 10%
Sizzle – Extend the brand online	Achieved through providing a new proposition and new experience online while at the same time appearing familiar	• Improve branding metrics such as: brand awareness, reach, brand favourability and purchase intent

Source: Smith and Chaffey, 2005

2 Services-oriented relationship-building web site

Provides information to stimulate purchase and build relationships. Products are not typically available for purchase online. Information is provided through the web site and e-newsletters to inform purchase decisions. The main business contribution is through encouraging offline sales and generating enquires or leads from potential customers. Such sites also add value to existing customers by providing them with detailed information to help them support them in their lives at work or at home.

Visit these examples: B2B management consultants such as PricewaterhouseCooper (**www.pwcglobal.com**) and Accenture (**www.accenture.com**), B2C portal for energy supplier British Gas (**www.house.co.uk**).

3 Brand-building site

Provide an experience to support the brand. Products are not typically available for online purchase. Their main focus is to support the brand by developing an online experience of the brand. They are typical for low-value, high-volume fast-moving consumer goods (FMCG) brands for consumers.

Visit these examples: Tango (**www.tango.com**), Guinness (**www.guinness.com**).

4 Portal or media site

Provide information or news about a range of topics. 'Portal' refers to a gateway of information. This is information both on the site and through links to other sites. Portals have a diversity of options for generating revenue including advertising, commission-based sales, sale of customer data (lists).

Visit these examples: Yahoo! (**www.yahoo.com**) (B2C) and Silicon (**www.silicon.com**) (B2B).

Each of these different types of sites tend to increase in sophistication as organisations develop their Internet marketing. Many organisations began the process of Internet marketing with the development of web sites in the form of brochureware sites or electronic brochures introducing their products and services, but are now enhancing them to add value to the full range of marketing functions. In Chapters 2 and 4 we look at stage models of the development of Internet marketing services, from static brochureware sites to dynamic transactional sites that support interactions with customers.

A powerful method of evaluating the strategic marketing opportunities of using the Internet is to apply the strategic marketing grid of Ansoff (1957) as discussed in the strategy formulation section of Chapter 4 (Figure 4.10). This shows how the Internet can potentially be used to achieve four strategic directions:

1 *Market penetration.* The Internet can be used to sell more existing products into existing markets.
2 *Market development.* Here the Internet is used to sell into new geographical markets, taking advantage of the low cost of advertising internationally without the necessity for a supporting sales infrastructure in the customers' countries.
3 *Product development.* New products or services are developed which can be delivered by the Internet. These are typically digital products.
4 *Diversification.* In this sector, the Internet supports selling new products which are developed and sold into new markets.

As well as assisting large corporate organisations develop their markets, perhaps the most exciting potential of the Internet is to help small and medium enterprises (SMEs) expand. Read Mini Case Study 1.1 'North West Supplies extends its reach online' which also illustrates some of the challenges of managing an online business and highlights the need for continual investment.

Brochureware site

A simple site with limited interaction with the user that replicates offline marketing literature.

Stage models

Models for the development of different levels of Internet marketing services.

Transactional sites

Sites that support online sales.

Mini Case Study 1.1   North West Supplies extends its reach online

NWS commenced operations in March 1999 when Andrew Camwell, a member of the RAF Volunteer Reserve at the time, spotted a gap in the UK market for mail-order supplies of military garments to people active in the Volunteer Reserve and the Air Cadet Force. Andrew, his wife Carys, and her sister Elaine Hughes, started running a mail-order business out of shop premises in the village of Cemaes Bay.

The web store at **www.northwestsupplies.co.uk** has been on-line since November 2002. As it can take several months for a web site to be indexed by search engines, NWS used pay-per-click advertising (PPC – see Chapter 8) as a method of very quickly increasing the web site's presence in the major search engines. This marketing method proved successful. The directors were pleasantly surprised as they had previously been somewhat dubious about the prospect of the Internet generating sales in their sector. Within six months of running the web site, the company had increased turnover by £20,000, but further advances would incur a high advertising cost. Following an eCommerce Review by Opportunity Wales, the company decided to tackle the issues by implementing search engine optimisation (SEO – see Chapter 8) and a site re-design which included:

- *Improved graphic design* – this was to be changed to a more professional and up-to-date look.
- *Best, featured and latest products* – the introduction of a dynamic front page to entice customers to re-visit the site on a regular basis. The contents of this page would feature the best sellers, and latest or featured products.
- *Reviews and ratings* – to provide confidence to consumers and allow some kind of interaction with them, which would allow users to review products they have purchased and give them a star rating.
- *Cross-selling* – when customers view a product there may be other products or categories that may be of interest or complementary, hence there was a proposal to allow staff to link products and categories so that these would be displayed.
- *Segmentation* – the site would be split into two sections emphasising the segmentation of product lines into military wear and outdoor wear sectors, thus being less confusing, and easier to use for the respective users (see Figure 1.8 under 'Best, featured and latest products').
- *Navigation by sub-categories* – as the product range had expanded, the additional pages created in each category made it harder for customers to find specific items or have to browse many pages before finding a suitable product. The introduction of sub-categories would provide a clear link to the areas of interest and contain fewer pages to browse thus helping the customer to make a choice more easily and more quickly. A new search tool and order tracking were also seen as important parts of the online customer experience (Chapter 8).

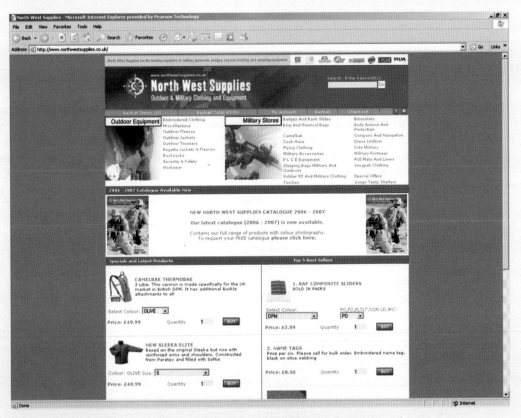

Figure 1.8 North West Supplies Ltd site (www.northwestsupplies.co.uk)
Source: Opportunity Wales

Benefits

The owners describe the benefits of the improvements to the site as follows:

- *Increased Direct Sales – 'The new launch increased sales and appealed to a broader audience – young and old'.* The annual turnover of the business has increased from £250,000 to £350,000 and this is mainly attributable to the new web site. The high profile launch aimed at existing customers, the greater visibility in search engines, and the greater usability of the site have all contributed to this.
- *Improved Promotion of the Whole Range of Stock – 'We started selling stuff that we hadn't sold before'.* The changes in navigation, particularly division into two market segments (military and outdoors) and greater use of sub-categories, meant that products were easier to find and hence easier to buy, leading to increased sales of products that had previously been slow sellers.
- *New Customers – 'We now send more items abroad'.* The better performance of the site in search engines has led to an increase in orders from new customers and from abroad. The company now has regular sales to Canada, Australia, New Zealand and various European states. 60% of orders are from new customers – not bad for a business that initially set up on the premise of a niche market for UK based cadet forces.
- *Adding Value to the Brand – 'New corporate clients could look at our Web site and see we weren't fly-by-night and that we meant business'.* Improvements to the design have raised confidence levels in visitors and this has led to increased sales. But perhaps more significantly, the professional image of the site was a good boost to confidence for potential business partners in the emerging business-to-business division that started to trade as North Star Contracts.

A strategic approach to Internet marketing

To realise the benefits of Internet marketing that we have described, an organisation needs to develop a planned, structured approach. As we will see in Chapter 4, which covers Internet marketing strategy, there are many risks if an ad-hoc rather than strategic approach to managing online channels is used. Some of the problems that we have commonly seen in organisations are:

- *Unclear responsibilities* for the many different Internet marketing activities shown in Figure 1;
- *No specific objectives* are set for Internet marketing;
- *Insufficient budget* is allocated for Internet marketing as *customer demand for online services is underestimated* and *competitors potentially gain market share* through superior online activities;
- *Budget is wasted* as different parts of an organisation experiment with using different tools or suppliers without achieving economies of scale;
- *New online value propositions for customers* are not developed since the Internet is treated as 'just another channel to market' without review of opportunities to offer improved, differentiated online services;
- *Results from digital marketing are not measured or reviewed* adequately, so actions cannot be taken to improve effectiveness;
- *An experimental rather than planned approach* is taken to using e-communications with *poor integration between online and offline marketing* communications.

Consequently, this book defines a strategic approach to Internet marketing which is intended to manage these risks and deliver the opportunities available from online channels. In Figure 1.9 we suggest a process for developing and implementing an Internet marketing which is based on our experience of strategy definition in a wide range of companies. This diagram highlights the key activities and their dependencies which are involved for creation of a typical Internet marketing. The purpose of strategic Internet marketing activities and the main point at which these topics are covered in this book are as follows:

A Defining the online opportunity

Setting objectives to define the potential is the core of this phase of strategy development. Key activities are:

- *1. Set e-marketing objectives (Chapter 4)*: Companies need to set specific numerical objectives for their online channels and then resource to deliver these objectives. These objectives should be informed by and influence the business objectives and also the following activities:
- *1.a. Evaluate e-marketing performance (Chapters 4 and 9)*: Applying web analytics tools to measure the contribution of leads, sales and brand involvement currently delivered by online communications such as search engine marketing, online advertising and e-mail marketing in conjunction with the web site.
- *1.b. Assess online marketplace (Chapters 2, 3 and 4)*: Situation analysis reviewing the micro-environment (customers, competitors, intermediaries, suppliers and internal capabilities and resources) and the broader macro-environment which influences strategy such as legal requirements and technology innovation.

B Selecting the strategic approach

- *2. Define e-marketing strategy (Chapter 4)*: Select appropriate strategies to achieve the objectives set at stage A1.
- *2a. Define customer value proposition (Chapters 4 to 7)*: Define the value proposition available through the online channel and how it relates to the core proposition delivered by the company. Reviewing the marketing mix and brand values to evaluate how they can be improved online.
- *2b. Define e-communications mix (Chapters 4 and 8)*: Selecting the offline and online communications tools to encourage usage of an organisation's online services and to generate leads and sales. Developing new outbound communications and event-triggered touch strategies to support customers through their relationship with the company.

C Delivering results online

- *3. Implement e-marketing plan (Part 3)*: This details the implementation of the strategy.
- *3a. Implement customer experience (Chapter 7)*: Build the web site and create the e-mail marketing communications' which form the online interactions customers make with a company. Create online customer relationship management capabilities to understand customers' characteristics, needs and behaviours and to deliver targeted, personalised value (Chapter 6).
- *3b. Execute e-communications (Chapter 8)*: Managing the continuous online marketing communications such as search engine marketing, partnerships, sponsorships and affiliate arrangements and campaign-based e-marketing communications such as

online advertising, e-mail marketing and microsites to encourage usage of the online service and to support customer acquisition and retention campaigns.

● *4. Customer profiling (Chapter 6), monitoring and improving online activities and maintaining the online activities (Chapter 9)*: Capturing profile and behavioural data on customer interactions with the company and summarising and disseminating reports and alerts about performance compared with objectives in order to drive performance improvement.

You will see that in the process diagram, Figure 1.9, many double-headed arrows are used, since the activities are often not sequential, but rather inform each other, so activity 1, set e-marketing objectives, is informed by the activities around it, but may also influence them. Similarly, activity 4, profile, measure and improve, is informed by the execution of online activities, but there should be a feedback loop to update the tactics and strategies used.

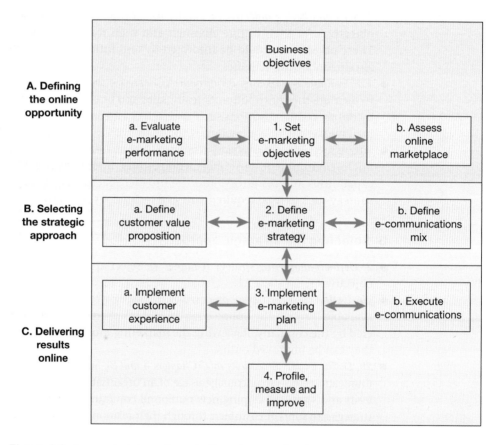

Figure 1.9 A generic Internet marketing strategy development process

How do Internet marketing communications differ from traditional marketing communications?

Internet marketing differs significantly from conventional marketing communications because of the digital medium used for communications. The Internet and other digital media such as digital television and mobile phones enable new forms of interaction and new models for information exchange. A useful summary of the differences between these new media and traditional media has been developed by McDonald and Wilson (1999) – they describe the '6 Is of the e-marketing mix'. Note that these can be used as a strategic analysis tool, but they are not used in this context here. The six Is are useful since they highlight factors that apply to practical aspects of Internet marketing such as personalisation, direct response and marketing research, but also strategic issues of industry restructuring and integrated channel communications.

1 Interactivity

John Deighton was one of the first authors to summarise this key characteristic of the Internet. He identified the following characteristics inherent in a digital medium (Deighton, 1996) which are true for much online marketing activity, but not all:

- the customer initiates contact;
- the customer is seeking information (*pull*);
- it is a high-intensity medium – the marketer will have 100 per cent of the individual's attention when he or she is viewing a web site;
- a company can gather and store the response of the individual;
- individual needs of the customer can be addressed and taken into account in future *dialogues*.

Figure 1.10(a) shows how traditional media are predominantly *push media* where the marketing message is broadcast from company *to* customer and other stakeholders. During this process, there is limited interaction with the customer, although interaction is encouraged in some cases such as the direct-response advert or mail-order campaign. On the Internet, it is often the customer who initiates contact and is *seeking* information through researching information on a web site. In other words it is a *'pull'* mechanism where it is particularly important to have good visibility in search engines such as Google, Yahoo! and MSN when customers are entering search terms relevant to a company's products or services. Note though, that outbound e-mail marketing and online advertising can be considered as 'push' broadcast techniques. Figure 1.10(b) shows how

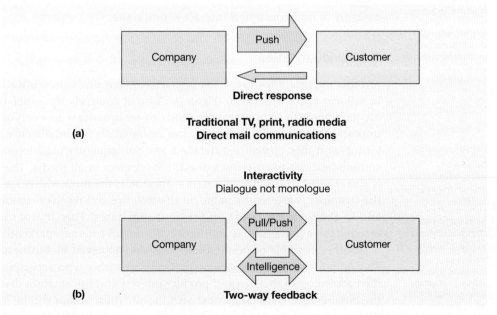

Figure 1.10 Summary of communication models for: (a) traditional media, (b) new media

the Internet should be used to encourage two-way communications, which may be extensions of the direct-response approach. For example, FMCG suppliers such as Nestlé (**www.nescafe.co.uk**) use their web site as a method of generating interaction by providing incentives such as competitions and sales promotions to encourage the customer to respond with their names, addresses and profile information such as age and sex.

Hoffman and Novak (1997) believe that digital media represent such a shift in the model of communication that it is a new model or paradigm for marketing communications. They suggest that the facilities of the Internet represent a computer-mediated environment in which the interactions are not between the sender and receiver of information, but with the medium itself. They say:

> consumers can interact with the medium, firms can provide content to the medium, and in the most radical departure from traditional marketing environments, consumers can provide commercially-oriented content to the media.

It has taken ten years of the growth in use of individual recommendations, auction sites, community sites and more recently blogs and podcasts for the full extent of this shift to become apparent. In 2005, a *Business Week* cover feature article referred to the 'Power of us' to explain this change and showed that although relatively few consumers are creating blogs (low single-figure percentages), a large proportion of Internet users are accessing them.

Podcasts

Individuals and organisations post online media (audio and video) which can be viewed in the appropriate players including the iPod which first sparked the growth in this technique.

2 Intelligence

The Internet can be used as a relatively low-cost method of collecting marketing research, particularly about customer perceptions of products and services. In the competitions referred to above, Nestlé are able to profile their customers' characteristics on the basis of questionnaire response.

A wealth of marketing research information is also available from the web site itself. Marketers use the web analytics approaches described in Chapter 9 to build their knowledge of customer preferences and behaviour according to the types of sites and content which they consume when online. Every time a web site visitor downloads content, this is recorded and analysed as 'site statistics' as described in Chapter 9 in order to build up a picture of how consumers interact with the site.

Web analytics

Techniques used to assess and improve the contribution of e-marketing to a business, including reviewing traffic volume, referrals, clickstreams, online reach data, customer satisfaction surveys, leads and sales.

3 Individualisation

Another important feature of the interactive marketing communications is that they can be tailored to the individual (Figure 1.11(b)) at relatively low costs, unlike in traditional media where the same message tends to be broadcast to everyone (Figure 1.11(a)). Importantly, this individualisation can be based on the intelligence collected about site visitors and then stored in a database and subsequently used to target and personalise communications to customers to achieve *relevance* in all media. The process of tailoring is also referred to as personalisation – Amazon is the most widely known example where the customer is greeted by name on the web site and receives recommendations on site and in their e-mails based on previous purchases. This ability to deliver 'sense and respond communications' is another key feature of Internet marketing.

Another example of personalisation is that achieved by business-to-business e-tailer RS Components (**www.rswww.com**). Every customer who accesses their system is profiled according to their area of product interest and information describing their role in the buying unit. When they next visit the site information will be displayed relevant to their product interest, for example office products and promotions if this is what was

Personalisation

Delivering individualised content through web pages or e-mail.

Sense and respond communications

Customer behaviour is monitored at an individual level and the marketer responds with communications tailored to the individual's need.

Mass customisation

Delivering customised content to groups of users through web pages or e-mail.

selected. This is an example of what is known as mass customisation where generic customer information is supplied for particular segments, i.e. the information is not unique to individuals, but is relevant to those with a common interest. Personalisation and mass customisation concepts are explored further in Chapter 6.

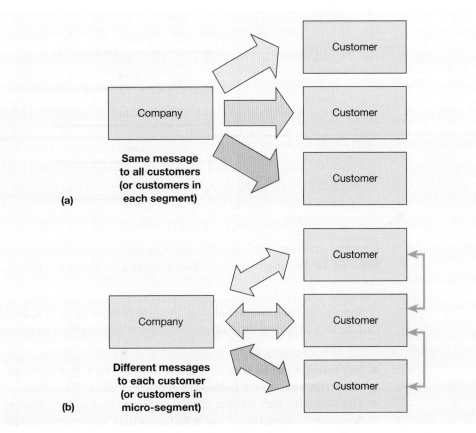

Figure 1.11 Summary of degree of individualisation for: (a) traditional media (same message), (b) new media (unique messages and more information exchange between customers)

4 Integration

Outbound Internet-based communications

The web site and e-mail marketing are used to send personalised communications to customers.

Inbound Internet-based communications

Customers enquire through web-based form and e-mail.

The Internet provides further scope for integrated marketing communications. Figure 1.12 shows the role of the Internet in multi-channel marketing. When assessing the marketing effectiveness of a web site, the role of the Internet in communicating with customers and other partners can best be considered from two perspectives. First, there is outbound Internet-based communications from *organisation to customer*. We need to ask how does the Internet complement other channels in communicating the proposition for the company's products and services to new and existing customers with a view to generating new leads and retaining existing customers? Second, inbound Internet-based communications *customer to organisation*: how can the Internet complement other channels to deliver customer service to these customers? Many companies have now integrated e-mail response and web site callback into their existing call-centre or customer service operation.

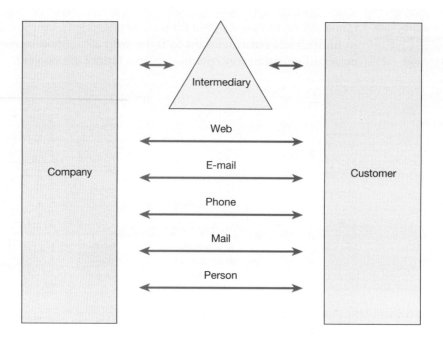

Figure 1.12 Channel requiring integration as part of integrated e-marketing strategy

Some practical examples of how the Internet can be used as an integrated communications tool as part of supporting a multi-channel customer journey (Figure 1.13) are the following:

- The Internet can be used as a direct-response tool, enabling customers to respond to offers and promotions publicised in other media.
- The web site can have a direct response or callback facility built into it. The Automobile Association has a feature where a customer service representative will contact a customer by phone when the customer fills in their name, phone number and a suitable time to ring.
- The Internet can be used to support the buying decision even if the purchase does not occur via the web site. For example, Dell has a prominent web-specific phone number on their web site that encourages customers to ring a representative in the call centre to place their order. This has the benefits that Dell is less likely to lose the business of customers who are anxious about the security of online ordering and Dell can track sales that result partly from the web site according to the number of callers on this line. Considering how a customer changes from one channel to another during the buying process, this is referred to as mixed-mode buying. It is a key aspect of devising online marketing communications since the customer should be supported in changing from one channel to another.
- Customer information delivered on the web site must be integrated with other databases of customer and order information such as those accessed via staff in the call centre to provide what Seybold (1999) calls a '360 degree view of the customer'.
- The Internet can be used to support customer service. For example easyJet (**www.easyjet.com**), which receives over half its orders electronically, encourages users to check a list of frequently asked questions (FAQ) compiled from previous customer enquiries before contacting customer support by phone.

Mixed-mode buying
The process by which a customer changes between online and offline channels during the buying process.

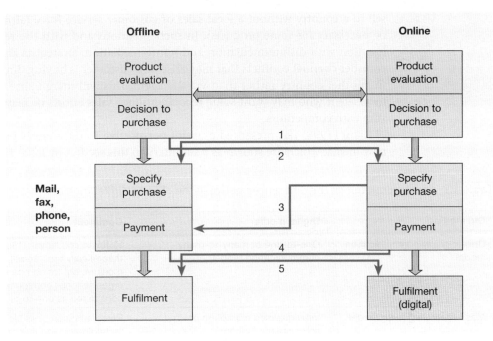

Figure 1.13 The role of mixed-mode buying in Internet marketing

---

Activity 1.3 | **Integrating online and offline communications**

Purpose

To highlight differences in marketing communications introduced through the use of the Internet as a channel and the need to integrate these communications with existing channels.

Activity

List communications between a PC vendor and a home customer over the lifetime of a product such as a PC. Include communications using both the Internet and traditional media. Refer to channel-swapping alternatives in the buying decision in Figure 1.13 to develop your answer.

---

5 Industry restructuring

Disintermediation

The removal of intermediaries such as distributors or brokers that formerly linked a company to its customers.

Reintermediation

The creation of new intermediaries between customers and suppliers providing services such as supplier search and product evaluation.

Disintermediation and reintermediation are key concepts of industry restructuring that should be considered by any company developing an e-marketing strategy and are explored in more detail in Chapters 2, 4 and 5.

For the marketer defining their company's communications strategy it becomes very important to consider the company's representation on these intermediary sites by answering questions such as 'Which intermediaries should we be represented on?' and 'How do our offerings compare to those of competitors in terms of features, benefits and price?'.

6 Independence of location

Electronic media also introduce the possibility of increasing the reach of company communications to the global market. This gives opportunities to sell into international markets that may not have been previously possible. The Internet makes it possible to sell to a country without a local sales or customer service force (although this may still be necessary for some products). In such situations and with the restructuring in conjunction with disintermediation and reintermediation, strategists also need to carefully consider channel conflicts that may arise. If a customer is buying direct from a company in another country rather than via the agent, this will marginalise the business of the local agent who may want some recompense for sales efforts or may look for a partnership with competitors.

Kiani (1998) has presented a useful perspective to differences between the old and new media, which are shown as a summary to this section in Table 1.2.

Table 1.2 An interpretation of the differences between the old and digital media

Old media	Digital media	Comment
One-to-many communication model	One-to-one or many-to-many communication model	Hoffman and Novak (1996) state that theoretically the Internet is a many-to-many medium, but for company-to-customer organisation(s) communications it is best considered as one-to-one or one-to-many
Mass-marketing push model	Individualised marketing or mass customisation. Pull model for web marketing	Personalisation possible because of technology to monitor preferences and tailor content (Deighton, 1996)
Monologue	Dialogue	Indicates the interactive nature of the World Wide Web, with the facility for feedback
Branding	Communication	Increased involvement of customer in defining brand characteristics. Opportunities for adding value to brand
Supply-side thinking	Demand-side thinking	Customer pull becomes more important
Customer as a target	Customer as a partner	Customer has more input into products and services required
Segmentation	Communities	Aggregations of like-minded consumers rather than arbitrarily defined target segments

Source: After Kiani (1998)

A short introduction to Internet technology

Internet

The physical network that links computers across the globe. It consists of the infrastructure of network servers and communication links between them that are used to hold and transport the vast amount of information on the Internet.

Marketers require a basic understanding of Internet technology in order to discuss the implementation of e-marketing with suppliers such as digital marketing agencies and with the internal IT team. In the final section of this chapter we provide a brief introduction to the technology, with which many readers will already be familiar. The Internet has existed since the late 1960s when a limited number of computers were connected for military and research purposes in the United States to form the ARPAnet.

Why then has the Internet only recently been widely adopted for business purposes? The recent dramatic growth in the use of the Internet has occurred because of the development of the World Wide Web. This became a commercial proposition in 1993 after development of the original concept by Tim Berners-Lee, a British scientist working at CERN in Switzerland in 1989. The World Wide Web changed the Internet from a difficult-to-use tool for academics and technicians to an easy-to-use tool for finding information for businesses and consumers. The World Wide Web is an interlinked

World Wide Web

The World Wide Web is
a medium for
publishing information
and providing services
on the Internet. It is
accessed through *web
browsers*, which display
site *content* on different
web pages. The content
making up *web sites* is
stored on *web servers*.

Web servers

Web servers are used
to store the web pages
accessed by web
browsers. They may
also contain databases
of customer or product
information, which can
be queried and
retrieved using a
browser.

Web browsers

Browsers such as
Mozilla Firefox and
Microsoft Internet
Explorer provide an easy
method of accessing and
viewing information
stored as HTML web
documents on different
web servers.

**Uniform (universal)
resource locator
(URL)**

A web address used to
locate a web page on a
web server.

Client–server

The client–server
architecture consists of
client computers such
as PCs sharing
resources such as a
database stored on a
more powerful server
computer.

**Internet service
provider (ISP)**

A provider enabling
home or business
users a connection to
access the Internet.
They can also host
web-based
applications.

Backbones

High-speed
communications links
used to enable Internet
communications across
a country and
internationally.

Static web page

A page on the web
server that is invariant.

publishing medium for displaying graphic and text information. This information is
stored on **web server** computers and then accessed by users who run **web browser** programs such as Microsoft Internet Explorer, Apple Safari or Mozilla Firefox which display
the information and allow users to select links to access other web sites.

Promoting web site addresses is important to marketing communications. The technical name for web addresses is **uniform or universal resource locators (URLs)**. URLs can be
thought of as a standard method of addressing similar to postal codes that make it
straightforward to find the name of a site.

Web addresses are structured in a standard way as follows:

http://www.domain-name.extension/filename.html

The domain name refers to the name of the web server and is usually selected to be
the same as the name of the company, and the extension will indicate its type. The
extension is also commonly known as the global top-level domain (gTLD). Note that
gTLDs are currently under discussion and there are proposals for adding new types such
as .store and .firm.

Common gTLDs are:

- **.com** represents an international or American company such as <u>www.travelocity.com</u>.
- **.co.uk** represents a company based in the UK such as <u>www.thomascook.co.uk</u>.
- **.ac.uk** is a UK-based university (e.g.<u>www.derby.ac.uk</u>).
- **.org.uk** and **.org** are not-for-profit organisations (e.g. <u>www.greenpeace.org</u>).
- **.net** is a network provider such as <u>www.demon.net</u>.

The 'filename.html' part of the web address refers to an individual web page, for example 'products.html' for a web page summarising a company's products. When a web
address is typed in without a filename, for example <u>www.bt.com</u>, the browser automatically assumes the user is looking for the home page, which by convention is referred to as
index.html. When creating sites, it is therefore vital to name the home page index.html
(or an equivalent). The file index.html can also be placed in sub-directories to ease access
to information. For example, to access a support page a customer would type
<u>www.bt.com/support</u> rather than <u>www.bt.com/support/index.htm</u>. In offline communica-
tions sub-directories are publicised as part of a company's URL strategy (see Chapter 8).

How does the Internet work?

The Internet enables communication between millions of connected computers worldwide. Information is transmitted from client PCs whose users request services from
server computers that hold information and host business applications that deliver the
services in response to requests. Thus, the Internet is a large-scale **client–server** system.
The client PCs within homes and businesses are connected to the Internet via local
Internet service providers (ISPs) which, in turn, are linked to larger ISPs with connection
to the major national and international infrastructure or **backbones**.

Infrastructure components of the Internet

Figure 1.14 shows the process by which web browsers communicate with web servers. A
request from the client PC is executed when the user types in a web address, clicks on a
hyperlink or fills in an online form such as a search. This request is then sent to the ISP
and routed across the Internet to the destination server. The server then returns the
requested web page if it is a **static (fixed) web page**, or if it requires reference to a database,

such as a request for product information, it will pass the query on to a database server and will then return this to the customer as a dynamically created web page. Information on all file requests such as images and pages is stored in a transaction log file which records the page requested, the time it was made and the source of the enquiry. This information can be analysed using a log file analyser along with different browser-based web analytics techniques to assess the success of the web site as explained in Chapter 9.

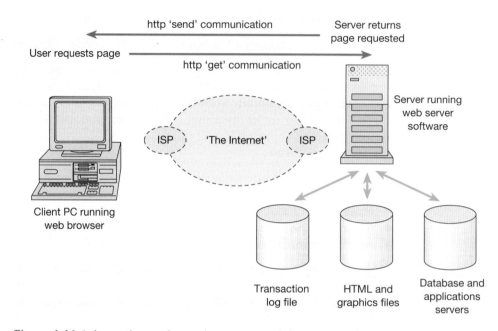

Figure 1.14 Information exchange between a web browser and a web server

Web page standards

The information, graphics and interactive elements that make up the web pages of a site are collectively referred to as content. Different standards exist for text, graphics and multimedia. The saying 'content is king' is still applied to the World Wide Web, since the content quality will determine the experience of the customer and whether they will return to that web site in the future.

Text information – HTML (Hypertext Markup Language)

Web page text has many of the formatting options available in a word processor. These include applying fonts, emphasis (bold, italic, underline) and placing information in tables. Formatting is possible since the web browser applies these formats according to instructions that are contained in the file that makes up the web page. This is usually written in HTML or Hypertext Markup Language. HTML is an international standard established by the World Wide Web Consortium (published at **www.w3.org**) and intended to ensure that any web page written according to the definitions in the standard will appear the same in any web browser.

A simple example of HTML is given for a simplified home page for a B2B company in Figure 1.15. The HTML code used to construct pages has codes or instruction tags such as <TITLE> to indicate to the browser what is displayed. The <TITLE> tag indicates what appears at the top of the web browser window. Each starting tag has a corresponding end tag, usually marked by a '/', for example <B>plastics</B> to embolden 'plastics'.

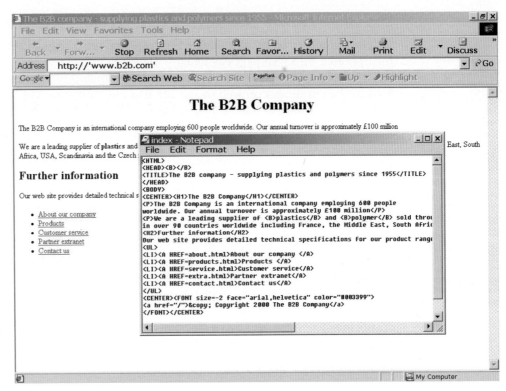

Figure 1.15 Home page index.html for The B2B Company in a web browser showing HTML source in text editor

Text information and data – XML (Extensible Markup Language)

When the early version of HTML was designed by Tim Berners-Lee at CERN, he based it on the existing standard for representation of documents. This standard was SGML, the Standard Generalised Markup Language which was ratified by the ISO in 1986. SGML uses tags to identify the different elements of a document such as title and chapters. HTML used a similar approach, for example the tag for title is <TITLE>. While HTML proved powerful in providing a standard method of displaying information that was easy to learn, it was purely presentational. It lacked the ability to describe the data on web pages. A metadata language providing data about data contained within pages would be much more powerful. These weaknesses have been acknowledged, and in an effort coordinated by the World Wide Web Consortium, the first XML or eXtensible Markup Language was produced in February 1998. This is also based on SGML. The key word describing XML is 'extensible'. This means that new markup tags can be created that facilitate the searching and exchange of information. For example, product information on a web page could use the XML tags <NAME>, <DESCRIPTION>, <COLOUR> and <PRICE>. The tags can effectively act as a standard set of database field descriptions so that data can be exchanged through B2B exchanges.

The importance of XML for data integration is indicated by its incorporation by Microsoft into its BizTalk server for B2B integration and the creation of the ebXML (electronic business XML) standard by their rival Sun Microsystems.

Metadata
Literally, data about data – a format describing the structure and content of data.

XML or eXtensible Markup Language
A standard for transferring structured data, unlike HTML which is purely presentational.

29

Graphical images (GIF, JPEG and PNG files)

Graphics produced by graphic designers or captured using digital cameras can be readily incorporated into web pages as images. GIF (Graphics Interchange Format) and JPEG (Joint Photographics Experts Group) refer to two standard file formats most commonly used to present images on web pages. GIF files are limited to 256 colours and are best used for small simple graphics, such as banner adverts, while JPEG is best used for larger images where image quality is important, such as photographs. Both formats use image compression technology to minimise the size of downloaded files. Portable Network Graphics is a patent and licence-free standard file format approved by the World Wide Web Consortium to replace the GIF file format.

Animated graphical information (GIFs and plug-ins)

GIF files can also be used for interactive banner adverts. Plug-ins are additional programs, sometimes referred to as 'helper applications', and work in association with the web browser to provide features not present in the basic web browser. The best-known plug-ins are probably that for Adobe Acrobat which is used to display documents in .pdf format (**www.adobe.com**) and the Macromedia Flash and Shockwave products for producing interactive graphics (**www.macromedia.com**).

Audio and video standards

Traditionally sound and video or 'rich media' have been stored as the Microsoft standards .WMA and .AVI. Alternative standards are MP3 and MPEG. These formats are used on some web sites, but they are less appropriate for sites such as that of the BBC (**www.bbc.co.uk**), since the user would have to wait for the whole clip to download before hearing or viewing it. Streaming media are now used for many multimedia sites since they enable video or audio to start playing within a few seconds – it is not necessary for the whole file to be downloaded before it can be played. Formats for streaming media have been established by Real Networks (**www.realnetworks.com**).

Internet-access software applications

Over its lifetime, many tools have been developed to help find, send and receive information across the Internet. Web browsers used to access the World Wide Web are the latest of these applications. These tools are summarised in Table 1.3. In this section we will briefly discuss the relevance of some of the more commonly used tools to the modern organisation. The other tools have either been superseded by the use of the World Wide Web or are of less relevance from a business perspective.

The application of the Internet for marketing in this book concentrates on the use of e-mail and the World Wide Web since these tools are now most commonly used by businesses for digital marketing. Many of the other tools such as IRC and newsgroups, which formerly needed special software to access them, are now available from the WWW.

Web 2.0

Since 2004, the Web 2.0 concept has increased in prominence amongst web site owners and developers. The main technologies and principles of Web 2.0 have been explained in an influential article by Tim O'Reilly (O'Reilly, 2005). It is important to realise that Web 2.0 isn't a new web standard or a 'paradigm shift' as the name implies, rather it's an

Table 1.3 Applications of different Internet tools

Internet tool	Summary
Electronic mail or e-mail	Sending messages or documents, such as news about a new product or sales promotion between individuals
Internet Relay Chat (IRC), Instant Messaging (IM)	These are synchronous communications tools for text-based 'chat' between different users who are logged on at the same time. IM from providers such as AOL, Yahoo! and MSN has largely replaced IRC and provides opportunities for advertising to users
Usenet newsgroups	Forums to discuss a particular topic such as a sport, hobby or business area. Traditionally accessed by special newsreader software, but can now be accessed via a web browser from www.deja.com (now part of Google – www.google.com)
FTP file transfer	The File Transfer Protocol is used as a standard for moving files across the Internet. FTP is still used for marketing applications such as downloading files such as product price lists or specifications. Also used to upload HTML files to web servers
Gophers, Archie and WAIS	These tools were important before the advent of the web for storing and searching documents on the Internet. They have largely been superseded by the web which provides better searching and more sophisticated document publishing
Telnet	This allows remote access to computer systems. For example, a retailer could check to see whether an item was in stock in a warehouse using a telnet application
Blogs	Web-based publishing of regularly updated information in an online diary type format using tools such as Blogger.com or Typepad
Really Simple Syndication (RSS)	An XML-based content distribution format commonly used for accessing blog information
Podcasting	A method of downloading and playing audio or visual clips for portable devices such as the iPod or MP3 players or fixed devices
World Wide Web	Widely used for publishing information and running business applications over the Internet, accessed through browsers such as Internet Explorer, Firefox, Safari and Opera

evolution of technologies and communications approaches which have grown in importance since 2004–5. The main characteristics of Web 2.0 are that it typically involves:

● Web services or interactive applications hosted on the web such as Flickr (www.flickr.com), Google Maps™ (http://maps.google.com) or blogging services such as Blogger.com or Typepad (www.typepad.com);

● Supporting participation – many of the applications are based on altruistic principles of community participation;

● Encouraging creation of user-generated content – blogs are the best example of this. Another example is the collaborative encyclopedia Wikipedia (www.wikipedia.com);

● Enabling rating of content and online services – services such as delicious (http://del.icio.us) and traceback comments on blogs support this. These services are useful given the millions of blogs that are available – rating and tagging (categorising) content help indicate the relevance and quality of the content;

● Ad funding of neutral sites – web services such as Google Mail/GMail™ and many blogs are based on contextual advertising such as Google Adsense™ or Overture/Yahoo! Content Match;

● Data exchange between sites through XML-based data standards. RSS is based on XML, but has relatively little semantic markup to describe the content. An attempt by Google to facilitate this which illustrates the principle of structured information exchange and searching is Google Base™ (http://base.google.com). This allows users to upload data about particular services such as training courses in a standardised format based on XML. New classes of content can also be defined;

● Rapid application development using interactive technology approaches known as 'Ajax' (Asynchronous JavaScript and XML). The best-known Ajax implementation is Google Maps which is responsive since it does not require refreshes to display maps.

From the Internet to intranets and extranets

Intranet

A network within a single company that enables access to company information using the familiar tools of the Internet such as email and web browsers. Only staff within the company can access the intranet, which will be password-protected.

Extranet

Formed by extending the intranet beyond a company to customers, suppliers, collaborators or even competitors. This is again password-protected to prevent access by general Internet users.

'Intranet' and 'extranet' are two terms that arose in the 1990s to describe applications of Internet technology with specific audiences rather than anyone with access to the Internet. Access to an **intranet** is limited by username and password to company staff, while an **extranet** can only be accessed by authorised third parties such as registered customers, suppliers and distributors. This relationship between the Internet, intranets and extranets is indicated by Figure 1.16. It can be seen that an intranet is effectively a private-company Internet with access available to staff only. An extranet permits access to trusted third parties, and the Internet provides global access.

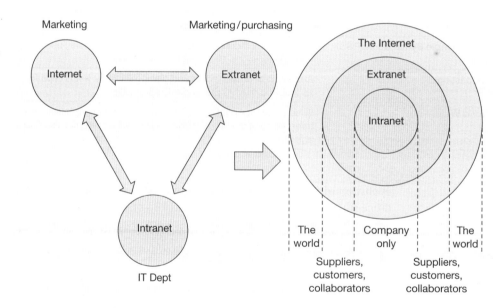

Figure 1.16 The relationship between access to intranets, extranets and the Internet

Extranets provide exciting opportunities to communicate with major customers since tailored information such as special promotions, electronic catalogues and order histories can be provided on a web page personalised for each customer. As well as using the Internet to communicate with customers, companies find that internal use of an intranet or use of an extranet facilitates communication and control between staff, suppliers and distributors. Second, the Internet, intranet and extranet can be applied at different levels of management within a company. Table 1.4 illustrates potential marketing applications of both Internet and intranet for supporting marketing at different levels of managerial decision making. Vlosky et al. (2000) examine in more detail how extranets impact business practices and relationships.

Table 1.4 Opportunities for using the Internet, extranets and intranets to support marketing functions

Level of management	Internet	Intranet and extranet
Strategic	Environmental scanning Competitor analysis Market analysis Customer analysis Strategic decision making Supply chain management	Internal data analysis Management information Marketing information Database Operations efficiency Business planning Monitoring and control Simulations Business intelligence (data warehouses)
Tactical and operational	Advertising/promotions Direct marketing Public relations Distribution/logistics Workgroups Marketing research Publishing	Electronic mail Data warehousing Relationship marketing Conferencing Training Technology information Product/service information Customer service Internet trading Sponsorship

To conclude this chapter, read Case Study 1 for the background on the success factors which have helped build one of the biggest online brands.

Case Study 1　eBay thrives in the global marketplace

Context

It's hard to believe that one of the most celebrated dot-coms has now celebrated its tenth birthday. Pierre Omidyar, a 28 year old French-born software engineer living in California coded the site while working for another company, eventually launching the site for business on Monday, 4 September, 1995 with the more direct name 'Auction Web'. Legend reports that the site attracted no visitors in its first 24 hours. The site became eBay in 1997 and site activity is rather different today; peak traffic in 2004 was 890 million page views per day and 7.7 gigabits of outbound data traffic per second. At the end of 2005, if eBay was a country it would be the 9th largest with its 157 million 'eBayers'.

Mission

eBay describes their purpose as to 'pioneer new communities around the world built on commerce, sustained by trust, and inspired by opportunity'.

At the time of writing eBay comprises three major businesses:

1 *The eBay Marketplace.* The mission for the core eBay business is to 'create the world's online marketplace'. eBay's SEC filing notes some of the success factors for this business for which eBay seeks to manage the functionality, safety, ease-of-use and reliability of the trading platform.
2 *PayPal.* The mission is to 'create the new global standard for online payments'. This company was acquired in 2003.
3 *Skype Internet telephony.* This company was acquired in 2005.

This case focuses on the best known, the eBay Marketplace.

Revenue model

The vast majority of eBay's revenue is for the listing and commission on completed sales. For PayPal purchases an additional commission fee is charged. Margin on each transaction is phenomenal since once the infrastructure is built, incremental costs on each transaction are tiny – all eBay is doing is transmitting bits and bytes between buyers and sellers.

Advertising and other non-transaction net revenues represent a relatively small proportion of total net revenues and the strategy is that this should remain the case. Advertising and other net revenues totalled $94.3 million in 2004 (just 3% of net revenue).

Proposition

The eBay marketplace is well known for its core service which enables sellers to list items for sale on an auction or fixed-price basis giving buyers the opportunity to bid for and purchase items of interest.

Software tools are provided, particularly for frequent traders including Turbo Lister, Seller's Assistant, Selling Manager and Selling Manager Pro, which help automate the selling process; the Shipping Calculator, Reporting tools, etc. Today over sixty per cent of listings are facilitated by software, showing the value of automating posting for frequent trading.

Fraud is a significant risk factor for eBay. BBC (2005) reported that around 1 in 10,000 transactions within the UK were fraudulent. 0.0001% is a small percentage, but scaling this up across the number of transactions, this is a significant volume.

eBay has developed 'Trust and Safety Programs' which are particularly important to reassure customers since online services are prone to fraud. For example, the eBay feedback forum can help establish credentials of sellers and buyers. There is also a Safe Harbor data protection method and a standard purchase protection system.

According to the SEC filing, eBay summarises the core messages to define its proposition as follows:

For buyers:

- Selection
- Value
- Convenience
- Entertainment

For sellers:

- Access to broad markets
- Efficient marketing and distribution costs
- Ability to maximise prices
- Opportunity to increase sales

Competition

Although there are now few direct competitors of online auction services in many countries, there are many indirect competitors. SEC (2005) describes competing channels as including online and offline retailers, distributors, liquidators, import and export companies, auctioneers, catalog and mail-order companies, classifieds, directories, search engines, products of search engines, virtually all online and offline commerce participants (consumer-to-consumer, business-to-consumer and business-to-business) and online and offline shopping channels and networks.

BBC (2005) reports that eBay are not complacent about competition. It has already pulled out of Japan due to competition from Yahoo! and within Asia and China is also facing tough competition by Yahoo! which has a portal with a broader range of services more likely to attract subscribers.

Before the advent of online auctions, competitors in the collectibles space included antique shops, car boot sales and charity shops. Anecdotal evidence suggests that all of these are now suffering at the hands of eBay. Some have taken the attitude of 'if you can't beat 'em, join 'em'. Many smaller traders who have previously run antique or car boot sales are now eBayers. Even charities such as Oxfam now have an eBay service where they sell high-value items contributed by donors. Other retailers such as Vodafone have used eBay as a means to distribute certain products within their range.

Objectives and strategy

The overall eBay aims are to increase the gross merchandise volume and net revenues from the eBay Marketplace. More detailed objectives are defined to achieve these aims, with strategies focusing on:

1 *Acquisition* – increasing the number of newly registered users on the eBay Marketplace.
2 *Activation* – increasing the number of registered users that become active bidders, buyers or sellers on the eBay Marketplace.
3 *Activity* – increasing the volume and value of transactions that are conducted by each active user on the eBay Marketplace

The focus on each of these 3 areas will vary according to strategic priorities in particular local markets.

eBay Marketplace growth is also driven by defining approaches to improve performance in these areas. First, category growth is achieved by increasing the number and size of categories within the marketplace, for example: Antiques, Art, Books and Business & Industrial. Second, formats for interaction. The traditional format is auction listings, but it has been refined now to include the 'Buy-It-Now' fixed price format. Another format is the 'Dutch Auction' format, where a seller can sell multiple identical items to the highest bidders. eBay Stores was developed to enable sellers with a wider range of products to showcase their products in a more traditional retail format. eBay say they are constantly exploring new formats for example through the acquisition in 2004 of mobile.de in Germany and Marktplaats.nl in the Netherlands, as well as investment in craigslist, the US-based classified ad format. Another acquisition is Rent.com, which enables expansion into the online housing and apartment rental category. Finally marketplace growth is achieved through delivering specific sites localised for different geographies as follows. You can see there is still potential for greater localisation, for example in parts of Scandinavia, Eastern Europe and Asia.

Localised eBay marketplaces:

- Australia
- Austria
- Belgium
- Canada
- China
- France
- Germany
- Hong Kong
- India
- Ireland
- Italy
- Malaysia
- The Netherlands
- New Zealand
- The Philippines
- Singapore
- South Korea
- Spain
- Sweden
- Switzerland
- Taiwan
- United Kingdom
- United States

In its SEC filing, success factors eBay believes are important to enable it to compete in its market include:

- ability to attract buyers and sellers;
- volume of transactions and price and selection of goods;

- customer service; and
- brand recognition.

It also notes that for its competitors, other factors it believes are important are:

- community cohesion, interaction and size;
- system reliability;
- reliability of delivery and payment;
- web site convenience and accessibility;
- level of service fees; and
- quality of search tools.

This implies that eBay believes it has optimised these factors, but its competitors still have opportunities for improving performance in these areas which will make the market more competitive.

Risk management

The SEC filing lists the risks and challenges of conducting business internationally as follows:

- regulatory requirements, including regulation of auctioneering, professional selling, distance selling, banking, and money transmitting;

Consolidated Statement of Income Data		Year Ended December 31				
	2000	2001	2002	2003	2004
	(In thousands, except per share amounts)				
Net revenues	$ 431,424	$ 748,821	$ 1,214,100	$ 2,165,096	$ 3,271,309
Cost of net revenues	95,453	134,816	213,876	416,058	614,415
Gross profit	335,971	614,005	1,000,224	1,749,038	2,656,894
Operating expenses:					
Sales and marketing	166,767	253,474	349,650	567,565	857,874
Product development	55,863	75,288	104,636	159,315	240,647
General and administrative	73,027	105,784	171,785	302,703	415,725
Patent litigation expense	–	–	–	29,965	–
Payroll tax on employee stock options	2,337	2,442	4,015	9,590	17,479
Amortisation of acquired intangible assets	1,433	36,591	15,941	50,659	65,927
Merger related costs	1,550	–	–	–	–
Total operating expenses	300,977	473,579	646,027	1,119,797	1,597,652
Income from operations	34,994	140,426	354,197	629,241	1,059,242
Interest and other income, net	46,337	41,613	49,209	37,803	77,867
Interest expense	(3,374)	(2,851)	(1,492)	(4,314)	(8,879)
Impairment of certain equity investments	–	(16,245)	(3,781)	(1,230)	–
Income before cumulative effect of accounting change, income taxes and minority interests	77,957	162,943	398,133	661,500	1,128,230
Provision for income taxes	(32,725)	(80,009)	(145,946)	(206,738)	(343,885)
Minority interests	3,062	7,514	(2,296)	(7,578)	(6,122)
Income before cumulative effect of accounting change	48,294	90,448	249,891	447,184	778,223
Cumulative effect of accounting change, net of tax	–	–	–	(5,413)	–
Net income	$ 48,294	$ 90,448	$ 249,891	$ 441,771	$ 778,223

Supplemental Operating Data

	2000	2001	2002	2003	2004
			(In millions)		
U.S. and International Marketplace Segments:					
Confirmed registered users	22.5	42.4	61.7	94.9	135.5
Active users	–	17.8	27.7	41.2	56.1
Number of non-stores listings	264.7	419.1	629.7	955.0	1,339.9
Number of stores listings	–	4.0	8.6	16.0	72.7
Gross merchandise volume	$ 5,422	$ 9,319	$ 14,868	$ 23,779	$ 34,168

Sources: BBC (2005), SEC (2005)

- legal uncertainty regarding liability for the listings and other content provided by users, including uncertainty as a result of less Internet-friendly legal systems, unique local laws, and lack of clear precedent or applicable law;
- difficulties in integrating with local payment providers, including banks, credit and debit card associations, and electronic fund transfer systems;
- differing levels of retail distribution, shipping, and communications infrastructures;
- different employee/employer relationships and the existence of workers' councils and labour unions;
- difficulties in staffing and managing foreign operations;
- longer payment cycles, different accounting practices, and greater problems in collecting accounts receivable;
- potentially adverse tax consequences, including local taxation of fees or of transactions on web sites;
- higher telecommunications and Internet service provider costs;
- strong local competitors;
- different and more stringent consumer protection, data protection and other laws;
- cultural ambivalence towards, or non-acceptance of, online trading;
- seasonal reductions in business activity;
- expenses associated with localising products, including offering customers the ability to transact business in the local currency;

- laws and business practices that favour local competitors or prohibit foreign ownership of certain businesses;
- profit repatriation restrictions, foreign currency exchange restrictions, and exchange rate fluctuations;
- volatility in a specific country's or region's political or economic conditions; and
- differing intellectual property laws and taxation laws.

Results

eBay's community of confirmed registered users has grown from around two million at the end of 1998 to more than 94 million at the end of 2003 and to more than 135 million at December 31, 2004. It is also useful to identify active users who contribute revenue to the business as a buyer or seller. eBay had 56 million active users at the end of 2004 who they define as any user who has bid, bought, or listed an item during a prior 12-month period.

Financial results are presented in the tables on p. 35 and above.

Question

Assess how the characteristics of the digital media and the Internet together with strategic decisions taken by its management team have supported eBay's continued growth.

Summary

1 Internet marketing refers to the use of Internet technologies, combined with traditional media, to achieve marketing objectives. E-marketing and digital marketing have a broader perspective and imply the use of other technologies such as databases and approaches such as customer relationship management (e-CRM).

2 A customer-centric approach to digital marketing considers the needs of a range of customers using techniques such as persona and customer scenarios (Chapter 2) to understand customer needs in a multi-channel buying process. Tailoring to individual customers may be practical using personalisation techniques.

3 Electronic commerce refers to both electronically mediated financial and informational transactions.

4 Sell-side e-commerce involves all electronic business transactions between an organisation and its customers, while buy-side e-commerce involves transactions between an organisation and its suppliers.

5 'Electronic business' is a broader term referring to how technology can benefit all internal business processes and interactions with third parties. This includes buy-side and sell-side e-commerce and the internal value chain.

6 E-commerce transactions include business-to-business (B2B), business-to-consumer (B2C), consumer-to-consumer (C2C) and consumer-to-business (C2B) transactions.

7 The Internet is used to develop existing markets through enabling an additional communications and/or sales channel with potential customers. It can be used to develop new international markets with a reduced need for new sales offices and agents. Companies can provide new services and possibly products using the Internet.

8 The Internet can support the full range of marketing functions and in doing so can help reduce costs, facilitate communication within and between organisations and improve customer service.

9 Interaction with customers, suppliers and distributors occurs across the Internet. The web and e-mail are particularly powerful if they can be used to create *relevant, personalised communications*. These communications are also interactive. If access is restricted to favoured third parties this is known as an *extranet*. If Internet technologies are used to facilitate internal company communications this is known as an *intranet* – a private company internet.

10 The marketing benefits the Internet confers are advantageous both to the large corporation and to the small or medium-sized enterprise. These include:

- a new medium for advertising and PR;
- a new channel for distributing products;
- opportunities for expansion into new markets;
- new ways of enhancing customer service;
- new ways of reducing costs by reducing the number of staff in order fulfilment.

Exercises

Self-assessment exercises

1 Which measures can companies use to assess the significance of the Internet to their organisation?

2 Why did companies only start to use the Internet widely for marketing in the 1990s, given that it had been in existence for over thirty years?

3 Distinguish between Internet marketing and e-marketing.

4 Explain what is meant by electronic commerce and electronic business. How do they relate to the marketing function?

5 What are the main differences and similarities between the Internet, intranets and extranets?

6 Summarise the differences between the Internet and traditional media using the six Is.

7 How is the Internet used to develop new markets and penetrate existing markets? What types of new products can be delivered by the Internet?

Essay and discussion questions

1 The Internet is primarily thought of as a means of advertising and selling products. What are the opportunities for use of the Internet in other marketing functions?

2 'The World Wide Web represents a *pull* medium for marketing rather than a *push* medium.' Discuss.

3 You are a newly installed marketing manager in a company selling products in the business-to-business sector. Currently, the company has only a limited web site containing electronic versions of its brochures. You want to convince the directors of the benefits of investing in the web site to provide more benefits to the company. How would you present your case?

4 Explain the main benefits that a company selling fast-moving consumer goods could derive by creating a web site.

Examination questions

1 Contrast electronic commerce to electronic business.

2 Internet technology is used by companies in three main contexts. Distinguish between the following types and explain their significance to marketers.

   (a) intranet
   (b) extranet
   (c) Internet.

3 An Internet marketing manager must seek to control and accommodate all the main methods by which consumers may visit a company web site. Describe these methods.

4 Imagine you are explaining the difference between the World Wide Web and the Internet to a marketing manager. How would you explain these two terms?

5 What is the relevance of 'conversion marketing' to the Internet?

6 Explain how the Internet can be used to increase market penetration in existing markets and develop new markets.

References

Ansoff, H. (1957) Strategies for diversification, *Harvard Business Review*, September–October, 113–24.

BBC (2005) eBay's 10-year rise to world fame. Robert Plummer story from BBC News, 2 September. **http://news.bbc.co.uk/go/pr/fr/-/1/hi/business/4207510.stm**. Published: 2005/09/02.

Business Week (2005) The Power of Us. Mass collaboration on the Internet is shaking up business. Feature, June 20, 2005. http://www.businessweek.com/magazine/content/05_25/63938601.htm

Chaffey, D. (2006) *E-Business and E-Commerce Management*, 3rd edn. Financial Times/Prentice Hall, Harlow.

Deighton, J. (1996) The future of interactive marketing, *Harvard Business Review*, November–December, 151–62.

Dibb, S., Simkin, S., Pride, W. and Ferrell, O. (2001) *Marketing. Concepts and Strategies*, 4th European edn. Houghton Mifflin, New York. *See* Chapter 1, An overview of the marketing concept.

Economist (2000) E-commerce survey. Define and sell, pp. 6–12. *Economist supplement*, 26 February.

EIAA (2005) European Advertising Association. European media research, October 2004. Research conducted by Millward Brown. Published at **www.eiaa.net** in 2005.

Hoffman, D.L. and Novak, T.P. (1996) Marketing in hypermedia computer-mediated environments: conceptual foundations, *Journal of Marketing*, 60 (July), 50–68.

IAB (2005) Internet Advertising Bureau. Bi-annual advertising spend study conducted with PricewaterhouseCoopers. Published at **www.iabuk.net**.

Kiani, G. (1998) Marketing opportunities in the digital world, *Internet Research: Electronic Networking Applications and Policy*, 8(2), 185–94.

McDonald, M. and Wilson, H. (1999) *E-Marketing: Improving Marketing Effectiveness in a Digital World*. Financial Times/Prentice Hall, Harlow.

O'Reilly, T. (2005) What Is Web 2? Design Patterns and Business Models for the Next Generation of Software. Web article, 30 September. O'Reilly Publishing, Sebastopol, CA.

SEC (2005) United States Securities and Exchange Commission submission Form 10-K. eBay submission for the fiscal year ended December 31, 2004.

Seybold, P. (1999) *Customers.com*. Century Business Books, Random House, London.

Smith, P.R. and Chaffey, D. (2005) *E-Marketing Excellence – at the Heart of EBusiness*, 2nd edn. Butterworth Heinemann, Oxford.

Svennivig, M. (2004) The interactive viewer: reality or myth? *Interactive Marketing*, 6(2), 151–64.

Vlosky, R., Fontenot, R. and Blalock, L. (2000) Extranets: impacts on business relationships, *Journal of Business and Industrial Marketing*, 15(6), 438–57.

Further reading

Deighton, J. (1996) The future of interactive marketing, *Harvard Business Review*, November–December, 151–62. One of the earliest articles to elucidate the significance of the Internet for marketers. Readable.

Hoffman, D.L. and Novak, T.P. (1997) A new marketing paradigm for electronic commerce, *The Information Society*, Special issue on electronic commerce, 13 (Jan.–Mar.), 43–54. This was the seminal paper on Internet marketing when it was published, and is still essential reading for its discussion of concepts. Available online at Vanderbilt University (**http://ecommerce.vanderbilt.edu/papers.html**).

Smith, P.R. and Chaffey, D. (2005) *E-Marketing Excellence: at the Heart of EBusiness*, 2nd edn. Butterworth Heinemann, Oxford. Chapter 1 gives more details on the benefits of Internet marketing.

Web links

- **ClickZ Experts** (www.clickz.com/experts). An excellent collection of articles on online marketing communications. US-focused.
- **ClickZ Stats** (www.clickz.com/stats). The definitive source of news on Internet developments, and reports on company and consumer adoption of Internet and characteristics in Europe and worldwide. A searchable digest of most analyst reports.
- **DaveChaffey.com** (www.davechaffey.com). A blog containing updates and articles on all aspects of digital marketing structured according to the chapters in Dave Chaffey's books.
- **Direct Marketing Association UK** (www.dma.org.uk). Source of up-to-date data protection advice and how-to guides about online direct marketing.
- **E-consultancy.com** (www.e-consultancy.com). UK-focused portal with extensive supplier directory, best-practice white papers and forum.
- **eMarketer** (www.emarketer.com). Includes reports on media spend based on compilations of other analysts. Fee-based service.
- **Interactive Advertising Bureau** (www.iab.net). Best practice on interactive advertising. See also www.iabuk.net.
- **Marketing Sherpa** (www.marketingsherpa.com). Case studies and news about online marketing.
- **Netimperative** (www.netimperative.com). News from the UK new media industry.

Print media

- **New Media Age** (www.newmediazero.com/nma). A weekly magazine reporting on the UK new media interest. Full content available online.
- **Revolution magazine** (www.revolutionmagazine.com). A monthly magazine on UK new media applications and approaches. Partial content available online.
- **Sloan Center for Internet Retailing** (http://ecommerce.vanderbilt.edu). Originally founded in 1994 as Project 2000 by Tom Novak and Donna Hoffman at School of Management, Vanderbilt University, to study marketing implications of the Internet. Useful links papers.
- **University of Strathclyde**, Department of Marketing, Marketing Resource Gateway (MRG) (www.marketing.strath.ac.uk/dcd/). A comprehensive directory of marketing-related links.

2

The Internet micro-environment

Learning objectives

After reading this chapter, the reader should be able to:

● Identify the different elements of the Internet environment that impact on an organisation's Internet marketing strategy

● Assess competitor, customer and intermediary use of the Internet

● Evaluate the relevance of changes in trading patterns and business models enabled by e-commerce

Questions for marketers

Key questions for marketing managers related to this chapter are:

● How are the competitive forces and value chain changed by the Internet?

● How do I assess the demand for Internet services from customers?

● How do I compare our online marketing with that of competitors?

● What is the relevance of the new intermediaries?

Links to other chapters

This chapter, together with the following one, provides a foundation for later chapters on Internet marketing strategy and implementation:

➤ Chapter 3, The Internet macro-environment complements this chapter

➤ Chapter 4, Internet marketing strategy explains how environment analysis is used as part of strategy development

➤ Chapter 5, The Internet and the marketing mix considers the role of 'Place' in the online marketing mix

Introduction

All organisations operate within an environment that influences the way in which they conduct business. Organisations that monitor, understand and respond appropriately to changes in the environment have the greatest opportunities to compete effectively in the competitive marketplace. Understanding an organisation's environment is a key part of situation analysis for the Internet marketing strategy development process introduced in Figure 1.9 and covered further in Chapter 4. There is also the need for a process to continually monitor the environment which is often referred to as environmental scanning.

In the next two chapters we look specifically at how organisations can assess and understand changes to the digital environment they operate in. The need to 'sense and respond' is particularly important for online marketers because of the rapid changes in customer behaviour we introduced in the first chapter. Let's look at two more examples of rapidly changing behaviour. First, complete Activity 2.1 to see how online media sites have increased in popularity over the past five years. An example of the changes is indicated by Figure 2.1 which shows the increasing number of visitors to Handbag.com over the last 10 years. Marketers at client organisations or their agencies who aren't aware of these changes in media consumption are missing an opportunity not only to advertise to these audiences, but also to interact with them by engaging them in polls or quizzes or games on microsites or destination sites, yet many of the marketers and their agencies continue with the status quo.

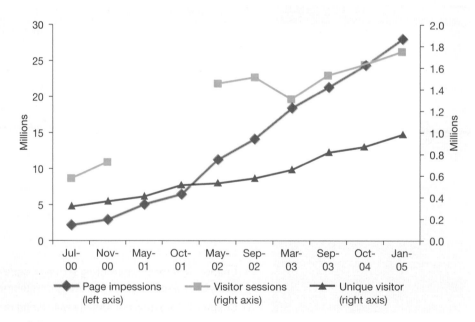

Figure 2.1 Increase in traffic volume at Handbag.com in selected months when audited. Page impressions are pages served to visitors, visitor sessions are visits up to a maximum of 30 minutes and unique visitors is the number of individuals visiting the site in a given month

Source: Compiled from ABC Electronic (www.abce.org.uk)

Reviewing the increase in popularity of online media sites

Purpose

To apply a tool to analyse the popularity of online media sites. The ABCe audit service is completed to prove the popularity of online sites to advertisers purchasing ad space on the site. It is the online equivalent of the audited bureau of circulation for magazines.

Activity

Visit the ABCe site and choose 'Database'. Select a media site that you might visit and plot its changes in visitors over the last 2 to 5 years. Visit the site to see how advertisers use the site to promote their products and interact with consumers.

In the second example of changing behaviour within the environment, we look at achieving sales rather than awareness. Look at Figure 2.2 which shows the index of online sales in the UK compared to an index of 100 in April 2000. Between April 2000 and June 2005, retail sales increased 17-fold! Masked within this general increase will be large variations in online sales figures for different companies according to the type of product and the Internet marketing capabilities developed in organisations during this period. It is important for companies to evaluate their relative performance in their market – an individual company's online sales may have increased by 20% in a period, which sounds positive, but it is not when compared to a competitor whose sales have increased by 100% in the same period.

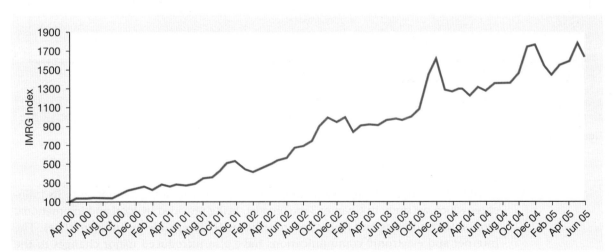

Figure 2.2 The IMRG retail index shows online sales volume in the UK relative to 100 in April 2000
Source: Interactive Media in Retail Group (www.imrg.org)

Different environment components

The Internet introduces new facets to the environment that must be considered by marketers since strategy development is strongly influenced by considering the environment the business operates in. Figure 2.3 illustrates the key elements of a business's environment that will influence the organisation. Many authors such as Porter (1980) on corporate strategy or Kotler et al. (2001) on marketing strategy make the distinction between

Micro-environment

Specific forces on an organisation generated by its stakeholders.

Macro-environment

Broader forces affecting all organisations in the marketplace including social, technological, economic, political and legal aspects.

micro-environment and macro-environment. The micro-environment, sometimes known as 'the operating environment' is the immediate marketplace of an organisation. For development of Internet marketing strategy, the most significant influences are arguably those of the micro-environment. This is shaped by the needs of customers and how services are provided to them through the competitors, intermediaries and upstream suppliers within the marketplace. The Internet and electronic communications have major implications for organisations and these must inform their Internet marketing strategy. We consider the changes to the micro-environment and their implications in this chapter.

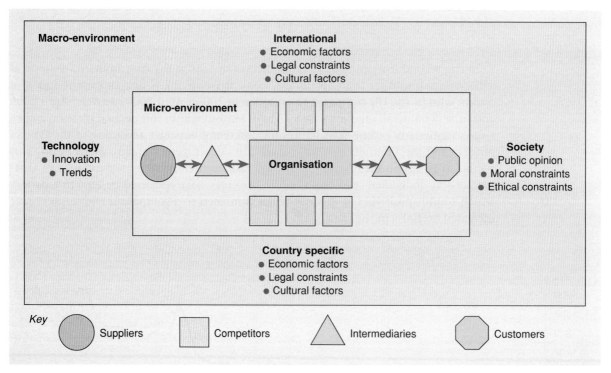

Figure 2.3 The Internet marketing environment

The macro-environment is sometimes known as 'the remote environment'; its influences which we study in Chapter 3 are broader, being provided by local and international economic conditions and legislation together with acceptable business practices. The Internet and electronic communications have also introduced major changes to the macro-environment. Reviewing the relevance of technological innovations to an organisation is vital in providing opportunities for superior services to competitors and to changing the shape of the marketplace. Another significant macro-environment influence is legal, specific laws have been enacted to control online marketing and of course the influence of new technologies.

In the current chapter, the impact of the Internet on the different elements of the micro-environment illustrated in Table 2.1 will be reviewed in turn. In the next chapter we then review the constraints and opportunities of the Internet macro-environment. For each of these elements we will highlight the issues that a marketing or Internet marketing manager needs to consider when developing e-marketing plans.

Table 2.1 Factors in the macro- and micro-environment of an organisation and Internet-marketing-related issues

Micro-environment	Macro-environment
The marketplace: • Competitive forces • Value chain analysis • New channel structures • Location of trading • Commercial arrangements for transactions • New business and revenue models	*Social:* • Privacy • Acceptable usage • Internet culture
The organisation: • Adaptability to change	*Technological:* • Selecting new technologies • Coping with technological change
Its customers: • Access levels to the Internet • Propensity to use and buy • Buyer behaviour	*Economic:* • The current and future economic situation
Its suppliers: • Access levels to the Internet • Propensity to use • Integration with existing systems	*Political, legal, ethical and taxation:* • Legal and tax constraints • Government incentives • Internet governance
Its competitors: • Competitor capabilities	
Intermediaries: • New capabilities • New intermediaries	

Internal organisation characteristics and capabilities

A review of the suitability of the characteristics and capabilities of an organisation to make increased use of electronic communications should occur as part of developing Internet marketing plans. This is sometimes known as the 'internal environment' of the organisation. The role of internal audits to assess the organisation as part of situation analysis for strategy development is discussed further in Chapter 4 including the 7S framework which was developed by consultants at McKinsey at the start of the 1980s and which stands for Strategy, Structure, Systems, Style, Staff, Skills and Superordinate goals.

Marketplace

The operation of an organisation's marketplace comprises the interactions between all elements of the micro-environment. In this section we review the great range of changes that the Internet has brought to the marketplace. The issues we will review include:

- *Competitive forces*. How are the major external forces on an organisation affected by the Internet?
- *From value chain to value network*. The value network concept describes a more dynamic version of the value chain with increased interaction between partners.
- *New channel structures*. What changes can occur to linkages to upstream and downstream partners in the supply chain? What is the role of new intermediaries?
- *Location of trading*. What are the options for location of trading online?
- *Commercial arrangements for transactions*. How are these changed?
- *New business and revenue models*. What business and revenue models can be adopted in the Internet marketplace?

Competitive forces

Michael Porter's classic 1980 model of the five main competitive forces that impact a company still provides a pertinent framework for reviewing threats arising in the e-business era. We will use it here to introduce the different competitive forces arising from the interplay between the different stakeholders of the micro-environment, each of which will be explored in more depth later in the chapter. Table 2.2 summarises the main impacts of the Internet on the five competitive forces affecting an organisation. Note that, as seen later in this chapter and in Chapter 4, this form of analysis does not directly emphasise the importance of neutral intermediaries and strategic partnerships in affecting the visibility of an organisation within the online marketplace. Intermediaries such as search engines, price comparison sites and even blogs often have a strong influence on the balance between the bargaining power of buyers and suppliers and tend to intensify rivalry between existing competitors.

Table 2.2 Impact of the Internet on the five competitive forces

Five forces				
Bargaining power of buyers	**Bargaining power of suppliers**	**Threat of substitute products and services**	**Barriers to entry**	**Rivalry between existing competitors**
• The power of online buyers is increased since they have a wider choice and prices are likely to be forced down through increased customer knowledge and price transparency (see Chapter 5).	• When an organisation purchases, the bargaining power of its suppliers is reduced since there is wider choice and increased commoditisation due to e-procurement and e-marketplaces.	• Substitution is a significant threat since new digital products or extended products can be readily introduced.	• Barriers to entry are reduced, enabling new competitors, particularly for retailers or service organisations that have traditionally required a high-street presence or a mobile sales force.	• The Internet encourages commoditisation which makes it less easy to differentiate products.
• For a B2B organisation, forming electronic links with customers may deepen a relationship and it may increase switching costs, leading to 'soft lock-in'.	• The reverse arguments regarding bargaining power of buyers.	• The introduction of new substitute products and services should be carefully monitored to avoid erosion of market share.	• New entrants must be carefully monitored to avoid erosion of market share.	• Rivalry becomes more intense as product lifecycles decrease and lead times for new product development decrease.
		• Internet technology enables faster introduction of products and services.	• Internet services are easier to imitate than traditional services, making it easy for 'fast followers'.	• The Internet facilitates the move to the global market, increasing the number of competitors.
		• This threat is related to new business models which are covered in a later section in this chapter.		

Activity 2.2	Assessing the impact of the Internet on competitive forces in different industries

Purpose

To assess how some of the changes to the competitive forces caused by electronic communications impact particular industries.

Activity

Referring to Table 2.2, assess the impact of the Internet on a sector you select from the options below. State which you feel are the most significant impacts.

1 Banking.
2 Grocery retail.
3 Book retail.
4 B2B engineering component manufacturer.
5 B2B software services company selling customer relationship management software.
6 Not-for-profit organisation such as hospital, local government or charity.

Examples of changes to the five forces

In this section further examples are given of changes to the five competitive forces.

Bargaining power of buyers

The increase in customer power and knowledge is perhaps the single biggest threat posed by electronic trading. The bargaining power of customers is greatly increased when they are using the Internet to evaluate products and compare prices. This is particularly true for standardised products for which offers from different suppliers can be readily compared through online intermediaries such as search engines and price comparison sites such as Kelkoo (**www.kelkoo.com**) or Pricerunner (**www.pricerunner.com**). For commodities, auctions on business-to-business exchanges can also have a similar effect of driving down price. Purchase of some products that have not traditionally been thought of as commodities, may become more price-sensitive. This process is known as commoditisation. Examples of goods that are becoming commoditised include electrical goods and cars.

> **Commoditisation**
> The process whereby product selection becomes more dependent on price than on differentiating features, benefits and value-added services.

In the business-to-business arena, a further issue is that the ease of use of the Internet channel makes it potentially easier for customers to swap between suppliers – switching costs are lower. With the Internet, which offers a more standard method for purchase through web browsers, the barriers to swapping to another supplier will be lower. With a specific EDI (electronic data interchange) link that has to be set up between one company and another, there may be reluctance to change this arrangement (soft lock-in due to switching costs). Commentators often glibly say 'online, your competitor is only a mouse click away', but it should be remembered that soft lock-in still exists on the web – there are still barriers and costs to switching between suppliers since, once a customer has invested time in understanding how to use a web site to select and purchase a particular type of products, they may not want to learn another service.

> **Soft lock-in**
> Electronic linkages between supplier and customer increase switching costs.

A significant downstream channel threat is the potential loss of partners or distributors if there is a channel conflict resulting from disintermediation (see section on new channel structures below). For example, a car distributor could switch to an alternative manufacturer if its profitability were threatened by direct sales from the manufacturer. The *Economist* (2000) reported that to avoid this type of conflict, Ford US are now using dealerships as part of the e-commerce solution and are still paying commission when sales are achieved online. This also helps protect their revenue from the lucrative parts and services market.

Bargaining power of suppliers

This can be considered as an opportunity rather than a threat. Companies can insist, for reasons of reducing cost and increasing supply chain efficiency, that their suppliers use electronic links such as EDI or Internet EDI to process orders. Additionally, the Internet tends to reduce the power of suppliers since barriers to migrating to a different supplier are reduced, particularly with the advent of business-to-business exchanges. However, if suppliers insist on proprietary technology to link companies, then this creates soft lock-in due to the cost or complexity of changing supppliers.

Barriers to entry reduced

For traditional companies, new online entrants have been a significant threat for retailers selling products such as books and financial services. For example, for the banking sector in Europe, traditional banks were threatened by the entry of completely new start-up competitors, such as First-e (**www.first-e.com**) (which later became financially unviable), or of traditional companies from one country that use the Internet to facilitate their entry into another country. US company Citibank (**www.citibank.com**) and ING Direct (**www.ingdirect.co.uk**) from the Netherlands used the latter approach. New companies were also created by traditional competitors, for example, Prudential created Egg (**www.egg.com**), the Abbey, Cahoot (**www.cahoot.com**), and the Co-Operative Bank, Smile (**www.smile.co.uk**). ING Direct has acquired millions of customers in new markets such as Canada, Australia and the UK through a combination of offline advertising, online advertising and an online or phone application process and account servicing.

These new entrants have been able to enter the market rapidly since they do not have the cost of developing and maintaining a distribution network to sell their products and these products do not require a manufacturing base.

However, to succeed, new entrants need to be market leaders in executing marketing and customer service. These are sometimes described as *barriers to success* or '*hygiene factors*' rather than barriers to entry. The costs of achieving these will be high, for example, First-e has not survived as an independent business. This competitive threat is less common in vertical business-to-business markets involving manufacture and process industries such as the chemical or oil industries since the investment barriers to entry are much higher.

Threat of substitute products and services

This threat can occur from established or new companies. The Internet is particularly good as a means of providing information-based services at a lower cost. The greatest threats are likely to occur where digital product and/or service fulfilment can occur over the Internet. These substitutes can involve the new online channel essentially replicating an existing service as is the case with online banking or e-books. But, often, online can involve adding to the proposition. For example, compared to traditional music retailers, online legal music services such as Napster (**www.napster.com**) offer a much wider choice of products with different delivery modes (real-time streaming to a PC or the capability to burn onto a CD or download to a portable music device such as an MP3 player). In banking, new facilities have been developed to help customers manage their finances online by aggregating services from different providers into one central account. Such added-value digital services can help lock customers into a particular supplier.

Internet EDI
Use of electronic data interchange standards delivered across non-proprietary Internet protocol networks.

Business-to-business exchanges or marketplaces
Virtual intermediaries with facilities to enable trading between buyers and sellers.

From this review of the competitive forces, it should be apparent that the extent of the threats will be dependent on the particular market a company operates in. Generally, the threats are greatest for companies that currently sell through retail distributors and have products that can be readily delivered to customers across the Internet or by parcel.

Value creation and value chain analysis

How businesses create value within their markets is fundamental to their success. Digital technologies have a significant role in changing the balance of value creation within a market, so the extent of this change and how well it has been implemented must be evaluated as part of environment analysis. Value delivered is dependent on the difference between the consumer benefit created by the business and the costs incurred in producing or delivering the value as suggested by Figure 2.4. You can see that arguably the biggest impact of the Internet is the capability to reduce costs through reducing intermediaries such as physical stores and also through changing the intangible benefits. Together, these combine to form the online value proposition, as explained in Chapter 4. To pass on the reduced costs of dealing direct it will be necessary for retailers, banks and other companies to change their structure and accounting practices to isolate online channels as a separate profit centre.

Value chain
A model that considers how supply chain activities can add value to products and services delivered to the customer.

Michael Porter's **value chain** (VC) is a well-established concept for considering key activities that an organisation can perform or manage with the intention of creating value for customers (Porter, 1980). We can identify an *internal* value chain within the boundaries of an organisation and an *external* value chain where activities are performed by partners. By analysing the different parts of the value chain managers can redesign internal and external processes to improve their efficiency and effectiveness. Traditional value chain analysis (Figure 2.5(a)) of the internal value chain distinguishes between *primary activities* which contribute directly to getting goods and services to the customer (such as inbound logistics, including procurement, manufacturing, marketing and delivery to buyers, support and servicing after sale) and *support activities* which provide the inputs and infrastructure that allow the primary activities to take place.

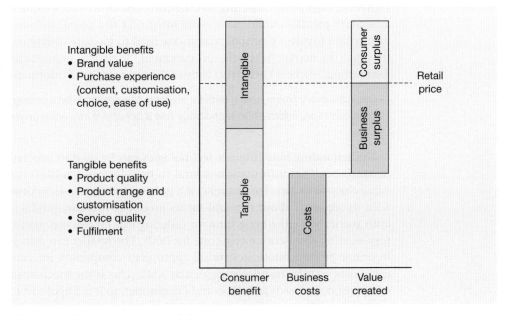

Figure 2.4 Value creation model

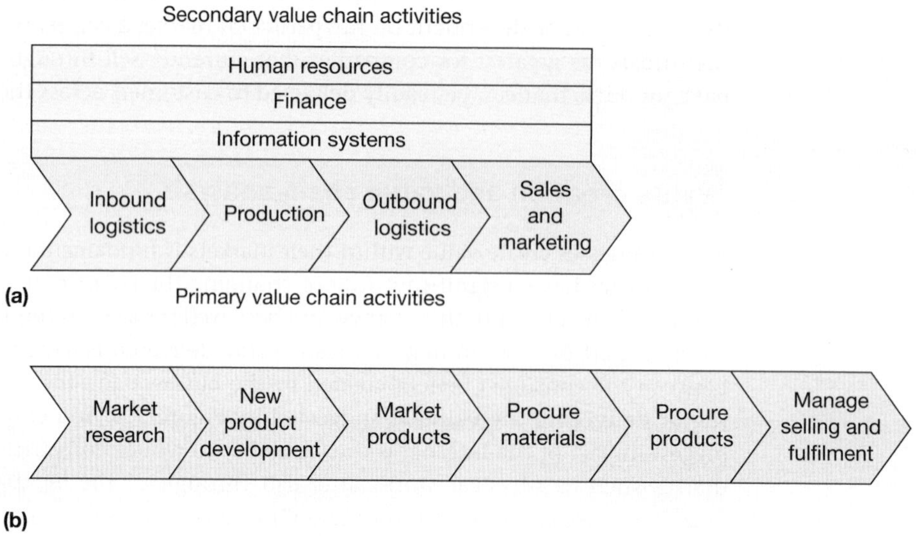

Secondary value chain activities

| Human resources |
| Finance |
| Information systems |

Inbound logistics → Production → Outbound logistics → Sales and marketing

(a) Primary value chain activities

Market research → New product development → Market products → Procure materials → Procure products → Manage selling and fulfilment

(b)

Figure 2.5 Two alternative models of the value chain: (a) traditional value chain model, (b) revised value chain model

Value can be created for the customer by reducing costs of providing goods and services *and* adding benefits for customers:

- *within each* element of the value chain such as procurement, manufacture, sales and distribution;
- *at the interface between* elements of the value chain such as between sales and distribution.

In equation form this is:

**Value = (Benefit of each VC activity – its cost) +
(Benefit of each interface between VC activities – its cost)**

Rayport and Sviokla (1996) contend that the Internet enables value to be created by gathering, organising, selecting, synthesising and distributing information. They refer to a separate parallel *virtual value chain* mirroring the physical value chain. The virtual value chain involves electronic commerce used to mediate traditional value chain activities such as market research, procurement, logistics, manufacture, marketing and distributing. Michael Porter also stresses the importance of information:

because every [value chain] activity involves the creation, processing and communication of information, information technology has a pervasive influence on the value chain.

Porter (2001)

Understanding how Internet technologies can be used to process, transfer and share marketing-related information is vital to help Internet marketers evaluate and revise value chain activities. For example, if a grocery retailer shares information electronically with its suppliers about demand for its products, this can enhance the value chain of both parties since the cycle time for ordering can be reduced, resulting in lower inventory holding and hence lower costs for both. The retailer can also set up links between its online product catalogues and all appropriate comparison intermediaries for products using data transfer technologies such as XML. This is the mechanism used by shopping comparison sites such as Kelkoo and Pricerunner, so it is important for online retailers to evaluate this integration. If this work is not seen as important since it is not a traditional marketing activity, then the opportunities of increased online visibility and hence number of visitors and sales will be reduced. Retailer Tesco has created its Price Check initiative (**www.tesco.com/pricecheck**) to highlight its competitiveness by making its competitor price survey available online. Of course, the most obvious examples of value creation occur directly through the interface between the web site and the customer, for example through detailed product information, product selection guides, personalised product recommendations and online customer support facilities which involve reducing cost to serve and may have intangible benefits for the customer such as improved recommendations or decreasing the purchase time.

Restructuring the internal value chain

Traditional models of the value chain (such as Figure 2.5(a)) have been re-evaluated with the advent of global electronic communications. It can be suggested that there are some key weaknesses in the traditional value chain model:

- It is most applicable to manufacturing of physical products as opposed to services.
- It is a one-way chain involving pushing products to the customer; it does not highlight the importance of understanding customer needs through market research and responsiveness through innovation and new product development.
- The internal value chain does not emphasise the importance of value networks (although Porter (1980) did produce a diagram that indicated network relationships).

A revised form of the value chain has been suggested by Deise et al. (2000); an adaptation of this model is presented in Figure 2.5(b). This digital value chain starts with the market research process, emphasising the importance of real-time environment scanning for decision making. For each of the different types of organisation site introduced in Chapter 1, there are opportunities to create value by processing information in new ways:

1 Customer information collected on a *transactional e-commerce site* can develop greater understanding of the purchasing behaviour of its target customers, which can also be analysed in terms of demographic profiles through tracking online shopping preferences and sequences.
2 *Service-oriented relationship building sites* can collect information as part of creating a dialogue using profiling forms, feedback forms and forums on the site enabling their owners to better understand customer characteristics and purchasing behaviour.
3 *Brand building sites* also have opportunities to collect information about the profiles and preferences of their site visitors or those in their target market using third-party sites.
4 *Portal or media sites* can potentially use visitors to contribute content. Think of the BBC web site which now has feedback on its news, sport and entertainment sites, so adding value to its visitors. Even well-known media owner Rupert Murdoch has suggested that online newspapers consider recruiting bloggers to add value to their audiences (Murdoch, 2005).

External value chains and value networks

Reduced time to market and increased customer responsiveness can be achieved through reviewing the efficiency of internal processes and how information systems are deployed. However, these goals are also achieved through consideration of how partners can be involved to outsource some processes that have traditionally been considered to

Value network

The links between an organisation and its strategic and non-strategic partners that form its external value chain.

be part of the internal value chain of a company. Porter's original work considered both the internal value chain and the external value chain or network. Since the 1980s there has been a tremendous increase in outsourcing of both core value-chain activities and support activities. As companies outsource more and more activities, management of the links between the company and its partners becomes more important. Deise et al. (2000) describe value network management as:

> the process of effectively deciding what to outsource in a constraint-based, real-time environment based on fluctuation.

Electronic communications have facilitated this shift to outsourcing, enabling the transfer of information necessary to create, manage and monitor partnerships. These links are not necessarily mediated directly through the company, but can take place through intermediaries known as value-chain integrators or directly between partners. In addition to changes in the efficiency of value-chain activities, electronic commerce also has implications for whether these activities are achieved under external control or internal control. These changes have been referred to as value-chain *disaggregation* (Kalakota and Robinson, 2000) or *deconstruction* (Timmers, 1999) and value-chain *reaggregation* (Kalakota and Robinson, 2000) or *reconstruction* (Timmers, 1999). Value-chain disaggregation can occur through deconstructing the primary activities of the value chain and then outsourcing as appropriate. Each of the elements can be approached in a new way, for instance by working differently with suppliers. In value-chain reaggregation the value chain is streamlined to increase efficiency between each of the value-chain stages.

The value network offers a different perspective which is intended to emphasise:

- the electronic interconnections between partners and the organisation and directly between partners that potentially enable real-time information exchange between partners;
- the dynamic nature of the network. The network can be readily modified according to market conditions or in response to customer demands. New partners can readily be introduced into the network and others removed if they are not performing well;
- different types of links can be formed between different types of partners. For example, EDI links may be established with key suppliers, while e-mail links may suffice for less significant suppliers.

Figure 2.6, which is adapted from the model of Deise et al. (2000), shows some of the partners of a value network that characterises partners as:

1. supply-side partners (upstream supply chain) such as suppliers, business-to-business exchanges, wholesalers and distributors;
2. partners who fulfil primary or core value-chain activities. The number of core value-chain activities that will have been outsourced to third parties will vary with different companies and the degree of virtualisation of an organisation which involves outsourcing non-core services;
3. sell-side partners (downstream supply chain) such as business-to-business exchanges, wholesalers, distributors and customers (not shown, since they are conceived as distinct from other partners);
4. value-chain integrators or partners who supply services that mediate the internal and external value chain. These companies typically provide the electronic infrastructure for a company and include strategic outsourcing partners, system integrators, ISPs and application service providers (ASPs).

Examples which illustrate the importance of value networks to Internet marketing are the affiliate networks and ad networks described in Chapter 8. Rather than working directly with individual publishers to drive visitors to a site, an online merchant will work with an affiliate network provider such as Commission Junction (**www.cj.com**) or ad network such as Miva (**www.miva.com**) which manages the links with the third parties.

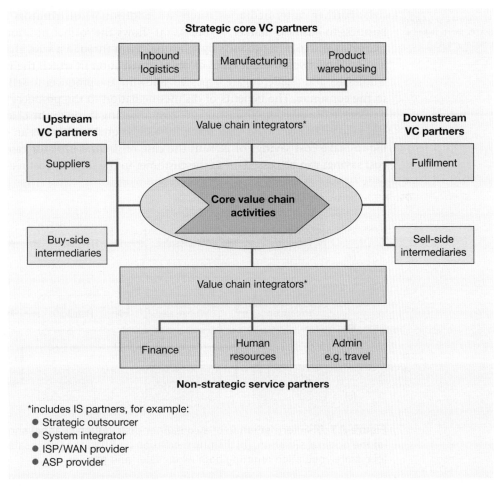

Figure 2.6 Members of the value network of an organisation
Source: Adapted from Deise et al. (2000)

New channel structures

Channel structure

The configuration of partners in a distribution channel.

Channel structures describe the way a manufacturer or selling organisation delivers products and services to its customers. The distribution channel will consist of one or more intermediaries such as wholesalers and retailers. For example, a music company is unlikely to distribute its CDs directly to retailers, but will use wholesalers which have a large warehouse of titles that are then distributed to individual branches according to demand. A company selling business products may have a longer distribution channel involving more intermediaries.

The relationship between a company and its channel partners can be dramatically altered by the opportunities afforded by the Internet. This occurs because the Internet offers a means of bypassing some of the channel partners. This process is known as disintermediation or, in plainer language, 'cutting out the middleman'.

Figure 2.7 illustrates disintermediation in a graphical form for a simplified retail channel. Further intermediaries such as additional distributors may occur in a business-to-business market. Figure 2.7(a) shows the former position where a company marketed and sold its products by 'pushing' them through a sales channel. Figures 2.7(b) and (c) show two different types of disintermediation in which the wholesaler (b) or the wholesaler and retailer (c) are bypassed, allowing the producer to sell and promote direct to the consumer. The benefits of disintermediation to the producer are clear – it is able to remove the sales and infrastructure cost of selling through the channel. Benjamin and Weigand (1995) calculate that, using the sale of quality shirts as an example, it is possible to make cost savings of 28% in the case of (b) and 62% for case (c). Some of these cost savings can be passed on to the customer in the form of cost reductions.

Disintermediation
The removal of intermediaries such as distributors or brokers that formerly linked a company to its customers.

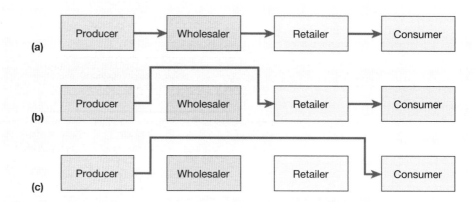

Figure 2.7 Disintermediation of a consumer distribution channel showing: (a) the original situation, (b) disintermediation omitting the wholesaler, and (c) disintermediation omitting both wholesaler and retailer

Reintermediation
The creation of new intermediaries between customers and suppliers providing services such as supplier search and product evaluation.

At the start of business hype about the Internet in the mid-1990s there was much speculation that widespread disintermediation would see the failure of many intermediary companies as direct selling occurred. While many companies have taken advantage of disintermediation, the changes have not been as significant as predicted. Since purchasers of products still require assistance in the selection of products this led to the creation of new intermediaries, a process referred to as reintermediation. In the UK Screentrade (www.screentrade.co.uk, Figure 2.8) was established as a broker to enable different insurance companies to sell direct. While it was in business for several years, it eventually failed as online purchasers turned to established brands. However, it was sold to an existing bank (Lloyds TSB) which continues to operate it as an independent intermediary.

Figure 2.8 Screentrade insurance intermediary (www.screentrade.com)

Figure 2.9 shows the operation of reintermediation in a graphical form. Following disintermediation, where the customer goes direct to different suppliers to select a product, this becomes inefficient for the consumer. Take, again, the example of someone buying insurance, to decide on the best price and offer, they would have to visit say five different insurers and then return to the one they decide to purchase from. Reintermediation removes this inefficiency by placing an intermediary between the purchaser and seller. This intermediary performs the price evaluation stage of fulfilment since its database has links updated from prices contained within the databases of different suppliers.

What are the implications of reintermediation for the Internet marketer? First, it is necessary to make sure that a company, as a supplier, is represented with the new intermediaries operating within your chosen market sector. This implies the need to integrate, using the Internet, databases containing price information with that of different intermediaries. Secondly, it is important to monitor the prices of other suppliers within this sector (possibly by using the intermediary web site for this purpose). Thirdly, long-term partnering arrangements such as sponsorships need to be considered. Finally, it may be appropriate to create your own intermediary to compete with existing intermediaries or to pre-empt similar intermediaries. For example, the Thomson Travel Group set up Latedeals.com (**www.latedeals.com**) in direct competition with Lastminute.com (**www.lastminute.com**). A further example is that, in the UK, Boots the Chemist set up its own intermediaries Handbag (**www.handbag.com**) and Wellbeing (**www.wellbeing.com**). This effectively created barriers to entry for other new intermediaries wishing to operate in this space. Such tactics to counter or take advantage of reintermediation are sometimes known as **countermediation**.

Countermediation
Creation of a new intermediary by an established company.

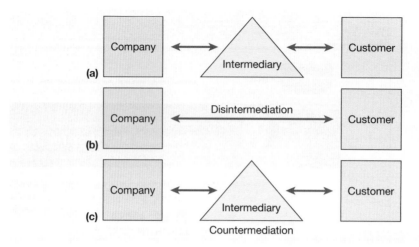

Figure 2.9 From (a) original situation to (b) disintermediation or (c) reintermediation or countermediation

Market mapping and developing channel chains is a powerful technique recommended by McDonald and Wilson (2002) for analysing the changes in a marketplace introduced by the Internet. A market map can be used to show the flow of revenue between a manufacturer or service provider and its customers through traditional intermediaries and new types of intermediaries. For example, Thomas and Sullivan (2005) give the example of a US multi-channel retailer that used cross-channel tracking of purchases through assigning each customer a unique identifier to calculate channel preferences as follow: 63% bricks-and-mortar store only, 12.4% Internet-only customers, 11.9% catalogue-only customers, 11.9% dual-channel customers and 1% three-channel customers.

A channel chain is similar – it shows different customer journeys for customers with different channel preferences. It can be used to assess the current and future importance of these different customer journeys. An example of a channel chain is shown in Figure 2.10.

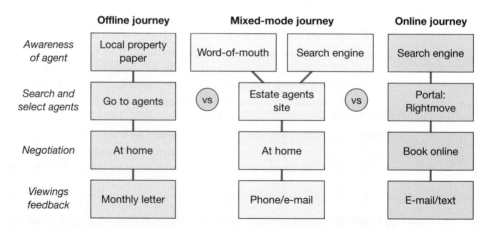

Figure 2.10 Example of a channel chain map for consumers selecting an estate agents to sell their property

Location of trading in marketplace

While traditional marketplaces have a physical location, Internet-based markets have no physical presence – it is a virtual marketplace. Rayport and Sviokla (1996) used this distinction to coin the new term electronic marketspace. This has implications for the way in which the relationships between the different actors in the marketplace occur.

The new electronic marketspace has many alternative virtual locations where an organisation needs to position itself to communicate and sell to its customers. Thus, one tactical marketing question is 'What representation do we have on the Internet?' A particular aspect of representation that needs to be reviewed is the different types of marketplace location. Berryman et al. (1998) have identified a simple framework for this. They identify three key online locations for promotion of services and for performing e-commerce transactions with customers (Figure 2.11). The three options are:

(a) *Supplier-controlled sites (sell-side at supplier site, one supplier to many customers).* This is the main web site of the company and is where the majority of transactions take place. Most e-tailers such as Amazon (**www.amazon.com**) or Dell (**www.dell.com**) fall into this category.

(b) *Buyer-controlled sites (buy-side at buyer site, many suppliers to one customer).* These are intermediaries that have been set up so that it is the buyer that initiates the market-making. This can occur through procurement posting where a purchaser specifies what they wish to purchase, it is sent by e-mail to suppliers registered on the system and

Electronic marketspace
A virtual marketplace such as the Internet in which no direct contact occurs between buyers and sellers.

Representation
The locations on the Internet where an organisation is located for promoting or selling its services.

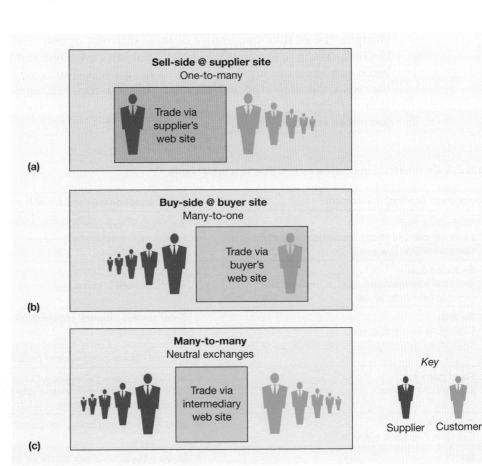

Figure 2.11 Different types of online trading location

then offers are awaited. Aggregators involve a group of purchasers combining to purchase a multiple order and thus reducing the purchase cost. General Electric Trading Post Network was the first to set up this type of arrangement (http://tpn.geis.com – site no longer available), but it remains uncommon in comparison to the other two alternatives.

(c) *Neutral sites or intermediaries (neutral location – many suppliers to many customers).* For consumers evaluator intermediaries that enable price and product comparison have become commonplace as we have seen. B2B intermediaries are known as *trading exchanges*, *marketplaces* or *hubs*. Examples of independent B2B exchanges mentioned in the previous edition are Vertical Net (www.vertical.net), Commerce One Marketsite (www.commerceone.com) and Covisint (www.covisint.net), none of which now exist in their original form. While some B2B intermediaries remain for some commodities or simple services (for example, EC21 (www.ec21.com), Elance (www.elance.com), eBay Business (http://business.ebay.com)) the new trading arrangements have not developed as predicted by many analysts due to the complexity of business purchase decisions and negotiations and their destabilising nature on markets.

Commercial arrangement for transactions

Markets can also be considered from another perspective – that of the type of commercial arrangement that is used to agree a sale and price between the buyer and supplier. The main alternative commercial arrangements are shown in Table 2.3.

It can be seen from Table 2.3 that each of these commercial arrangements is similar to a traditional arrangement. Although the mechanism cannot be considered to have changed, the relative importance of these different options has changed with the Internet. Owing to the ability to rapidly publish new offers and prices, auction has become an important means of selling on the Internet. A turnover of billions of dollars has been achieved by eBay from consumers offering items ranging from cars to antiques. Many airlines have successfully trialled auctions to sell seats remaining on an aircraft just before a flight.

Table 2.3 Commercial mechanisms and online transactions

Commercial (trading) mechanism	Online transaction mechanism of Nunes et al. (2000)
1 Negotiated deal Example: can use similar mechanism to auction as on Commerce One (www.ec21.com)	● Negotiation – bargaining between single seller and buyer ● Continuous replenishment – ongoing fulfilment of orders under preset terms
2 Brokered deal Example: intermediaries such as Screentrade (www.screentrade.co.uk)	● Achieved through online intermediaries offering auction and pure markets online
3 Auction C2C: eBay (www.ebay.com) B2B: eBay business (http://business.ebay.com)	● Seller auction – buyers' bids determine final price of sellers' offerings ● Buyer auction – buyers request prices from multiple sellers ● Reverse – buyer posts desired price for seller acceptance
4 Fixed price sale Example: All e-tailers	● Static call – online catalogue with fixed prices ● Dynamic call – online catalogue with continuously updated prices and features
5 Pure markets Example: Electronic share dealing	● Spot – buyers' and sellers' bids clear instantly
6 Barter Example: www.intagio.com	● Barter – buyer and seller exchange goods

Business models in e-commerce

A consideration of the different business models made available through e-commerce is of particular importance to both existing and start-up companies. Venkatraman (2000) points out that existing businesses need to use the Internet to build on current business models while at the same time experimenting with new business models. New business models may be important to gain a competitive advantage over existing competitors and at the same time head off similar business models created by new entrants. For start-ups or dot-coms the viability of a business model will be crucial to funding from venture capitalists. But what is a business model? Timmers (1999) defines a 'business model' as:

An architecture for product, service and information flows, including a description of the various business actors and their roles; and a description of the potential benefits for the various business actors; and a description of the sources of revenue.

It can be suggested that a business model for e-commerce requires consideration of the marketplace from several different perspectives:

- Does the company operate in the B2B or B2C arena, or a combination?
- How is the company positioned in the value chain between customers and suppliers?
- What is its value proposition and for which target customers?
- What are the specific revenue models that will generate different income streams?
- What is its representation in the physical and virtual world, i.e. high-street presence, online only, intermediary, mixture?

Timmers (1999) identifies no less than eleven different types of business model that can be facilitated by the web as follows:

1 *e-shop* – marketing of a company or shop via the web;
2 *e-procurement* – electronic tendering and procurement of goods and services;
3 *e-mall* – a collection of e-shops such as BarclaySquare (**www.barclays-square.com**);
4 *e-auctions* – these can be for B2C, e.g. eBay (**www.ebay.com**), or B2B, e.g. QXL (**www.qxl.com**);
5 *virtual communities* – these can be B2C communities such as Habbo Hotel for teenagers (**www.habbo.com**) or B2B communities such as Clearlybusiness (**www.clearlybusiness.com/community**) which are both important for their potential in e-marketing and are described in the virtual communities section in Chapter 6;
6 *collaboration platforms* – these enable collaboration between businesses or individuals, e.g. E-groups (**www.egroups.com**), now part of Yahoo! (**www.yahoo.com**) services;
7 *third-party marketplaces* – marketplaces are intermediaries that facilitate online trading by putting buyers and sellers in contact. They are sometimes also referred to as 'exchanges' or 'hubs';
8 *value-chain integrators* – offer a range of services across the value chain;
9 *value-chain service providers* – specialise in providing functions for a specific part of the value chain such as the logistics company UPS (**www.ups.com**);
10 *information brokerage* – providing information for consumers and businesses, often to assist in making the buying decision or for business operations or leisure;
11 *trust and other services* – examples of trust services include Internet Shopping is Safe (ISIS) (**www.imrg.org/isis**) or TRUSTe (**www.truste.org**) which authenticate the quality of service and privacy protection provided by companies trading on the web.

Figure 2.12 suggests a different perspective for reviewing alternative business models. There are three different perspectives from which a business model can be viewed. Any individual organisation can operate in different categories, as the examples below show,

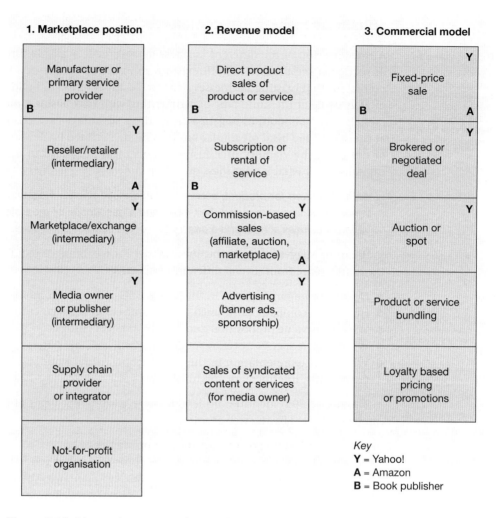

Figure 2.12 Alternative perspectives on business models

but most will focus on a single category for each perspective. Such a categorisation of business models can be used as a tool for formulating e-business strategy. The three perspectives, with examples are:

1 *Marketplace position perspective.* The book publisher is the manufacturer, Amazon is a retailer and MSN is a retailer, marketplace intermediary and media owner.
2 *Revenue model perspective.* The book publisher can use the web to sell direct and MSN and Amazon can take commission-based sales. Yahoo! also has advertising as a revenue model.
3 *Commercial model perspective.* All three companies offer fixed-price sales, but in its place as a marketplace intermediary, MSN also offers other alternatives.

Michael Porter (2001) urges caution against overemphasis on new business or revenue models and attacks those who have suggested that the Internet invalidates his well-known strategy models. He says:

Many have assumed that the Internet changes everything, rendering all the old rules about companies and competition obsolete. That may be a natural reaction, but it is a dangerous one . . . [companies have taken] decisions that have eroded the attractiveness of their industries and undermined their own competitive advantages.

He gives the example of some industries using the Internet to change the basis of competition away from quality, features and service and towards price, making it harder for anyone in their industries to turn a profit.

Revenue models

Revenue models
Describe methods of generating income for an organisation.

Revenue models specifically describe different techniques for generation of income. The main revenue models are shown in the second column of Figure 2.12. For existing companies, revenue models have been based upon the income from sales of products or services. This may be either for selling direct from the manufacturer or supplier of the service or through an intermediary that will take a cut of the selling price. Both of these revenue models are, of course, still crucial in online trading. There may, however, be options for other methods of generating revenue: perhaps a manufacturer may be able to sell advertising space or sell digital services that were not previously possible. Activity 2.3 explores some of the revenue models that are possible.

Activity 2.3 | **Revenue models at Yahoo!**

visit the
w.w.w.

Purpose

To illustrate the range of revenue generating opportunities for a company operating as an Internet pure-play.

Yahoo! (**www.yahoo.com**) is a well-known intermediary with local content available for many countries.

Activity

Visit the local Yahoo! site for your region, e.g. **www.yahoo.co.uk**, and explore the different site services which generate revenue. Reference the investor relations reports to gain an indication of the relative importance of these revenue sources.

Customers

Customer insight
Knowledge about customers' needs, characteristics, preferences and behaviours based on analysis of qualitative and quantitative data. Specific insights can be used to inform marketing tactics directed at groups of customers with shared characteristics.

Situation analysis related to customers is very important to setting realistic objectives estimates for online customers and developing appropriate propositions for customers online. Customer-related analysis can be divided into two. First, understanding the potential and actual volume of visitors to a site (demand analysis) and the extent to which they convert to outcomes on the site such as leads and sales (conversion modelling). Secondly, we need to understand the needs, characteristics and buyer behaviour of online customers (also covered in Chapter 7), often collectively referred to as customer insight.

Demand analysis and conversion modelling

It is essential for Internet marketing and e-marketing managers to understand the current levels and trends in usage of the Internet for different services and the factors that affect how many people actively use these services. This evaluation process is demand analysis. If customer usage of online media is evaluated for customers in a target market,

Demand analysis

Quantitative
determination of the
potential usage and
business value
achieved from online
customers of an
organisation.
Qualitative analysis of
perceptions of online
channels is also
assessed.

companies can identify the opportunity for influencing and delivering sales online. They can also understand the drivers to usage and barriers to increased usage and so encourage adoption of online channels by emphasising the benefits in their communications and explaining why some of the barriers may not be valid. For example, marketing communications can be used to explain the value proposition (see Chapter 4) and reduce fears of complexity and security.

Surveys reported in the social factors section of the next chapter show that the following are important factors in governing adoption of the Internet:

1 *Cost of access.*
2 *Value proposition.*
3 *Perception of ease of use.*
4 *Perception of security.*

Assessing demand for e-commerce services

To set realistic strategic objectives such as leads or sales levels for online revenue contributions for digital channels (as described in Chapter 4), e-marketing managers need to assess the level of customer Internet access and activity for different markets and the online market share that a particular organisation has achieved. For each customer segment and for each digital channel such as Internet, interactive digital TV or mobile we need to work to assess the volume and share of customers who:

1 Have access to the digital channel;
2 Are influenced by using the digital channel but purchase using another channel as part of the multi-channel buyer behaviour;
3 Purchase using the digital channel.

This can be simplified to the ratios: 'Access : Choose : Buy'. This information can be gathered as secondary research by the researcher by accessing published research for different sectors. Primary research can be used to better understand these characteristics in the target market.

Conversion models

**Conversion
marketing**

Using marketing
communications to
maximise conversion of
potential customers to
actual customers.

As part of situation analysis and objective setting, experienced online marketers build conversion or waterfall models of the efficiency of their web marketing. Using this approach, the total online demand for a service in a particular market can be estimated and then the success of the company in achieving a share of this market determined. Conversion marketing tactics can then be create as many *potential* site visitors into *actual* visitors and then convert these into leads, customers and repeat visitors. A widely quoted conceptual measurement framework based on the industrial marketing concepts of purchasing decision processes and hierarchy of effects models, which can be applied for conversion marketing, was proposed by Berthon et al. (1998). The model assesses efficiency of offline and online communications in drawing the prospect through different stages of the buying decision. The main measures defined in the model are the following ratios:

● *Awareness efficiency*: target web-users/all web-users.
● *Locatability or attractability efficiency*: number of individual visits/number of seekers.
● *Contact efficiency*: number of active visitors/number of visits.
● *Conversion efficiency*: number of purchases/number of active visits.
● *Retention efficiency*: number of repurchases/number of purchases.

This model is instructive for improving Internet marketing within an organisation since these different types of conversion efficiency are key to understanding how effective online and offline marketing communications are in achieving marketing outcomes. Figure 2.13 is an adaptation of the original model of Berthon et al. (1998) from Chaffey (2001), which highlights the key conversion metrics of attraction efficiency and conversion efficiency. It shows key traffic or audience measures (Q_0 to Q_4) and key conversion efficiency ratios. The model has been revised to reflect current nomenclature. Also, the original work was focused on conversion to purchase – the model is more widely applicable since it applies to any marketing outcome achieved on site, whether this be a new lead from a potential customer, an e-mail registration from a competition entrant or a sale. Additionally, it has been modified to distinguish between first-time visitors (Q_2) and repeat visitors (Q_{2R}). E-marketers need to know how conversion effectiveness differs between first-time users and repeat users. An additional important aspect of online buyer behaviour not shown in the figure is the site path or clickstream for different audience types or segments.

Clickstream

The sequence of clicks made by a visitor to the site to make a purchase.

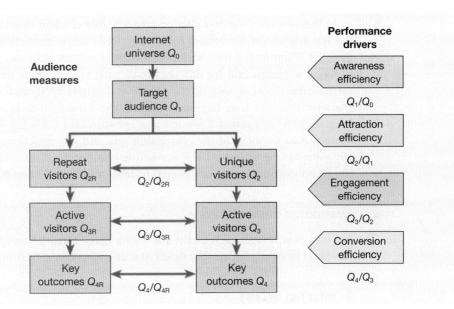

Figure 2.13 A model of the Internet marketing conversion process

Figure 2.14 shows an example of how measuring conversion rates can be used to improve web marketing. Numbers are across a fixed time period of one month. If for a particular market there is a potential audience (market) of 250 000 (Q_1), then if online and offline promotion techniques (Chapter 8) achieve 100 000 visitors to the site (Q_2), marketers have achieved an impressive conversion rate of 50%. The online marketers are then looking to convert these visitors to action. Before this is achieved, the visitors must be engaged. Data from log files show that many visitors leave when they first visit the home page of a site if they do not find the site acceptable or they are not happy with the experience. The number of visitors engaged (Q_3) is 50 000, which is half of all visitors. For the visitors that are engaged, the next step is to convert them to action. This is achieved for 500 visitors (Q_4), giving a conversion rate (Q_4/Q_3) of 1%. If what is calculated (as is most common) is (Q_4/Q_2), this gives a conversion rate of 0.5%.

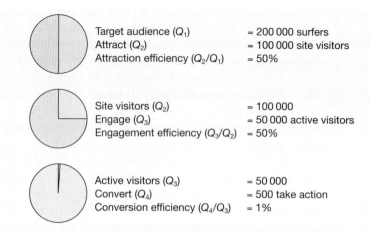

Figure 2.14 An example of a conversion model

In this example, the organisation seems highly efficient in attracting visitors to the site, but less efficient at converting them to action – future marketing improvements could be directed at improving this. Some organisations will measure different conversion rates for different segments and for different goals such as generating new leads, responding to a sales promotion or signing up for a seminar. Analysis by Agrawal et al. (2001) suggests that the strongest sites may have conversion rates from visit to sale for e-commerce sites as high as 12%, as against 2.5% for average sites and 0.4% for poorly performing ones. Clearly, measurement of the conversion rate and taking actions to improve this rate are key e-marketing activities. The marketing communications techniques used to increase these conversion rates are considered further in Chapters 7 and 8.

Evaluating demand levels

We will now review each of the following three factors that affect demand for e-commerce services in a little more detail, starting with consumers in the B2C marketplace.

1 Internet access

E-commerce provides a global marketplace, and this means we must review access and usage of the Internet channel at many different geographic levels: worldwide and between and within continents and countries.

On a worldwide basis, a relatively small proportion of the population has access to the Internet. The compilation of statistics prepared by ClickZ (www.clickz.com/stats/web_worldwide) suggests that despite rapid growth from the mid-1990s to about one billion users by 2005–6 this only represents less than 20% of the global population although there are initiatives such as the $100 PC that are intended to redress this.

If we look at individual countries, the proportion of consumers and businesses accessing the Internet is startling. If we take the United Kingdom, National Statistics (2005) showed that by 2005 over 55% of households had access to the Internet. To look at the scale of variation between different countries and continents complete Activity 2.4. When you complete this activity, you will see that often growth will plateau in most countries since there is a significant majority of the population who do not wish to or cannot afford to access the Internet. For example, Figure 2.15 shows that Internet access is now increasing less rapidly in Europe. As we will see at the start of the next chapter, there is a significant group that have no perceived need for the Internet.

Activity 2.4

Global variation in Internet provision

visit the w.w.w.

Visit the web site of the International Telecommunications Union (ITU) (**www.itu.int/ti/industryoverview/index.htm**). Choose Internet indicators. This presents data on Internet and PC penetration in over 200 countries. A summary of the indicators for different continents is presented in Figure 2.15.

Questions

1. Find your country and compare the number of PCs per hundred population and percentage Internet access compared with other countries in your region and on a global basis.
2. Now attempt to explain reasons for the disparity between your country and other countries.
3. Can you see your country equalling or exceeding the USA in terms of these indicators?

Note that PCs are recorded as PCs per hundred population. This figure may be skewed in developed countries by people with more than one PC (e.g. at home and at work).

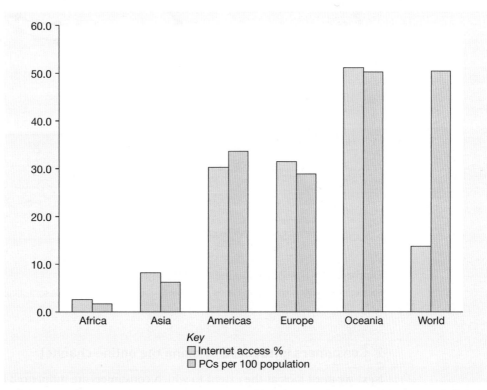

Figure 2.15 Global variation in number of PCs per hundred population and percentage Internet access in 2004

Source: ITU (www.itu.int)

An additional factor relating to consumer Internet usage is the type of Internet access. Some countries now have significant levels of high-speed, always-on, broadband access. For example, in the UK, over a quarter of households have broadband access (which exceeds dial-up access) and in South Korea over three-quarters of households have it. Broadband access permits more sophisticated sites and streaming media such as music and video. Usage of the Internet also tends to increase because of the 'always-on' connection.

Other digital access platforms

Although we focus on Internet usage in this book, technology offerings for consumers are in constant flux, so e-marketers need to assess how well new technologies fulfil their objectives. Already, interactive digital TV and mobile Internet access are used by more people than the web (Figure 2.16). These technologies are studied in more detail in Chapter 3.

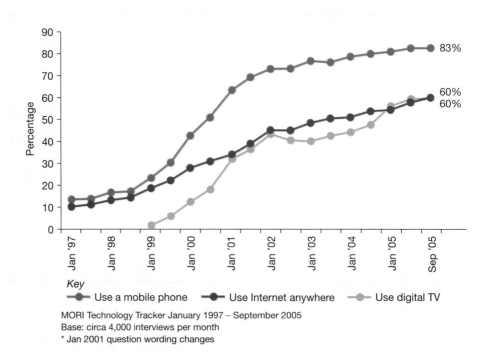

MORI Technology Tracker January 1997 – September 2005
Base: circa 4,000 interviews per month
* Jan 2001 question wording changes

Figure 2.16 UK rate of adoption of different digital media
Source: MORI Technology Tracker, September 2006. See www.mori.com/technology/techtracker.shtml for details

2 Consumers influenced by using the online channel

Next we must look at the extent to which consumers are influenced by online media – a key aspect of buyer behaviour. We saw at the start of Chapter 1 that many Internet users now research products online, but they may buy through offline channels such as phone or in store. Research summarised in the AOL-sponsored BrandNewWorld (2004) study showed that:

1 The Internet is a vital part of the research process, with 73% of Internet users agreeing that they now spend longer researching products. The purchase process is generally now more considered and is more convoluted.

2 The Internet is used at every stage of the research process from the initial scan to the more detailed comparison and final check before purchase.

3 Consumers are more informed from a multiplicity of sources; price is not exclusively the primary driver.

4 Online information and experience (and modified brand opinions) also translate into offline purchase.

There is also a wide variation in influence according to type of product, so it is important to assess the role of the web in supporting buying decisions for a particular market. Understanding the potential reach of a web site and its role in influencing purchase is clearly important in setting e-marketing budgets. A different perspective on this is indicated by Figure 2.17 which shows the proportion of people who purchase offline after online research.

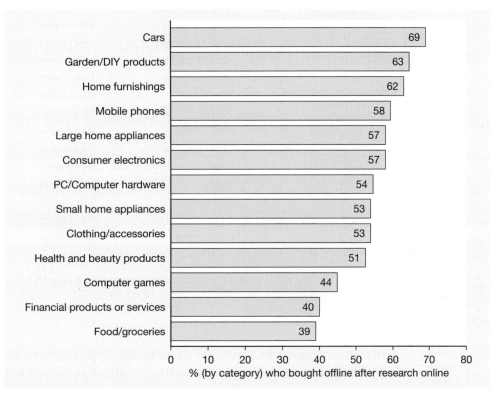

Figure 2.17 Percentage (by category) who bought offline after researching online
Source: BrandNewWorld (2004)

Calculating demand through search term volumes

Search engines are the primary method of finding information about a company and its products. Research compiled by Searchenginewatch (**www.searchenginewatch.com**) shows that over 90% of web users state that they use search engines to find information online. Savvy e-marketers use tools provided by search engine service providers such as Google (**www.google.com**), Yahoo! (**www.yahoo.com**) and Miva (**www.miva.com**) to evaluate the demand for their products or services based on the volume of different search terms typed in by search engine users (see Chaffey (2006) for a listing of these keyphrase analysis tools). Hitwise also provides this type of information – Figure 2.18 shows

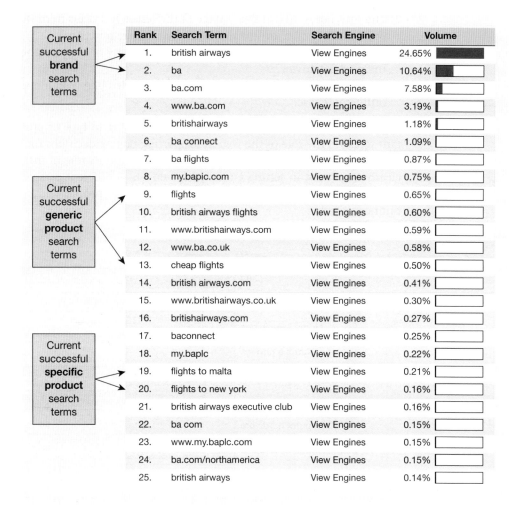

	Rank	Search Term	Search Engine	Volume	
Current successful **brand** search terms	1.	british airways	View Engines	24.65%	
	2.	ba	View Engines	10.64%	
	3.	ba.com	View Engines	7.58%	
	4.	www.ba.com	View Engines	3.19%	
	5.	britishairways	View Engines	1.18%	
	6.	ba connect	View Engines	1.09%	
	7.	ba flights	View Engines	0.87%	
	8.	my.bapic.com	View Engines	0.75%	
Current successful **generic product** search terms	9.	flights	View Engines	0.65%	
	10.	british airways flights	View Engines	0.60%	
	11.	www.britishairways.com	View Engines	0.59%	
	12.	www.ba.co.uk	View Engines	0.58%	
	13.	cheap flights	View Engines	0.50%	
	14.	british airways.com	View Engines	0.41%	
	15.	www.britishairways.co.uk	View Engines	0.30%	
	16.	britishairways.com	View Engines	0.27%	
	17.	baconnect	View Engines	0.25%	
Current successful **specific product** search terms	18.	my.baplc	View Engines	0.22%	
	19.	flights to malta	View Engines	0.21%	
	20.	flights to new york	View Engines	0.16%	
	21.	british airways executive club	View Engines	0.16%	
	22.	ba com	View Engines	0.15%	
	23.	www.my.baplc.com	View Engines	0.15%	
	24.	ba.com/northamerica	View Engines	0.15%	
	25.	british airways	View Engines	0.14%	

Figure 2.18 The most popular search terms typed into a search engine that resulted in traffic to www.ba.com, four weeks ending 18.03.06

Source: Hitwise (www.hitwise.co.uk)

that these types of tools provide an incredible opportunity to understand customer search behaviour together with assessing a company's success in reaching these customers searching online. Through evaluating the volume of phrases used to search for products in a given market it is possible to calculate the total potential opportunity and the current share of search terms for a company. 'Share of search' can be determined from web analytics reports from the company site which indicate the precise key phrases used by visitors to actually reach a site from different search engines. We explore the techniques of search engine marketing in more detail in Chapter 8.

Share of search

The audience share of Internet searchers achieved by a particular audience in a particular market.

3 Purchased online

The proportion of Internet users who will purchase different types of product online will vary dramatically according to product type, as we saw at the start of Chapter 1. The propensity to purchase online is dependent on different variables over which the marketer has relatively little control. However, factors which affect the propensity to purchase can be estimated for different types of products. De Kare-Silver (2000) developed a framework known as The Electronic Shopping Test in which he suggests that the criteria for purchase include product characteristics, familiarity and confidence and consumer attributes. Typical results from the evaluation are: groceries (27/50), mortgages (15/50), travel (31/50) and books (38/50). De Kare-Silver states that any product scoring over 20 has good potential, since the score for consumer attributes is likely to increase through time. Given this, he suggests companies will regularly need to review the score for their products. The effectiveness of this test is now demonstrated by data for online purchases in different product categories (Figure 2.19, page 70).

Mini Case Study 2.1 The Electronic Shopping or ES Test

The ES Test was developed by de Kare-Silver (2000) to assess the extent to which consumers are likely to purchase a retail product using the Internet. De Kare-Silver suggests factors that should be considered in the ES Test:

1 *Product characteristics*. Does the product need to be physically tried, or touched, before it is bought?
2 *Familiarity and confidence*. Considers the degree to which the consumer recognises and trusts the product and brand.
3 *Consumer attributes*. These shape the buyer's behaviour – is he or she amenable to online purchases (i.e. in terms of access to the technology and skills available) and does he or she no longer wish to shop for a product in a traditional retail environment? For example, a student familiar with technology may buy a CD online because they are comfortable with the technology. An elderly person looking for a classical CD would probably not have access to the technology and might prefer to purchase the item in person.

In his book, de Kare-Silver describes a method for ranking products. Product characteristics and familiarity and confidence are marked out of 10, and consumer attributes are marked out of 30. Using this method, he scores products as shown in Table 2.4.

De Kare-Silver states that any product scoring over 20 has good potential, since the score for consumer attributes is likely to increase through time. Given this, he suggests companies will regularly need to review the score for their products.

Table 2.4 Product scores in de Kare-Silver's (2000) Electronic Shopping (ES) potential test

Product	Product characteristics (10)	Familiarity and confidence (10)	Consumer attributes (30)	Total
1 Groceries	4	8	15	27
2 Mortgages	10	1	4	15
3 Travel	10	6	15	31
4 Books	8	7	23	38

Understanding of customer buyer behaviour is important to designing a site and other communications. Variations in behaviour are discussed later in this chapter.

Customer characteristics

Understanding the nature of customers is fundamental to marketing practice and it is equally important online. We will see in Chapter 4 on strategy development that traditional segmentation approaches can be used successfully to understand the range of audiences. A further technique that can be used as part of situation analysis is customer scenario and persona analysis which is an online technique for user- or customer-centric

Psychographic segmentation for transactional e-commerce

Market research firm BMRB (2004) has developed this segmentation which is used to represent different attitudes to purchasing online.

1 *Realistic Enthusiasts* (14% 2004, 15% 1999) – characterised by an enthusiastic approach toward e-commerce but they typically like to see the product in real life before making a purchase and they often consider that finding the product to purchase is a difficult process. Examples of this include a willingness to use the Internet for purchases in excess of £500; they are prepared to purchase products from an unknown company and consider the convenience of Internet shopping to be more important than price.

2 *Confident Brand Shoppers* (18% 2004, 16% 1999) – members of this group are happy to use the Internet for the next time they want to make a purchase in excess of £500, with this confidence stemming from the importance they lay on purchasing well-known brands and the necessity to shop around.

3 *Carefree Spenders* (19% 2004, 15% 1999) – these consumers are prepared to purchase from unknown companies and do not consider that purchases should be restricted to well-known brands. Furthermore, they are willing to make the purchase without seeing the product first.

4 *Cautious Shoppers* (14% 2004, 20% 1999) – these shoppers are not likely to purchase goods through an online auction, have concerns over the quality of products they purchase and would like to see the product prior to making a purchase.

5 *Bargain Hunters* (21% 2004, 16% 1999) – this group would buy from an unknown company or any web site as long as it was the cheapest and is driven not by the convenience of the medium but by price.

6 *Unfulfilled* (14% 2004, 17% 1999) – this group finds it too difficult to find the products they wish to purchase on the Internet, they would not buy from any web site or through an auction and they think it takes too long for products purchased online to be delivered.

Psychographic segmentation
A breakdown of customers according to different characteristics.

web site design (see Chapter 7 for a discussion of this approach). This is an extension of the traditional marketing approach of **psychographic segmentation**. See the box 'Psychographic segmentation for transactional e-commerce' for an example of this type of segmentation applied to online purchase behaviour. Which profile do you fit?

Demographic characteristics

Demographic characteristics
Variations in attributes of the populations such as age, sex and social class.

Within each country, adoption of the Internet also varies significantly according to individual **demographic characteristics** such as sex, age and social class or income. This analysis is important as part of the segmentation of different groups within a target

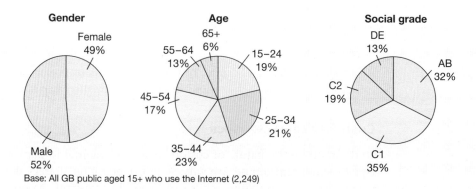

Base: All GB public aged 15+ who use the Internet (2,249)

Figure 2.19 Summary of demographic characteristics of Internet users
Source: (September 2003) MORI Technology Tracker. See www.mori.com/technology/techtracker.shtml for details

market. Since these factors will vary throughout each country there will also be regional differences. Access is usually much higher in capital cities.

From Activity 2.5 it can be seen that the stereotype of the typical Internet user as male, around 30 years of age and with high disposable income no longer holds true. Many females and more senior 'silver surfers' are also active.

To fully understand online customer access we also need to consider the user's access location, access device and 'webographics', all of which are significant for segmentation and constraints on site design. '*Webographics*' is a term coined by Grossnickle and Raskin (2001). According to these authors webographics includes:

Activity 2.5 | **Adoption of the Internet and other new media according to demographic characteristics**

visit the
w.w.w.

Purpose

To highlight variation in Internet access according to individual consumer characteristics. See **www.mori.com/technology/techtracker.shtml** for up-to-date data on demographics in the UK.

Activity

1 Refer to Figure 2.19 opposite, which is typical for most countries with Internet use at more than 50% of the population. What differences are there in the demographics compared to those for the national population?
2 Now refer to Figure 2.20. Summarise the variation in different access platforms for digital media across different social groups. Attempt to explain this variation and suggest its implications for marketers.

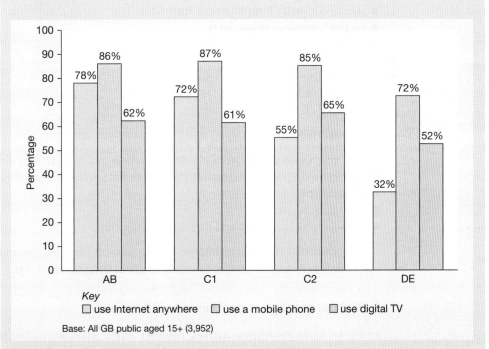

Figure 2.20 Summary of variation in access to the digital media according to social group

Source: (September 2005) MORI Technology Tracker. See www.mori.com/technology/techtracker.shtml for details

- *Usage location*. In most countries, many users access either from home or from work, with home being the more common location. Work access places constraints on Internet marketers since firewalls will not permit some plug-ins or rich e-mail to be accepted.
- *Access device*. For example, browser type, screen resolution and computer platform (available from web analytics services as described in Chapter 9), digital TV or mobile phone access.
- *Connection speed* – dial-up or different choice of broadband speed.
- *ISP* – a portal-based ISP such as AOL or Wanadoo, or an ISP which does not provide any additional content.
- *Experience level* – length of time using the web and their familiarity with online purchase.
- *Usage type* – mode of usage, for example, work, social, entertainment.
- *Usage level* – frequency of use and length of sessions giving total usage level in minutes per month.

Online demand for business services

We now turn our attention to how we assess online customer demand and characteristics for business services. The B2B market is more complex than that for B2C in that variation in online demand or research in the buying process will occur according to different types of organisation and people within the buying unit in the organisation. We need to profile business demand according to:

Variation in organisation characteristics

- size of company (employees or turnover)
- industry sector and products
- organisation type (private, public, government, not-for-profit)
- application of service (which business activities do purchased products and services support?)
- country and region.

Individual role

- role and responsibility from job title, function or number of staff managed
- role in buying decision (purchasing influence)
- department
- product interest
- demographics: age, sex and possibly social group.

For generating demand estimates, we can also profile business users of the Internet in a similar way to consumers by assessing the following three factors.

1 The percentage of companies with access

In the business-to-business market, Internet access levels are higher than for business-to-consumer. The DTI International Benchmarking Study for 2004 (DTI, 2004) shows that around 95% of businesses in the majority of countries surveyed have Internet access although this figure masks lower levels of access for SMEs (small and medium-sized enterprises) and particularly micro-businesses. Understanding access for different members of the organisational buying unit amongst their customers is also important for marketers. Although the Internet seems to be used by many companies we also need to ask whether it reaches the right people in the buying unit. The answer is 'not necessarily' – access is not available to all employees. This can be an issue if marketing to particular types of staff who have shared PC access such as healthcare professionals for example.

2 Influenced online

In B2B marketing, the high level of access is consistent with a high level of using the Internet to identify suppliers.

Figure 2.21 indicates that for many companies the Internet is important in identifying online suppliers, with the majority identifying some suppliers online, especially in the larger companies.

3 Purchase online

The DTI (2004) survey reveals that there is a large variation between how businesses in different countries order online (Figure 2.21) with the figure substantially higher in some countries such as Sweden and Germany in comparison to Italy and France for example. This shows the importance of understanding differences in the environment for e-commerce in different countries since this will dramatically affect the volume of leads and orders.

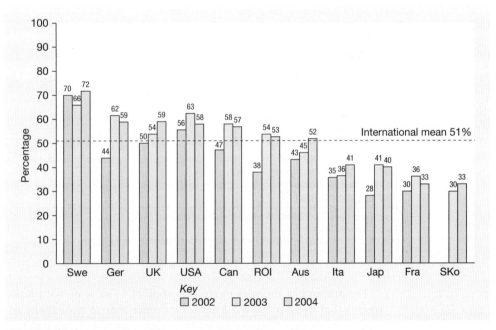

Figure 2.21 Percentage of businesses that order online
Source: DTI (2004)

Online buyer behaviour

As part of situation analysis either for a campaign or a longer-term plan it is important that marketers and agencies gain an appreciation of how the Internet supports the multi-channel buying process. In this section we will review different models of online buyer behaviour that have been developed to help marketers better understand this.

Insights into the different ways in which consumers use the Internet are provided by Table 2.5. It is apparent that, as we saw from Figure 2.17, using the Internet to inform buying decisions is the most common activity – almost twice as common as purchasing online. Investment of campaign budgets should reflect this. In some, such as the car market, they do, with BMW reputedly now spending over a quarter of its marketing budget on digital media in the UK. The popularity of e-mail use and general browsing show that socialising and entertainment are also common activities and suggest that FMCG (fast-moving consumer goods) brands can also use the Internet to reach their customers through supporting these activities.

Table 2.5 Internet usage activities in the UK

Purpose of Internet use: by age,[1] 2003/04

Great Britain				Percentages
	16–34	35–54	55 and over	All adults
Using e-mail	83	84	85	84
Searching for information about goods or services	80	84	74	80
Searching for information about travel and accommodation	63	74	70	69
General browsing or surfing	76	66	49	67
Buying goods, tickets or services	51	52	42	50
Internet banking	34	39	33	36
Activities related specifically to employment	39	37	17	35
Reading or downloading online news	37	34	25	34
Activities related to an education course	38	23	11	28
Playing or downloading music	37	18	12	25
Other educational activities	26	26	18	25
Downloading other software	27	22	18	23
Listening to web radios	20	13	9	15
Other financial services	7	9	9	8

[1] Adults who have used the Internet in the last three months.
Source: National Statistics, 2004:
www.statistics.gov.uk/downloads/theme_social/Social_Trends35/Social_Trends_35_Ch13.pdf

The amount of Internet usage also appears to increase with familiarity. BMRB (2001) reports that those using the Internet for more than 2 years spent an average of 20 hours online per month. This compares to 14 hours for those who had been using the Internet for less than 2 years. Similarly, the activities that consumers get involved with increase in involvement and risk through time. Figure 2.22 shows that initially Internet users may restrict themselves to searching for information or using e-mail. As their confidence grows their use of the Internet for purchase is likely to increase with a move to higher-value items and more frequent purchases. This is often coupled with the use of broadband. For this reason, there is still good potential for e-retail sales, even if the percentage of the population with access to the Internet plateaus.

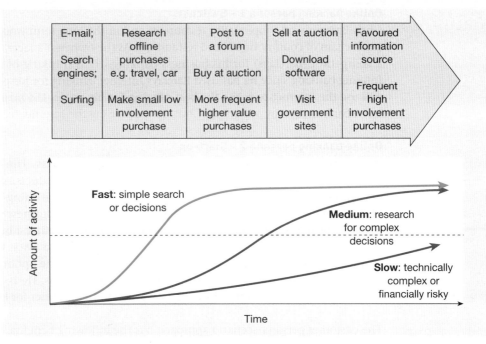

Figure 2.22 Development of experience in Internet usage

Customer persona and scenario analysis

Personas

A thumbnail summary of the characteristics, needs, motivations and environment of typical web site users.

Creating **personas** for typical site visitors is a powerful technique for influencing the planning of online campaigns and the usability and customer centricity of a web site.

Personas are essentially a 'thumbnail' description of a type of person. They have been used for a long time in research for segmentation and advertising, but in recent years have also proved effective for improving web site design by companies that have applied the technique.

Customer scenarios (user journeys)

Alternative tasks or outcomes required by a visitor to a web site. Typically accomplished in a series of stages of different tasks involving different information needs or experiences.

Customer scenarios are developed for different personas. Patricia Seybold, in her book with Ronni Marshak, *The Customer Revolution* (2001), explains them as follows:

A customer scenario is a set of tasks that a particular customer wants or needs to do in order to accomplish his or her desired outcome.

You will see that scenarios can be developed for each persona. For an online bank, scenarios might include:

1 New customer – opening online account
2 Existing customer – transferring an account online
3 Existing customer – finding an additional product.

Each scenario is split up into a series of steps or tasks before the scenario is completed. These steps can be best thought of as a series of questions a visitor asks. By identifying questions web site designers identify the different information needs of different customer types at different stages in the buying process.

The use of scenarios is a simple, but very powerful, web design technique that is still relatively rare in web site design. They can also be used when benchmarking competitor sites as part of situation analysis.

Here are two simple examples of a commercial bank offering business services which show an experienced user (persona 1) and less experienced user (persona 2).

Online banking persona 1 – Switcher

Chris Barber owns a top-quality restaurant, and in the long term would like to build up a small chain of country hotels and restaurants. As the owner–manager, Chris currently uses a competitor (Barclays) for his business banking. He is thinking of moving to business Internet banking since he has used Barclays Internet banking for his personal banking. He will use the Internet to select the best offering for his needs. His main interest is to minimise bank charges by switching. Chris has been using the Internet for five years.

Online banking persona 2 – Start-up

John Smith has just registered Gifts-R-Us as a new business. The company will be a wholesale gift supplier, selling a range of imported gift products, such as candles and decorations to small shops and stores. He has worked as a marketing director in a similar business previously, but is now seeking to start up his own business with the operations manager of the other company as his partner. John is selecting a business bank, but is not sure whether to use Internet banking or not. He wants to assess the benefits. He has no preferences for a business bank – he wants to review all the options and find the easiest to use. He also wants one with favourable banking rates. He is not an experienced Internet user since previously his secretary accessed the Internet for him.

The customer persona/scenario approach has the following benefits:

- Fostering customer-centricity;
- Identifies detailed information needs and steps required by customers;
- Can be used to both test existing web site designs or prototypes and to devise new designs;
- Can be used to compare and test the strength and clarity of communication of proposition on different web sites;
- Can be linked to specific marketing outcomes required by site owners.

These are some guidelines and ideas on what can be included when developing a persona. The start or end point is to give each persona a name. The detailed stages are:

1 Build personal attributes into personas:
   - Demographic: Age, sex, education, occupation and, for B2B, company size, position in buying unit;
   - Psychographic: Goals, tasks, motivation;
   - Webographics: Web experience (months), usage location (home or work), usage platform (dial-up, broadband), usage frequency, favourite sites.

2 Remember that personas are only models of characteristics and environment:
   - Design targets;
   - Stereotypes;
   - 3 or 4 usually suffice to improve general usability, but more needed for specific behaviours;
   - Choose one primary persona whom, if satisfied means others are likely to be satisfied.

Primary persona

A representation of the typical site user.

3 Different scenarios can be developed for each persona as explained further below. Write 3 or 4, for example:
   - Information-seeking scenario (leads to site registration);
   - Purchase scenario – new customer (leads to sale);
   - Purchase scenario – existing customer (leads to sale).

Once different personas have been developed that are representative of key site-visitor types or customer types, a primary persona is sometimes identified. Wodtke (2002) says:

> *Your primary persona needs to be a common user type who is both important to the business success of the product and needy from a design point of view – in other words, a beginner user or a technologically challenged one.*

She also says that secondary personas can also be developed, such as super-users or complete novices. Complementary personas are those that don't fit into the main categories and which display unusual behaviour. Such complementary personas help 'out-of-box thinking' and offer choices or content that may appeal to all users.

Multi-channel customer experiences

Remember that the customer scenario or user journey on the web site is only part of a wider customer experience which involves multiple channels. The importance of multi-channel strategies should also be built into assessing customer behaviour and their perception of the online customer experience. The importance of digital channels in influencing the overall customer experience is indicated in Mini Case Study 2.2 'Lexus assesses multi-channel experience consistency'.

Mini Case Study 2.2 — Lexus assesses multi-channel experience consistency

The luxury car brand Lexus has worked with the Multi-channel Marketing Best Practice Club at the Cranfield School of Management, UK to assess the relative importance of consistency between channels. The pertinent results of this study are presented in Table 2.6. It can be seen that, as might be expected, the showroom experience is very important to the overall attitude towards the brand and purchase intent. The importance of the web site experience quality is also notable and especially its role in the propensity to recommend – the Lexus customer can readily recommend the web site to a friend or a colleague. So, it is the interactive channels that deliver the best experience, as would be expected.

Table 2.6 The impact of channel experience on customer relationship

Lexus communication channel	Attitude towards the brand	Future purchase intention	Propensity to recommend
TV experience quality	0.362**	0.360**	0.185
Print experience quality	0.203	0.133	0.023
Direct mail experience quality	0.343*	0.204	0.072
Showroom experience quality	0.447**	0.292*	0.217
Contact centre experience quality	0.431*	0.566	0.147
Web site experience quality	0.452**	0.315*	0.309*

Source: Menteth et al. (2005)
* Correlation is significant at the 0.05 level
** Correlation is significant at the 0.01 level

Models of online buyer behaviour

Standard models of consumer buyer behaviour have been developed by Bettman (1979) and Booms and Bitner (1981). In these models, consumers process marketing stimuli such as the 4 Ps and environmental stimuli according to their personal characteristics such as their culture, social group and personal and psychological make-up. Together these characteristics will affect the consumers' response to marketing messages. For the Internet marketer, a review of the factors influencing behaviour is especially important since a single web site may need to accommodate consumers with different needs at different stages of the buying process. Users will also have different levels of experience of using the web.

Specific behavioural traits are evident on the Internet. Studies show that the World Wide Web is used quite differently by different groups of people. Lewis and Lewis (1997) identified five different types of web users or rather modes of usage of the Internet which remain valid today:

- *Directed information-seekers*. These users will be looking for product, market or leisure information such as details of their football club's fixtures. They are not typically planning to buy online.
- *Undirected information-seekers*. These are the users, usually referred to as 'surfers', who like to browse and change sites by following hyperlinks. Members of this group tend to be novice users (but not exclusively so) and they may be more likely to click on banner advertisements.
- *Directed buyers*. These buyers are online to purchase specific products online. For such users, brokers or cybermediaries that compare product features and prices will be important locations to visit.
- *Bargain hunters*. These users (sometimes known as 'compers') want to find the offers available from sales promotions such as free samples or competitions. For example, the MyOffers site (**www.myoffers.co.uk**) is used by many brands to generate awareness and interest from consumers.
- *Entertainment seekers*. These are users looking to interact with the Web for enjoyment through entering contests such as quizzes, puzzles or interactive multi-player games.

Styler (2001) describes four consumer buying behaviours derived from in-depth home interviews researching behaviour across a range of media, including the Internet. These behaviours are brand-focused, price-sensitive, feature-savvy and advice-led. As Moe (2003) has pointed out, in the bricks-and-mortar environment, stores employ sales people who can distinguish between shoppers based on their in-store behaviour. Some shoppers appear to be very focused in looking for a specific product. In those cases, sales people may try to help the shopper find what they are looking for. In other cases, the shopper is just browsing 'window shopping'. The experienced sales person can identify these shoppers and either ignore them and let them continue or can try to stimulate a purchase. Although there is no sales person to perform this role online, Moe and Fader (2004) believe that through analysing clickstream behaviour and patterns of repeated visits, it may be possible to identify directed buying, browsing or searching behaviour and make prompts accordingly online.

In a report on benchmarking the user experience of UK retail sites, E-consultancy (2004) identified a useful classification of online shopping behaviour to test how well web site design matches different consumer behaviours. In a similar way to previous studies, three types of potential behaviour were identified which are trackers, hunters and explorers. Note that these do not equate to different people, since according to the type of product or occasion, the behaviour of an individual may differ. Indeed, as they research a product they are likely to become more directed.

1 Tracker

Knows exactly which product they wish to buy and uses an online shopping site to track it down and check its price, availability, delivery time, delivery charges or after-sales support.

That is, the tracker is looking for specific information about a particular product. The report says:

If they get the answers they are seeking they need little further persuasion or purchase-justification before completing the purchase.

While this may not be true since they may compare on other sites, this type of shopper will be relatively easy to convert.

2 Hunter

Doesn't have a specific product in mind but knows what type of product they are looking for (e.g. digital camera, cooker) and probably has one or more product features they are looking for. The hunter uses an online shopping site to find a range of suitable products, compare them and decide which one to buy. The hunter needs more help, support and guidance to reach a purchasing decision.

The report says:

Once a potential purchase is found, they then need to justify that purchase in their own minds, and possibly to justify their purchase to others. Only then will confirmation of the purchase become a possibility.

3 Explorer

Doesn't even have a particular type of product in mind. They may have a well-defined shopping objective (buying a present for someone or treating themselves), a less-resolved shopping objective (buying something to 'brighten up' the lounge) or no shopping objective at all (they like the High Street store and thought they would have a look at the online site).

The report suggests that the explorer has a range of possible needs and many uncertainties to be resolved before committing to purchase, but the following may be helpful in persuading these shoppers to convert:

Certain types of information, however, are particularly relevant. Suggested gift ideas, guides to product categories, lists of top selling products and information-rich promotions (What's New? What's Hot?) – these could all propel them towards a purchasing decision.

From this brief review of online buyer behaviours, we can suggest that online marketers need to take into account the range of behaviours shown in Table 2.7 both when developing an Internet marketing strategy and when executing it through site design.

Table 2.7 Alternative perspectives on online buyer behaviours

Range of behavioural traits	Sources referred to
1 Directed to undirected information-seekers	Lewis and Lewis (1997), Kothari et al. (2001)
2 Brand-knowledgeable to not knowledgeable	Kothari et al. (2001), Styler (2001)
3 Feature-led to not feature-led	Styler (2001)
4 Price-led to not price-led	Styler (2001)
5 Service-quality-led to not service-quality-led	—
6 Require advice to do not require advice	Styler (2001)
7 Brand-loyal to opportunistic	Clemons and Row (2000), Styler (2001)

Hierarchy of response models

An alternative view of consumer behaviour in using the Internet during the buying process relates to the well-documented 'hierarchy of response model', summarised for example by Kotler et al. (2001), as made up of the following stages:

● awareness;
● interest;
● evaluation;
● trial;
● adoption.

Breitenbach and van Doren (1998) also suggest that audience members of an individual web site tend to pass through these stages.

Figure 2.23 indicates how the Internet can be used to support the different stages in the buying process. The boxes on the left show the typical stages that a new prospect passes through, according to, for example, Robinson et al. (1967). A similar analysis was performed by Berthon et al. (1998), who speculated that the relative communications effectiveness of using a web site in this process gradually increased from 1 to 6.

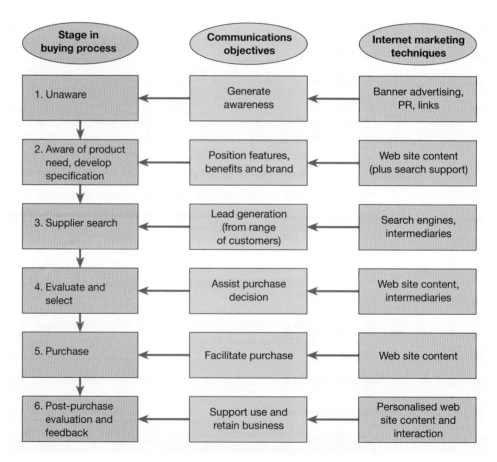

Figure 2.23 A summary of how the Internet can impact on the buying process for a new purchaser

It is worthwhile reviewing each of the stages in the buying process referred to in Figure 2.23 in order to highlight how effective the Internet can be when used at different stages to support the marketing communications objectives. Of course, the exact stage of the buying decision varies for different products and different types of customers, so an alternative approach is to develop channel chains (Figure 2.10) which reflect these differences. In general, digital media support the consumer buying process as follows.

1 Consumer: unaware. Company: generates awareness (of need, product or service)
Generating awareness of need is conventionally achieved principally through the mass media used in offline advertising. The Internet is relatively ineffective at this since it tends to have a more limited impact and reach than television, radio or print media. However, display advertising or paid search marketing can be used to supplement offline awareness-building as explained in Chapter 8. Some companies such as Zopa (see Case Study 2 below) have effectively developed brand awareness by means of PR and media mentions concerning their success on the Internet, with the result that even if a customer does not have a current need for a product, that customer may be aware of the source when the need develops. Examples of e-businesses that have developed a well-known brand include Amazon for books, Dell for computers, CDWOW for music, Microsoft Expedia for Holidays and AutoByTel for cars. In more specialised business-to-business sectors it may also be possible for a company to establish a reputation as a preferred web site as a source of expertise in its sector (for example, **www.siebel.com** for CRM and **www.tektronix.com** for test and measurement).

2 Consumer: aware of need, develops specification. Company: position features, benefits and brand
Once a consumer is aware of a need and is considering what features and benefits he or she requires from a product, then they may turn straight to the web to start identifying the range of features available from a particular type of product through using a generic search. Online, search engines such as Google, MSN and Yahoo! are important at this stage and effectively increase comparison at an early stage in the buying processes. Specification development effectively happens at the same time as supplier search and more suppliers can be evaluated in greater depth than traditionally. For example, Figure 2.24 shows e-retailers available in paid search for an initial product search on fridges. Retailers such as Comet are displayed in the natural listings (see Chapter 8) while others such as Tesco are displayed in the sponsored links.

Intermediaries well known within a sector are very important in supplier search and can also help in evaluation. For example, Shopgenie (**www.shopgenie.co.uk**) in the example in Figure 2.24 or CNET (**www.computers.com**) provides detailed information and reviews on computers to help consumers make the choice. The prospect will likely also click through to destination sites to find out about, for example, features available in a digital television or characteristics of a place to go on holiday. If a company is fortunate enough to achieve interest at this point, then it has an early opportunity to enter a dialogue with a customer and build the product's brand and generate a lead.

3 Consumer: supplier search. Company: generate leads (engage and capture interest)
Once customers are actively searching for products (the directed information-seeker of Lewis and Lewis, 1997), the web provides an excellent medium to help them do this. It also provides a good opportunity for companies to describe the benefits of their web sites and obtain qualified leads. The Internet marketer must consider the methods that a

Figure 2.24 Initial product search showing e-retailers available

customer will choose for searching and then ensure that the company or its product is featured prominently.

4 Consumer: evaluate and select. Supplier: assist purchase decision

One of the most powerful features of web sites is their facility to carry a large amount of content at relatively low cost. This can be turned to advantage when customers are looking to identify the best product. By providing relevant information in a form that is easy to find and digest, a company can use its web site to help in persuading the customer. For example, the Comet site (Figure 2.25) enables customers to readily compare product features side-by-side, so the customer can decide on the best products for them. Thanks to the web, this stage can now overlap with earlier stages. Brand issues are important here, as proved by research in the branding section of Chapter 5, since a new buyer naturally prefers to buy from a familiar supplier with a good reputation – it will be difficult for a company to portray itself in this way if it has a slow, poorly designed or shoddy web site.

5 Consumer: purchase. Company: facilitate purchase

Once a customer has decided to purchase, then the company will not want to lose the custom at this stage! The web site should enable standard credit-card payment mechanisms with the option to place the order by phone or mail. Online retailers pay great attention to identifying factors that encourage customers to convert once they have added a product to their 'shopping basket'. Security guarantees, delivery choices and free delivery offers, for example, can help increase conversion rates.

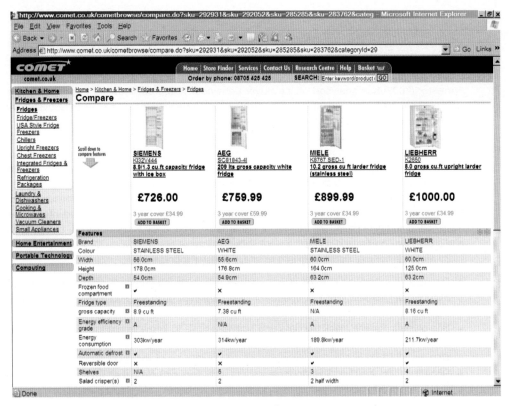

Figure 2.25 Comet product comparison facility (www.comet.co.uk)

6 Consumer: post-purchase service, evaluation and feedback. Company: support product use and retain business

The Internet also provides great potential for retaining customers, as explained in Chapter 6 since:

- value-added services such as free customer support can be provided by the web site and these encourage repeat visits and provide value-added features;
- feedback on products can be provided to customers; the provision of such information will indicate to customers that the company is looking to improve its service;
- e-mail can be used to give regular updates on products and promotions and encourage customers to revisit the site;
- repeat visits to sites provide opportunities for cross-selling and repeat selling through personalised sales promotions messages based on previous purchase behaviour.

In this section we have reviewed simple models of the online buying process that can help Internet marketers convert more site visitors to lead and sale; however, in many cases, the situation is not as simple as the models. Mini Case Study 2.3 *'Multi-site online car purchase behaviour'* indicates the complexity of online buyer behaviour, suggesting that it is difficult to develop general models that define online buyer behaviour.

Mini Case Study 2.3 · Multi-site online car purchase behaviour

Forrester (2002) has analysed online buyer behaviour in the car industry in detail. They estimate that different sites such as car manufacturers, dealers, and independent auto sites collectively invest more than $1 billion each year trying to turn online auto shoppers into buyers. They recommend that to effectively identify serious car buyers from the millions of site visitors, auto site owners must correlate car buyers' *multi-site* behaviour to near-term (within three months) vehicle purchases. In the research, Forrester analysed behaviour across sites from three months of continuous online behaviour data and buyer-reported purchase data provided by comScore Networks, extracted from comScore's Global Network of more than 1.5 million opt-in Internet users. To find the correlation between online shopping behaviour and car buying, Forrester observed 78,000 individual consumers' paths through 170 auto sites and interviewed 17 auto site owners and software providers. Behaviour patterns like frequency and intensity of online research sessions and cross-site comparison-shopping were strong purchase predictors.

By researching user paths from site to site, Forrester found that:

- Online auto marketing and retailing continues to see strong growth despite weak demand in 2001 from the car market. While independent sites remain popular with consumers, manufacturer sites saw a 59 per cent increase in traffic in 2001.
- Site owners currently lack the data and software tools to know where they fit in the online auto retail landscape – or even how individual customers use their sites.
- Roughly one in four auto site visitors buys a car within three months.
- Repeat visitors are rare. Sixty-four per cent of all buyers complete their research in five sessions or less.
- Auto shoppers' web research paths predict their probability of vehicle purchase; on some paths, 46 per cent are near-term buyers.
- The theory of a 'marketing funnel' doesn't map to actual car buyer behaviour. Conventional wisdom suggests that shoppers first visit information sites, then manufacturers', then e-retailers' or dealer sites, as they go from awareness to interest, desire, and action. Mapping consumer data reveals a messier, more complex consideration process.

Summarising the research Mark Dixon Bünger, senior analyst, Forrester Research says:

Common assumptions about customer behavior when shopping for vehicles online are wrong. For example, loyalty and repeat visits are actually an anti-predictor of purchase. Most people who buy come in short, intense bursts, and don't hang out on auto sites. Single-site traffic analysis is not enough to understand and influence multisite, multisession auto shoppers. Today's Web site analysis tools weren't created to measure the complex nature of online auto shopping, which involves many sites over several episodes.

A segmentation of car buying profiles

Forrester developed what they call a 'site owner road map' to help car site owners better understand their customers and segment them into four distinct car buying profiles. Since this segmentation is not predictive, Forrester suggests that to sell more cars through a better site experience, companies need to help each type of buyer reach its different goals. The four types are:

- *Explorers.* Forrester suggests that car buying is a 'journey of discovery' for these users, so suggests giving them a guide tour or user guides. This should lead them through a convenient, explicit buying process.
- *Offroaders.* These perform detailed research before visiting showrooms, but often leave without purchasing. If dealers can identify these visitors through the number of configurations, comparisons and number of page views they have, then dealers should quickly respond to the number of quotes they require.
- *Drive-bys.* These are the largest segment of car site visitors. They visit four sites or fewer, but only 20 per cent buy online. Forrester suggests profiling these customers by incentivising them in order to better understand their purchase intentions.
- *Cruisers.* Frequent visitors, but only 15 per cent buy a car in the short term. These are influencers who have a great interest in cars, but are not necessarily interested in purchase.

Competitors

Competitor analysis

Review of Internet marketing services offered by existing and new competitors and adoption by their customers.

Competitor analysis or the monitoring of competitor use of Internet marketing for acquisition and retention of customers is especially important because of the dynamic nature of the Internet medium. As Porter (2001) has pointed out, this dynamism enables new services to be launched and elements of the marketing mix such as price and promotion changed much more frequently than was traditionally the case. Copying of concepts and approaches may be possible, but can on some occasions be controlled through patenting. For example, Amazon.com has patented the 'One Click' approach to purchase, so this term and approach is not seen on other sites. The implications of this dynamism are that competitor benchmarking is not a one-off activity while developing a strategy, but needs to be continuous.

'Benchmarking' is the term used for structured comparison of e-commerce services within a market. Its purpose is to identify threats posed by changes to competitor offerings, but also to identify opportunities for enhancing a company's own web services through looking at innovative approaches in non-competing companies. Competitor benchmarking is closely related to developing the customer experience and is informed by understanding the requirements of different customer personas as introduced earlier in this chapter.

Traditionally competitors will be well known. With the Internet and the global marketplace there may be new entrants that have the potential to achieve significant market share. This is particularly the case with retail sales. For example, successful new companies have developed on the Internet who sell books, music, CDs and electronic components. As a consequence, companies need to review the Internet-based performance of both existing and new players. Companies should review:

- well-known local competitors (for example, UK or European competitors for British companies);
- well-known international competitors;
- new Internet companies local and worldwide (within sector and out of sector).

Chase (1998) advocates that when benchmarking, companies should review competitors' sites, identifying best practices, worst practices and 'next practices'. Next practices are where a company looks beyond its industry sector at what leading Internet companies such as Amazon (**www.amazon.com**) and Cisco (**www.cisco.com**) are doing. For instance, a company in the financial services industry could look at what portal sites are providing and see if there are any lessons to be learnt on ways to make information provision easier. When undertaking scanning of competitor sites, the key differences that should be watched out for are:

- new approaches from existing companies;
- new companies starting on the Internet;
- new technologies, design techniques and customer support on the site which may give a competitive advantage.

As well as assessing competitors on performance criteria, it is also worthwhile categorising them in terms of their capability to respond. Deise et al. (2000) suggest an equation that can be used in combination to assess the capability of competitors to respond:

$$\text{Competitive capability} = \frac{Agility \times Reach}{Time\text{-}to\text{-}market}$$

'Agility' refers to the speed at which a company is able to change strategic direction and respond to new customer demands. 'Reach' is the ability to connect to or to promote products and generate new business in new markets. 'Time-to-market' is the product life-cycle from concept through to revenue generation. Companies with a high competitive capability within their market and competitive markets are arguably the most important ones to watch.

Companies can also turn to benchmarking organisations such as Gomez (**www.gomez.com**) to review e-commerce scorecards. In some sectors such as banking, competitors share data with a benchmarking organisation, enabling them to see their relative performance (without knowing actual sales or efficiency levels). An example is eBenchmarkers, which in the UK produces reports for different financial services markets. Performance criteria are related to the conversion efficiency introduced earlier – companies are ranked relative to each other on their capacity to attract, convert and retain customers to use their e-commerce services.

To assess the success of competitors in generating visitors to their web sites, a variety of data sources can be used; the methods of collection are explained further in Chapter 9.

- Panel data can be used to compare number and type of visitors to competitor sites through time.
- Summaries of ISP data such as Hitwise (**www.hitwise.co.uk**) can be used to assess visitor rankings for different competitors.
- Audits of web site traffic such as that produced by ABCelectronic (**www.abce.org**) can be used for basic comparison of visitors.

We revisit competitor benchmarking in more detail in Chapters 4 and 7.

Suppliers

The most significant aspect of monitoring suppliers in the context of Internet marketing is with respect to the effect suppliers have on the value of quality of product or service delivered to the end customer. Key issues include the effect of suppliers on product price, availability and features. This topic is not discussed further since it is less significant than other factors in an Internet marketing context.

Intermediaries

Marketing intermediaries
Firms that can help a company to promote, sell and distribute its products or services.

Destination sites
Sites typically owned by merchants, product manufacturers or retailers, providing product information.

Marketing intermediaries are firms that can help a company to promote, sell and distribute its products or services. In the Internet context, online intermediaries can be contrasted with destination sites which are typically merchant sites owned by manufacturers or retailers which offer information and products (in reality any type of site can be a destination site, but the term is generally used to refer to merchant and brand sites).

Online intermediary sites provide information about destination sites and provide a means of connecting Internet users with product information. The best known online intermediaries are the most popular sites such as Google, MSN and Yahoo! These are known as 'portals' and are described further below. Other consumer intermediaries such as Kelkoo (**www.kelkoo.com**) and Bizrate (**www.bizrate.com**) provide price comparison

Online intermediary sites
Web sites that facilitate exchanges between consumer and business suppliers.

Online social network
A service facilitating the connection, collaboration and exchange of information between individuals.

for products, as described earlier in this chapter. Most newspaper and magazine publishers such as VNU (**www.vnu.com**) and Emap (**www.emap.com**) now provide online versions of their publications. These are as important in the online world in promoting products as newspapers and magazines are in the offline world.

Online intermediaries are businesses which support business and consumer audiences, so they can serve both B2B and B2C information exchanges. Auction sites are another type of online intermediary that support the B2B and the C2C exchanges introduced in Chapter 1. Online intermediaries sometimes support online social networks which are a form of online community described in more detail in the section on virtual communities at the end of Chapter 6. The Google Orkut service (**www.orkut.com**) is an example of a personal social network, while Linked In (**www.linkedin.com**) and Eacademy (**www.eacademy.com**) are examples of business networks. A business-to-business community serving the interest of Internet marketers is the E-consultancy forums (**www.e-consultancy.com/forum**).

Online intermediaries are typically independent of merchants and brands, but can be owned by brands. In business-to-business marketing examples of such intermediaries include Clearly Business (**www.clearlybusiness.com**) from Barclays or bCentral (**www.bcentral.co.uk**) from Microsoft. These are examples of 'countermediaries' referred to earlier in the chapter which are created by a service provider to provide valuable content or services to their audience with a view to enhancing their brand, so they are not truly independent.

Sarkar et al. (1996) identified many different types of potential online intermediaries (mainly from a B2C perspective) which they refer to as 'cybermediaries'. Some of the main intermediaries identified by Sarkar et al. (1996), listed with current examples, are:

- Directories (such as Yahoo! directory, Open Directory, Business.com).
- Search engines (Google, Yahoo! Search).
- Malls (now replaced by comparison sites such as Kelkoo and Pricerunner).
- Virtual resellers (own inventory and sells direct, e.g. Amazon, CDWOW).
- Financial intermediaries (offering digital cash and payment services such as PayPal which is now part of eBay).
- Forums, fan clubs and user groups (referred to collectively as 'virtual communities' or social networks such as HabboHotel for youth audiences).
- Evaluators (sites which act as reviewers or comparison of services such as Kelkoo).

Search engines, spiders and robots
Automatic tools known as 'spiders' or 'robots' index registered sites. Users search by typing keywords and are presented with a list of pages.

Directories or catalogues
Structured listings of registered sites in different categories.

At the time that Sarkar et al. (1996) listed the different types of intermediaries given above, there were many separate web sites offering these types of services. For example, AltaVista (**www.altavista.com**) offered search engine facilities and Yahoo! (**www.yahoo.com**) offered a directory of different web sites. Since this time, such sites have diversified the services offered. Yahoo! now offers all these services and additional types such as dating, communities and auctions. Diversification has occurred through the introduction of new intermediaries that provide services to other intermediaries and also through acquisition and merger. Since Google issued shares it has increasingly acquired or developed new services in its Google Labs (**http://labs.google.com**) to integrate into its services as Yahoo! has done throughout its history. For example, it has purchased provider Blogger (**www.blogger.com**) and has introduced the Gmail e-mail service and Orkut social networking service.

Activity 2.6 highlights the alternative revenue models available to these new intermediaries, in this case an evaluator, and speculates on their future.

Activity 2.6	Kelkoo.com, an example of revenue models for new intermediaries

visit the w.w.w.

Purpose

To provide an example of the services provided by cybermediaries and explore their viability as businesses.

Figure 2.26 Kelkoo.com, a European price comparison site

Questions

1 Visit the Kelkoo web site (www.kelkoo.com) shown in Figure 2.26 and search for this book, a CD or anything else you fancy. Explain the service that is being offered to customers.
2 Write down the different revenue opportunities for this site (some may be evident from the site, but others may not); write down your ideas also.
3 Given that there are other competing sites in this intermediary category, such as Shopsmart (www.shopsmart.com), assess the future of this online business using press releases and comments from other sites such as Moreover (www.moreover.com).

Infomediary

An intermediary business whose main source of revenue derives from capturing consumer information and developing detailed profiles of individual customers for use by third parties.

Hagel and Rayport (1997) use 'infomediary' specifically to refer to sale of customer information, although it is sometimes used more widely to refer to sites offering detailed information about any topic. Traditional infomediaries are Experian (www.experian.com) and Claritas (www.claritas.com) which provide customer data for direct marketing or credit scoring. Such companies now use the web to collect additional customer information from prize draw sites such as Email Inform (www.emailinform.com). An example of an infomediary providing detailed information about a sector, in this case e-marketing topics, is E-consultancy (www.e-consultancy.com).

A further type of intermediary is the *virtual marketplace* or virtual B2B trading community mentioned earlier in the chapter.

Portals

Portal

A web site that acts as a gateway to information and services available on the Internet by providing search engines, directories and other services such as personalised news or free e-mail.

An Internet **portal** is a web site that acts as a gateway to information and services available on the Internet. Essentially, it is an alternative term for online intermediary, but the main emphasis is on providing access to information on the portal site and other sites.

Portals are important to Internet marketers since portals are where users spend the bulk of their time online when they are not on merchant or brand sites. Situation analysis involves assessing which portals target customers with different demographics and psychographics use. It also relates to competitor benchmarking, since the sponsorship deals and co-branding arrangements set up by competitors should also be reviewed.

For marketers to extend the visibility or reach of their company online, they need to be well represented on a range of portals through using sponsorships, online adverts and search marketing, as explained in Chapter 8. Portals also enable targeted communications. Specialist portals enable markets to target a particular audience through advertising, sponsorship and PR while general portals often have sections or 'channels' which indicate a particular product interest. For example, financial services provider Alliance and Leicester uses a Loan calculator to sponsor the Money, Loans channel on ISP portal Wanadoo (www.wanadoo.com.uk) and web measurement company NetIQ sponsors the relevant channel on ClickZ (www.clickz.com) to reach their target audiences. Main portals such as newspapers and trade magazines also have registration, so can provide options for delivering messages via e-mail also.

Activity 2.7 **Which are the top portals?**

→ visit the w.w.w.

To see the most important portals in your region, visit Nielsen//NetRatings (www.netratings.com) and choose 'Top Rankings'. This gives the top 10 most popular sites in the countries listed. You will see that the largest portals such as MSN and Google can be used to reach over 50% of the Internet audience in a country. The pattern of top sites is different in each country, so international marketers need to ensure they are equally visible in different countries.

Many portals are related to Internet service providers – ISPs such as AOL (www.aol.com) and Wanadoo (www.wandadoo.com) have created a portal as the default home page for their users. The Microsoft Network (www.msn.com) is a popular portal since when users install the Internet Explorer browser it will be set up so that the home page is a Microsoft page.

Types of portals

Portals vary in scope and in the services they offer, so naturally terms have evolved to describe the different types of portals. It is useful, in particular, for marketers to understand these terms since they act as a checklist that companies are represented on the different types of portals. Table 2.8 shows different types of portals. It is apparent that there is overlap between the different types of portal. Yahoo! for instance, is a horizontal portal since it offers a range of services, but it has also been developed as a geographical portal for different countries and, in the USA, even for different cities. Many vertical and marketplace portals such as Chemdex and many Vertical Net sites (now VertMarkets (www.vertmarkets.com)) which were created at the height of the dot-com boom proved unsustainable and have largely been replaced by online versions of trader magazines for these markets.

Table 2.8 Portal characteristics

Type of portal	Characteristics	Example
Access portal	Associated with ISP	Wanadoo (www.wanadoo.com) AOL (www.aol.com)
Horizontal or functional portal	Range of services: search engines, directories, news recruitment, personal information management, shopping, etc.	Yahoo! (www.yahoo.com) MSN (www.msn.com) Lycos (www.lycos.com)
Vertical	A vertical portal covers a particular market such as construction with news and other services	Construction Plus (www.constructionplus.co.uk) Chem Industry (www.chemindustry.com)
Media portal	Main focus is on consumer or business news or entertainment	BBC (www.bbc.co.uk) Guardian (www.guardian.co.uk) ITWeek (www.itweek.co.uk)
Geographical (region, country, local)	May be: ● horizontal ● vertical	Yahoo! country and city versions Countyweb (www.countyweb.com)
Marketplace	May be: ● horizontal ● vertical ● geographical	EC21 (www.ec21.com) eBay (www.eBay.com)
Search portal	Main focus is on search	Google (www.google.com) Ask Jeeves (www.ask.com)
Media type	May be: ● voice ● video Delivered by streaming media or downloads of files	BBC (www.bbc.co.uk) Silicon (www.silicon.com)

The following case study is an example of a new business model and gives you an opportunity to review the marketplace for this product.

Case Study 2 · Zopa launches a new lending model

Context

It might be thought that innovation in business models was left behind in the dot-com era, but still fledgling businesses are launching new online services. Zopa is an interesting example launched in March 2005.

Zopa is an online service which enables borrowers and lenders to bypass the big high street banks. It is an example of a consumer-to-consumer exchange intermediary. It illustrates the challenges and opportunities of launching a new business online, especially a business with a new business model.

Zopa stands for 'Zone of Possible Agreement' which is a term from business theory. It refers to the overlap between one person's bottom line (the lowest they're prepared to receive for something they are offering) and another person's top line (the most they're prepared to pay for something). In practice, this approach underpins negotiations about the majority types of products and services.

The business model

The exchange provides a matching facility between people who want to borrow and people who want to lend. Significantly, each lender's money is parcelled out between at least 50 borrowers. Zopa revenue is based on charging borrowers 1 per cent of their loan as a fee, and from commission on any repayment protection insurance that the borrower selects. At the time of writing, Zopa estimates it needs to gain just a 0.2 per cent share of the UK loan market to break even, which it could achieve within 18 months of launch.

The main benefit for borrowers is that they can borrow relatively cheaply over shorter periods for small amounts. This is the reverse of banks, where if you borrow more and for longer it gets cheaper. The service will also appeal to borrowers who have difficulty gaining credit ratings from traditional financial services providers.

For lenders, higher returns are possible than through traditional savings accounts if there are no bad debts. These are in the range of 20 to 30% higher than putting money in a deposit account, but of course, there is the risk of bad debt. Lenders choose the minimum interest rate that they are prepared to accept after bad debt has been taken into account for different markets within Zopa. Borrowers are placed in different risk categories with different interest rates according to their credit histories (using the same Equifax-based credit ratings as used by the banks) and lenders can decide which balance of risk against return they require.

Borrowers who fail to pay are pursued through the same mechanism as banks use and also get a black mark against their credit histories. But for the lender, their investment is not protected by any compensation scheme, unless they have been defrauded.

The *Financial Times* reported that banks don't currently see Zopa as a threat to their high street business. One financial analyst said Zopa was 'one of these things that could catch on but probably won't'.

Zopa does not have a contact centre. According to its web site, enquiries to Zopa are restricted to e-mail in order to keep its costs down. However, there is a service promise of answering e-mails within 3 hours during working hours.

Although the service was launched initially in the UK in 2005, *Financial Times* (2005) reported that Zopa has 20 countries where people want to set up franchises. These include the US, where Zopa has a team trying to develop the business through the regulatory hurdles. Other countries include China, New Zealand, India and South American countries.

About the founders

The three founders of Zopa are chief executive Richard Duvall, chief financial officer James Alexander and David Nicholson. All were involved with Egg, with Richard Duvall creating the online bank for Prudential in 1998. Mr Alexander had been strategy director at Egg after joining in 2000, and previously had written the business plan for Smile, another online bank owned by the Co-operative. The founders were also joined by Sarah Matthews, who was Egg's brand development director.

Target market

The idea for the business was developed from market research that showed there was a potential market of 'freeformers' to be tapped.

Freeformers are typically not in standard employment, rather they are self-employed or complete work that is project-based or freelance. Examples include consultants and entrepreneurs. Consequently, their incomes and lifestyles may be irregular, although they may still be assessed as creditworthy. According to James Alexander, '*they're people who are not understood by banks, which value stability in people's lives and income over everything else*'. The Institute of Directors (IOD) (2005) reported that the research showed that freeformers had '*much less of a spending model of money and much more of an asset model*'.

Surprisingly, the research indicated a large number of freeformers. *New Media Age* reported Duvall as estimating that in the UK there may be around 6 million freeformers (of a population of around 60 million). Duvall is quoted as saying: '*it's a group that's growing really quickly. I think that in 10 or 15 years time most people will work this way. It's happening right across the developing world. We've been doing some research in the US and we think there are some 30 or 40 million people there with these attitudes and behaviours*'.

Some of the directors see themselves as freeformers, they have multiple interests and do not only work for Zopa; James Alexander works for one day a week in a charity and Sarah Matthews works just 3 days a week for Zopa. You can see example personas of typical borrowers and lenders on the web site: **www.zopa.com/ZopaWeb/public/how/zopamembers.shtml**.

From reviewing the customer base, lenders and borrowers are often united by a desire to distance themselves from conventional institutions. James Alexander says: '*I spend a lot of time talking to members and have found enormous goodwill towards the idea, which is really like lending to family members or within a community*'. But he also says that some of the lenders are simply entrepreneurs who have the funds, understand portfolio diversification and risk and are lending on Zopa alongside other investments.

Business status

The *Financial Times* (2005) reported that Zopa had just 300 members at launch, but within 4 months it had 26,000 members. According to James Alexander, around 35 per cent are lenders, who between them have £3m of capital waiting to be distributed. The company has not, to date, revealed how much has been lent, but average loans have been between £2,000 and £5,000. Moneyfacts.co.uk isn't showing any current accounts with more than 5 per cent interest, but Zopa is a riskier product, so you'd expect better rates. Unlike a deposit account, it's not covered by any compensation schemes.

Marketing communications

The launch of Zopa has been quite different from Egg and other dot-coms at the turn of the millennium. Many companies at that time invested large amounts in offline media such as TV and print to rapidly grow awareness and to explain their proposition to customers.

Instead Zopa has followed a different communications strategy, which has relied on word-of-mouth and PR with some online marketing activities where the cost of customer acquisition can be controlled. The launch of such a model and the history of its founders, makes it relatively easy to have major pieces about the item in relevant newspapers and magazines such as the *Guardian*, the *Financial Times*, the *Economist* and the Institute of Directors house magazine, which its target audience may read. Around launch, IOD (2005) reports that Duvall's PR agency, Sputnik, achieved 200 million opportunities for the new company to be read about. Of course, not all coverage is favourable, many of the articles explored the risk of lending and the viability of the start-up. However, others have pointed out that the rates for the best-rated 'A category' borrowers are better than any commercial loan offered by a bank and for lenders, rates are better than any savings account. The main online marketing activities that Zopa uses are search engine marketing and affiliate marketing.

Funding

Zopa initially received funding from two private equity groups, Munich-based Wellington Partners and Benchmark Capital of the US. Although the model was unique within financial services, its appeal was increased by the well-publicised success of other peer-to-peer Internet services such as Betfair, the gambling web site, and eBay, the auction site.

Sources: *Financial Times* (2005), *New Media Age* (2005), Institute of Directors (2005), Zopa web site (www.zopa.com) and blog (http://blog.zopa.com).

Question

Imagine you are a member of the team at the investors reviewing the viability of the Zopa business. On which criteria would you assess the future potential of the business and the returns in your investment based on Zopa's position in the marketplace and its internal capabilities?

Summary

1 The constantly changing Internet environment should be monitored by all organisations in order to be able to respond to changes in the micro-environment or the immediate marketplace.

2 The Internet has created major changes to the competitive environment. Organisations should deploy tools such as Porter's five forces and the value chain and value network models in order to assess opportunities and potential threats posed by the Internet.

3 The Internet can encourage the formation of new channel structures. These include *disintermediation* within the marketplace as organisations' channel partners such as wholesalers or retailers are bypassed. Alternatively, the Internet can cause *reintermediation* as new intermediaries with a different purpose are formed to help bring buyers and sellers together in a *virtual marketplace* or *marketspace*.

4 Trading in the marketplace can be sell-side (seller-controlled), buy-side (buyer-controlled) or at a neutral marketplace.

5 A business model is a summary of how a company will generate revenue, identifying its product offering, value-added services, revenue sources and target customers. Exploiting the range of business models made available through the Internet is important to both existing companies and start-ups.

6 The Internet may also offer opportunities for new revenue models such as commission on affiliate referrals to other sites or banner advertising.

7 The opportunity for new commercial arrangements for transactions includes negoti-ated deals, brokered deals, auctions, fixed-price sales, and pure spot markets; and barters should also be considered.

8 Customer analysis is an important part of situation analysis. It involves assessing demand for online services, characteristics of existing online customers and the multi-channel behaviour of customers as they select and purchase products.

9 Regular competitive benchmarking should be conducted to compare services.

10 The role of intermediaries in promoting an organisation's services should also be carefully assessed.

Exercises

Self-assessment exercises

1 Why is environmental scanning necessary?

2 Summarise how each of the micro-environment factors may directly drive the content and services provided by a web site.

3 What are the main aspects of customer adoption of the Internet that managers should be aware of?

4 What are the main changes to channel structures that are facilitated through the Internet?

5 What are the different elements and different types of business model?

6 How should a marketing manager benchmark the online performance of competitors?

7 Describe two different models of online buyer behaviour.

8 How can the Internet be used to support the different stages of the buying process?

Essay and discussion questions

1 Discuss, using examples, how the Internet may change the five competitive forces of Michael Porter.

2 'Internet access levels will never exceed 50% in most countries.' Discuss.

3 What are the options, for an existing organisation, for using new business models through the Internet?

4 Perform a demand analysis for e-commerce services for a product sector and geographical market of your choice.

5 Perform competitor benchmarking for online services for an organisation of your choice.

6 What are the alternatives for modified channel structures for the Internet? Illustrate through different organisations in different sectors.

→

Examination questions

1 What options are available to a supplier, currently fulfilling to customers through a reseller, to use the Internet to change this relationship?

2 What types of channel conflicts are caused by the Internet?

3 What are virtual organisations and how can the Internet support them?

4 Name three options for a company's representation on the Internet in different types of marketplace.

5 Explain the term 'virtual value-chain'.

6 What are the three key factors that affect consumer adoption of the Internet?

7 Summarise how the bargaining power of buyers may be changed by the Internet for a commodity product.

8 How can the internal value chain be modified when an organisation deploys Internet technologies?

References

Agrawal, V., Arjona, V. and Lemmens, R. (2001) E-performance: the path to rational exuberance, *McKinsey Quarterly*, No 1, 31–43.

Benjamin, R. and Wigand, R. (1995) Electronic markets and virtual value-chains on the information superhighway, *Sloan Management Review*, Winter, 62–72.

Berryman, K., Harrington, L., Layton-Rodin, D. and Rerolle, V. (1998) Electronic commerce: three emerging strategies, *McKinsey Quarterly*, No. 1, 152–9.

Berthon, P., Lane, N., Pitt, L. and Watson, R. (1998) The World Wide Web as an industrial marketing communications tool: models for the identification and assessment of opportunities, *Journal of Marketing Management*, 14, 691–704.

Bettman, J. (1979) *An Information Processing Theory of Consumer Choice*. Addison-Wesley, Reading, MA.

BMRB (2001, 2004) *Internet monitor, November*. BMRB International, Manchester. Available online at www.bmrb.co.uk.

Booms, B. and Bitner, M. (1981) Marketing strategies and organisation structure for service firms. In J. Donelly and W. George (eds) *Marketing of Services*. American Marketing Association, New York.

BrandNewWorld (2004) AOL research published at www.aolbrandnewworld.co.uk.

Breitenbach, C. and van Doren, D. (1998) Value-added marketing in the digital domain: enhancing the utility of the Internet, *Journal of Consumer Marketing*, 15(6), 559–75.

Chaffey, D. (2001) Optimising e-marketing performance – a review of approaches and tools. In *Proceedings of IBM Workshop on Business Intelligence and E-marketing*. Warwick, 6 December.

Chaffey, D. (2006) Compilation of search engine keyphrase analysis tools. Page maintained at: www.davechaffey.com/Internet-Marketing/C8-Communications/E-tools/Search-marketing/Search-marketing-keyphrase-tools.

Chase, L. (1998) *Essential Business Tactics for the Net*. Wiley, New York.

Clemons, E. and Row, M. (2000) Behaviour is key to web retailing. *Financial Times*, Mastering Management Supplement, 13 November.

Consumers' Association (2001) Annual UK Internet survey, July (available online at www.which.net/surveys/intro.htm).

Deise, M., Nowikow, C., King, P. and Wright, A. (2000) *Executive's Guide to E-Business. From Tactics to Strategy*. Wiley, New York.

de Kare-Silver, M. (2000) *EShock 2000. The Electronic Shopping Revolution: Strategies for Retailers and Manufacturers*. Macmillan, London.

DTI (2004) *Business in the Information Age – International Benchmarking Study 2004*. UK Department of Trade and Industry. **www.ukonlineforbusiness.gov.uk**.

Economist (2000) Enter the ecosystem, *The Economist*, 11 November.

E-consultancy (2004) Online Retail 2004, benchmarking the user experience of UK retail sites. Report, July, London. Available online from **www.e-consultancy.com**.

Financial Times (2005) Lending exchange bypasses high street banks. Paul J. Davies, *Financial Times*, 22 August.

Forrester Research (2002) Mapping customer paths across multiple sites helps site owners predict which consumers are likely to buy and when. Forrester Research Press Release, Cambridge, MA, 19 February.

Grossnickle, J. and Raskin, O. (2001) *The Handbook of Online Marketing Research: Knowing your Customer Using the Net*. McGraw-Hill, New York.

Hagel, J. III and Rayport, J. (1997) The new infomediaries, *McKinsey Quarterly*, No. 4, 54–70.

Institute of Directors (2005) Profile – Richard Duvall, *Director*, September, 51–5.

Kalakota, R. and Robinson, M. (2000) *E-Business. Roadmap for Success*. Addison-Wesley, Reading, MA.

Kothari, D., Jain, S., Khurana, A. and Saxena, A. (2001) Developing a marketing strategy for global online customer management, *International Journal of Customer Relationship Management*, 4(1), 53–8.

Kotler, P., Armstrong, G., Saunders, J. and Wong, V. (2001) *Principles of Marketing*, 3rd European edn. Financial Times/Prentice Hall, Harlow.

Lewis, H. and Lewis, R. (1997) Give your customers what they want, selling on the Net. *Executive Book Summaries*, 19(3), March.

McDonald, M. and Wilson, H. (2002) *New Marketing: Transforming the Corporate Future*. Butterworth Heinemann, Oxford.

Menteth, H., Arbuthnot, S. and Wilson, H. (2005) Multi-channel experience consistency: evidence from Lexus, *Interactive Marketing*, 6 (4) 317–25.

Moe, W. (2003) Buying, searching, or browsing: differentiating between online shoppers using in-store navigational clickstream. *Journal of Consumer Psychology*, 13 (1/2), 29.

Moe, W. and Fader, P. (2004) Dynamic conversion behavior at e-commerce sites. *Management Science*, 50 (3), 326–35.

MORI (2002) Technology Tracker, January. Available online at: **www.mori.com/technology/techtracker.shtml**.

Murdoch, R. (2005) Speech to the American Society of Newspaper editors, 13 April. Available online at **www.newscorp.com**.

National Statistics (2005) National Statistics Omnibus Survey – Internet access section, May, **www.statistics.gov.uk**.

New Media Age (2005) Personal Lender, Dominic Dudley, 18 August.

Nunes, P., Kambil, A. and Wilson, D. (2000) The all in one market, *Harvard Business Review*, May–June, 2–3.

Porter, M. (1980) *Competitive Strategy*. Free Press, New York.

Porter, M. (2001) Strategy and the Internet, *Harvard Business Review*, March, 62–78.

Rayport, J. and Sviokla, J. (1996) Exploiting the virtual value-chain, *McKinsey Quarterly*, No. 1, 20–32.

Robinson, P., Faris, C. and Wind, Y. (1967) *Industrial Buying and Creative Marketing*. Allyn and Bacon, Boston.

Sarkar, M., Butler, B. and Steinfield, C. (1996) Intermediaries and cybermediaries. A continuing role for mediating players in the electronic marketplace, *Journal of Computer Mediated Communication*, issue 1.

Seybold, P. and Marshak, R. (2001) *The Customer Revolution*. Crown Business, New York.

Styler, A. (2001) Understanding buyer behaviour in the 21st century, *Admap*, September, 23–6.

Thomas, J. and Sullivan, U. (2005) Managing marketing communications with multichannel customers, *Journal of Marketing*, 69 (October), 239–51.

Timmers, P. (1999) *Electronic Commerce Strategies and Models for Business-to-Business Trading*. Wiley, Chichester.

Venkatraman, N. (2000) Five steps to a dot-com strategy: how to find your footing on the web, *Sloan Management Review*, Spring, 15–28.

Wodtke, C. (2002) *Information Architecture: Blueprints for the Web*. New Riders, IN.

Further reading

Dibb, S., Simkin, S., Pride, W. and Ferrel, O. (2001) *Marketing. Concepts and Strategies*, 4th European edn. Houghton Mifflin, New York. *See* Chapter 2, The marketing environment.

Kotler, P., Armstrong, G., Saunders, J. and Wong, V. (2001) *Principles of Marketing*, 3rd European edn. Financial Times/Prentice Hall, Harlow. *See* Chapter 4, The marketing environment.

Porter, M. (2001) Strategy and the Internet, *Harvard Business Review*, March, 62–78. A retrospective assessment of how the Internet has changed Porter's model, first proposed in the 1980s.

Timmers, P. (1999) *Electronic Commerce Strategies and Models for Business-to-Business Trading*. Wiley, Chichester. Detailed descriptions of different B2B models are available in this book.

Web links

A directory of Internet marketing links, including sources for statistics from the Internet environment, is maintained by Dave Chaffey at **www.davechaffey.com**.

Digests of reports and surveys concerned with e-commerce

1 *Digests of published MR data*
   - ClickZ Internet research (**www.clickz.com/stats**)
   - Market Research.com (**www.marketresearch.com**)
   - MR Web (**www.mrweb.co.uk**)

2 *Directories of MR companies*
   - British Market Research Association (**www.bmra.org.uk**)
   - Market Research Society (**www.mrs.org.uk**)
   - International MR agencies (**www.greenbook.org**)

3 *Traditional market research agencies*
   - MORI (**www.mori.com/emori**)
   - NOP (**www.nopworld.com**)
   - Nielsen (**www.nielsen.com**)

4 *Government sources*
   - European government (**http://europa.eu.int/comm/eurostat**)
   - OECD (**www.oecd.org**)
   - UK government (**www.open.gov.uk**, **www.ons.gov.uk**)
   - US government (**www.stat-usa.gov**)

5 *Online audience data*
   - Comscore (**www.comscore.com**)
   - Hitwise (**www.hitwise.com**)
   - Mori (**www.mori.com/emori**)
   - Netratings (**www.netratings.com**)
   - NOP World (**www.nopworld.com**)

3

The Internet macro-environment

Learning objectives

After reading this chapter, the reader should be able to:

● Identify the different elements of the Internet macro-environment that impact on an organisation's Internet marketing strategy and execution

● Assess the impact of legal, moral and ethical constraints and opportunities on an organisation and devise solutions to accommodate them

● Evaluate the significance of other macro-factors such as economics, taxation and legal constraints

Questions for marketers

Key questions for marketing managers related to this chapter are:

● Which factors affect the environment for online trading in a country?

● How do I make sure my online marketing is consistent with evolving online culture and ethics?

● How do I assess new technological innovations?

● Which laws am I subject to when trading online?

Links to other chapters

Like the previous chapter, this one provides a foundation for later chapters on Internet marketing strategy and implementation:

➤ Chapter 4, Internet marketing strategy

➤ Chapter 5, The Internet and the marketing mix

➤ Chapter 6, Relationship marketing using the Internet

➤ Chapter 7, Delivering the online customer experience

➤ Chapter 8, Interactive marketing communications

Introduction

In the last chapter we reviewed the micro-economic factors that an organisation must consider in order to assess the impact of the Internet. In this chapter, we will review how the macro-economic factors can influence the way in which the Internet is used to support marketing.

We present the macro-environment factors using the widely used SLEPT framework. SLEPT stands for Social, Legal, Economic, Political and Technological factors. Often, these factors are known as the PEST factors, but we use SLEPT since it is useful to stress the importance of the Law in influencing Internet marketing practices. The SLEPT factors are:

- *Social factors* – these include the influence of consumer perceptions in determining usage of the Internet for different activities.
- *Legal and ethical factors* – determine the method by which products can be promoted and sold online. Governments, on behalf of society, seek to safeguard individuals' rights to privacy.
- *Economic factors* – variations in the economic performance in different countries and regions affect spending patterns and international trade.
- *Political* – national governments and transnational organisations have an important role in determining the future adoption and control of the Internet and the rules by which it is governed.
- *Technological factors* – changes in technology offer new opportunities to the way products can be marketed.

Together, these macro-economic factors will determine the overall characteristics of the micro-environment described in the previous chapter. For example, the social, legal, economic, political and technological environment in any country will directly affect the demand for e-commerce services by both consumers and businesses. Governments may promote the use of e-commerce while social conventions may limit its popularity. For instance, some southern European countries traditionally do not have a culture suited to catalogue shopping since consumers tend to prefer personal contact. In these countries there will be a lower propensity to buy online.

While it can be considered that the macro-economic factors will influence all competitors in a marketplace, this doesn't mean that the macro-environment factors are unimportant. Changes in the macro-environment such as changes in social behaviour, new laws and the introduction of new technologies can all present opportunities or threats. Organisations that monitor and respond best to their macro-environment can use it as a source of differentiation and competitive advantage.

An indication of the challenge of assessing the macro-environment factors is presented in Figure 3.1. This figure of the 'waves of change' shows how fluctuations in the characteristics of different aspects of the environment vary at different rates through time. The manager has to constantly scan the environment and assess which changes are relevant to their sphere of influence. Changes in social culture and particularly pop culture (what's 'hot' and what's not) tend to be very rapid. Introduction of new technologies and changes in their popularity tend to be frequent too and need to be assessed. Government and legal changes tend to happen over longer time scales, although since this is only a generalisation new laws can be introduced relatively fast. The trick for Internet marketers is to identify those factors which are important in the context of Internet marketing which are critical to competitiveness and service delivery and monitor these. We believe it is the technological and legal factors which are most important to the Internet marketer, so we focus on these.

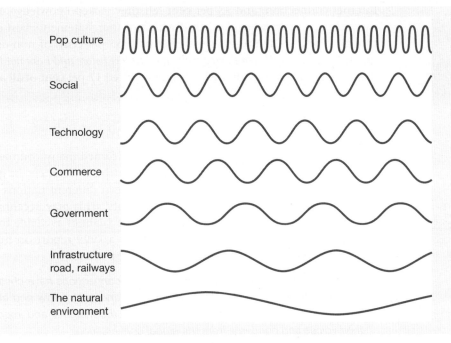

Figure 3.1 'Waves of change' – different timescales for change in the environment

Social factors

In the last chapter, in the sections on customer adoption of Internet technology, we looked at how Internet usage varies across different countries in terms of levels of access, amount of usage, its influence on offline purchase and the proportion of online purchases. These variations are in part dependent on how the Internet is perceived in society. An indication of how social perceptions shape access is clear from a UK government-sponsored survey (Booz Allen Hamilton, 2002) of perceptions in different countries. It noted that social barriers to adoption of the Internet included:

● No perceived benefit
● Lack of trust
● Security problems
● Lack of skills
● Cost.

These factors combine to mean that there is a significant group in each national population of around a third of the adult population that does not envisage ever using the Internet. Clearly, the lack of demand for Internet services from this group needs to be taken into account when forecasting future demand. It is not sufficient to simply extrapolate past rates of Internet adoption growth, since in many developed countries it appears that penetration within households is reaching a plateau as saturation of services amongst those who require them is reached. Taking the UK as an example of possible saturation of fixed PC-based Internet access, National Statistics (2005) reports that in the UK, just under one third (32 per cent) of adults had never used the Internet as of May 2005. Of those who had not used the Internet, 43 per cent stated that they did not want to use, or had no need for, or no interest in, the Internet; 38 per cent had no

Internet connection; and 33 per cent felt they lacked knowledge or the confidence to use it. These adults were also asked which of four statements best described what they thought about using the Internet. Over half (55 per cent) of non-users chose the statement *'I have not really considered using the Internet before and I am not likely to in the future'*. This core group of non-Internet users represented 17 per cent of all adults in the UK.

Social exclusion

The social impact of the Internet has also concerned many commentators because the Internet has the potential effect of accentuating differences in quality of life, both within a society in a single country, and between different nations, essentially creating 'information haves' and 'information have-nots'. This may accentuate social exclusion where one part of society is excluded from the facilities available to the remainder and so becomes isolated. The United Nations, in a 1999 report on human development (p. 63), noted that parallel worlds are developing where

> those with income, education and – literally – connections have cheap and instantaneous access to information. The rest are left with uncertain, slow and costly access . . . the advantage of being connected will overpower the marginal and impoverished, cutting off their voices and concerns from the global conversation.

While the problem is easy to identify, it is clearly difficult to rectify. Developed countries with the economies to support it are promoting the use of IT and the Internet through social programmes such as the UK government's UK Online initiative, which operated between 2000 and 2004 to promote the use of the Internet by business and consumers. In some developing countries, the Internet is seen as a catalyst for change. The *Guardian* (2005) reported how Ethiopia has developed a high-speed broadband infrastructure to facilitate education and commerce.

Like other innovations such as mechanised transport, electricity or the phone, the Internet has been used to support social progress. Those with special needs and interests can now communicate on a global basis and empowering information sources are readily available to all. For example, visually impaired people are no longer restricted to Braille books, but can use screen readers to hear information available to sighted people on the web. As we will see, this has implications for disability discrimination laws which impact accessibility. However, these same technologies, including the Internet, can have negative social impacts such as changing traditional social ideals and being used as a conduit for crime. The Internet has facilitated the publication of and access to information, which has led to many benefits, but it has also led to publication of and access to information which most in society would deem inappropriate. Well-known problems include the use of the Internet to incite racial hatred and terrorism, support child pornography and for identity theft. Such social problems can have implications for marketers who need to respond to laws or the morals established by society and respond to the fears generated. For example, portals such as MSN (**www.msn.com**) and Yahoo! (**www.yahoo.com**) discontinued their use of unmoderated chatrooms in 2003 since paedophiles were using them to 'groom' children for later real-world meetings.

Social exclusion

Part of society is excluded from the facilities available to the remainder.

Legal and ethical issues of Internet usage

Ethical standards
Practices or behaviours which are morally acceptable to society.

Ethical standards are personal or business practices or behaviours which are generally considered acceptable by society. A simple test is that acceptable ethics can be described as moral or just and unethical practices as immoral or unjust.

Ethical issues and the associated laws developed to control the ethical approach to Internet marketing is an important consideration of the Internet business environment for marketers. Privacy of consumers is a key ethical issue on which we will concentrate since many laws have been enacted and it affects all types of organisation regardless of whether they have a transactional e-commerce service. A further ethical issue for which laws have been enacted in many countries is providing an accessible level of Internet services for disabled users. We will also review other laws that have been developed for managing commerce and distance-selling online.

Privacy legislation

Privacy
A moral right of individuals to avoid intrusion into their personal affairs.

Identity theft
The misappropriation of the identity of another person, without their knowledge or consent.

Privacy refers to a moral right of individuals to avoid intrusion into their personal affairs by third parties. Privacy of personal data such as our identities, likes and dislikes is a major concern to consumers, particularly with the dramatic increase in **identity theft**. According to the *Guardian* (2003a), quoting the Credit Industry Fraud Avoidance System (CIFAS), the UK's fraud prevention service, it is the fastest-growing white-collar crime, generating a criminal cashflow of £10m a day. In 1999, there were 20,264 reported cases of identity theft in the UK; but by 2002, that figure had reached 74,766, and in 2003, the figure was 101,000. Identity fraud involving credit and debit cards rose by 45 per cent in 2003.

Yet, for marketers to better understand their customers' needs, this type of information is very valuable. Through collecting such information it will also be possible to use more targeted communications and develop products that are more consistent with users' needs. How should marketers respond to this dilemma? An obvious step is to ensure that marketing activities are consistent with the latest data protection and privacy laws. Although compliance with the laws may sound straightforward, in practice different interpretations of the law are possible and since these are new laws they have not been tested in court. As a result, companies have to take their own business decision based on the business benefits of applying particular marketing practices, against the financial and reputational risks of less strict compliance.

Effective e-commerce requires a delicate balance to be struck between the benefits the individual customer will gain to their online experience through providing personal information and the amount and type of information that they are prepared for companies to hold about them.

What are the main information types used by the Internet marketer which are governed by ethics and legislation? The information needs are:

1 *Contact information.* This is the name, postal address, e-mail address and, for B2B companies, web site address.
2 *Profile information.* This is information about a customer's characteristics that can be used for segmentation. They include age, sex and social group for consumers, and company characteristics and individual role for business customers. The specific types of information and how they are used is referenced in Chapters 2 and 6. The willingness of consumers to give this information and the effectiveness of incentives have

been researched for Australian consumers by Ward et al. (2005). They found that consumers are willing to give non-financial data if there is an appropriate incentive.

3 *Behavioural information (on a single site)*. This is purchase history, but also includes the whole buying process. Web analytics (Chapter 9) can be used to assess the web and e-mail content accessed by individuals.

4 *Behavioural information (across multiple sites)*. This can potentially show how a user accesses multiple sites and responds to ads across sites.

Table 3.1 summarises how these different types of customer information are collected and used through technology.

Table 3.1 Types of information collected online and related technologies

Type of information	Approach and technology used to capture and use information
Contact information	Collected through online forms in response to an incentive for the customer. Stored in databases linking to web site. Cookies are used to remember a specific person on subsequent visits.
Profile information	Also collected through online forms. Cookies can be used to assign a person to a particular segment by linking the cookie to a customer database record and then offering content consistent with their segment.
Behavioural information on a single site	Purchase histories are stored in the sales order database. Web logs are used to store clickstreams of the sequence of web pages visited. A single pixel GIF is used to assess whether a reader had opened an e-mail. Cookies are also used for monitoring visitor behaviour during a site visit and on subsequent visits.
Behavioural information across multiple sites	Web logs can tell the previous site visited by a customer. Banner advertising networks (Chapter 8) and ISPs can potentially assess all sites visited.

Ethical issues concerned with personal information ownership have been usefully summarised by Mason (1986) into four areas:

● *Privacy* – what information is held about the individual?
● *Accuracy* – is it correct?
● *Property* – who owns it and how can ownership be transferred?
● *Accessibility* – who is allowed to access this information, and under which conditions?

Fletcher (2001) provides an alternative perspective, raising these issues of concern for both the individual and the marketer:

● *Transparency* – who is collecting what information?
● *Security* – how is information protected once it has been collected by a company?
● *Liability* – who is responsible if data are abused?

All of these issues arise in the next section which reviews actions marketers should take to achieve privacy and trust.

Data protection legislation is enacted to protect the individual, to protect their privacy and to prevent misuse of their personal data. Indeed, the first article of the European Union Directive 95/46/EC on which legislation in individual European countries is based, specifically refers to personal data. It says:

Personal data
Any information about an individual stored by companies concerning their customers or employees.

Member states shall protect the fundamental rights and freedoms of natural persons [i.e. a named individual at home or at work], and in particular their right to privacy with respect to the processing of personal data.

In the UK, the enactment of the European legislation is the Data Protection Act 1984, 1998 (DPA), which is managed by the legal requirements of the 1998 UK data protection act and summarised at **www.informationcommissioner.gov.uk**. This law is typical of what has evolved in many countries to help protect personal information. Any company that holds personal data on computers or on file about customers or employees must be registered with a data protection registrar (although there are some exceptions which may exclude small businesses). This process is known as notification.

The guidelines on the eight data protection principles are produced by Information Commissioner (1998) on which this overview is based. These principles state that personal data should be:

Notification
The process whereby companies register with the data protection register to inform about their data holdings.

1 Fairly and lawfully processed

In full:

> *Personal data shall be processed fairly and lawfully and, in particular, shall not be processed unless – at least one of the conditions in Schedule 2 is met; and in the case of sensitive personal data, at least one of the conditions in Schedule 3 is also met.*

The Information Commissioner has produced a 'fair processing code' which suggests how an organisation needs to achieve 'fair and lawful processing' under the details of Schedules 2 and 3 of the Act. This requires:

Data controller
Each company must have a defined person responsible for data protection.

Data subject
The legal term to refer to the individual whose data are held.

- Appointment of a data controller who is a person with defined responsibility for data protection within a company.
- Clear details in communications such as on a web site or direct mail of how a 'data subject' can contact the data controller or a representative.
- Before data processing 'the data subject has given his consent' or the processing must be *necessary* either for a 'contract to which the data subject is a party' (for example as part of a sale of a product) or because it is required by other laws. Consent is defined in the published guidelines as '*any freely given specific and informed indication of his wishes by which the data subject signifies his agreement to personal data relating to him being processed*'.
- Sensitive personal data requires particular care, this includes:
  - the racial or ethnic origin of the data subject;
  - political opinions;
  - religious beliefs or other beliefs of a similar nature;
  - membership of a trade union;
  - physical or mental health or condition;
  - sexual life;
  - the commission or alleged commission or proceedings of any offence.
- No other laws must be broken in processing the data.

2 Processed for limited purposes

In full:

> *Personal data shall be obtained only for one or more specified and lawful purposes, and shall not be further processed in any manner incompatible with that purpose or those purposes.*

This implies that the organisation must make it clear why and how the data will be processed at the point of collection. For example, an organisation has to explain how your data will be used if you provide your details on a web site when entering a prize draw. You would also have to agree (give consent) for further communications from the company.

Figure 3.2 suggests some of the issues that should be considered when a data subject is informed of how the data will be used. Important issues are:

- Whether future communications will be sent to the individual (explicit consent is required for this in online channels; this is clarified by the related Privacy and Electronic Communications Regulation Act which is referred to below);
- Whether the data will be passed on to third parties (again explicit consent is required);
- How long the data will be kept.

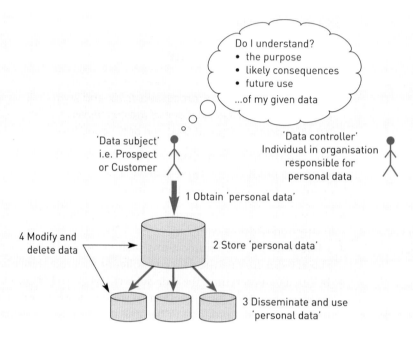

Figure 3.2 Information flows that need to be understood for compliance with data protection legislation

3 Adequate, relevant and not excessive
In full:

Personal data shall be adequate, relevant and not excessive in relation to the purpose or purposes for which they are processed.

This specifies that the minimum necessary amount of data is requested for processing. There is difficulty in reconciling this provision between the needs of the individual and the needs of the company. The more details that an organisation has about a customer, then the better they can understand that customer and so develop products and marketing communications specific to that customer which they are more likely to respond to.

4 Accurate
In full:

Personal data shall be accurate and, where necessary, kept up to date.

It is clearly also in the interest of an organisation in an ongoing relationship with a partner that the data be kept accurate and up-to-date. The guidelines on the Act suggest that additional steps should be taken to check data are accurate, in case they are in error, for example due to mis-keying by the data subject or the organisation or for some other reason. Inaccurate data are defined in the guidelines as: 'incorrect or misleading as to any matter of fact'.

The guidelines go on to discuss the importance of keeping information up-to-date. This is only necessary where there is an ongoing relationship and the rights of the individual may be affected if they are not up-to-date. This implies, for example, that a credit-checking agency should keep credit scores up-to-date.

5 Not kept longer than necessary

In full:

Personal data processed for any purpose or purposes shall not be kept for longer than is necessary for that purpose or those purposes.

The guidelines state:

To comply with this Principle, data controllers will need to review their personal data regularly and to delete the information which is no longer required for their purposes.

It might be in a company's interests to 'clean data' so that records that are not relevant are archived or deleted, for example if a customer has not purchased for ten years. However, there is the possibility that the customer may still buy again, in which case the information would be useful.

If a relationship between the organisation and the data subject ends, then data should be deleted. This will be clear in some instances, for example when an employee leaves a company their personal data should be deleted. With a consumer who has purchased products from a company this is less clear since frequency of purchase will vary, for example a car manufacturer could justifiably hold data for several years.

6 Processed in accordance with the data subject's rights

In full:

Personal data shall be processed in accordance with the rights of data subjects under this Act.

One aspect of the data subject's rights is the option to request a copy of their personal data from an organisation; this is known as a 'subject access request'. For payment of a small fee such as £10 or £30, an individual can request information which must be supplied by the organisation within 40 days. This includes all information on paper files and on computer. If you requested this information from your bank there might be several boxes of transactions!

Other aspects of a data subject's rights which the law upholds are designed to prevent or control processing which:

Subject access request
A request by a data subject to view personal data from an organisation.

- causes damage or distress (for example repeatedly sending mailshots to someone who has died);
- is used for direct marketing (for example, in the UK consumers can subscribe to the mail, e-mail or telephone preference services to avoid unsolicited mailings, e-mails or phone calls). This invaluable service is provided by the Direct Marketing Association (**www.dmaconsumers.org**). If you subscribe to these services organisations must check against these 'exclusion lists' before contacting you. If they don't, and some don't, they are breaking the law;
- is used for automatic decision taking – automated credit checks, for example, may result in unjust decisions on taking a loan. These can be investigated if you feel the decision is unfair.

7 Secure

In full:

Appropriate technical and organisational measures shall be taken against unauthorised or unlawful processing of personal data and against accidental loss or destruction of, or damage to, personal data.

This guideline places a legal imperative on organisations to prevent unauthorised internal or external access to information and also its modification or destruction. Of course, most organisations would want to do this anyway since the information has value to their organisation.

Of course, the cost of security measures will vary according to the level of security required. The Act allows for this through this provision:

(i) Taking into account the state of technological development at any time and the cost of implementing any measures, the measures must ensure a level of security appropriate to: (a) the harm that might result from a breach of security; and (b) the nature of the data to be protected. (ii) The data controller must take reasonable steps to ensure the reliability of staff having access to the personal data.

8 Not transferred to countries without adequate protection

In full:

Personal data shall not be transferred to a country or territory outside the European Economic Area, unless that country or territory ensures an adequate level of protection of the rights and freedoms of data subjects in relation to the processing of personal data.

Transfer of data beyond Europe is likely for multinational companies. This principle prevents export of data to countries that do not have sound data processing laws. If the transfer is required in concluding a sale or contract or if the data subject agrees to it, then transfer is legal.

Anti-spam legislation

Laws have been enacted in different countries to protect individual privacy and with the intention of reducing spam or unsolicited commercial e-mail (UCE). Originally, the best-known 'spam' was tinned meat (a contraction of 'spiced ham'), but a modern version of this acronym is '*sending persistent annoying e-mail*'. Spammers rely on sending out millions of e-mails in the hope that even if there is only a 0.01% response they may make some money, if not get rich.

Anti-spam laws do not mean that e-mail cannot be used as a marketing tool. As explained below, opt-in is the key to successful e-mail marketing. Before starting an e-mail dialogue with customers, according to European and American law and in many countries in the Asia–Pacific region, companies must ask customers to provide their e-mail address and then give them the option of 'opting into' further communications. Ideally they should proactively opt in by checking a box. E-mail lists can also be purchased where customers have opted in to receive e-mail. Data held about individuals are commonly used for marketing products to potential or existing customers through e-mail.

Legal opt-in e-mail addresses and customer profile information are available for purchase or rental from a database traditionally known by marketers as a cold list, so called because the company that purchases the data from a third party does not know you. Your name will also potentially be stored on an opt-in house list within companies you have purchased from where you have given your consent to be contacted by the company or given additional consent to be contacted by its partners.

Spam
Unsolicited e-mail (usually bulk-mailed and untargeted).

Cold list
Data about individuals that are rented or sold by a third party.

House list
Data about existing customers used to market products to encourage future purchase.

Regulations on privacy and electronic communications

While the Data Protection Directive 95/46 and Data Protection Act afford a reasonable level of protection for consumers, they were quickly superseded by advances in technology and the rapid growth in spam. As a result, in 2002 the European Union passed the '2002/58/EC Directive on Privacy and Electronic Communications' to complement previous data protection law. This Act is significant from an information technology perspective since it applies specifically to electronic communications such as e-mail and the monitoring of web sites.

As with other European laws, this law was implemented differently in different countries. Some countries considered infringements more seriously. A company which is in breach of the directive in Italy is threatened by fines of up to €66,000 while in the UK the maximum fine is £5,000. It is clearly important for managers to have access to legal advice which applies not only to their own country, but also to other European countries.

In the US in January 2004, a new federal law known as the CAN-SPAM Act was introduced to assist in the control of unsolicited e-mail. CAN SPAM stands for 'Controlling the Assault of Non-Solicited Pornography and Marketing' (an ironic juxtaposition between pornography and marketing). This harmonised separate laws in different US states, but was less strict than in some states such as California. The Act requires unsolicited commercial e-mail messages to be labelled (though not by a standard method) and to include opt-out instructions and the sender's physical address. It prohibits the use of deceptive subject lines and false headers in such messages. Anti-spam legislation in other countries can be accessed at **www.spamlaws.com**.

As an example of European privacy law, we will now review the implications for managers of the UK enactment of 2002/58/EC Directive on Privacy and Electronic Communications. This came into force in the UK on 11 December 2003 as the **Privacy and Electronic Communications Regulations (PECR) Act**. The law is published at: **www.hmso.gov.uk/si/si2003/20032426.htm**. Consumer marketers in the UK also need to heed the Code of Advertising Practice from the Advertising Standards Agency (ASA CAP code, **www.asa.org.uk/the_codes**). This has broadly similar aims and places similar restrictions on marketers to the PECR law.

It is a surprisingly accessible and commonsense document – many marketers will be practising similar principles already. Clauses 22 to 24 are the main clauses relevant to e-mail communications. We will summarise the main implications of the law by picking out key phrases. The new PECR law:

1 Applies to consumer marketing using e-mail or SMS text messages

22(1) applies to *individual subscribers*. 'Individual subscribers' means consumers, although the Information Commissioner has stated that this may be reviewed in future to include business subscribers as is the case in some other countries such as Italy and Germany.

Although this sounds like great news for business-to-business (B2B) marketers and some take the view *'great, the new law doesn't apply to us'*, this could be dangerous. There has been adjudication by the Advertising Standards Agency which found against a B2B organisation which had unwittingly e-mailed consumers from what they believed was an in-house list of B2B customers.

2 Is an 'opt-in' regime

The new law applies to *'unsolicited communications'* (22(1)). It was introduced with a view to reducing spam, although we all know its impact will be limited on spammers beyond Europe. The relevant phrase is part of 22(2) where the recipient must have *'previously notified the sender that he consents'* or has proactively agreed to receiving commercial

Privacy and Electronic Communications Regulations Act
A law intended to control the distribution of e-mail and other online communications including cookies.

Opt-in

A customer proactively agrees to receive further information.

e-mail. This is opt-in. Opt-in can be achieved online or offline through asking people whether they want to receive e-mail. Online this is often done through a tick box.

The main options are shown in Figure 3.3. Figure 3.3(a) is opt-out and it can be considered this is against the spirit of the law since someone may sign up to receive e-mail communications without realising it. Figure 3.3(b) is opt-in since the subscriber has to explicitly check the box. Figure 3.3(c) is also opt-in, but it is a more subtle approach. The consumer cannot enter the prize draw unless they complete the form. In fact, the PECR law does not mandate a tick box option provided consent is clearly indicated.

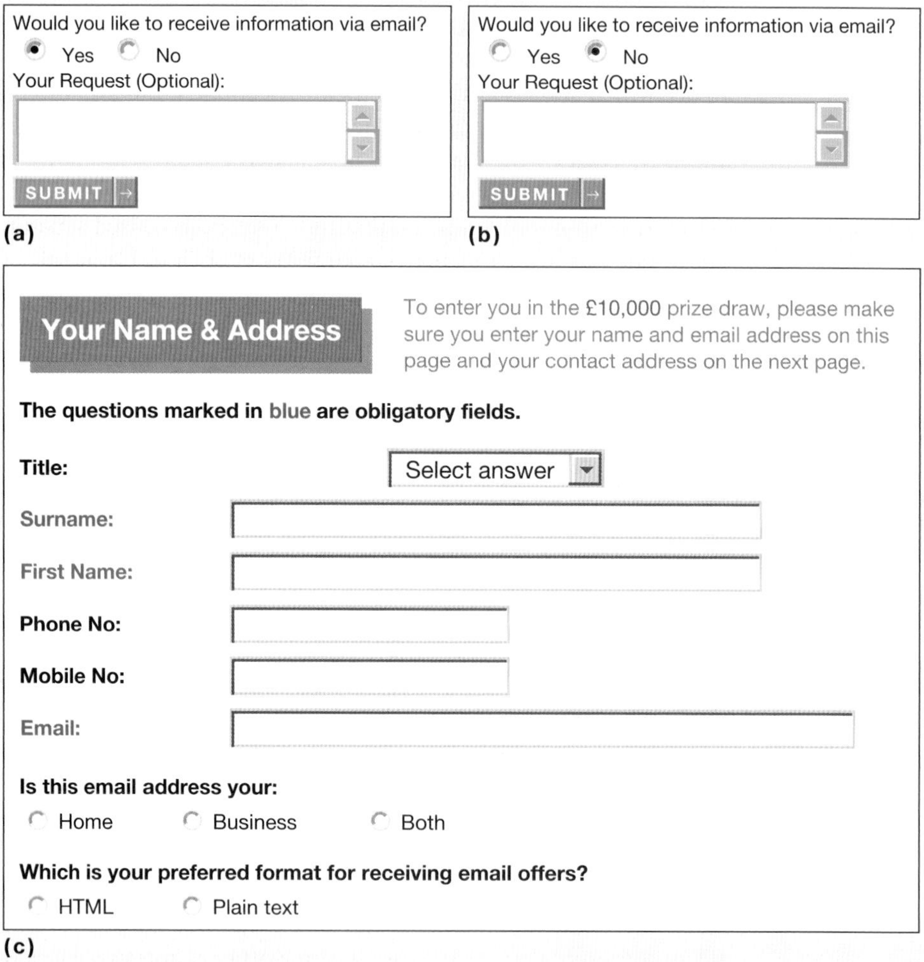

(a)

Would you like to receive information via email?
● Yes ○ No
Your Request (Optional):

SUBMIT →

(b)

Would you like to receive information via email?
○ Yes ● No
Your Request (Optional):

SUBMIT →

(c)

Your Name & Address

To enter you in the £10,000 prize draw, please make sure you enter your name and email address on this page and your contact address on the next page.

The questions marked in blue are obligatory fields.

Title: [Select answer ▼]

Surname:

First Name:

Phone No:

Mobile No:

Email:

Is this email address your:
○ Home   ○ Business   ○ Both

Which is your preferred format for receiving email offers?
○ HTML   ○ Plain text

Figure 3.3 Online forms: (a) opt-out, (b) opt-in, (c) implicit opt-in

Permission marketing

Customers agree (opt-in) to be involved in an organisation's marketing activities, usually as a result of an incentive.

The approach required by the law has, in common with many aspects of data protection and privacy law, been used by many organisations for some time. In other words, sending unsolicited e-mails was thought to be unethical and also not in the best interests of the company because of the risk of annoying customers. In fact, the law conforms to an established approach known as 'permission marketing', a term coined by US commentator Seth Godin (1999, Chapter 6 – first four chapters available free from www.permission.com).

3 Requires an opt-out option in all communications

An opt-out or method of 'unsubscribing' is required so that the recipient does not receive future communications. In a database this means that a 'do not e-mail' field must be created to avoid e-mailing these customers. The law states that a 'simple means of refusing' future communications is required both when the details were first collected and in each subsequent communication.

4 Does not apply to existing customers when marketing similar products

This commonsense clause (22 (3) (a)) states that previous opt-in is not required if the contact details were obtained during the course of the sale or negotiations for the sale of a product or service. This is sometimes known as 'soft opt-in'. While this is great news for retailers, it is less clear where this leaves not-for-profit organisations such as charities or public-sector organisations where the concept of a sale does not apply.

Clause 22 (3) (b) adds that when marketing to existing customers the marketer may market 'similar products and services only'. Case law will help in clarifying this. For example, for a bank, it is not clear whether a customer with an insurance policy could be targeted for a loan.

5 Requires contact details must be provided

It is not sufficient to send an e-mail with a simple sign-off from 'the marketing team' or 'the web team' with no further contact details. The law requires a name, address or phone number to whom a recipient can complain.

6 Requires the 'from' identification of the sender must be clear

Spammers aim to disguise the e-mail originator. The law says that the identity of the person who sends the communication must not be 'disguised or concealed' and that a valid address to 'send a request that such communications cease' should be provided.

7 Applies to direct marketing communications

The communications that the legislation refers to are for 'direct marketing'. This suggests that other communications involved with customer service such as an e-mail about a monthly phone statement are not covered, so the opt-out choice may not be required here.

8 Restricts the use of cookies

Cookies
Cookies are small text files stored on an end-user's computer to enable web sites to identify the user.

Some privacy campaigners consider that the user's privacy is invaded by planting cookies or electronic tags on the end-user's computer. The concept of the cookie and its associated law is not straightforward, so it warrants separate discussion.

Understanding cookies

A cookie is a data file placed on your computer that identifies that individual computer. 'Cookie' derives from the Unix operating system term 'magic cookie' which meant something passed between routines or programs that enables the receiver to perform some operation.

Types of cookies

The main cookie types are:

Persistent cookies
Cookies that remain on the computer after a visitor session has ended. Used to recognise returning visitors.

- Persistent cookies – these stay on a user's computer between multiple sessions and are most valuable for marketers to identify repeat visits to sites;

Session cookies
A cookie used to manage a single visitor session.

- Temporary or session cookies (single-session) – useful for tracking within pages of a session such as on an e-commerce site;

First-party cookies

Served by the site currently in use – typical for e-commerce sites.

Third-party cookies

Served by another site to the one being viewed – typical for portals where an ad network will track remotely or where the web analytics software places a cookie.

- **First-party cookies** – served by the site currently in use, typical for e-commerce sites. These can be persistent or session cookies;
- **Third-party cookies** – served by another site to the one being viewed, typical for portals where an ad network will track remotely or where the web analytics software places a cookie. These are typically persistent cookies.

Cookies are stored as individual text files in a directory on a personal computer. There is usually one file per web site. For example: dave_chaffey@british-airways.txt. This file contains encoded information as follows:

> FLT_VIS IK:bapzRnGdxBYUUID:Jul-25-1999I british-airways.com/ 0 425259904 29357426 1170747936 29284034 *

The information in the cookie file is essentially just an identification number and a date of the last visit although other information can be stored.

Cookies are specific to a particular browser and computer, so if a user connects from a different computer such as at work or starts using a different browser, the web site will not identify him or her as a similar user.

What are cookies used for?

Common marketing applications of cookies include:

- *Personalising a site for an individual*. Cookies are used to identify individual users and retrieve their preferences from a database according to an identifier stored in the cookie. For example, I subscribe to the E-consultancy service (www.e-consultancy.com) for the latest information about e-business; each time I return I do not have the annoyance of having to log in because it remembers my previous visit. Many sites feature a 'Remember Me' option which implies using a cookie to remember a returning visitor. Retailers such as Amazon can use cookies to recognise returning visitors and can recommend related books purchased by other readers. This approach generally has good benefits for both the individual (it is a hassle to sign in again and relevant content can be delivered) and the company (tailored marketing messages can be delivered).
- *Online ordering systems*. This enables a site such as Tesco.com to track what is in your basket as you order different products.
- *Tracking within a site*. Web analytics software such as Webtrends (www.webtrends.com) which analyses statistics on visitors to web sites relies on persistent cookies to find the proportion of repeat visitors to a web site. Webtrends and other tools increasingly use first-party cookies since they are more accurate and less likely to be blocked. Marketers should check whether use of first-party cookies is possible on their site.
- *Tracking across sites*. Advertising networks use cookies to track the number of times a particular computer user has been shown a particular banner advertisement; they can also track adverts served on sites across an ad network. There was an individual rights outcry in the late 1990s since Doubleclick was using this to profile customers. Doubleclick no longer operates an ad network, partly due to this.

Affiliate networks and pay-per-click ad networks such as Google Adwords and Yahoo! Search services (Overture) may also use cookies to track through from a click on a third-party site to a sale or lead being generated on a destination or merchant site. These approaches tend to use third-party cookies. For example, if conversion tracking is enabled in Google Adwords, Google sets a cookie when a user clicks through on an ad. If this user buys the product, then the purchase confirmation page will include script code supplied by Google to make a check for a cookie placed by Google. If there is a match, the sale is attributed to Adwords. An alternative approach using third-party tracking is that different online campaigns have different tracking parameters or codes within the links through to the destination site and when the user arrives on a site from a particular source (such as Google Adwords) this is identified and a cookie set.

When purchase confirmation occurs, this can then be attributed back to the original source, e.g. Google Adwords and the particular referrer.

Owing to the large investments made now in pay-per-click marketing and affiliate marketing by many companies, this is the area of most concern for marketers since the tracking can become inaccurate. However, a sale should still occur even if the cookies are blocked or deleted, so the main consequence is that the ROI (return on investment) of online advertising or pay-per-click marketing may look lower than expected. In affiliate marketing, this phenomenon may benefit the marketer in that payment may not need to be made to the third party if a cookie has been deleted (or blocked) between the time of original clickthrough and sale.

Privacy issues with cookie use

The problem for Internet marketers is that, despite these important applications, blocking by browsers, such as Internet Explorer, or security software and deletion by users has increased dramatically. In 2005 Jupiter Research claimed that 39% of online users may be deleting cookies from their primary computer monthly, although this is debated.

Many distrust cookies since they indicate a 'big brother' is monitoring your actions. Others fear that their personal details or credit card details may be accessed by other web sites. This is very unlikely since all the cookies contain is a short identifier or number that is used to link you to your record in a database. Anyone who found the cookie wouldn't be able to log on to the database without your password. Cookies do not contain passwords, credit card information or any personal details as many people seem to think. These are held on the site servers, protected by firewalls and usernames and passwords. In most cases, the worst that someone can do who gets access to your cookies is to find out which sites you have been visiting.

It is possible to block cookies if the user finds out how to block them, but this is not straight-forward and many customers either do not know or do not mind that their privacy may be infringed. In 2003 an interesting survey on the perception and behaviour with regards to cookies was conducted on cookie use in the UK (RedEye, 2003). Of the 1000 respondents:

- 50% had used more than one computer in the last three months;
- 70% said that their computer was used by more than one person;
- 94% said they either accepted cookies or did not know what they were, although 20% said they only accepted session cookies;
- 71% were aware of cookies and accepted them. Of these only 18% did not know how to delete cookies, and 55% of them were deleting them on a monthly basis;
- 89% knew what cookies were and how to delete them and said that they had deleted them once in the last three months.

Legal constraints on cookies

The new PECR law limits the use of cookies. It states:

> a person shall **not** use an electronic communications **network to store information**, or to **gain access** to information stored, in the terminal equipment of a subscriber or user unless the following requirements are met.

The requirements are:

(a) the user is provided with **clear and comprehensive information about the purposes of the storage** of, or access to, that information; and

(b) is **given the opportunity to refuse the storage** of or access to that information.

Privacy statement
Information on a web site explaining how and why individuals' data are collected, processed and stored.

(a) suggests that it is important that there is a clear privacy statement and (b) suggests that opt-in to cookies is required. In other words, on the first visit to the site, a box would have to be ticked to agree to the use of cookies. This was thought by many commentators to be a curious provision since this facility is already available in the web browser. A further

$\rightarrow$

provision clarifies this. The law states: *'where such storage or access is **strictly necessary** for the provision of an information society service requested by the subscriber or user'*. This indicates that for an e-commerce service session cookies are legitimate without the need for opt-in. It is arguable whether the identification of return visitors is 'strictly necessary' and this is why some sites have a 'remember me' tick box next to the log-in. Through doing this they are compliant with the law. Using cookies for tracking return visits alone would seem to be outlawed, but we will have to see how case law develops over the coming years before this is resolved.

Viral e-mail marketing

Viral marketing
A marketing message is communicated from one person to another, facilitated by different media, such as word of mouth, e-mail or web sites. Implies rapid transmission of messages is intended.

One widespread business practice that is not covered explicitly in the PECR law is 'viral marketing'. The network of people referred to in the definition is more powerful in an online context where e-mail is used to transmit the virus – rather like a cold or flu virus. The combination of the viral offer and the transmission medium is sometimes referred to as the 'viral agent'. Different types of viral marketing are reviewed in Chapter 8.

Privacy verification bodies

There are several initiatives that are being taken by industry groups to reassure web users about threats to their personal information. The first of these is TRUSTe (**www.truste.org**), sponsored by IBM and with sites validated by PricewaterhouseCoopers and KPMG (Figure 3.2). The validators will audit the site to check each site's privacy statement to see whether it is valid. For example, a privacy statement will describe:

- how a site collects information;
- how the information is used;
- who the information is shared with;
- how users can access and correct information;
- how users can decide to deactivate themselves from the site or withhold information from third parties.

A UK initiative coordinated by the Internet Media in Retail Group is ISIS (Internet Shopping is Safe) (**www.imrg.org/ISIS**). Government initiatives will also define best practice in this area and may introduce laws to ensure guidelines are followed. In the UK, the Data Protection Act covers some of these issues and the 1999 European Data Protection Act also has draft laws to help maintain personal privacy on the Internet.

We conclude this section on privacy legislation with a checklist summary of the practical steps that are required to audit a company's compliance with data protection and privacy legislation. Companies should:

1 Follow privacy and consumer protection guidelines and laws in all local markets. Use local privacy and security certification where available.
2 Inform the user, before asking for information on:
 - who the company is;
 - what personal data are collected, processed and stored;
 - what is the purpose of collection.
3 Ask for consent for collecting sensitive personal data, and it is good practice to ask before collecting any type of data.
4 Reassure customers by providing clear and effective privacy statements and explaining the purpose of data collection.
5 Let individuals know when 'cookies' or other covert software are used to collect information about them.

6 Never collect or retain personal data unless it is strictly necessary for the organisation's purposes. For example, a person's name and full address should not be required to provide an online quotation. If extra information is required for marketing purposes this should be made clear and the provision of such information should be optional.

7 Amend incorrect data when informed and tell others. Enable correction on-site.

8 Only use data for marketing (by the company, or third parties) when a user has been informed this is the case and has agreed to this. (This is opt-in.)

9 Provide the option for customers to stop receiving information. (This is opt-out.)

10 Use appropriate security technology to protect the customer information on your site.

Other e-commerce legislation

Sparrow (2000) identified eight areas of law which need to concern online marketers. Although laws have been refined since then, this is still a useful framework for considering the laws to which digital marketers are subject.

1 Marketing your e-commerce business

Domain name

The domain name refers to the name of the web server and it is usually selected to be the same as the name of the company, e.g. **www.company-name.com**, and the extension will indicate its type.

At the time of writing, Sparrow used this category to refer to purchasing a domain name for its web site. There are now other legal constraints that also fall under this category.

Domain name registration

Most companies are likely to own several domains (see end of Chapter 1 for an introduction), perhaps for different product lines or countries or for specific marketing campaigns. Domain name disputes can arise when an individual or company has registered a domain name which another company claims they have the right to. This is sometimes referred to as 'cybersquatting'.

One of the best-known cases was brought in 1998 by Marks and Spencer and other high-street retailers, since another company, 'One In a Million Limited', had registered names such as marks&spencer.com, britishtelecom.net and sainsbury.com. It then tried to sell these names for a profit. The companies already had sites with more familiar addresses such as marksandspencers.co.uk, but had not taken the precaution of registering all related domains with different forms of spelling and different top-level domains such as .net. Unsurprisingly, an injunction was issued against One in a Million which was no longer able to use these names.

The problem of companies' names being misappropriated was common during the 1990s, but companies still need to be sure to register all related domain names for each brand since new top-level domain names are created through time such as .biz and .eu.

If you are responsible for web sites, you need to check that domain names are automatically renewed by your hosting company (as most are today). For example, the .co.uk domain must be renewed every two years. Companies that don't manage this process potentially risk losing their domain name since another company could potentially register it if the domain name lapsed.

Using competitor names and trademarks in meta-tags (for search engine optimisation)

Meta-tags, which are part of the HTML code of a site are used to market web sites by enabling them to appear more prominently in search engines as part of search engine optimisation (SEO) (see Chapter 8). Some companies have tried putting the name of a competitor company name within the meta-tags. This is not legal since case law has found against companies that have used this approach. A further issue of marketing-related law is privacy law for e-mail marketing which was considered in the previous section.

Using competitor names and trademarks in pay-per-click advertising

A similar approach can potentially be used in pay-per-click marketing (see Chapter 8) to advertise on competitors' names and trademarks. For example, if a search user types 'Dell laptop' can an advertiser bid to place an ad offering an 'HP laptop'? There is less case law in this area and differing findings have occurred in the US and France (such advertising is not permitted in France).

Accessibility law

Web accessibility refers to enabling all users of a web site to interact with it regardless of disabilities they may have or the web browser or platform they are using to access the site. The visually impaired or blind are the main audience that designing an accessible web site can help.

Many countries now have specific accessibility legislation. This is often contained within disability and discrimination acts. In the UK, the relevant act is the Disability and Discrimination Act 1995.

2 Forming an electronic contract (contract law and distance-selling law)

We will look at two aspects of forming an electronic contract.

Country of origin principle

The contract formed between a buyer and a seller on a web site will be subject to the laws of a particular country. In Europe, many such laws are specified at the regional (European Union) level, but are interpreted differently in different countries. This raises the issue of which law applies – is it that for the buyer, for example located in Germany, or the seller (merchant), whose site is based in France? Although this has been unclear, in 2002 attempts were made by the EU to adopt the '*country of origin principle*'. This means that the law for the contract will be that where the merchant is located.

Distance-selling law

Sparrow (2000) advises different forms of disclaimers to protect the retailer. For example, if a retailer made an error with the price or the product details were in error, then the retailer is not bound to honour a contract, since it was only displaying the products as 'an invitation to treat', not a fixed offer.

A well-known case was when an e-retailer offered televisions for £2.99 due to an error in pricing a £299 product. Numerous purchases were made, but the e-retailer claimed that a contract had not been established simply by accepting the online order, although the customers did not see it that way! Unfortunately, no legal precedent was established in this case since the case did not come to trial.

Disclaimers can also be used to limit liability if the web site service causes a problem for the user, such as a financial loss resulting from an action based on erroneous content. Furthermore, Sparrow suggests that terms and conditions should be developed to refer to issues such as timing of delivery and damage or loss of goods.

The distance-selling directive also has a bearing on e-commerce contracts in the European Union. It was originally developed to protect people using mail-order (by post or phone). The main requirements, which are consistent with what most reputable e-retailers would do anyway, are that e-commerce sites must contain easily accessible content which clearly states:

- The company's identity including address;
- The main features of the goods or services;
- Prices information, including tax and, if appropriate, delivery costs;
- The period for which the offer or price remains valid;
- Payment, delivery and fulfilment performance arrangements;
- Right of the consumer to withdraw, i.e. cancellation terms;
- The minimum duration of the contract and whether the contract for the supply of products or services is to be permanent or recurrent, if appropriate;
- Whether an equivalent product or service might be substituted, and confirmation as to whether the seller pays the return costs in this event.

After the contract has been entered into, the supplier is required to provide written confirmation of the information provided. An e-mail confirmation is now legally binding provided both parties have agreed that e-mail is an acceptable form for the contract. It is always advisable to obtain an electronic signature to confirm that both parties have agreed the contract, and this is especially valuable in the event of a dispute. The default position for services is that there is no cancellation right once services begin.

3 Making and accepting payment

For transactional e-commerce sites, the relevant laws are those referring to liability between a credit card issuer, the merchant and the buyer. Merchants need to be aware of their liability for different situations such as the customer making a fraudulent transaction.

4 Authenticating contracts concluded over the Internet

'Authentication' refers to establishing the identity of the purchaser. For example, to help prove a credit card owner is the valid owner, many sites now ask for a 3-digit authentication code which is separate from the credit card number. This helps reduce the risk of someone buying fraudulently who has, for instance, found a credit card number from a traditional shopping purchase. Using digital signatures is another method of helping to prove the identity of purchasers (and merchants).

5 E-mail risks

One of the main risks with e-mail is infringing an individual's privacy. Specific laws have been developed in many countries to reduce the volume of unsolicited commercial e-mail or spam, as explained in the previous section on privacy.

A further issue with e-mail is defamation. This is where someone makes a statement that is potentially damaging to an individual or a company. A well-known example from 2000 involved a statement made on the Norwich Union Healthcare internal e-mail system in England which was defamatory towards a rival company, WPA. The statement falsely alleged that WPA was under investigation and that regulators had forced them to stop accepting new business. The posting was published on the internal e-mail system to various members of Norwich Union Healthcare staff. Although this was only on an internal system, it was not contained and became more widespread. WPA sued for libel and the case was settled in an out-of-court settlement when Norwich Union paid £415,000 to WPA. Such cases are relatively rare.

6 Protecting intellectual property (IP)

Intellectual property rights (IPRs) protect designs, ideas and inventions and include content and services developed for e-commerce sites. Closely related is copyright law which is designed to protect authors, producers, broadcasters and performers through ensuring they see some returns from their works every time they are experienced. The European Directive of Copyright (2001/29/EC) came into force in many countries in 2003. This is a significant update to the law which covers new technologies and approaches such as streaming a broadcast via the Internet.

IP can be misappropriated in two senses online.

First, an organisation's IP may be misappropriated and you need to protect against this. For example, it is relatively easy to copy web content and re-publish on another site, and this practice is not unknown amongst smaller businesses. Reputation management services can be used to assess how an organisation's content, logos and trademarks are being used on other web sites.

Secondly, an organisation may misappropriate content inadvertently. Some employees may infringe copyright if they are not aware of the law. Additionally, some methods of designing transactional web sites have been patented. For example, Amazon has patented its 'One-click' purchasing option which is why you do not see this labelling and process on other sites.

7 Advertising on the Internet

Advertising standards that are enforced by independent agencies such as the UK's Advertising Standards Authority Code also apply in the Internet environment (although they are traditionally less strongly policed, leading to more 'edgy' creative executions online.

8 Data protection

Data protection has been referred to in depth in the previous section.

Technological factors

Electronic communications are disruptive technologies that have, as we saw in Chapter 2, already caused major changes in industry structure, marketplace structure and business models. Consider a B2B organisation. Traditionally it has sold its products through a network of distributors. With the advent of e-commerce it now has the opportunity to bypass distributors and trade directly with customers via a web site; it also has the opportunity to reach customers through new B2B marketplaces. Knowledge of the opportunities and threats presented by these changes is essential to those involved in defining marketing strategy.

One of the great challenges for Internet marketers is to be able to successfully assess which new technological innovations can be applied to give competitive advantage. For example, personalisation technology (Chapter 6) is intended to enhance the customer's online experience and increase their loyalty. However, a technique such as personalisation may require a large investment in proprietary software and hardware technology to be able to implement it effectively. How does the manager decide whether to proceed and which solution to adopt? In addition to technologies deployed on the web site, the suitability of new approaches for attracting visitors to the site must be evaluated – for example, should registration at a paid-for search engine, or new forms of banner adverts or e-mail marketing be used? Deciding on the best mix of traffic building techniques is discussed further in Chapter 8.

The manager may have read articles in the trade and general press or spoken to colleagues which has highlighted the potential of a new technology-enabled marketing technique. They then face a difficult decision as to whether to:

- ignore the use of the technique completely, perhaps because it is felt to be too expensive or untried, or because they simply don't believe the benefits will outweigh the costs;
- ignore the technique for now, but keep an eye on the results of other companies that are starting to use it;
- evaluate the technique in a structured manner and then take a decision whether to adopt it according to the evaluation;
- enthusiastically adopt the technique without a detailed evaluation since the hype alone convinces the manager that the technique should be adopted.

Depending on the attitude of the manager, this behaviour can be summarised as:

1 cautious, 'wait and see' approach;
2 intermediate approach, sometimes referred to as 'fast-follower'. Let others take the majority of the risk, but if they are proving successful, then rapidly adopt the technique, i.e. copy them;
3 risk-taking, early-adopter approach.

Early adopters

Companies or departments that invest in new technologies and techniques.

Different behaviours by different adopters will result in different numbers of adopters through time. This diffusion–adoption process (represented by the bell curve in Figure 3.4) was identified by Rogers (1983) who classified those trialling new products from innovators, early adopters, early majority, late majority, through to the laggards.

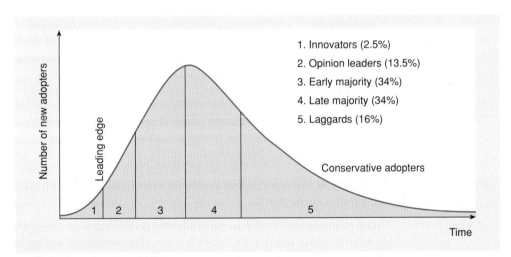

Figure 3.4 Diffusion–adoption curve

Figure 3.4 can be used in two main ways as an analytical tool to help managers. First, it can be used to understand the stage at which customers are in adoption of a technology, or any product. For example, the Internet is now a well-established tool and in many developed countries we are into the late majority phase of adoption with large numbers of users of services. This suggests it is essential to use this medium for marketing purposes. But if we look at WAP technology (see below) it can be seen that we are in the innovator phase, so investment now may be wasted since it is not clear how many will adopt the product. Secondly, managers can look at adoption of a new technique by other businesses – from an organisational perspective. For example, an online supermarket could look at how many other e-tailers have adopted personalisation to evaluate whether it is worthwhile adopting the technique.

Trott (1998) looks at this organisational perspective to technology adoption. He identifies different requirements that are necessary within an organisation to be able to respond effectively to technological change or innovation. These are:

- growth orientation – a long- rather than short-term vision;
- vigilance – the capability of environment scanning;
- commitment to technology – willingness to invest in technology;
- acceptance of risk – willingness to take managed risks;
- cross-functional cooperation – capability for collaboration across functional areas;
- receptivity – the ability to respond to externally developed technology;
- slack – allowing time to investigate new technological opportunities;
- adaptability – a readiness to accept change;
- diverse range of skills – technical and business skills and experience.

Hype cycle

A graphic representation of the maturity, adoption and business application of specific technologies.

A commercial application of the diffusion of innovation curve was developed by technology analyst Gartner and has been applied to different technologies since 1995. They describe a hype cycle as a graphic representation of the maturity, adoption and business application of specific technologies.

Gartner (2005) recognises the following stages within a hype cycle, an example of which is given for current trends in 2005 (Figure 3.5):

1 *Technology Trigger* – The first phase of a Hype Cycle is the 'technology trigger' or breakthrough, product launch or other event that generates significant press and interest.
2 *Peak of Inflated Expectations* – In the next phase, a frenzy of publicity typically generates over-enthusiasm and unrealistic expectations. There may be some successful applications of a technology, but there are typically more failures.
3 *Trough of Disillusionment* – Technologies enter the 'trough of disillusionment' because they fail to meet expectations and quickly become unfashionable. Consequently, the press usually abandons the topic and the technology.
4 *Slope of Enlightenment* – Although the press may have stopped covering the technology, some businesses continue through the 'slope of enlightenment' and experiment to understand the benefits and practical application of the technology.
5 *Plateau of Productivity* – A technology reaches the 'plateau of productivity' as the benefits of it become widely demonstrated and accepted. The technology becomes increasingly stable and evolves in second and third generations. The final height of the plateau varies according to whether the technology is broadly applicable or benefits only a niche market.

The problem with being an early adopter (as an organisation) is that being at the leading edge of using new technologies is often also referred to as the 'bleeding edge' due to the risk of failure. New technologies will have bugs, may integrate poorly with the existing systems or the marketing benefits may simply not live up to their promise. Of course, the reason for risk taking is that the rewards are high – if you are using a technique that your competitors are not, then you will gain an edge on your rivals. For example, RS Components (www.rswww.com) was one of the first UK suppliers of industrial components to adopt personalisation as part of their e-commerce system. They have learnt the strengths and weaknesses of the product and now know how to position it to appeal to customers. It offers facilities such as customised pages, access to previous order history and the facility to place repeat orders or modified re-buys. This has enabled them to build up a base of customers who are familiar with using the RS Components online services and are then less likely to swap to rival services in the future.

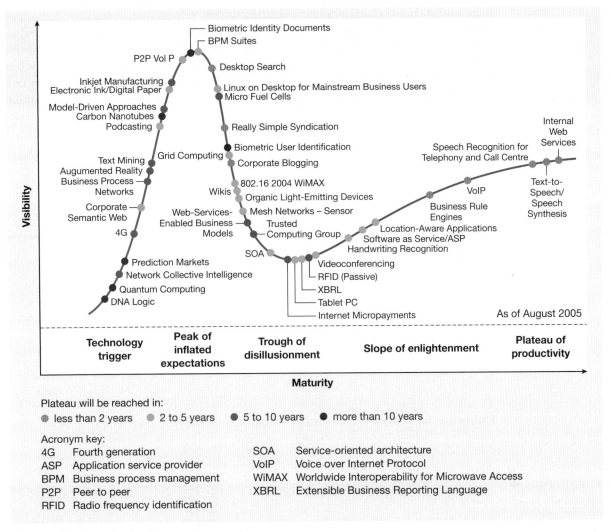

Figure 3.5 Example of a Gartner hype cycle

Source: Gartner (2005) Gartner's Hype Cycle Special Report for 2005

It may also be useful to identify how rapidly a new concept is being adopted. When a product or service is adopted rapidly this is known as *rapid diffusion*. The access to the Internet is an example of this. In developed countries the use of the Internet has become widespread more rapidly than the use of TV, for example. It seems that interactive digital TV and Internet-enabled mobile phones are relatively slow-diffusion products! Activity 3.1, later in this chapter, considers this issue further.

So, what action should e-commerce managers take when confronted by new techniques and technologies? There is no straightforward rule of thumb, other than that a balanced approach must be taken. It would be easy to dismiss many new techniques as fads, or classify them as 'not relevant to my market'. However, competitors are likely to be reviewing new techniques and incorporating some, so a careful review of new techniques is required. This indicates that benchmarking of 'best of breed' sites within sector and in different sectors is essential as part of environmental scanning. However, by waiting for others to innovate and review the results on their web site, a company has probably already lost 6 to 12 months. Figure 3.6 summarises the choices. The stepped curve I shows the variations in technology through time. Some changes may be small incremental changes such as a new operating system; others, such as the introduction of personalisation technology, are more significant in delivering value to customers and so improving business performance. Line A is a company that is using innovative business techniques, adopts technology early, or is even in advance of what the technology can currently deliver. Curve C shows the conservative adopter whose use of technology lags behind the available potential. Curve B, the middle ground, is probably the ideal situation where a company monitors new ideas as early adopters, trials them and then adopts those that will positively impact the business.

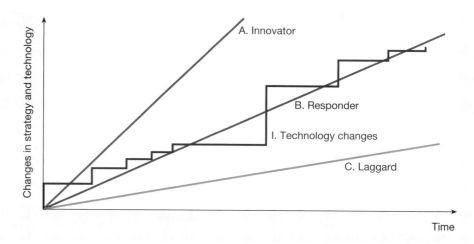

Figure 3.6 Alternative responses to changes in technology

Access platform
A method for customers to access digital media.

Alternative digital technologies

In this section we introduce three alternative or complementary digital media **access platforms** to PC-based fixed Internet access, which provide many similar advantages. These access platforms or environments are mobile or wireless, interactive digital TV and digital radio.

Mobile or wireless access devices

Mobile technologies are not new – it has been possible for many years to access the Internet for e-mail using a laptop connected via a modem. However, the need for large devices directly connected to the Internet was overcome with the development of personal digital assistants (PDAs) such as the PocketPC or RIM Blackberry and mobile phones. These access the Internet using a wireless connection.

The characteristics that mobile or wireless connections offer to their users are ubiquity (can be accessed from anywhere), reachability (their users can be reached when not in their normal location) and convenience (it is not necessary to have access to a power supply or fixed-line connection). In addition to these obvious benefits, there are additional benefits that are less obvious: they provide security – each user can be authenticated since each wireless device has a unique identification code; their location can be used to tailor content; and they provide a degree of privacy compared with a desktop PC – looking for jobs on a wireless device might be better than under the gaze of

Table 3.2 Summary of mobile or wireless Internet access consumer proposition

Element of proposition	Evaluation
Not fixed location	The user is freed from the need to access via the desktop, making access possible when commuting, for example
Location-based services	Mobiles can be used to give geographically based services, e.g. an offer in a particular shopping centre. Future mobiles will have global positioning services integrated
Instant access/convenience	The latest GPRS and 3G services are always on, avoiding the need for lengthy connection (see section on alternative digital technologies)
Privacy	Mobiles are more private than desktop access, making them more suitable for social use or for certain activities such as an alert service for looking for a new job
Personalisation	As with PC access, personal information and services can be requested by the user, although these often need to be set up via PC access
Security	In the future mobile may become a form of wallet, but thefts of mobiles make this a source of concern

a boss. An additional advantage is that of instant access or 'always-on'; here there is no need to dial up a wireless connection. Table 3.2 provides a summary of the mobile or wireless Internet access proposition. There are considerable advantages in comparison to PC-based Internet access, but it is currently limited by the display limitations such as small screen size and limited graphics.

Technology convergence

Technology convergence
A trend in which different hardware devices such as TVs, computers and phones merge and have similar functions.

Technology convergence is an important phenomenon as digital marketers consider how they can evolve their propositions for consumers. As you know, today a mobile phone is not just a phone, it is likely also a text messaging system, music playing system, e-mail reading platform, camera, personal organiser, Internet access device and Global Positioning System (GPS). Of course, just because a technology is possible does not mean it is widely used. So, for marketers, it is important to assess new technologies and support them once they reach critical mass, or if there is a niche which can be exploited. For example, Mintel reported in 2005 that the downloadable content for ringtones and games is now a $1 billion market in the UK. Many users now use phones or PDAs for accessing e-mails, so it is important that marketers ensure their messages are received on these devices.

SMS messaging

Short Message Service (SMS)
The formal name for text messaging.

In addition to offering voice calls and data transfer, mobile phones have increasingly been used for e-mail and **Short Message Service (SMS)**, commonly known as 'texting' (Figure 3.7). SMS is, of course, a simple form of e-mail that enables messages to be transferred between mobile phones.

Texting has proved useful for business in some niche applications. For example, banks now notify customers when they approach an overdraft and provide weekly statements using SMS. Text has also been used by consumer brands to market their products, particularly to a younger audience as the case studies at text agency Flytxt (**www.flytxt.com**) and Text.It, the organisation promoting text messaging (**www.text.it**), show. Texting can also be used in supply chain management applications for notifying managers of problems or deliveries.

121

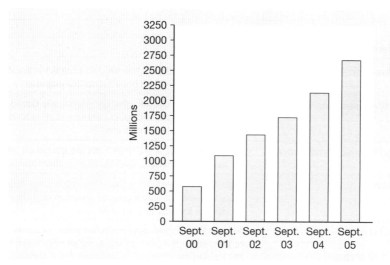

Figure 3.7 Number of text messages sent monthly in the UK, 2001 to 2005
Source: Mobile data association

SMS applications

For the creative marketer who respects opt-in and privacy legislation, SMS has proved a great way to get closer to customers, particularly those in the youth market who are difficult to reach with other media. These are some of the applications showcased on Text.it (**www.text.it**):

1 *Database building/direct response to ads/direct mail or on-pack*. This is one of the most significant applications. For example, Ford engaged its audience when promoting the Ford Ka by offering consumers to text in a unique code printed on their postcard for entry into a prize draw.
2 *Location-based services*. Text for the nearest pub, club, shop or taxi. In London you can now text for the nearest available taxi and pay the congestion charge through texting once accounts are set up via the web!
3 *Sampling/trial*. Nestlé used an opt-in SMS database to offer samples for a new chocolate bar to consumers in its target group.
4 *Sales promotions*. Timed e-coupons can be sent out to encourage footfall in real and virtual stores. Drinks brand WKD offered its consumers to 'Peel Off and Win' on its bottles. The competition offered prizes of 3,000 football club shirts, mini footballs, 10,000 referee cards, and 1m exclusive ringtones and logos designed by WKD. Half a million people played the game, a campaign response rate of 3%. A 3,000-strong opt-in database of the company's 18–24-year-old customer base was created. The company plans to use this database to trial new WKD variety Silver.
5 *Rewarding with offers for brand engagement*. Valuable content on mobiles can be offered via SMS, for example free ringtones, wallpaper, Java games or credits can be offered to consumers via text.
6 *Short codes*. These are easy to remember 5-digit numbers combined with text that can be used by advertisers or broadcasters for response.
7 *Offering paid for WAP services and content*. Any service such as a ringtone delivered by WAP can be invoked from a text message. For example, Parker's Car Guides now prints ad text 'go parkers' to 89080 (a short code) for quick access to the Parker's WAP site which provides car prices on-the-go, at £1 for 10 minutes.

SMS Messaging has recently been augmented by Picture Messaging or Multimedia Messaging Services (MMS). While volumes have been relatively low initially, the overlap between text messaging and e-mail marketing will decrease as there are more handsets with larger screens.

Mini Case Study 3.1   How impt is txt msging?

In 2004, 25 billion text messages were sent in the UK alone. The top texting days for 2002–4 show the importance of this medium for consumers.

1   26 August 2004: 79 million text messages were sent on the day that GCSE results were announced;

2   New Year's Day 2004: on New Year's Day 2004, the number of text messages reached 111 million, the highest recorded daily total;

3   14 February 2003: 78 million text messages were sent by Britons on Valentine's Day 2003, six times more than traditional cards and a 37% increase on text figures for 2002;

4   22 November 2003: 76 million messages were sent on the day England won the Rugby World Cup;

5   17 March 2003: 65.7 million messages were sent exchanging St Patrick's Day greetings;

6   11 May 2003: 65 million text messages were sent on the last day of the 2002/3 season's Premiership;

7   7 June 2002: England v Argentina, World Cup group match – 58 million messages sent.

Mobile services

The services delivered for consumers, to date, have included transactional and informational. Consumer applications to date include retail (WH Smith Online books, the Carphone Warehouse), ticketing (lastminute.com), brokering, banking (the Woolwich), gambling (Ladbrokes), bill payment and job searching. Some informational services based on personalisation such as those of Excite UK and Yahoo! have also been launched. These include information such as sports news, stock prices, news, cinemas, weather, horoscopes and reminders.

Services for businesses delivered by WAP are currently less developed, but are forecast to centre on supply-chain integration where there will be facilities to place orders, check stock availability, notify of dispatch and track orders.

Wi-Fi ('wireless fidelity')
....
A high-speed wireless local-area network enabling wireless access to the Internet for mobile, office and home users.

Wi-Fi ('wireless fidelity') is the shorthand often used to describe a high-speed wireless local-area network. Wi-Fi can be deployed in an office or home environment where it removes the need for cabling and adds flexibility. However, it has attracted most attention for its potential for offering wireless access in cities and towns without the need for a fixed connection. The Intel Centrino mobile chip launched in 2003 offers facilities to make Wi-Fi access easier for laptop users.

For example, in 2002 some airports, cafés and hotels started offering Wi-Fi 'hotspots' which allowed customers access to the Internet from their laptops or other mobile devices without the need to connect using a wire. This helped differentiate themselves from other services without this facility. Wireless LANs are appearing everywhere. In the US, network operators are expected to install over 55,000 new hotspots in the next five years. At the end of 2002, there were 4200 Wi-Fi locations.

There was extensive media coverage of Wi-Fi when it was launched and, as is often the case with new technologies, the technology does not appear to satisfy a demand. The *Guardian* (2003b) quotes Lars Godell, a telecoms analyst at Forrester Research. In a recent research note, he said

It's as if the dotcom boom and bust never happened – this bubble seems ready to burst. I agree there is some need, but think there has been very pointed exaggeration of the need for internet access around the clock, and on top of that the willingness to pay for it. And that is the critical issue when you create a business plan.

He also noted that 'The usage rates of wireless Lan have been appallingly low'. He cites the case of Amsterdam's Schipol airport, through which 41m passengers pass every year, but where there are only a dozen Wi-Fi hotspot users a day. Other hotspot operators confirm, in private, that they see similarly low usage numbers.

Despite the media hype about public wireless networks it appears as if the main applications for wireless networks are at home and at work.

Some marketers are now considering Bluejacking which involves sending a message from a mobile phone (or other transmitter) to another mobile phone which is in close range via Bluetooth technology. It has potential for: (1) viral communication; (2) community activities (dating or gaming events); (3) location-based services – electronic coupons as you pass a store.

Whether WAP, I-mode or other forms of phone are used, users can now surf or browse specially built sites, extending the 5S benefits derived from web sites, although constrained by the smaller screen and limited graphics.

Now we're moving into location-based marketing where customers receive messages on their mobiles relevant to their geographic location (whether passing a store or arriving in an airport).

Current levels of usage of mobile commerce

Mobile commerce (m-commerce) refers to the use of wireless devices such as mobile phones for informational or monetary transactions. Levels of product purchase by mobile phone have proved very low in comparison with the Internet, even for standardised products such as books and CDs. Many m-commerce providers such as Sweden's M-box went into receivership. However, analysts expect that with new access platforms, such as 3G (third-generation mobile devices which will have higher access speeds offering video transmissions), this will change. Consider the example of travel, which is the leading e-commerce category in Europe by revenue for the fixed Internet.

IT Week (2005), quoting a JupiterResearch report, estimated that although in 2004 there were 5.1 million 3G devices, by 2010 this would increase dramatically to 184 million.

The Japanese experience with i-Mode suggests that with suitable access devices coupled with the right content and services that support colour images, the impact of 3G could be significant. Mobile phone ringtones and other music downloads are the most popular i-Mode purchase, followed by other paid-for information services. The strength of the proposition is indicated by the fact that over 30 million Japanese were using this service despite a launch less than two years previously. The i-Mode service has now been launched in Europe.

Strategies for mobile commerce

Different types of strategy can be identified for two main different types of organisations. For portal and media owners the options are to migrate their own portal to WAP/SMS (the option followed by Excite and the *Guardian*) or to partner with other WAP portals and provide content for these. Revenue models may include sponsorship or subscription for individual content items or on a subscription basis. Options for advertising are also being explored – **www.247europe.com** is one of the first companies to offer WAP-based advertisements. For destination sites such as banks and retailers, the options available include:

Bluejacking

Sending a message from a mobile phone or transmitter to another mobile phone which is in close range via Bluetooth technology.

Bluetooth

A standard for wireless transmission of data between devices, e.g. a mobile phone and a PDA.

Mobile commerce (m-commerce)

The use of wireless devices such as mobile phones for informational or monetary transactions.

I-Mode

A mobile access platform that enables display of colour graphics and content subscription services.

- marketing communications (to support purchase and support);
- e-commerce (sale of products on-site);
- brand building – improving brand image by being one of the first suppliers to offer an innovative service.

Future mobile services

In 2001 new services became available on GPRS (General Packet Radio Service). This is approximately five times faster than GSM (Global System for Mobile Communications) and is an 'always-on' service which is charged according to usage. Display is still largely text-based and based on the WAP protocol. Later, a completely new generation (3G) of services became available in 2003 by UMTS (Universal Mobile Telecommunications System); with this delivery of sound and images should be possible, enabling continuous, instant access to the Internet ('always on'). In the UK auctions for the licence to operate on these frequencies have exceeded £20 billion – such is the perceived importance of these services to the telecommunications companies (telcos). Many commentators now believe it will be difficult for the telcos to recoup this money, and this has resulted in large falls in their share prices.

4G
Fourth-generation wireless, expected to deliver wireless broadband at 20-40 Mbps (about 10-20 times the current rates of ADSL broadband service).

In the longer term **4G** broadband mobile communications are under development and are expected to be introduced first in Japan as early as 2006. As would be expected, the main distinction over 3G is transmission rates. 4G is currently estimated to yield increases, reaching 20–40 Mbps (about 10–20 times the current rates of ADSL high-speed wire-based broadband service).

Figure 3.8 summarises these new standards for mobile access of the Internet. For each new technology there is a significant range between the lowest and highest possible transmission speeds. Very often the hype is based on the upper limit, but when implemented only the lower limit is achieved.

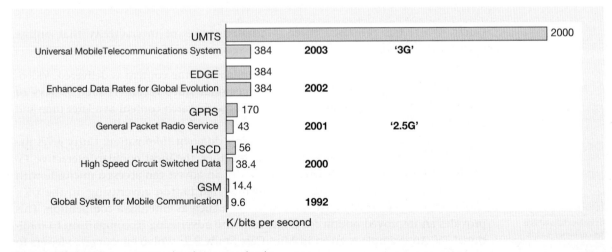

Figure 3.8 Mobile access technology standards

Interactive digital television

Interactive digital TV (iDTV)

Television displayed using a digital signal delivered by a range of media – cable, satellite, terrestrial (aerial). Interactions can be provided through phone line or cable service.

Interactive digital television (iDTV) has now been used in Europe for nearly ten years to deliver broadcasting to homes and offer new interactive services. In France, Canal Plus launched iDTV in 1996, Télévision par satellite launched in 1997 and Spain, Italy and Germany have had these facilities since 1996 or 1997. In the UK, levels of access to interactive digital TV rival those of the Internet. All three main new media are tracked by the MORI Technology Tracker (**www.e-mori.co.uk**) (Figure 2.16). The importance of digital TV is indicated by these figures, which in 2005 were equal to Internet access at 60% household penetration.

Interactive digital TV offers similar e-commerce facilities to the Internet, but is provided with a simpler interface with more limited content that can be operated from a remote control. The amount of information available from providers is lower because of limited bandwidth shared between channels.

Table 3.3 summarises the proposition for interactive digital TV. It is evident that it is more similar to PC-based Internet access than to mobile access. A key difference is that TV viewing is more likely to involve several members of a family while PC usage is more individual. This may cause conflict in use of some individualised iDTV services.

Table 3.3 Summary of interactive digital TV consumer proposition

Element of proposition	Evaluation
Instant access/convenience	Interactive services are available quite rapidly, but return path connections using phone lines for purchase are slower
Personalisation	This is less practical for PC and mobile since there are usually several viewers
Security	Credit card details can be held by the iDTV provider, making it theoretically unnecessary to repeatedly enter personal details

Curry (2001) has proposed three alternative types of interactivity that online marketers can exploit:

1 *Distribution interactivity.* Here the user controls when the content is delivered. Video-on-demand is an example of this. Using personal video recorders such as Sky+ or TiVO is a further example, since users can choose to watch content at a later time and possibly omit adverts.

2 *Information interactivity.* Here the user can select different information. Curry gives the example of teletext and games which are, together, the most popular interactive TV activity. A further example is where a viewer of an advert can access a microsite with further information on the advert (known as 'red button advertising' in the UK). Information can be exchanged via a **return path** such as entering a competition. This provides an improved option for direct response advertising in comparison to traditional TV. An example is given in Mini Case Study 3.2: 'Volvo encourages viewers to "Press Red" for their "Mystery of Dalaro" campaign'. Interaction with interactive TV is often combined with text messaging in quiz and reality TV programmes.

Return path

An interaction where the customer sends information to the iDTV provider using a phone line or cable.

3 *Participation activity.* This is where the user can select different options during a programme such as choosing a different camera angle in a football match or different news stories. There is no return path in this case.

Mini Case Study 3.2	Volvo encourages viewers to 'Press Red' for their 'Mystery of Dalaro' campaign

This innovative campaign, supporting the launch of the Volvo S40, was shot in the style of a documentary purporting to be a real account of the Swedish village Dalaro where 32 people all bought a new Volvo S40 on the same day.

But Volvo has now revealed that it is Spike Jonze, the director of the films 'Being John Malkovich' and 'Adaptation' as well as the legendary Beastie Boys video 'Sabotage', who made the documentary. However, it has said that the characters in the campaign are real residents of Dalaro and not actors.

This campaign shows how offline ad executions naturally drive visitors online. During the campaign, visits to the Volvo UK web site doubled and 435,000 digital viewers of the ad selected the red button option to view the documentary via interactive TV.

Those pressing red on iTV saw a longer eight minute version of the documentary, made by director Spike Jonze, featuring interviews with residents of Dalaro talking about the spooky phenomenon and had the opportunity to download brochures, thus interacting much more closely with the brand than was possible before the advent of iTV. The documentary was also available from the web site which received 96,000 visits with 64% accessing the video and several thousand requesting a brochure.

Source: *Revolution Magazine*, 19 March 2004 (www.revolutionmagazine.com)

Svennivig (2004), in his research on use of interactive media, points out some of the limitations of interactive TV when he says: 'Television may not, however, be the ideal route for delivering interactive services in terms of volume of use. For a start, the medium has a central social function … This social role is not particularly compatible with the range of existing or potential services.' The research summarised by Svennevig (2004) in Figure 3.9 shows that the usage of web-based services is currently much more important than using iDTV services amongst UK audiences.

How does interactive digital TV work?

Figure 3.10 shows that a set-top box is an important component of the interactive digital TV system. This is used to receive and decode the message from a satellite dish or cable that is then displayed on a conventional TV. The set-top box also includes a modem that is used to pass back selections made on the interactive shopping channel to the company across the Internet using standard phone lines for the connection. For digital cable connections, there is a continuous connection between the set-top box and the provider which means that more detailed information on customer behaviour is available. The image displayed is lower-resolution than a PC and each supplier uses a different display standard. This means that HTML web content cannot readily be transferred to iDTV and needs to be **repurposed**.

Repurposing
Developing for a new access platform content that was previously used for a different platform such as the web.

Sky interactive services have previously been limited to a small number of e-commerce sites such as Domino Pizza and BlueSquare paying premium fees. This 'walled garden' has now been extended to any site with the 2005 launch of SiteControl (Beta version) **https://control.skyinteractive.com**. You can think of this as 'web over TV' although Sky is keen not to position it as such since the reality is that content does need to be repurposed for the lower resolution. The benefits of this new service as defined at the launch are:

Any web site operator can now extend their service to include over 7 million interactive TV Sky boxes reaching new customers and audiences efficiently and cost-effectively using Sky's new e-business portal. All you need to do is build a site using WTVML (that's Worldwide TV Mark-up Language), use SiteControl to tell Sky where the site is and configure any special options you want.

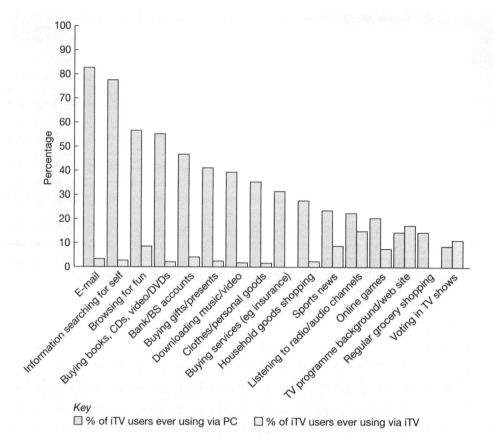

Figure 3.9 Relative use of the Internet and interactive TV

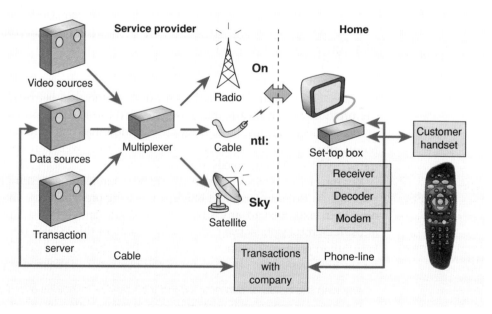

Figure 3.10 Components of an interactive digital TV system

When a company decides how to respond to iDTV several levels of commitment can be identified:

- *promotion* – using interactive ads;
- *content* – repurposing web site for interactive TV;
- *content* – new interactive services;
- *e-commerce* – transactional services, typically for a limited range of products.

Other new digital access devices may affect the future infrastructure requirements. These include digital home storage. Its promoters are describing this as 'The biggest change in conventional broadcasting since the industry began'. Variously referred to as 'personal video recorders', 'home media servers' or 'content refrigerators', they all involve recording a TV programme direct to a magnetic disk which gives 20 hours of recording time. Examples are Sky+ and TiVo. These offer the opportunity to pause a programme while it is being transmitted, record it and return to it later. It may also be possible to filter out adverts. There is likely to be convergence of these devices with the PC. Home entertainment PCs running Windows MediaCenter are gradually growing in importance.

As a conclusion to this section complete Activity 3.1, which illustrates the type of technology dilemma marketers face as new technologies are introduced. Case Study 3 can be used to support Activity 3.1.

Activity 3.1 — Assessing new technology options

Purpose

To illustrate the process for reviewing the relevance of new technology options.

Activity

You work for an FMCG (fast-moving consumer goods) brand and are attending an industry trade show where you see a presentation about the next-generation (3G) mobile phones which are due to launch in your country in one year's time. You need to decide whether your organisation adopts the new phone and if so when. Complete the following:

1 How would you assess the significance of this new technology?
2 Summarise the proposition of the new access devices for both consumers and your organisation.
3 What recommendations would you make about when to adopt and which services to offer?

Digital radio
All types of radio broadcast as a digital signal.

Digital audio broadcasting (DAB) radio
Digital radio with clear sound quality with the facility to transmit text, images and video.

Web radio
Or 'Internet radio' is when existing broadcasts are streamed via the Internet and listened to using plug-ins such as Real Media or Windows Media Player.

Digital radio

We can identify two types of digital radio – digital radio and web radio. Both are interactive. Digital radio is also available through interactive TV, mobile and in-car.

Digital radio requires buying a new digital radio although it can be streamed just like a 'traditional analogue web radio'. Digital radio is often accompanied by a big liquid crystal 4" × 5" display and is transactional 2-way. Digital radio is now widely known as digital audio broadcasting (DAB) radio.

Web radio or Internet radio is when existing broadcasts are streamed via the Internet and listened to using plug-ins such as Real Media or Windows Media Player. This is an important trend, with radio-listener auditing service Rajar reporting that in 2004 nearly 20% of adults had listened to radio on the web. 'Streamies' are people who listen to web radio at home or at work. For many it means logging on to a web radio station and leaving it to play as you work. In fact, once you log on to a station it accompanies you wherever you go on the net – so you can carry on listening wherever you go online. And if you like a particular track or broadcast feature you can order it there and then. A variant of web radio is that provided by music downloading services such as iTunes and Napster. Here, listeners can define their own sequence of tracks to listen to, or listen to prepared selections of tracks – currently without presenters, so there are limited opportunities for advertising between tracks.

According to the World DAB Forum (**www.worlddab.org**), the trade association promoting DAB, the benefits of DAB for the consumer are:

Aside from distortion-free reception digital sound quality, DAB offers further advantages as it has been designed for the multimedia age. DAB can carry not only audio, but also text, pictures, data and even videos – all on your radio at home and on the move!

One of the limitations of DAB is that a 'return path' isn't available, so a direct response has to be achieved through other e-tools such as a web site or SMS.

Web radio can be used successfully for integrated campaigns. Listeners may first see an ad in the newspaper or on TV, register it, but not respond. When they then hear about it online, response is more seamless – they just type in the company or campaign code into their browser. For example, for Christmas 2004 eBay UK ran a treasure hunt to showcase the range of products on sale through clues on the home page which prompted a search. It was advertised both in print and on streaming radio stations.

Mini Case Study 3.3	Comet uses Virgin Radio for positioning and response

In 2004 Virgin Radio was the most popular commercial radio station in the UK. Its web site receives over 1,000,000 unique visitors per month. The Comet campaign is a typical cross-media campaign that uses on-air and web site messaging and interaction.

Campaign objectives
- Support awareness of Comet's Price Promise that they provide low prices all year round.
- Communicate that Comet has great Christmas gifts for all the family.
- Drive traffic to Comet's gift finder at comet.co.uk.
- Create competitive standout through engaging activity.

Implementation
- Listeners were invited to play 'The Price is Right' with Comet in a weeklong Drivetime Show promotion.
- Each day, a prize package demonstrating Comet's wide product range was up for grabs with a higher than normal starting price.
- Two listeners then guessed ever-decreasing prices to guess the package's true low Comet price.
- The first listener to get the price right won, or the first to get the price too low lost (and the other won by default).
- On-air mentions directed listeners to Comet's Gift Finder which was built into a co-branded micro-site on virginradio.co.uk.
- Banner ads and a competitions area on the web site were used to direct visitors to Gift Finder.

Source: Virgin Radio (**www.virginradio.co.uk**)

Radio has always been a good brand builder for the marketer. Now it is beginning to offer additional routes via new syndication and content deals which, in turn, may mean new programmes which means new sponsorship opportunities, and even new radio station opportunities. Some radio stations now offer audio ads with a banner ad or 'buy now' button when listening to web radio – you hear the ad, you click the button. Web radio also offers to do partner deals delivering niche radio to other web sites. This adds to the branding and also offers new revenue-generating channels as affiliates share ad revenues and merchandise sales from the partner web radio company.

Another benefit of web radio is that, as with traditional radio, there is already a dialogue – people phone in, e-mail in and snail-mail in. Today, they can click and respond instantaneously, continuing the conversation later or joining in a group discussion.

Security

We now focus on security technology, which is, like privacy, a major concern for Internet users. Security fears are a major barrier to e-commerce adoption, by both businesses and consumers. When a customer of an e-commerce site enters their credit card details, these are typically stored on servers of the merchant (retailer) of the third party. Once here, they are vulnerable to downloading by hackers who can use the numbers for fraudulent purchase. Customers may lose the first £50, if the credit card issuer does not cover them, but for larger amounts the risk lies with the credit card issuer. As a result, Internet-related fraud is now the largest source of fraud affecting credit card companies such as Visa and Mastercard. To summarise we can identify the following security risks from the customer or merchant perspective:

A transaction or credit card details stolen in transit;
B customer's credit card details stolen from merchant's server;
C merchant or customer are not who they claim to be.

In this section we assess the measures that can be taken to reduce the risk of these breaches of e-commerce security. We start by reviewing some of the theory of online security and then review the techniques used.

Principles of secure systems

Before we look at the principles of secure systems, it is worth reviewing the standard terminology for the different parties involved in the transaction:

- *Purchasers*. These are the consumers buying the goods.
- *Merchants*. These are the retailers.
- *Certification authority (CA)*. This is a body that issues digital certificates that confirm the identity of purchasers and merchants.
- *Banks*. These are traditional banks.
- *Electronic token issuer*. A virtual bank that issues digital currency.

The basic requirements for security systems from these different parties to the transaction are as follows:

1 *Authentication* – are parties to the transaction who they claim to be (risk C above)?
2 *Privacy and confidentiality* – is the transaction data-protected? The consumer may want to make an anonymous purchase. Are all non-essential traces of a transaction removed from the public network and all intermediary records eliminated (risks B and C above)?

3 *Integrity* – checks that the message sent is complete, i.e. that it isn't corrupted.

4 *Non-repudiability* – ensures sender cannot deny sending message.

5 *Availability* – how can threats to the continuity and performance of the system be eliminated?

Approaches to developing secure systems

Digital certificates

There are two main methods of encryption using digital certificates or 'keys':

Digital certificates (keys)

Consist of keys made up of large numbers that are used to uniquely identify individuals.

Symmetric encryption

Both parties to a transaction use the same key to encode and decode messages.

Asymmetric encryption

Both parties use a related but different key to encode and decode messages.

1 Secret-key (symmetric) encryption. This involves both parties having an identical (shared) key that is known only to them. Only this key can be used to encrypt and decrypt messages. The secret key has to be passed from one party to the other before use in much the same way a copy of a secure attaché case key would have to be sent to a receiver of information. This approach has traditionally been used to achieve security between two separate parties, such as major companies conducting EDI. Here the private key is sent out electronically or by courier to ensure it is not copied.

This method is not practical for general e-commerce since it would not be safe for a purchaser to give a secret key to a merchant since control of it would be lost and it could not then be used for other purposes. A merchant would also have to manage many customer keys.

2 Public-key (asymmetric) encryption. Asymmetric encryption is so called since the keys used by the sender and receiver of information are different. The two keys are related by a numerical code, so only the pair of keys can be used in combination to encrypt and decrypt information. Figure 3.11 shows how public-key encryption works in an e-commerce context. A customer can place an order with a merchant by automatically looking up the public key of the merchant and then using this key to encrypt the message containing their order. The scrambled message is then sent across the Internet and on receipt by the merchant is read using the merchant's private key. In this way only the merchant who has the only copy of the private key can read the order. In the reverse case the merchant could confirm the customer's identity by reading identity information such as a digital signature encrypted with the private key of the customer using their public key.

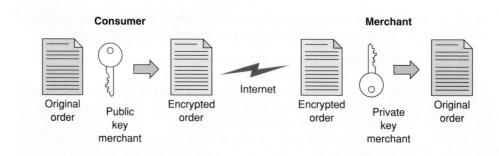

Figure 3.11 Public-key or asymmetric encryption

Digital signatures

A method of identifying individuals or companies using public-key encryption.

Digital signatures

Digital signatures can be used to create commercial systems by using public-key encryption to achieve authentication: the merchant and purchaser can prove they are genuine. The purchaser's digital signature is encrypted before sending a message using their private key and on receipt the public key of the purchaser is used to decrypt the digital signature. This proves the customer is genuine. Digital signatures are not widely used currently due to the difficulty of setting up transactions, but will become more widespread as the public-key infrastructure (PKI) stabilises and use of certificate authorities increases.

The public-key infrastructure (PKI) and certificate authorities

Certificates and certificate authorities (CAs)
A certificate is a valid copy of a public key of an individual or organisation together with identification information. It is issued by a trusted third party (TTP) or certificate authority (CA). CAs make public keys available and also issue private keys.

In order for digital signatures and public-key encryption to be effective it is necessary to be sure that the public key intended for decryption of a document actually belongs to the person you believe is sending you the document. The developing solution to this problem is the issuance by a trusted third party (TTP) of a message containing owner identification information and a copy of the public key of that person. The TTPs are usually referred to as certificate authorities (CAs) – an example is Verisign (www.verisign.com). The message is called a certificate. In reality, as asymmetric encryption is rather slow, it is often only a sample of the message that is encrypted and used as the representative digital signature.

Examples of certificate information are:

- user identification data;
- issuing authority identification and digital signature;
- user's public key;
- expiry date of this certificate;
- class of certificate;
- digital identification code of this certificate.

Virtual private networks

Virtual private network
Private network created using the public network infrastructure of the Internet.

A virtual private network (VPN) is a private wide-area network (WAN) that runs over the public network, rather than a more expensive private network. The technique by which a VPN operates is sometimes referred to as *tunnelling*, and involves encrypting both packet headers and content using a secure form of the Internet protocol known as IPSec. VPNs enable the global organisation to conduct its business securely, but using the public Internet rather than more expensive proprietary systems.

Current approaches to e-commerce security

In this section we review the approaches used by e-commerce sites to achieve security using the techniques described above.

Secure Sockets Layer protocol (SSL)

Secure Sockets Layer (SSL)
A commonly used encryption technique for scrambling data as they are passed across the Internet from a customer's web browser to a merchant's web server.

SSL is a security protocol, originally developed by Netscape, but now supported by all web browsers such as Microsoft Internet Explorer. SSL is used in the majority of B2C e-commerce transactions since it is easy for the customer to use without the need to download additional software or a certificate.

When a customer enters a secure checkout area of an e-commerce site SSL is used and the customer is prompted that 'you are about to view information over a secure connection' and a key symbol is used to denote this security. When encryption is occurring they will see that the web address prefix in the browser changes from 'http://' to 'https://' and a padlock appears at the bottom of the browser window.

How does SSL relate to the different security concepts described above? The main facility it provides is security and confidentiality. SSL enables a private link to be set up between customer and merchant. Encryption is used to scramble the details of an e-commerce transaction as it is passed between the sender and receiver and also when the details are held on the computers at each end. It would require a determined attempt to intercept such a message and decrypt it. SSL is more widely used than the rival S-HTTP method.

The detailed stages of SSL are as follows:

1 Client browser sends request for a secure connection.
2 Server responds with a digital certificate which is sent for authentication.
3 Client and server negotiate *session keys*, which are symmetrical keys used only for the duration of the transaction.

Since, with enough computing power, time and motivation, it is possible to decrypt messages encrypted using SSL, much effort is being put into more secure methods of encryption such as SET. From a merchant's point of view there is also the problem that authentication of the customer is not possible without resorting to other methods such as credit checks.

Secure Electronic Transaction (SET)

Secure Electronic Transaction (SET)
A standard for public-key encryption intended to enable secure e-commerce transactions lead-developed by Mastercard and Visa.

Secure Electronic Transaction (SET) was once touted as the way forward for increasing Internet security, but adoption was limited due to the difficulty of exchanging keys and the time of transaction, with most e-commerce sites still using SSL. SET is a security protocol based on digital certificates, developed by a consortium led by Mastercard and Visa, which allows parties to a transaction to confirm each other's identity. By employing digital certificates, SET allows a purchaser to confirm that the merchant is legitimate and conversely allows the merchant to verify that the credit card is being used by its owner. It also requires that each purchase request include a digital signature, further identifying the cardholder to the retailer. The digital signature and the merchant's digital certificate provide a certain level of trust.

Alternative payment systems

Payment systems
Methods of transferring funds from a customer to a merchant.

Micropayments
Small-denomination payments.

The preceding discussion has focused on payment using credit card systems since this is the prevalent method for e-commerce purchases. Throughout the 1990s there were many attempts to develop alternative payment systems to credit cards. These focused on micropayments or electronic coinage such as downloading an online newspaper, for which the overhead and fee of using a credit card was too high. One system that has succeeded is PayPal (**www.paypal.com**) which was purchased by eBay and is a major part of their revenue stream since it is used for payment by those who don't have access to credit cards. BT has launched BT 'Click and Buy' for micropayments which is successful within the UK.

Reassuring the customer

Once the security measures are in place, content on the merchant's site can be used to reassure the customer, for example Amazon (**www.amazon.com**) takes customer fears about security seriously judging by the prominence and amount of content it devotes to this issue. Some of the approaches used indicate good practice in allaying customers' fears. These include:

● use of customer guarantee to safeguard purchase;
● clear explanation of SSL security measures used;
● highlighting the rarity of fraud ('ten million customers have shopped safely without credit card fraud');

- the use of alternative ordering mechanisms such as phone or fax;
- the prominence of information to allay fears – the guarantee is one of the main menu options.

Companies can also use independent third parties that set guidelines for online privacy and security. The best-known international bodies are TRUSTe (**www.truste.org**) and Verisign for payment authentication (**www.verisign.com**). Within particular countries there may be other bodies such as, in the UK, ISIS (**www.imrg.org.uk/isis**).

Malicious threats to e-commerce security

Hackers can use techniques such as 'spoofing' to hack into a system and find credit card details. Spoofing, as its name suggests, involves someone masquerading as someone else. Spoofing can be of two sorts:

- IP spoofing is used to gain access to confidential information by creating false identification data such as the originating network (IP) address. The objective of this access can be espionage, theft or simply to cause mischief, generate confusion and damage corporate public image or political campaigns. Firewalls can be used to reduce this threat.
- Site spoofing, i.e. fooling the organisation's customers: using a similar URL such as **www.amazno.com** can divert customers to a site which is not the bona fide retailer.

Firewall
A specialised software application mounted on a server at the point where the company is connected to the Internet. Its purpose is to prevent unauthorised access into the company from outsiders.

Firewalls can be used to minimise the risk of security breaches by hackers and viruses. Firewalls are usually created as software mounted on a separate server at the point the company is connected to the Internet. Firewall software can then be configured to accept only links from trusted domains representing other offices in the company or key account customers. A firewall has implication for marketers since staff accessing a web site from work may not be able to access some content such as graphics plug-ins.

Denial-of-service attacks

The risk to companies of these attacks was highlighted in the spring of 2000, when the top web sites were targeted. The performance of these sites such as Yahoo! (**www.yahoo.com**) and eBay (**www.ebay.com**) was severely degraded as millions of data packets flooded the site from a number of servers. This was a distributed attack where the sites were bombarded from rogue software installed on many servers, so it was difficult for the e-tailers to counter. Since then, fraudsters have attempted to blackmail online merchants at critical times, for example online betting companies before a major sporting event or e-retailers before Christmas. These are often very sophisticated attacks which involve using viruses to compromise many 'zombie' computers around the world which are not adequately protected by firewalls and are then subsequently used to broadcast messages. Such attacks are very difficult to counter.

Phishing
Obtaining personal details online through sites and e-mails masquerading as legitimate businesses.

'Phishing'

Phishing (pronounced 'fishing') is a specialised form of online identity theft. The most common form of 'phishing' is where a spam e-mail is sent out purporting to be from an organisation such as a bank or payment service. In 2004, the sites barclaysprivate.com and eurocitibank.com – neither of them anything to do with existing banks – were shut down, having been used to garner ID details for fraud. Recipients are then invited to visit a web site to update their details after entering their username and password. The web address directs them to a false site appearing the same as the organisation's site. When the username and password are entered these are then collected and used for removing money from the recipient's real account. Such scams are a modern version of the scam devised by criminals where they install a false ATM in a wall with a card reader to access someone's account details. This form of scam is difficult to counter since the e-mail and web site can be made to appear identical to those of the organisation through copying. The main countermeasure is education of users, so banks for instance will tell their customers that they would never send this form of e-mail. However, this will not eradicate the problem since with millions of online customers some will always respond to such scams. A further approach is the use of multiple passwords, such that when an account is first accessed from a new system an additional password is required which can only be obtained through mail or by phone. Of course, this will only work if identity theft hasn't occurred. So, for organisations subject to phishing attacks, options for e-mail marketing are limited.

Economic factors

The economic prosperity and competitive environment in different countries will determine the e-commerce potential of each. Managers developing e-commerce strategies will target the countries that are most developed in the use of the technology. Knowledge of different economic conditions is also part of budgeting for revenue from different countries. For example, Fisher (2000) noted that the Asian market for e-commerce is predicted to triple within three years. However, within this marketplace there are large variations. Relative to income, the cost of a PC is still high in many parts of Asia for people on low incomes. In China there is regulation on foreign ownership of Internet portals and ISPs which could hamper development. User access to certain content is also restricted. Despite this, access in China is doubling every 6 months and at this rate China could have the largest user base within 10 years!

The trend to globalisation can arguably insulate a company to some extent from fluctuations in regional markets, but is of course no protection from a global recession. Managers can also study e-commerce in leading countries to help predict future e-commerce trends in their own country.

In Chapter 2 we saw that there is wide variation in the level of use of the Internet in different continents and countries, particularly for consumer use. According to Roussel (2000), economic, regulatory and cultural issues are among the factors affecting use of the Internet for commercial transactions. The relative importance of these means e-commerce will develop differently in every country. Roussel (2000) rated different countries according to their readiness to use the Internet for business (Figure 3.12). This was based on two factors – propensity for e-commerce and Internet penetration. To calculate the propensity of a country for e-commerce transactions, the business environment was evaluated using the Economic Intelligence Unit (**www.eiu.com**) rating of countries according to 70 different indicators, such as the strength of the economy, political stability, the regulatory climate, taxation policies and openness to trade and investment. Cultural factors were also considered, including language and the attitude to online purchasing as opposed to browsing. The two graphed factors do not correspond in all countries, for example, Scandinavian users frequently use the Internet to gain information, helped by widespread English usage, but they are less keen to purchase online due to concerns about security. Internet penetration varies widely and is surprisingly low in some countries, for example in France, which was earlier a leader in e-commerce through its Minitel system, and in Japan.

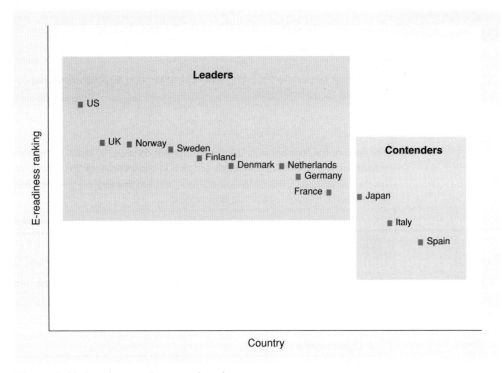

Figure 3.12 Leaders and contenders in e-commerce

Source: Adapted from the Economist Intelligence Unit/Pyramid Research e-readiness ranking (www.eiu.com)

Globalisation

Globalisation refers to the move towards international trading in a single global market-place and the blurring of social and cultural differences between countries. Some perceive it as 'Westernisation' or even 'Americanisation'.

Quelch and Klein (1996) point out some of the consequences for organisations that wish to compete in the global marketplace. They say a company must have:

● *a 24-hour order-taking and customer service response capability;*
● *regulatory and customs-handling experience to ship internationally;*
● *in-depth understanding of foreign marketing environments to assess the advantages of its own products and services.*

Language and cultural understanding may also present a problem and a small or medium-sized company is unlikely to possess the resources to develop a multi-language version of its site or employ staff with language skills. On the other hand, Quelch and Klein (1996) note that the growth of the use of the Internet for business will accelerate the trend of English becoming the lingua franca of commerce.

Hamill and Gregory (1997) highlight the strategic implications of e-commerce for business-to-business exchanges conducted internationally. They note that there will be increasing standardisation of prices across borders as businesses become more aware of price differentials. Secondly, they predict that the importance of traditional intermediaries such as agents and distributors will be reduced by Internet-enabled direct marketing and sales.

Larger organisations typically already compete in the global marketplace, or have the financial resources to achieve this. But what about the smaller organisation? Most

Activity 3.2	Overcoming SME resistance to e-commerce

Purpose

To highlight barriers to exporting amongst SMEs and suggest measures by which they may be overcome by governments.

Activity

For each of the four barriers to internationalisation given in Table 3.4 suggest the management reasons why the barriers may exist and actions governments can take to overcome these barriers. Evaluate how well the government in your country communicates the benefits of e-commerce through education and training.

Table 3.4 Issues in SME resistance to exporting (barriers from Hamill and Gregory (1997) and Poon and Jevons (1997))

Barrier	Management issues	How can barrier be overcome?
1 Psychological		
2 Operational		
3 Organisational		
4 Product/market		

governments are looking to encourage SMEs to use electronic commerce to tap into the international market. Advice from governments must reassure SMEs wishing to export. Hamill and Gregory (1997) identify the barriers to SME internationalisation in Table 3.4. Complete Activity 3.2 to look at the actions that can be taken to overcome these barriers.

Political factors

The political and regulatory environment is shaped by the interplay of government agencies, public opinion and consumer pressure groups such as CAUCE (the coalition against unsolicited e-mail) which were active in the mid-1990s and helped in pressurising for laws, **www.cauce.org**, and industry-backed organisations such as TRUSTe (**www.truste.org**) that promote best practice amongst companies. The political environment is one of the drivers for establishing the laws to ensure privacy and to collect taxes, as described in previous sections.

Political action enacted through government agencies to control the adoption of the Internet can include:

● promoting the benefits of adopting the Internet for consumers and business to improve a country's economic prosperity;
● sponsoring research leading to dissemination of best practice amongst companies, for example the DTI international benchmarking survey;
● enacting legislation to regulate the environment, for example to protect privacy or control taxation;

- setting up international bodies to coordinate the Internet such as ICANN (the Internet Corporation for Assigned Names and Numbers, www.icann.com) which has introduced new domains such as .biz and .info.

Some examples of the role of government organisations in promoting and regulating e-commerce is given by these examples from the European Commission:

- In 1998 new data protection guidelines were enacted, as is described in the section on privacy, to help protect consumers and increase the adoption of e-commerce by reducing security fears.
- In May 2000 the eEurope Action Plan was launched with objectives of 'a cheaper, faster, more secure Internet; investing in people's skills and access; and stimulating the use of the Internet'. The Commission intends to increase Internet access relative to the USA, in order to make Europe more competitive.
- Also in May 2000 the Commission announced that it wants the supply of local loops, the copper cables that link homes to telephone exchanges, to be unbundled so that newer companies can compete with traditional telecommunications suppliers. The objective here is the provision of widespread broadband services as a major aim of the EU.
- In June 2000 an e-commerce directive was adopted by the European Union. Pullen and Robinson (2001) note that the most fundamental provision of the Act is in Article 3 which defines the principles of country of origin and mutual recognition. This means that any company trading in an EU member state is subject in that country to the laws of that country and not those of the other member states. This prevents the need for companies to adhere to specific advertising or data protection laws in the countries in which they operate.

The type of initiative launched by governments is highlighted by the launch in the UK in September 1999 of a new 'UK online' campaign, a raft of initiatives and investment aimed at moving people, business and government itself online (e-government). E-envoy posts and an e-minister have also been appointed. The prime minister said in 1999:

E-government
The use of Internet technologies to provide government services to citizens.

> There is a revolution going on in our economy. A fundamental change, not a dot.com fad, but a real transformation towards a knowledge economy. So, today, I am announcing a new campaign. Its goal is to get the UK on-line. To meet the three stretching targets we have set: for Britain to be the best place in the world for e-commerce, with universal access to the Internet and all Government services on the net. In short, the UK on-line campaign aims to get business, people and government on-line.

Specific targets have been set for the proportion of people and businesses that have access, including public access points for those who cannot currently afford the technology. Managers who are aware of these initiatives can tap into sources of funding for development or free training to support their online initiatives.

Internet governance

Internet governance
Control of the operation and use of the Internet.

Internet governance describes the control put in place to manage the growth of the Internet and its usage. Governance is traditionally undertaken by government, but the global nature of the Internet makes it less practical for a government to control cyberspace. Dyson (1998) says:

> Now, with the advent of the Net, we are privatising government in a new way – not only in the traditional sense of selling things off to the private sector, but by allowing organisations independent of traditional governments to take on certain 'government' regulatory

roles. These new international regulatory agencies will perform former government functions in counterpoint to increasingly global large companies and also to individuals and smaller private organisations who can operate globally over the Net.

The US approach to governance, formalised in the Framework for Global Electronic Commerce in 1997 is to avoid any single country taking control.

Dyson (1998) describes different layers of jurisdiction. These are:

1 physical space comprising each individual country where their own laws such as those governing taxation, privacy and trading and advertising standards hold;
2 ISPs – the connection between the physical world and the virtual world;
3 domain name control (**www.icann.net**) and communities;
4 agencies such as TRUSTe (**www.truste.org**).

Taxation

How to change tax laws to reflect the globalisation through the Internet is a problem that many governments are grappling with. The fear is that the Internet may cause significant reductions in tax revenues to national or local governments if existing laws do not cover changes in purchasing patterns. In Europe, the use of online betting in lower-tax areas such as Gibraltar has resulted in lower revenues to governments in the countries where consumers would have formerly paid gaming tax to the government via a betting shop. Large UK bookmakers such as William Hill and Victor Chandler are offering Internet-based betting from 'offshore' locations such as Gibraltar. The lower duties in these countries offer the companies the opportunity to make betting significantly cheaper than if they were operating under a higher-tax regime. This trend has been dubbed LOCI or Location Optimised Commerce on the Internet by Mougayer (1998). Meanwhile, the government of the country from which a person places the bet will face a drop in its tax revenues. In the UK the government has sought to reduce the revenue shortfall by reducing the differential between UK and overseas costs.

The extent of the taxation problem for governments is illustrated by the US ABC News (2000) reporting that between $300 million and $3.8 billion of potential tax revenue was lost by authorities in 2000 in the USA as more consumers purchased online. The revenue shortfall occurs because online retailers need to impose sales or use tax only when goods are being sent to a consumer who lives in a state (or country) where the retailer has a bricks-and-mortar store. Buyers are supposed to voluntarily pay the appropriate sales taxes when buying online, but this rarely happens in practice. This makes the Internet a largely tax-free area in the USA.

Since the Internet supports the global marketplace it could be argued that it makes little sense to introduce tariffs on goods and services delivered over the Internet. Such instruments would, in any case, be impossible to apply over products delivered electronically. This position is currently that of the USA. In the document 'A Framework for Global Electronic Commerce', President Clinton stated that:

The United States will advocate in the World Trade Organisation (WTO) and other appropriate international fora that the Internet be declared a tariff-free zone.

Tax jurisdiction

Tax jurisdiction determines which country gets tax income from a transaction. Under the current system of international tax treaties, the right to tax is divided between the country where the enterprise that receives the income is resident ('residence' country) and that from which the enterprise derives that income ('source' country). Laws on taxation are rapidly evolving and vary dramatically between countries. A proposed EU directive intends to deal with these issues by defining the place of establishment of a merchant as where they pursue an economic activity from a fixed physical location. At the time of writing the general principle that is being applied is that tax rules are similar to those for a conventional mail-order sale; for the UK, the tax principles are as follows:

(a) if the supplier (residence) and the customer (source) are both in the UK, VAT will be chargeable;
(b) exports to private customers in the EU will attract either UK VAT or local VAT;
(c) exports outside the EU will be zero-rated (but tax may be levied on import);
(d) imports into the UK from the EU or beyond will attract local VAT, or UK import tax when received through customs;
(e) services attract VAT according to where the supplier is located. This is different from products and causes anomalies if online services are created. For example, a betting service located in Gibraltar enables UK customers to gamble at a lower tax rate than with the same company in the UK.

Case Study 3 — Boo hoo – learning from the largest European dot-com failure

Context

'*Unless we raise $20 million by midnight, boo.com is dead.*' So said Boo.com CEO Ernst Malmsten, on 18 May 2000. Half the investment was raised, but this was too little, too late, and at midnight, less than a year after its launch, Boo.com closed. The headlines in the *Financial Times*, the next day read: '*Boo.com collapses as Investors refuse funds. Online Sports retailer becomes Europe's first big Internet casualty.*'

The Boo.com case remains a valuable case study for all types of businesses, since it doesn't only illustrate the challenges of managing e-commerce for a clothes retailer, but rather highlights failings in e-commerce strategy and management that can be made in any type of organisation.

Company background

Boo.com was a European company founded in 1998 and operating out of a London head office, which was founded by three Swedish entrepreneurs, Ernst Malmsten, Kajsa Leander and Patrik Hedelin. Malmsten and Leander had previous business experience in publishing where they created a specialist publisher and had also created an online bookstore, bokus.com, which in 1997 became the world's third largest book e-retailer behind Amazon and Barnes & Noble. They became millionaires when they sold the company in 1998. At Boo.com, they were joined by Patrik Hedelin who was also the financial director at bokus, and at the time they were perceived as experienced European Internet entrepreneurs by the investors who backed them in their new venture.

Company vision

The vision for Boo.com was for it to become the world's first online global sports retail site. It would be a European brand, but with a global appeal. Think of it as a sports and fashion retail version of Amazon. At launch it would open its virtual doors in both Europe and America with a view to 'amazoning the sector'. Note though that, in contrast, Amazon did not launch simultaneously in all markets. Rather it became established in the US before providing local European distribution through acquisition and re-branding of other e-retailers in the United Kingdom for example.

The boo.com brand name

According to Malmsten et al. (2001), the Boo brand name originated from film star Bo Derek, best known for her role in the movie *10*. The domain name 'Bo.com' was unavailable, but adding an 'o', they managed to procure the domain 'Boo.com' for $2,500 from a domain name dealer. According to Rob Talbot, director of marketing for Boo.com, Boo were 'looking for a name that was easy to spell across all the different countries and easy to remember ... something that didn't have a particular meaning'.

Target market

The audience targeted by Boo.com can be characterised as 'young, well-off and fashion-conscious' 18-to-24-year-olds. The concept was that globally the target market would be interested in sports and fashion brands stocked by Boo.com.

The market for clothing in this area was viewed as very large, so the thought was that capture of only a small part of this market was required for Boo.com to be successful. The view at this time on the scale of this market and the basis for success is indicated by *New Media Age* (1999) where it was described as

> The $60b USD industry is dominated by Gen X'ers who are online and according to market research in need of knowing what is in, what is not and a way to receive such goods quickly. If boo.com becomes known as the place to keep up with fashion and can supply the latest trends then there is no doubt that there is a market, a highly profitable one at that for profits to grow from.

The growth in market was also supported by retail analysts, with Verdict predicting online shopping in the United Kingdom to grow from £600 million in 1999 to £12.5 billion in 2005.

However, *New Media Age* (1999) does note some reservations about this market, saying

> Clothes and trainers have a high rate of return in the mail order/home shopping world. Twenty year olds may be online and may have disposable income but they are not the main market associated with mail order. To date there is no one else doing anything similar to boo.com.

The Boo.com proposition

In their proposal to investors, the company stated that 'their business idea is to become the world-leading Internet-based retailer of prestigious brand leisure and sportswear names'. They listed brands such as Polo, Ralph Lauren, Tommy Hilfiger, Nike, Fila, Lacoste and Adidas. The proposition involved sports and fashion goods alongside each other. The thinking was than sports clothing has more standardised sizes with less need for a precise fit than designer clothing.

The owners of Boo.com wanted to develop an easy to use experience which re-created the offline shopping experience as far as possible. As part of the branding strategy, an idea was developed of a virtual salesperson, initially named Jenny and later Miss Boo. She would guide users through the site and give helpful tips. When selecting products, users could drag them on to models, zoom in and rotate them in 3D to visualise them from different angles. The technology to achieve this was built from scratch along with the stock control and distribution software. A large investment was required in technology with several suppliers being replaced before launch, which was 6 months later than promised to investors, largely due to problems with implementing the technology.

Clothing the mannequin and populating the catalogue was also an expensive challenge. For 2000, about $6 million was spent on content about spring/summer fashionwear. It cost $200 to photograph each product, representing a monthly cost of more than $500,000.

Although the user experience of Boo.com is often criticised for its speed, it does seem to have had that wow factor that influenced investors. Analyst Nik Margolis, writing in *New Media Age* (1999), illustrates this by saying:

> What I saw at boo.com is simply the most clever web experience I have seen in quite a while. The presentation of products and content are both imaginative and offer an experience. Sure everything loads up fast in an office but I was assured by those at boo.com that they will keep to a limit of 8 seconds for a page to download. Eight seconds is not great but the question is will it be worth waiting for?

Of course, today, the majority of European users have broadband, but in the late 1990s the majority were on dial-up and had to download the software to view products.

Communicating the Boo.com proposition

Early plans referred to extensive 'high-impact' marketing campaigns on TV and in newspapers. Public relations were important in leveraging the novelty of the concept and human side of the business – Leander was previously a professional model and had formerly been Malmsten's partner. This PR was initially focused within the fashion and sportswear trade and then rolled out to publications likely to be read by the target audience. The success of this PR initiative can be judged by the 350,000 e-mail pre-registrations who wanted to be notified of launch. For the launch Malmsten et al. (2001) explains that 'with a marketing and PR spend of only $22.4 million we had managed to create a worldwide brand'.

To help create the values of the Boo.com brand, *Boom* a lavish online fashion magazine, was created, which required substantial staff for different language versions. The magazine wasn't a catalogue which directly supported sales, rather it was a publishing venture competing with established fashion titles. For existing customers the *Look Book*, a 44-page print catalogue was produced which showcased different products each month.

The challenges of building a global brand in months

The challenges of creating a global brand in months are illustrated well by Malmsten et al. (2001). After an initial round of funding, including investment from JP Morgan, LMVH Investment and the Benetton family, which generated around $9 million, the founders planned towards launch by identifying thousands of individual tasks, many of which needed to be completed by staff yet to be recruited. These tasks were divided into twenty-seven areas of responsibility familiar to many organisations including office infrastructure, logistics, product information, pricing, front-end applications, call centres, packaging, suppliers, designing logos, advertising/PR, legal issues, and recruitment. At its zenith, Boo.com had 350 staff, with over one hundred in London and new offices in Munich, New York, Paris and Stockholm. Initially, Boo.com was available in UK English, US English, German, Swedish, Danish and Finnish with localised versions for France, Spain and Italy added after launch. The web site was tailored for individual countries using the local language and currency and also local prices. Orders were fulfilled and shipped out of one of two warehouses: one in Louisville, Kentucky and the other in Cologne, Germany. This side of the business was relatively successful with on-time delivery rates approaching 100% achieved.

Boo possessed classic channel conflicts. Initially, it was difficult getting fashion and sports brands to offer their products through Boo.com. Manufacturers already had a well-established distribution network through large high-street sports and fashion retailers and many smaller retailers. If clothing brands permitted Boo.com to sell their clothes online at discounted prices, then this would conflict with retailers' interests and would also portray the brands in a negative light if their goods were in an online 'bargain bucket'. A further pricing issue is where local or *zone pricing* in different markets exists, for example lower prices often exist in the US than Europe and there are variations in different European countries.

Making the business case to investors

Today it seems incredible that investors were confident enough to invest $130 million in the company and that at the high point the company was valued at $390 million. Yet much of this investment was based on the vision of the founders to be a global brand and achieve 'first-mover advantage'. Although there were naturally revenue projections, these were not always based on an accurate detailed analysis of market potential. Immediately before launch, Malmsten et al. (2001) explains a meeting with would-be investor Pequot Capital, represented by Larry Lenihan who had made successful investments in AOL and Yahoo! The Boo.com management team were able to provide revenue forecasts, but were unable to answer fundamental questions for modelling the potential of the business, such as 'How many visitors are you aiming for? What kind of conversion rate are you aiming for? How much does each customer have to spend? What's your customer acquisition cost. And what's your payback time on customer acquisition cost?' When these figures were obtained, the analyst found them to be 'far-fetched' and reputedly ended the meeting with the words, 'I'm not interested. Sorry for my bluntness, but I think you're going to be out of business by Christmas'.

When the site launched on 3 November 1999, around 50,000 unique visitors were achieved on the first day, but only 4 in 1000 placed orders (a 0.25% conversion rate), showing the importance of modelling conversion rate accurately in modelling business potential. This low conversion rate was also symptomatic of problems with technology. It also gave rise to negative PR. One reviewer explained how he waited:

'Eighty-one minutes to pay too much money for a pair of shoes that I still have to wait a week to get?'

These rates did improve as problems were ironed out – by the end of the week 228,848 visits had resulted in 609 orders with a value of $64,000. In the 6 weeks from launch, sales of $353,000 were made and conversion rates had more than doubled to 0.98% before Christmas. However, a relaunch was required within 6 months to cut download times and to introduce a 'low-bandwidth version' for users using dial-up connections. This led to conversion rates of nearly 3% on sales promotion. Sales results were disappointing in some regions, with US sales accounting for 20% compared to the planned 40%.

The management team felt that further substantial investment was required to grow the business from a presence in 18 countries and 22 brands in November to 31 countries and 40 brands the following spring. Turnover was forecast to rise from $100 million in 2000/01 to $1350 million by 2003/4, which would be driven by $102.3 million in marketing in 2003/4. Profit was forecast to be $51.9 million by 2003/4.

The end of Boo.com

The end of Boo.com came on 18 May 2000, when investor funds could not be raised to meet the spiralling marketing, technology and wage bills.

Source: Prepared by Dave Chaffey from original sources including Malmsten et al. (2001) and *New Media Age* (1999)

Questions

1 Which strategic marketing assumptions and decisions arguably made Boo.com's failure inevitable? Contrast these with other dot-com era survivors that are still in business, for example, Lastminute.com, Egg.com and Firebox.com.

2 Using the framework of the marketing mix, appraise the marketing tactics of Boo.com in the areas of product, pricing, place, promotion, process, people and physical evidence.

3 In many ways, the vision of Boo's founders were 'ideas before their time'. Give examples of e-retail techniques used to create an engaging online customer experience which Boo adopted that are now becoming commonplace.

Summary

1 Environmental scanning and analysis of the macro-environment are necessary in order that a company can respond to environmental changes and act on legal and ethical constraints on its activities.

2 Social factors include variation in usage of the Internet while ethical issues include the need to safeguard consumer privacy and security of details. Privacy issues include collection and dissemination of customer information, cookies and the use of direct e-mail. Marketers must act within current law, reassure customers about their privacy and explain the benefits of collection of personal information.

3 Rapid variation in technology requires constant monitoring of adoption of the technology by customers and competitors and appropriate responses.

4 Economic factors considered in this chapter include the regional differences in the use of the Internet for trade. Different economic conditions in different markets are considered in developing e-commerce budgets.

5 Political factors involve the role of governments in promoting e-commerce, but also in trying to restrict it.

6 Legal factors to be considered by e-commerce managers include taxation, domain name registration, copyright and data protection.

Exercises

Self-assessment exercises

1 Summarise the key elements of the macro-environment that should be scanned by an e-commerce manager.

2 Give an example of how each of the macro-environment factors may directly drive the content and services provided by a web site.

3 What actions should e-commerce managers take to safeguard consumer privacy and security?

4 Give three examples of techniques web sites can use to protect the user's privacy.

5 How do governments attempt to control the adoption of the Internet?

6 Suggest approaches to managing technological innovation.

Essay and discussion questions

1 You recently started a job as e-commerce manager for a bank. Produce a checklist of all the different legal and ethical issues that you need to check for compliance on the existing web site of the bank.

2 How should the e-commerce manager monitor and respond to technological innovation?

3 Benchmark different approaches to achieving and reassuring customers about their privacy and security using three or four examples for a retail sector such as travel, books, toys or clothing.

4 Select a new Internet-access technology (such as phone, kiosks or TV) that has been introduced in the last two years and assess whether it will become a significant method of access.

Examination questions

1 Explain the different layers of governance of the Internet.

2 Summarise the macro-environment variables a company needs to monitor when operating an e-commerce site.

3 Explain the purpose of environmental scanning in an e-commerce context.

4 Give three examples of how web sites can use techniques to protect the user's privacy.

5 Explain the significance of the diffusion–adoption concept to the adoption of new technologies to:

(a) consumers purchasing using technological innovations;

(b) businesses deploying technological innovations.

6 What action should an e-commerce manager take to ensure compliance with ethical and legal standards of their site?

References

ABC News (2000) *Ecommerce Causes Tax Shortfall in US.* News story on ABC.com. 27/07/00, http://abcnews.go.com/sections/business/DailyNews/internettaxes000725.html.

Booz Allen Hamilton (2002) *International E-Economy Benchmarking The World's Most Effective Policies for the E-Economy.* Report published 19 November, London, www.e-envoy.gov.uk/assetRoot/04/00/08/19/04000819.pdf.

Curry, A. (2001) What's next for interactive television?, *Interactive Marketing*, 3(2), October/December, 114–28.

Dyson, E. (1998) *Release 2.1. A Design for Living in the Digital Age.* Penguin, London.

Fisher, A. (2000) Gap widens between the 'haves' and 'have-nots', *Financial Times*, 5 December.

Fletcher, K. (2001) Privacy: the Achilles heel of the new marketing, *Interactive Marketing*, 3(2), October/December, 128–41.

Gartner (2005) Gartner's Hype Cycle Special Report for 2005. Report summary available at www.gartner.com: ID Number: G00130115.

Godin, S. (1999) *Permission Marketing.* Simon and Schuster, New York.

Guardian (2003a) Hijacked your bank balance, your identity, your life. The *Guardian*, Saturday, 25 October, www.guardian.co.uk/weekend/story/0,3605,1069646,00.html.

Guardian (2003b) Will Wi-Fi fly? Neil McIntosh, Thursday, 14 August. www.guardian.co.uk/online/story/0,3605,1017664,00.html.

Guardian (2005) Ethiopia's digital dream. Michael Cross, Thursday, 4 August.

Hamill, J. and Gregory, K. (1997) Internet marketing in the internationalisation of UK SMEs, *Journal of Marketing Management*, Special edition on internationalisation, J. Hamill (ed.), 13 (1–3).

IT Week (2005) Need for speed leaves GSM in the past, 1 August. *IT Week*, 8(30), 13, **www.itweek.co.uk**.

Malmsten, E., Portanger, E. and Drazin, C. (2001) *Boo Hoo. A Dot.com Story from Concept to Catastrophe*. Random House, London.

Mason, R. (1986) Four ethical issues of the information age, *MIS Quarterly*, March.

MobileCommerceWorld (2002) British SMS records smashed in December. 24 January, Press release based on data from the mobile data association, **www.mobilecommerceworld.com**.

Mougayer, W. (1998) *Opening Digital Markets – Battle Plans and Strategies for Internet Commerce*, 2nd edn. CommerceNet Press, McGraw-Hill, New York.

National Statistics (2005) Individuals accessing the Internet – Report from the National Statistics Omnibus Survey. Published October 2005.

New Media Age (1999) Will boo.com scare off the competition? Budd Margolis, 22 July.

Poon, S. and Jevons, C. (1997) Internet-enabled international marketing: a small business network perspective, *Journal of Marketing Management*, 13, 29–41.

Pullen, M. and Robinson, J. (2001) The e-commerce directive and its impact on pan-European interactive marketing, *Interactive Marketing*, 2(3), 272–5.

Quelch, J. and Klein, L. (1996) The Internet and international marketing, *Sloan Management Review*, Spring, 61–75.

RedEye (2003) A study into the accuracy of IP and cookie-based online management information, The RedEye Report, available online at **www.redeye.com**.

Rogers, E. (1983) *Diffusion of Innovations*, 3rd edn. Free Press, New York.

Roussel, A. (2000) Leaders and laggards in B2C commerce. Gartner Group report. 4 August. SPA-11-5334, **www.gartner.com**.

Sparrow, A. (2000) *E-Commerce and the Law. The Legal Implications of Doing Business Online*. Financial Times Executive Briefings.

Svennevig, M. (2004) The interactive viewer: reality or myth? *Interactive Marketing*, 6(2), 151–64.

Trott, P. (1998) *Innovation Management and New Product Development*. Financial Times/Prentice Hall, Harlow.

United Nations (1999) New technologies and the global race for knowledge. In *Human Development Report*. United Nations, New York.

Ward, S., Bridges, K. and Chitty, B. (2005) Do incentives matter? An examination of on-line privacy concerns and willingness to provide personal and financial information, *Journal of Marketing Communications*, 11(1), 21–40.

Further reading

Dyson, E. (1998) *Release 2.1. A Design for Living in the Digital Age*. Penguin, London. Chapters 5 Governance, 8 Privacy, 9 Anonymity and 10 Security are of particular relevance.

Garfinkel, S. (2000) *Database Nation*. O'Reilly, Sebastopol, CA. This book is subtitled 'the death of privacy in the 21st century' and this is the issue on which it focuses (includes Internet- and non-Internet-related privacy).

Slevin, J. (2000) *The Internet and Society*. Polity Press, Cambridge. A book about the Internet that combines social theory, communications analysis and case studies from both academic and applied perspectives.

Zugelder, M., Flaherty, T. and Johnson, J. (2000) Legal issues associated with international Internet marketing, *International Marketing Review*, 17(3), 253–71. Gives a detailed review of legal issues associated with Internet marketing including consumer rights, defamation and disparagement, intellectual property protection, and jurisdiction.

Web links

- **Mobile Commerce World** (www.mobilecommerceworld.com). Source on usage of m-commerce.
- **MORI Technology Tracker** (www.mori.com/technology/techtracker.shtml). Provides a summary of access to new media platforms.
- **New Media Age** (www.newmediazero.com/nma). A weekly magazine reporting on the UK new media interest. Content now available online.
- **New Television Strategies** (www.newmediazero.com/ntvs). Sister publication to *New Media Age*.
- **Revolution magazine** (www.revolutionmagazine.com). A weekly magazine available for the UK, covering a range of new media platforms.

New law development

Two of the best legal sources to stay up-to-date are:

- **iCompli** (www.icompli.co.uk). Portal and e-newsletter concentrating on e-commerce law.
- **Marketing Law** (www.marketinglaw.co.uk). Up-to-date source on all forms of law related to marketing activities.

Part 2

INTERNET STRATEGY DEVELOPMENT

In Part 2 approaches for developing an Internet marketing strategy are explored. These combine traditional approaches to strategic marketing planning with specific Internet-related issues that need to be considered by Internet marketers. In Chapter 4 a strategy framework is described, Chapter 5 discusses the opportunities for varying the marketing mix online and Chapter 6 reviews strategies for online customer relationship management.

4

Internet marketing strategy

Learning objectives

After reading this chapter, the reader should be able to:

● Relate Internet marketing strategy to marketing and business strategy

● Identify opportunities and threats arising from the Internet

● Evaluate alternative strategic approaches to the Internet

Questions for marketers

Key questions for marketing managers related to this chapter are:

● What approaches can be used to develop Internet marketing strategy?

● How does Internet marketing strategy relate to other strategy development?

● What are the key strategic options for Internet marketing?

Links to other chapters

This chapter is related to other chapters as follows:

➤ It builds on the evaluation of the Internet environment from Chapters 2 and 3

➤ Chapter 5 describes the potential for varying different elements of the marketing mix as part of Internet marketing strategy

➤ Chapter 6 describes customer relationship management strategies

Introduction

The importance of the Internet to modern business strategy was underlined by Michael Porter, who famously said:

The key question is not whether to deploy Internet technology – companies have no choice if they want to stay competitive – but how to deploy it.   Porter (2001)

Internet marketing strategy

Definition of the approach by which Internet marketing will support marketing and business objectives.

An **Internet marketing strategy** is needed to provide consistent direction for an organisation's e-marketing activities so that they integrate with its other marketing activities and supports its objectives. We can suggest that the Internet marketing strategy has many similarities to the typical aims of traditional marketing strategies, in that it will:

- provide a future direction to Internet marketing activities;
- involve analysis of the organisation's external environment and internal resources to inform strategy;
- articulate Internet marketing objectives that support marketing objectives;
- involve selection of strategic options to achieve Internet marketing objectives and create sustainable differential competitive advantage;
- include strategy formulation to include typical marketing strategy options such as target markets, positioning and specification of the marketing mix;
- specify how resources will be deployed and the organisation will be structured to achieve the strategy.

This chapter examines each of these elements of strategy. We start by considering, in more detail, an appropriate process for developing an Internet marketing strategy, and then consider the following aspects of strategy:

1 situation review (drawing on our coverage in Chapters 2 and 3);
2 goal setting;
3 strategy formulation.

Figure 4.1 indicates the context for Internet marketing strategy development. The internal influences include corporate objectives and strategy, and these in turn influence marketing strategy that should directly influence the Internet marketing strategy. Key external influences include the market structure and demand, competitor strategies and the current and evolving opportunities and threats. Methods for monitoring the external environment to anticipate external opportunities and threats and competitors' actions have been introduced in Chapters 2 and 3, as were methods of assessing the demand of the market for Internet-delivered services.

Channel marketing strategy

Defines how a company should set specific objectives for a channel such as the Internet and vary its proposition and communications for this channel.

Customer touchpoints

Communications channels with which companies interact directly with prospects and customers. Traditional touchpoints include face-to-face (in-store or with sales representatives), phone and mail. Digital touchpoints include web services, e-mail and potentially mobile phone.

Internet strategy is a channel marketing strategy

We need to remember that an Internet marketing strategy is a channel marketing strategy which defines how a company should set *channel-specific objectives* and develop a *differential channel-proposition* and *channel-specific communications* consistent with the characteristics of the channel and consumer usage of it. The Internet marketing strategy determines the strategic significance of the Internet relative to other communications channels which are used to communicate directly with customers at different customer touchpoints. Some organisations such as low-cost airlines will decide to primarily use virtual channels such as the web site and e-mail marketing for delivering services and communicating with customers. Others may follow a strategy where the use of face-to-face, phone or direct mail communications remain important for the time being.

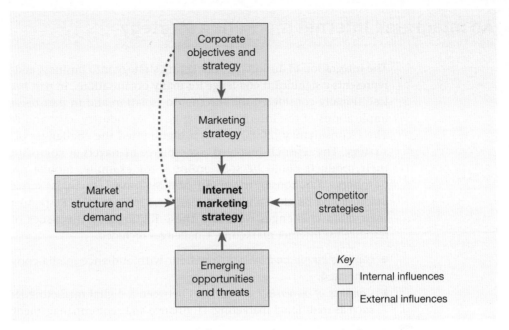

Figure 4.1 Internal and external influences on Internet marketing strategy

So the focus of Internet marketing strategy is decisions about how to use the channel to support existing marketing strategies, how to exploit its strengths and manage its weaknesses and to use it in conjunction with other channels as part of a multi-channel marketing strategy. This multi-channel marketing strategy defines how different marketing channels should integrate and support each other in terms of their proposition development and communications based on their relative merits for the customer and the company.

Multi-channel marketing strategy
Defines how different marketing channels should integrate and support each other in terms of their proposition development and communications based on their relative merits for the customer and the company.

The scope of Internet marketing strategy

When reviewing options for Internet marketing strategy, it is also useful to keep in mind that Internet strategy involves much more than the narrow focus of a strategy to develop web site services. Although this is part of Internet marketing strategy, marketers also examine broader issues of using the web, e-mail and databases strategically as communications and relationship-building tools which must integrate with other marketing communications. Internet strategy may also involve redesigning business processes to integrate with partners such as suppliers and distributors in new ways. Figure 1 in the Preface suggests the range of digital marketing activities that must be managed within an Internet marketing strategy. The figure shows that the operational activities which need to be managed can be usefully divided into those for (1) acquisition, (2) conversion and proposition development and (3) retention and growth. Many of these activities and much of Internet marketing strategy development involve developing a digital marketing communications strategy. The acquisition activities such as search engine marketing and online advertising and the retention activities such as e-mail marketing in Figure 4.2 are covered in Chapter 8. Conversion and proposition development is covered in Chapter 7. Proposition development, or the definition of the services that a company offers and how they are used for relationship building, is core to this chapter and is considered further in Chapter 5 on developing the online marketing mix and Chapter 6 on relationship building. The supporting operating processes and the management processes form the core of Internet marketing strategy.

An integrated Internet marketing strategy

The integration of an Internet marketing strategy into business and marketing strategies represents a significant challenge for many organisations, in part because they may have traditionally considered the Internet in isolation and in part because of the profound implications of the Internet for change at an industry level and within organisations. The E-consultancy (2005) research highlighted the challenges of Internet marketing strategy. The research involved e-commerce managers at companies in markets where their products could be sold online – for example, mobile phones (Orange, The Carphone Warehouse), travel (Tui and MyTravel), financial services (Lloyds TSB and Bradford and Bingley) and direct marketers such as BCA. Respondents were asked what their main challenges were and these highlighted the issues of gaining sufficient resource for Internet marketing. Challenges included:

- *Gaining buy-in and budget* consistent with audience media consumption and value generated;
- *Conflicts of ownership and tensions* between a digital marketing team and other teams such as traditional marketing, IT, finance and senior management;
- *Coordination with different channels* in conjunction with teams managing marketing programmes elsewhere in the business;
- *Managing and integrating customer information* about characteristics and behaviours collected online;
- *Achieving consistent reporting*, review, analysis and follow-up actions of digital marketing results throughout the business;
- *Structuring the specialist digital team* and integrating into the organisation by changing responsibilities elsewhere in the organisation;
- *In-sourcing vs outsourcing online marketing tactics*, i.e. search, affiliate, e-mail marketing, PR;
- *Staff recruitment and retention.*

Is a separate Internet marketing plan needed?

Should an organisation have a separate e-marketing plan defining its strategic approach to the Internet, either for the organisation as a whole or for specific markets or brands? Consider Figure 4.2. You will be familiar with the hierarchy of plans for an organisation, from a corporate or business plan which informs a marketing plan which in turn informs a communications plan and campaign briefs for different markets or brands. But where does the e-marketing plan fit? Does the organisation need one? Figure 4.2 suggests that an e-marketing plan may be useful to manage the 'e-campaign components' which refers to online communications tools such as online advertising or e-mail marketing or continuous e-marketing activities which may be conducted throughout the year to drive traffic, for example search engine marketing, affiliate marketing or online sponsorship.

You may be thinking that the marketer already has enough plans to deal with. Surely the practical approach for companies that are embracing e-marketing is to integrate e-marketing activities within their existing planning frameworks? But we believe that in many organisations, a distinct e-marketing plan is initially essential if the organisation is to effectively harness digital marketing. Since online channels are new, it is even more imperative to have clarity within the organisation. An e-marketing specialist can create an e-marketing plan to help inform and influence not only senior managers or directors and other non-marketing functions, but also to achieve buy-in from fellow marketers.

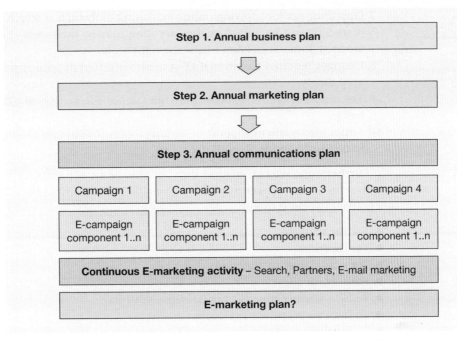

Figure 4.2 Hierarchy of organisation plans including e-marketing plans

Our rationale is that online channels are still in their infancy, yet they have had and will have dramatic effects on how customers select and use products. We sometimes hear that the Internet is 'just another channel to market'. However, the potential significance of the Internet as an influencer and direct contributor to sales is such that often it does warrant separate attention. Strategies to increase the contribution of digital channels to a business are required and the e-marketing plan can help define these strategies.

In the longer term, once an organisation has successfully defined its approaches to Internet marketing, it is likely that a separate Internet marketing strategy or e-marketing plan *will not* need to be developed each year since the Internet can be considered as any other communications medium.

These problems are typical and commonplace when there is no clear planning or control for e-marketing:

1 Customer demand for online services will be underestimated if this has not been researched and it is under-resourced and no or unrealistic objectives are set to achieve online marketing share.
2 Existing and start-up competitors will gain market share if insufficient resources are devoted to e-marketing and no clear strategies are defined.
3 Duplication of resources will occur, for example different parts of the marketing organisation purchasing different tools or different agencies for performing similar online marketing tasks.
4 Insufficient resource will be devoted to planning and executing e-marketing and there is likely to be a lack of specific specialist e-marketing skills, making it difficult to respond to competitive threats effectively.
5 Insufficient customer data are collected online as part of relationship building and these data are not integrated well with existing systems.
6 Efficiencies available through online marketing will be missed, for example lower communications costs and enhanced conversion rates in customer acquisition and retention campaigns.

7 Opportunities for applying online marketing tools such as search marketing or e-mail marketing will be missed or the execution may be inefficient if the wrong resources are used or marketers don't have the right tools.

8 Changes required to internal IT systems by different groups will not be prioritised accordingly.

9 The results of online marketing are not tracked adequately on a detailed or high-level basis.

10 Senior management support of e-marketing is inadequate to drive what often needs to be a major strategic initiative.

Furthermore, we can suggest that benefits of an e-marketing plan are in common with those of any marketing plan. McDonald (2003) describes the following reasons why a marketing plan is useful:

● For the marketer
● For superiors
● For non-marketing functions
● For subordinates
● To help identify sources of competitive advantage
● To force an organised approach
● To develop specificity
● To ensure consistent relationships
● To inform
● To get resources
● To get support
● To gain commitment
● To set objectives and strategies.

Managers responsible for a substantial investment in an Internet web site and associated e-marketing communications will naturally want to ensure that the correct amount of money is invested and that it is used effectively. For these reasons and others given in this section, many leading adopters of e-commerce do have a distinct e-marketing plan, as the E-consultancy survey of UK e-commerce managers shows (Figure 4.3).

For smaller organisations, the digital plan need not be exhaustive – a two-page summary defining objectives and outlining strategies may be sufficient. The important thing

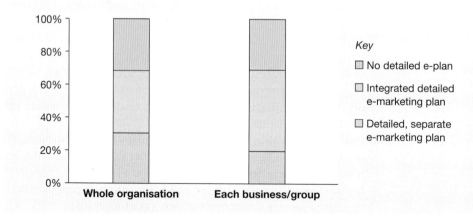

Figure 4.3 Usage of detailed e-marketing plans in UK e-commerce organisations
Source: E-consultancy (2005)

is to set clear objectives and strategies showing how the digital presence should contribute to the sales and marketing process. Specific initiatives that are required such as search marketing, e-mail marketing or features of web site redesign can be specified.

A generic strategic approach

Strategy process model
A framework for approaching strategy development.

Marketing planning
A logical sequence and a series of activities leading to the setting of marketing objectives and the formulation of plans for achieving them.

A **strategy process model** provides a framework that gives a logical sequence or 'roadmap' to follow to ensure inclusion of all key activities of strategy development and implementation. In a marketing context, these strategy development and implementation activities are coordinated through a marketing plan, and the process of creating this is known as '**marketing planning**'. McDonald (2003) defines marketing planning simply as:

> *The planned application of marketing resources to achieve marketing objectives ... Marketing planning is simply a logical sequence and a series of activities leading to the setting of marketing objectives and the formulation of plans for achieving them.*

McDonald (2003) distinguishes between strategic marketing plans which cover a period beyond the next financial year (typically three to five years) and tactical marketing plans which cover detailed actions over a shorter time period of one year or less.

For Internet marketing, a similar distinction is useful. We suggest that a longer-term strategic Internet marketing plan should be developed in large organisations, which places emphasis on three key areas. First, early identification of changes to competitive forces in the micro-environment and significant changes in the macro-environment. Second, developing value propositions for customers using online services as part of their buying process. Third, definition of the technology infrastructure and information architecture to deliver these value propositions as a customer experience. It could be argued that the third issue is part of tactical planning, but the reality is that new technologies and new information architectures such as a customer relationship management system are major investments which can take several years to specify, select and implement. This long-term plan provides a two-to-four-year roadmap of the infrastructure for e-commerce as noted by some interviewees in E-consultancy (2005) research.

Figure 4.4 shows an overall strategy process model for strategic Internet marketing. An alternative perspective was presented in Figure 1.9 in order to introduce the role of strategy development into the first three chapters.

Shorter-term, tactical or operational Internet marketing plans then address actions specific to the current time such as specification of Internet marketing activities to support current marketing objectives. Alternative shorter-term plans include:

- *Web site design and build plan*. A plan to relaunch an existing web site or to create a new company web site or campaign microsite. Includes specification of online and offline marketing communications to support a web site launch or relaunch.
- *Specialist online marketing communications plans*. These are plans for specific digital marketing tools, featured in more details in Chapters 6 to 9. They include:
  - search marketing plan
  - affiliate marketing plan
  - e-mail communications or e-newsletter plan
  - e-CRM plan
  - interactive advertising and sponsorship
  - mobile marketing campaign
  - web analytics plan.

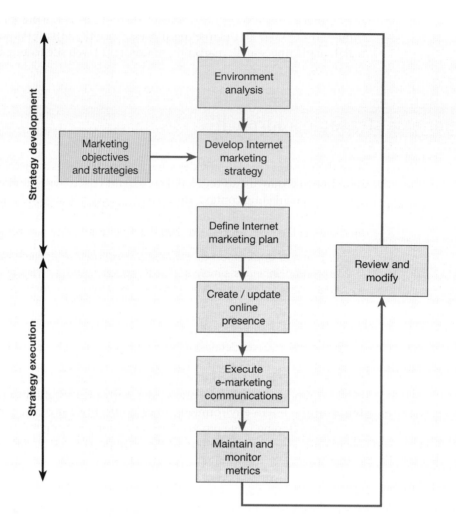

Figure 4.4 A simple framework for Internet marketing strategy development

It can be argued, however, that there is a need for more responsive strategic process models where reaction can occur to events in the marketplace. Mintzberg and Quinn (1991) and other authors commenting on corporate strategy, such as Lynch (2000), distinguish between prescriptive and emergent strategy approaches. In the prescriptive strategy approach, similar to Figure 4.4, Lynch identifies three elements of strategy – strategic analysis, strategic development and strategy implementation, and these are linked together sequentially. Strategic analysis is used to develop a strategy, and it is then implemented. In other words, the strategy is prescribed in advance. Alternatively, the distinction between the three elements of strategy may be less clear. This is the emergent strategy approach where strategic analysis, strategic development and strategy implementation are interrelated. It can be suggested that the emergent strategy approach is an essential part of any e-business strategy to enable response in a highly dynamic environment. This approach is best able to respond to sudden environmental changes which can open strategic windows. Strategic windows may occur through changes such as introduction of new technology (the Internet is the obvious example here!), changes in regulation of an industry, changes to distribution channels in the industry (again the Internet has had this impact), development of a new segment or redefinitions of markets (an example is the growth in leisure and health clubs during the 1990s).

Based on preliminary findings by Brian Smith, Daniel et al. (2002) have suggested that planning styles adopted by organisations for e-commerce will be governed by a combination of market complexity and turbulence. Smith identifies three main modes of strategy development:

1 *Logical rational planning.* Uses analytical tools and frameworks to formulate and implement strategy.
2 *Pragmatic incremental.* Strategy develops in response to minor adjustments to the external environment.
3 *Subjective visionary.* Strategy is the result of a leader, typically dominant or charismatic.

Daniel et al. suggest that in low-complexity high-turbulence markets vision and incrementalism will be dominant, that in high-complexity low-turbulence markets rational planning approaches are dominant, and that in highly complex, turbulent markets all three styles may be required.

Kalakota and Robinson (2000) recommend a dynamic, emergent strategy process specific to e-business. The elements of this strategy approach are shown in Figure 4.5. The emphasis is on responsiveness with continuous review and prioritisation of investment in new Internet applications. Clearly, the quality of environment scanning and information collection, dissemination and analysis and the speed of response will be key for organisations following such a responsive, emergent approach. One example of an approach to collecting this market event data is competitive intelligence or CI.

We will now start reviewing the four main stages of Internet marketing strategy development.

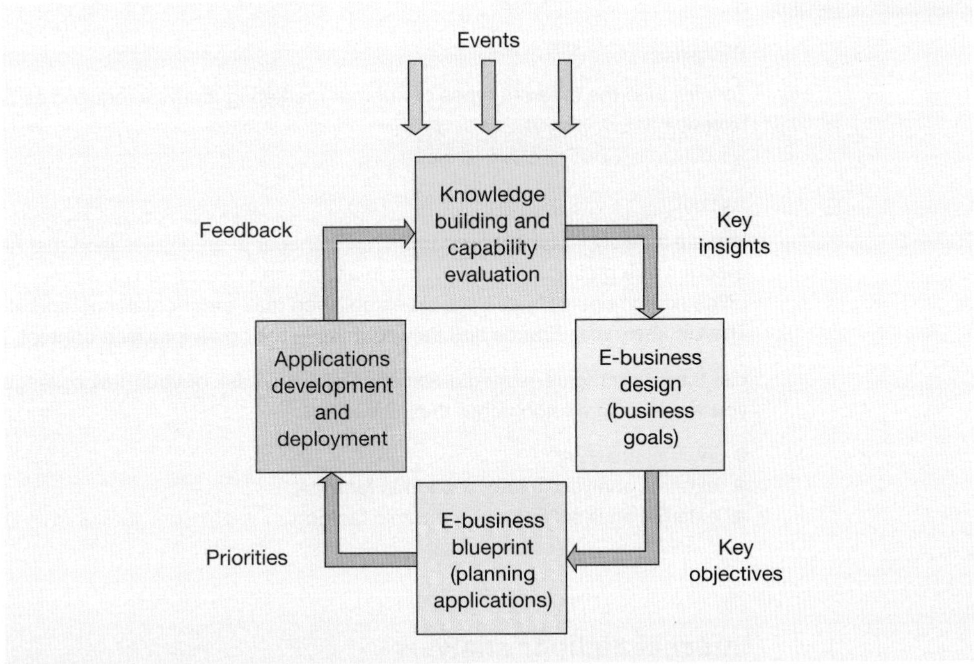

Competitive intelligence (CI)

A process that transforms disaggregated information into relevant, accurate and usable strategic knowledge about competitors, position, performance, capabilities and intentions.

Figure 4.5 Dynamic e-business strategy model

Source: Adapted from description in Kalakota and Robinson (2000)

Situation review

Strategic analysis
Collection and review of information about an organisation's internal processes and resources and external marketplace factors in order to inform strategy definition.

The situation review or analysis is best known as a marketing audit of the current effectiveness of marketing activities within a company together with environmental factors outside the company that should govern the way the strategy is developed. These principles can be readily applied to review online marketing effectiveness and internal capabilities. Strategic analysis or situation analysis involves review of:

● the internal capabilities, resources and processes of the company and a review of its activity in the marketplace;
● the immediate competitive environment (micro-environment) including customer demand and behaviour, competitor activity, marketplace structure and relationships with suppliers and partners. These micro-environment factors were reviewed in Chapter 2 and are not considered in detail in this chapter;
● the wider environment (macro-environment) in which a company operates, which includes economic development and regulation by governments in the form of law and taxes together with social and ethical constraints such as the demand for privacy. These macro-environment factors including the social, legal, economic and political factors were reviewed in Chapter 3 and are not considered further in this chapter.

Now complete Activity 4.1, which illustrates the type of analysis that needs to be performed for an Internet marketing situation analysis.

Activity 4.1 — Situation analysis for an e-commerce operation

Purpose

To introduce the different types of Internet marketing analysis required as part of situation review.

Activity

You are a newly incumbent e-commerce manager in an organisation that has operated a B2B e-commerce presence for two years in all the major European countries. The organisation sells office equipment and has been an established mail-order catalogue operation for 25 years. The UK, Germany, France and Italy each have their own localised content.

List the e-commerce-related questions you would ask of your new colleagues and research you would commission under these headings:

● internal analysis;
● external analysis (micro-economic factors);
● external analysis (macro-economic factors).

Internal audit or analysis

The internal audit will review the existing contribution that the Internet marketing channel is currently delivering in relation to other channels and in relation to the resources used.

Assessing the current contribution of the Internet to the organisation

To assess the contribution and the effectiveness of Internet marketing involves the company in reviewing how well its online presence is meeting its goals. So this activity overlaps with that on strategic goal setting discussed in the next section. Assessing effectiveness also requires a performance measurement or web analytics system to collect and report on data effectiveness. We cover this topic in more detail in Chapter 9. At this point, note that these different levels of measures can be usefully used to assess effectiveness:

1 Business effectiveness

This will include the contribution of the site directly or indirectly to sales and how well it is supporting business objectives. The relative costs of producing, updating and promoting the site will also be reviewed as part of a cost–benefit analysis.

2 Marketing effectiveness

These measures may include:

- leads (qualified enquiries);
- sales;
- customer retention and loyalty;
- online market (or audience share);
- brand enhancement;
- customer service.

For large organisations, these measures can be assessed for each of the different markets a company operates in or for product lines produced on the web site. The way in which the elements of the marketing mix are utilised will also be reviewed.

3 Internet effectiveness

These are specific measures that are used to assess the way in which the web site is used, and the characteristics of the audience. They are described in more detail in Chapter 9. According to Smith and Chaffey (2005) key performance indicators (KPIs) include:

- *unique visitors* – the number of separate, individual visitors who visit the site;
- total numbers of *sessions* or *visits* to a web site;
- *repeat visits* – average number of visits per individual;
- *duration* – average length of time visitors spend on a site;
- *subscription rates* such as the number of visitors subscribing for services such as an opt-in e-mail and newsletters;
- *conversion rates* – the percentage of visitors converting to subscribers (or becoming customers);
- *attrition rates* through the online buying process;
- *churn rates* – percentage of subscribers withdrawing or unsubscribing;
- *click-through rates (CTR)* from third-party sites to your own.

Resource analysis

Resource analysis
Review of the technological, financial and human resources of an organisation and how they are utilised in business processes.

The internal audit will also include a resource analysis. This involves assessing the capabilities of the organisation to deliver its online services. Aspects that can be reviewed include:

- *Financial resources* – the cost components of running an online presence, including site development, promotion and maintenance. Mismatch between current spend and required spend to achieve visibility within the online marketplace should be reviewed using tools such as Hitwise and Netratings which can be used to assess online market share.

- *Technology infrastructure resources* – availability and performance (speed) of web site and service-level agreements with the ISP. The need for different applications to enhance the customer experience can be assessed (e.g. on-site search, customisation facilities or customer relationship management facilities).
- *Human resources* – availability for an e-retailer includes service and fulfilment resources for answering customer queries and dispatching goods. For all companies there is a challenge of possibly recruiting new staff or reskilling marketing staff to manage online marketing activities such as web site services, search engine marketing, affiliate marketing and e-mail marketing. We return to this topic later in this chapter.
- *Structure* – what are the responsibilities and control mechanisms used to coordinate Internet marketing across different departments and business units? We again return to this topic later in the chapter.
- *Strengths and weaknesses* – SWOT analysis is referred to in the next section where generic strengths and weaknesses are summarised in Figure 4.7. Companies will also assess their distinctive competencies. Chaston (2000) suggests a resource–advantage matrix should be produced which compares the costs of different online services against the value they provide to customers. These can then be evaluated to select strategic options. For example, a high-cost, low-value service might be terminated while a medium-cost, high-value service might be extended. This is a form of portfolio analysis where different e-commerce services are assessed for future potential. See also the strategy formulation section later in this chapter.

Portfolio analysis

Evaluation of value of current e-commerce services or applications.

Stage models of the Internet marketing capability

A further perspective on assessing current usage of the Internet channel is to assess the current level of Internet services and integration of Internet marketing with other marketing activities. Stage models of capability delivered through the online presence assist in this evaluation. Companies that operate in a particular market tend to follow a natural progression in developing their web site to support their marketing activities. The following levels of Internet marketing can be identified:

- **Level 0.** No web site.
- **Level 1.** Company places an entry in a web site that lists company names such as Yellow Pages (www.yell.co.uk) to make people searching the web aware of the existence of the company or its products. There is no web site at this stage.
- **Level 2.** Simple static web site created containing basic company and product information (sometimes referred to as 'brochureware').
- **Level 3.** Simple interactive site where users are able to search the site and make queries to retrieve information such as product availability and pricing. Enquiries submitted by a form and transmitted by e-mail may also be supported.
- **Level 4.** Interactive site supporting transactions with users. The functions offered will vary according to the company. If products can be sold direct then an electronic commerce option for online sales will be available. Other functions might include an interactive customer-service helpdesk.
- **Level 5.** Fully interactive site providing relationship marketing with individual customers and facilitating the full range of marketing functions relevant for the sector.

Brochureware

A web site in which a company has simply transferred ('migrated') its existing paper-based promotional literature on to the Internet without recognising the differences required by this medium.

A variety of online stage models have been produced since Quelch and Klein (1996) noted the sequence in which web sites develop for different types of company. They distinguish between existing major companies (see Figure 4.6(a)) and start-up companies (see Figure 4.6(b)) that start as Internet companies. The main difference is that Internet start-ups are likely to introduce transaction facilities earlier than existing companies.

However, they may take longer to develop suitable customer service facilities. Stage models can be usefully applied to SME businesses and Levy and Powell (2003) have reviewed different adoption ladders which broadly speaking have four stages of (1) publish, (2) interact, (3) transact and (4) integrate.

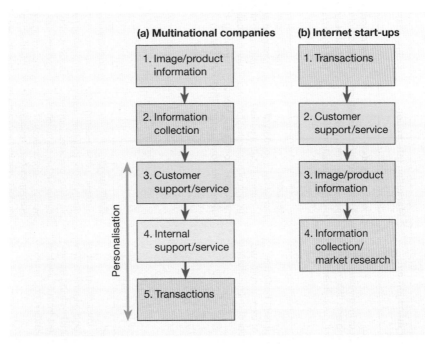

Figure 4.6 Levels of web site development in: (a) the information to transaction model and (b) the transaction to information model of Quelch and Klein (1996)

Stage models have been criticised for a variety of reasons. First, as a generic model they typically apply to businesses that have products which are suitable for online sale, but may not apply to the full range of businesses such as the four types of online presence introduced in Chapter 1. Secondly, these stage models are externally focused and do not address the broader development of Internet marketing capabilities within an organisation. Dave Chaffey writing for E-consultancy (2005) has recently developed a framework for assessing internal digital marketing capabilities across a range of companies (Table 4.1). In the Internet marketing context, 'capabilities' refers to the processes, structures and skills adopted for planning and implementation of digital marketing. This was inspired by the capability maturity models devised by the Carnegie Mellon Software Engineering Institute (**www.sei.cmu.edu/cmm/cmm.html**) to help organisations improve their software development practices. Table 4.1 is intended to help:

1 Review current approaches to digital marketing to identify areas for improvement;
2 Benchmark with competitors who are in the same market sector or industry and in different sectors;
3 Identify best practice from more advanced adopters;
4 Set targets and develop strategies for improving capabilities.

Of the companies assessed within the research, the majority were at Level 3 or 4 overall, although companies may occupy different levels according to different criteria. We return to assessing capabilities using the 7 Ss to implement Internet marketing strategy at the end of the chapter.

Table 4.1 Capability maturity model of E-commerce adoption based on E-consultancy (2005) research

Level	Strategy process and performance improvement	Structure: Location of e-commerce	Senior management buy-in	Marketing integration	Online marketing focus
1 Unplanned	*Limited.* Online channels not part of business planning process. Web analytics data collected, but unlikely to be reviewed or actioned	*Experimentation.* No clear centralised e-commerce resources in business. Main responsibility typically within IT	*Limited.* No direct involvement in planning and little necessity seen for involvement	*Poor integration.* Some interested marketers may experiment with e-communications tools	*Content focus.* Creation of online brochures and catalogues. Adoption of first style guidelines
2 Diffuse management	*Low-level.* Online referenced in planning, but with limited channel-specific objectives. Some campaign analysis by interested staff	*Diffuse.* Small central e-commerce group or single manager, possibly with steering group controlled by marketing. Many separate web sites, separate online initiatives, e.g. tools adopted and agencies for search marketing, e-mail marketing. E-communications funding from brands/businesses may be limited	*Aware.* Management becomes aware of expenditure and potential of online channels	*Separate.* Increased adoption of e-communications tools and growth of separate sites and microsites continues. Media spend still dominantly offline	*Traffic focus.* Increased emphasis on driving visitors to site through pay-per-click search marketing and affiliate marketing
3 Centralised management	*Specific.* Specific channel objectives set. Web analytics capability not integrated to give unified reporting of campaign effectiveness	*Centralised.* Common platform for content management, web analytics. Preferred-supplier list of digital agencies. Centralised, independent e-commerce function, but with some digital-specific responsibilities by country/product/brand	*Involved.* Directly involved in annual review and ensures review structure involving senior managers from Marketing, IT, operations and finance	*Arm's-length.* Marketing and e-commerce mainly work together during planning process. Limited review within campaigns. Senior e-commerce team-members responsible for encouraging adoption of digital marketing throughout organisation	*Conversion and customer experience focus.* Initiatives for usability, accessibility and revision of content management system (including search engine optimisation) are common at this stage

Level	Strategy process and performance improvement	Structure: Location of e-commerce	Senior management buy-in	Marketing integration	Online marketing focus
4 Decentralised operations	*Refined.* Close cooperation between e-commerce and marketing. Targets and performance reviewed monthly. Towards unified reporting. Project debriefs	*Decentralised.* Digital marketing skills more developed in business with integration of e-commerce into planning and execution at business or country level. e-retailers commonly adopt direct-channel organisation of which e-commerce is one channel. Online channel profit and loss accountability sometimes controlled by businesses/brands, but with central budget for continuous e-communications spend (search, affiliates, e-communications)	*Driving performance.* Involved in review at least monthly	*Partnership.* Marketing and e-commerce work closely together through year. Digital media spend starts to reflect importance of online channels to business and consumers	*Retention focus.* Initiatives on analysis of customer purchase and response behaviour and implementation of well-defined touch strategies with emphasis on e-mail marketing. Loyalty drivers well known and managed
5 Integrated and optimised	*Multi-channel process.* The interactions and financial contribution of different channels are well understood and resourced and improved accordingly	*Integrated.* Majority of digital skills within business and e-commerce team commonly positioned within marketing or direct sales operation. 'Front-end' systems development skills typically retained in e-commerce team	*Integral.* Less frequent in-depth involvement required. Annual planning and six-monthly or quarterly review.	*Complete.* Marketing has full complement of digital marketing skills, but calls on specialist resource from agencies or central e-commerce resource as required. Online potential not constrained by traditional budgeting processes	*Optimisation focus.* Initiatives to improve acquisition, conversion and retention according to developments in access platform and customer experience technologies. May use temporary multi-disciplinary team to drive performance

External audits or analysis

External audits consider the business and economic environment in which the company operates. These include the economic, political, fiscal, legal, social, cultural and technological factors usually referred to by the SLEPT acronym and reviewed in Chapter 3. Of these various factors, it is worth noting how three of them are particularly relevant to the Internet and should be monitored regularly since the way in which they vary will directly affect the viability of the Internet channel. The three most significant factors, described in more depth in Chapter 3, are:

1 *Legal constraints.* What are the legal limitations to online promotion and trade such as privacy, disability discrimination (see Chapter 7 section on accessibility) and distance-selling regulations?
2 *Ethical constraints.* What are the ethical implications in areas such as privacy which have not yet been legislated for?
3 *Technological constraints.* What is the current availability of technology to access the Internet and to deliver services and what are the emerging opportunities which need to be planned for?

The external audit should also consider the state of the market in terms of customers and competitors. Pertinent factors for the Internet include demand analysis, competitor analysis, intermediary analysis and channel structure. These are described only briefly here since they were discusssed in more depth in Chapter 2.

Demand analysis for e-commerce
Assessment of the demand for e-commerce services amongst existing and potential customer segments using the ratio Access : Choose : Buy online.

Demand analysis

A key factor driving e-marketing and e-business strategy objectives is the current level and future projections of customer demand for e-commerce services in different market segments. Demand analysis indicates the scale of opportunity for making or influences sales online and this, in turn, should govern the objectives defined and resources allocated to online channels. In Chapter 2, we saw how companies can model the number of consumers in a particular demographic who use the Internet and even the volume and type of key phrases they type into search engines.

An alternative perspective on e-commerce demand analysis is to review demand from existing customers who migrate online, and those who are new to the company. But, for some companies whose strategy has been to launch an online brand variant, the e-commerce service may have more new customers than those who migrate online from the current user base. For example, 80% of customers of the Co-operative Bank's online bank Smile (**www.smile.co.uk**) were new customers.

Personas
A thumbnail summary of the characteristics, needs, motivations and environment of typical web site users.

Customer scenarios
Alternative tasks or outcomes required by a visitor to a web site. Typically accomplished in a series of stages of different tasks involving different information needs or experiences.

Qualitative customer research

It is important that customer analysis is not restricted to quantitative demand analysis. Varianini and Vaturi (2000) point out that qualitative research provides insights that can be used to inform strategy. They suggest using graphic profiling, which is an attempt to capture the core characteristics of target customers – not only demographics, but also their needs and attitudes and how comfortable they are with the Internet. In Chapter 2 we reviewed how customer personas and scenarios are developed to help inform understanding of online buyer behaviour.

Competitor analysis

Competitor analysis or the monitoring of competitor use of e-commerce to acquire and retain customers is especially important in the e-marketplace due to the dynamic nature of the Internet medium. This enables new services to be launched and prices and promotions changed much more rapidly than through print communications. Activity 4.2 highlights some of the issues in competitor benchmarking, and this topic is referred to in more detail in Chapter 2.

Activity 4.2 | **Competitor benchmarking**

visit the w.w.w.

Purpose

To understand the characteristics of competitor web sites it is useful to know how to benchmark and to assess the value of benchmarking.

Activity

Choose a B2C industry sector such as airlines, book retailers, book publishers, CDs or clothing, or a B2B sector such as oil companies, chemical companies, construction industry companies or B2B exchanges. Work individually or in groups to identify the type of information that should be available from the web site (and which parts of the site you will access it from) and will be useful in terms of competitor benchmarking. Once your criteria have been developed, you should then benchmark companies and summarise which you feel is making best use of the Internet medium.

Intermediary analysis

Chapter 2 highlighted the importance of web-based intermediaries such as portals in driving traffic to an organisation's web site. Situation analysis will also involve identifying relevant intermediaries for a particular marketplace and look at how the organisation and its competitors are using the intermediaries to build traffic and provide services. For example, an e-tailer needs to assess which comparison services such as Kelkoo (**www.kelkoo.com**) and Pricerunner (**www.pricerunner.com**) it and its competitors are represented on. Do competitors have any special sponsorship arrangements or microsites created with intermediaries? The other aspect of situation analysis for intermediaries is to consider the way in which the marketplace is operating. To what extent are competitors using disintermediation or reintermediation? How are existing channel arrangements being changed?

Assessing opportunities and threats

Companies should conduct a structured analysis of the external opportunities and threats that are presented by the Internet environment. They should also consider their own strengths and weaknesses in the Internet marketing environment. Summarising the results through Internet-specific SWOT analysis (internal Strengths and Weaknesses and external Opportunities and Threats) will clearly highlight the opportunities and threats. Appropriate planning to counter the threats and take advantage of the opportunities can then be built into the Internet marketing plan. An example of a typical SWOT analysis of Internet-marketing-related strengths and weaknesses is shown in Figure 4.7. As is often the case with SWOT analysis, the opportunities available to a company are the opposites

The organisation	Stengths – S 1. Existing brand 2. Existing customer base 3. Existing distribution	Weaknesses – W 1. Brand perception 2. Intermediary use 3. Technology/skills 4. X-channel support
Opportunities – O 1. Cross-selling 2. New markets 3. New services 4. Alliances/Co-branding	SO strategies Leverage strengths to maximise opportunities = **Attacking strategy**	WO strategies Counter weaknesses through exploiting opportunities = **Build strengths for attacking strategy**
Threats – T 1. Customer choice 2. New entrants 3. New competitive products 4. Channel conflicts	ST strategies Leverage strengths to minimise threats = **Defensive strategy**	WT strategies Counter weaknesses and threats = **Build strengths for defensive strategy**

Figure 4.7 A generic SWOT analysis showing typical opportunities and threats presented by the Internet

of the threats presented by other companies. The strengths and weaknesses will vary according to the company involved, but many of the strengths and weaknesses are dependent on the capacity of senior management to acknowledge and act on change.

The presentation of the Internet-specific SWOT shown in Figure 4.7 is a powerful technique since it not only indicates the SWOT, but can be used to generate appropriate strategies. Often, the most rewarding strategies combine Strengths and Opportunities or counter Threats through Strengths.

Strategic goal setting

Any marketing strategy should be based on clearly defined corporate objectives, but there has been a tendency for Internet marketing to be conducted separately from other business and marketing objectives. Porter (2001) has criticised the lack of goal setting when many organisations have developed Internet strategies. He notes that many companies, responding to distorted market signals, have used 'rampant experimentation' that is not economically sustainable. This has resulted in the failure of many 'dot-com' companies and also poor investments by many established companies. He suggests that economic value or sustained profitability for a company is the final arbiter of business success.

It is best, of course, if the Internet marketing strategy is consistent with and supports business and marketing objectives. For example, business objectives such as increasing market share in an overseas market or introducing a new product to market can and should be supported by the Internet communications channel.

Scenario-based analysis

Models of the future environment are developed from different starting points.

Goal setting for the Internet will be based on managers' view of the future relevance of the Internet to their industry. Scenario-based analysis is a useful approach to discussing alternative visions of the future prior to objective setting. Lynch (2000) explains that scenario-based analysis is concerned with possible models of the future of an organisation's environment. He says:

The aim is not to predict, but to explore a set of possibilities; scenarios take different situations with different starting points.

Lynch distinguishes qualitative scenario-based planning from quantitative prediction such as that of Activity 4.3 (see page 171). In an Internet marketing perspective, scenarios that could be explored include:

1 One player in our industry becomes dominant through use of the Internet ('Amazoning' the sector).
2 Major customers do not adopt e-commerce because of organisational barriers.
3 Major disintermediation (Chapter 2) occurs in our industry.
4 B2B marketplaces do or do not become dominant in our industry.
5 New entrants or substitute products change our industry.

Through performing this analysis, better understanding of the drivers for different views of the future will result, new strategies can be generated and strategic risks can be assessed. It is clear that the scenarios above will differ between worst-case and best-case scenarios.

As a starting point for setting specific objectives, it is useful to think through the benefits of the Internet channel so that these benefits can be converted into objectives. It is useful to identify both *tangible benefits*, for which monetary savings or revenues can be identified, and *intangible benefits*, for which it is more difficult to calculate financial benefits and costs, but are still important, for example customer service quality. Table 4.2 presents a summary of typical benefits of Internet marketing.

Table 4.2 Tangible and intangible benefits from Internet marketing

Tangible benefits	Intangible benefits
Increased sales from new sales leads giving rise to increased revenue from: • new customers, new markets • existing customers (repeat-selling) • existing customers (cross-selling) Cost reductions from: • reduced time in customer service • online sales • reduced printing and distribution costs of marketing communications	• Corporate image communication • Enhance brand • More rapid, more responsive marketing communications including PR • Improved customer service • Learning for the future • Meeting customer expectations to have a web site • Identify new partners, support existing partners better • Better management of marketing information and customer information • Feedback from customers on products

An alternative way of thinking through the benefits, is to review the 5 Ss of Smith and Chaffey (2005) who suggest there are five broad benefits of e-marketing:

● *Sell* – grow sales (through wider distribution to customers you can't service offline, or perhaps through a wider product range than in-store, or better prices).
● *Serve* – add value (give customers extra benefits online, or inform them of product development through online dialogue and feedback).
● *Speak* – get closer to customers by tracking them, asking them questions, conducting online interviews, creating a dialogue, monitoring chat rooms, learning about them.
● *Save* – save costs of service, sales transactions and administration, print and post. Can you reduce transaction costs and therefore either make online sales more profitable or

use cost savings to enable you to cut prices, which in turn could enable you to generate greater market share?

● *Sizzle* – extend the brand online. Reinforce brand values in a totally new medium. The web scores very highly as a medium for creating brand awareness, recognition and involvement, as explained further in Chapter 5.

The online revenue contribution

Online revenue contribution
An assessment of the direct contribution of the Internet or other digital media to sales, usually expressed as a percentage of overall sales revenue.

A key objective for Internet marketing is the online revenue contribution. This is a measure of the extent to which a company's online presence directly impacts the sales revenue of the organisation and can be used to influence resource allocation to the online channels. Online revenue contribution objectives can be specified for different types of products, customer segments and geographic markets. For example, in 1997, low-cost airline easyJet set an online contribution objective of 50% by the year 2000. This established a clear vision and resources could be put in place to achieve this. EasyJet now has an online revenue contribution of 95%. Forrester (2005) provides benchmark figures of direct online revenue contribution for different sectors in the US (forecasts for 2010 are in brackets):

● Services 15% (32%)
● Manufacturers 15% (32%)
● Financial services 15% (28%)
● Retail 14% (21%)
● Total 15% (29%).

The significant growth of these average figures over the next four years shows the importance of setting objectives for the online revenue contribution.

For some companies such as an FMCG manufacturer, a beverage company or a B2B manufacturer, it is unrealistic to expect a direct online revenue contribution. In this case, an indirect online contribution can be stated. This considers the Internet as part of the promotional mix and its role in reaching and influencing a proportion of customers to purchase the product, generating trials, or in the case of a B2B company, leads. In this

Online promotion contribution
An assessment of the proportion of customers (new or retained) who are reached by online communications and are influenced as a result.

case a company could set an online promotion contribution or indirect online revenue contribution of 5% of its target market visiting the web site and interacting with the brand. Bazett et al. (2005) give the example of a high-street chain that for every £1 of revenue it takes on the web, £3 are spent in the store after browsing online – so it has objectives for this and works equally hard to help these customers through such facilities as store locators and information on the nearest store with a particular product in stock. Complete Activity 4.3 to explore the factors that impact online revenue contribution in different markets.

Setting SMART objectives

You have probably heard before that effective objectives and measures to assess performance are SMART. SMART is used to assess the suitability of objectives set to drive different strategies or the improvement of the full range of business processes.

● *Specific.* Is the objective sufficiently detailed to measure real-world problems and opportunities?
● *Measurable.* Can a quantitative or qualitative attribute be applied to create a metric?
● *Actionable.* Can the information be used to improve performance? If the objective doesn't change behaviour in staff to help them improve performance, there is little point in it!
● *Relevant.* Can the information be applied to the specific problem faced by the manager?
● *Time-related.* Can the information be constrained through time?

Activity 4.3   **Assessing the significance of digital channels**

Purpose

To illustrate the issues involved with assessing the suitability of the Internet for e-commerce.

Activity

For each of the products and services in Table 4.3, assess the suitability of the Internet for delivery of the product or service and position it on the grid in Figure 4.8 with justification. Make estimates in Table 4.3 for the direct and indirect online revenue contribution in 5 and 10 years' time for different products in your country. Choose specific products within each category.

Table 4.3 Vision of online revenue contribution for different types of company

Products/services	Now	2 years' time	5 years' time	10 years' time
Example: Cars, US Direct online sales Indirect online sales	 5% 50%	 10% 70%	 25% 90%	 50% 95%
Financial services Direct online sales Indirect online sales				
Clothing Direct online sales Indirect online sales				
Business office supplies Direct online sales Indirect online sales				

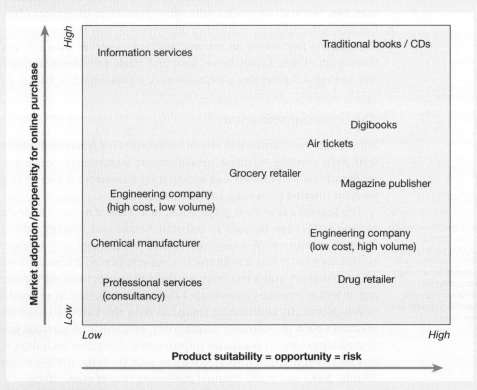

Figure 4.8 Grid of product suitability against market adoption for transactional e-commerce (online purchases)

171

With SMART objectives everyone is sure exactly what the target is and progresses towards it and, if appropriate, action can be taken to put the company back on target. Typical examples of SMART objectives to support goal-setting for Internet marketing strategy include:

- achieve 10 per cent online revenue contribution within 2 years;
- migrate 40% of customers to online services and e-mail communications within 3 years;
- achieve first or second position in category penetration in the countries within which the company operates (this is effectively online audience or market share and can be measured through visitor rankings such as Hitwise or Netratings (Chapter 2) or, better, by online revenue share);
- achieve a cost reduction of 10 per cent in marketing communications within 2 years;
- increase retention of online customers by 10 per cent;
- increase by 20 per cent within one year the number of sales arising from a certain target market, e.g. 18–25-year-olds;
- create value-added customer services not currently available;
- improve customer service by providing a response to a query within 2 hours, 24 hours per day, 7 days a week.

Specific digital communications objectives are also described in Chapter 8.

Frameworks for objective setting

A significant challenge of objective setting for Internet marketing is that there will potentially be many different measures such as those in the list above and these will have be to grouped to be meaningful. Categorisation of objectives into groups is also useful since it can be used to identify suitable objectives. In this chapter, we have already seen two methods of categorising objectives. First, objectives can be set at the level of business effectiveness, marketing effectiveness and Internet marketing effectiveness as explained in the section on internal auditing as part of situation analysis. Second, the 5S framework of Sell, Speak, Serve, Save and Sizzle provides a simple framework for objective setting. A further five-part framework is presented in Chapter 9.

The balanced scorecard

Some larger companies will identify objectives for Internet marketing which are consistent with existing business measurement frameworks. Since the balanced business scorecard is a well-known and widely used framework it can be helpful to define objectives for Internet marketing in these categories.

Balanced scorecard
A framework for setting and monitoring business performance. Metrics are structured according to customer issues, internal efficiency measures, financial measures and innovation.

The balanced scorecard, popularised in a *Harvard Business Review* article by Kaplan and Norton (1993) can be used to translate vision and strategy into objectives and, then, through measurement assessing whether the strategy and its implementation are successful. In part, it was a response to over-reliance on financial metrics such as turnover and profitability and a tendency for these measures to be retrospective rather than looking at future potential as indicated by innovation, customer satisfaction and employee development. In addition to financial data the balanced scorecard uses operational measures such as customer satisfaction, efficiency of internal processes and also the organisation's innovation and improvement activities including staff development. It has since been applied to IT (Der Zee and De Jong, 1999), e-commerce (Hasan and Tibbits, 2000) and multi-channel marketing (Bazett et al., 2005).

Table 4.4 illustrates specific Internet marketing measures within the four main areas of organisational performance managed through the balanced scorecard. In our presentation we have placed objectives within the areas of efficiency ('doing the thing right') and effectiveness ('doing the right thing'). For example, efficiency involves increasing conversion rates and reducing costs of acquisition. Effectiveness involves supporting broader marketing objectives and often indicates the contribution of the online channel. It is useful to identify efficiency and effectiveness measures separately, since often online marketing and web analytics tend to focus on efficiency. Hasan and Tibbits (2000) note that the internal process measures in particular are concerned with the efficiency and the customer and business value perspectives are indicated with effectiveness, but these measures can be applied across all four areas as we have shown.

Efficiency

Minimising resources or time needed to complete a process. 'Doing the thing right'.

Effectiveness

Meeting process objectives, delivering the required outputs and outcomes. 'Doing the right thing'.

Table 4.4 Example allocation of Internet marketing objectives within the balanced scorecard framework for a transactional e-commerce site

Balanced scorecard sector	Efficiency	Effectiveness
Financial results (Business value)	• Channel costs • Channel profitability	• Online contribution (direct) • Online contribution (indirect) • Profit contributed
Customer value	• Online reach (unique visitors as % of potential visitors) • Cost of acquisition or cost per sale (CPA / CPS) • Customer propensity to defect	• Sales and sales per customer • New customers • Online market share • Customer satisfaction ratings • Customer loyalty index
Operational processes	• Conversion rates • Average order value • List size and quality • E-mail active %	• Fulfilment times • Support response times
Innovation and learning (people and knowledge)	• Novel approaches tested • Internal e-marketing education • Internal satisfaction ratings	• Novel approaches deployed • Performance appraisal review

Performance drivers

Performance metrics

Measures that are used to evaluate and improve the efficiency and effectiveness of business processes.

Key performance indicators (KPIs)

Metrics used to assess the performance of a process and/or whether goals set are achieved.

Specific performance metrics are used to evaluate and improve the efficiency and effectiveness of a process. Key performance indicators (KPIs) are a special type of performance metric which indicate the overall performance of a process or its sub-processes. An example of KPIs for an online electrical goods retailer is shown in Figure 4.9. Improving the results from the e-commerce site involves using the techniques on the left of the diagram to improve the performance drivers and so the KPI. The KPI is the total online sales figure. For a traditional retailer, this could be compared as a percentage to other retail channels such as mail order or retail stores. It can be seen that this KPI is dependent on performance drivers such as number of site visits or average order value which combine to govern this KPI. Note that the definition of KPI is arbitrary and is dependent on scope. So, overall conversion rate could be a KPI and this is then supported by other performance drivers such as engagement rate, conversion to opportunity and conversion to sale.

A further objective-setting or metrics framework, the online lifecycle management grid, is presented at the end of the chapter as a summary since this integrates objectives, strategies and tactics.

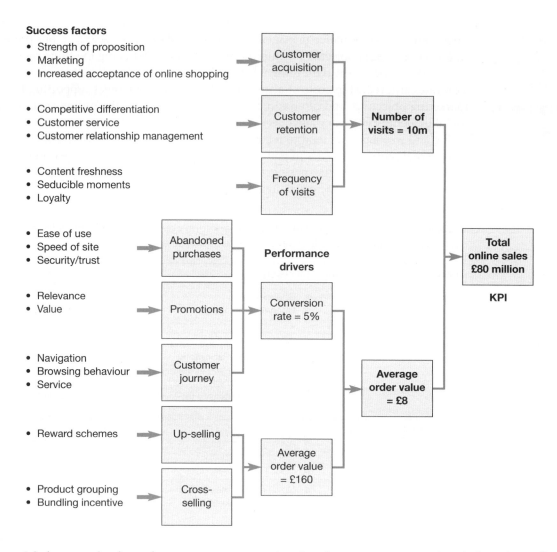

Figure 4.9 An example of a performance measurement system for an e-commerce electrical goods retailer
Source: Friedlein (2002)

Strategy formulation

Strategy formulation
Generation, review and selection of strategies to achieve strategic objectives.

Strategy formulation involves the identification of alternative strategies, a review of their merits and then selection of the best candidate strategies. Since the Internet is a relatively new medium, and many companies are developing a strategy for the first time, a range of strategic factors must be considered in order to make the best use of it. In this section we shall cover the main strategic options by defining eight key decisions.

Although at the height of the dot-com bubble it was suggested by some commentators that companies should entirely re-invent themselves, for most companies Internet marketing strategy formulation typically involves making *adjustments* to marketing strategy to take advantage of the benefits of online channels rather than wholescale changes. Michael Porter (2001) attacks those who have suggested that the Internet invalidates well-known approaches to strategy. He says:

Many have assumed that the Internet changes everything, rendering all the old rules about companies and competition obsolete. That may be a natural reaction, but it is a dangerous one . . . [resulting in] decisions that have eroded the attractiveness of their industries and undermined their own competitive advantages.

The key strategic decisions for e-marketing are the same as strategic decisions for traditional marketing. They involve selecting target customer groups and specifying how to deliver value to these groups. Segmentation, targeting, differentiation and positioning are all key to effective digital marketing.

The main thrust of Internet marketing strategy is taking decisions on the selective targeting of customer groups and different forms of value delivery for online channels. Rather than selective targeting, another strategic option is to replicate existing offline segmentation, targeting, differentiation and positioning in the online channels. While this is relatively easy to implement, the company is likely to lose market share relative to more nimble competitors that modify their approach for online channels. An example of where companies have followed a 'do-nothing strategy' is grocery shopping where some have not rolled out home shopping to all parts of the country or do not offer the service at all. These supermarkets will lose customers to the most enthusiastic adopters of online channels such as Tesco.com and Sainsbury which will be difficult to win back in the future (see Case Study 4 for examples).

As mentioned at the start of the chapter, we should remember that Internet marketing strategy is a channel marketing strategy and it needs to operate in the context of multi-channel marketing. It follows that it is important that the Internet marketing strategy should:

- Be based on objectives for online contribution of leads and sales for this channel;
- Be consistent with the types of customers that use and can be effectively reached through the channel;
- Support the customer journey as they select and purchase products using this channel in combination with other channels;
- Define a unique, differential proposition for the channel;
- Specify how we communicate this proposition to persuade customers to use online services in conjunction with other channels;
- Manage the online customer lifecycle through the stages of attracting visitors to the web site, converting them to customers and retention and growth.

This said, many of the decisions related to Internet marketing strategy development involve reappraising a company's approach to strategy based on familiar elements of marketing strategy. We will review these decisions:

- Decision 1: Market and product development strategies
- Decision 2: Business and revenue models strategies
- Decision 3: Target marketing strategy
- Decision 4: Positioning and differentiation strategy (including the marketing mix)
- Decision 5: Multi-channel distribution strategy
- Decision 6: Multi-channel communications strategy
- Decision 7: Online communications mix and budget
- Decision 8: Organisational capabilities (7S).

The first four decisions are concerned with fundamental questions of how an organisation delivers value to customers online and which products are offered to which markets online. The next four decisions are more concerned with the mix of marketing communications used to communicate with customers across multiple channels.

Decision 1: Market and product development strategies

In Chapter 1, we introduced the Ansoff matrix as a useful analytic tool for assessing online strategies for manufacturers and retailers. This tool is also fundamental to marketing planning and it should be the first decision point since it can help companies think about how online channels can support their marketing objectives, but also suggest innovative use of these channels to deliver new products and more markets (the boxes help stimulate 'out-of-box' thinking which is often missing with Internet marketing strategy). Fundamentally, the market and product development matrix (Figure 4.10) can help identify strategies to grow sales volume through varying what is sold (the product dimension on the horizontal axis of Figure 4.10) and who it is sold to (the market dimension on the *y* axis). Specific objectives need to be set for sales generated via these strategies, so this decision relates closely to that of objective setting. Let us now review these strategies in more detail.

Figure 4.10 Using the Internet to support different growth strategies

1 Market penetration

This strategy involves using digital channels to sell more existing products into existing markets. The Internet has great potential for achieving sales growth or maintaining sales by the market penetration strategy. As a starting point, many companies will use the Internet to help sell existing products into existing markets, although they may miss opportunities indicated by the strategies in other parts of the matrix. Figure 4.10 indicates some of the main ways in which the Internet can be used for market penetration:

- *Market share growth* – companies can compete more effectively online if they have web sites that are efficient at converting visitors to sale as explained in Chapter 7 and mastery of the online marketing communications techniques reviewed in Chapter 8 such as search engine marketing, affiliate marketing and online advertising.
- *Customer loyalty improvement* – companies can increase their value to customers and so increase loyalty by migrating existing customers online (see the mini case study on BA later in the chapter) by adding value to existing products, services and brand by developing their online value proposition (see Decision 4).
- *Customer value improvement* – the value delivered by customers to the company can be increased by increasing customer profitability by decreasing cost to serve (and so price to customers) and at the same time increasing purchase or usage frequency and quantity. These combined effects should drive up sales.

2 Market development

Here online channels are used to sell into new markets, taking advantage of the low cost of advertising internationally without the necessity for a supporting sales infrastructure in the customer's country. The Internet has helped low-cost airlines such as easyJet and Ryanair to enter new markets served by their routes cost-effectively. This is a relatively conservative use of the Internet, but is a great opportunity for SMEs to increase exports at a low cost, though it does require overcoming the barriers to exporting.

Existing products can also be sold to new market segments or different types of customers. This may happen simply as a by-product of having a web site. For example, RS Components (**www.rswww.com**), a supplier of a range of MRO (maintenance, repair and operations) items, found that 10% of the web-based sales were to individual consumers rather than traditional business customers. The UK retailer Argos found the opposite was true with 10% of web site sales being from businesses, when their traditional market was consumer-based. EasyJet also has a section of its web site to serve business customers. The Internet may offer further opportunities for selling to market sub-segments that have not been previously targeted. For example, a product sold to large businesses may also appeal to SMEs that they have previously been unable to serve because of the cost of sales via a specialist sales force. Alternatively a product targeted at young people could also appeal to some members of an older audience and vice versa. Many companies have found that the audience and customers of their web site are quite different from their traditional audience.

3 Product development

The web can be used to add value to or extend existing products for many companies. For example, a car manufacturer can potentially provide car performance and service information via a web site. But truly new products or services that can be delivered by the Internet only apply for some types of products. These are typically digital media or information products, for example, online trade magazine *Construction Weekly* has diversified to a B2B portal Construction Plus (**www.constructionplus.com**) which has new revenue streams. Similarly, music and book publishing companies have found new ways to deliver products through the new development and usage model such as subscription and pay-per-use as explained in Chapter 5 in the section on the product element of the marketing mix. Retailers can extend their product range and provide new bundling options online also.

4 Diversification

In this sector, new products are developed which are sold into new markets. The Internet alone cannot facilitate these high-risk business strategies, but it can facilitate them at lower costs than have previously been possible. The options include:

- *Diversification into related businesses* (for example, a low-cost airline can use the web site and customer e-mails to promote travel-related services such as hotel booking, car rental or travel insurance at relatively low costs);
- *Diversification into unrelated businesses* – again the web site can be used to promote less-related products to customers, which is the approach used by the Virgin brand, although it is relatively rare;
- *Upstream integration* – with suppliers – achieved through data exchange between a manufacturer or retailer and its suppliers to enable a company to take more control of the supply chain;
- *Downstream integration* – with intermediaries – again achieved through data exchange with distributors such as online intermediaries.

The benefits and risks of market and product development are highlighted by the creation of **smile** (www.smile.co.uk), an Internet-specific bank set up by the Co-operative Bank in the UK. **smile** opened for business in October 1999 and its first year added 200,000 customers at a rate of 20,000 per month. Significantly, 80% of these customers were market development in the context of the parent, since they were not existing Co-op Bank customers and typically belonged to a higher income segment.

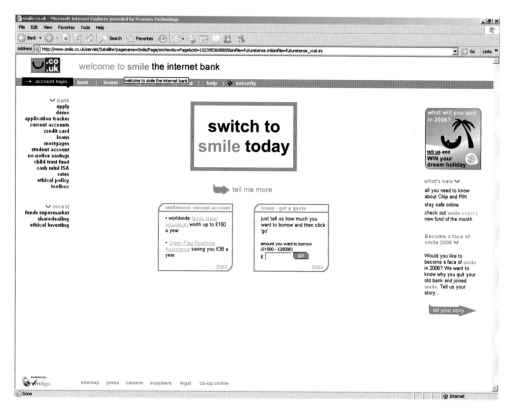

Figure 4.11 Smile (www.smile.co.uk)

The risks of the new approach to banking were highlighted by the cost of innovation; with it being estimated that in its first year, costs of creation and promotion of **smile** increased overall costs at The Co-operative Bank by 5%. However, within five years, **smile** was on target, profitable and growing strongly, and continues to do so today.

Decision 2: Business and revenue models strategies

Business model
A summary of how a company will generate revenue, identifying its product offering, value-added services, revenue sources and target customers.

Revenue models
Describe methods of generating income for an organisation.

Early (first) mover advantage
An early entrant into the marketplace.

A further aspect of Internet strategy formulation closely related to product development options is the review of opportunities from new business and revenue models, (first introduced in Chapter 2 and discussed further in the next chapter in the sections on product and price). Evaluating new models is important since if companies do not review opportunities to innovate then competitors and new entrants certainly will. Andy Grove of Intel famously said: *'Only the paranoid will survive'*, alluding to the need to review new revenue opportunities and competitor innovations. A willingness to test and experiment with new business models is also required. Dell is another example of a technology company that regularly reviews and modifies its business model as shown in Mini Case Study 4.1 'Innovation in the Dell business model'. Companies at the bleeding edge of technology such as Google and Yahoo! constantly innovate through acquiring other companies and internal research and development (Witness Google Labs (http://labs.google.com) and Yahoo! Research (http://research.google.com)). The case study on Tesco.com at the end of this chapter also highlights innovation in the Tesco business model facilitated through online channels.

Mini Case Study 4.1 — Innovation in the Dell business model

One example of how companies can review and revise their business model is provided by Dell Computer. Dell gained early-mover advantage in the mid-1990s when it became one of the first companies to offer PCs for sale online. Its sales of PCs and peripherals grew from the mid-1990s with online sales of $1 million per day to 2000 sales of $50 million per day. Based on this success it has looked at new business models it can use in combination with its powerful brand to provide new services to its existing customer base and also to generate revenue through new customers. In September 2000, Dell announced plans to become a supplier of IT consulting services through linking with enterprise resource planning specialists such as software suppliers, systems integrators and business consulting firms. This venture will enable the facility of Dell's PremierPages to be integrated into the procurement component of ERP systems such as SAP and Baan, thus avoiding the need for rekeying and reducing costs.

In a separate initiative, Dell launched a B2B marketplace (formerly www.dellmarketplace.com) aimed at discounted office goods and services procurements including PCs, peripherals, software, stationery and travel. This strategic option did not prove sustainable.

To sound a note of caution, flexibility in the business model should not be to the company's detriment through losing focus on the core business. A 2000 survey of CEOs of leading UK Internet companies such as Autonomy, Freeserve, NetBenefit and QXL (Durlacher, 2000) indicates that although flexibility is useful this may not apply to business models. The report states:

A widely held belief in the new economy in the past, has been that change and flexibility is good, but these interviews suggest that it is actually those companies who have stuck to a single business model that have been to date more successful . . . CEOs were not moving far from their starting vision, but that it was in the marketing, scope and partnerships where new economy companies had to be flexible.

So with all strategy options, managers should also consider the 'do-nothing option'. Here, a company will not risk a new business model, but adopt a 'wait-and-see' or 'fast-follower' approach to see how competitors perform and respond rapidly if the new business model proves sustainable.

Finally, we can note that companies can make less radical changes to their revenue models through the Internet which are less far-reaching, but may nevertheless be worthwhile. For example:

- Transactional e-commerce sites (e.g. Tesco.com and Lastminute.com) can sell advertising space or run co-branded promotions on site or through their e-mail newsletters or lists to sell access to their audience to third parties.
- Retailers or media owners can sell-on white-labelled services through their online presence such as ISP, e-mail services or photo-sharing services.
- Companies can gain commission through selling products which are complementary (but not competitive to their own). For example, a publisher can sell its books through an affiliate arrangement through an e-retailer.

Decision 3: Target marketing strategy

Target marketing strategy
Evaluation and selection of appropriate segments and the development of appropriate offers.

Deciding on which markets to target is a key strategic consideration for Internet marketing strategy in the same way it is key to marketing strategy. Target marketing strategy involves the four stages shown in Figure 4.12, but the most important decisions are:

- *Segmentation/targeting strategy* – a company's online customers have different demographic characteristics, needs and behaviours from its offline customers. It follows that different approaches to segmentation may be required and specific segments may need to be selectively targeted.
- *Positioning/differentiation strategy* – competitors' product and service offerings will often differ in the online environment. Developing an appropriate online value proposition as described below is an important aspect of this strategy.

In an Internet context, organisations need to target those customer groupings with the highest propensity to access, choose and buy online.

Segmentation
Identification of different groups within a target market in order to develop different offerings for each group.

The first stage in Figure 4.12 is segmentation. Segmentation involves understanding the groupings of customers in the target market in order to understand their needs and potential as a revenue source so as to develop a strategy to satisfy these segments while maximising revenue. Dibb et al. (2001) say that:

Market segmentation is the key of robust marketing strategy development . . . it involves more than simply grouping customers into segments . . . identifying segments, targeting, positioning and developing a differential advantage over rivals is the foundation of marketing strategy.

In an Internet marketing planning context, market segments will be analysed to assess:

1 their current market size or value, future projections of size and the organisation's current and future market share within the segment;
2 competitor market shares within segment;

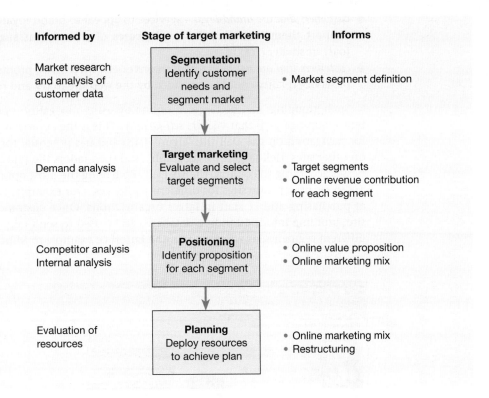

Figure 4.12 Stages in target marketing strategy development

3 needs of each segment, in particular, unmet needs;

4 organisation and competitor offers and proposition for each segment across all aspects of the buying process.

Stage 2 in Figure 4.12 is target marketing. Here we select segments for targeting online that are most attractive in terms of growth and profitability. These may be similar or different compared with groups targeted offline. Some examples of customer segments that are targeted online include:

- *the most profitable customers* – using the Internet to provide tailored offers to the top 20 per cent of customers by profit may result in more repeat business and cross-sales;
- *larger companies (B2B)* – an extranet could be produced to service these customers, and increase their loyalty;
- *smaller companies (B2B)* – large companies are traditionally serviced through sales representatives and account managers, but smaller companies may not warrant the expense of account managers. However, the Internet can be used to reach smaller companies more cost-effectively. The number of smaller companies that can be reached in this way may be significant, so although the individual revenue of each one is relatively small, the collective revenue achieved through Internet servicing can be large;
- *particular members of the buying unit (B2B)* – the site should provide detailed information for different interests which supports the buying decision, for example technical documentation for users of products, information on savings from e-procurement for IS or purchasing managers, and information to establish the credibility of the company for decision makers;
- *customers that are difficult to reach using other media* – an insurance company looking to target younger drivers could use the web as a vehicle for this;

- *customers that are brand-loyal* – services to appeal to brand loyalists can be provided to support them in their role as advocates of a brand, as suggested by Aaker and Joachimsthaler (2000);
- *customers that are not brand-loyal* – conversely, incentives, promotion and a good level of service quality could be provided by the web site to try and retain such customers.

Such groupings can be targeted online by using navigation options to different content groupings such that visitors *self-identify*. This is the approach used as the main basis for navigation on the Dell site (Figure 4.13) and has potential for subsidiary navigation on other sites. Dell targets by geography and then tailors the types of consumers or businesses according to country, the US Dell site having the most options. Other alternatives are to set up separate sites for different audiences – for example, Dell Premier is targeted at purchasing and IT staff in larger organisations. Once customers are registered on a site, profiling information in a database can be used to send tailored e-mail messages to different segments, as we explain in the Euroffice example in Mini Case Study 4.2 below.

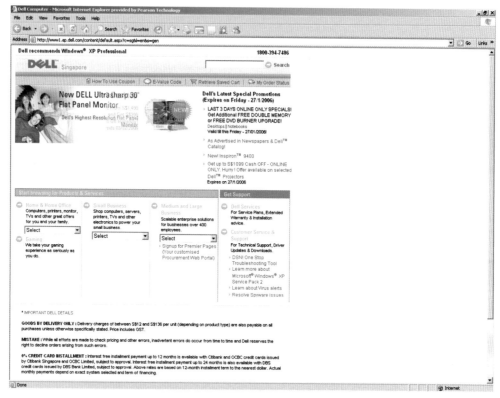

Figure 4.13 Dell Singapore site segmentation
Source: http://www.ap.dell.com/content/default.aspx?c=sg&1=en&s=gen

The most sophisticated segmentation and targeting schemes are often used by e-retailers, which have detailed customer profiling information and purchase history data and seek to increase customer lifetime value through encouraging increased use of online services through time. However, the general principles of this approach can also be used by other types of companies online. The segmentation and targeting approach used by e-retailers is based on five main elements which in effect are layered on top of each other. The number of options used, and so the sophistication of the approach will depend on resources available, technology capabilities and opportunities afforded by the list:

1 Identify customer lifecycle groups

Figure 4.14 illustrates this approach. As visitors use online services they can potentially pass through seven or more stages. Once companies have defined these groups and set up the customer relationship management infrastructure to categorise customers in this way, they can then deliver targeted messages, either by personalised on-site messaging or through e-mails that are triggered automatically by different rules. First-time visitors can be identified by whether they have a cookie placed on their PC. Once visitors have registered, they can be tracked through the remaining stages. Two particularly important groups are customers that have purchased one or more times. For many e-retailers, encouraging customers to move from the first purchase to the second purchase and then on to the third purchase is a key challenge. Specific promotions can be used to encourage further purchases. Similarly, once customers become inactive, i.e. they have not purchased for a defined period such as 3 months, they become inactive and further follow-ups are required.

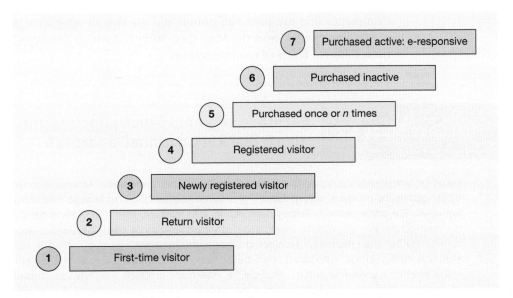

Figure 4.14 Customer lifecycle segmentation

2 Identify customer profile characteristics

This is a traditional segmentation based on the type of customer. For B2C e-retailers this will include age, sex and geography. For B2B companies, it will include size of company and the industry sector or application they operate in.

3 Identify behaviour in response and purchase

As customers progress through the lifecycle shown in Figure 4.14, by analysis of their database, the marketer will be able to build up a detailed response and purchase history which considers the details of recency, frequency, monetary value and category of products purchased. This approach, which is known as RFM or FRAC analysis, is reviewed in more detail in Chapter 6. See Tesco.com Case Study 4 for how Tesco targets its online customers.

4 Identify multi-channel behaviour (channel preference)

Regardless of the enthusiasm of the company for online channels, some customers will prefer using online channels and others will prefer traditional channels. This will, to an extent be indicated by RFM and response analysis since customers with a preference for online channels will be more responsive and will make more purchases online. Drawing a channel chain (Figure 2.10) for different customers is useful to help understand this. It is also useful to have a flag within the database which indicates the customers' channel preference and, by implication, the best channel to target them by. Customers that prefer online channels can be targeted mainly by online communications such as e-mail, while customers that prefer traditional channels can be targeted by traditional communications such as direct mail or phone.

5 Tone and style preference

In a similar manner to channel preference, customers will respond differently to different types of message. Some may like a more rational appeal, in which case a detailed e-mail explaining the benefits of the offer may work best. Others will prefer an emotional appeal based on images and with warmer, less formal copy. Sophisticated companies will test for this in customers or infer it using profile characteristics and response behaviour and then develop different creative treatments accordingly. Companies that use polls can potentially use this to infer style preferences. To summarise this section, read the Mini Case Study 4.2 which illustrates the combination of these different forms of communication.

Mini Case Study 4.2	Euroffice segment office supplies purchasers using 'touch marketing funnel' approach

Euroffice (www.euroffice.co.uk) targets small and mid-sized companies. According to George Karibian, CEO, 'getting the message across effectively required segmentation' to engage different people in different ways. The office sector is fiercely competitive, with relatively little loyalty since company purchasers will often simply buy on price. However, targeted incentives can be used to reward or encourage buyers' loyalty. Rather than manually developing campaigns for each segment which is time-consuming, Euroffice mainly uses an automated event-based targeting approach based on the system identifying the stage at which a consumer is in the lifecycle, i.e. how many products they have purchased and the types of product within their purchase history. Karibian calls this a 'touch marketing funnel' approach, i.e. the touch strategy is determined by customer segmentation and response. Three main groups of customers are identified in the lifecycle and these are broken down further according to purchase category. Also layered on this segmentation is breakdown into buyer type – are they a small home-user, an operations manager at a mid-size company or a purchasing manager at a larger company? Each will respond to different promotions.

The first group, at the top of the funnel and the largest, are 'Group 1. Trial customers' who have made one or two purchases. For the first group, Euroffice believes that creating impulse buying through price promotions is most important. These will be based on categories purchased in the past. The second group, 'Group 2. The nursery', have made three to eight purchases. A particular issue, as with many e-retailers is encouraging customers from the third to fourth purchase – there is a more significant drop-out at this point which the company uses marketing to control. Karibian says: 'When they get to group two, it's about creating frequency of purchase to ensure they don't forget you'. Euroffice sends a printed catalogue to Group 2 separately from their merchandise as a reminder about the company. The final group, 'Group 3. Key accounts or 'Crown Jewels', have made nine or more orders. They also tend to have a higher basket value. These people are 'the Crown Jewels' and will spend an average of £135 per order compared to an average of £55 for trial customers. They have a 90% probability of re-ordering within a six-month period. For this group, tools have been developed on the site to make it easier for them to shop. The intention is that these customers find these tools help them in making their orders and they become reliant on them, so achieving 'soft lock-in'.

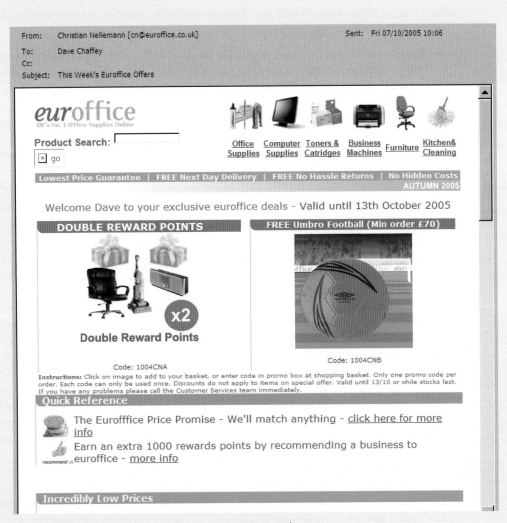

Figure 4.15 Euroffice e-mail (www.euroffice.co.uk)

Source: Adapted from the company web site press releases and *Revolution* (2005a)

Decision 4: Positioning and differentiation strategy (including the marketing mix)

Positioning

Customers' perception of the product offer relative to those of competitors.

Stage 3 in Figure 4.12 is **positioning**. Deise et al. (2000) suggest that in an online context, companies can position their products relative to competitor offerings according to four main variables: product quality, service quality, price and fulfilment time. They suggest it is useful to review these through an equation of how they combine to influence customer perceptions of value or brand:

$$Customer\ value\ (brand\ perception) = \frac{Product\ quality \times Service\ quality}{Price \times Fulfilment\ time}$$

Strategies should review the extent to which increases in product and service quality can be balanced against variations in price and fulfilment time. Chaston (2000) argues that there are four options for strategic focus to position a company in the online marketplace.

It is evident that these are related to the different elements of Deise et al. (2000). He says that online these should build on existing strengths, and can use the online facilities to enhance the positioning as follows:

- *Product performance excellence.* Enhance by providing online product customisation.
- *Price performance excellence.* Use the facilities of the Internet to offer favourable pricing to loyal customers or to reduce prices where demand is low (for example, British Midland Airlines uses auctions to sell underused capacity on flights).
- *Transactional excellence.* A site such as that of software and hardware e-tailer dabs.com offers transactional excellence through combining pricing information with dynamic availability information on products, listing number in stock, number on order and when they are expected.
- *Relationship excellence* – personalisation features to enable customers to review sales order history and place repeat orders. An example is RS Components (**www.rswww.com**).

These positioning options have much in common with Porter's generic competitive strategies of cost leadership or differentiation in a broad market and a market segmentation approach focusing on a more limited target market (Porter, 1980). Porter has been criticised since many commentators believe that to remain competitive it is necessary to combine excellence in all of these areas. It can be suggested that the same is true for sell-side e-commerce. These are not mutually exclusive strategic options, rather they are prerequisites for success. Customers will be unlikely to judge on a single criterion, but on the balance of multiple criteria. This is the view of Kim et al. (2004) who concluded that for online businesses, *'integrated strategies that combine elements of cost leadership and differentiation will outperform cost leadership or differentiation strategies'*. It can be seen that Porter's original criteria are similar to the strategic positioning options of Chaston (2000) and Deise et al. (2000). Figure 4.16 summarises the positioning options described in this section, showing the emphasis on the three main variables for online differentiation – price, product and relationship-building services. The diagram can be used to show the mix of the three elements of positionings. EasyJet has an emphasis on price performance, but with a component of product innovation. Amazon is not positioned on price performance, but rather on relationship building and product innovation. We will see in Chapter 5, in the section on price, that although it would be expected that pricing is a key aspect determining online retail sales, there are other factors about a retail brand such as familiarity, trust and service which are also important.

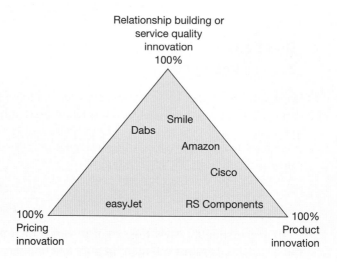

Figure 4.16 Alternative positionings for online services

An alternative perspective on positioning strategies has been suggested by Picardi (2000). The three main approaches suggested are generic:

1 *Attack e-tailing.* As suggested by the name, this is an aggressive competitive approach that involves frequent comparison with competitors' prices and then matching or bettering them. This approach is important on the Internet because of the transparency of pricing and availability of information made possible through shopping comparison sites such as PriceRunner (**www.pricerunner.com**) and Kelkoo (**www.kelkoo.com**).

2 *Defend e-tailing.* This is a strategic approach that traditional companies can use in response to 'attack e-tailing'. It involves differentiation based on other aspects of brand beyond price. It will often be used by multi-channel e-retailers such as Debenhams (**www.debenhams.com**) and John Lewis (**www.johnlewis.com**). Such retailers may not want to eat into sales from their high-street stores, or may believe that the strength of their brands is such that they do not need to offer differential online prices. They may use a mixed approach with some 'attack e-tailing' approaches such as competitive pricing on the most popular items or special promotions.

3 *E2E (end-to-end) integration.* This is an efficiency strategy that uses the Internet to decrease costs and increase product quality and shorten delivery times. This strategy is achieved by moving towards an automated supply chain and internal value chain. This approach is used by e-retailiers such as dabs.com (**www.dabs.com**) and E-buyer (**www.ebuyer.com**).

The online value proposition

Differential advantage
A desirable attribute of a product offering that is not currently matched by competitor offerings.

The aim of positioning is to develop a differential advantage over rivals' products as perceived by the customer. Many examples of differentiated online offerings are based on the lower costs in acquiring and retaining online customers which are then passed on to customers – to do this requires creation of a different profit centre for e-commerce operations. Examples include:

● *Retailers* offering lower prices online. Examples: Tesco.com (price promotions on selected products), Comet (discounts relative to in-store on some products);
● *Airlines* offering lower-cost flights for online bookings. Examples: easyJet, Ryanair, BA;
● *Financial services* companies offering higher interest rates on savings products and lower interest rates on credit products such as credit cards and loans. Examples: Nationwide, Alliance and Leicester;
● *Mobile phone* network providers or utilities offering lower-cost tariffs or discounts for customers accounts who are managed online without paper billing. Examples: O_2, British Gas.

Online value proposition (OVP)
A statement of the benefits of online services reinforces the core proposition and differentiates from an organisation's offline offering and those of competitors.

Other options for differentiation are available online for companies where their products are not appropriate for sale online such as high-value or complex products or FMCG (fast-moving consumer goods) brands sold through retailers. These companies can use online services to add value to the brand or product through providing different services or experiences from those available elsewhere.

In an e-marketing context the differential advantage and positioning can be clarified and communicated by developing an online value proposition (OVP). Developing an OVP, involves:

● Developing messages which:
  ● reinforce core brand proposition and credibility,
  ● communicate what a visitor can get from an online brand that …
    – they can't get from the brand offline;
    – they can't get from competitors or intermediaries.

● Communicating these messages to all appropriate online and offline customers touch points in different levels of detail from straplines to more detailed content on the web site or in print.

Communicating the OVP on the site can help create a customer-centric web site. Look at how Autotrader does this for different types of visitors and services in Figure 4.17. Virgin Wines uses an OVP to communicate its service promise as follows:

● And what if ... *You are out during the day*? We promise: our drivers will find a safe place to leave your wine; but if it does get stolen, we just replace it;

● *You find it cheaper elsewhere*? We will refund the difference if you are lucky enough to find a wine cheaper elsewhere;

● *You live somewhere obscure*? We deliver anywhere in the UK, including Northern Ireland, the Highlands and Islands, and the Scilly Isles, for £5.99;

● *You are in a hurry*? We deliver within 7 days, or your delivery is free.

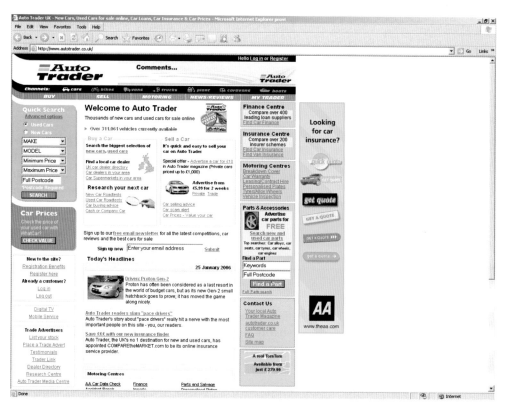

Figure 4.17 Autotrader site (www.autotrader.co.uk) clearly communicates its proposition

Mini Case Study 4.3 'BA asks "Have you clicked yet?"' gives an example of an ad campaign to communicate an OVP. This is a good example since it explains the benefits of online services and e-mail communications and also positions these benefits within the customer buying process.

Varianini and Vaturi (2000) conducted a review of failures in B2C dot-com companies in order to highlight lessons that can be learned. They believe that many of the problems have resulted from a failure to apply established marketing orientation approaches.

They summarise their guidelines as follows:

First identify customer needs and define a distinctive value proposition that will meet them, at a profit. The value proposition must then be delivered through the right product and service and the right channels and it must be communicated consistently. The ultimate aim is to build a strong, long-lasting brand that delivers value to the company marketing it.

Likewise, Agrawal et al. (2001) suggest that the success of leading e-commerce companies is often due to matching value propositions to segments successfully.

McDonald and Wilson (2002) suggest that to determine a value proposition marketers should first assess changes in an industry's structure (see Chapter 2) since channel innovations

Mini Case Study 4.3   BA asks 'Have you clicked yet?'

In 2004, British Airways launched online services which allowed customers to take control of the booking process, so combining new services with reduced costs. BA decided to develop a specific online ad campaign to create awareness and encourage usage of its Online Value Proposition. BA's UK marketing manager said about the objective:

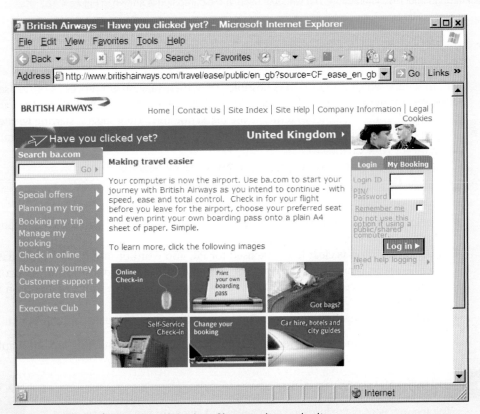

Figure 4.18 BA 'Have you clicked yet?' campaign web site

British Airways is leading the way in innovating technology to simplify our customer's journey through the airport. The role of this campaign was to give a strong message about what is now available online, over and above booking tickets.

The aim was to develop a campaign that educated and changed the way in which BA's customers behave before, during and after their travel. The campaign focused on the key benefits of the new online services – speed, ease and convenience – and promoted the ability to check in online and print out a boarding pass. The two main target audiences were quite different, early-adopters and those who use the web occasionally but don't rely on it. Early-adopters were targeted on sites such as T3.co.uk, Newscientist.com and DigitalHomeMag.com. Occasional users were reached through ads on sites such as JazzFM.com, Vogue.com and Menshealth.com.

Traditional media used to deliver the 'Have you clicked yet?' message included print, TV and outdoor media. The print ad copy, which details the OVP was:

Your computer is now the airport. Check in online, print your own boarding pass, choose your seat, change your booking card and even find hire cars and hotels. Simple.

A range of digital media were used, including ATMs, outdoor LCD transvision screens such as those in London rail stations which included Blue-casting where commuters could receive a video on their Bluetooth enabled mobile phone, digital escalator panels. More than 650,000 consumers interacted with the ATM screen creative. Online ads included overlays and skyscrapers which showed a consumer at his computer, printing out a ticket and walking across the screen to the airport. Such rich-media campaigns generated 17 per cent clickthrough and 15% interaction. The web site used in the campaign is shown in Figure 4.18.

Source: *Revolution* (2005b)

will influence which proposition is possible. They then suggest sub-processes of first setting objectives for market share, volume or value by each segment and then defining the value to be delivered to the customer in terms of the marketing mix. They suggest starting with defining the price and value proposition using the 4 Cs and then defining marketing strategies using the 4 Ps (see Chapter 5).

Having a clear online value proposition has several benefits:

- it helps distinguish an e-commerce site from its competitors (this should be a web site design objective);
- it helps provide a focus to marketing efforts so that company staff are clear about the purpose of the site;
- if the proposition is clear it can be used for PR, and word-of-mouth recommendations may be made about the company. For example, the clear proposition of Amazon on its site is that prices are reduced by up to 40% and that a wide range of 3 million titles are available;
- it can be linked to the normal product propositions of a company or its product.

We look further into options for varying the proposition and marketing mix in Chapter 5.

Activity 4.4   Online value proposition

visit the w.w.w.

Visit the web sites of the following companies and, in one or two sentences each, summarise their Internet value proposition. You should also explain how they use the content of the web site to indicate their value proposition to customers.

1 Tektronix (www.tektronix.com).
2 Handbag.com (www.handbag.com).
3 Harrods (www.harrods.com).
4 Guinness (www.guinness.com).

Decision 5: Multi-channel distribution strategy

Decisions 5 and 6 relate to multi-channel prioritisation which assesses the strategic significance of the Internet relative to other communications channels. In making this prioritisation it is helpful to distinguish between customer communications channels and distribution channels. Customer communications channels, which we review as decision 6, refer to how an organisation influences its customers to select products and suppliers through the different stages of the buying process through inbound and outbound communications. For a retailer, it refers to selection of the mix of channels such as in-store, inbound contact-centre, web and outbound direct messaging used to communicate with prospects and customers.

'Distribution channels' refers to flow of products from a manufacturer or service provider to the end customer. These may be direct to consumer channels or, more often, intermediaries such as retailers are involved. Internet distribution channel priorities have been summarised by Gulati and Garino (2000) as 'getting the right mix of bricks and clicks'. This expression has been used to refer to traditional 'bricks and mortar' enterprises with a physical presence, but limited Internet presence. In the UK, an example of a 'bricks and mortar' store would be the bookseller Waterstones (www.waterstones.co.uk), which when it ventured online became 'clicks and mortar'. It initially followed a strategy of creating its own online presence, but now delivers its online channel through a partnering arrangement based on the Amazon.com infrastructure which is an example of the partnering strategy suggested by Gulati and Garino (2000). Internet pureplays or 'e-businesses' such as dabs.com which operate solely through their online representation are relatively rare. Dabs.com, which is featured in Case Study 7, uses its web site and e-mail marketing as the primary interactions with the customers. Other e-retailers such as Virgin Wines.com make more use of phone contact and physical mail with customers. Even dabs.com uses these channels where appropriate – for large-volume business customers.

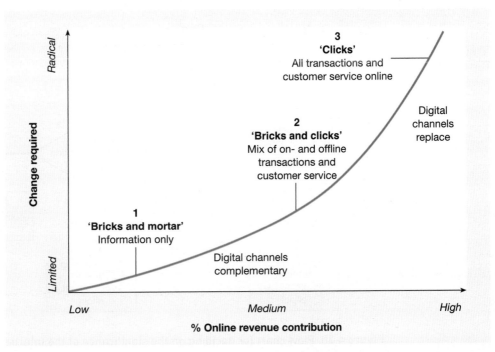

Figure 4.19 Strategic options for a company in relation to the importance of the Internet as a channel

191

The general options for the mix of 'bricks and clicks' are shown in Figure 4.19. The online revenue contribution estimate is informed by the customer demand analysis of propensity to purchase a particular type of product. A similar diagram was produced by de Kare-Silver (2000) who suggested that strategic e-commerce alternatives for companies should be selected according to the percentage of the target market using the channel and the commitment of the company. The idea is that the commitment should mirror the readiness of consumers to use the new medium. If the objective is to achieve a high online revenue contribution of greater than 70% then this will require fundamental change for the company to transform to a 'bricks and clicks' or 'clicks-only' company.

Kumar (1999) suggests that a company should decide whether the Internet will primarily *complement* the company's other channels or primarily *replace* other channels. Clearly, if it is believed that the Internet will primarily replace other channels, then it is important to invest in the promotion and infrastructure to achieve this. This is a key decision as the company is essentially deciding whether the Internet is 'just another communications and/or sales channel' or whether it will fundamentally change the way it communicates and sells to its customers.

Figure 4.20 summarises the main decisions on which a company should base its commitment to the Internet. Kumar (1999) suggests that replacement is most likely to happen when:

● customer access to the Internet is high;
● the Internet can offer a better value proposition than other media;
● the product can be delivered over the Internet (it can be argued that this condition is not essential for replacement, so it is not shown in the figure);
● the product can be standardised (the user does not usually need to view to purchase).

Only if all four conditions are met will there be primarily a replacement effect. The fewer the conditions met, the more likely is it that there will be a complementary effect.

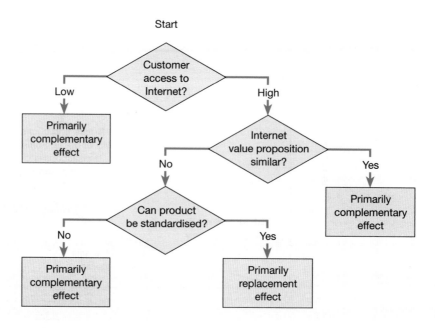

Figure 4.20 Flow chart for deciding on the significance of the Internet to a business
Source: After Kumar (1999)

From an analysis such as that in Figure 4.20 it should be possible to state whether the company strategy should be directed as a complementary or as a replacement scenario. As mentioned in relation to the question of the contribution of the Internet to its business, the company should repeat the analysis for different product segments and different markets. It will then be possible to state the company's overall commitment to the Internet. If the future strategic importance of the Internet is high, with replacement likely, then a significant investment needs to be made in the Internet, and a company's mission needs to be directed towards replacement. If the future strategic importance of the Internet is low then this still needs to be recognised, and appropriate investment made.

Poon and Joseph (2000) have suggested that frameworks assessing the suitability of the Internet for sales, based solely on product characteristics are likely to be misleading. They surveyed Australian firms to assess the importance of product characteristics in determining online sales. They found that there was not a significant difference between physical goods and standardised digital goods such as software.

They conclude:

Although it is logical to believe that firms who are selling search goods of low tangibility have a natural advantage in Internet commerce, it is important to understand that all products have some degree of tangibility and a mixture of search and experience components. The only difference is the relative ratio of such characteristics. For example, a pair of jeans is an experience good with high tangibility, but the size and fit can be easily described using standard descriptions. Similarly, a piece of software is a search good with low tangibility, but the functionality of a software package cannot be fully appreciated without 'test-driving' a beta release.

Changes to marketplace structure

Strategies to take advantage of changes in marketplace structure should also be developed. These options are created through disintermediation and reintermediation (Chapter 2) within a marketplace. The strategic options for the sell-side downstream channels which have been discussed in Chapter 2 are:

- disintermediation (sell direct);
- create new online intermediary (countermediation);
- partner with new online or existing intermediaries;
- do nothing!

Prioritising strategic partnerships as part of the move from a value chain to a value network should also occur as part of this decision. For all options tactics will be needed to manage the channel conflicts that may occur as a result of restructuring.

Technological integration

To achieve strategic Internet marketing goals, B2B organisations will have to plan for integration with customers' and suppliers' systems. Chaffey (2006) describes how a supplier may have to support technical integration with a range of customer e-procurement needs, for example:

1 *Links with single customers.* Organisations will decide whether a single customer is large enough to enforce such linkage. For example, supermarkets often insist that their suppliers trade with them electronically. However, the supplier may be faced with the cost of setting up different types of links with different supermarket customers.
2 *Links with intermediaries.* Organisations have to assess which are the dominant intermediaries such as B2B marketplaces or exchanges and then evaluate whether the trade resulting from the intermediary is sufficient to set up links with this intermediary.

Decision 6: Multi-channel communications strategy

As part of creating an Internet marketing strategy, it is vital to define how the Internet integrates with other inbound communications channels used to process customer enquiries and orders and outbound channels which use direct marketing to encourage retention and growth or deliver customer service messages. For a retailer, these channels include in-store, contact-centre, web and outbound direct messaging used to communicate with prospects and customers. Some of these channels may be broken down further into different media – for example, the contact-centre may involve inbound phone enquiries, e-mail enquiries or real-time chat. Outbound direct messaging may involve direct mail, e-mail media or web-based personalisation. Mini Case Study 2.2 'Lexus assesses multi-channel experience consistency' in Chapter 2 shows the importance of the quality of multiple channels in influencing customer experiences.

The multi-channel communications strategy must review different types of customer contact with the company and then determine how online channels will best support these channels. The main types of customer contact and corresponding strategies will typically be:

- Inbound sales-related enquiries (customer acquisition or conversion strategy);
- Inbound customer-support enquiries (customer service strategy);
- Outbound contact strategy (customer retention and development strategy).

For each of these strategies, the most efficient mix and sequence of media to support the business objectives must be determined. Typically the short-term objective will be conversion to outcome such as sale or satisfactorily resolved service enquiry in the shortest possible time with the minimum cost. However, longer-term objectives of customer loyalty and growth also need to be considered. If the initial experience is efficient, but unsatisfactory to the customer, then they may not remain a customer!

The multi-channel communications strategy must assess the balance between:

- *customer channel preferences* – some customers will prefer online channels for product selection or making enquiries while others will prefer traditional channels;
- *organisation channel preferences* – traditional channels tend to be more expensive to service than digital channels for the company; however, they may not be as effective in converting the customer to sale (for example, a customer who responds to a TV ad to buy car insurance may be more likely to purchase if they enquire by phone in comparison to web enquiry) or in developing customer loyalty (the personal touch available through face-to-face or phone contact may result in a better experience for some customers which engenders loyalty).

Myers et al. (2004) say:

customers may always be right, but allowing them to follow their own preferences often increases a company's costs while leaving untapped opportunities to boost revenues. Instead customers [segments with different characteristics and value] must be guided to the right mix of channels for each product or service.

They suggest companies need to use data to assess a mismatch between the company's actual customer channel preferences and those of the market at large. Thomas and Sullivan (2005) give the example of a US multi-channel retailer that used cross-channel tracking of purchases through assigning each customer a unique identifier to calculate channel preferences as follow: 63% bricks-and-mortar store-only customers, 12.4% Internet-only customers, 11.9% catalogue-only customers, 11.9% dual-channel customers and 1% three-channel customers. This analysis shows the potential for multi-channel sales since Myers et al. (2004) state that these multi-channel customers spend 20 to 30% more.

So, the multi-channel communications strategy needs to specify the extent of communications choices made available to customers and the degree to which a company persuades customers to use particular channels. Deciding on the best combination of channels is a complex challenge for organisations. Consider your mobile phone company. When purchasing you may make your decision about handset and network supplier in-store, on the web or through phoning the contact centre. Any of these contact points may either be direct with the network provider or through a retail intermediary. After purchase, if you have support questions about billing, handset upgrades or new tariffs you may again use any of these touchpoints to resolve your questions. Managing this multi-channel challenge is vital for the phone company for two reasons, both concerned with customer retention. First, the experience delivered through these channels is vital to the decision whether to remain with the network supplier when their contract expires – price is not the only consideration. Second, outbound communications delivered via web site, e-mail, direct mail and phone are critical to getting the customer to stay with the company by recommending the most appropriate tariff and handset with appropriate promotions, but which is the most appropriate mix of channels for the company (each channel has a different level of cost-effectiveness for customers which contributes different levels of value to the customer) and the customer (each customer will have a preference for the combinations of channels they will use for different decisions)?

McDonald and Wilson (2002) suggest evaluating different distribution channels using the channel curve which is a similar tool to the electronic shopping test of de Kare-Silver (2000) described in Chapter 2. For a particular product category they suggest evaluating the customer's preference for each channel against store, mail and phone ordering channels and in terms of cost, convenience, added-value, viewing and accessibility for the customer.

To review strategic options for the role of the Internet in multi-channel marketing the channel coverage map (Figure 4.21), popularised by Friedman and Furey (1999), is a useful tool. This model is best applied to a business-to-business context. Considering an organisation such as Dell, customers will vary by value within and between segments. Low-value segments will be smaller businesses and consumers while large organisations placing many purchases will be higher-value. For consumers, Dell's preferred channel preference will be the low-cost online channel. For medium-sized companies, the preference will be a combination of desk-based sales agents in a call centre supported by the web. Through using phone contact, Dell can better explain the options available for multiple purchases. For the highest-value, large companies, the most important effective

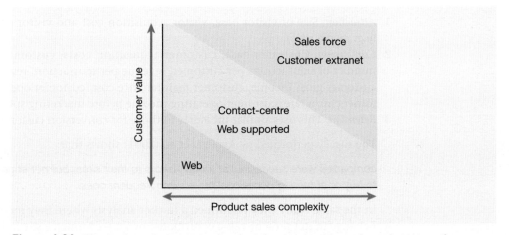

Figure 4.21 Channel coverage map showing the company's preferred strategy for communications with different customer segments with different value

approach will be through field staff such as account managers. Specific web applications such as the Dell Premier extranets will form part of the strategy to support these customers. The model considers the different type of products a company sells from lower-cost standardised products through to higher-cost customised products and services such as network management.

We will return to this key decision about implementing customer contact strategies in later chapters in the book.

Decision 7: Online communications mix and budget

The decision on the amount of spending on online communications and the mix between the different communications techniques such as search engine marketing, e-mail marketing and online advertising is closely related to the previous one.

Varianini and Vaturi (2000) suggest that many e-commerce failures have resulted from poor control of media spending. They suggest that many companies spend too much on poorly targeted communications. They suggest the communications mix should be optimised to minimise the cost of acquisition of customers. It can also be suggested that optimisation of the conversion to action on site is important to the success of marketing. The strategy will fail if the site design, quality of service and marketing communications are not effective in converting visitors to prospects or buyers.

A further strategic decision is the balance of investment between customer acquisition and retention. Many start-up companies will invest primarily on customer acquisition. This can be a strategic error since customer retention through repeat purchases will be vital to the success of the online service. For existing companies, there is a decision on whether to focus expenditure on customer acquisition or on customer retention or to use a balanced approach.

Agrawal et al. (2001) suggest that the success of e-commerce sites can be modelled and controlled based on the customer lifecycle of customer relationship management (Chapter 6). They suggest using a scorecard, assessed using a longitudinal study analysing hundreds of e-commerce sites in the USA and Europe. The scorecard is based on the performance drivers or critical success factors for e-commerce such as the costs for acquisition and retention, conversion rates of visitors to buyers to repeat buyers, together with churn rates. Note that to maximise retention and minimise churn (customers who don't continue to use the service) there will need to be measures that assess the quality of service including customer satisfaction ratings. These are discussed in Chapter 7. There are three main parts to their scorecard:

Performance drivers
Critical success factors that determine whether business and marketing objectives are met.

1 *Attraction.* Size of visitor base, visitor acquisition cost and visitor advertising revenue (e.g. media sites).
2 *Conversion.* Customer base, customer acquisition costs, customer conversion rate, number of transactions per customer, revenue per transaction, revenue per customer, customer gross income, customer maintenance cost, customer operating income, customer churn rate, customer operating income before marketing spending.
3 *Retention.* This uses similar measures to those for conversion customers.

The survey performed by Agrawal et al. (2001) shows that:

companies were successful at luring visitors to their sites, but not at getting these visitors to buy or at turning occasional buyers into frequent ones.

In the same study they performed a further analysis where they modelled the theoretical change in net present value contributed by an e-commerce site in response to a 10%

change in these performance drivers. This shows the relative importance of these drivers or 'levers', as they refer to them:

1 **Attraction**
   - Visitor acquisition cost: 0.74% change in NPV
   - Visitor growth: 3.09% change in NPV.

2 **Conversion**
   - Customer conversion rate: 0.84% change in NPV
   - Revenue per customer: 2.32% change in NPV.

3 **Retention**
   - Cost of repeat customer: 0.69% change in NPV
   - Revenue per repeat customer: 5.78% change in NPV
   - Repeat customer churn rate: 6.65% change in NPV
   - Repeat customer conversion rate: 9.49% change in NPV.

Campaign-based e-communications
E-marketing communications that are executed to support a specific marketing campaign such as a product launch, price promotion or a web site launch.

Continuous e-communications
Long-term use of e-marketing communications for customer acquisition (such as, search engine and affiliate marketing) and retention (for example, e-newsletter marketing).

This modelling highlights the importance of on-site marketing communications and the quality of service delivery in converting browsers to buyers and buyers into repeat buyers. It is apparent that marketing spend is large relative to turnover initially, to achieve customer growth, but is then carefully controlled to achieve profitability.

We will return to this topic in Chapter 8, where we will review the balance between campaign-based e-communications which are often tied into a particular event such as the launch or re-launch of a web site or a product. For example, an interactive (banner) advert campaign may last for a period of 2 months following a site re-launch or for a 5-month period around a new product launch.

In addition to campaign-based e-communications we also need continuous e-communications. Organisations need to ensure that there is sufficient investment in continuous online marketing activities such as search marketing, affiliate marketing and sponsorship.

We observe that there is a significant change in mindset required to change budget allocations from a traditional campaign-based approach to an increased proportion of expenditure on continuous communications.

Decision 8: Organisational capabilities (7S)

A useful framework for reviewing an organisation's capabilities to implement Internet marketing strategy is shown in Table 4.5 applied to Internet marketing. This 7S framework was developed by McKinsey consultants in the 1980s and summarised by Waterman *et al.* (1980).

Which are the main challenges in implementing strategy? E-consultancy (2005) surveyed UK e-commerce managers to assess their views on the main challenges of managing e-commerce within an organisation. Their responses are summarised in Figure 4.22. In the context of the 7Ss, we can summarise the main challenges as follows:

- *Strategy* – limited capabilities to integrate into Internet strategy within core marketing and business strategy as discussed earlier in this chapter is indicated by frustration on gaining appropriate budgets;
- *Structure* – structural and process issues are indicated by the challenges of gaining resource and buy-in from traditional marketing and IT functions;
- *Skills and staff* – these issues were indicated by difficulties in finding specialist staff or agencies.

Table 4.5 The 7S strategic framework and its application to digital marketing management

Element of 7S model	Relevance to Internet marketing capability	Key issues
Strategy	The contribution of digital marketing in influencing and supporting organisations' strategy	● Gaining appropriate budgets and demonstrating or delivering value and return on investment from budgets. Annual planning approach ● Techniques for using Internet marketing to impact organisation strategy ● Techniques for aligning Internet marketing strategy with organisational and marketing strategy
Structure	The modification of organisational structure to support Internet marketing	● Integration of team with other management, marketing (corporate communications, brand marketing, direct marketing) and IT staff ● Use of cross-functional teams and steering groups ● Insourcing vs outsourcing
Systems	The development of specific processes, procedures or information systems to support Internet marketing	● Campaign planning approach-integration ● Managing/sharing customer information ● Managing content quality ● Unified reporting of digital marketing effectiveness ● In-house vs external best-of-breed vs external integrated technology solutions
Staff	The breakdown of staff in terms of their background, age and sex and characteristics such as IT vs marketing Use of contractors/consultants	● Insourcing vs outsourcing ● Achieving senior management buy-in/involvement with digital marketing ● Staff recruitment and retention ● Virtual working ● Staff development and training
Style	Includes both the way in which key managers behave in achieving the organisation's goals and the cultural style of the organisation as a whole	● Relates to role of the Internet marketing team in influencing strategy – is it dynamic and influential or conservative and looking for a voice?
Skills	Distinctive capabilities of key staff, but can be interpreted as specific skill-sets of team members	● Staff skills in specific areas: supplier selection, project management, content management, specific e-marketing approaches (search engine marketing, affiliate marketing, e-mail marketing, online advertising)
Superordinate goals	The guiding concepts of the Internet marketing organisation which are also part of shared values and culture. The internal and external perception of these goals may vary	● Improving the perception of the importance and effectiveness of the digital marketing team amongst senior managers and staff it works with (marketing generalists and IT)

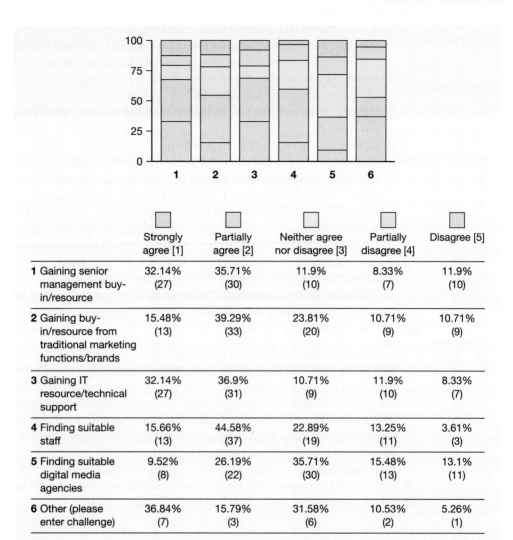

	Strongly agree [1]	Partially agree [2]	Neither agree nor disagree [3]	Partially disagree [4]	Disagree [5]
1 Gaining senior management buy-in/resource	32.14% (27)	35.71% (30)	11.9% (10)	8.33% (7)	11.9% (10)
2 Gaining buy-in/resource from traditional marketing functions/brands	15.48% (13)	39.29% (33)	23.81% (20)	10.71% (9)	10.71% (9)
3 Gaining IT resource/technical support	32.14% (27)	36.9% (31)	10.71% (9)	11.9% (10)	8.33% (7)
4 Finding suitable staff	15.66% (13)	44.58% (37)	22.89% (19)	13.25% (11)	3.61% (3)
5 Finding suitable digital media agencies	9.52% (8)	26.19% (22)	35.71% (30)	15.48% (13)	13.1% (11)
6 Other (please enter challenge)	36.84% (7)	15.79% (3)	31.58% (6)	10.53% (2)	5.26% (1)

Figure 4.22 The main challenges of e-marketing (*n* = 84)
Source: E-consultancy (2005)

Change management
Controls to minimise the risks of project-based and organisational change.

Organisational structure decisions form two main questions. The first is 'How should internal structures be changed to deliver e-marketing?' and the second 'How should the structure of links with partner organisations be changed to achieve e-marketing objectives?'. Once structural decisions have been made attention should be focused on effective change management. Many e-commerce initiatives fail, not in their conceptualisation, but in their implementation. Chaffey (2007) describes approaches to change management and risk management in Chapter 10.

Internal structures

There are several alternative options for restructuring within a business such as the creation of an in-house digital marketing or e-commerce group. This issue has been considered by Parsons et al. (1996) from a sell-side e-commerce perspective. They recognise four stages in the growth of what they refer to as 'the digital marketing organisation' which are still useful for benchmarking digital marketing capabilities. A more sophisticated e-commerce capability assessment was presented earlier in this chapter in the section on situation review (Table 4.1). The stages are:

1 *Ad-hoc activity*. At this stage there is no formal organisation related to e-commerce and the skills are dispersed around the organisation. It is likely that there is poor integration between online and offline marketing communications. The web site may not reflect the offline brand, and the web site services may not be featured in the offline marketing communications. A further problem with ad-hoc activity is that the maintenance of the web site will be informal and errors may occur as information becomes out-of-date.

2 *Focusing the effort*. At this stage, efforts are made to introduce a controlling mechanism for Internet marketing. Parsons et al. (1996) suggest that this is often achieved through a senior executive setting up a steering group which may include interested parties from marketing and IT and legal experts. At this stage the efforts to control the site will be experimental, with different approaches being tried to build, promote and manage the site.

3 *Formalisation*. At this stage the authors suggest that Internet marketing will have reached a critical mass and there will be a defined group or separate business unit within the company that will manage all digital marketing.

4 *Institutionalising capability*. This stage also involves a formal grouping within the organisation, but is distinguished from the previous stage in that there are formal links created between digital marketing and the company's core activities.

Although this is presented as a stage model with evolution implying all companies will move from one stage to the next, many companies will find that true formalisation with the creation of a separate e-commerce or e-business department is unnecessary. For small and medium companies with a marketing department numbering a few people and an IT department perhaps consisting of two people, it will not be practical to have a separate group. Even large companies may find it is sufficient to have a single person or small team responsible for e-commerce with their role being to coordinate the different activities within the company using a matrix management approach.

Activity 4.5 reviews different types of organisational structures for e-commerce. Table 4.6 reviews some of the advantages and disadvantages of each.

Table 4.6 Advantages and disadvantages of the organisational structures shown in Figure 4.23

Organisational structure	Circumstances	Advantages	Disadvantages
(a) No formal structure for e-commerce	Initial response to e-commerce or poor leadership with no identification of need for change	Can achieve rapid response to e-commerce	Poor-quality site in terms of content quality and customer service responses (e-mail, phone). Priorities not decided logically. Insufficient resources
(b) A separate committee or department manages and coordinates e-commerce	Identification of problem and response in (a)	Coordination and budgeting and resource allocation possible	May be difficult to get different departments to deliver their input because of other commitments
(c) A separate business unit with independent budgets	Internet contribution (Chapter 6) is sizeable (>20%)	As for (b), but can set own targets and not be constrained by resources. Lower-risk option than (d)	Has to respond to corporate strategy. Conflict of interests between department and traditional business
(d) A separate operating company	Major revenue potential or flotation. Need to differentiate from parent	As for (c), but can set strategy independently. Can maximise market potential	High risk if market potential is overestimated due to start-up costs

| Activity 4.5 | **Which is the best organisation structure for e-commerce?** |

Purpose

To review alternative organisational structures for e-commerce.

Activity

1 Match the four types of companies and situations to the structures (a) to (d) in Figure 4.23.
   ● A separate operating company. Example: Prudential and Egg (www.egg.com).
   ● A separate business unit with independent budgets. Example: RS Components Internet Trading Channel (www.rswww.com).
   ● A separate committee or department manages and coordinates e-commerce. Example: Derbyshire Building Society (www.derbyshire.co.uk).
   ● No formal structure for e-commerce. Examples: many small businesses.
2 Under which circumstances would each structure be appropriate?
3 Summarise the advantages and disadvantages of each approach.

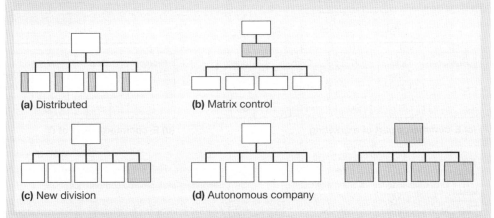

(a) Distributed **(b)** Matrix control **(c)** New division **(d)** Autonomous company

Figure 4.23 Summary of alternative organisational structures for e-commerce suggested in Parsons et al. (1996)

Where the main e-commerce function is internal, the E-consultancy (2005) research suggested that it was typically located in one of four areas (see Figure 4.24) in approximate decreasing order of frequency:

(a) Main e-commerce function in separate team.
(b) Main e-commerce function part of operations or direct channel.
(c) Main e-commerce function part of marketing, corporate communications or other central marketing function.
(d) Main e-commerce function part of information technology (IT).

There is also often one or several secondary areas of e-commerce competence and resource. For example, IT may have a role in applications development and site build and each business, brand or country may have one or more e-commerce specialists responsible for managing e-commerce in their unit. Which was appropriate depended strongly on the market(s) the company operated in and their existing channel structures.

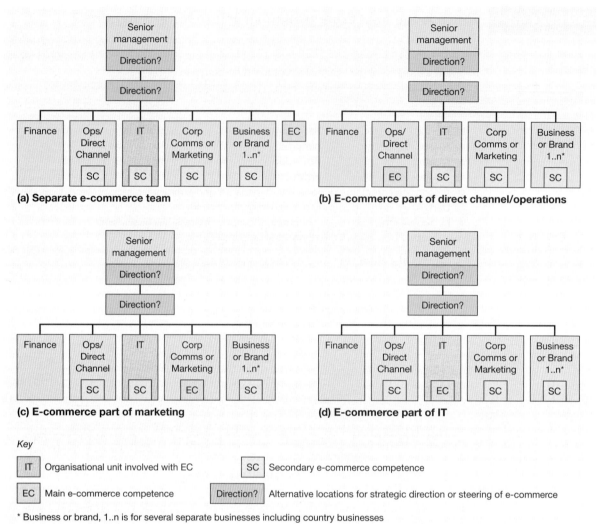

Figure 4.24 Options for location of control of e-commerce
Source: E-consultancy (2005)

Links with other organisations

Gulati and Garino (2000) identify a continuum of approaches from integration to separation for delivering e-marketing through working with outside partners. The choices are:

1 *In-house division (integration).* Example: RS Components Internet Trading Channel (**www.rswww.com**).
2 *Joint venture (mixed).* The company creates an online presence in association with another player.
3 *Strategic partnership (mixed).* This may also be achieved through purchase of existing dot-coms, for example, in the UK Great Universal Stores acquired e-tailer Jungle.com for its strength in selling technology products and strong brand while John Lewis purchased Buy.com's UK operations.
4 *Spin-off (separation).* Example: Egg bank is a spin-off from Prudential Financial Services Company.

Skills

There is a wide range of new skills required for e-commerce. Figure 4.25 gives an indication of typical roles within an e-commerce team, placed within a customer-lifecyle-based structure. Each grouping of roles is placed in a dotted box which indicates the other teams this group needs to work with, or potentially where in the organisation or outside this work is completed. For example, e-CRM activities such as e-mail marketing could be potentially undertaken in a particular business unit or country. Similarly, many activities of development planning and implementation can be completed within IT or a specialist agency.

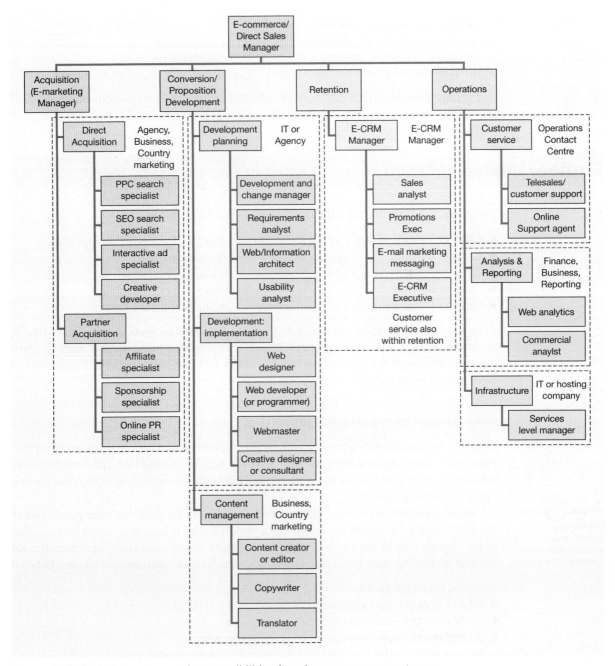

Figure 4.25 Typical structure and responsibilities for a large e-commerce team

Source: E-consultancy (2005)

For the skills indicated in Figure 4.25 it may be more efficient to outsource some skills. These are some of the main options for external suppliers for these Internet marketing skills:

1 Full-service digital agency.
2 Specialist digital agency.
3 Traditional agency.
4 In-house resource.

When deciding on supplier or resource, suppliers need to consider the level and type of marketing activities they will be covering.

The level typically ranges through:

1 Strategy
2 Analysis and creative concepts
3 Creative or content development
4 Executing campaign, including reporting analysis and adjustment
5 Infrastructure (e.g. web hosting, ad-serving, e-mail broadcasting, evaluation).

Options for outsourcing different e-marketing activities are reviewed in Activity 7.1.

Strategy implementation

This forms the topic for subsequent chapters in this book:

● Chapter 5 – options for varying the marketing mix in the Internet environment;
● Chapter 6 – implementing customer relationship management;
● Chapter 7 – delivering online services via a web site;
● Chapter 8 – interactive marketing communications;
● Chapter 9 – monitoring and maintaining the online presence.

In each of these areas such as CRM or development of web site functionality, it is common that different initiatives will compete for budget. The next section reviews techniques for prioritising these projects and deciding on the best portfolio of e-commerce applications.

Assessing different Internet projects

A further organisational capability issue is the decision about different information systems marketing applications. Typically, there will be a range of different Internet marketing alternatives to be evaluated. Limited resources will dictate that only some applications are practical.

Portfolio analysis
Identification,
evaluation and
selection of desirable
marketing applications.

Portfolio analysis can be used to select the most suitable projects. For example, Daniel et al. (2001) suggest that potential e-commerce opportunities should be assessed for the value of the opportunity to the company against its ability to deliver. Typical opportunities for Internet marketing strategy for an organisation which has a brochureware site might be:

● online catalogue facility;
● e-CRM system – lead generation system;
● e-CRM system – customer service management;
● e-CRM system – personalisation of content for users;
● partner relationship management extranet for distributors or agents;
● transactional e-commerce facility.

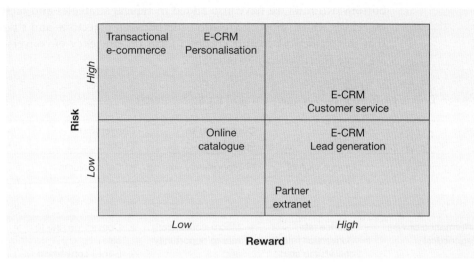

Figure 4.26 Example of risk–reward analysis

Such alternatives can then be evaluated in terms of their risk against reward. Figure 4.26 shows a possible evaluation of strategic options. It is apparent that with limited resources, the e-CRM lead generation, partner extranet and customer services options offer the best mix of risk and reward.

For information systems investments, the model of McFarlan (1984) has been used extensively to assess the future strategic importance applications in a portfolio. This model has been applied to the e-commerce applications by Daniel et al. (2001) and Chaffey (2006). Potential e-commerce applications can be assessed as:

1 *Key operational* – essential to remain competitive. Example: partner relationship management extranet for distributors or agents;
2 *Support* – deliver improved performance, but not critical to strategy. Example: e-CRM system – personalisation of content for users;
3 *High-potential* – may be important to achieving future success. Example: e-CRM system – customer service management;
4 *Strategic* – critical to future business strategy. Example: e-CRM system – lead generation system is vital to developing new business.

A further portfolio analysis suggested by McDonald and Wilson (2002) is a matrix of attractiveness to customer against attractiveness to company, which will give a similar result to the risk–reward matrix. Finally, Tjan (2001) has suggested a matrix approach of viability (return on investment) against fit (with the organisation's capabilities) for Internet applications. He presents five metrics for assessing each of viability and fit.

The online lifecycle management grid

Earlier in the chapter, in the section on objective setting, we reviewed different frameworks for identifying objectives and metrics to assess whether they are achieved. We consider the online lifecycle management grid at this point since Table 4.7 acts as a good summary that integrates objectives, strategies and tactics.

The columns isolate the key performance areas of site visitor acquisition, conversion to opportunity, conversion to sale and retention. The rows isolate more detailed metrics such as the tracking metrics and performance drivers from higher-level metrics such as the customer-centric key performance indicators (KPIs) and business-value KPIs. In the bottom two rows we have also added in typical strategies and tactics used to achieve objectives which show the relationship between objectives and strategy. Note, though, that this framework mainly creates a focus on efficiency of conversion, although there are some effectiveness measures also.

Table 4.7 Online performance management grid for an e-retailer

Metric	Visitor acquisition	Conversion to opportunity	Conversion to sale	Customer retention and growth
Tracking metrics	• Unique visitors • New visitors	• Opportunity volume	• Sales volume	• E-mail list quality • E-mail response quality • Transactions
Performance drivers (diagnostics)	• Bounce rate • Conversion rate: new visit to start quote	• Macro-conversion rate to opportunity and micro-conversion efficiency	• Conversion rate to sale • E-mail conversion rate	• Active customers % (site and e-mail active) • Repeat conversion rate for different purchases
Customer centric KPIs	• Cost per click and per sale • Brand awareness	• Cost per opportunity • Customer satisfaction	• Cost per sale • Customer satisfaction • Average order value (AOV)	• Lifetime value • Customer loyalty index • Products per customer
Business value KPIs	• Audience share	• Online product requests (n, £, % of total)	• Online originated sales (n, £, % of total)	• Retained sales growth and volume
Strategy	• Online targeted reach strategy • Offline targeted reach strategy	• Lead generation strategy	• Online sales generation strategy • Offline sales impact strategy	• Retention and customer growth strategy
Tactics	• Continuous communications mix • Campaign communications mix • Online value proposition	• Usability • Personalisation • Inbound contact strategy (customer service)	• Usability • Personalisation • Inbound contact strategy (customer service) • Merchandising • Triggered e-mails	• Database / list quality • Targeting • Outbound contact strategy (e-mail) • Personalisation

Source: adapted from Neil Mason's Applied Insights (www.applied-insights.co.uk) Acquisition, Conversion, Retention approach

These are some of the generic Internet marketing main strategies to achieve the objectives in the grid which apply to a range of organisations:

● *Online value proposition strategy* – defining the value proposition for acquisition and retention to engage with customers online. Includes informational and promotional incentives used to encourage trial. Also defines programme of value creation through time – e.g. business white papers published on partner sites.

● *Online targeted reach strategy* – the aim is to communicate with relevant audiences online to achieve communications objectives. The communications commonly include campaign communications such as online advertising, PR, e-mail, viral campaigns and continuous communications such as search engine marketing or sponsorship or partnership arrangements. The strategy may involve (1) driving new, potential customers to the company site, (2) migrating existing customers to online channels or (3) achieving reach to enhance brand awareness, favourability and purchase intent through ads and sponsorships on third-party sites. Building brand awareness, favourability and purchase intent on third-party sites may be a more effective strategy for low-involvement FMCG brands where it will be difficult to encourage visitors to the site.

- *Offline targeted reach strategy* – the objective is to encourage potential customers to use online channels, i.e. visit web site and transact where relevant. The strategy is to communicate with selected customer segments offline through direct mail, media buys, PR and sponsorship.
- *Online sales efficiency strategy* – the objective is to convert site visitors to engage and become leads (for example, through registering for an e-newsletter or placing the first item in the shopping basket) to convert them to buy products and maximise the purchase transaction value.
- *Offline sales impact strategy* – the aim is to achieve sales offline from new or existing customers. Strategy defines how online communications through the web site and e-mail can influence sales offline, i.e. by phone, mail-order or in-store.

| Case Study 4 | Tesco.com uses the Internet to support its diversification strategy |

Context

Tesco, well known as Britain's leading food retail group with a presence also in Europe and Asia has also been a pioneer online. By September 2005 online sales in the first half of the year were £401 million, a 31% year-on-year increase, and profit increased by 37% to £21 million. Tesco.com now receives 170,000 orders each week. Soon it should reach an annual turnover of £1 billion online and is generally recognised as the world's largest online grocer.

Product ranges

The Tesco.com site acts as a portal to most of Tesco's products, including various non-food ranges (for example, books, DVDs and electrical items under the 'Extra' banner), Tesco Personal Finance and the telecoms businesses, as well as services offered in partnership with specialist companies, such as dieting clubs, flights and holidays, music downloads, gas, electricity and DVD rentals. It does not currently sell clothing online but in May 2005 it introduced a clothing web site (www.clothing attesco.com), initially to showcase Tesco's clothing brands and link customers to their nearest store with this range.

Competitors

Tesco currently leads the UK's other leading grocery retailers in terms of market share. This pattern is repeated online. The compilation below is from Hitwise (2005) and the figures in brackets show market share for traditional offline retail formats from the Taylor Nelson Softres Super Panel (see http://superpanel.tns-global.com):

1 Tesco Superstore, 27.28% (29% of retail trade)
2 ASDA, 13.36%
3 ASDA @t Home, 10.13% (17.1%)
4 Sainsbury's, 8.42%
5 Tesco Wine Warehouse, 8.19%
6 Sainsbury's to You, 5.86% (15.9%)
7 Waitrose.com, 3.42% (3.6%)
8 Ocado, 3.32% (owned by Waitrose, 3.6%)
9 Lidl, 2.49% (1.8%)
10 ALDI – UK, 2.10% (2.3%)

Some companies are repeated since their main site and the online shopping site are reported on separately. Asda.com now seems to be performing in a consistent manner online to its offline presence. However, Sainsbury's online performance seems to be significantly lower compared to its offline performance. Some providers such as Ocado which originally just operated within the London area have a strong local performance.

Notably, some of Tesco.com's competitors are absent from the Hitwise listing since their strategy has been to focus on retail formats. These are Morrisons (12.5% retail share), Somerfield (5.5%) and Co-op (5.0%).

Promotion of service

As with other online retailers, Tesco.com relies on in-store advertising and marketing to the supermarket's Clubcard loyalty scheme's customer base to persuade customers to shop online. *New Media Age* (2005) quotes Nigel Dodd, marketing director at Tesco.com, as saying: '*These are invaluable sources as we have such a strong customer base*'. However, for non-food goods the supermarket does advertise online using keyword targeted ads.

For existing customers, e-mail marketing and direct mail marketing to provide special offers and promotions to customers is important.

According to Humby and Hunt (2003), e-retailer Tesco.com uses what he describes as a 'commitment-based segmentation' or 'loyalty ladder' which is based on recency of purchase, frequency of purchase and value which is used to identify six lifecycle categories which are then further divided to target communications:

- 'Logged-on'
- 'Cautionary'
- 'Developing'
- 'Established'
- 'Dedicated'
- 'Logged-off' (the aim here is to win back).

Tesco then uses automated event-triggered messaging which can be created to encourage continued purchase. For example, Tesco.com has a touch strategy which includes a sequence of follow-up communications triggered after different events in the customer lifecycle. In the example given below, communications after event 1 are intended to achieve the objective of converting a web site visitor to action; communications after event 2 are intended to move the customer from a first-time purchaser to a regular purchaser and for event 3 to reactivate lapsed purchasers.

Trigger event 1: Customer first registers on site (but does not buy)
Auto-response (AR) 1: Two days after registration e-mail sent offering phone assistance and £5 discount off first purchase to encourage trial.

Trigger event 2: Customer first purchases online
AR1: Immediate order confirmation.

AR2: Five days after purchase e-mail sent with link to online customer satisfaction survey asking about quality of service from driver and picker (e.g. item quality and substitutions).

AR3: Two weeks after first purchase – direct mail offering tips on how to use service and £5 discount on next purchases intended to encourage re-use of online services.

AR4: Generic monthly e-newsletter with online exclusive offers encouraging cross-selling.

AR5: Bi-weekly alert with personalised offers for customer.

AR6: After two months – £5 discount for next shop.

AR7: Quarterly mailing of coupons encouraging repeat sales and cross-sales.

Trigger event 3: Customer does not purchase for an extended period
AR1: Dormancy detected – reactivation e-mail with survey of how the customer is finding the service (to identify any problems) and a £5 incentive.

AR2: A further discount incentive is used in order to encourage continued usage to shop after the first shop after a break.

Tesco's online product strategy

NMA (2005) ran a profile of Laura Wade-Gery, CEO of Tesco.com since January 2004, which provides an interesting insight into how the business has run. In her first year, total sales were increased 24% to £719 million. Laura is 40 years old, a keen athlete and has followed a varied career developing from a MA in History at Magdalen College, Oxford, an MBA from Insead; manager and partner in Kleinwort Benson; manager and senior consultant, Gemini Consulting; targeted marketing director (Tesco Clubcard), and group strategy director, Tesco Stores.

The growth overseen by Wade-Gery has been achieved through a combination of initiatives. Product range development is one key area. In early 2005, Tesco.com fulfilled 150,000 grocery orders a week but now also offers more intangible offerings, such as e-diets and music downloads.

Laura has also focused on improving the customer experience online – the time it takes for a new customer to complete their first order has been decreased from over an hour to 35 minutes through usability work culminating in a major site revision.

To support the business as it diversifies into new areas, Wade-Gery's strategy was 'to make home delivery part of the DNA of Tesco' according to NMA (2005). She continues: 'What we offer is delivery to your home of a Tesco service – it's an obvious extension of the home-delivered groceries concept.' By May 2005, Tesco.com had 30,000 customers signed up for DVD rental, through partner Video Island (which runs the rival Screenselect service). Over the next year, her target is to treble this total, while also extending home-delivery services to the likes of bulk wine and white goods.

Wade-Gery looks to achieve synergy between the range of services offered. For example, its partnership with eDiets can be promoted through the Tesco Clubcard loyalty scheme, with mailings to 10m customers a year. In July 2004, Tesco.com Limited paid £2 million for the exclusive licence to eDiets.com in the UK and Ireland under the URLs www.eDietsUK.com and www.eDiets.ie. Through promoting these services through these URLs, Tesco can use the dieting business to grow use of the Tesco.com service and in-store sales.

To help keep focus on home retail-delivery, Wade-Gery sold women's portal iVillage (www.ivillage.co.uk) back to its US owners for an undisclosed sum in March 2004. She explained to NMA:

It's a very different sort of product to the other services that we're embarking on. In my mind, we stand for providing services and products that you buy, which is slightly different to the world of providing information.

The implication is that there was insufficient revenue from ad sales on iVillage and insufficient opportunities to promote Tesco.com sales. However, iVillage was a useful learning experience in that there are some parallels with iVillage, such as message boards and community advisers.

Wade-Gery is also director of Tesco Mobile, the joint 'pay-as-you-go' venture with O_2 which is mainly serviced online, although promoted in-store and via direct mail. Tesco also offers broadband and dial-up ISP services, but believe the market for Internet telephony (provided through Skype and Vonage, for example) is not sufficiently developed. Tesco.com has concentrated on more traditional services which have the demand, for example, Tesco Telecom fixed-line services attracted over a million customers in their first year.

However, this is not to say that Tesco.com will not invest in relatively new services. In November 2004, Tesco introduced a music download service and just six months later, Wade-Gery estimates they have around 10% market share – one of the benefits of launching relatively early. Again, there is synergy, this time with hardware sales. NMA (2005) reported that as MP3 players were unwrapped, sales went up – even on Christmas Day! She says:

The exciting thing about digital is where you can take it in the future. As the technology grows, we'll be able to turn Tesco.com into a digital download store of all

sorts, rather than just music. Clearly, film [through video on demand] would be next.

But it has to be based firmly on analysis of customer demand. She says:

The number one thing for us is whether the product is something that customers are saying they want, has it reached a point where mass-market customers are interested?

There also has to be scope for simplification. NMA (2005) notes that Tesco is built on a core premise of convenience and value and Wade-Gery believes what it's already done with mobile tariffs, broadband packages and music downloads are good examples of the retailer's knack for streamlining propositions. She says:

'We've actually managed to get people joining broadband who have never even had a dial-up service'.

Sources: Humby and Hunt (2003), NMA (2005), Hitwise (2005), Wikipedia (2005)

Question

Based on the case study and your own research on competitors, summarise the strategic approaches which have helped Tesco.com achieve success online.

Summary

1 The development of the online presence follows stage models from basic static 'brochureware' sites through simple interactive sites with query facilities to dynamic sites offering personalisation of services for customers.

2 The Internet marketing strategy should follow a similar form to a traditional strategic marketing planning process and should include:

- goal setting;
- situation review;
- strategy formulation;
- resource allocation and monitoring.

A feedback loop should be established to ensure the site is monitored and modifications are fed back into the strategy development.

3 Strategic goal setting should involve:

- setting business objectives that the Internet can help achieve;
- assessing and stating the contribution that the Internet will make to the business in the future, both as a proportion of revenue and in terms of whether the Internet will complement or replace other media;
- stating the full range of business benefits that are sought, such as improved corporate image, cost reduction, more leads and sales, and improved customer service.

4 The situation review will include assessing internal resources and assets, including the services available through the existing web site. External analysis will involve customer demand analysis, competitor benchmarking and review of the macro-environment SLEPT factors.

5 Strategy formulation will involve defining a company's commitment to the Internet; setting an appropriate value proposition for customers of the web site; and identifying the role of the Internet in exploiting new markets, marketplaces and distribution channels and in delivering new products and services. In summary:

- Decision 1: Market and product development strategies
- Decision 2: Business and revenue models strategies
- Decision 3: Target market strategy
- Decision 4: Positioning and differentiation strategy (including the marketing mix)
- Decision 5: Multi-channel distribution strategy
- Decision 6: Multi-channel communications strategy
- Decision 7: Online communications mix and budget
- Decision 8: Organisational capabilities (7S)

Exercises

Self-assessment exercises

1 Draw a diagram that summarises the stages through which a company's web site may evolve.

2 What is meant by the 'Internet contribution', and what is its relevance to strategy?

3 What is the role of monitoring in the strategic planning process?

4 Summarise the main tangible and intangible business benefits of the Internet to a company.

5 What is the purpose of an Internet marketing audit? What should it involve?

6 What does a company need in order to be able to state clearly in the mission statement its strategic position relative to the Internet?

7 What are the market and product positioning opportunities offered by the Internet?

8 What are the distribution channel options for a manufacturing company?

Essay and discussion questions

1 Discuss the frequency with which an Internet marketing strategy should be updated for a company to remain competitive.

2 'Setting long-term strategic objectives for a web site is unrealistic since the rate of change in the marketplace is so rapid.' Discuss.

3 Explain the essential elements of an Internet marketing strategy.

4 Summarise the role of strategy tools and models in formulating a company's strategic approach to the Internet.

Examination questions

1 When evaluating the business benefits of a web site, which factors are likely to be common to most companies?

2 Use Porter's five forces model to discuss the competitive threats presented to a company by other web sites.

3 Which factors will affect whether the Internet has primarily a complementary effect or a replacement effect on a company?

4 Describe different stages in the sophistication of development of a web site, giving examples of the services provided at each stage.

5 Briefly explain the purpose and activities involved in an external audit conducted as part of the development of an Internet marketing strategy.

6 What is the importance of measurement within the Internet marketing process?

7 Which factors would a retail company consider when assessing the suitability of its product for Internet sales?

8 Explain what is meant by the online value proposition, and give two examples of the value proposition for web sites with which you are familiar.

References

Aaker, D. and Joachimsthaler, E. (2000) *Brand Leadership*. Free Press, New York.

Agrawal, V., Arjona, V. and Lemmens, R. (2001) E-performance: the path to rational exuberance, *McKinsey Quarterly*, No. 1, 31–43.

Bazett, M., Bowden, I., Love, J., Street, R. and Wilson, H. (2005) Measuring multichannel effectiveness using the balanced scorecard. *Interactive Marketing*, 6(3) (January–March), 224–31.

Chaffey, D. (2007) *E-Business and E-Commerce Management*, 3rd edn. Financial Times/Prentice Hall, Harlow.

Chaston, I. (2000) *E-Marketing Strategy*. McGraw-Hill, Maidenhead.

Daniel, E., Wilson, H., McDonald, M. and Ward, J. (2001) *Marketing Strategy in the Digital Age*. Financial Times/Prentice Hall, Harlow.

Daniel, E., Wilson, H., Ward, J. and McDonald, M. (2002) Innovation @nd integration: developing an integrated e-enabled business strategy. Preliminary findings from an industry-sponsored research project for the Information Systems Research Centre and the Centre for E-marketing. Cranfield University School of Management, January.

Deise, M., Nowikow, C., King, P. and Wright, A. (2000) *Executive's Guide to E-Business. From Tactics to Strategy*. Wiley, New York.

de Kare-Silver, M. (2000) *EShock 2000. The Electronic Shopping Revolution: Strategies for Retailers and Manufacturers*. Macmillan, London.

Der Zee, J. and De Jong, B. (1999) Alignment is not enough: integrating business and information technology management with the balanced business scorecard, *Journal of Management Information Systems*, 16(2), 137–57.

Dibb, S., Simkin, S., Pride, W. and Ferrell, O. (2001) *Marketing. Concepts and Strategies*, 4th European edn. Houghton Mifflin, New York.

Durlacher (2000) Trends in the UK new economy, *Durlacher Quarterly Internet Report*, November, 1–12.

E-consultancy (2005) Managing an E-commerce team. Integrating digital marketing into your organisation. 60-page report. Author: Dave Chaffey. Available from www.e-consultancy.com.

Forrester Research (2005) Press release: Forrester research US eCommerce Forecast: online retail sales to reach $329 billion by 2010. Cambridge, MA, 19 September.

Friedlein, A. (2002) *Maintaining and Evolving Successful Commercial Web Sites*. Morgan Kaufmann, San Francisco.

Friedman, L. and Furey, T. (1999) *The Channel Advantage*. Butterworth Heinemann, Oxford.

Gulati, R. and Garino, J. (2000) Getting the right mix of bricks and clicks for your company, *Harvard Business Review*, May–June, 107–14.

Hasan, H. and Tibbits, H. (2000) Strategic management of electronic commerce: an adaptation of the balanced scorecard, *Internet Research*, 10(5), 439–50.

Hitwise (2005) Press release: The top UK Grocery and Alcohol websites week ending October 1st, ranked by market share of web site visits, from Hitwise.co.uk. Press release available at **www.hitwise.co.uk**.

Humby, C. and Hunt, T. (2003) *Scoring points. How Tesco Is Winning Customer Loyalty*. Kogan Page, London.

Kalakota, R. and Robinson, M. (2000) *E-Business. Roadmap for Success*. Addison-Wesley, Reading, MA.

Kaplan, R.S. and Norton, D.P. (1993) Putting the balanced scorecard to work, *Harvard Business Review*, September–October, 134–42.

Kim, E., Nam, D. and Stimpert, D. (2004) The applicability of Porter's generic strategies in the digital age: assumptions, conjectures and suggestions, *Journal of Management*, 30(5).

Kumar, N. (1999) Internet distribution strategies: dilemmas for the incumbent, *Financial Times*, Special Issue on Mastering Information Management, no 7. Electronic Commerce (**www.ftmastering.com**).

Levy, M. and Powell, P. (2003) Exploring SME Internet adoption: towards a contingent model, *Electronic Markets*, 13 (2), 173–81. **www.electronicmarkets.org**.

Lynch, R. (2000) *Corporate Strategy*. Financial Times/Prentice Hall, Harlow.

McDonald, M. (2003) *Marketing Plans. How to Prepare them, how to Use them*, 5th edn. Butterworth Heinemann, Oxford.

McDonald, M. and Wilson, H. (2002) *New Marketing: Transforming the Corporate Future*. Butterworth Heinemann, Oxford.

McFarlan, F.W. (1984) Information technology changes the way you compete, *Harvard Business Review*, May–June, 54–61.

Mintzberg, H. and Quinn, J.B. (1991) *The Strategy Process*, 2nd edn. Prentice Hall, Upper Saddle River, NJ.

Myers, J., Pickersgill, A, and Van Metre, E. (2004) Steering customers to the right channels, *McKinsey Quarterly*, No. 4.

New Media Age (2005) Delivering the goods, *New Media Age*, Article by Nic Howell, 5 May.

Parsons, A., Zeisser, M. and Waitman, R. (1996) Organizing for digital marketing, *McKinsey Quarterly*, No. 4, 183–92.

Picardi, R. (2000) *EBusiness Speed: Six Strategies for ECommerce Intelligence*. IDC Research Report. IDC, Framlington, MA.

Poon, S. and Joseph, M. (2000) A preliminary study of product nature and electronic commerce, *Marketing Intelligence and Planning*, 19(7), 493–9.

Porter, M. (1980) *Competitive Strategy*. Free Press, New York.

Porter, M. (2001) Strategy and the Internet, *Harvard Business Review*, March, 62–78.

Quelch, J. and Klein, L. (1996) The Internet and international marketing, *Sloan Management Review*, Spring, 61–75.

Revolution (2005a) E-mail marketing report, by Justin Pugsley. *Revolution*, September, 58–60.

Revolution (2005b) Campaign of the month, by Emma Rigby, *Revolution*, October, p. 69.

Smith, P.R. and Chaffey, D. (2005) *EMarketing Excellence: at the Heart of EBusiness*, 2nd edn. Butterworth Heinemann, Oxford.

Thomas, J. and Sullivan, U. (2005) Managing marketing communications with multichannel customers, *Journal of Marketing*, 69 (October), 239–51.

Tjan, A. (2001) Finally, a way to put your Internet portfolio in order, *Harvard Business Review*, February, 78–85.

Varianini, V. and Vaturi, D. (2000) Marketing lessons from e-failures, *McKinsey Quarterly*, No. 4, 86–97.

Waterman, R.H., Peters, T.J. and Phillips, J.R. (1980) Structure is not organisation, *McKinsey Quarterly*, Summer, 2–21.

Wikipedia (2005). Tesco, *Wikipedia*, the free encyclopedia. **http://en.wikipedia.org/wiki/Tesco**.

Further reading

Brassington, F. and Petitt, S. (2000) *Principles of Marketing*, 2nd edn. Financial Times/Prentice Hall, Harlow. *See* companion Prentice Hall web site (**www.booksites.net/brassington2**). Chapters 10 and 11 describe pricing issues in much more detail than that given in this chapter. Chapters 20, Strategic management, and 21, Marketing planning, management and control, describe the integration of marketing strategy with business strategy.

Daniel, E., Wilson, H., McDonald, M. and Ward, J. (2001) *Marketing Strategy in the Digital Age*. Financial Times/Prentice Hall, Harlow. Clear guidelines on strategy development based on and including industry case studies.

Deise, M., Nowikow, C., King, P. and Wright, A. (2000) *Executive's Guide to E-Business*. From Tactics to Strategy. Wiley, New York. An excellent practitioners' guide.

Friedlein, A. (2002) *Maintaining and Evolving Successful Commercial Web Sites*. Morgan Kaufmann, San Francisco. An excellent book for professionals covering managing change, content, customer relationships and site measurement.

Ghosh, S. (1998) Making business sense of the Internet, *Harvard Business Review*, March–April, 127–35. This paper gives many examples of how US companies have adapted to the Internet and asks key questions that should govern the strategy adopted. It is an excellent introduction to strategic approaches.

Gulati, R. and Garino, J. (2000) Getting the right mix of bricks and clicks for your company, *Harvard Business Review*, May–June, 107–14. A different perspective on the six strategy decisions given in the strategic definition section with a roadmap through the decision process.

Hackbarth, G. and Kettinger, W. (2000) Building an e-business strategy, *Information Systems Management*, Summer, 78–93. An information systems perspective to e-business strategy.

Willcocks, L. and Sauer, C. (2000) Moving to e-business: an introduction. In L. Willcocks and C. Sauer (eds) *Moving to E-Business*, pp. 1–18. Random House, London. Combines traditional IS-strategy-based approaches with up-to-date case studies.

Web links

- **BRINT.com** (**www.brint.com**). A Business Researcher's Interests. Extensive portal with articles on e-business, e-commerce and knowledge management.

- **CIO Magazine E-commerce resource centre** (**www.cio.com/forums/ec**). One of the best online magazines from business technical perspective – see other research centres also, e.g. intranets, knowledge management.

- **DaveChaffey.com** (**www.davechaffey.com**). Updates about all aspects of digital marketing including strategy.

- **E-commerce innovation centre** (**www.ecommerce.ac.uk**) at Cardiff University. Interesting case studies for SMEs and basic explanations of concepts and terms.

- **E-commerce Times** (**www.ecommercetimes.com**). An online newspaper specific to e-commerce developments.

- **E-consultancy.com** (**www.e-consultancy.com**). A good compilation of reports and white papers many of which are strategy-related.

- **Financial Times Digital Business** (**http://news.ft.com/reports/digitalbusiness**). Excellent monthly articles based on case studies.

- **Mohansawney.com** (**www.mohansawney.com**). Case studies and white papers from one of the leading IS authorities on e-commerce.

- **US center for e-business** (**www.ebusiness.mit.edu**). Useful collection of articles.

5

The Internet and the marketing mix

Learning objectives

After reading this chapter, the reader should be able to:

● Apply the elements of the marketing mix in an online context

● Evaluate the opportunities that the Internet makes available for varying the marketing mix

● Define the characteristics of an online brand

Questions for marketers

Key questions for marketing managers related to this chapter are:

● How are the elements of the marketing mix varied online?

● What are the implications of the Internet for brand development?

● Can the product component of the mix be varied online?

● How are companies developing online pricing strategies?

● Does 'place' have relevance online?

Links to other chapters

This chapter is related to other chapters as follows:

➤ Chapter 2 introduces the impact of the Internet on market structure and distribution channels

➤ Chapter 4 describes how Internet marketing strategies can be developed

➤ Chapters 6 and 7 explain the service elements of the mix in more detail

➤ Chapter 8 explains the promotion elements of the mix in more detail

Introduction

Marketing mix

The series of seven key variables – Product, Price, Place, Promotion, People, Process and Physical evidence – that are varied by marketers as part of the customer offering.

Online branding

How online channels are used to support brands that, in essence, are the sum of the characteristics of a product or service as perceived by a user.

This chapter shows how the well-established strategic framework of the marketing mix can be applied by marketers to inform their Internet marketing strategy. It explores this key issue of Internet marketing strategy in more detail than was possible in Chapter 4. As well as the marketing mix, another major topic is covered in Chapter 5, online branding. As part of our discussion of product we will review how the Internet can be used to support and impact the way brands are developed.

The marketing mix – widely referred to as the 4 Ps of Product, Price, Place and Promotion – was originally proposed by Jerome McCarthy (1960) and is still used as an essential part of formulating and implementing marketing strategy by many practitioners. The 4 Ps have since been extended to the 7 Ps, which include three further elements that better reflect service delivery: People, Process and Physical evidence (Booms and Bitner, 1981), although others argue that these are subsumed within the 4 Ps. Figure 5.1 summarises the different sub-elements of the 7 Ps.

The marketing mix is applied frequently in discussion of marketing strategy since it provides a simple strategic framework for varying different elements of an organisation's product offering to influence the demand for products within target markets. For example, if the aim is to increase sales of a product, options include decreasing the price and changing the amount or type of promotion, or some combination of these elements.

E-commerce provides many new opportunities for the marketer to vary the marketing mix, as suggested by Figure 5.1 and Activity 5.1. E-commerce also has far-reaching implications for the relative importance of different elements of the mix for many markets regardless of whether an organisation is involved directly in e-commerce. Consequently, the marketing mix is a useful framework to inform strategy development. First, it gives a framework for comparing an organisation's existing services with competitors' in and out of sector as part of the benchmarking process described in Chapter 1. As well as a tool for benchmarking, it can also be used as a mechanism for generating alternative strategic approaches.

Given the potential implications of the Internet on the marketing mix, a whole chapter is devoted to examining its impact and strategies companies can develop to best manage this situation.

Using the Internet to vary the marketing mix						
Product	**Promotion**	**Price**	**Place**	**People**	**Process**	**Physical evidence**
• Quality	• Marketing communications	• Positioning	• Trade channels	• Individuals on marketing activities	• Customer focus	• Sales/staff contact experience of brand
• Image	• Personal promotion	• List	• Sales support	• Individuals on customer contact	• Business-led	• Product packaging
• Branding	• Sales promotion	• Discounts	• Channel number	• Recruitment	• IT-supported	• Online experience
• Features	• PR	• Credit	• Segmented channels	• Culture/ image	• Design features	
• Variants	• Branding	• Payment methods		• Training and skills	• Research and development	
• Mix	• Direct marketing	• Free or value-added elements		• Remuneration		
• Support						
• Customer service						
• Use occasion						
• Availability						
• Warranties						

Figure 5.1 The elements of the marketing mix

Activity 5.1	How can the Internet be used to vary the marketing mix?

Purpose

An introductory activity which highlights the vast number of areas which the Internet impacts.

Activity

Review Figure 5.1 and select the *two* most important ways in which the Internet gives new potential for varying the marketing mix *for each* of product, price, promotion, place, people and processes. State:

- new opportunities for varying the mix;
- examples of companies that have achieved this;
- possible negative implications (threats) for each opportunity.

The key issues related to different elements of the marketing mix that are discussed in this chapter are:

- *Product* – are there opportunities for modifying the core or extended product online?
- *Price* – the implications of the Internet for pricing and the adoption of new pricing models or strategies.
- *Place* – the implications for distribution.
- *Promotion* (what new promotional tools can be applied) – this is only discussed briefly in this chapter since it is described in more detail in Chapter 8.
- *People, process and physical evidence* – these are not discussed in detail in this chapter since their online application is covered in more detail in Chapters 6, 7 and 9 in connection with customer relationship management and managing and maintaining the online presence.

Before embarking on a review of the role of the Internet on each of the 7 Ps, it is worth briefly restating some of the well-known criticisms of applying the marketing mix as a solitary tool for marketing strategy. First and perhaps most importantly, the marketing mix, because of its origins in the 1960s, is symptomatic of a push approach to marketing and does not explicitly acknowledge the needs of customers. As a consequence, the marketing mix tends to lead to a product orientation rather than customer orientation – a key concept of market orientation and indeed a key Internet marketing concept (see Chapter 8, for example). To mitigate this effect, Lautenborn (1990) suggested the 4 Cs framework which considers the 4 Ps from a customer perspective. In brief, the 4 Cs are:

- customer needs and wants (from the product);
- cost to the customer (price);
- convenience (relative to place);
- communication (promotion).

This customer-centric approach also lends itself well online, since the customer is often in an active comparison mode rather than a passive media consumption mode.

It follows that the selection of the marketing mix is based on detailed knowledge of buyer behaviour collected through market research. Furthermore, it should be remembered that the mix is often adjusted according to different target markets or segments to better meet the needs of these customer groupings.

Although it is useful to apply existing frameworks to new channels, the emphasis of the importance of different parts of a framework may vary. As you read this chapter, you should consider which are the key elements of the mix which can be varied online for the different types of online presence introduced in Chapter 1, i.e. transactional e-commerce, relationship-building, brand-building and media owner portal. Allen and Fjermestad (2001) and Harridge-March (2004) have reviewed how the Internet has impacted the main elements of the marketing mix. There is no denying that all of the elements are still important, but Smith and Chaffey (2005) have said that, online, Partnerships is the eighth P since this is so important in achieving reach and affiliation. In this text, though, Partnerships will be considered as part of Place and Promotion.

Product

Product variable

The element of the marketing mix that involves researching customers' needs and developing appropriate products.

Core product

The fundamental features of the product that meet the user's needs.

Extended product

Additional features and benefits beyond the core product.

The product element of the marketing mix refers to characteristics of a product, service or brand. Product decisions are informed by market research where customers' needs are assessed and the feedback is used to modify existing products or develop new products. There are many alternatives for varying the product in the online context when a company is developing its online strategy. Internet-related product decisions can be usefully divided into decisions affecting the core product and the extended product. The core product refers to the main product purchased by the consumer to fulfil their needs, while the extended or augmented product refers to additional services and benefits that are built around the core of the product.

The main implications of the Internet for the product aspect of the mix, which we will review in this section, are:

1 options for varying the core product;
2 options for changing the extended product;
3 conducting research online;
4 velocity of new product development;
5 velocity of new product diffusion.

There is also a subsection which looks at the implications for migrating a brand online.

1 Options for varying the core product

For some companies, there may be options for new digital products which will typically be information products that can be delivered over the web. Ghosh (1998) talks about developing new products or adding 'digital value' to customers. The questions he posed still prove useful today:

1 *Can I offer additional information or transaction services to my existing customer base?* [For example, for a bookseller, providing reviews of customer books, previews of books or selling books online. For a travel company, providing video tours of resorts and accommodation.]
2 *Can I address the needs of new customer segments by repackaging my current information assets or by creating new business propositions using the Internet?* [For an online bookseller, creating an electronic book service, or a DVD rental service as has been achieved by Amazon.]
3 *Can I use my ability to attract customers to generate new sources of revenue such as advertising or sales of complementary products?* [Lastminute.com which sells travel-related services has a significant advertising revenue; it can also sell non-travel services.]
4 *Will my current business be significantly harmed by other companies providing some of the value I currently offer?* [Considers the consequences if other companies use some of the product strategies described above.]

Of course, the markets transformed most by the Internet are those where products themselves can be transformed into digital services. Such products include music (download or streaming of digital tracks – see the Napster case study at the end of the chapter), books (electronic books), newspaper and magazine publishing (online access to articles) and software (digital downloads and online subscription services).

Rayport and Sviokla (1994) describe transactions where the actual product has been replaced by information about the product, for example a company providing oil drilling equipment focusing instead on analysis and dissemination of information about drilling.

The Internet also introduces options for mass customisation of products. Levi's provide a truly personal service that dates back to 1994, when Levi Strauss initiated its 'Personal Pair' programme. Women who were prepared to pay up to $15 more than the standard price and wait for delivery could go to Levi's Stores and have themselves digitised – that is, have their measurements taken and a pair of custom jeans made and then have their measurements stored on a database for future purchases.

The programme achieved a repeat purchase rate significantly higher than the usual 10–12 per cent rate, and by 1997 accounted for a quarter of women's jeans sales at Levi's Stores. In 1998 the programme was expanded to include men's jeans and the number of styles for each was doubled – to 1500 styles. This service has now migrated to the web and is branded as Original Spin.

Mass customisation or personalisation of products in which a customer takes a more active role in product design is part of the move to the prosumer. An example is provided in Figure 5.2. Further details are given in the box.

Mass customisation

Using economies of scale enabled by technology to offer tailored versions of products to individual customers or groups of customers.

Prosumer

'Producer + consumer'. The customer is closely involved in specifying their requirements in a product.

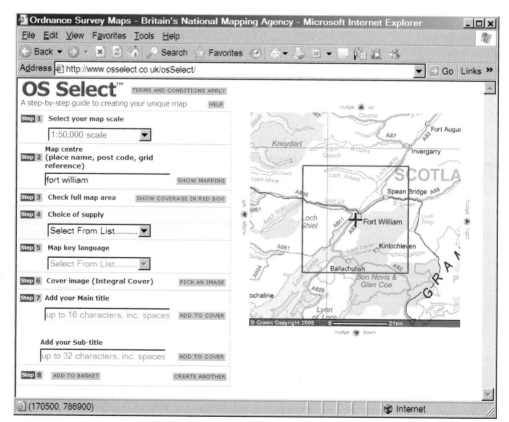

Figure 5.2 Customising maps according to customers' preferences

Source: Ordnance Survey OS Select (www.osselect.co.uk)

The prosumer

The prosumer concept was introduced in 1980 by futurist Alvin Toffler in his book *The Third Wave*. According to Toffler, the future would once again combine production with consumption. In *The Third Wave*, Toffler saw a world where interconnected users would collaboratively 'create' products. Note that he foresaw this over 10 years before the web was invented!

Alternative notions of the prosumer, all of which are applicable to e-marketing, are catalogued at Logophilia WordSpy (**www.wordspy.com**):

1 A consumer who is an amateur in a particular field, but who is knowledgeable enough to require equipment that has some professional features:
('**professional**' + '**consumer**').
2 A person who helps to design or customise the products they purchase:
('**producer**' + '**consumer**').
3 A person who creates goods for their own use and also possibly to sell:
('**producing**' + '**consumer**').
4 A person who takes steps to correct difficulties with consumer companies or markets and to anticipate future problems:
('**proactive**' + '**consumer**').

An example of the application of the prosumer is provided by BMW who used an interactive web site prior to launch of their Z3 roadster where users could design their own preferred features. The information collected was linked to a database and as BMW had previously collected data on its most loyal customers, the database could give a very accurate indication of which combinations of features were the most sought after and should therefore be put into production.

Companies can also consider how the Internet can be used to change the range or combination of products offered. Some companies only offer a subset of products online – for example, WH Smith launched an interactive TV service which offered bestsellers only at a discount. Alternatively, a company may have a fuller catalogue available online than is available through offline brochures. **Bundling** is a further alternative. For example, easyJet has developed a range of complementary travel-related services including flights, packages and car hire. McDonald and Wilson (2002) note how the potential for substituted or reconfigured products should be assessed for each marketplace.

Bundling
Offering complementary services.

Finally, it should also be noted that information about the core features of the product becomes more readily available online, as pointed out by Allen and Fjermestad (2001). However, this has the greatest implications for price (downwards pressure caused by price transparency) and place and promotion (marketers must ensure they are represented favourably on the portal intermediaries) where the products will be compared with others in terms of core features, extended features and price.

2 Options for changing the extended product

When a customer buys a new computer, it consists not only of the tangible computer, monitor and cables, but also the information provided by the computer salesperson, the instruction manual, the packaging, the warranty and the follow-up technical service. These are elements of the extended product. Smith and Chaffey (2005) suggest these examples of how the Internet can be used to vary the extended product:

- endorsements
- awards
- testimonies

- customer lists
- customer comments
- warranties
- guarantees
- money-back offers
- customer service (see people, process and physical evidence)
- incorporating tools to help users during their selection and use of the product.

Figure 5.3 shows a site developed by Fisher-Price, which rather than just being a toy catalogue, instead shows how children develop through play and how their carers can assist in this.

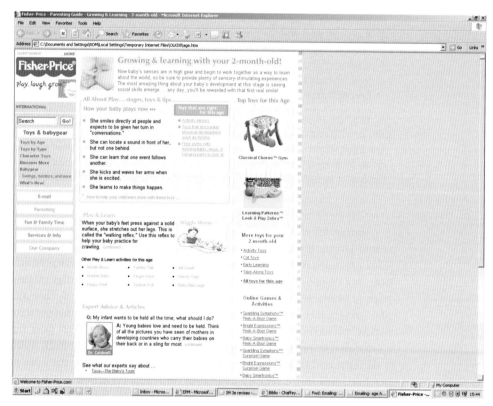

Figure 5.3 Play Laugh Grow (www.fisher-price.com/uk/myfp/age.asp?age=2month) child development resource site from Fisher-Price

The digital value referred to by Ghosh (1998) will often be free, in which case it will be part of the extended product. He suggests that companies should provide free digital value to help build an audience which can then be converted into customers. He refers to this process as 'building a customer magnet'; today this would be known as a 'portal' or 'community'. There is good potential for customer magnets in specialised vertical markets served by business-to-business companies where there is a need for industry-specific information to assist individuals in their day-to-day work. For example, a customer magnet could be developed for the construction industry, agrochemicals, biotechnology or independent financial advisers. Examples include resource centres at Siebel (**www.siebel.com**) and DoubleClick (**www.doubleclick.com**). Alternatively the portal could be branded as an 'extranet' that is only available to key accounts to help differentiate the service. Dell Premier is an example of such an extranet.

Extended product is not necessarily provided free of charge. In other cases a premium may be charged. Amazon (www.amazon.com), for instance, charges for its wrapping service.

3 Conducting research online

The Internet provides many options for learning about products. It can be used as a relatively low-cost method of collecting marketing research, particularly about customer perceptions of products and services. Typically these will complement rather than replace offline research. Options include:

- *Online focus group.* A moderated focus group can be conducted to compare customers' experience of product use.
- *Online questionnaire survey.* These typically focus on the site visitors' experience, but can also include questions relating to products.
- *Customer feedback or support forums.* Comments posted to the site or independent sites may give information on future product innovation.
- *Web logs.* A wealth of marketing research information is also available from the web site itself, since every time a user clicks on a link this is recorded in a transaction log file summarising what information on the site the customer is interested in. Such information can be used to indirectly assess customers' product preferences.

Approaches for undertaking these types of research are briefly reviewed in Chapter 9.

4 Velocity of new product development

Quelch and Klein (1996) note that the Internet can also be used to accelerate new product development since different product options can be tested online more rapidly as part of market research. Companies can use their own panels of consumers to test opinion more rapidly and often at lower costs than for traditional market research. In Chapter 1, Figure 1.7, we saw how the Dubit Informer is used by brands to research the opinions of the youth market.

Another aspect of the velocity of new product development is that the network effect of the Internet enables companies to form partnerships more readily to launch new products. The subsection on virtual organisations in the section on 'Place' below discusses this in a little more detail.

5 Velocity of new product diffusion

Quelch and Klein (1996) also noted that the implication of the Internet and concomitant globalisation is that to remain competitive, organisations will have to roll out new products more rapidly to international markets. More recently, Malcolm Gladwell in his book *The Tipping Point* (2000) has shown how word-of-mouth communication has a tremendous impact on the rate of adoption of new products and we can suggest this effect is often enhanced or facilitated through the Internet. In Chapter 8, we will see how marketers seek to influence this effect through what is known as 'viral marketing'. Marsden (2004) provides a good summary of the implications of the tipping point for marketers. He says that 'using the science of social epidemics, *The Tipping Point* explains the three simple principles that underpin the rapid spread of ideas, products and behaviours through a population'. He advises how marketers should help create a 'tipping point' for a new product or service, the moment when a domino effect is triggered and an epidemic of demand sweeps through a population like a highly contagious virus.

There are three main laws that are relevant from *The Tipping Point*:

Tipping point
Using the science of social epidemics explains principles that underpin the rapid spread of ideas, products and behaviours through a population.

221

1 The law of the few

This suggests that the spread of any new product or service is dependent on the initial adoption by 'connectors' who are socially connected and who encourage adoption through word-of-mouth and copycat behaviour. In an online context, these connectors may use personal blogs, e-mail newsletters and podcasts to propagate their opinions.

2 The stickiness factor

Typically, this refers to how 'glued' we are to a medium such as a TV channel or a web site, but in this context it refers to attachment to the characteristics and attributes of a product or a brand. Gladwell stresses the importance of testing and market research to make the product effective. Marsden suggests that there are key cross-category attributes which are key drivers for product success and he commends the work of Morris and Martin (2000) which summarises these attributes as:

- *Excellence*: perceived as best of breed
- *Uniqueness*: clear one-of-a-kind differentiation
- *Aesthetics*: perceived aesthetic appeal
- *Association*: generates positive associations
- *Engagement*: fosters emotional involvement
- *Expressive value*: visible sign of user values
- *Functional value*: addresses functional needs
- *Nostalgic value*: evokes sentimental linkages
- *Personification*: has character, personality
- *Cost*: perceived value for money.

Incidentally, you can see that this list is also a useful prompt about the ideal characteristics of a web site or online service.

3 The power of context

Gladwell suggests that like infectious diseases, products and behaviours spread far and wide only when they fit the physical, social and mental context into which they are launched. He gives the example of a wave of crime in the New York subway that came to an abrupt halt by simply removing the graffiti from trains and clamping down on fare-dodging. It can be suggested that products should be devised and tested to fit their context, situation or occasion of use.

Activity 5.2 | **Assessing options online to vary product using the Internet**

Purpose

To illustrate the options for varying the product element of the marketing mix online.

visit the w.w.w.

Activity

Select one of the sectors below. Use a search engine to find three competitors with similar product offerings. List ways in which each has used the Internet to vary its core and extended product. Which of the companies do you think makes best use of the Internet?

- Computer manufacturers
- Management consultants
- Children's toy sector
- Higher education.

The long tail concept

The long tail concept

A frequency distribution suggesting the relative variation in popularity of items selected by consumers.

The long tail concept is useful for considering the role of Product, Place, Price and Promotion online. The phenomenon now referred to as the 'long tail', following an article by Anderson (2004), was arguably first applied to human behaviour by George Kingsley Zipf, professor of linguistics at Harvard who observed the phenomenon in word usage (see **http://en.wikipedia.org/wiki/Zipf%27s_law**). He found that if the variation in popularity of different words in a language is considered, there is a systematic pattern in the frequency of usage or popularity. Zipf's 'law' suggests that if a collection of items is ordered or ranked by popularity, the second item will have around half the popularity of the first one and the third item will have about a third of the popularity of the first one and so on. In general:

The kth item is 1/k the popularity of the first.

Look at Figure 5.4 which shows how the 'relative popularity' of items is predicted to decline according to Zipf's law from a maximum count of 1000 for the most popular item to 20 for the 50th item.

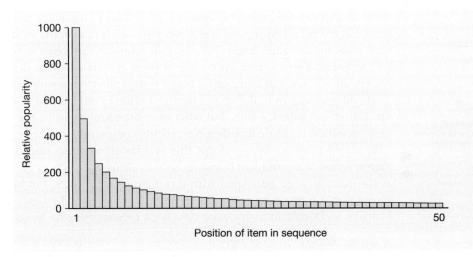

Figure 5.4 Zipf's law, showing decrease in popularity of items within an ordered sequence

In an online context, application of this 'law' is now known as 'the long tail' thanks to Anderson (2004). It can be applied to the relatively popularity of a group of web sites or web pages or products on an individual site, since they tend to show a similar pattern of popularity. There are a small number of sites (or pages within sites) which are very popular (the head which may account for 80% of the volume) and a much larger number of sites or pages that are less popular individually, but still collectively important. Returning to the product context, Anderson (2004) argued that for a company such as Amazon, the long tail or Zipf's law can be applied to describe the variation in preferences for selecting or purchasing from a choice for products as varied as books, CDs, electronic items, travel or financial services. This pattern has also been identified by Brynjolfsson et al. (2003) who present a framework that quantifies the economic impact of increased product variety made available through electronic markets. They say:

One reason for increased product variety on the Internet is the ability of online retailers to catalog, recommend, and provide a large number of products for sale. For example, the number of book titles available at Amazon.com is more than 23 times larger than the number of books on the shelves of a typical Barnes & Noble superstore, and 57 times greater than the number of books stocked in a typical large independent bookstore.

Looking at the issue from another perspective, they estimate that 40% of sales are from relatively obscure books with a sales rank of more than 100,000 (if you visit Amazon, you will see that every book has a sales rank from 1 for the most popular to over 1 million for the least popular). This indicates the importance of the long tail for online retailers like Amazon, since 40% of sales are from these less popular books which cannot be stocked in a conventional bookstore (a large real-world book store would typically hold 100,000 books). In a Pricing context, another benefit for online retailers is that less popular products cannot be readily obtained in the real world, so Amazon can justify higher prices for these books. Brynjolfsson et al. (2003) estimated that average Amazon prices for an item in the top 100,000 is $29.26 and in less popular titles $41.60.

The Internet and branding

What constitutes a successful online brand? Is it an e-commerce site with high levels of traffic? Is it a brand with good name recognition? Is it a profitable brand? Or is it a site with more modest sales levels, but one that customers perceive as providing good service? Although sites meeting only some of these criteria are often described as successful brands, we will see that a successful brand is dependent on a wide range of factors.

The importance of building an effective online brand is often referred to when start-ups launch e-commerce sites, but what does branding mean in the online context and how important is online branding for existing companies?

Branding seems to be a concept that is difficult to grasp since it is often used in a narrow sense. Many think of branding only in terms of aspects of the brand identity such as the name or logo associated with a company or products, but branding gurus seem agreed that it is much more than that. A brand is described by Leslie de Chernatony and Malcolm McDonald in their classic 1992 book *Creating Powerful Brands* as

an identifiable product or service augmented in such a way that the buyer or user perceives relevant unique added values which match their needs most closely. Furthermore, its success results from being able to sustain these added values in the face of competition.

This definition highlights three essential characteristics of a successful brand:

- brand is dependent on customer perception;
- perception is influenced by the added-value characteristics of the product;
- the added-value characteristics need to be sustainable.

To summarise, a brand is dependent on a customer's psychological affinity for a product, and is much more than physical name or symbol elements of brand identity.

De Chernatony (2001) has evaluated the relevance of the brand concept on the Internet. He also believes that the main elements of brand values and brand strategy are the same in the Internet environment. However, he suggests that the classical branding model of the Internet where consumers are passive recipients of value is challenged online. Instead he suggests that consumers on the Internet become active co-producers of value where consumers can contribute feedback through discussion groups to add value to a brand. De Chernatony argues for a looser form of brand control where the company facilitates rather than controls customer discussion.

Branding

The process of creating and evolving successful brands.

Brand

The sum of the characteristics of a product or service perceived by a user.

A further method by which the Internet can change branding that was suggested by Jevons and Gabbott (2000) is that online, 'the first-hand experience of the brand is a more powerful token of trust than the perception of the brand'. In the online environment, the customer can experience or interact with the brand more frequently and to a greater depth. As Dayal et al. (2000) say, 'on the world wide web, the brand is the experience and the experience is the brand'. They suggest that to build successful online brands, organisations should consider how their proposition can build on these possible brand promises:

Brand experience
The frequency and depth of interactions with a brand can be enhanced through the Internet.

- *the promise of convenience* – making a purchase experience more convenient than the real-world one, or that with rivals;
- *the promise of achievement* – to assist consumers in achieving their goals, for example supporting online investors in their decision or supporting business people in their day-to-day work;
- *the promise of fun and adventure* – this is clearly more relevant for B2C services;
- *the promise of self-expression and recognition* – provided by personalisation services such as Yahoo! Geocities where consumers can build their own web site;
- *the promise of belonging* – provided by online communities.

Summarising the elements of online branding, de Chernatony (2001) suggests successful online branding requires delivering three aspects of a brand: rational values, emotional values and promised experience (based on rational and emotional values). We return to the notion of brand promise at the start of Chapter 7 since this is closely related to delivering customer experience.

An alternative perspective on branding is provided by Aaker and Joachimsthaler (2000) who refer to brand equity, which they define as:

a set of brand assets and liabilities linked to a brand, its name and symbol, that add to or subtract from the value provided by a product or service to a firm and/or to that firm's customers.

Brand equity
The assets (or liabilities) linked to a brand's name and symbol that add to (or subtract from) a service.

So, brand equity indicates the value provided to a company, or its customers through a brand. Assessing brand equity on the web needs to address the unique characteristics of computer-mediated environments as Christodoulides and de Chernatony (2004) have pointed out. These researchers set out to explore whether additional measures of brand equity were required online. Based on expert interviews they have identified the additional measures of brand equity which are important online, as summarised in Table 5.1. As we would expect, this includes attributes of the digital medium such as interactivity and customisation which combine to form relevance and a great online brand experience. Content is not stressed separately, which is surprising, although they do mention its importance under site design and it is also a key aspect of other attributes such as customisation, relevance and the overall experience.

Table 5.1 Traditional measures of brand equity and online measures of brand equity

Traditional measures of brand equity (Aaker and Joachimsthaler, 2000)	Online measures of brand equity (from Christodoulides and de Chernatony, 2004)
• Price premium	• Online brand experience
• Satisfaction/loyalty	• Interactivity
• Perceived quality	• Customisation
• Leadership popularity	• Relevance
• Perceived value	• Site design
• Brand personality	• Customer service
• Organisational associations	• Order fulfilment
• Brand awareness	• Quality of brand relationships
• Market share	• Communities
• Market price and distribution coverage	• Web site logs (see Chapter 9)

Brand identity

Aaker and Joachimsthaler (2000) also emphasise the importance of developing a plan to communicate the key features of the brand identity and increase brand awareness. Brand identity is again more than the name. These authors refer to it as a set of brand associations that imply a promise to customers from an organisation. See Mini Case Study 5.1 to see the different elements of brand identity which are effectively a checklist of what many e-tailers are looking to achieve.

Brand identity

The totality of brand associations including name and symbols that must be communicated.

Mini Case Study 5.1   Napster.com's brand identity

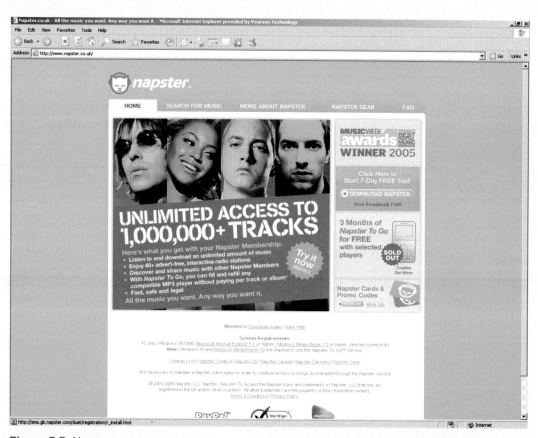

Figure 5.5 Napster.com

Aaker and Joachimsthaler (2000) suggest that the following characteristics of identity need to be defined at the start of a brand building campaign. Marketing communications can then be developed that create and reinforce this identity. Here, we will apply them to Napster which is revisited in the main case study at the end of this chapter.

- *Brand essence (a summary of what the brand represents)*
  This is not necessarily a tag line, but for Napster it has been described as an 'All you can eat music service which is fun and affordable'

- *Core identity (its key features)*
  - choice – millions of tracks
  - value for money – under £10 per month subscription for as many tracks as you can listen to
  - easy-to-use – Napster runs as a separate application built for purpose
  - listen anywhere – on a PC or other computer, MP3 player or mobile phone
  - listen on anything – unlike iPod, Napster is compatible with most MP3 players rather than being tied into a specific hardware manufacturer
- *Extended identity*
  - personality – flaunts what is standard for existing music providers thanks to its heritage as a peer-to-peer file-sharing service
  - personalisation – Napster Radio based on particular genres or based on other songs you have downloaded
  - community – facility to share tracks with friends or other Napster members
  - symbols – Napster cat logo
- *Value proposition*
  - functional benefits – ease of use and personalisation
  - emotional benefits – community, non-conformist
  - self-expressive benefit – build your own collection of your tastes
- *Relationship*

Options for changing brand identity online

A further decision for marketing managers is whether to redefine the name element of brand identity and how to vary associated positioning messages to support the move online. Brands that were newly created for the Internet such as Expedia.com and Zopa.com do not risk damaging existing brands. Existing organisations need to think about how they differentiate their online services, and changing the brand identity is part of that. There are four main options for existing organisations migrating their brands online. When a company launches or relaunches an online presence, it has the following choices with regards to brand identity:

1 Transfer traditional brand online

This is probably the most common approach. Companies with brands that are well established in the real world can build on the brand by duplicating it online. Sites from companies such as Ford, Argos and Guinness (Figure 5.6) all have consistent brand identities and values that would be expected from experience of their offline brands. The Guinness site has additional brand messages to explain the online value proposition including online merchandise sales. Increasingly, companies will also replicate their offline branding campaigns online. Mobile operator Orange has achieved this since the first edition of this book and others such as Ford have become adept at doing it, but this unified messaging across channels is often not achieved by many companies, due to the organisational and technical challenges of integrating messages into the web site. The only risk of migrating existing brands online is that the brand equity may be reduced if the site is of poor quality in terms of performance, structure or information content. There may also be a missed opportunity to use the online channel to add to the experience of the brand, as explained below.

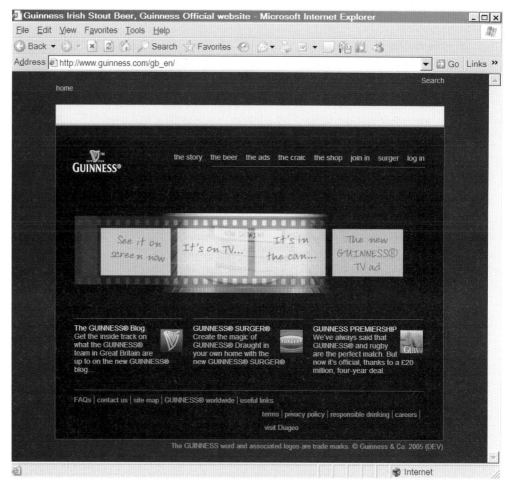

Figure 5.6 Guinness brand site (www.guinness.com)

2 Extend traditional brand: variant

Some companies decide to create a slightly different version of their brand when they create their web site. An early version of the DHL couriers site (**www.dhl.co.uk**) was based on an online brand 'Red Planet' which was part of a spaceship concept. Through using this approach, the company was able to differentiate itself from similar competing services and this can be used in online and offline promotion to distinguish the site from its rivals. BA used a similar approach with its 2005 'Have You Clicked Yet?' campaign, which sought to showcase arranging a flight and checking in online. The use of an online brand variant helps raise the profile of the web site and helps the customer think of the site in association with the company. Aaker and Joachimsthaler (2000) suggest that when a brand variant is created there may still be problems with recognition and also brand trust and quality associations may be damaged.

3 Partner with existing digital brand

It may be that a company can best promote its products in association with a strong existing digital or Internet brand such as Yahoo! or MSN. For example, the shopping options for record and book sales on Freeserve are branded as Freeserve although they are actually based on sites from other companies such as record seller Audiostreet.com. Freeserve is given brand prominence since this is to the advantage of both companies.

4 Create a new digital brand

It may be necessary to create an entirely new digital brand if the existing offline brand has negative connotations or is too traditional for the new medium. An example of an entirely new digital brand was the Egg banking service which is part of Prudential, a well-established company. Egg can take new approaches without damaging Prudential's brand, and at the same time not be inhibited by the Prudential brand. Egg is not an entirely online brand since it is primarily accessed by phone. Egg now encourages some of its million-plus customers to perform all their transactions online. Another example of a new digital brand was the Go portal which was created by Disney, who desired to be able to 'own' some of the many online customers who are loyal to one portal. It was felt they could achieve this best through using a completely new brand. The Disney brand might be thought to appeal to a limited younger audience. However, the new brand was not sufficiently powerful to compete with the existing Yahoo! brand and has now failed.

Some of the characteristics of a successful brand name are suggested by de Chernatony and McDonald (1992): ideally it should be simple, distinctive, meaningful and compatible with the product. These principles can be readily applied to web-based brands. Examples of brands that fulfil most of these characteristics are CDNow, CarPoint, BUY.COM and e-STEEL. Others suggest that distinctiveness is most important: Amazon, Yahoo!, Expedia, Quokka.com (extreme sports), E*Trade, and FireandWater (HarperCollins) books.

Ries and Ries (2000) suggest two rules for naming brands. (a) The Law of the Common Name – they say 'The kiss of death for an Internet brand is a common name'. This argues that common names such as Art.com or Advertising.com are poor since they are not sufficiently distinctive. (b) The Law of the Proper Name – they say 'Your name stands alone on the Internet, so you'd better have a good one'. This suggests that proper names are to be preferred to generic names, e.g. Handbag.com against Woman.com or Moreover.com against Business.com. The authors suggest that the best names will follow most of these eight principles: (1) short, (2) simple, (3) suggestive of the category, (4) unique, (5) alliterative, (6) speakable, (7) shocking and (8) personalised. Although these are cast as 'immutable laws' there will of course be exceptions!

The importance of brand online

The Internet presents a 'double-edged sword' to existing brands. We have seen that a consumer who already has knowledge of a brand is more likely to trust it. However, loyalty can be decreased because it encourages consumers to trial other brands. This is suggested by Figure 5.7. This trial may well lead to purchase of brands that have not been previously considered.

The BrandNewWorld (2004) survey showed that in some categories, a large proportion of buyers have purchased different brands from those they initially considered for example:

- Large home appliances, 47%
- Financial products and services, 39%
- Holidays and travel, 31%
- Mobile phones, 28%
- Cars, 26%.

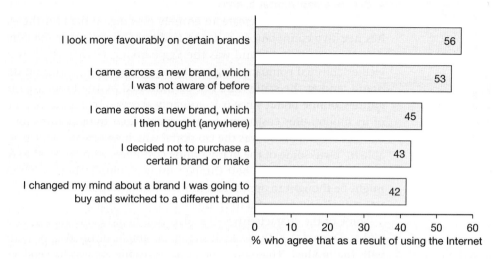

Figure 5.7 Changes to brand perception and behaviour as a result of using the Internet for research

Source: BrandNewWorld (2004)

But, for other types of products, existing brand preferences appear to be more important:

● Clothing/accessories, 22%
● Computer hardware, 21%
● Garden/DIY products, 17%
● Home furnishings, 6%.

The survey also suggested that experienced Internet users were more likely to switch brands (52% agreed they were more likely to switch after researching online) compared to less-experienced users (33%).

Of course, the likelihood of a consumer purchasing will depend upon their knowledge of the retailer brand or the product brand. Figure 5.8 shows that many customers will still buy an unknown manufacturer brand if they are familiar with the retailer brand. This is less true if they don't know the retailer. Significantly, if they don't know the retailer or the brand, it is fairly unlikely they will buy.

When buying online, I will buy a product if...

I am familiar with the *retailer*	Yes	Yes	No	No
I am familiar with the *product brand*	Yes	No	Yes	No
	90%	82%	54%	13%

Figure 5.8 The influence of brand knowledge on purchase. Matrix for question 'I will buy a product if ...'

Source: BrandNewWorld (2004)

Price

Price variable

The element of the marketing mix that involves defining product prices and pricing models.

Pricing models

Describe the form of payment such as outright purchase, auction, rental, volume purchases and credit terms.

The price variable of the marketing mix refers to an organisation's pricing policies which are used to define pricing models and, of course, to set prices for products and services. The Internet has dramatic implications for pricing in many sectors and there is a lot of literature in this area. Baker et al. (2000) noted two approaches that have been commonly adopted for pricing on the Internet: start-up companies have tended to use low prices to gain a customer base, while many existing companies have transferred their existing prices to the web. Other existing companies have used differential pricing with lower prices for some of their products online. This has been the approach followed by online electrical retailers such as Comet (**www.comet.co.uk**). The Pricing element mix will often relate to the Product element since online pricing depends on the range of products offered. Extending the product range may allow these products to be discounted online. Some organisations have launched new products online which have a lower Price element, for example banks have launched 'eSavings' products where higher interest rates are offered to online customers. Often these agreements are dependent on the customer servicing their account online, which helps reduce the cost-base of the bank. This then relates to the service elements of the mix since service has to be delivered online. Although much of the discussion in this chapter refers to reducing prices online, it should be remembered that offering very low prices implies reducing the level of customer service available. While this may be acceptable for managing a bank account it may not be acceptable for customers of a retailer who have poor support and a bad experience may stop them using the service again. Remember that Amazon, one of the most successful online companies, established its brand through being known for its range of products and quality of service rather than having the lowest prices.

The main implications of the Internet for the price aspect of the mix, which we will review in this section, are:

1 increased price transparency and its implications on differential pricing;
2 downward pressure on price (including commoditisation);
3 new pricing approaches (including dynamic pricing and auctions);
4 alternative pricing structure or policies.

Price transparency

Customer knowledge about pricing increases due to increased availability of pricing information.

Differential pricing

Identical products are priced differently for different types of customers, markets or buying situations.

Price elasticity of demand

Measure of consumer behaviour that indicates the change in demand for a product or service in response to changes in price.

1 Increased price transparency

Quelch and Klein (1996) describe two contradictory effects of the Internet on price that are related to price transparency. First, a supplier can use the technology for differential pricing, for example, for customers in different countries. However, if precautions are not taken about price, the customers may be able to quickly find out about the price discrimination and they will object to it.

Pricing online has to take into account the concept of price elasticity of demand. This is a measure of consumer behaviour based on economic theory that indicates the change in demand for a product or service in response to changes in price. Price elasticity of demand is determined by the price of the product, availability of alternative goods from alternative suppliers and consumer income. A product is said to be 'elastic' (or responsive to price changes) if a small change in price increases or reduces the demand substantially. A product is 'inelastic' if a large change in price is accompanied by a small amount of change in demand.

Although, intuitively, we would think that price transparency enabled through the Internet price comparison services such as Pricerunner (Figure 5.9) would lead to common comparisons of price and the selection of the cheapest product, the reality seems different. Pricing online is relatively inelastic. There are two main reasons for this, first, pricing is only one variable – consumers also decide on suppliers according to other aspects about the brand such as familiarity, trust and perceived service levels. Secondly, consumers often display satisficing behaviour. The term 'satisfice' was coined by Herbert Simon in 1957 when he said that people are only 'rational enough' and that they suspend or relax their rationality if they feel it is no longer required. This is called 'bounded rationality' by cognitive psychologists. In other words, although consumers may seek to minimise some variable (such as price) when making a product or supplier selection, most may not try too hard. Online, this is supported by research by Johnson et al. (2004) who showed that by analysing panel data from over 10,000 Internet households and three commodity-like products (books, compact discs (CDs) and air travel services) the amount of online search is actually quite limited. On average, households visit only 1.2 book sites, 1.3 CD sites and 1.8 travel sites during a typical active month in each category. Of course, these averages will reflect a range of behaviour. This is consistent with earlier research quoted by Marn (2000) which suggested that only around 8% of active online consumers are 'aggressive price shoppers'. Furthermore, he notes that Internet price bands have remained broad. Online booksellers' prices varied by an average of 33% and those of CD sellers by 25%.

One strategy for companies in the face of increased price transparency is to highlight the other features of the brand, to reduce the emphasis on cost as a differentiator. In October 2000, *Revolution* magazine reported a dispute between Abbey National and financial comparison site Moneysupermarket.com (**www.moneysupermarket.com**). The bank had reportedly requested that several comparison sites including Moneysupermarket not list them and a legal dispute ensued.

For business commodities, auctions on business-to-business exchanges can also have a similar effect of driving down price. Purchase of some products that have not traditionally been thought of as commodities may become more price-sensitive. This process is known as commoditisation. Examples of goods that are becoming commoditised include electrical goods and cars.

Satisficing behaviour
Consumers do not behave entirely rationally in product or supplier selection. They will compare alternatives, but then may make their choice given imperfect information.

Commoditisation
The process whereby product selection becomes more dependent on price than on differentiating features, benefits and value-added services.

Activity 5.3 · Assessing price ranges on the Internet

visit the w.w.w.

Purpose

To illustrate the concept of price transparency.

Activity

Visit a price comparison site such as Kelkoo (**www.kelkoo.com**) or Pricerunner (**www.pricerunner.com**). Choose one of the products below and write down the range of prices from lowest to highest. What is the percentage premium charged for a product by the most expensive company?

- Low-involvement purchase – CD or book.
- Higher-involvement purchase – household appliance.

Figure 5.9 Pricerunner (www.pricerunner.com)

2 Downward pressure on price

Price transparency is one reason for downward pressure on price. The Internet also tends to drive down prices since Internet-only retailers which do not have a physical presence do not have the overhead of operating stores and a retailer distribution network. This means that online companies can offer lower prices than offline rivals. This phenomenon is marked in the banking sector where many banks have set up online companies offering better rates of interest on savings products.

A further reason for downward pressure on price is that companies looking to compete online may discount online prices. For example, easyJet discounted online prices in an effort to meet its growth objectives of online revenue contribution. Such discounts are possible since there is a lower overhead of processing a customer transaction online than for phone transactions. Note that there may be a danger in channel conflicts resulting from this approach.

Similarly, to acquire customers, online booksellers may decide to offer a discount of 50% on the top 25 best-selling books in each category, for which no profit is made, but offer a smaller discount on less popular books to give a profit margin.

Diamantopoulos and Matthews (1993) suggest there are two aspects of competition that affect an organisation's pricing. The first is the structure of the market – the greater the number of competitors and the visibility of their prices the nearer the market is to being a perfect market. The implication of a perfect market is that an organisation will be less able to control prices, but must respond to competitors' pricing strategies. It is clear that since the Internet is a global phenomenon and, as we have seen, it facilitates

Perfect market

An efficient market where there are an infinite number of suppliers and buyers and complete price transparency.

233

price transparency, it does lead to a move towards a perfect market. The second is the perceived value of the product. If a brand is differentiated in some way, it may be less subject to downward pressure on price. As well as making pricing more transparent, the Internet does lead to opportunities to differentiate in information describing products or through added-value services. Whatever the relative importance of these factors in influencing purchase decisions, it seems clear that the Internet will lead to more competition-based pricing.

Baker et al. (2000) suggest that companies should use the following three factors to assist in pricing.

1 *Precision.* Each product has a price-indifference band, where varying price has little or no impact on sales. Baker et al. (2000) report that these bands can be as wide as 17% for branded consumer beauty products, 10% for engineered industrial components, but less than 10% for some financial products. The authors suggest that while the cost of undertaking a survey to calculate price indifference is very expensive in the real world, it is more effective online. They give the example of Zilliant, a software supplier that, in a price discovery exercise, reduced prices on four products by 7%. While this increased volumes of three of those by 5–20%, this was not sufficient to warrant the lower prices. However, for the fourth product, sales increased by 100%. It was found that this was occurring through sales to the educational sector, so this price reduction was just introduced for customers in that sector.

2 *Adaptablity.* This refers simply to the fact that it is possible to respond more quickly to the demands of the marketplace with online pricing. For some product areas such as ticketing it may be possible to dynamically alter prices in line with demand. Tickets.com adjusts concert ticket prices according to demand and has been able to achieve 45% more revenue per event as a result. The authors suggest that in this case and for other sought-after items such as video games or luxury cars, the Internet can actually increase the price since there it is possible to reach more people.

3 *Segmentation.* This refers to pricing differently for different groups of customers. This has not traditionally been practical for B2C markets since at the point of sale, information is not known about the customer, although it is widely practised for B2B markets. One example of pricing by segments would be for a car manufacturer to vary promotional pricing, so that rather than offering every purchaser discount purchasing or cash-back, it is only offered to those for whom it is thought necessary to make the sale. A further example is where a company can identify regular customers and fill-in customers who only buy from the supplier when their needs can't be met elsewhere. In the latter case, up to 20% higher prices are levied.

What then are the options available to marketers given this downward pressure on pricing? We will start by looking at traditional methods for pricing and how they are affected by the Internet. Bickerton et al. (2000) identify a range of options that are available for setting pricing.

1 *Cost-plus pricing.* This involves adding on a profit margin based on production costs. As we have seen above, a reduction in this margin may be required in the Internet era.

2 *Target-profit pricing.* This is a more sophisticated pricing method that involves looking at the fixed and variable costs in relation to income for different sales volumes and unit prices. Using this method the breakeven amount for different combinations can be calculated. For e-commerce sales the variable selling cost, i.e the cost for each transaction, is small. This means that once breakeven is achieved each sale has a large margin. With this model differential pricing is often used in a B2B context according to the volume of goods sold. Care needs to be taken that differential prices are not

evident to different customers. One company, through an error on their web site, made prices for different customers available for all to see, with disastrous results.

3 *Competition-based pricing.* This approach is common online. The advent of price-comparison engines such as Kelkoo (**www.kelkoo.com**) for B2C consumables has increased price competition and companies need to develop online pricing strategies that are flexible enough to compete in the marketplace, but are still sufficient to achieve profitability in the channel. This approach may be used for the most popular products, e.g. the Top 25 CDs, but other methods such as target-profit pricing used for other products.

4 *Market-oriented pricing.* Here the response to price changes by customers making up the market are considered. This is known as 'the elasticity of demand'. There are two approaches. *Premium pricing* (or *skimming the market*) involves setting a higher price than the competition to reflect the positioning of the product as a high-quality item. *Penetration pricing* is when a price is set below the competitors' prices to either stimulate demand or increase penetration. This approach was commonly used by dot-com companies to acquire customers. The difficulty with this approach is that if customers are price-sensitive then the low price has to be sustained – otherwise customers may change to a rival supplier. This has happened with online banks – some customers regularly move to reduce costs of overdrafts for example. Alternatively if a customer is concerned by other aspects such as service quality it may be necessary to create a large price differential in order to encourage the customer to change supplier.

Kotler (1997) suggests that in the face of price cuts from competitors in a market, a company has the following choices which can be applied to e-commerce:

(a) Maintain the price (assuming that e-commerce-derived sales are unlikely to decrease greatly with price since other factors such as customer service are equally or more important).
(b) Reduce the price (to avoid losing market share).
(c) Raise perceived quality or differentiate product further by adding-value services.
(d) Introduce new lower-priced product lines.

3 New pricing approaches (including auctions)

Forward auctions
Item purchased by highest bid made in bidding period.

Reverse auctions
Item purchased from lowest-bidding supplier in bidding period.

Offer
A commitment by a trader to *sell* under certain conditions.

Bid
A commitment by a trader to *purchase* under certain conditions.

Aggregated buying
A form of customer union where buyers collectively purchase a number of items at the same price and receive a volume discount.

Figure 5.10 summarises different pricing mechanisms. While many of these were available before the advent of the Internet and are not new, the Internet has made some models more tenable. In particular, the volume of users makes traditional or forward auctions (B2C) and reverse auctions (B2B) more tenable – these have become more widely used than previously. Emiliani (2001) reviews the implications of B2B reverse auctions in detail, and Mini Case Study 5.2 provides an example. To understand auctions it is important to distinguish between offers and bids. An offer is a commitment for a trader to sell under certain conditions such as a minimum price. A bid is made by a trader to buy under the conditions of the bid such as a commitment to purchase at a particular price.

A further approach, not indicated in Figure 5.10, is aggregated buying. This approach was promoted by LetsBuyit.com, but the business model did not prove viable – the cost of creating awareness for the brand and explaining the concept was not offset by the revenue from each transaction.

Pitt et al. (2001) suggest that when developing a pricing strategy, the options will be limited by relative strengths of the seller and buyer. Where the buyer is powerful then reverse auctions are possible. Major car manufacturers fall into this category. See also Mini Case Study 5.2. Where the seller is more powerful then a negotiation may be more likely where the seller can counter-offer. Nextag.com provides such a service.

235

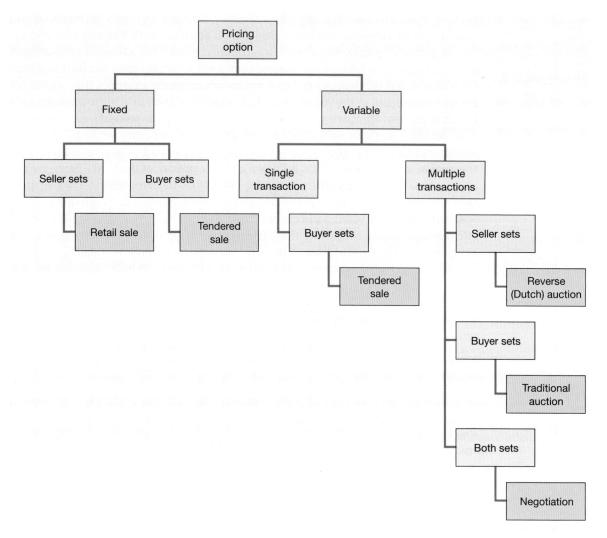

Figure 5.10 Alternative pricing mechanisms

Marn (2000) suggests that the Internet can be used to test new pricing policies. For example, if a company wants to know the sales impact of a 3 per cent price increase, it can try this on every 50th visitor to the site and compare the buy rates.

Dynamic pricing

Prices can be updated in real time according to the type of customer or current market conditions.

The Internet introduces new opportunities for dynamic pricing, for example, new customers could be automatically given discounted purchases for the first three items. Care has to be taken with differential pricing since established customers will be unhappy if significant discounts are given to new customers. Amazon trialled such a discounting scheme in 2000 and it received negative press and had to be withdrawn when people found out that their friends or colleagues had paid less. If the scheme had been a clear introductory promotion this problem may not have arisen.

Mini Case Study 5.2	GlaxoSmithKline reduces prices through reverse auctions

Healthcare company GlaxoSmithKline (GSK) started using online reverse auctions in 2000 to drive down the price of its supplies. For example, it bought supplies of a basic solvent for a price 15 per cent lower than the day's spot price in the commodity market, and Queree (2000) reported that on other purchases of highly specified solvents and chemicals, SmithKline Beecham (prior to formation of GSK) regularly beat its own historic pricing by between 7 and 25 per cent. She says:

> FreeMarkets, the company that manages the SmithKline Beecham auctions, quotes examples of savings achieved by other clients in these virtual marketplaces: 42 per cent on orders for printed circuit boards, 41 per cent on labels, 24 per cent on commercial machinings and so on.

The reverse auction process starts with a particularly detailed Request for Proposals (RFP) from which suppliers ask to take part, and then selected suppliers are invited to take part in the auction. Once the bidding starts, the participants see every bid, but not the names of the bidders. In the final stages of the auction, each last bid extends the bidding time by one more minute. One auction scheduled for 2 hours ran for 4 hours and 20 minutes and attracted more than 700 bids!

4 Alternative pricing structure or policies

Different types of pricing may be possible on the Internet, particularly for digital, downloadable products. Software and music have traditionally been sold for a continuous right to use. The Internet offers new options such as payment per use, rental at a fixed cost per month or a lease arrangement. Bundling options may also be more possible. The use of applications service providers (ASPs) to deliver service such as web site traffic monitoring also gives new methods of volume pricing. Web analytics companies such as Indextools (**www.indextools.com**) and Webtrends (**www.webtrendslive.com**) charge in price bands based on the number of visitors to the purchaser's site.

Further pricing options which could be varied online include:

- basic price
- discounts
- add-ons and extra products and services
- guarantees and warranties
- refund policies
- order cancellation terms.

Place

Place

The element of the marketing mix that involves distributing products to customers in line with demand and minimising cost of inventory, transport and storage.

The **place** element of the marketing mix refers to how the product is distributed to customers. Typically, for offline channels, the aim of Place is to maximise the reach of distribution to achieve widespread availability of products while minimising the costs of inventory, transport and storage. In an online context, thanks to ease of navigating from one site to another through the humble hyperlink, the scope of 'Place' is less clear since Place also relates to Promotion and Partnerships. Take the example of a retailer of mobile phones. For this retailer to reach its potential audience to sell and distribute its product, it has to think beyond its own web site to third-party web sites where it can promote its services. Successful retailers are those that maximise their representation or visibility on third-party sites which are used by their target audiences. These third-party sites will include search engines, online portals about mobile phones and product comparison sites. When thinking about representation on third-party sites, it is useful to think of the long-tail concept (Anderson, 2004) referenced in Figure 5.4. Across all Internet sites, there are a small number of sites including portals such as Google, MSN and Yahoo! which are very popular (the head which may theoretically account for 80% of the volume of visitors) and a much larger number of sites that are less popular individually, but still collectively important. Similarly within a category of sites, such as automotive, there will be a few very popular sites, and then many niche sites which are collectively important in volume and may be more effective at reaching a niche target audience. When considering Place and Promotion, it is important to target both the head and the tail to maximise reach and to attract quality visitors to the destination site.

The main implications of the Internet for the Place aspect of the mix, which we will review in this section, are:

1 place of purchase;
2 new channel structures;
3 channel conflicts;
4 virtual organisations.

1 Place of purchase

Although the concept of place may seem peculiar for what is a global medium that transcends geographical boundaries, nevertheless, marketers still have several options for managing the place of purchase. Allen and Fjermestad (2001) argue that the Internet has the greatest implications for place in the marketing mix since the Internet has a global reach.

The framework of Berryman et al. (1998), introduced in Chapter 2, is a simple framework for reviewing different places of promotion and/or distribution and purchase. However, McDonald and Wilson (2002) introduce two additional locations for purchase which are useful (Table 5.2):

(A) *Seller-controlled sites* are those that are the main site of the supplier company and are e-commerce-enabled.
(B) *Seller-oriented sites* are controlled by third parties and are representing the seller rather than providing a full range of options.
(C) *Neutral sites* are independent evaluator intermediaries that enable price and product comparison and will result in the purchase being fulfilled on the target site.
(D) *Buyer-oriented sites* are controlled by third parties on behalf of the buyer.
(E) *Buyer-controlled sites* usually involve either procurement posting on buyer-company sites or on those of intermediaries that have been set up in such a way that it is the buyer that initiates the market-making. This can occur through procurement posting, whereby a purchaser specifies what he or she wishes to purchase, this request being sent by e-mail to suppliers registered on the system and then offers are awaited. Aggregators are groups of purchasers who combine to purchase in bulk and thus benefit from a lower purchase cost.

Evans and Wurster (1999) have argued that there are three aspects of 'navigational advantage' that are key to achieving competitive advantage online. These three, which all relate to the Place elements of the mix, are:

Table 5.2 Different places for cyberspace representation

Place of purchase	Examples of sites
A Seller-controlled	• Vendor sites, i.e. home site of organisation selling products, e.g. www.dell.com
B Seller-oriented	• Intermediaries controlled by third parties to the seller such as distributors and agents, e.g. Opodo (www.opodo.com) represents the main air carriers
C Neutral	• Intermediaries not controlled by buyer's industry, e.g. EC21 (www.ec21.com) • Product-specific search engines, e.g. CNET (www.computer.com) • Comparison sites, e.g. uSwitch (www.uswitch.com) • Auction space, e.g. eBay (www.eBay.com)
D Buyer-oriented	• Intermediaries controlled by buyers, e.g. the remaining parts of the Covisint network of motor manufacturers • Purchasing agents and aggregators
E Buyer-controlled	• Web site procurement posting on company's own site, e.g. GE Trading Process Network (www.tpn.geis.com)

- *Reach*. Evans and Wurster say: 'It [Reach] means, simply, how many customers a business can connect with and how many products it can offer to those customers'. Reach can be increased by moving from a single site to representation with a large number of different intermediaries. Allen and Fjermestad (2001) suggest that niche suppliers can readily reach a much wider market due to search-engine marketing (Chapter 8). Evans and Wurster also suggest that reach refers to the range of products and services that can be offered since this will increase the number of people the company can appeal to.
- *Richness*. This is the depth or detail of information which is both collected about the customer and provided to the customer. The latter is related to the richness of product information and how well it can be personalised to be relevant to the individual needs.
- *Affiliation*. This refers to whose interest the selling organisation represents – consumers or suppliers – and stresses the importance of forming the right partnerships. This particularly applies to retailers. The authors suggest that successful online retailers will provide customers who provide them with the richest information on comparing competitive products. They suggest this tilts the balance in favour of the customer.

Localisation

Providing a local site, with or without a language-specific version, is referred to as localisation. A site may need to support customers from a range of countries with:

- different product needs;
- language differences;
- cultural differences.

Localisation

Tailoring of web site information for individual countries or regions.

Localisation will address all these issues. It may be that products will be similar in different countries and localisation will simply involve converting the web site to suit another country. However, in order to be effective, this often needs more than translation, since different promotion concepts may be needed for different countries. Examples of localised sites include Durex, B2C, and Gestetner, B2B. Note that each company prioritises different countries according to the size of the market, and this priority then governs the amount of work it puts into localisation.

Activity 5.4   Place of purchase on the Internet

visit the
w.w.w.

Purpose

To illustrate the concept of representation and reach on the Internet.

Activity

For the same sector as you selected in Activity 5.2, find out which company has the best reach in terms of numbers of links from other sites. Go to a search engine such as Google and use the advanced search to find the number of sites that link to that site. Alternatively use the syntax: link:URL in the search box.

2 New channel structures

New channel structures enabled by the Internet have been described in detail in Chapters 2 and 4. The main types of phenomena that companies need to develop strategies for are:

(a) *Distintermediation*. Is there an option for selling direct? Selling direct can lead to the channel conflicts mentioned in the next section. When assessing this option there will be a number of barriers and facilitators to this change. Research by Mols (2001) in the banking sector in Denmark suggests that important factors are senior management support, a willingness to accept some cannibalisation of existing channels and perceived customer benefits.

(b) *Reintermediation*. The new intermediaries created through reintermediation described by Sarkar et al. (1996) should be evaluated for suitability for partnering with for affiliate arrangements. The intermediaries receive a commission on each sale resulting from a referral from their site.

(c) *Countermediation*. Should the organisation partner with another independent intermediary, or set up its own independent intermediary? For example, a group of European airlines have joined forces to form Opodo (**www.opodo.com**) which is intended to counter independent companies such as Lastminute.com (**www.lastminute.com**) or eBookers (**www.ebookers.com**) in offering discount fares.

The distribution channel will also be affected. For instance, grocery retailers have had to identify the best strategy for picking customers' goods prior to home delivery. Options include in-store picking (selection of items on customer orders) and regional picking centres. The former is proving more cost-effective.

3 Channel conflicts

A significant threat arising from the introduction of an Internet channel is that while disintermediation gives a company the opportunity to sell direct and increase profitability on products, it can also threaten distribution arrangements with existing partners. Such channel conflicts are described by Frazier (1999), and need to be carefully managed. Frazier (1999) identifies some situations when the Internet should only be used as a communications channel. This is particularly the case where manufacturers offer an exclusive, or highly selective, distribution approach. To take an example, a company manufacturing expensive watches costing thousands of pounds will not in the past have sold direct, but will have used a wholesaler to distribute watches via retailers. If this wholesaler is a major player in watch distribution, then it is powerful, and will react against the watch manufacturer selling direct. The wholesaler may even refuse to act as distributor and may threaten to distribute only a competitor's watches, which are not available over the Internet. Furthermore, direct sales may damage the product's brand or change its price positioning.

Further channel conflicts involve other stakeholders including sales representatives and customers. Sales representatives may see the Internet as a direct threat to their livelihood. In some cases such as Avon cosmetics and Enyclopaedia Britannica this has proved to be the case, with this sales model being partly or completely replaced by the Internet. For many B2B purchases, sales representatives remain an essential method of reaching the customer to support them in the purchase decision. Here, following training of sales staff, the Internet can be used as a sales support and customer education tool. Customers who do not use the online channels may also respond negatively if lower prices are available to their online counterparts. This is less serious than other types of channel conflict.

To assess channel conflicts it is necessary to consider the different forms of channel the Internet can take. These are:

1 a communication channel only;
2 a distribution channel to intermediaries;
3 a direct sales channel to customers;
4 any combination of the above.

To avoid channel conflicts, the appropriate combination of channels must be arrived at. For example, Frazier (1999) notes that using the Internet as a direct sales channel may not be wise when a product's price varies considerably across global markets. In the watch manufacturer example, it may be best to use the Internet as a communication channel only.

Internet channel strategy will, of course, depend on the existing arrangements for the market. If a geographical market is new and there are no existing agents or distributors, there is unlikely to be channel conflict in that there is a choice of distribution through the Internet only or appointments of new agents to support Internet sales, or a combination of the two. Often SMEs will attempt to use the Internet to sell products without appointing agents, but this strategy will only be possible for retail products that need limited pre-sales and after-sales support. For higher-value products such as engineering equipment, which will require skilled sales staff to support the sale and after-sales servicing, agents will have to be appointed.

For existing geographical markets in which a company already has a mechanism for distribution in the form of agents and distributors, the situation is more complex, and there is the threat of channel conflict. The strategic options that are available when an existing reseller arrangement is in place have been described by Kumar (1999):

1 *No Internet sales*. Neither the company nor any of its resellers makes sales over the Internet. This will be the option to follow when a company, or its resellers, feel that the number of buyers has not reached the critical mass thought to warrant the investment in an online sales capability.
2 *Internet sales by reseller only*. A reseller who is selling products from many companies may have sufficient aggregated demand (through selling products for other companies) to justify the expenditure of setting up online sales. The manufacturer may also not have the infrastructure to fulfil orders direct to customers without further investment, whereas the reseller will be set up for this already. In this case it is unlikely that a manufacturer would want to block sales via the Internet channel.

3 *Internet sales by manufacturer only*. It would be unusual if a manufacturer chose this option if it already had existing resellers in place. Were the manufacturer to do so, it would probably lead to lost sales as the reseller would perhaps stop selling through traditional channels.

4 *Internet sales by all*. This option is arguably the logical future for Internet sales. It is also likely to be the result if the manufacturer does not take a proactive approach to controlling Internet sales.

Strategy will need to be reviewed annually and the sales channels changed as thought appropriate. Given the fast rate of change of e-commerce, it will probably not be possible to create a five-year plan! Kumar (1999) notes that history suggests that most companies have a tendency to use existing distribution networks for too long. The reason for this is that resellers may be powerful within a channel and the company does not want to alienate them, for fear of losing sales.

4 Virtual organisations

Benjamin and Wigand (1995) state that 'it is becoming increasingly difficult to delineate accurately the borders of today's organisations'. A further implication of the introduction of electronic networks such as the Internet is that it becomes easier to outsource aspects of the production and distribution of goods to third parties (Kraut et al., 1998). This can lead to the boundaries within an organisation becoming blurred. Employees may work in any time zone, and customers are able to purchase tailored products from any location. The absence of any rigid boundary or hierarchy within the organisation should lead to a company becoming more responsive and flexible, and having a greater market orientation.

Davidow and Malone (1992) describe the virtual corporation as follows:

To the outside observer, it will appear almost edgeless, with permeable and continuously changing interfaces between company, supplier and customer. From inside the firm, the view will be no less amorphous, with traditional offices, departments, and operating divisions constantly reforming according to need. Job responsibilities will regularly shift.

Virtual organisation and virtualisation

A virtual organisation uses information and communications technology to allow it to operate without clearly defined physical boundaries between different functions. It provides customised services by outsourcing production and other functions to third parties. Virtualisation is the process whereby a company develops more of the characteristics of a virtual organisation.

Kraut et al. (1998) suggest the following features of a virtual organisation:

1 Processes transcend the boundaries of a single form and are not controlled by a single organisational hierarchy.
2 Production processes are flexible, with different parties involved at different times.
3 Parties involved in the production of a single product are often geographically dispersed.
4 Given this dispersion, coordination is heavily dependent on telecommunications and data networks.

Introna (2001) notes that a key aspect of the virtual organisation is strategic alliances or partnering. The ease of forming such alliances in the value network as described in Chapter 2 is one of the factors that has given rise to the virtual organisation.

All companies tend to have some elements of the virtual organisation. The process whereby these characteristics increase is known as virtualisation. Malone et al. (1987) argued that the presence of electronic networks tends to lead to virtualisation since they enable the governance and coordination of business transactions to be conducted effectively at lower cost.

What are the implications for a marketing strategist of this trend towards virtualisation? Initially it may appear that outsourcing does not have direct relevance to market orientation. However, an example shows the relevance. Michael Dell relates (in Magretta, 1998) that Dell does not see outsourcing as getting rid of a process that does not add value, rather it sees it as a way of 'coordinating their activity to create the most value for customers'. Dell has improved customer service by changing the way it works with both its suppliers and its distributors to build a computer to the customer's specific order within just six days. This *vertical integration* has been achieved by creating a contractual vertical marketing system in which members of a channel retain their independence, but work together by sharing contracts.

So, one aspect of virtualisation is that companies should identify opportunities for providing new services and products to customers that are looking to outsource their external processes. The corollary of this is that it may offer companies opportunities to outsource some marketing activities that were previously conducted in-house. For example, marketing research to assess the impact of a web site can now be conducted in a virtual environment by an outside company rather than by having employees conduct a focus group.

Marshall et al. (2001) provide useful examples of different structures for the virtual organisation. These are:

1 *Co-alliance model*. Effort and risk are shared equally by partners.
2 *Star alliance model*. Here the effort and risk are centred on one organisation that subcontracts other virtual partners as required.
3 *Value alliance model*. This is a partnership where elements are contributed across a supply chain for a particular industry. This is effectively the value network of Chapter 2.
4 *Market alliance model*. This is similar to the value alliance, but is more likely to serve several different marketplaces.

Using the Internet to facilitate such alliances can provide competitive advantage to organisations operating in business-to-business markets since their core competences can be complemented by partnerships with third parties. This can potentially help organisations broaden their range of services or compete for work which on their own, they may be unable to deliver. Such approaches can also be used to support business-to-consumer markets. For example, Dell can compete on price and quality in its consumer markets through its use of a star alliance model where other organisations are responsible for peripherals such as monitors or printers or distribution.

Promotion

Promotion variable
The element of the marketing mix that involves communication with customers and other stakeholders to inform them about the product and the organisation.

The promotion element of the marketing mix refers to how marketing communications are used to inform customers and other stakeholders about an organisation and its products. This topic is discussed in more detail in Chapter 8 – it is only introduced here.

Promotion is the element of the marketing mix that is concerned with communicating the existence of products or services to a target market. Burnett (1993) defines it as:

the marketing function concerned with persuasively communicating to target audiences the components of the marketing program in order to facilitate exchange.

A broader view of promotion is given by Wilmshurst (1993):

Promotion unfortunately has a range of meanings. It can be used to describe the market-ing communications aspect of the marketing mix or, more narrowly, as in sales promotion. In its very broad sense it includes the personal methods of communications, such as face to face or telephone selling, as well as the impersonal ones such as advertising. When we use a range of different types of promotion – direct mail, exhibitions, publicity etc. we describe it as the promotional mix.

The main elements of the promotional or communications mix can be considered to be (as stated by, for example, Fill (2000)):

1 advertising;
2 sales promotion;
3 personal selling;
4 public relations;
5 direct marketing.

Specification of the Promotion element of the mix is usually part of a communications strategy. This will include selection of target markets, positioning and integration of differ-ent communications tools. The Internet offers a new, additional marketing communications channel to inform customers of the benefits of a product and assist in the buying decision. These are different approaches for looking at how the Internet can be used to vary the Promotion element of the mix:

1 reviewing new ways of applying each of the elements of the communications mix such as advertising, sales promotions, PR and direct marketing;
2 assessing how the Internet can be used at different stages of the buying process;
3 using promotional tools to assist in different stages of customer relationship manage-ment from customer acquisition to retention. In a web context this includes gaining initial visitors to the site and gaining repeat visits through these types of communica-tions techniques:
   - reminders in traditional media campaigns why a site is worth visiting, such as online services and unique online offers and competitions;
   - direct e-mail reminders of site proposition – new offers;
   - frequently updated content including promotional offers or information that helps your customer do their job or reminds them to visit.

The Promotion element of a marketing plan also requires three important decisions about investment for the online promotion or the online communications mix:

1 *Investment in site promotion compared to site creation and maintenance.* Since there is often a fixed budget for site creation, maintenance and promotion, the e-marketing plan should specify the budget for each to ensure there is a sensible balance and the promotion of the site is not underfunded.
2 *Investment in online promotion techniques in comparison to offline promotion.* A balance must be struck between these techniques. Typically, offline promotion investment often exceeds that for online promotion investment. For existing companies tradi-tional media such as print are used to advertise the sites, while print and TV will also be widely used by dot-com companies to drive traffic to their sites.
3 *Investment in different online promotion techniques.* For example, how much should be paid for banner advertising as against online PR about online presence, and how much for search engine registration?

These issues are explored further in Chapter 8.

People, process and physical evidence

People

The **people** element of the marketing mix refers to how an organisation's staff interact with customers and other stakeholders during sales and pre- and post-sales communications with them.

Smith and Chaffey (2005) suggest that, online, the main consideration for the People element of the mix is the review of how staff involvement in the buying is changed, either through new roles such as replying to e-mails or online chat enquiries or through them being replaced through automated online services. These are some of the options:

- *Autoresponders*. These automatically immediately generate a response when a company e-mails an organisation with an enquiry or submits an online form.
- *E-mail notification*. Automatically generated by a company's systems to update customers on the status of their order, for example, order received, item now in stock, order dispatched.
- *Callback facility*. Customers fill in their phone number on a form and specify a convenient time to be contacted. Dialling from a representative in the call centre occurs automatically at the appointed time, and the company pays, which is popular.
- *Online chat*. A real-time chat session is initiated by the customer with customer service staff to discuss questions about the product or service. For example, One Account (**www.oneaccount.com**) offers this facility once the customer is on an enquiry path (this facility could not be offered on the home page since this would generate a volume of enquiries that is too high for staff to respond to sufficiently quickly).
- *Co-browsing*. Similar to online chat, but in this case the customer support staff share the customer's desktop to explain how they should use the site. This is often combined with a phone call. Such a situation has technical limitations since it requires a broadband connection and software needs to be downloaded onto the end-user's machine to manage the session.
- *Frequently asked questions (FAQ)*. For these, the art is in compiling and categorising the questions so customers can easily find (a) the question and (b) a helpful answer.
- *On-site search engines*. These help customers find what they're looking for quickly, and are popular when available. Advanced online retailers invest in optimising online search so that the customer's queries are answered with relevant results, rather than be presented with a blank page. Site maps are a related feature.
- *Product selection tools*. Guide the customer through a range of choices to recommend the best product for them, based on criteria defined by the customer.
- *Virtual assistants* or 'avatars' are representations of customer service staff. Boo.com featured Miss Boo who was an avatar that advised on products. One specialised company creating avatars is German company Kiwilogic (**www.kiwilogic.de**) which is distributed in the UK by Creative Virtual (**www.creativevirtual.com**). They create avatars or virtual customer-service staff for Ikea and Cahoot which they call 'Lingubots'. These operate using natural language processing. After a question is answered the visitor is directed to the relevant page of the site.

Organisations can test actions needed at each stage for different types of scenario, e.g. enquiry from a new or existing customer, enquiry about the web site or e-mails from different stages in the buying process such as pre-sales, sales or post-sales.

To manage service quality organisations must devise plans to accommodate the five stages shown in Figure 5.11. The stages are as follows.

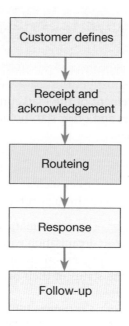

Figure 5.11 Stages in managing inbound e-mail

Stage 1: Customer defines support query

Companies should consider how easily the customer can find contact points and compose a support request on site. Best practice is clearly to find e-mail support options. Often, finding contact and support information on a web site is surprisingly difficult. Standardised terminology on site is 'Contact Us' or 'Support'. Options should be available for the customer to specify the type of query on a web form or provide alternative e-mail addresses such as **products@company.com** or **returns@company.com** on-site, or in offline communications such as a catalogue. Providing FAQs or automated diagnostic tools should be considered at this stage to reduce the number of inbound enquiries. Epson (**www.epson.co.uk**) provides an online tool to diagnose problems with printers and to suggest solutions.

Finally, the web site should determine expectations about the level of service quality. For example, inform the customer that 'your enquiry will be responded to within 24 hours'.

Stage 2: Receipt of e-mail and acknowledgement

Autoresponders or 'mailbots'

Software tools or 'agents' running on web servers that automatically send a standard reply to the sender of an e-mail message.

Best practice is that automatic message acknowledgement occurs. This is usually provided by autoresponder software. While many autoresponders only provide a simple acknowledgement, more sophisticated responses can reassure the customer about when the response will occur and highlight other sources of information.

Stage 3: Routeing of e-mail

Best practice involves automated routeing or workflow. Routeing the e-mail to the right person is made easier if the type of query has been identified through the techniques described for Stage 1. It is also possible to use pattern recognition to identify the type of enquiry. For example, Nationwide (**www.nationwide.co.uk**), see Mini Case Study 5.3, use

Brightware's 'skill-based message routeing' so that messages are sent to a specialist adviser where specific enquiries are made. Such software can also be used at Stage 1 to give an autoresponse appropriate for the enquiry.

Mini Case Study 5.3   Customer service at the Nationwide

The Nationwide is a financial services organisation which has been active in using the Internet as a customer service tool. Bicknell (2002) reports that the volume of customer service is as follows:

- 900,000 registrants on site with 2.4 million visits to the site in August 2001.
- Of the 1.2 million who entered the online bank, 900,000 made transactions resulting in 60,000 online contracts which require customer service.

These figures highlight the number of transactions that will have reduced customer contacts in real-world branches and by phone, but this still leaves 60,000 online contacts. The Nationwide believed that customers should expect service to be fast and accurate. Mark Cromack, operations manager, said:

> There was a hugh demand for more and more information and an explosion in the level of information that people wanted. That had implications for staff morale. What we needed was an autoresponse facility which provided quality, compliant and consistent answers.

To reduce the volume of calls, Frequently Answered Questions (FAQ) was not sufficient. The company purchased two products from Firepond to improve service. *Concierge* is provided on the home page to provide a facility with natural language searching to help customers find the answers to their queries more rapidly. *Answer* is an automated message routeing tool that provides automated answers to simple questions which can be reviewed by contact centre staff before dispatch and yet is able to spot the phrasing of more complex queries for completion by call centre operators.

Using these solutions, the quality of answers improved to give a first-time resolution rate of 94%. With the reduced staff time involved, the cost per contact had been reduced from £4 to £2.

Stage 4: Compose response

Best practice is to use a library of pre-prepared templates for different types of query. These can then be tailored and personalised by the contact centre employee as appropriate. The right type of template can again be selected automatically using the software referred to in Stage 2. Through using such auto-suggestion, the Nationwide has seen e-mail handling times reduced by 25% for messages requiring adviser intervention. Sony Europe identifies all new support issues and adds them with the appropriate response to a central knowledge base.

Stage 5: Follow-up

Best practice is that if the employee does not successfully answer the first response, then the e-mail should suggest callback from an employee or a live-chat. Indeed, to avoid the problem of 'e-mail ping-pong' where several e-mails may be exchanged, the company may want to proactively ring the customer to increase the speed of problem resolution, and so solve the problem. Finally, the e-mail follow-up may provide the opportunity for outbound contact and marketing, perhaps advising about complementary products or offers.

Process

Process variable

The element of the marketing mix that involves the methods and procedures companies use to achieve all marketing functions.

The Process element of the marketing mix refers to the methods and procedures companies use to achieve all marketing functions such as new product development, promotion, sales and customer service (as described in the previous section). The restructuring of the organisation and channel structures to accommodate online marketing which were described in the previous chapter are part of Process.

Physical evidence

Physical evidence variable

The element of the marketing mix that involves the tangible expression of a product and how it is purchased and used.

The Physical evidence element of the marketing mix refers to the tangible expression of a product and how it is purchased and used. In an online context, 'physical evidence' refers to the customers' experience of the company through the web site. It includes issues such as site ease of use or navigation, availability and performance, which are discussed further in Chapter 7.

Case Study 5 — The re-launched Napster changes the music marketing mix

This case about online music subscription service Napster illustrates how different elements of the mix can be varied online. It also highlights success factors for developing an online marketing strategy since Napster's proposition, objectives, competitors and risk factors are all reviewed.

The Napster brand has had a varied history. Its initial incarnation was as the first widely used service for 'free' peer-to-peer (P2P) music sharing. The record companies mounted a legal challenge to Napster due to lost revenues on music sales which eventually forced it to close. But the Napster brand was purchased and its second incarnation offers a legal music download service in direct competition with Apple's iTunes.

The original Napster

Napster was initially created between 1998 and 1999 by a 19-year-old called Shawn Fanning while he attended Boston's Northeastern University. He wrote the program initially as a way of solving a problem for a friend who wanted to find music downloads more easily online. The name 'Napster' came from Fanning's nickname.

The system was known as peer-to-peer since it enabled music tracks stored on other Internet user's hard disks in MP3 format to be searched and shared with other Internet users. Strictly speaking, the service was not a pure P2P since central services indexed the tracks available and their locations in a similar way to which instant messaging (IM) works.

The capability to try a range of tracks proved irresistible and Napster use peaked with 26.4 million users worldwide in February 2001.

It was not long before several major recording companies backed by the RIAA (Recording Industry Association of America) launched a lawsuit. Of course, such an action also gave Napster tremendous PR and more users trialled the service. Some individual bands also responded with lawsuits. Rock band Metallica found that a demo of their song 'I disappear' began circulating on the Napster network and was eventually played on the radio. Other well-known artists who vented their ire on Napster included Madonna and Eminem by posting false 'cuckoo egg' files instead of music; Madonna asked the downloader: 'What the fuck do you think you're doing?'! However, not all artists felt the service was negative for them. UK band Radiohead pre-released some tracks of their album *Kid A* on to Napster and subsequently became Number 1 in the US despite failing to achieve this previously.

Eventually as a result of legal action an injunction was issued on 5 March 2001 ordering Napster to cease trading of copyrighted material. Napster complied with this injunction, but tried to make a deal with the record companies to pay past copyright fees and to turn the service into a legal subscription service.

In the following year, a deal was agreed with German media company Bertelsmann AG to purchase Napster's assets for $8 million as part of an agreement when Napster filed for Chapter 11 bankruptcy in the United States. This sale was blocked and the web site closed. Eventually, the Napster brand was purchased by Roxio, Inc which used the brand to rebrand their PressPlay service.

Since this time, other P2P services such as Gnutella, Grokster and Kazaa have prospered which have been more difficult for the copyright owners to pursue in court;

however, many individuals have now been sued in the US and Europe and the associations of these services with spyware and adware has damaged them, which has reduced the popularity of these services.

New Napster in 2005

Fast forward to 2005 and Napster now has around 410,000 subscribers in the United States, Canada and the United Kingdom who pay up to £14.95 each month to gain access to about 1.5 million songs. The company is seeking to launch in other countries such as Japan through partnerships.

The online music download environment has also changed with legal music downloading propelled through increasing adoption of broadband, the success of Apple iTunes and its portable music player, the iPod, which by 2005 had achieved around half a billion sales.

Napster gains its main revenues from online subscriptions and permanent music downloads. The Napster service offers subscribers on-demand access to over 1 million tracks that can be streamed or downloaded as well as the ability to purchase individual tracks or albums on an *à la carte* basis. Subscription and permanent download fees are paid by end-user customers in advance via credit card, online payment systems or redemption of pre-paid cards, gift certificates or promotional codes. Napster also periodically licenses merchandising rights and resells hardware that its end-users use to store and replay their music.

BBC (2005) estimated that the global music market is now worth $33 billion (£18.3 billion) a year while the online music market accounted for around 5% of all sales in the first half of 2005. Napster (2005), quoting Forrester Research estimates that United States purchases of downloadable digital music will exceed $1.9 billion by 2007 and that revenues from online music subscription services such as Napster will exceed $800 million by 2007.

BBC (2005) reports Brad Duea, president of Napster, as saying:

The number one brand attribute at the time Napster was shut down was innovation. The second highest characteristic was actually 'free'. The difference now is that the number one attribute is still innovation. Free is now way down on the list. People are able to search for more music than was ever possible at retail, even in the largest megastore.

The Napster proposition

Napster subscribers can listen to as many tracks as they wish which are contained within the catalogue of over 1 million tracks (the service is sometimes described as 'all you can eat' rather than '*à la carte*'). Napster users can listen to tracks on any compatible device that includes Windows Digital Rights Management software, which includes MP3 players, computers, PDAs and mobile phones.

Duea describes Napster as an 'experience' rather than a retailer. He says this because of features available such as:

- Napster recommendations;
- Napster radio based around songs by particular artists;
- Napster radio playlists based on the songs you have downloaded;
- swapping playlists and recommendations with other users.

iTunes and Napster are probably the two highest profile services, but they have a quite different model of operating. There are no subscribers to iTunes, where users purchase songs either on a per-track basis or in the form of albums. By mid-2005, over half a billion tracks had been purchased on Napster. Some feel that iTunes locks people into purchasing Apple hardware; as one would expect, Duea of Napster says that Steve Jobs of Apple 'has tricked people into buying a hardware trap'.

But Napster's subscription model has also been criticised since it is service where subscribers do not 'own' the music unless they purchase it at additional cost, for example to burn it to CD. The music is theirs to play either on a PC or on a portable player, but for only as long as they continue to subscribe to Napster. So it could be argued that Napster achieves lock-in in another form and requires a different approach to music ownership than some of its competitors.

Napster strategy

Napster (2005) describe their strategy as follows. The overall objective is to become the 'leading global provider of consumer digital music services'. They see these strategic initiatives as being important to achieving this:

- *Continue to build the Napster consumer brand* – as well as increasing awareness of the Napster brand identity, this also includes promoting the subscription service which encourages discovery of new music. Napster (2005) say 'We market our Napster service directly to consumers through an integrated offline and online marketing program consistent with the existing strong awareness and perception of the Napster brand. The marketing message is focused on our subscription service, which differentiates our offering from those of many of our competitors. Offline marketing channels include television (including direct-response TV), radio and print advertising. Our online marketing program includes advertising placements on a number of web sites (including affiliate partners) and search engines'.
- *Continue to innovate by investing in new services and technologies* – this initiative encourages support of a wide range of platforms from portable MP3 players, PCs, cars, mobile phones, etc. The large technical team in Napster shows the importance of this strategy. In the longer term, access to other forms of content such as video may be offered. Napster see their ability to compete depend substantially upon their intellectual property. They have a number of patents issued, but are also in dispute with other organisations over their patents.
- *Continue to pursue and execute strategic partnerships* – Napster has already entered strategic partnerships with technology companies (Microsoft and Intel), hardware companies (iRiver, Dell, Creative, Toshiba and IBM), retailers (Best Buy, Blockbuster, Radio Shack,

Dixons Group, The Link, PC World, Currys, Target), and others (Molson, Miller, Energizer, Nestlé).

- *Continue to pursue strategic acquisitions and complementary technologies* – this is another route to innovation and developing new services.

Customers

The Register (2005) reported that in the UK, by mid-2005, Napster UK's 750,000 users have downloaded or streamed 55m tracks since the service launched in May 2004. The company said 80 per cent of its subscribers are over the age of 25, and half of them have kids. Some three-quarters of them are male. Its subscribers buy more music online than folk who buy one-off downloads do and research shows that one in five of them no longer buy CDs, apparently.

Distribution

Napster's online music services are sold directly to end-users through the web site (www.napster.com). Affiliate networks and universities have procured site licences (in the US, a significant proportion of subscribers are university users). Prepaid cards are also available through retail partners such as Dixons in the UK, who also promote the service.

Napster also bundles its service with hardware manufacturers such as iRiver, Dell, Creative Labs, Gateway and Samsung.

Competition

Napster see their competitors for online music services in the US as Apple Computer's iTunes, Amazon, RealNetworks, Inc.'s Rhapsody, Yahoo! Unlimited, Sony Connect, AOL Music, MusicNet and MusicNow. In the UK, in 2005, new services with a subscription model were launched by retailers HMV and Virgin. They expect other competitors such as MTV Networks to enter the market soon.

Napster (2005) believe that the main competitive factors affecting their market include programming and features, price and performance, quality of customer support, compatibility with popular hardware devices and brand.

Employees

As of 31 March 2005, Napster had 135 employees, of which 10 directly supported the online music service (maintaining content and providing customer care), 25 were in sales and marketing, 63 were in engineering and product development and 37 were in finance, administration and operations. The costs of managing these staff is evident in Table 5.3.

Risk factors

In their annual report submission to the United States Securities and Exchange Commission, Napster is required to give its risk factors, which also give an indication of success factors for the business. Napster (2005) summarises the main risk factors as follows:

Table 5.3 Summary of Napster finances from Napster (2005)

	Year Ended March 31	
	2005	2004
(in thousands, except per share amounts)		
Net revenues	$46,729	$ 11,964
Cost of revenues	37,550	10,530
Gross profit	9,179	1,434
Operating expenses:		
Research and development	12,107	11,940
Sales and marketing	39,215	15,647
General and administrative	23,316	21,217
Restructuring charges	—	1,119
Amortisation of intangible assets	1,936	2,172
Stock-based compensation charges(1)	676	904
Total operating expenses	77,250	52,999
Loss from continuing operations	(68,071)	(51,565)
Other income, net	1,091	634
Loss before provision for income taxes	(66,980)	(50,931)
Income tax benefit	15,547	4,515
Loss from continuing operations, after provision for income taxes	(51,433)	(46,416)
Net loss	$(29,506)	$(44,413)

1 The success of our Napster service depends upon our ability to add new subscribers and reduce churn.
2 Our online music distribution business has lower margins than our former consumer software products business. Costs of our online music distribution business as a percentage of the revenue generated by that business are higher than those of our former consumer software products business. The cost of third-party content, in particular, is a substantial portion of revenues we receive from subscribers and end-users and is unlikely to decrease significantly over time as a percentage of revenue.
3 We rely on the value of the Napster brand, and our revenues could suffer if we are not able to maintain its high level of recognition in the digital music sector.
4 We face significant competition from traditional retail music distributors, from emerging paid online music services delivered electronically such as ours, and from 'free' peer-to-peer services.
5 Online music distribution services in general are new and rapidly evolving and may not prove to be a profitable or even viable business model.
6 We rely on content provided by third parties, which may not be available to us on commercially reasonable terms or at all.
7 We must provide digital rights management solutions that are acceptable to both content providers and consumers.
8 Our business could be harmed by a lack of availability of popular content.
9 Our success depends on our music service's interoperability with our customers' music playback hardware.
10 We may not successfully develop new products and services.
11 We must maintain and add to our strategic marketing relationships in order to be successful.

12 The growth of our business depends on the increased use of the Internet for communications, electronic commerce and advertising.
13 If broadband technologies do not become widely available or widely adopted, our online music distribution services may not achieve broad market acceptance, and our business may be harmed.
14 Our network is subject to security and stability risks that could harm our business and reputation and expose us to litigation or liability.
15 If we fail to manage expansion effectively, we may not be able to successfully manage our business, which could cause us to fail to meet our customer demand or to attract new customers, which would adversely affect our revenue.
16 We may be subject to intellectual property infringement claims, such as those claimed by SightSound Technologies, which are costly to defend and could limit our ability to use certain technologies in the future.

Finances
Despite growth in subscribers and revenue, Napster has experienced significant net losses since its inception and according to the SEC filing Napster (2005), 'we expect to incur net losses for at least the next twelve months and likely continue to experience net losses thereafter'. Since 1 April 2003, Napster have incurred approximately $97.8 million of after tax losses from continuing operations. A summary of the finances is presented in Table 5.3.

Sources: BBC (2005), Napster (2005), Wikipedia (2005), The Register (2005) and Wired (2002)

Question
Evaluate how Napster has varied each element of the marketing mix to compete with traditional and online music retailers.

Summary

1 Evaluating the opportunities provided by the Internet for varying the marketing mix is a useful framework for assessing current and future Internet marketing strategy.

2 *Product.* Opportunities for varying the core product through new information-based services and also the extended product should be reviewed.

3 *Price.* The Internet leads to price transparency and commoditisation and hence lower prices. Dynamic pricing gives the ability to test prices or to offer differential pricing for different segments or in response to variations in demand. New pricing models such as auctions are available.

4 *Place.* Place refers to place of purchase and channel structure on the Internet. There are three main locations for e-commerce transactions: seller site, buyer site and

intermediary. New channel structures are available through direct sales and linking to new intermediaries. Steps must be taken to minimise channel conflict.

5 *Promotion.* This aspect of the mix is discussed in more detail in Chapter 8.

6 *People, process and physical evidence.* These aspects of the mix are discussed in more detail in Chapters 6 and 7 where customer relationship management and service delivery are discussed.

Exercises

Self-assessment exercises

1 Select the two most important changes introduced by the Internet for each of the 4 Ps.

2 What types of product are most amenable to changes to the core and extended product?

3 Explain the differences in concepts between online B2C and B2B auctions.

4 Explain the implications of the Internet for Price.

5 What are the implications of the Internet for Place?

Essay and discussion questions

1 'The marketing mix developed as part of annual planning is no longer a valid concept in the Internet era.' Discuss.

2 Critically evaluate the impact of the Internet on the marketing mix for an industry sector of your choice.

3 Write an essay on pricing options for e-commerce.

4 Does 'Place' have any meaning for marketers in the global marketplace enabled by the Internet?

Examination questions

1 Describe three alternative locations for transactions for a B2B company on the Internet.

2 Explain two applications of dynamic pricing on the Internet.

3 How does the Internet impact an organisation's options for core and extended (augmented) product?

4 Briefly summarise the implications of the Internet on each of these elements of the marketing mix:
   (a) Product
   (b) Price
   (c) Place
   (d) Promotion.

5 Explain the reasons why the Internet could be expected to decrease prices online.

6 How can an organisation vary its promotional mix using the Internet?

References

Aaker, D. and Joachimsthaler, E. (2000) *Brand Leadership*. Free Press, New York.

Allen, E. and Fjermestad, J. (2001) E-commerce marketing strategies: a framework and case analysis, *Logistics Information Management*, 14(1/2), 14–23.

Anderson, C. (2004) The Long Tail. *Wired*. 12.10. October. www.wired.com/wired/archive/12.10/tail.html.

Baker, W., Marn, M. and Zawada, C. (2000) Price smarter on the Net, *Harvard Business Review*, February, 2–7.

BBC (2005) Napster boss on life after piracy. *BBC*. By Derren Waters, 22 August. http://news.bbc.co.uk/1/hi/entertainment/music/4165868.stm.

Benjamin, R. and Wigand, R. (1995) Electronic markets and virtual value-chains on the information superhighway, *Sloan Management Review*, Winter, 62–72.

Berryman, K., Harrington, L., Layton-Rodin, D. and Rerolle, V. (1998) Electronic commerce: three emerging strategies, *McKinsey Quarterly*, No. 1, 152–9.

Bickerton, P., Bickerton, M. and Pardesi, U. (2000) *CyberMarketing*, 2nd edn. Butterworth Heinemann, Oxford.

Bicknell, D. (2002) Banking on customer service, *e.Businessreview*, January, 21–2.

Booms, B. and Bitner, M. (1981) Marketing strategies and organisation structures for service firms. In J. Donnelly and W. George (eds), *Marketing of Services*. American Marketing Association, New York.

BrandNewWorld (2004) AOL research published at www.brandnewworld.co.uk.

Brynjolfsson, E., Smith, D. and Hu, Y. (2003) Consumer surplus in the digital economy: estimating the value of increased product variety at online booksellers, *Management Science*, 49(11), 1580–96. http://ebusiness.mit.edu/research/papers/176_ErikB_OnlineBooksellers2.pdf.

Burnett, J. (1993) *Promotional Management*. Houghton Mifflin, Boston.

Christodoulides, G. and de Chernatony, L. (2004) Dimensionalising on- and offline brands' composite equity, *Journal of Product and Brand Management*, 13(3), 168–79.

Davidow, W.H. and Malone, M.S. (1992) *The Virtual Corporation. Structuring and Revitalizing the Corporation for the 21st Century*. HarperCollins, New York.

Dayal, S., Landesberg, H. and Zeissberg, M. (2000) Building digital brands, *McKinsey Quarterly*, No. 2.

de Chernatony, L. (2001) Succeeding with brands on the Internet, *Journal of Brand Management*, 8(3), 186–95.

de Chernatony, L. and McDonald, M. (1992) *Creating Powerful Brands*. Butterworth Heinemann, Oxford.

Diamantopoulos, A. and Matthews, B. (1993) *Making Pricing Decisions. A Study of Managerial Practice*. Chapman & Hall, London.

Emiliani, V. (2001) Business-to-business online auctions: key issues for purchasing process improvement, *Supply Chain Management: An International Journal*, 5(4), 176–86.

Evans, P. and Wurster, T. S. (1999) Getting real about virtual commerce, *Harvard Business Review*, November, 84–94.

Fill, C. (2000) *Marketing Communications – Contexts, Contents and Strategies*, 3rd edn. Financial Times/Prentice Hall, Harlow.

Frazier, G. (1999) Organising and managing channels of distribution, *Journal of the Academy of Marketing Science*, 27(2), 222–40.

Ghosh, S. (1998) Making business sense of the Internet, *Harvard Business Review*, March–April, 127–35.

Gladwell, M. (2000) *The Tipping Point: How Little Things can Make a Big Difference*. Little, Brown, New York.

Harridge-March, S. (2004) Electronic marketing, the new kid on the block. *Marketing Intelligence and Planning*, 22(3), 297–309.

Introna, L. (2001) Defining the virtual organisation. In S. Barnes and B. Hunt (eds). *E-Commerce and V-Business. Business Models for Global Success*. Butterworth Heinemann, Oxford.

Jevons, C. and Gabbott, M. (2000) Trust, brand equity and brand reality in Internet business relationships: an interdisciplinary approach, *Journal of Marketing Management*, 16, 619–34.

Johnson, E., Moe, W., Fader, P., Bellman, S. and Lohse, G. (2004) On the depth and dynamics of online search behavior, *Management Science*, 50(3), 299–308.

Kotler, P. (1997) *Marketing Management: Analysis, Planning, Implementation and Control*, 9th international edn. Prentice-Hall, Upper Saddle River, NJ.

Kraut, R., Chan, A., Butler, B. and Hong, A. (1998) Coordination and virtualisation: the role of electronic networks and personal relationships, *Journal of Computer Mediated Communications*, 3(4).

Kumar, N. (1999) Internet distribution strategies: dilemmas for the incumbent, *Financial Times*, Special Issue on Mastering Information Management, no 7. Electronic Commerce (**www.ftmastering.com**).

Lautenborn, R. (1990) New marketing litany: 4Ps passes; C-words take over, *Advertising Age*, 1 October, p. 26.

McCarthy, J. (1960) *Basic Marketing: A Managerial Approach*. Irwin, Homewood, IL.

McDonald, M. and Wilson, H. (2002) *New Marketing: Transforming the Corporate Future*. Butterworth Heinemann, Oxford.

Magretta, J. (1998) The power of virtual integration. An interview with Michael Dell, *Harvard Business Review*, March–April, 72–84.

Malone, T., Yates, J. and Benjamin, R. (1987) Electronic markets and electronic hierarchies: effects of information technology on market structure and corporate strategies, *Communications of the ACM*, 30(6), 484–97.

Marn, M. (2000) Virtual pricing, *McKinsey Quarterly*, No. 4.

Marsden, P. (2004) Tipping point marketing: a primer, *Brand strategy*, April. Available at: **www.viralculture.com/pubs/tippingpoint2.htm**.

Marshall, P., McKay, J. and Burn J. (2001) Structure, strategy and success factors in the virtual organisation. In S. Barnes and B. Hunt (eds), *E-Commerce and V-Business. Business Models for Global Success*. Butterworth Heinemann, Oxford.

Mols, N. (2001) Organising for the effective introduction of new distribution channels in retail banking, *European Journal of Marketing*, 35(5/6), 661–86.

Morris, R.J. and Martin, C.L. (2000) Beanie Babies: a case study in the engineering of a high involvement/relationship-prone brand, *Journal of Product and Brand Management*, 9(2), 78–98.

Napster (2005) Annual Report, pubished at Investor relations site (**http://investor.napster.com**).

Pitt, L., Berthorn, P., Watson, R. and Ewing, M. (2001) Pricing strategy and the Net, *Business Horizons*, March–April, 45–54.

Quelch, J. and Klein, L. (1996) The Internet and international marketing, *Sloan Management Review*, Spring, 61–75.

Queree, A. (2000) *Financial Times*, Technology Supplement, 1 March.

Rayport, J. and Sviokla, J. (1994) Managing in the marketspace, *Harvard Business Review*, July, 141–50.

The Register (2005) Napster UK touts subscriber numbers. *The Register*. Tony Smith, 5 September. **www.theregister.co.uk/2005/09/05/napster_numbers**.

Ries, A. and Ries, L. (2000) *The 11 Immutable Laws of Internet Branding*. HarperCollins Business, London.

Sarkar, M., Butler, B. and Steinfield, C. (1996) Intermediaries and cybermediaries. A continuing role for mediating players in the electronic marketplace, *Journal of Computer Mediated Communication*, 1(3).

Smith, P.R. and Chaffey, D. (2005) *E-Marketing Excellence: at the Heart of EBusiness*, 2nd edn. Butterworth Heinemann, Oxford.

Wikipedia (2005) Napster. Wikipedia. Wikipedia entry at **http://en.wikipedia.org/wiki/Napster**.

Wilmshurst, J. (1993) *Below the Line Promotion*. Butterworth Heinemann, Oxford.

Wired (2002) The Day Napster Died. *Wired magazine*. Brad King, May 2002. **www.wired.com/news/mp3/0,1285,52540,00.html**.

Further reading

Allen, E. and Fjermestad, J. (2001) E-commerce marketing strategies: a framework and case analysis, *Logistics Information Management*, 14(1/2), 14–23. Includes an analysis of how the 4 Ps are impacted by the Internet.

Baker, W., Marn, M. and Zawada, C. (2000) Price smarter on the Net, *Harvard Business Review*, February, 2–7. This gives a clear summary of the challenges and opportunities of Internet pricing.

Ghosh, S. (1998) Making business sense of the Internet, *Harvard Business Review*, March–April, 127–35. This paper gives many examples of how US companies have adapted their products to the Internet and asks key questions that should govern the strategy adopted.

Harridge-March, S. (2004) Electronic marketing, the new kid on the block. *Marketing Intelligence and Planning*, 22(3), 297–309. Like the Allen and Fjermestad (2001) paper, this gives a review of the impact of the Internet on different aspects of the marketing mix.

Kumar, N. (1999) Internet distribution strategies: dilemmas for the incumbent, *Financial Times*, Special Issue on Mastering Information Management, no. 7. Electronic Commerce (**www.ftmastering.com**). This article assesses the impact of the Internet on manufacturers and their distribution channels. The other articles in this special issue are also interesting.

Smith, P.R. and Chaffey, D. (2005) *E-Marketing Excellence: at the Heart of EBusiness*, 2nd edn. Butterworth Heinemann, Oxford. Chapter 2 is devoted to applying the marketing mix to Internet marketing.

Web links

- **Chris Anderson** has a blog site (**www.thelongtail.com**), the Long Tail, to support his book on the topic published in 2006 by Hyperion, New York.
- **ClickZ** (**www.clickz.com**). An excellent collection of articles on online marketing communications, US-focused. Relevant section for this chapter: Brand marketing.
- **Gladwell.com** (**www.gladwell.com**). Author's site with extracts from *The Tipping Point* and other books.
- **Marketing on the internet (MOTI)** by Greg Rich and colleagues from OhioLink educational establishments (**http://iws.ohiolink.edu/moti/**). This site provides a succinct summary, with examples, of how each of the 4 Ps of the Internet can be applied online.
- **Paul Marsden's Viral Culture site** (**www.viralculture.com**). Articles related to the tipping point and connected marketing.

6

Relationship marketing using the Internet

Chapter at a glance

Learning objectives

After reading this chapter, the reader should be able to:

● Assess the relevance of the concepts of relationship, direct and database marketing on the Internet

● Evaluate the potential of the Internet to support one-to-one marketing and the range of techniques and systems available to support dialogue with the customer over the Internet

● Assess the characteristics required of tools to implement one-to-one marketing

Questions for marketers

Key questions for marketing managers related to this chapter are:

● How can the Internet be used to support the different stages of the customer lifecycle?

● How do I implement permission marketing?

● What do personalisation and mass customisation mean and how should I apply them in my marketing?

Links to other chapters

Related chapters are:

➤ Chapter 4 introduces customer lifecycle-based segmentation models

➤ Chapter 7 has guidelines on how to develop the right customer experience to assist in forming and maintaining relationships

➤ Chapter 8 describes methods of acquiring customers for one-to-one marketing

➤ Chapters 10 and 11 give examples of relationship marketing in the business-to-consumer and business-to-business markets

Introduction

Building long-term relationships with customers is essential for any sustainable business, and this applies equally to online elements of a business. Failure to build relationships largely caused the failures of many dot-coms following huge expenditure on customer acquisition. Research summarised by Reichheld and Schefter (2000) showed that acquiring online customers is so expensive (20–30% higher than for traditional businesses) that start-up companies may remain unprofitable for at least 2 to 3 years. The research also shows that by retaining just 5% more customers, online companies can boost their profits by 25% to 95%.

Over the last decade or more, relationship marketing, direct marketing and database marketing have combined to create a powerful new marketing paradigm. This paradigm is often referred to as customer relationship management (CRM). A related approach is known as one-to-one marketing, where in theory, relationships are managed on an individual basis. But, owing to the costs of managing relationships on an individual level, many companies will apply CRM by approaches which tailor services to develop relationships with particular customer segments or groups, rather than individuals. This involves a company in developing a long-term relationship with each customer in order to better understand that customer's needs and then deliver services that meet these individual needs.

The interactive nature of the web combined with e-mail communications provides an ideal environment in which to develop customer relationships, and databases provide a foundation for storing information about the relationship and providing information to strengthen it by improved, personalised services. This online approach to CRM is often known as e-CRM or electronic customer relationship management, and it is on this we focus in this chapter.

Figure 6.1 summarises the linkages between CRM and existing marketing approaches. Direct marketing provides the tactics that deliver the marketing communications and sometimes the product itself to the individual customer. Relationship marketing theory provides the conceptual underpinning of CRM since it emphasises enhanced customer service through knowledge of the customer, and deals with markets segmented to the level of the individual. Database marketing provides the technological enabler, allowing vast quantities of customer-related data to be stored and accessed in ways that create strategic and tactical marketing opportunities.

Customer relationship management (CRM)
A marketing-led approach to building and sustaining long-term business with customers.

One-to-one marketing
A unique dialogue occurs between a company and individual customers (or groups of customers with similar needs).

Electronic customer relationship management
Using digital communications technologies to maximise sales to existing customers and encourage continued usage of online services.

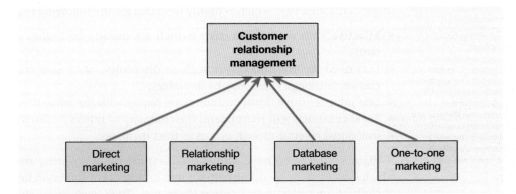

Figure 6.1 Linkages between customer relationship management and related marketing approaches

This chapter begins by introducing the key concepts of relationship marketing and e-CRM. We then review, in more detail how e-CRM can be implemented using techniques such as permission marketing, personalisation and e-mail. E-CRM operates within the context of multi-channel marketing. Since this concept has been covered as a major concept within Chapter 4 we mainly focus on online relationship marketing concepts in this chapter.

Key concepts of relationship marketing

Relationship marketing

'Consistent application of up to date knowledge of individual customers to product and service design which is communicated interactively in order to develop a continuous and long term relationship which is mutually beneficial' (Cram, 1994).

Mass marketing

One-to-many communication between a company and potential customers, with limited tailoring of the message.

Customer-centric marketing

The approach to Internet marketing function is based on customer behaviour within the target audience and then seeks to fulfil the needs and wants of each individual customer.

Sense and respond communications

Delivering timely, relevant communications to customers as part of a contact strategy based on assessment of their position in the customer lifecycle and monitoring specific interactions with a company's web site, e-mails and staff.

Relationship marketing is best understood within the context of the historical development of marketing. The Industrial Revolution, the large-scale production of more widely distributed, standardised products changed the nature of marketing. Whereas marketing had previously been largely by word of mouth and based on personal relationships, it became an impersonal mass-marketing monologue. During the twentieth century, differentiation of products and services became more important, and this highlighted the need for feedback from customers about the type of product features required. Sharma and Sheth (2004) have stressed the importance of this trend from mass marketing to what is now widely known as 'one-to-one' or 'customer-centric marketing' (although many would regard the latter as a tautology since the modern marketing concept places the customer at the heart of marketing activity). These authors give the example of the Dell model where each PC is manufactured and distributed 'on demand' according to the need for a specific customer. This is an example of what they refer to as 'reverse marketing' with the change in emphasis on marketing execution from product supply to customer need. Another aspect of this transformation is that online, web marketers can track the past behaviours of customers in order to customise communications to encourage future purchases. This approach, which is another aspect of reverse marketing and also a key concept with e-CRM, can be characterised as 'sense and respond communications'. The classic example of this is the personalisation facilities provided by Amazon where personal recommendations are provided.

Benefits of relationship marketing

Relationship marketing is aimed at increasing customer loyalty or retention within a current customer base which is highly desirable for the following reasons:

- Effectively no acquisition costs (which are usually far higher than 'maintenance' costs);
- Less need to offer incentives such as discounts, or to give vouchers to maintain custom (although these may be desirable);
- Less price-sensitive (loyal customers are happy with the value they are getting);
- Loyal customers will recommend the company to others ('referrals');
- Individual revenue growth occurs as trust increases.

Rigby et al. (2000) have summarised a study by Mainspring and Bain & Company which evaluated the spending patterns and loyalty of consumers in online retail categories of clothing, groceries and consumer electronics. Their work shows that e-tailers could not

Table 6.1 A summary of different concepts for the transactional and relationship paradigms

Transactional paradigm concept	Relationship paradigm concept	Comments and examples
Market segment	Individual customer	Raphel (1997) describes the success story of AMC Kabuki 8 movie theatres in San Francisco. Despite the competition from the giant multiplexes, AMC is flourishing because of its understanding of the cinematic preferences of its customers so they can be informed in advance of ticket sales.
		'The most failure-prone fault-line in transactional marketing is the statistical customer – the hypothetical human who is composed of statistically averaged attributes drawn form research'. (Wolfe, 1998)
Duration of transaction	Lifetime relationship	The pursuit of customer loyalty 'is a perpetual one – more of a journey than a destination'. (Duffy, 1998)
Margin	Lifetime value	To support the Huggies product in the 1970s, Kimberley-Clark spent over $10m to construct a database that could identify 75 per cent of the four million expectant mothers every year in the USA, using information obtained from doctors, hospitals and childbirth trainers. During the pregnancy, mothers received a magazine and letters with advice on baby care. When the baby arrived a coded coupon was sent, which was tracked to learn which mothers had tried the product. The justification was the lifetime value of these prospective customers, not the unit sale. (Shaw, 1996)
Market share	Most valued customers and customer share	Rather than waging expensive 'trench warfare' where profit objectives are linked automatically to overall market share, companies have now realised that, as 80 per cent of their business often comes from 20 per cent of their customers (the famous Pareto law), then retaining and delighting that 20 per cent will be much more cost-effective than trying to retain the loyalty of the 80 per cent. Reichheld (1996) conducted research indicating that an increase in customer retention of 5 per cent could improve profitability by as much as 125 per cent.
Mass market monologue	Direct marketing dialogue	'The new marketing requires a feedback loop'. (McKenna, 1993)
Passive consumers	Empowered clients	'Transactional marketing is all about seduction and propaganda and it depends on a passive, narcotized receptor, the legendary "couch potato".' (Rosenfield, 1998)

breakeven on 'one-time' shoppers. For grocery e-tailers, customers have to be retained for 18 months for breakeven. The study also shows that repeat purchasers tend to spend more in a given time period and generate larger transactions. For example, online grocery shoppers spend 23% more in months 31–36 than in the first 6 months; this includes products in other categories (cross- and up-selling). A final effect is that repeat customers tend to refer more people, to bring in greater business. The impact of these referrals can be signficant – over a 3-year period, in each product category, more than 50% additional revenue of the referrer was generated. Each referrer also has a lower acquisition cost.

Table 6.1 summarises the differences between the two paradigms discussed in this section. Figure 6.16 shows that to build relationships and loyalty online, the quality of the online experience is significant. The topic of loyalty drivers is discussed further in Chapter 7.

Differentiating customers by value

A core approach to relationship marketing is to focus our limited resources and marketing activities on the most valuable customers. Figure 6.2 gives a visual indication of this approach using the terminology suggested by Peppers and Rogers (2002). They identify three groups of customers with corresponding strategies as follows:

1 Most-valuable customers (MVCs)

These are the customers who contribute the most profit and are typically a small proportion of the total customer base as suggested by their position in the pyramid. These customers will likely have purchased more or higher-value products. The strategy for these customers focuses on retention rather than extension. In the case of a bank, personal relationship managers would be appointed for customers in this category to provide them with guidance and advice and to make sure they remain loyal. Often this strategy will work best using direct personal contact as the primary communication channel, but using online marketing for support where the customer has a propensity to use online channels.

2 Most-growable customers (MGCs)

Customers who show potential to become more valuable customers. They are profitable when assessed in terms of lifetime value, but the number of product holdings or lifetime value is relatively low compared with the MVCs.

Strategies for these customers centre on extension, through making recommendations about relevant products based on previous purchases. Encouraging similar re-purchases could also be part of this. Online marketing offers great opportunities to make personalised recommendations through the web site and e-mail.

3 Below-zero customers (BZCs)

BZCs are simply unprofitable customers. The strategy for these customers may vary – they can be encouraged to develop towards MGCs, but more typically expenditure will be minimised if it is felt that it will be difficult to change their loyalty behaviour or the source of their being unprofitable. Again, digital media can be used as a lower-cost form of marketing expenditure to encourage these customers to make repeat purchases or to allow them to self-serve online.

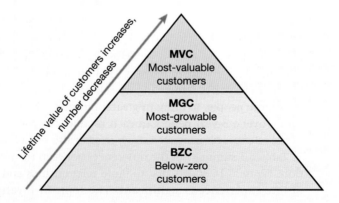

Figure 6.2 Categorising customers according to value

Customer loyalty

Another core facet of relationship marketing is its focus on increasing customer loyalty, particularly of the MVCs and MGCs. Sargeant and West (2001) describe loyalty as:

The desire on the part of the customer to continue to do business with a given supplier over time.

To successfully develop retention strategies, it is useful to acknowledge that there are two types of loyalty, behavioural loyalty and emotional loyalty. Behavioural loyalty is the name given to behaviour that proves loyalty to the brand through sales. It means that the customer behaves in the way the brand wants, i.e. by spending money. Measures of behavioural loyalty include response rates to direct marketing to the customer base, 'share of wallet' and market share. Emotional loyalty acknowledges that perceptions and emotions drive behaviour. A customer who is emotionally loyal has empathy and attachment with a brand and company and is more likely to recommend it to potential customers.

This distinction, which is not always acknowledged, is critical to retention marketing. The two types of loyalty reinforce each other if they can be achieved together and strategies need to be developed to achieve both. On the other hand, customers who are only behaviourally loyal are at risk of lapsing as soon as they become aware of or can readily switch to another supplier. Likewise there is relatively little value from an emotionally loyal customer who does not exhibit behavioural loyalty!

Sargeant and West (2001) extend the concept of behavioural and emotional loyalty through categorising customers into one of these four types:

1 *No loyalty.* Customers in a category move from one supplier to another for reasons such as cost or price promotions or because they don't discern any difference in supplier.
2 *Spurious loyalty.* In this case the customer does not switch supplier due to inertia although they have limited emotional loyalty.
3 *Latent loyalty.* A buyer does have an emotional loyalty but it doesn't necessarily translate to behavioural loyalty – they may still 'shop around'.
4 *True loyalty.* The behavioural pattern indicates a single favoured supplier or product in a given category.

The relationship between satisfaction and loyalty

Although the terms 'satisfaction' and 'loyalty' are sometimes used interchangeably, we have seen that they do not necessarily correspond. 'Customer satisfaction' refers to the degree a customer is happy about the quality of products and services. As a customer's satisfaction with products and/or services increases, so should their behavioural and emotional loyalty.

As we have seen, though, there may be customers with a high degree of satisfaction who don't exhibit behavioural loyalty, and conversely, customers who are behaviourally loyal may be at risk of defection since they are not satisfied. The implications are that it is important not only to measure satisfaction with online services, but loyalty also. In this way we are able to identify customers at risk of defection who are likely to choose an alternative and those in the zone of indifference. These are an important category of customers who, although they may have a high degree of satisfaction, are not necessarily loyal.

Mini Case Study 6.1	How car manufacturers use loyalty-based segmentation

An approach to reconciling customer satisfaction, loyalty, value and potential is to use a value-based segmentation. This modeling approach is often used by car manufacturers and other companies who are assessing strategies to enhance the future value of their customer segments. This approach involves creating a segmentation model combining real data for each customer about their current value and satisfaction and modeled values for future loyalty and value. Each customer is scored according to these four variables:

- Current satisfaction
- Current value
- Repurchase loyalty
- Future potential.

Table 6.2 Loyalty-based segmentation for car manufacturer

SLVP score	Nature of customer	Segment strategy
Moderate satisfaction and loyalty. Moderate current and future potential value.	An owner of average loyalty who replaces their car every three to four years and has a tendency to repurchase from brand.	Not a key segment to influence. But should encourage to subscribe to e-newsletter club and deliver targeted messages around time of renewal.
High satisfaction, moderate loyalty. Low future and potential value.	A satisfied owner but tends to buy second-hand and keeps cars until they have a high mileage.	Engage in dialogue via e-mail newsletter and use this to encourage advocacy and make aware of benefits of buying new.
Low satisfaction and loyalty. High current and future potential value.	A dissatisfied owner of luxury cars who is at risk of switching.	A key target segment who needs to be contacted to understand issues and reassure about quality and performance.

Key concepts of electronic customer relationship management (e-CRM)

Electronic customer relationship management

Using digital communications technologies to maximise sales to existing customers and encourage continued usage of online services.

E-CRM or electronic customer relationship management involves creating strategies and plans for how digital technology and digital data can support CRM. Some specialists in e-commerce teams have this as their job title or in their job description.

But what is e-CRM? This is what Smith and Chaffey (2005) say:

What is e-CRM? Customer Relations Management with an 'e'? Ultimately, E-CRM cannot be separated from CRM, it needs to be integrated and seamlessly. However, many organisations do have specific E-CRM initiatives or staff responsible for E-CRM. Both CRM and E-CRM are not just about technology and databases, it's not just a process or a way of doing things, it requires, in fact, a complete customer culture.

More specifically, we can say that important e-CRM challenges and activities which require management are:

- Using the *web site for customer development* from generating leads through to conversion to an online or offline sale using e-mail and web-based information to encourage purchase;

- *Managing e-mail list quality* (coverage of e-mail addresses and integration of customer profile information from other databases to enable targeting);
- Applying *e-mail marketing* to support upsell and cross-sell;
- *Data mining* to improve targeting;
- Providing online personalisation or *mass customisation* facilities to automatically recommend the 'next-best product';
- Providing *online customer service facilities* (such as frequently asked questions, callback and chat support);
- Managing *online service quality* to ensure that first-time buyers have a great customer experience that encourages them to buy again;
- Managing the *multi-channel customer experience* as they use different media as part of the buying process and customer lifecycle.

Benefits of e-CRM

Using the Internet for relationship marketing involves integrating the customer database with web sites to make the relationship targeted and personalised. Through doing this marketing can be improved as follows.

- *Targeting more cost-effectively*. Traditional targeting, for direct mail for instance, is often based on mailing lists compiled according to criteria that mean that not everyone contacted is in the target market. For example, a company wishing to acquire new affluent consumers may use postcodes to target areas with appropriate demographics, but within the postal district the population may be heterogeneous. The result of poor targeting will be low response rates, perhaps less than 1 per cent. The Internet has the benefit that the list of contacts is *self-selecting* or pre-qualified. A company will only aim to build relationships with those who have visited a web site and expressed an interest in its products by registering their name and address. The mere act of visiting the web site and browsing indicates a target customer. Thus the approach to acquiring new customers with whom to build relationships is fundamentally different, as it involves attracting the customers to the web site, where the company provides an offer to make them register.
- *Achieve mass customisation of the marketing messages* (and possibly the product). This tailoring process is described in a subsequent section. Technology makes it possible to send tailored e-mails at much lower costs than is possible with direct mail and also to provide tailored web pages to smaller groups of customers (micro-segments).
- *Increase depth and breadth and improve the nature of relationship*. The nature of the Internet medium enables more information to be supplied to customers as required. For example, special pages such as Dell's Premier can be set up to provide customers with specific information. The nature of the relationship can be changed in that contact with a customer can be made more frequently. The frequency of contact with the customer can be determined by customers – whenever they have the need to visit their personalised pages – or they can be contacted by e-mail by the company.
- *A learning relationship can be achieved using different tools throughout the customer lifecycle.* For example: tools summarise products purchased on-site and the searching behaviour that occurred before these products were bought; online feedback forms about the site or products are completed when a customer requests free information; questions asked through forms or e-mails to the online customer service facilities; online questionnaires asking about product category interests and opinions on competitors; new product development evaluation – commenting on prototypes of new products.
- *Lower cost*. Contacting customers by e-mail or through their viewing web pages costs less than using physical mail, but perhaps more importantly, information only needs to be sent to those customers who have expressed a preference for it, resulting in fewer mail-outs. Once personalisation technology has been purchased, much of the targeting and communications can be implemented automatically.

Marketing applications of CRM

A CRM system supports the following marketing applications:

1 *Sales force automation (SFA).* Sales representatives are supported in their account management through tools to arrange and record customer visits.
2 *Customer service management.* Representatives in contact centres respond to customer requests for information by using an intranet to access databases containing information on the customer, products and previous queries. It is more efficient and may increase customer convenience if customers are given the option of web self-service, i.e. accessing support data through a web interface.
3 *Managing the sales process.* This can be achieved through e-commerce sites, or in a B2B context by supporting sales representatives by recording the sales process (SFA).
4 *Campaign management.* Managing advertising, direct mail, e-mail and other campaigns.
5 *Analysis.* Through technologies such as data warehouses and approaches such as data mining, which are explained further later in the chapter, customers' characteristics, their purchase behaviour and campaigns can be analysed in order to optimise the marketing mix.

Web self-service

Customers perform information requests and transactions through a web interface rather than by contact with customer support staff.

CRM technologies and data

Database technology is at the heart of delivering these CRM applications. Often the database is accessible through an intranet web site accessed by employees or an extranet accessed by customers or partners provides an interface onto the entire customer relationship management system. E-mail is used to manage many of the inbound, outbound and internal communications managed by the CRM system. A workflow system is often used for automating CRM processes. For example, a workflow system can remind sales representatives about customer contacts or can be used to manage service delivery such as the many stages of arranging a mortgage. The three main types of customer data held as tables in customer databases for CRM are typically:

1 *Personal and profile data.* These include contact details and characteristics for profiling customers such as age and sex (B2C), and business size, industry sector and individual's role in the buying decision (B2B).
2 *Transaction data.* A record of each purchase transaction including specific product purchased, quantities, category, location, date and time and channel where purchased.
3 *Communications data.* A record of which customers have been targeted by campaigns, and their response to them (outbound communications). Also includes a record of inbound enquiries and sales representative visits and reports (B2B).

The behavioural data available through 2 and 3 are very important for targeting customers to more closely meet their needs.

Research completed by Stone et al. (2001) illustrates how customer data collected through CRM applications can be used for marketing. The types of data that are held, together with the frequency of their usage, are:

- basic customer information (75%);
- campaign history (62.5%);
- purchase patterns (sales histories) (50%);
- market information (42.5%);
- competitor information (42.5%);
- forecasts (25%).

The data within CRM systems were reported to be used for marketing applications as follows:

- targeted marketing, 80%;
- segmentation, 65%;
- keeping the right customers, 47.5%;
- trend analysis, 45%;
- increased loyalty, 42.5%;
- customised offers, 32.5%;
- increase share of customer, 27.5%.

Despite these benefits, it should be noted that in 2000, it was reported that around 75% of CRM projects failed in terms of delivering a return on investment or completion on time. This is not necessarily indicative of weaknesses in the CRM concept, rather it indicates the difficulty of implementing a complex information system that requires substantial changes to organisations' processes and major impacts on the staff that conduct them. Such failure rates occur in many other information systems projects.

Read Mini Case Study 6.2 'Customer data management at Deutsche Bank' for an example of the practical realities of managing customer data in a large organisation.

Mini Case Study 6.2   Customer data management at Deutsche Bank

Deutsche Bank is one of the largest financial institutions in Europe, with assets under management worth 100 billion euros (£60 billion). It operates in seven different countries under different names, although the company is considering consolidating into a single brand operating as a pan-European bank.

In 1999 its chairman, Dr Walther, said the company had to improve its cost-to-revenue ratio to 70 per cent from 90 per cent and add 10 million customers over the next four to eight years. That would be achieved by increasing revenues through growing customer value by cross- and up-selling, reducing costs through more targeted communications, and by getting more new customers based on meaningful data analysis.

Central to this programme has been the introduction of an enterprise-wide database, analysis and campaign management system called DataSmart. This has brought significant changes to its marketing processes and effectiveness. Achieving this new IT infrastructure has been no mean feat – Deutsche Bank has 73 million customers, of which 800,000 are on-line and 190,000 use its online brokerage service, it has 19,300 employees, 1250 branches and 250 financial centres, plus three call centres supporting Deutsche Bank 24, its telebanking service. It also has e-commerce alliances with Yahoo!, e-Bay and AOL.

'DataSmart works on four levels – providing a technical infrastructure across the enterprise, consolidating data, allowing effective data analyses and segmentations, and managing multi-channel marketing campaigns', says Jens Fruehling, head of the marketing database automation project, Deutsche Bank 24. The new database runs on the largest Sun server in Europe with 20 processors, 10 Gb of RAM and 5 terabytes of data storage. It is also mirrored. The software used comprises Oracle for the database, Prime Response for campaign management, SAS for data mining, Cognos for OLAP reporting, plus a data extraction, transformation, modelling and loading tool.

'Before DataSmart, we had a problem of how to get data from our operating systems where it was held in a variety of different ways and was designed only for use as transactional data. There are 400 million data sets created every month. We had a data warehouse which was good, but was not right for campaign management or data mining', says Fruehling.

→

The new data environment was developed to facilitate all of those things. It also brings in external data such as Experian's Mosaic. 'We have less information on new prospects, so we bought third party data on every household – the type of house, the number of householders, status, risk, lifestyle data, financial status, age, plus GIS coding', he says.

For every customer, over 1000 fields of data are now held. These allow the bank to understand customers' product needs, profile, risk, loyalty, revenue and lifetime value. That required a very sophisticated system. For every customer, there is also a whole bundle of statistical models, such as affinity for a product and channel, profitability overall and by type of product.

'These are calculated monthly so we can perform time-series analyses, so if their profitability is falling, we can target a mailing to them', says Fruehling. DataSmart has allowed Deutsche Bank to makes some important changes in its marketing process, allowing it to operate more quickly and effectively.

'We have a sales support system called BTV in our branches to communicate with each bank manager. They can see the customer data and are able to add information, such as lists of customers who should be part of a branch campaign, who to include or exclude, and response analyses', he says.

Previously, typical marketing support activity involved segmenting and selecting customers, sending these lists through BTV for veto by branch managers, making the final selection, then sending those lists to BTV and the lettershop for production. 'There were many disconnects in that process – we had no campaign history, nothing was automated. Our programmers had to write SAS code for every selection, which is not the best way to work. We had no event-driven campaigns', says Fruehling.

An interface has been developed between PrimeVantage, BTV and each system supporting the seven key channels to market. Now the database marketing unit simply selects a template for one of its output channels. This has allowed Deutsche Bank to become more targeted in its marketing activities, and also faster.

'Regular selections are very important because local branches do our campaigns. We may have up to 20 separate mailings per week for different channels. That is now much more profitable', says Fruehling. Customer surveys are a central part of the bank's measurement culture and these have also become much easier to run.

'Every month we run a customer opinion poll on a sample of 10,000. Every customer is surveyed twice in a year. That takes half a day to run, whereas previously it took one week and 30 people using SAS. If a customer responds, their name is then suppressed, if they do not, they are called by the call centre', he says.

The bank's customer acquisition programme, called AKM, now uses up to 30 mailings per year with as many as 12 different target groups and very complex selection criteria. 'We flag customers using SAS and PrimeVantage recognises those flags', he says. 'We are now looking to move to a higher communications frequency so every customer gets a relevant offer.'

Source: European Centre for Customer Strategies case study (www.eccs.uk.com), 2001

Question

Summarise the data types that Deutsche Bank collects and how they are used for customer relationship management.

Customer lifecycle management

As was explained in Chapter 4 in the section on target marketing strategy and through Mini Case Study 4.2 on Euroffice, assessing and understanding the position of the customer in their relationship with an organisation is key to online marketing strategy. In this section we review methods of assessing the position of customers in the lifecycle and the use of 'sense and respond' communications to build customer loyalty at each stage of the customer lifecycle.

A high-level view of the classic customer lifecycle of select, acquire, retain, extend is shown in Figure 6.3.

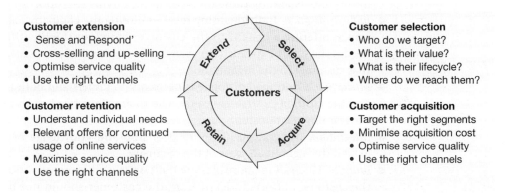

Figure 6.3 The four classic marketing activities of customer relationship management

1 Customer selection means defining the types of customers that a company will market to. It means identifying different groups of customers for which to develop offerings and to target during acquisition, retention and extension. Different ways of segmenting customers by value and by their detailed lifecycle with the company are reviewed.

2 Customer acquisition refers to marketing activities to form relationships with new customers while minimising acquisition costs and targeting high value customers. Service quality and selecting the right channels for different customers are important at this stage and throughout the lifecycle.

3 Customer retention refers to the marketing activities taken by an organisation to keep its existing customers. Identifying relevant offerings based on their individual needs and detailed position in the customer lifecycle (e.g. number and value of purchases) is key.

4 Customer extension refers to increasing the depth or range of products that a customer purchases from a company. This is often referred to as 'customer development'.

There are a range of customer extension techniques that are particularly important to online retailers:

(a) *Re-sell*. Selling similar products to existing customers – particularly important in some B2B contexts as rebuys or modified rebuys.

(b) *Cross-sell*. Selling additional products which may be closely related to the original purchase, but not necessarily so.

(c) *Up-sell*. A subset of cross-selling, but in this case, selling more expensive products.

(d) *Reactivation*. Customers who have not purchased for some time, or have lapsed can be encouraged to purchase again.

(e) *Referrals*. Generating sales from recommendations from existing customers. For example, member-get-member deals.

You can see that this framework distinguishes between customer retention and customer extension. Retention involves keeping the most valuable customers by selecting relevant customers for retention, understanding their loyalty factors that keep them buying and then developing strategies that encourage loyalty and cement the relationship. Customer extension is about developing customers to try a broader range of products to convert the most growable customers into the most valuable customers. You will also see that there are common features to each area – balancing cost and quality of service through the channels used according to the anticipated value of customers.

Peppers and Rogers (1997) recommend the following stages to achieve these goals, which they popularise as the 5 Is (as distinct from the 4 Ps):

- *Identification*. It is necessary to learn the characteristics of customers in as much detail as possible to be able to conduct the dialogue. In a business-to-business context, this means understanding those involved in the buying decision.
- *Individualisation*. Individualising means tailoring the company's approach to each customer, offering a benefit to the customer based on the identification of customer needs. The effort expended on each customer should be consistent with the value of that customer to the organisation.
- *Interaction*. Continued dialogue is necessary to understand both the customer's needs and the customer's strategic value. The interactions need to be recorded to facilitate the learning relationship.
- *Integration*. Integration of the relationship and knowledge of the customer must extend throughout all parts of the company.
- *Integrity*. Since all relationships are built on trust it is essential not to lose the trust of the customer. Efforts to learn from the customer should not be seen as intrusive, and privacy should be maintained. (See Chapter 3 for coverage of privacy issues related to e-CRM.)

Permission marketing

Permission marketing

Customers agree (opt-in) to be involved in an organisation's marketing activities, usually as a result of an incentive.

Permission marketing is a significant concept that underpins online CRM throughout management of the customer lifecycle. 'Permission marketing' is a term coined by Seth Godin. It is best characterised with just three (or four) words:

Permission marketing is …
anticipated, relevant and personal [and timely].

Godin (1999) notes that while research used to show we were bombarded by 500 marketing messages a day, with the advent of the web and digital TV this has now increased to over 3000 a day! From the marketing organisation's viewpoint, this leads to a dilution in the effectiveness of the messages – how can the communications of any one company stand out? From the customer's viewpoint, time is seemingly in ever-shorter supply, customers are losing patience and expect reward for their attention, time and information.

Interruption marketing

Marketing communications that disrupt customers' activities.

Godin refers to the traditional approach as 'interruption marketing'. Permission marketing is about seeking the customer's permission before engaging them in a relationship and providing something in exchange. The classic exchange is based on information or entertainment – a B2B site can offer a free report in exchange for a customer sharing their e-mail address which will be used to maintain a dialogue; a B2C site can offer a screensaver in exchange.

From a practical e-commerce perspective, we can think of a customer agreeing to engage in a relationship when they check a box on a web form to indicate that they agree

Opt-in
A customer proactively agrees to receive further information.

Opt-out
A customer declines the offer to receive further information.

to receive further communications from a company (see Figure 3.3 for further examples). This approach is referred to as 'opt-in'. This is preferable to opt-out, the situation where a customer has to consciously agree not to receive further information.

The importance of incentivisation in permission marketing has also been emphasised by Seth Godin who likens the process of acquisition and retention to dating someone. Likening customer relationship building to social behaviour is not new, as O'Malley and Tynan (2001) note; the analogy of marriage has been used since the 1980s at least. They also report on consumer research that indicates that while marriage may be analogous to business relationships, it is less appropriate for B2C relationships. Moller and Halinen (2000) have also suggested that due to the complexity of the exchange, longer-term relationships are more readily formed for interorganisational exchanges. So, the description of the approaches that follow are perhaps more appropriate for B2B applications.

Godin (1999) suggests that dating the customer involves:

1 offering the prospect an *incentive* to volunteer;
2 using the attention offered by the prospect, offering a curriculum over time, teaching the consumer about your product or service;
3 reinforcing the *incentive* to guarantee that the prospect maintains the permission;
4 offering additional *incentives* to get even more permission from the consumer;
5 over time, using the permission to change consumer behaviour towards profits.

Notice the importance of incentives at each stage. The use of incentives at the start of the relationship and throughout it are key to successful relationships. As we shall see in a later section, e-mail is very important in permission marketing to maintain the dialogue between company and customer.

Writing for *What's New in Marketing* e-newsletter, Chaffey (2004) has extended Godin's principles to e-CRM with his 'e-permission marketing principles':

● **Principle 1**. '*Consider selective opt-in to communications.*' In other words, offer choice in *communications preferences* to the customer to ensure more relevant communications. Some customers may not want a weekly e-newsletter, rather they may only want to hear about new product releases. Remember opt-in is a legal requirement in many countries. Four key communications preferences options, selected by tick box are:

 – Content – news, products, offers, events
 – Frequency – weekly, monthly, quarterly, or alerts
 – Channel – e-mail, direct mail, phone or SMS
 – Format – text vs HTML.

Make sure though that through providing choice you do not overstretch your resources, or on the other hand limit your capabilities to market to customers (for example if customers only opt in to an annual communication such as a catalogue update) you still need to find a way to control the frequency and type of communications.

● **Principle 2**. *Create a 'common customer profile'*. A structured approach to customer data capture is needed otherwise some data will be missed, as is the case with the utility company that collected 80,000 e-mail addresses, but forgot to ask for the postcode for geo-targeting! This can be achieved through a common customer profile – a definition of all the database fields that are relevant to the marketer in order to understand and target the customer with a relevant offering. The customer profile can have different levels to set targets for data quality (Level 1 is contact details and key profile fields only, Level 2 includes preferences and Level 3 includes full purchase and response behaviour).

- **Principle 3.** *Offer a range of opt-in incentives.* Many web sites now have 'free-win-save' incentives to encourage opt-in, but often it is one incentive fits all visitors. Different incentives for different audiences will generate a higher volume of permission, particularly for business-to-business web sites. We can also gauge the characteristics of the respondent by the type of incentives or communications they have requested, without the need to ask them.

- **Principle 4.** *'Don't make opt-out too easy.'* Often marketers make it too easy to unsubscribe. Although offering some form of opt-out is now a legal requirement in many countries due to privacy laws, a single click to unsubscribe is making it too easy. Instead, wise e-permission marketers such as Amazon use the concept of 'My Profile' or a 'selective opt-out'. Instead of unsubscribe, they offer a link to a 'communications preferences' web form to update a profile, which includes the options to reduce communications which may be the option taken rather than unsubscribing completely.

- **Principle 5.** *'Watch, don't ask.'* The need to ask interruptive questions can be reduced through the use of monitoring clicks to better understand customer needs and to trigger follow-up communications. Some examples:
  - Monitoring clickthrough to different types of content or offer.
  - Monitoring the engagement of individual customers with e-mail communications.
  - Follow-up reminder to those who don't open the e-mail first time.

- **Principle 6.** *Create an outbound contact strategy.* Online permission marketers need a plan for the number, frequency and type of online and offline communications and offers. This is a contact or touch strategy which is particularly important for large organisations with several marketers responsible for e-mail communications. The contact strategy should indicate the following. (1) Frequency (e.g. minimum once per quarter and maximum once per month). (2) Interval (e.g. there must be a gap of at least one week or one month between communications). (3) Content and offers (we may want to limit or achieve a certain number of prize draws or information-led offers). (4) Links between online communications and offline communications. (5) A control strategy (a mechanism to make sure these guidelines are adhered to, for example using a single 'focal point' for checking all communications before creation dispatch).

Examples of contact strategies for Euroffice and Tesco.com were discussed in Chapter 4.

Personalisation and mass customisation

The potential power of personalisation is suggested by these quotes from Evans et al. (2000) that show the negative effects of lack of targeting of traditional direct mail:

'Don't like unsolicited mail ... haven't asked for it and I'm not interested.'

(Female, 25–34)

'Most isn't wanted, it's not relevant and just clutters up the table ... you have to sort through it to get to the "real mail".'

(Male, 45–54)

'It's annoying to be sent things that you are not interested in. Even more annoying when they phone you up. ... If you wanted something you would go and find out about it.'

(Female, 45–54)

Personalisation and mass customisation can be used to tailor information content on a web site and opt-in e-mail can be used to deliver it to add value and at the same time remind the customer about a product. 'Personalisation' and 'mass customisation' are terms that are often used interchangeably. In the strict sense, personalisation refers to

Contact or touch strategy

Definition of the sequence and type of outbound communications required at different points in the customer lifecycle.

Personalisation

Web-based personalisation involves delivering customised content for the individual, through web pages, e-mail or push technology.

Mass customisation

Mass customisation is the creation of tailored marketing messages or products for individual customers or groups of customers typically using technology to retain the economies of scale and the capacity of mass marketing or production.

customisation of information requested by a site customer at an *individual* level. Mass customisation involves providing tailored content to a *group or individual* with similar interests. It uses technology to achieve this on an economical basis. An example of mass customisation is when Amazon recommends similar books according to what others in a segment have offered, or if it sent a similar e-mail to customers who had an interest in a particular topic such as e-commerce.

Other methods of profiling customers include collaborative filtering and monitoring the content they view. With collaborative filtering, customers are openly asked what their interests are, typically by checking boxes that correspond to their interests. A database then compares the customer's preferences with those of other customers in its database, and then makes recommendations or delivers information accordingly. The more information a database contains about an individual customer, the more useful its recommendations can be. The best-known example of this technology in action can be found on the Amazon web site (**www.amazon.com**), where the database reveals that customers who bought book 'x' also bought books 'y' and 'z'.

Figure 6.4 summarises the options available to organisations wishing to use the Internet for mass customisation or personalisation. If there is little information available about the customer and it is not integrated with the web site then no mass customisation is possible (A). To achieve mass customisation or personalisation, the organisation must have sufficient information about the customer. For limited tailoring to groups of customers (B), it is necessary to have basic profiling information such as age, sex, social group, product category interest or, for B2B, role in the buying unit. This information must be contained in a database system that is directly linked to the system used to display web site content. For personalisation on a one-to-one level (C) more detailed information about specific interests, perhaps available from a purchase history, should be available.

An organisation can use Figure 6.4 to plan their relationship marketing strategy. The symbols X_1 to X_3 show a typical path for an organisation. At X_1 information collected about customers is limited. At X_2 detailed information is available about customers, but it is in discrete databases that are not integrated with the web site. At X_3 the strategy is to provide mass customisation of information and offers to major segments, since it is felt that the expense of full personalisation is not warranted.

Collaborative filtering

Profiling of customer interest coupled with delivery of specific information and offers, often based on the interests of similar customers.

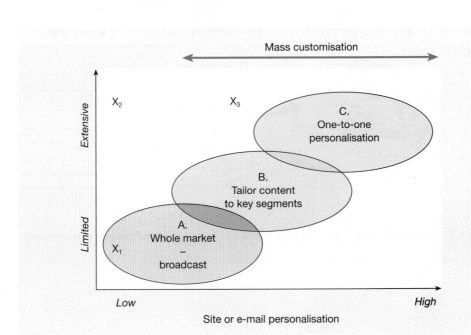

Figure 6.4 Options for mass customisation and personalisation using the Internet

Online and multi-channel service quality

In the last part of Chapter 7, we review how the online presence can be managed in order to achieve online service quality which is also a key element leading to customer satisfaction and loyalty (Figure 6.16).

Approaches to implementing e-CRM

E-CRM uses common approaches or processes to achieve online customer acquisition and retention. Refer to Figure 6.5 for a summary of a common, effective process for online relationship building to achieve the different stages of the customer lifecycle.

In the following sections we proceed through the different stages in more detail.

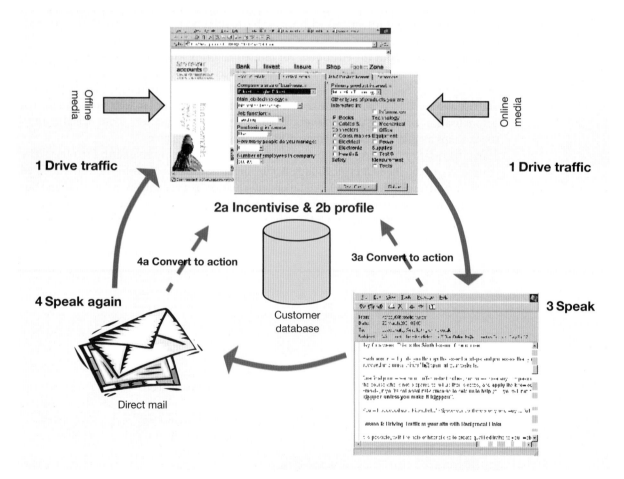

Figure 6.5 A summary of an effective process of permission-based online relationship building

Stage 1: Attract new and existing customers to site

For new customers, the goal is to attract quality visitors who are likely to convert to the site using all the online and offline methods of site promotion described in Chapter 8, such as search engines, portals and banner advertisements. These promotion methods should aim to highlight the value proposition of the site and it is important to communicate a range of incentives such as free information or competitions (and others shown in top left box of Figure 6.7). To encourage new users to use the one-to-one facilities of the web site, information about the web site or incentives to visit it can be built into existing direct marketing campaigns such as catalogue mailshots.

Stage 2a: Incentivise visitors to action

Lead generation offers
....
Offered in return for customers providing their contact details and characteristics. Commonly used in B2B marketing where free information such as a report or a seminar will be offered.

Sales generation offers
....
Offers that encourage product trial. A coupon redeemed against a purchase is a classic example.

The first time a visitor arrives at a site is the most important since if he or she does not find the desired information or experience, they may not return. We need to move from using the customer using the Internet in pull mode, to the marketer using the Internet in push mode through e-mail and traditional direct mail communications (Chapter 8). The quality and credibility of the site must be sufficient to retain the visitor's interest so that he or she stays on the site. To initiate one-to-one, offers or incentives must be prominent, ideally on the home page. It can be argued that converting unprofiled visitors to profiled visitors is a major design objective of a web site. Two types of incentives can be identified: lead generation offers and sales generation offers.

Types of offers marketers can devise include information value, entertainment value, monetary value and privileged access to information (such as that only available on an extranet).

Stage 2b: Capture customer information to maintain relationship

Capturing profile information is commonly achieved through an online form such as Figure 6.6 which the customer must complete to receive the offer. It is important to design these forms to maximise their completion. Factors which are important are:

- Branding to reassure the customer;
- *Key profile fields* to capture the most important information to segment the customer for future communications, in this case, postcode, airport and preferred activities (not too many questions must be asked);
- *Mandatory fields* – mark fields which must be completed, or as in this case, only include mandatory figures;
- *Privacy* – 'we will not share' is the magic phrase to counter the customer's main fear of their details being passed on. A full privacy statement should be available for those who need it;
- *KISS* – 'Keep It Simple, Stupid' is a well-known American phrase;
- *WIFM* – 'What's in it for me?' Explain why the customer's data is being captured – which benefits it will give them;
- Validate e-mail, postcode – check data as far as possible to make it accurate.

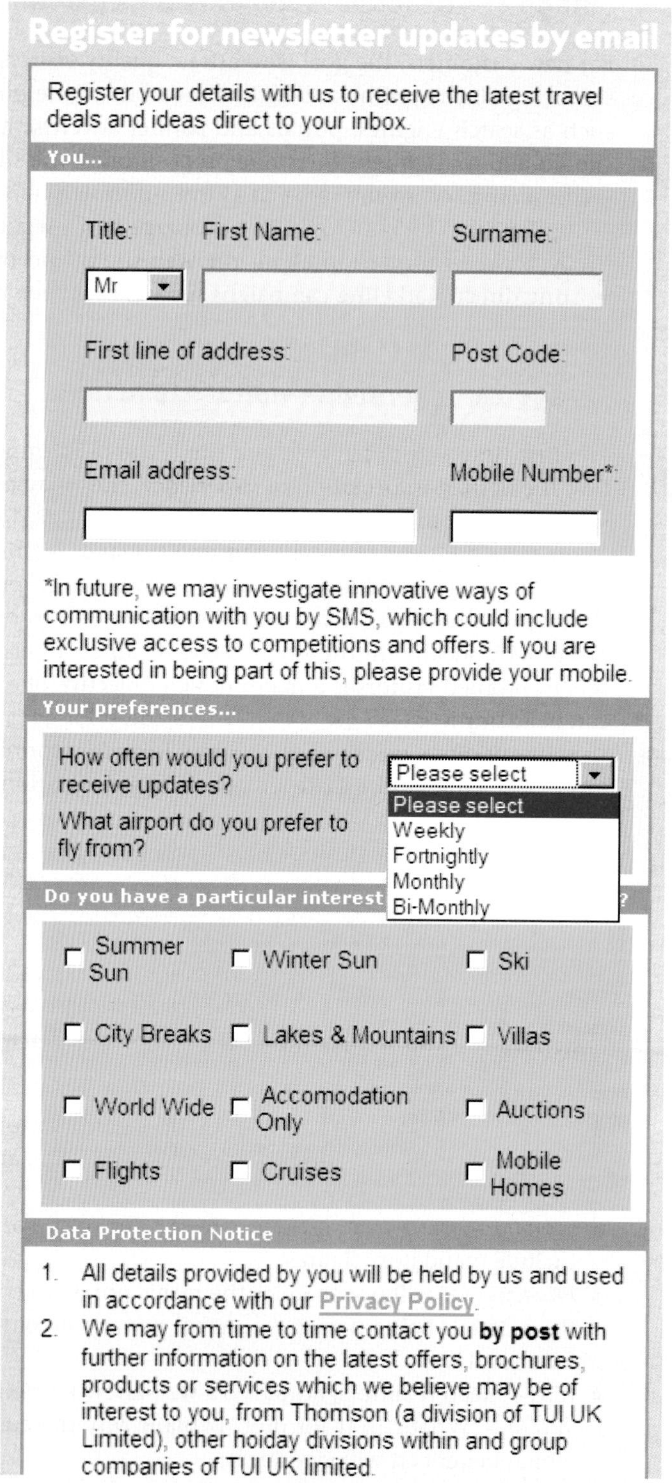

Register for newsletter updates by email

Register your details with us to receive the latest travel deals and ideas direct to your inbox.

You...

Title: First Name: Surname:

[Mr ▼] [   ] [   ]

First line of address: Post Code:

[   ] [   ]

Email address: Mobile Number*:

[   ] [   ]

*In future, we may investigate innovative ways of communication with you by SMS, which could include exclusive access to competitions and offers. If you are interested in being part of this, please provide your mobile.

Your preferences...

How often would you prefer to receive updates? [Please select ▼]

What airport do you prefer to fly from?

- Please select
- Weekly
- Fortnightly
- Monthly
- Bi-Monthly

Do you have a particular interest

☐ Summer Sun ☐ Winter Sun ☐ Ski

☐ City Breaks ☐ Lakes & Mountains ☐ Villas

☐ World Wide ☐ Accomodation Only ☐ Auctions

☐ Flights ☐ Cruises ☐ Mobile Homes

Data Protection Notice

1. All details provided by you will be held by us and used in accordance with our Privacy Policy.
2. We may from time to time contact you **by post** with further information on the latest offers, brochures, products or services which we believe may be of interest to you, from Thomson (a division of TUI UK Limited), other hoiday divisions within and group companies of TUI UK limited.

Figure 6.6 Opt-in customer profiling form

As well as online data capture, it is important to use all customer touchpoints to capture information and keep it up-to-date since this affects our capabilities to target customers accurately. Figure 6.7 provides a good way for a company to review all the possible methods of capturing e-mail addresses and other profile information:

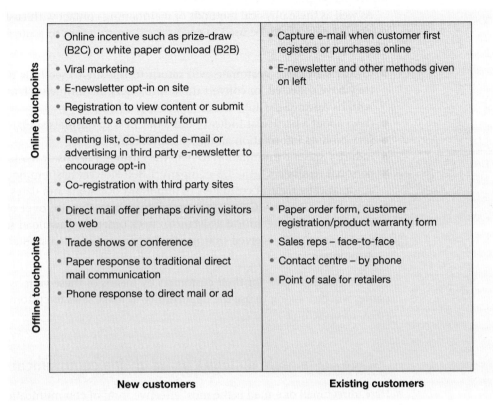

Figure 6.7 Matrix of customer touchpoints for collecting and updating customer e-mail contact and other profile information

Apart from the contact information, the other important information to collect is a method of profiling the customer so that appropriate information can be delivered to them. For example, B2B company RS Components asks for:

- industry sector;
- purchasing influence;
- specific areas of product interest;
- how many people you manage;
- total number of employees in company.

Stage 3: Maintain dialogue using online communication

To build the relationship between company and customer there are three main Internet-based methods of physically making the communication. These are:

1 Send e-mail to customer.
2 Display specific information on web site when the customer logs in. This is referred to as 'personalisation'.
3 Use push technology to deliver information to the individual.

Dialogue will also be supplemented by other tools such as mailshots, phone calls or personal visits, depending on the context. For example, after a customer registers on the RS Components web site, the company sends out a letter to the customer with promotional offers and a credit-card-sized reminder of the user name and password to use to log in to the site.

As well as these physical methods of maintaining contact with customers, many other marketing devices can be used to encourage users to return to a site (see also Chapter 8). These include:

- loyalty schemes – customers will return to the site to see how many loyalty points they have collected, or convert them into offers. An airline such as American Airlines, with its Advantage Club, is a good example of this;
- news about a particular industry (for a business-to-business site);
- new product information and price promotions;
- industry-specific information to help the customer do his or her job;
- personal reminders – the US company 1-800-Flowers has reminder programmes that automatically remind customers of important occasions and dates;
- customer support – Cisco's customers log on to the site over one million times a month to receive technical assistance, check orders or download software. The online service is so well received that nearly 70 per cent of all customer enquiries are handled online.

While adding value for their customers by means of these various mechanisms, companies will be looking to use the opportunity to make sales to customers by, for example, cross- or up-selling.

Stage 4: Maintain dialogue using offline communication

Here, direct mail or e-mail is the most effective form of communication since this can be tailored to be consistent with the user's preference. The aim here may be to drive traffic to the web site as follows:

- online competition;
- online web seminar (webinar);
- sales promotion.

When e-mail addresses are captured offline a common problem is the level of errors in the address – this can often reach a double-figure percentage. Plan for this also – staff should be trained in the importance of getting the e-mail address correct and how to check for an invalid address format. Some call centres have even incentivised staff according to the number of valid e-mail addresses they collect. When collecting addresses on paper, some practical steps can help, such as allowing sufficient space for the e-mail address and asking for it to be written in CAPS.

A further objective in stage 3 and 4 is to improve customer information quality. In particular, e-mails may bounce – in which case offline touchpoints as indicated in Figure 6.7 need to be planned to collect these e-mail addresses.

The balance between online communications (stage 3) and offline communications (stage 4) should be determined by how responsive customers are to different communications channels since stage 3 is a lower-cost route.

The IDIC approach to relationship building

An alternative process for building customer relationships online has been suggested by Peppers and Rogers (1998) and Peppers et al. (1999). They suggest the IDIC approach as a framework for customer relationship management and using the web effectively to form and build relationships (Figure 6.8). Examples of the application of IDIC include:

1 *Customer identification*. This stresses the need to identify each customer on their first visit and subsequent visits. Common methods for identification are use of cookies or asking a customer to log on to a site. In subsequent customer contacts, additional customer information should be obtained using a process known as '**drip irrigation**'. Since information will become out-of-date through time, it is important to verify, update and delete customer information.

2 *Customer differentiation*. This refers to building a profile to help segment customers. Appropriate services are then developed for each customer. Activities suggested are identifying the top customers, non-profitable customers, large customers that have ordered less in recent years and customers that buy more products from competitors.

3 *Customer interaction*. These are interactions provided on-site such as customer service questions or creating a tailored product. More generally, companies should listen to the needs and experiences of major customers. Interactions should be in the customer-preferred channel, for example e-mail, phone or post.

4 *Customer communication*. This refers to dynamic personalisation or mass customisation of content or e-mails according to the segmentation achieved at the acquisition stage. This stage also involves further market research to find out if products can be further tailored to meet customers' needs.

Drip irrigation

Collecting information about customer needs through their lifetime.

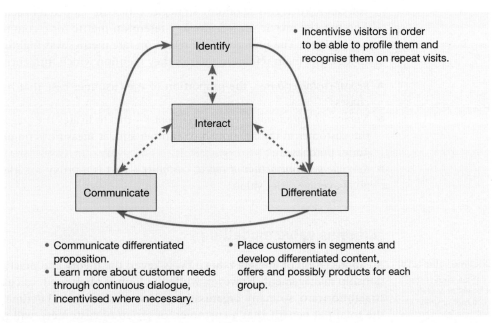

Figure 6.8 The elements of the IDIC framework

Techniques for managing customer activity and value

Within the online customer base of an organisation, there will be customers that have different levels of activity in usage of online services or in sales. A good example is a bank – some customers may use the online account once a week, others much less frequently and some not at all. Figure 6.9 illustrates the different levels of activity. A key part of e-CRM strategy is to define measures which indicate activity levels and then develop tactics to increase activity levels through more frequent use. An online magazine could segment its customers in this way, also based on returning visitors. Even for companies without transactional service a similar concept can apply if they use e-mail marketing – some customers will regularly read and interact with the e-mail and others will not.

Objectives and corresponding tactics can be set for:

- Increasing number of new users per month and annually (separate objectives will be set for existing bank customers and new bank customers) through promoting online services to drive visitors to the web site.
- Increasing percentage of active users (an appropriate threshold can be used – for some other organisations could be set at 7, 30 or 90 days). Using direct communications such as e-mail, personalised web site messages, direct mail and phone communications to new, dormant and inactive users increases the percentage of active users.
- Decreasing percentage of dormant users (were once new or active – could be sub-categories), but have not used the service or responded to communications within a defined time period such as three months.
- Decreasing percentage of inactive users (or non-activated) users. These are those who signed up for a service such as online banking and had a username issued, but they have not used the service.

You can see that corresponding strategies can be developed for each of these objectives.

Another key metric, in fact the key retention metric for e-commerce sites, refers to repeat business. The importance of retention rate metrics was highlighted by Agrawal et al. (2001). The main retention metrics they mention which influence profitability are:

- *Repeat-customer base* – the proportion of the customer base that has made repeat purchases;
- *Number of transactions per repeat customer* – this indicates the stage of development of the customer in the relationship (another similar measure is number of product categories purchased);
- *Revenue per transaction of repeat customer* – this is a proxy for lifetime value since it gives average order value.

Lifetime value modelling

Lifetime value (LTV)

Lifetime value is the total net benefit that a customer or group of customers will provide a company over their total relationship with a company.

An appreciation of lifetime value (LTV) is key to the theory and practice of customer relationship management. However, while the term is often used, calculation of LTV is not straightforward, so many organisations do not calculate it. Lifetime value is defined as the total net benefit that a customer, or group of customers, will provide a company over their total relationship with the company. Modelling is based on estimating the income and costs associated with each customer over a period of time and then calculating the net present value in current monetary terms using a discount rate value applied over the period.

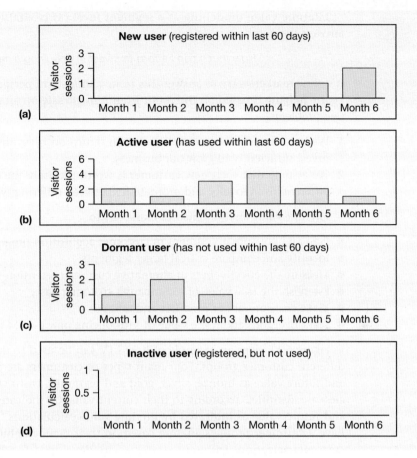

Figure 6.9 Activity segmentation of a site requiring registration

There are different degrees of sophistication in calculating LTV. These are indicated in Figure 6.10. Option 1 is a practical way or approximate proxy for future LTV, but the true LTV is the future value of the customer at an individual level.

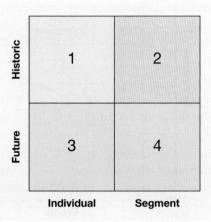

Figure 6.10 Different representations of lifetime value calculation

Lifetime value modelling at a segment level (4) is vital within marketing since it answers the question:

How much can I afford to invest in acquiring a new customer?

If online marketers try to answer this from a short-term perspective, as is often the case, i.e. by judging it based on the profit from a single sale on an e-commerce site, there are two problems:

1 We become very focused on short-term return on investment (ROI) and so may not invest sufficiently to grow our business.
2 We assume that each new customer is worth precisely the same to us and we ignore differentials in loyalty and profitability between differing types of customer.

Lifetime value analysis enables marketers to:

● Plan and measure investment in customer acquisition programmes;
● Identify and compare critical target segments;
● Measure the effectiveness of alternative customer retention strategies;
● Establish the true value of a company's customer base;
● Make decisions about products and offers;
● Make decisions about the value of introducing new e-CRM technologies.

Figure 6.11 gives an example of how LTV can be used to develop a CRM strategy for different customer groups. Four main types of customers are indicated by their current and future value as bronze, silver, gold and platinum. Distinct customer groupings (circles) are identified according to their current value (as indicated by current profitability) and future value as indicated by lifetime value calculations. Each of these groups will have a customer profile signature based on their demographics, so this can be used for customer selection. Different strategies are developed for different customer groups within the four main value groupings. Some bronze customers such as groups A and B realistically do not have development potential and are typically unprofitable, so the

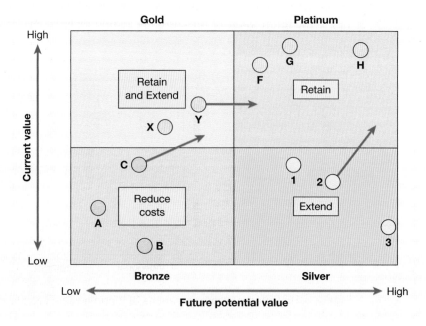

Figure 6.11 An example of an LTV-based segmentation plan

aim is to reduce costs in communications and if they do not remain as customers this is acceptable. Some bronze customers such as group C may have potential for growth so for these the strategy is to extend their purchases. Silver customers are targeted with customer extension offers and gold customers are extended where possible although they have relatively little growth potential. Platinum customers are the best customers, so it is important to understand the communication preferences of these customers and to not over-communicate unless there is evidence that they may defect.

To illustrate another application of LTV and how it is calculated, take a look at the last example in Activity 6.1.

| Activity 6.1 | Charity uses lifetime value modelling to assess returns from new e-CRM system |

A charity is considering implementing a new e-mail marketing system to increase donations from its donors. The charity's main role is as a relief agency which aims to reduce poverty through providing aid, particularly to the regions that need it most. Currently, its only e-mail activity is a monthly e-newsletter received by its 200,000 subscribers which features its current campaigns and appeals. It hopes to increase donations by using a more targeted approach to increase donations based on previous customer behaviour. The e-mail system will integrate with the donor database which contains information on customer profiles and previous donations.

The company is considering three solutions which will cost between £50,000 and £100,000 in the first year. In the charity, all such investments are assessed using lifetime value modelling.

Table 6.3 is a lifetime value model showing customer value derived from using the current system and marketing activities.

Table 6.3 Lifetime value model for customer base for current system

		Year 1	Year 2	Year 3	Year 4	Year 5
A	Donors	100,000	50,000	27,500	16,500	10,725
B	Retention	50%	55%	60%	65%	70%
C	Donations per annum	£100	£120	£140	£160	£180
D	Total donations	£10,000,000	£6,000,000	£3,850,000	£2,640,000	£1,930,500
E	Net profit (at 20% margin)	£2,000,000.0	£1,200,000.0	£770,000.0	£528,000.0	£386,100.0
F	Discount rate	1	0.86	0.7396	0.636	0.547
G	NPV contribution	£2,000,000.0	£1,032,000.0	£569,492.0	£335,808.0	£211,196.7
H	Cumulative NPV contribution	£2,000,000.0	£3,032,000.0	£3,601,492.0	£3,937,300.0	£4,148,496.7
I	Lifetime value at net present value	£20.0	£30.3	£36.0	£39.4	£41.5

A *Donors* – this is the number of initial donors. It declines each year dependent on the retention rate (row B).

B *Retention rate* – in lifetime value modelling it is usually found to increase year-on-year, since customers who stay loyal are more likely to remain loyal.

C *Donations per annum* – likewise, the charity finds that the average contributions per year increase through time within this group of customers.

D *Total donations* – calculated through multiplying rows B and C.

E *Net profit (at 20% margin)* – LTV modelling is based on profit contributed by this group of customers, row D is multiplied by 0.2.

F *Discount rate* – since the value of money held at a point in time will decrease due to inflation, a discount rate is applied to calculate the value of future returns in terms of current day value.

G *NPV contribution* – this is the profitability after taking the discount factor into account to give net present value in future years. This is calculated by multiplying row E by row F.

H *Cumulative NPV contribution* – this adds the previous year's NPV for each year.

I *Lifetime value at net present value* – this is a value per customer calculated by dividing row H by the initial number of donors in Year 1.

Based on preliminary tests with improved targeting, it is estimated that with the new system retention rates will increase from 50% to 51% in the first year, increasing by 5% per year as currently. It is estimated that in Year 1 donations per annum will increase from £100 per annum to £102 per annum, increasing by £20 per year as currently.

Question

Using the example of the lifetime value for the current donor base with the current system, calculate the LTV with the new system.

Sense, respond, adjust – delivering relevant e-communications through monitoring customer behaviour

To be able to identify customers in the categories of value, growth, responsiveness or defection risk we need to characterise them using information about them which indicates their purchase and campaign-response *behaviour*. This is because the past and current actual behaviour is often the best predictor of future behaviour. We can then seek to influence this future behaviour.

Digital marketing enables marketers to create a cycle of:

- Monitoring customer actions or behaviours and then ...
- Reacting with appropriate messages and offers to encourage desired behaviours
- Monitoring response to these messages and continuing with additional communications and monitoring.

Or if you prefer, simply:

Sense → Respond → Adjust

The sensing is done through using technology to monitor visits to particular content on a web site or clicking on particular links in an e-mail. Purchase history can also be monitored, but since purchase information is often stored in a legacy sales system it is important to integrate this with systems used for communicating with customers. The response can be done through messages on-site, or in e-mail and then adjustment occurs through further sensing and responding.

This 'sense and respond' technique has traditionally been completed by catalogue retailers such as Argos or Littlewoods Index using a technique known as 'RFM analysis'. This technique tends to be little known outside retail circles, but e-CRM gives great potential to apply it in a range of techniques since we can use it not only to analyse purchase history, but also visit or log-in frequency to a site or online service and response rates to e-mail communications.

Recency Frequency Monetary value (RFM) analysis

RFM is sometimes known as FRAC, which stands for: Frequency, Recency, Amount, (obviously equivalent to monetary value), Category (types of product purchased – not included within RFM). We will now give an overview of how RFM approaches can be applied, with special reference to online marketing. We will also look at the related concepts of latency and hurdle rates.

Recency

This is the **Recency** of customer action, e.g. purchase, site visit, account access, e-mail response, e.g. 3 months ago. Novo (2003) stresses the importance of recency when he says:

> Recency, or the number of days that have gone by since a customer completed an action (purchase, log-in, download, etc.) is the most powerful predictor of the customer repeating an action … Recency is why you receive another catalogue from the company shortly after you make your first purchase from them.

Online applications of analysis of recency include: monitoring through time to identify vulnerable customers, scoring customers to preferentially target more responsive customers for cost savings.

Frequency

Frequency is the number of times an action is completed in a period of a customer action, e.g. purchase, visit, e-mail response, e.g. 5 purchases per year, 5 visits per month, 5 log-ins per week, 5 e-mail opens per month, 5 e-mail clicks per year. Online applications of this analysis include combining with recency for 'RF targeting'.

Monetary value

The **Monetary** value of purchase(s) can be measured in different ways, e.g. average order value of £50, total annual purchase value of £5,000. Generally, customers with higher monetary values tend to have a higher loyalty and potential future value since they have purchased more items historically. One example application would be to exclude these customers from special promotions if their RF scores suggested they were actively purchasing. Frequency is often a proxy for monetary value per year since the more products purchased, the higher the overall monetary value. It is possible, then, to simplify analysis by just using Recency and Frequency. Monetary value can also skew the analysis with high-value initial purchases.

Latency

Latency is related to Frequency – it is the average time between customer events in the customer lifecycle. Examples include the average time between web site visits, second and third purchase and e-mail clickthroughs. Online applications of latency include putting in place triggers that alert companies to customer behaviour outside the norm, for example increased interest or disinterest, and then to manage this behaviour using e-communications or traditional communications. For example, if a B2B or B2C organisation with a long interval between purchases would find that the average latency increased for a particular customer, then they may be investigating an additional purchase (their recency and frequency would likely increase also). E-mails, phone calls or direct mail could then be used to target this person with relevant offers according to what they were searching for.

Hurdle rate

According to Novo (2003), 'hurdle rate' refers to the percentage of customers in a group (such as in a segment or on a list) who have completed an action. It is a useful concept, although the terminology doesn't really describe its application. Its value is that it can be used to compare the engagement of different groups or to set targets to increase engagement with online channels as the examples below show:

- 20% of customers have visited in past 6 months
- 5% of customers have made 3 or more purchases in year
- 60% of registrants have logged on to system in year
- 30% have clicked through on e-mail in year.

Grouping customers into different RFM categories

In the examples above, each division for Recency, Frequency and Monetary value is placed in an arbitrary position to place a roughly equal number of customers in each group. This approach is also useful since the marketer can set thresholds of value relevant to their understanding of their customers.

RFM analysis involves two techniques for grouping customers

1 Statistical RFM analysis

This involves placing an equal number of customers in each RFM category using quintiles of 20% (10 deciles can also be used for larger databases) as shown in Figure 6.12. The figure also shows one application of RFM with a view to using communications channels more effectively. Lower-cost e-communications can be used to correspond with customers who use only services more frequently since they prefer these channels while more expensive offline communications can be used for customers who seem to prefer traditional channels.

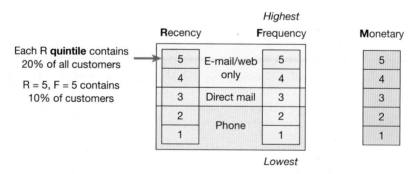

Note here boundaries are arbitrary in order to place an equal number into each group

Figure 6.12 RFM analysis

2 Arbitrary divisions of customer database

This approach is also useful since the marketer can set thresholds of value relevant to their understanding of their customers.

For example, RFM analysis can be applied for targeting using e-mail according to how a customer interacts with an e-commerce site. Values could be assigned to each customer as follows:

Recency:
1 – Over 12 months
2 – Within last 12 months
3 – Within last 6 months
4 – Within last 3 months
5 – Within last 1 month

Frequency:
1 – More than once every 6 months
2 – Every 6 months
3 – Every 3 months
4 – Every 2 months
5 – Monthly

Monetary value:
1 – Less than £10
2 – £10–£50
3 – £50–£100
4 – £100–£200
5 – More than £200

Simplified versions of this analysis can be created to make it more manageable, for example a theatre group uses these nine categories for its direct marketing:

Oncers (attended theatre once)
- Recent oncer   attended <12 months
- Rusty oncer   attended >12 <36 months
- Very rusty oncer   attended in 36+ months

Twicers:
- Recent twicer   attended < 12 months
- Rusty twicer   attended >12, < 36 months
- Very rusty twicer   attended in 36+ months

2+ subscribers:
- Current subscribers   booked 2+ events in current season
- Recent   booked 2+ last season
- Very rusty   booked 2+ more than a season ago

Another example, with real-world data is shown in Figure 6.13. You can see that plotting customer numbers against recency and frequency in this way for an online company gives a great visual indication of the health of the business and groups that can be targeted to encourage greater repeat purchases.

Product recommendations and propensity modelling

Propensity modelling
A name given to the approach of evaluating customer characteristics and behaviour and then making recommendations for future products.

'Propensity modelling' is one name given to the approach of evaluating customer characteristics and behaviour, in particular previous products or services purchased, and then making recommendations for the next suitable product. However, it is best known as recommending the 'Next Best Product' to existing customers.

A related acquisition approach is to target potential customers with similar characteristics through renting direct mail or e-mail lists or advertising online in similar locations.

The following recommendations are based on those in van Duyne et al. (2003).

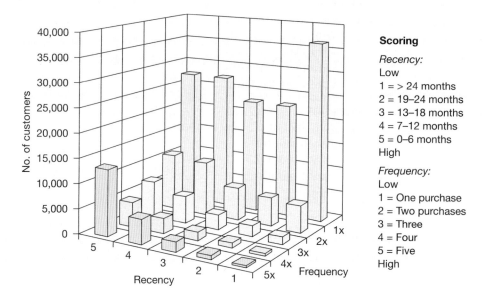

Figure 6.13 Example of RF analysis
Source: Patron (2004)

1 *Create automatic product relationships* [i.e. Next Best Product]. A low-tech approach to this is, for each product, to group together products, previously purchased together. Then for each product rank product by number of times purchased together to find relationships.

2 *Cordon off and minimise the 'real estate' devoted to related products.* An area of screen should be reserved for 'Next-best product prompts' for up-selling and cross-selling. However, if these can be made part of the current product they may be more effective.

3 *Use familiar 'trigger words'.* That is, familiar from using other sites such as Amazon. Such phrases include: 'Related products', 'Your recommendations', 'Similar', 'Customers who bought ...', 'Top 3 related products'.

4 *Editorialise about related products.* That is, within copy about a product.

5 *Allow quick purchase of related products.*

6 *Sell-related product during checkout.* And also on post-transaction pages, i.e. after one item has been added to basket or purchased.

Note that techniques do not necessarily require an expensive recommendations engine except for very large sites.

An example of a site that has simple rules to show related products is UK dot-com Firebox (**www.firebox.com**), shown in Figure 6.14.

An example of an e-retailer that uses many of the techniques described in this section is Debenhams (see Case Study 6).

Loyalty schemes

Loyalty schemes are often used to encourage customer extension and retention. You will be familiar with schemes run by retailers such as the Tesco Clubcard or Nectar schemes or those of airlines and hotel chains. Such schemes are often used for e-CRM purposes as follows:

- Initial bonus points for sign-up to online services or initial registration;
- Points for customer development or extension – more points awarded to encourage second or third online purchase;
- Additional points to encourage reactivation of online services;
- Popular products are offered for a relatively low number of points to encourage repeat purchases.

Figure 6.14 Firebox.com

If customers have lapsed in using online services, it is often necessary to contact them by direct mail or phone to make these offers.

As well as loyalty schemes operated by retailers and their partners, there are also some online-specific loyalty schemes which are operated independently. While early attempts at developing the online currency Beenz (www.beenz.com) failed, others such as iPoints (www.ipoints.co.uk) have survived. New ones are still being launched, for example, Pigs Back has worked well in Ireland and was launched in the UK in 2005 (www.pigsback.co.uk).

Virtual communities

Virtual community

An Internet-based forum for special-interest groups to communicate.

Virtual communities also provide opportunities for some companies to develop relationships with their customers. Since the publication of the article by Armstrong and Hagel in 1996 entitled 'The real value of online communities' and John Hagel's subsequent book (Hagel, 1997) there has been much discussion about the suitability of the web for virtual communities.

The power of the virtual communities, according to Hagel (1997), is that they exhibit a number of positive-feedback loops (or 'virtuous circles'). Focused content attracts new members, who in turn contribute to the quantity and quality of the community's pooled knowledge. Member loyalty grows as the community grows and evolves. The purchasing power of the community grows and thus the community attracts more vendors. The growing revenue potential attracts yet more vendors, providing more choice and attracting more members. As the size and sophistication of the community grow (while it still remains tightly focused) its data gathering and profiling capabilities increase – thus enabling better targeted marketing and attracting more vendors . . . and so on. In such positive-feedback loops there is an initial start-up period of slow and uneven growth until critical mass in members, content, vendors and transactions is reached. The potential for growth is then exponential – until the limits of the focus of the community as it defines itself are reached.

From this description of virtual communities it can be seen that they provide many of the attributes for effective relationship marketing – they can be used to learn about customers and provide information and offers to a group of customers.

When deciding on a strategic approach to virtual communities, companies have two basic choices if they decide to use them as part of their efforts in relationship building. First, they can provide community facilities on the site, or they can monitor and become involved in relevant communities set up by other organisations.

If a company sets up a community facility on its site, it has the advantage that it can improve its brand by adding value to its products. Sterne (1999) suggests that minimal intrusion should occur, but it may be necessary for the company to seed discussion and moderate out some negative comments. It may also be instrumental in increasing word-of-mouth promotion of the site. The community will provide customer feedback on the company and its products as part of the learning relationship. However, the brand may be damaged if customers criticise products. The company may also be unable to get sufficient people to contribute to a company-hosted community. An example where this approach has been used successfully is shown in Figure 6.15. Communities are best suited to high-involvement brands such as a professional body like CIPD or those related to sports and hobbies and business-to-business.

What is the reality behind Hagel and Armstrong's original vision of communities? How can companies deliver the promise of community? The key to a successful community is customer-centred communication. It is a customer-to-customer (C2C) interaction (Chapter 1). Consumers, not businesses, generate the content of the site, e-mail list or bulletin board.

According to Durlacher (1999), depending on market sector, an organisation has a choice of developing different types of community: communities of purpose, position and interest for B2C, and of profession for B2B.

1 *Purpose* – people who are going through the same process or trying to achieve a particular objective. Examples include those researching cars, e.g. at Autotrader (**www.autotrader.co.uk**) or stocks online, e.g. at the Motley Fool (**www.motleyfool.co.uk**).

Price or product comparison services such as Bizrate (**www.bizrate.com**) are also in this category.

2 *Position* – people who are in a certain circumstance such as a health disorder or in a certain stage of life, such as communities set up specifically for young people or old people. Examples are teenage chat site Habbo Hotel (**www.habbohotel.com**), Cennet, **www.cennet.co.uk** 'New horizons for the over 50s' and parenting sites such as Baby Center (**www.babycenter.com**).

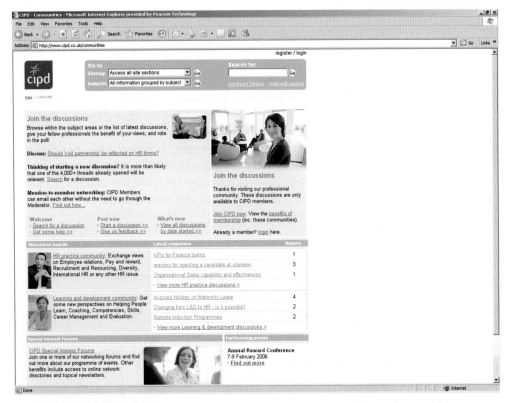

Figure 6.15 CIPD forums – a forum operated by a company to keep closer to its customers

3 *Interest.* This community is for people who share an interest or passion such as sport (**www.football365.com**), music (**www.pepsi.com**) or leisure (**www.walkingworld.com**).
4 *Profession.* These are important for companies promoting B2B services.

A further classification of communities is that of Armstrong and Hagel (1996) which is arguably less useful and identifies communities of transaction, communities of interest, communities of fantasy and communities of relationship.

What tactics can organisations use to foster community? Despite the hype and potential, many communities fail to generate activity, and a silent community isn't a community. Parker (2000) suggests eight questions organisations should ask when considering how to create a customer community:

1 What interests, needs or passions do many of your customers have in common?
2 What topics or concerns might your customers like to share with each other?
3 What information is likely to appeal to your customers' friends or colleagues?
4 What other types of business in your area appeal to buyers of your products and services?

5 How can you create packages or offers based on combining offers from two or more affinity partners?

6 What price, delivery, financing or incentives can you afford to offer to friends (or colleagues) that your current customers recommend?

7 What types of incentives or rewards can you afford to provide customers who recommend friends (or colleagues) who make a purchase?

8 How can you best track purchases resulting from word-of-mouth recommendations from friends?

Customer experience – the missing element required for customer loyalty

We have in this chapter shown how delivering relevant timely communications as part of permission marketing is important to developing loyalty. However, even the most relevant communications will fail if another key factor is not taken into account – this is the customer experience. If a first-time or repeat customer experience is poor due to a slow-to-download difficult-to-use site, then it is unlikely loyalty from the online customer will develop. The relationship between the drivers of customer satisfaction and loyalty is shown in Figure 6.16. In the next chapter we review techniques used to help develop this experience.

Figure 6.16 The relationship between service quality, customer satisfaction and loyalty

Case Study 6   Boots mine diamonds in their customer data

The high street retailer Boots launched its Advantage loyalty card in 1997. Today, there are over 15 million card holders of which 10 million are active. Boots describes the benefits for its card-holders as follows:

> The scheme offers the most generous base reward rate of all UK retailers of 4 points per £1 spent on products, with average card holders receiving 6.5 points per £1 when taking into account all other tactical points offers.

There are 23 analysts in the Customer Insight team run by Helen James who mine the data available about card users and their transactional behaviour. They use tools including MicroStrategy's DSS Agent and Andyne's GQL which are used for the majority of queries. IBM's Intelligent Miner for Data is used for more advanced data mining such as segmentation and predictive modelling. Helen James describes the benefits of data mining as follows:

> From our traditional Electronic Point-of-sale data we knew what was being sold, but now [through data mining] we can determine what different groups of customers are buying and monitor their behaviour over time.

The IBM case study gives these examples of the applications of data mining:

> What interests the analysts most is the behaviour of groups of customers. They are interested, for example, in the effect of Boots' marketing activity on customers – such as the impact of promotional offers on buying patterns over time. They can make a valuable input to decisions about layout, ranging and promotions by using market basket analysis to provide insight into the product purchasing repertoires of different groups of customers.

Like others, Boots has made a feature of multi-buy promotional schemes in recent years with numerous 'three for the price of two' and even 'two for the price of one' offers. Using the card data the Insight team has now been able to identify four groups of promotion buyers:

- the deal seekers who only ever buy promotional lines;
- the stockpilers who buy in bulk when goods are on offer and then don't visit the store for weeks;
- the loyalists – existing buyers who will buy a little more of a line when it is on offer but soon revert to their usual buying patterns;
- the new market – customers who start buying items when on promotion and then continue to purchase the same product once it reverts to normal price.

'This sort of analysis helps marketeers to understand what they are achieving via their promotions, rather than just identifying the uplift. They can see whether they are attracting new long term business or just generating short term uplift and also the extent to which they are cannibalising existing lines,' says Helen. Analysing market basket trends by shopper over time is also providing Boots with a new view of its traditional product categories and departmental spanides. Customers buying skin-care products, for example, often buy hair-care products as well so this is a good link to use in promotions, direct mail and in-store activity.

Other linkings which emerge from the data – as Helen says, quite obvious when one thinks about them – include films and suntan lotion; sensitive skin products – be they washing up gloves, cosmetics or skincare; and films and photograph frames with new baby products. 'Like many large retailers we are still organised along product category lines,' she says, 'so it would never really occur to the baby products buyers to create a special offer linked to picture frames – yet these are the very thing which new parents are likely to want.'

'We're also able to see how much shoppers participate in a particular range,' says Helen. 'They may buy toothbrushes, but do they also buy toothpaste and dental floss?' It may well be more profitable to encourage existing customers to buy deeper in the range than to attract new ones.

Monitoring purchases over time is also helping to identify buying patterns which fuel further marketing effort. Disposable nappy purchases, for example, are generally limited by the number of packs a customer can carry. A shopper visiting Boots once a fortnight and buying nappies is probably buying from a number of supply sources whereas one calling at the store twice a week probably gets most of her baby's nappy needs from Boots. Encouraging the first shopper to visit more would probably also increase nappy sales. Boots combines its basic customer demographic data (data such as age, gender, number of children and postcode) with externally available data. However, according to Helen 'the real power comes from being able to combine this with detailed purchase behaviour data – and this is now being used to fuel business decisions outside of the marketing arena.'

An analysis of how Boots customers shop a group of stores in a particular geographical area has led to a greatly improved understanding of the role different stores play within that area and the repertoire of goods that should be offered across the stores. For example, Boots stores have typically been grouped and merchandised according to their physical size. This leads to large stores competing with smaller stores for trade in the same area. 'We quickly learned that our most valuable customers shop across many stores in their area,' says Helen, 'and that there is a lot to be gained by managing stores as local areas and focusing on getting the overall customer offer right.'

Gaining a greater understanding of how customers shop product areas and stores offers really valuable insights.

However, as Helen says, 'the real prize is in gaining a really good overall understanding of your customers'. For a retailer with a very broad customer base it is too simple just to focus all efforts on the most valuable customers. Boots build up their understanding by combining data from a number of customer dimensions: RFM (Recency, Frequency and Monetary value) analysis enhanced with profitability. This helps Boots to understand the main drivers of customer value and identify which customers they should value and retain and which could be more valuable if they focussed on them more.

Lifestage analysis – This provides insight into how a customer's value changes over their lifetime. Using it, Boots can identify which are the potentially valuable customers of the future. They can also see the point at which a customer might become less valuable and try to prevent this. It is also clear that some messages become very important at certain times (for example, vitamins to people over 35 who have realised they may not be immortal) and irrelevant at others (what mother is concerned about cosmetics within a couple of weeks of the birth of her child?). This informs the mix of messages the customer receives, for instance via direct mail.

Attitudinal insight from market research surveys and questionnaires gives Boots an understanding of the attitudes driving the behaviour they see on their database. It is pointless directing a lot of marketing effort at people whose attitudes mean that they are unlikely to become more valuable to Boots.

This diversity of data is being used to build up a multi-dimensional picture of customers that gets to the heart of what drives customer value both today and into the future. Analysis of attitudes and customer repertoires offers Boots pointers to influencing customer value in a positive way. This understanding of customers has many applications within Boots from the way the Boots brand is communicated to specific cross-selling activities for store staff. One of the first applications of this segmentation was as a driver of the Boots relationship marketing programme enabled by the Advantage Card.

The segmentation provides a framework for relationship marketing. Specific campaigns help Boots to deliver that framework. These could encourage customers to shop along different themes – summer holidays, Christmas shopping – and incentivise them to make a visit. They may simply raise awareness of a particular new product or service – Boots Health & Travel Cover

launched in April is a good example of this. They could be an invitation to an exclusive shopping event where the customer can shop in peace and perhaps earn extra points as well.

To make all this happen Boots needed a campaign management system that could involve customers in the relationship marketing programme most relevant to them. The 'campaign management' component has been fully integrated within CDAS through a bespoke development by IBM. This means that direct marketing analysts are able to develop their target customer profiles without having to first create a separate extract of the data and are also able to base these profiles on the full richness of information held within the database. Having defined these criteria, the system will automatically come up with a mailing list of matching card holders with no further intervention. The system not only automates the measurement of basic campaign response analysis, but also makes the list of customers actually mailed available within the analysis environment so that more sophisticated response analysis can be performed. 'The close integration of the Campaign Management System within the analytic environment of CDAS is one of its main strengths,' says Ian, 'not only are we able to drive high response rates by tightly targeting relevant customer groups, but we are able to close the loop from initial customer analysis, through customer selection and campaign execution back to campaign response measurement and further campaign analysis.'

'When we announced the Advantage loyalty scheme we knew that the incremental sales generated by it would pay for the initial investment, but that the long-term value would come from the application of customer insights across the business,' says Helen. 'We are already proving that we can add significant value from doing this. But you do not obtain these benefits unless you get the base of detailed information right – and couple this with an ability to thoroughly exploit it.'

Computer Weekly (2001b) Interactive Being. *Computer Weekly*, 2 May 2001. Article by Lindsay Nicolle.

Question

Based on the case study, for the scenario below, answer these questions:

1. Summarise the potential benefits a loyalty scheme can deliver in terms of improved knowledge about customers.

2. Summarise changes to organisational structure and responsibilities which may be necessary for introduction of such a scheme.

3. Assess potential reaction to change amongst staff and outline approaches through which this could be managed.

Summary

1 The three areas of relationship marketing, direct marketing and database marketing have converged to create a powerful new marketing paradigm known as 'customer relationship management'.

2 Relationship marketing theory provides the conceptual underpinning of one-to-one marketing and customer relationship management since it emphasises enhanced customer service through customer knowledge.

3 The objective of customer relationship management (CRM) is to increase customer loyalty in order to increase profitability over customers' lifetime value (LTV). It is aimed at improving all aspects of the level of customer service.

4 CRM tactics can be based around the acquisition, retention, extension model of the ideal relationship between company and customer. Marketers can use 'sense and respond' techniques such as RFM analysis to target customers for retention and extension.

5 Direct marketing provides the tactics that deliver the marketing communications (and sometimes the product itself) to the individual customer. This approach is evolving rapidly with the advent of the Internet, the rise of call centres and advances in logistics.

6 Database marketing provides the technological enabler, allowing vast amounts of data to be stored and accessed in ways that create business opportunities.

7 Online relationship marketing is effective since it provides an interactive, multimedia environment in which the customer opts in to the relationship.

8 Steps in implementing one-to-one on the Internet are:

- Step 1. Attract customers to site.
- Step 2a. Incentivise in order to gain contact and profile information.
- Step 2b. Capture customer information to maintain the relationship and profile the customer.
- Step 3. Maintain dialogue through using online communications to achieve repeat site visits.
- Step 4. Maintain dialogue consistent with customer's profile using direct mail.

9 Personalisation technologies enable customised e-mails to be sent to each individual (or related groups) and customised web content to be displayed or distributed using push technology.

10 Integration with databases is important for profiling the customer and recording the relationship.

11 Virtual communities have an important role to play in fostering relationships.

12 Marketers must be aware of the risk of infringing customer privacy since this is damaging to the relationship. Providing customers with the option to opt in and opt out of marketing communications is a legal requirement in many countries.

13 Internet-based one-to-one marketing needs to be integrated with traditional communications by mail and phone as described in Chapter 8.

Exercises

Self-assessment exercises

1 Why is the Internet a suitable medium for relationship marketing?

2 Explain personalisation in an Internet marketing context.

3 What is meant by 'customer profiling'?

4 Explain the concept and benefits of the 'sense and respond' approach to customer communications.

5 How can customer concerns about privacy be responded to when conducting one-to-one marketing using the Internet?

6 Explain the relationship between database marketing, direct marketing and relationship marketing.

7 Explain the concept and applications of RFM analysis to different types of web presence.

8 How can a web site integrate with telemarketing?

Essay and discussion questions

1 Explain the factors that influence the development of multi-channel customer contact strategies.

2 Compare and contrast traditional transaction-oriented marketing with one-to-one marketing using the Internet.

3 Write a report summarising for a manager the necessary stages for transforming a brochureware site to a one-to-one interactive site and the benefits that can be expected.

4 Explore the legal and ethical constraints upon implementing relationship marketing using the Internet.

Examination questions

1 Define and explain direct marketing within the Internet context.

2 What characteristics of the Internet make it so conducive to the direct marketing approach?

3 How does a company initiate one-to-one marketing with a company using the Internet?

4 Explain the concept of a 'virtual community' and how such communities can be used as part of relationship marketing.

5 Suggest three measures a company can take to ensure a customer's privacy is not infringed when conducting one-to-one marketing.

6 What is the role of a database when conducting one-to-one marketing on the Internet?

7 What is 'web self-service'? What are typical challenges in managing this?

8 Explore opportunities and methods for personalising the interactive web session and adding value for that individual customer.

References

Agrawal, V., Arjona, V. and Lemmens, R. (2001) E-performance: the path to rational exuberance, *McKinsey Quarterly*, No. 1, 31–43.

Armstrong, A. and Hagel, J. (1996) The real value of online communities, *Harvard Business Review*, May–June, 134–41.

Chaffey, D. (2004) E-permission marketing. Chartered Institute of Marketing 'What's new in marketing' e-newsletter, Issue 25. (**www.wnim.com**).

Cram, T. (1994) *The Power of Relationship Marketing: Keeping Customers for Life*. Financial Times Management, London.

Duffy, D. (1998) Customer loyalty strategies, *Journal of Consumer Marketing*, 15(5), 435–48.

Durlacher (1999) UK online community, *Durlacher Quarterly Internet Report*, Q3, 7–11, London.

Evans, M., Patterson, M. and O'Malley, L. (2000) Bridging the direct marketing–direct consumer gap: some solutions from qualitative research, *Proceedings of the Academy of Marketing Annual Conference*, 2000, Derby, UK.

Godin, S. (1999) *Permission Marketing*. Simon and Schuster, New York.

Hagel, J. (1997) *Net Gain: Expanding Markets through Virtual Communities*. Harvard Business School Press, Boston.

McKenna, R. (1993) *Relationship Marketing: Successful Strategies for the Age of the Customer*. Addison-Wesley, Reading, MA.

Moller, K. and Halinen, A. (2000) Relationship marketing theory: its roots and direction, *Journal of Marketing Management*, 16, 29–54.

Novo, J. (2003) *Drilling Down: Turning customer data into profits with a spreadsheet*. Available from **www.jimnovo.com**.

O'Malley, L. and Tynan, C. (2001) Reframing relationship marketing for consumer markets, *Interactive Marketing*, 2(3), 240–6.

Parker, R. (2000) *Relationship Marketing on the Web*. Adams Streetwise, Cincinnati, OH.

Patron, M. (2004) Case study: applying RFM segmentation to the SilverMinds catalogue, *Interactive Marketing*, 5(3), 269–75.

Peppers, D. and Rogers, M. (1997) *Enterprise One-to-One: Tools for Building Unbreakable Customer Relationships in the Interactive Age*. Piatkus, London.

Peppers, D. and Rogers, M. (1998) *One-to-One Fieldbook*. Doubleday, New York.

Peppers, D. and Rogers, M. (2002) *One to One B2B: Customer Relationship Management Strategies for the Real Economy*. Cupstone, Oxford.

Peppers, D., Rogers, M. and Dorf, B. (1999) Is your company ready for one-to-one marketing? *Harvard Business Review*, January–February, 3–12.

Raphel, M. (1997) How a San Francisco movie complex breaks attendance records with database marketing, *Direct Marketing*, 59(11), 52–5.

Reichheld, F.F. (1996) *The Loyalty Effect*. Harvard Business School Press, Boston.

Reichheld, F. and Schefter, P. (2000) E-loyalty, your secret weapon, *Harvard Business Review*, July–August, 105–13.

Rigby, D., Bavega, S., Rastoi, S., Zook, C. and Hancock, S. (2000) The value of customer loyalty and how you can capture it. Bain and Company/Mainspring Whitepaper, 17 March. Published at www.mainspring.com.

Rosenfield, J.R. (1998) The future of database marketing, *Direct Marketing*, 60(10), 28–31.

Sargeant, A. and West, D. (2001) *Direct and Interactive Marketing*. Oxford University Press, Oxford.

Sharma, A., and Sheth, J. (2004) Web-based marketing: the coming revolution in marketing thought and strategy, *Journal of Business Research*, 57(7), 696–702.

Shaw, R. (1996) How to transform marketing through IT, *Management Today*, Special Report.

Smith, P.R. and Chaffey, D. (2005) *E-Marketing Excellence: at the Heart of Business*, 2nd edn. Butterworth Heinemann, Oxford.

Sterne, J. (1999) *World Wide Web Marketing*, 2nd edn. Wiley, New York.

Stone, M., Abbott, J. and Buttle, F. (2001) Integrating customer data into CRM strategy. In B. Foss and M. Stone (eds) *Successful Customer Relationship Marketing*. Wiley, Chichester.

van Duyne, D., Landay, J. and Hong, J. (2003). *The Design of Sites. Patterns, Principles, and Processes for Crafting a Customer-centered Web Experience*. Addison-Wesley, Reading, MA.

Wolfe, D.B. (1998) Developmental relationship marketing: connecting messages with mind, an empathetic marketing system, *Journal of Consumer Marketing*, 15(5), 449–67.

Further reading

Chaffey, D. (2003) *Total E-mail Marketing*. Butterworth Heinemann, Elsevier, Oxford. A detailed, practical guide to permission-based e-mail marketing.

Peppers, D., Rogers, M. and Dorf, B. (1999) Is your company ready for one-to-one marketing? *Harvard Business Review*, January–February, 3–12. A fairly detailed summary of the IDIC approach.

Reichheld, F. and Schefter, P. (2000) E-loyalty, your secret weapon, *Harvard Business Review*, July–August, 105–13. An excellent review of the importance of achieving online loyalty and approaches to achieving it.

Tapp, A. (2005) *Principles of Direct and Database Marketing*, 3rd edn. Financial Times/Prentice Hall, Harlow. A well-structured guide to best practice in direct and interactive marketing.

Web links

- **ClickZ (www.clickz.com).** An excellent collection of articles on online marketing communications. US-focused. Relevant section for this chapter: CRM strategies.

- **CRM Today (www.crm2day.com).** A portal with articles about the practical aspects of deploying CRM technology.

- **Database Marketing Institute (www.dbmarketing.com).** Useful collection of articles on best practice.

- **Jim Novo** (www.jimnovo.com). A site by a US consultant that has a lot of detail on techniques to profile customers online.

- **Peppers and Rogers One-to-One marketing web site** (www.1to1.com). A site containing a lot of information on the techniques and tools of relationship marketing.

Part 3

INTERNET MARKETING: IMPLEMENTATION AND PRACTICE

In Part 3 particular issues of the execution of an Internet marketing strategy are described, including development of a web site and ensuring a quality customer experience (Chapter 7), marketing communications to promote a site (Chapter 8) and the maintenance and evaluation of an online presence (Chapter 9). In Chapters 10 and 11, specific examples are given of how business-to-consumer and business-to-business companies are using the Internet.

7

Delivering the online customer experience

Learning objectives

After reading this chapter, the reader should be able to:

● Describe the different stages involved in creating a new site or relaunching an existing site

● Describe the design elements that contribute to effective web site content

● Define the factors that are combined to deliver an effective online customer experience

Questions for marketers

Key questions for marketing managers related to this chapter are:

● Which activities are involved in building a new site or updating an existing site?

● What are the key factors of online service quality and site design that will encourage repeat visitors?

● Which techniques can I use to determine visitors' requirements?

● Which forms of buyer behaviour do consumers exhibit online?

● What are the accepted standards of site design needed for an effective site?

Links to other chapters

Related chapters are:

➤ Chapters 4 and 5, which describe the development of the strategy and tactics that inform the design of the web site

➤ Chapter 8, which describes approaches to promoting web sites

➤ Chapter 9, which describes the maintenance of a site once it is created

Introduction

Developing the capability to create and maintain an effective online presence through a web site is a key part of Internet marketing. 'Effective' means that the web site and related communications must deliver relevance to its audience, whether this be through news content for a portal, product and service information for a business-to-business site or relevant products and offers for an e-commerce site. At the same time, 'effective' means the web site must deliver results for the company.

However, delivering relevant content for the audience is only part of the story. Interacting with web content is not a static experience, it is an interactive experience. So Internet marketers also have to work hard to develop consumer trust and deliver a great experience for their audience. In their book *Managing the Customer Experience*, Shaun Smith and Joe Wheeler (2002) suggest that companies should ask afresh 'what experience must we provide to meet the needs and expectations of customers'. They note that some companies use online channels to replicate existing services, whereas others have extended the experience online. In Chapter 5, in the section on the contribution of branding as part of the Product element of the mix, we explained how it is important to provide a promise of what the online representation of the brand will deliver to customers. The concept of online brand promise is closely related to that of delivering online customer experience. In this chapter, we will explore different practical actions that companies can take to create and maintain satisfactory online experiences. An indication of the effort required to produce a customer-centric online presence is given by Alison Lancaster, head of marketing and catalogues at John Lewis Direct, who says:

> *A good site should always begin with the user. Understand who the customer is, how they use the channel to shop, and understand how the marketplace works in that category. This includes understanding who your competitors are and how they operate online. You need continuous research, feedback and usability testing to continue to monitor and evolve the customer experience online. Customers want convenience and ease of ordering. They want a site that is quick to download, well-structured and easy to navigate.*

You can see that creating effective online experiences is a challenge since there are many practical issues to consider which we present in Figure 7.1. This is based on a diagram by de Chernatony (2001) who suggested that delivering the online experience promised by a brand requires delivering rational values, emotional values and promised experience (based on rational and emotional values). The diagram also highlights the importance of delivering service quality online, as has been indicated by Trocchia and Janda (2003).

The factors that influence the online customer experience can be presented in a pyramid form of success factors as is shown in Figure 7.1 (the different success factors reflect current best-practice and differ from those of de Chernatony). The diagram incorporates many of the factors that are relevant for a transactional e-retail site, but you can see that many of the rational and emotional values are important to any web site. Some of the terms such as 'usability' and 'accessibility' (which are delivered through an effective web site design) you may not be familiar with, but these will all be explained later in this chapter.

In the figure these factors are all associated with using the web site, but the online customer experience extends beyond this, and Internet marketing should also consider these issues:

Online customer experience

The combination of rational and emotional factors of using a company's online services that influences customers' perceptions of a brand online.

- Ease of locating the site through search engines (Chapter 8);
- Services provided by partners online on other web sites;
- Quality of outbound communications such as e-newsletters;
- Quality of processing inbound e-mail communications from customers;
- Integration with offline communications.

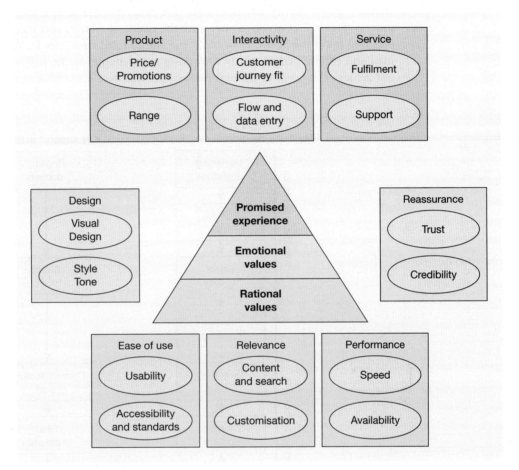

Figure 7.1 The online customer experience pyramid – success factors

We start the chapter by considering how we create the web site to deliver appropriate rational and emotional values since web site design is a core part of creating the online customer experience. We also look at the stages in managing a project to improve the customer experience. Our coverage on web site design is integrated with consideration of researching online buyer behaviour since an appropriate experience can only be delivered if it is consistent with customer behaviour, needs and wants. We then go on to review delivery of service quality online. This includes aspects such as speed and availability of the site itself which support the rational values and also fulfilment and support which are a core part of the promised experience.

Planning web site design and build

In the past, it has been a common mistake amongst those creating a new web site for the first time to 'dive in' and start creating web pages without sufficient forward planning. Planning is necessary since design of a site must occur before creation of web pages – to ensure a good-quality site that does not need reworking at a later stage. The design process (Figure 7.2) involves analysing the needs of owners and users of a site and then deciding upon the best way to build the site to fulfil these needs. Without a structured plan and careful design, costly reworking is inevitable, as the first version of a site will not achieve the needs of the end-users or the business.

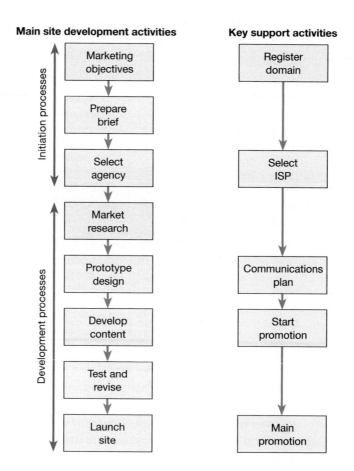

Figure 7.2 Summary of process of web site development

Of the stages shown in Figure 7.2, those of market research and design are described in most detail in this chapter since the nature of the web site content is, of course, vital in providing a satisfactory experience for the customer which leads to repeat visits. Testing and promotion of the web site are described in subsequent chapters. An alternative model can be found in a practical 'Internet marketing framework' presented by Ong (1995) and summarised by Morgan (1996).

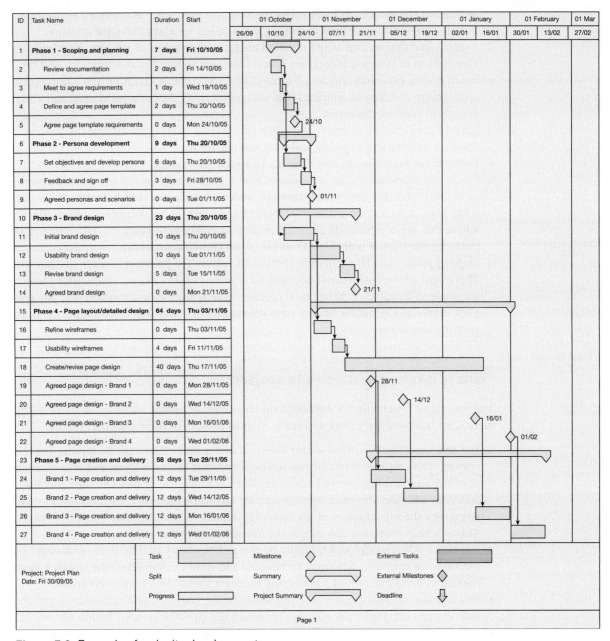

Figure 7.3 Example of web site development

The process of web site development summarised in Figure 7.2 is idealised, since, for efficiency, many of these activities have to occur in parallel. Figure 7.3 gives an indication of the relationship between these tasks, and how long they may take, for a typical web site project. We will explain some of the specialist design terminology later in this chapter. The content planning and development stages overlap in that HTML and graphics development are necessary to produce the prototypes. As a consequence, some development has to occur while analysis and design are under way. The main development tasks which need to be scheduled as part of the planning process are as follows:

1 *Pre-development tasks*. For a new site, these include domain name registration and deciding on the company (ISP) to host the web site. They also include preparing a brief

setting out the aims and objectives of the site, and then – if it is intended to outsource the site – presenting the brief to rival agencies to bid for and pitch their offering.

2 *Analysis and design.* This is the detailed analysis and design of the site, and includes clarification of business objectives, market research to identify the audience and typical customer personas and user journeys and their needs, defining the information architecture of different content types and prototyping different functional and visual designs to support the brand.

3 *Content development and testing.* Writing the HTML pages, producing the graphics, database integration, usability and performance testing.

4 *Publishing or launching the site.* This is a relatively short stage.

5 *Pre-launch promotion or communications.* Search engine registration and optimisation is most important for new sites. Although search engines can readily index a new site, some place a penalty on a new site (sometimes known as 'the Google sandbox effect'), where the site is effectively on trial until is established. Briefing the PR company to publicise the launch is another example of pre-launch promotion.

6 *Ongoing promotion.* The schedule should also allow for promotion after site launch. This might involve structured discount promotions on the site or competitions which are planned in advance. Many now consider search engine optimisation and pay-per-click marketing (Chapter 8) as a continuous process, and will often employ a third party to help achieve this.

Who is involved in a web site project?

The success of a web site is dependent on the range of people involved in its development, and how well they work as a team. Typical profiles of team members follow:

- *Site sponsors.* These will be senior managers who will effectively be paying for the system. They will understand the strategic benefits of the system and will be keen that the site is implemented successfully to achieve the objectives they have set. Sponsors will also aim to encourage staff by means of their own enthusiasm and will stress why the introduction of the system is important to the business and its workers. This will help overcome any barriers to introduction of the web site.

- *Site owner.* 'Ownership' will typically be the responsibility of a marketing manager or e-commerce manager, who may be devoted full-time to overseeing the site in a large company; it may be part of a marketing manager's remit in a smaller company.

- *Project manager.* This person is responsible for the planning and coordination of the web site project. He or she will aim to ensure the site is developed within the budget and time constraints that have been agreed at the start of the project, and that the site delivers the planned-for benefits for the company and its customers.

- *Site designer.* The site designer will define the 'look and feel' of the site, including its layout and how company brand values are transferred to the web.

- *Content developer.* The content developer will write the copy for the web site and convert it to a form suitable for the site. In medium or large companies this role may be split between marketing staff or staff from elsewhere in the organisation who write the copy and a technical member of staff who converts it to the graphics and HTML documents forming the web page and does the programming for interactive content.

- *Webmaster.* This is a technical role. The webmaster is responsible for ensuring the quality of the site. This means achieving suitable availability, speed, working links between pages and connections to company databases. In small companies the webmaster may take on graphic design and content developer roles also.

● *Stakeholders*. The impact of the web site on other members of the organisation should not be underestimated. Internal staff may need to refer to some of the information on the web site or use its services.

While the site sponsor and site owner will work within the company, many organisations outsource the other resources since full-time staff cannot be justified in these roles. There are a range of different choices for outsourcing which are summarised in Activity 7.1.

We are seeing a gradual blurring between these different types of supplier as they recruit expertise so as to deliver a 'one-stop shop' or 'full-service agency', but they still tend to be

---

Activity 7.1 — Options for outsourcing different e-marketing activities

Purpose

To highlight the outsourcing available for e-business implementation and to gain an appreciation of how to choose suppliers.

Activity

A B2C company is trying to decide which of its e-business activities it should outsource. Select a single supplier that you think can best deliver each of these services indicated in Table 7.1. Justify your decision.

Table 7.1 Options for outsourcing different e-business activities

E-marketing function	Traditional marketing agency	Digital marketing agency	ISP or traditional IT supplier	Management consultants
1 Strategy				
2 Design				
3 Content and service development				
4 Online promotion				
5 Offline promotion				
6 Infrastructure				

---

strongest in particular areas. Companies need to decide whether to partner with the best of breed in each, or to perhaps compromise and choose the one-stop shop that gives the best balance and is most likely to achieve integration across different marketing activities – this would arguably be the new media agency or perhaps a traditional marketing agency that has an established new media division. Which approach do you think is best?

Observation of the practice of outsourcing suggests that two conflicting patterns are evident:

1 *Outside-in*. A company starts an e-business initiative by outsourcing some activities where there is insufficient in-house expertise. These may be areas such as strategy or online promotion. The company then builds up skills internally to manage these areas as e-business becomes an important contributor to the business. The company initially partnered with a new media agency to offer online services, but once the online contribution to sales exceeded 20% the management of e-commerce was taken inside. The new media agency was, however, retained for strategy guidance. An out-

side-in approach will probably be driven by the need to reduce the costs of outsourcing, poor delivery of services by the supplier or simply a need to concentrate a strategic core resource in-house.

2 *Inside-out.* A company starts to implement e-business using existing resources within the IT department and marketing department in conjunction with recruitment of new media staff. They may then find that there are problems in developing a site that meets customers' needs or in building traffic to the site. At this point they may turn to outsourcing to solve the problems.

These approaches are not mutually exclusive, and an outside-in approach may be used for some e-commerce functions such as content development while an inside-out approach is used for other functions such as site promotion. It can also be suggested that these approaches are not planned – they are simply a response to prevailing conditions. However, in order to cost e-business and manage it as a strategic asset it can be argued that the e-business manager should have a long-term picture of which functions to outsource and when to bring them in-house.

Web site prototyping

Prototypes are trial versions of a web site that are gradually refined through an iterative process to become closer to the final version. Initial prototypes may simply be paper prototypes, perhaps of a 'wireframe' or screen layout. These may then be extended to include some visuals of key static pages using a tool such as Adobe Photoshop. Finally, working prototypes will be produced as HTML code is developed. The idea is that the design agency or development team and the marketing staff who commissioned the work can review and comment on prototypes, and changes can then be made to the site to incorporate these comments. Prototyping should result in a more effective final site which can be developed more rapidly than a more traditional approach with a long period of requirements determination.

Each iteration of the prototype typically passes through the stages shown in Figure 7.4, which are:

Prototype
A preliminary version of part or a framework of all of a web site, which can be reviewed by its target audience or the marketing team. Prototyping is an iterative process in which web site users suggest modifications before further prototypes and the final version of the site are developed.

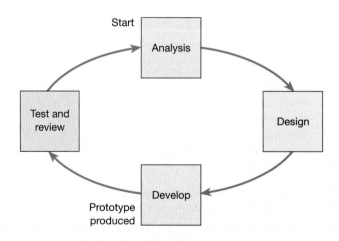

Figure 7.4 Four stages of web site prototyping

1 *Analysis.* Understanding the requirements of the audience of the site and the requirements of the business, defined by business and marketing strategy (and comments input from previous prototypes).
2 *Design.* Specifying different features of the site that will fulfil the requirements of the users and the business as identified during analysis.
3 *Develop.* The creation of the web pages and the dynamic content of the web site.
4 *Test and review.* Structured checks are conducted to ensure that different aspects of the site meet the original requirements and work correctly.

When using the prototyping approach for a web site, a company has to decide whether to implement the complete version of the web site before making it available to its target audience (hard launch) or to make available a more limited version of the site (soft launch). If it is necessary to establish a presence rapidly, the second approach could be used. This also has the benefit that feedback can be solicited from users and incorporated into later versions.

Before the analysis, design and creation of the web site, all major projects will have an initial phase in which the aims and objectives of the web site are reviewed, to assess whether it is worthwhile investing in the web site, and to decide on the amount to

Hard launch

A site is launched once fully complete with full promotional effort.

Soft launch

A trial version of a site is launched with limited publicity.

Initiation of the web site project

Initiation of the web site project

This phase of the project should involve a structured review of the costs and benefits of developing a web site (or making a major revision to an existing web site). A successful outcome to initiation will be a decision to proceed with the site development phase, with an agreed budget and target completion date.

invest. This is part of the strategic planning process described in Chapters 4 and 5. This provides a framework for the project that ensures:

(a) there is management and staff commitment to the project;
(b) objectives are clearly defined;
(c) the costs and benefits are reviewed in order that the appropriate amount of investment in the site occurs;
(d) the project will follow a structured path, with clearly identified responsibilities for different aspects such as project management, analysis, promotion and maintenance;
(e) the implementation phase will ensure that important aspects of the project such as testing and promotion are not skimped.

Domain name registration

If the project involves a new site rather than an upgrade, it will be necessary to register a new domain name, more usually referred to as a 'web address' or 'uniform (or universal) resource locator (URL)'.

Domain names are registered using an ISP or direct with one of the domain name services, such as:

Domain name registration

The process of reserving a unique web address that can be used to refer to the company web site, in the form of **www.<companyname>.com** or **www.<companyname>.co.uk**.

1 *InterNIC* (**www.internic.net**). Registration for the .com, .org and .net domains.
2 *Nominet* (**www.nominet.org.uk**). Registration for the .co.uk domain. All country-specific domains such as .fr (France) or .de (Germany) have their own domain registration authority.
3 *Nomination* (**www.nomination.uk.com**). An alternative registration service for the UK, allowing registration in the (uk.com) pseudo-domain.

The following guidelines should be borne in mind when registering domain names:

1 *Register the domain name as early as possible.* This is necessary since the precedent in the emerging law is that the first company to register the name is the one that takes ownership if it has a valid claim to ownership.

2 *Register multiple domain names* if this helps the potential audience to find the site. For example, British Midland may register its name as **www.britishmidland.com** and **www.britishmidland.co.uk**.

3 *Use the potential of non-company brand names* to help promote a product. For example, a 1998 traditional media campaign for British Midland used **www.iflybritishmidland.com** as a memorable address to help users find its site.

Selecting an Internet service provider (ISP)

Internet service provider (ISP)

Company that provides home or business users with a connection to access the Internet. It can also host web sites or provide a link from web servers to allow other companies and consumers access to a corporate web site.

Selecting the right partner to host a web site is an important decision since the quality of service provided will directly impact on the quality of service delivered to a company's customers. The partner that hosts the content will usually be an Internet service provider (or ISP) for the majority of small and medium companies, but for larger companies the web server used to host the content may be inside the company and managed by the company's IT department.

The quality of service of hosted content is essentially dependent on two factors: the performance of the web site and its availability.

The performance of the web site

Bandwidth

Indicates the speed at which data are transferred using a particular network medium. It is measured in bits per second (bps).

The important measure in relation to performance is the speed with which a web page is delivered to users from the time when it is requested by clicking on a hyperlink (see Table 7.2 for examples). The length of time is dependent on a number of factors, some of which cannot be controlled (such as the number of users accessing the Internet), but primarily depends on the bandwidth of the ISP's connection to the Internet and the performance of the web server hardware and software. It also depends on the 'page weight' of the site's pages measured in kilobytes (which is dependent on the number and complexity of images and animations). Table 7.2 shows that the top 5 sites with the lowest download speeds tend to have a much smaller page size compared with the slower sites from 95 to 100. However, viewing these slower sites over a broadband connection shows that this is perhaps less of an issue than in the days when the majority, rather than the minority, were dial-up Internet users.

Table 7.2 Variation in download speed (across a 56.6 kbps modem) and page size for the top 5 and bottom 6 UK sites week starting 6 October 2005

Web site		Avg. download speed	Page size
1	Thomas Cook	4.65 sec	18.46 kb
2	British Airways	5.15 sec	23.46 kb
3	Next On-Line Shopping	5.64 sec	26.90 kb
4	EasyJet	6.09 sec	27.88 kb
5	NTL	6.66 sec	29.77 kb
95	Nokia UK	37.60 sec	180.98 kb
96	The Salvation Army	37.68 sec	171.07 kb
97	Rail Track	38.14 sec	111.00 kb
98	workthing.com	38.77 sec	187.35 kb
99	Orange	40.01 sec	194.16 kb
100	FT.com	44.39 sec	211.55 kb

Source: Site Confidence (www.siteconfidence.co.uk)

A major factor for a company to consider when choosing an ISP is whether the server is *dedicated* to one company or whether content from several companies is located on the same server. A dedicated server is best, but it will attract a premium price.

The availability of the web site

The availability of a web site is an indication of how easy it is for a user to connect to it. In theory this figure should be 100 per cent, but sometimes, for technical reasons such as failures in the server hardware or upgrades to software, the figure can drop substantially below this.

The extent of the problem of e-commerce service levels was indicated by The Register (2004) in an article titled 'Wobbly shopping carts blight UK e-commerce'. The research showed that failure of transactions once customers have decided to buy is often a problem. As the article said, 'UK E-commerce sites are slapping customers in the face, rather than shaking them by the hand. Turning consumers away once they have made a decision to buy is commercial suicide'. The research showed this level of problems:

- 20% of shopping carts did not function for 12 hours a month or more.
- 75% failed the standard service level availability of 99.9% uptime.
- 80% performed inconsistently with widely varying response times, time-outs and errors – leaving customers at best wondering what to do next and at worst unable to complete their purchases.

Similarly, SciVisum, a web testing specialist found that three-quarters of Internet marketing campaigns are impacted by web site failures, with 14 per cent of failures so severe that they prevented the campaign meeting its objectives. The company surveyed marketing professionals from 100 UK-based organisations across the retail, financial, travel and online gaming sectors. More than a third of failures were rated as 'serious to severe', with many customers complaining or unable to complete web transactions. These are often seen by marketers as technology issues which are owned by others in the business, but marketers need to ask the right questions. The SciVisum (2005) research showed that nearly two-thirds of marketing professionals did not know how many users making transactions their web sites could support, despite an average transaction value of £50 to £100, so they were not able to factor this into campaign plans. Thirty-seven per cent could not put a monetary value on losses caused by customers abandoning web transactions. A quarter of organisations experienced web site overloads and crashes as a direct result of a lack of communication between the two departments.

SciVisum recommends that companies do the following:

1 Define the peak visitor throughput requirements for each customer journey on the site. For example, the site should be able to support at the same time: approximately ten checkout journeys per second, 30 add-to-basket journeys per second, five registration journeys per second, two check-my-order-status journeys per second.
2 Service-level agreement. More detailed technical requirements need to be agreed for each of the transactions stages. Home-page delivery time and server uptime are insufficiently detailed.
3 Set up a monitoring programme that measures and reports on the agreed journeys 24/7.

Researching site users' requirements

Analysis phase

The identification of the requirements of a web site. Techniques to achieve this may include focus groups, questionnaires sent to existing customers or interviews with key accounts.

Analysis involves using different marketing research techniques to find out the needs of the site audience. These needs can then be used to drive the design and content of the web site.

It is not a 'one-off' exercise, but is likely to be repeated for each iteration of the prototype. Although analysis and design are separate activities, there tends to be considerable overlap between the two phases. In analysis we are seeking to answer the following types of 'who, what, why, how' questions:

- Who are the key audiences for the site?
- Why should they use the site (what will appeal to them)?
- What should the content of site be? Which services will be provided?
- How will the content of the site be structured (information architecture)?
- How will navigation around the site occur?
- What are the main marketing outcomes we want the site to deliver (registrations, leads, sales)?

User-centred design

A design approach which is based on research of user characteristics and needs.

Persuasion marketing

Using design elements such as layout, copy and typography together with promotional messages to encourage site users to follow particular paths and specific actions rather than giving them complete choice in their navigation

To help answer these questions, web designers commonly use an approach known as **user-centred design** which uses a range of techniques to ensure the site meets user needs. Within this design process, usability and accessibility are goals which we will now study further. It is now generally agreed that web site designers also need to add **persuasion marketing** into the design mix; to create a design that is not only easy to use, but also delivers results for the business. This approach is essential since usability which will often lead to giving the user choice, may conflict with using a web site to meet business objectives which will often need to persuade customers to register or buy a product. Most web sites should not give total business choice in which sections they use, but, as with any marketing communication, should influence the recipient of the communication to encourage them to take particular actions or follow particular paths. You can see that this concept of user-centred design is similar to the concept of customer orientation or customer-centricity which we have covered in preceding chapters.

Consultant Bryan Eisenberg of Future Now (www.futurenowinc.com) is an advocate of persuasion marketing alongside other design principles such as usability and accessibility. He says:

> during the wireframe and storyboard phase we ask three critical questions of every page a visitor will see:
>
> 1 What action needs to be taken?
> 2 Who needs to take that action?
> 3 How do we persuade that person to take the action we desire?

Usability

Usability

An approach to web site design intended to enable the completion of user tasks.

Usability is a concept that can be applied to the analysis and design for a range of products which defines how easy they are to use. The British Standard/ISO Standard: Human Centred design processes for interactive systems defines usability as the:

> extent to which a product can be used by specified users to achieve specified goals with effectiveness, efficiency and satisfaction in a specified context of use.

(BSI, 1999)

You can see how the concept can be readily applied to web site design – web visitors often have defined *goals* such as finding particular information or completing an action such as booking a flight or viewing an account balance.

In Jakob Nielsen's classic book *Designing Web Usability* (Nielsen, 2000b), he describes usability as follows.

> *An engineering approach to website design to ensure the user interface of the site is learnable, memorable, error free, efficient and gives user satisfaction. It incorporates testing and evaluation to ensure the best use of navigation and links to access information in the shortest possible time. A companion process to information architecture.*

In practice, usability involves two key project activities. Expert reviews are often performed at the beginning of a redesign project as a way of identifying problems with a previous design. Usability testing involves:

1 Identifying representative users of the site (see, for example, Table 7.3) and identifying typical tasks;
2 Asking them to perform specific tasks such as finding a product or completing an order;
3 Observing what they do and how they succeed.

For a site to be successful, the user tasks or actions need to be completed:

- Effectively – web usability specialists measure task completion, for example, only 3 out of 10 visitors to a web site may be able to find a telephone number or other piece of information.
- Efficiently – web usability specialists also measure how long it takes to complete a task on-site, or the number of clicks it takes.

Jakob Nielsen explains the imperative for usability best in his 'Usability 101' (**www.useit.com/alertbox/20030825.html**). He says:

> *On the Web, usability is a necessary condition for survival. If a website is difficult to use, people **leave**. If the **homepage** fails to clearly state what a company offers and what users can do on the site, people **leave**. If users get lost on a website, they **leave**. If a website's information is hard to read or doesn't answer users' key questions, they **leave**. Note a pattern here?*

For these reasons, Nielsen suggests that around 10% of a design project budget should be spent on usability, but often actual spend is significantly less.

Some would also extend usability to include testing of the visual or brand design of a site in focus groups, to assess how consumers perceive it reflects the brand. Often, alternative visual designs are developed to identify those which are most appropriate.

Expert reviews
An analysis of an existing site or prototype, by an experienced usability expert who will identify deficiencies and improvements to a site based on their knowledge of web design principles and best practice.

Usability/user testing
Representative users are observed performing representative tasks using a system.

Table 7.3 Different potential audiences for a web site

Customers vary by	Staff	Third parties
New or existing prospects	New or existing	New or existing
Size of prospect companies (e.g. small, medium or large)	Different departments	Suppliers
Market type (e.g. different vertical markets)	Sales staff for different markets	Distributors
Location (by country)	Location (by country)	Investors
Members of buying process (decision makers, influencers, buyers)		Media
Familiarity (with using the web, the company, its products and services or its web site)		Students

Additional web site design research activities include the use of *personas* and *scenario-based design* as introduced in Chapter 2.

Web accessibility

Accessibility

An approach to site design intended to accommodate site usage using different browsers and settings particularly required by the visually impaired.

General Packet Radio Services (GPRS)

A standard offering mobile data transfer and WAP access approximately 5 to 10 times faster than traditional GSM access.

Accessibility legislation

Legislation intended to protect users of web sites with disabilities including visual disability.

Web accessibility is another core requirement for web sites. It is about allowing all users of a web site to interact with it regardless of disabilities they may have or the web browser or platform they are using to access the site. The visually impaired are the main audience that designing an accessible web site can help. However, increased usage of mobile or wireless access devices such as personal digital assistants (PDAs) and GPRS or 3G phones also make consideration of accessibility important.

The following quote shows the importance of accessibility to a visually impaired user who uses a screen-reader which reads out the navigation options and content on a web site.

For me being online is everything. It's my hi-fi, it's my source of income, it's my super-market, it's my telephone. It's my way in.

(Lynn Holdsworth, screen-reader user, web developer and programmer)
Source: RNIB

Remember that many countries now have specific accessibility legislation to which web site owners are subject. This is often contained within disability and discrimination acts. In the UK, the relevant act is the Disability and Discrimination Act (DDA) 1995. Recent amendments to the DDA make it unlawful to discriminate against disabled people in the way in which a company recruits and employs people, provides services, or provides education. Providing services is the part of the law that applies to web site design. Providing accessible web sites is a requirement of Part II of the Disability and Discrimination Act published in 1999 and required by law from 2002. In the 2002 code of practice there is a legal requirement for web sites to be accessible. This is most important for sites which provide a service; for example, the code of practice gives this example:

An airline company provides a flight reservation and booking service to the public on its website. This is a provision of a service and is subject to the Act.

Although there is a moral imperative for accessibility, there is also a business imperative to encourage companies to make their web sites accessible. The main arguments in favour of accessibility are:

1 *Number of visually impaired people.* In many countries there are millions of visually impaired people varying from 'colour blind' to partially sighted to blind.
2 *Number of users of less popular browsers or variation in screen display resolution.* Microsoft Internet Explorer is now the dominant browser, but there are less well-known browsers which have a loyal following amongst the visually impaired (for example, screen-readers and Lynx, a text-only browser) and early-adopters (for example, Mozilla Firefox, Safari and Opera). If a web site does not display well in these browsers, then you may lose these audiences. Complete Activity 7.2 to review how much access has varied since this book was first published.
3 *More visitors from natural listings of search engines.* Many of the techniques used to make sites more usable also assist in search engine optimisation. For example, clearer navigation, text alternatives for images and site maps can all help improve a site's position in the search engine rankings.
4 *Legal requirements.* In many countries it is a legal requirement to make web sites accessible. For example, the UK has a Disability Discrimination Act that requires this.

Activity 7.2 — Allowing for the range in access devices

One of the benefits of accessibility requirements is that they help web site owners and web agencies consider the variation in platforms used to access web sites.

Questions

1 Update the compilation in Table 7.4 to the latest values using Onestat.com or other data from web analytics providers.
2 Explain the variations. Which browsers and screen resolutions do you think should be supported?

Table 7.4 Summarises the range in browsers and screen resolutions used at the time of writing

Web browser popularity		Screen resolution popularity	
1 Microsoft IE	86.63 %	1 1024 768	57.38%
2 Mozilla Firefox	8.69 %	2 800 600	18.23%
3 Apple Safari	1.26 %	3 1280 1024	14.18%
4 Netscape	1.08 %	4 1152 864	4.95%
5 Opera	1.03 %	5 1600 1200	1.67%

Source: Onestat press releases (www.onestat.com)

Guidelines for creating accessible web sites are produced by the governments of different countries and non-government organisations such as charities. Internet standards organisations such as the World Wide Web Consortium have been active in promoting guidelines for web accessibility through the Website Accessibility Initiative (see **www.w3.org/WAI**). This describes common accessibility problems such as:

images without alternative text; lack of alternative text for imagemap hot-spots; misleading use of structural elements on pages; uncaptioned audio or undescribed video; lack of alternative information for users who cannot access frames or scripts; tables that are difficult to decipher when linearized; or sites with poor color contrast.

A fuller checklist for acessibility compliance for web site design and coding using HTML is available from the World Wide Web Consortium (**www.w3.org/TR/WCAG10/full-checklist.html**).

There are three different priority levels which it describes as follows:

- *Priority 1 (Level A).* A web content developer must satisfy this checkpoint. Otherwise, one or more groups will find it impossible to access information in the document. Satisfying this checkpoint is a basic requirement for some groups to be able to use web documents.
- *Priority 2 (Level AA).* A web content developer should satisfy this checkpoint. Otherwise, one or more groups will find it difficult to access information in the document. Satisfying this checkpoint will remove significant barriers to accessing web documents.
- *Priority 3 (Level AAA).* A web content developer may address this checkpoint. Otherwise, one or more groups will find it somewhat difficult to access information in the document. Satisfying this checkpoint will improve access to web documents.

So, for many companies the standard is to meet Priority 1 and Priority 2 or 3 where practical.

Some of the most important Priority 1 elements are indicated by these 'Quick Tips' from the WAI:

Alt tags

Alt tags appear after an image tag and contain a phrase associated with that image. For example: ‹img src="logo.gif" alt="Company name, company products"/›

● Images and animations: use **alt tags** to describe the function of each visual.
● Image maps: use the client-side map and text for hotspots.
● Multimedia: provide captioning and transcripts of audio, and descriptions of video.
● Hypertext links: use text that makes sense when read out of context, for example avoid 'click here'.
● Page organisation: use headings, lists, and consistent structure. Use CSS for layout and style where possible.
● Graphs and charts: summarise or use the longdesc attribute.
● Scripts, applets and plug-ins: provide alternative content in case active features are inaccessible or unsupported.
● Frames: use the noframes element and meaningful titles.
● Tables: make line-by-line reading sensible. Summarise.
● Check your work. Validate: Use tools, checklist, and guidelines at **www.w3.org/TR/WCAG**.

Figure 7.5 is an example of an accessible site which still meets brand and business objectives while supporting accessibility through resizing of screen resolution, text resizing and alternative image text.

Figure 7.5 HSBC Global home page (www.hsbc.com)

Localisation

A further aspect of customer-centricity for web site design is the decision whether to include specific content for particular countries. This is referred to as 'localisation'. A site may need to support customers from a range of countries with:

- different product needs;
- language differences;
- cultural differences.

Localisation will address all these issues. It may be that products will be similar in different countries and localisation will simply involve converting the web site to suit another country. However, in order to be effective, this often needs more than translation, since different promotion concepts may be needed for different countries.

Reviewing competitors' web sites

Benchmarking of competitors' web sites is vital in positioning your web site to compete effectively with competitors that already have web sites. Given the importance of this activity, criteria for performing benchmarking have been described in Chapters 2 and 4.

Benchmarking should not only be based on the obvious tangible features of a web site such as its ease of use and the impact of its design. Benchmarking criteria should include those that define the companies' marketing performance in the industry and those that are specific to web marketing as follows:

- *Financial performance* (available from About Us, investor relations and electronic copies of company reports) – this information is also available from intermediary sites such as finance information or share dealing sites such as Interactive Trader International (**www.iii.com**) or Bloomberg (**www.bloomberg.com**) for major quoted companies.
- *Marketplace performance* – market share and sales trends and, significantly, the proportion of sales achieved through the Internet. This may not be available directly on the web site, but may need the use of other online sources. For example, new entrant to European aviation easyJet (**www.easyjet.com**) achieved over two-thirds of its sales via the web site and competitors needed to respond to this.
- *Business and revenue models (see Chapter 6)* – do these differ from other marketplace players?
- *Marketing communications techniques* – is the customer value proposition of the site clear? Does the site support all stages of the buying decision from customers who are unfamiliar with the company through to existing customers? Are special promotions used on a monthly or periodic basis? Beyond the competitor's site, how do they make use of intermediary sites to promote and deliver their services?
- *Services offered* – what is offered beyond brochureware? Is online purchase possible? What is the level of online customer support and how much technical information is available?
- *Implementation of services* – these are the practical features of site design that are described in this chapter, such as aesthetics, ease of use, personalisation, navigation, availability and speed.

A review of corporate web sites suggests that, for most companies, the type of information that can be included on a web site will be fairly similar. Many commentators such as Sterne (2001) make the point that some sites miss out the basic information that someone who is unfamiliar with a company may want to know, such as:

- Who are you? 'About Us' is now a standard menu option.
- What do you do? What products or services are available?
- Where do you do it? Are the products and services available internationally?

Designing the information architecture

Information architecture

The combination of organisation, labelling and navigation schemes constituting an information system.

Rosenfeld and Morville (2002) emphasise the importance of information architecture to an effective web site design. They say:

It is important to recognize that every information system, be it a book or an intranet, has an information architecture. 'Well developed' is the key here, as most sites don't have a planned information architecture at all. They are analogous to buildings that weren't architected in advance. Design decisions reflect the personal biases of designers, the space doesn't scale over time, technologies drive the design and not the other way around.

In their book, Rosenfeld and Morville give alternative definitions of an information architecture. They say it is:

1 *The combination of organization, labelling, and navigation schemes within an information system.*

2 *The structural design of an information space to facilitate task completion and intuitive access to content.*

3 *The art and science of structuring and classifying web sites and intranets to help people find and manage information.*

4 *An emerging discipline and community of practice focused on bringing principles of design and architecture to the digital landscape.*

Rosenfeld and Morville (2002)

Site map

A graphical or text depiction of the relationship between different groups of content on a web site.

Essentially, in practice, creation of an information architecture involves creating a plan to group information logically – it involves creating a site structure which is often represented as a site map. Note, though, that whole books have been written on information architecture, so this is necessarily a simplification! A well-developed information architecture is very important to usability since it determines navigation options. It is also important to search engine optimisation (Chapter 8), since it determines how different types of content that users may search for are labelled and grouped.

A planned information architecture is essential to large-scale web sites such as transactional e-commerce sites, media owner sites and relationship-building sites that include a large volume of product or support documentation. Information architectures are less important to small-scale web sites and brand sites, but even here, the principles can be readily applied and can help make the site more visible to search engines and usable.

The benefits of creating an information architecture include:

- A defined structure and categorisation of information will support user and organisation goals, i.e. it is a vital aspect of usability.
- It helps increase 'flow' on the site – a user's mental model of where to find content should mirror that of the content on the web site.
- Search engine optimisation – a higher listing in the search rankings can often be used through structuring and labelling information in a structured way.
- Applicable for integrating offline communications – offline communications such as ads or direct mail can link to a product or campaign landing page to help achieve direct response, sometimes known as 'web response'. A sound URL strategy, as explained in Chapter 8, can help this.

● Related content can be grouped to measure the effectiveness of a web site as part of design for analysis, which is also explained below.

Card sorting

Card sorting or web classification

The process of arranging a way of organising objects on the web site in a consistent manner.

Using card sorting is a way in which users can become actively involved in the development process of information architecture.

Card sorting is a useful approach since web sites are frequently designed from the perspective of the designer rather than the information user, leading to labels, subject grouping and categories that are not intuitive to the user. Card sorting or web classification should categorise web objects (e.g documents) in order to facilitate information task completion or information goals the user has set.

Robertson (2003) explains an approach to card sorting which identifies the following questions when using card sorting to aid the process of modelling web classification systems:

● Do the users want to see the information grouped by: subject, task, business or customer groupings, or type of information?
● What are the most important items to put on the main menu?
● How many menu items should there be, and how deep should it go?
● How similar or different are the needs of the users throughout the organisation?

Selected groups of users or representatives will be given index cards with the following written on them, depending on the aim of the card sorting process.

● Types of documents
● Organisational key words and concepts
● Document titles
● Descriptions of documents
● Navigation labels.

The user groups may then be asked to:

● Group together cards that they feel relate to each other;
● Select cards that accurately reflect a given topic or area;
● Organise cards in terms of hierarchy – high-level terms (broad) to low-level terms.

At the end of the session the analyst must take the cards away and map the results into a spreadsheet to find out the most popular terms, descriptions and relationships. If two or more different groups are used the results should be compared and reasons for differences should be analysed.

Blueprints

Blueprints

Show the relationships between pages and other content components, and can be used to portray organisation, navigation and labelling systems

According to Rosenfeld and Morville (2002), blueprints:

Show the relationships between pages and other content components, and can be used to portray organization, navigation and labelling systems.

They are often thought of, and referred to, as 'site maps' or 'site structure diagrams' and have much in common with these, except that they are used as a design device clearly showing grouping of information and linkages between pages, rather than a page on the web site to assist navigation.

Refer to Figure 7.6 for an example of a site structure diagram for a toy manufacturer web site which shows the groupings of content and an indication of the process of task completion also.

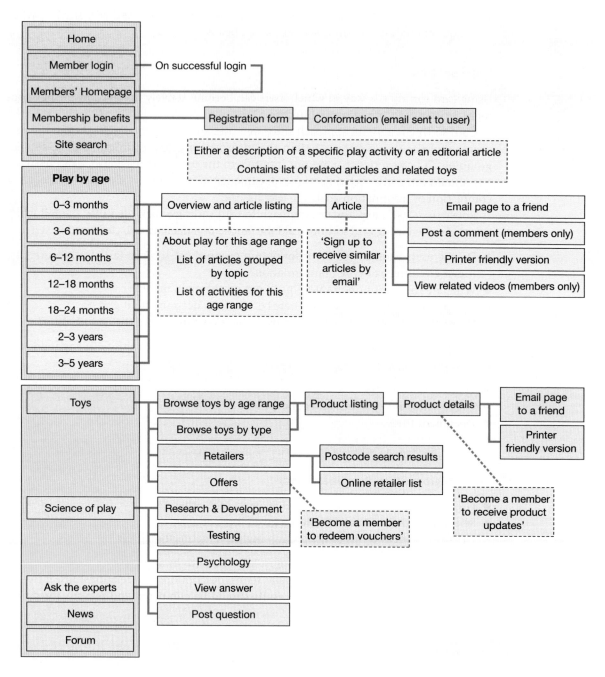

Figure 7.6 Site structure diagram (blueprint) showing layout and relationship between pages

Wireframes

Wireframe

Also known as 'schematics', a way of illustrating the layout of an individual web page.

A related technique to blueprints is the wireframes which are used by web designers to indicate the eventual layout of a web page. Figure 7.7 shows that the wireframe is so called because it just consists of an outline of the page with the 'wires' of content separating different areas of content or navigation shown by white space.

Wodtke (2002) describes a wireframe (sometimes known as a 'schematic') as:

a basic outline of an individual page, drawn to indicate the elements of a page, their relationships, and their relative importance.

A wireframe will be created for all types of similar page groups, identified at the blueprint (site map) stage of creating the information architecture.

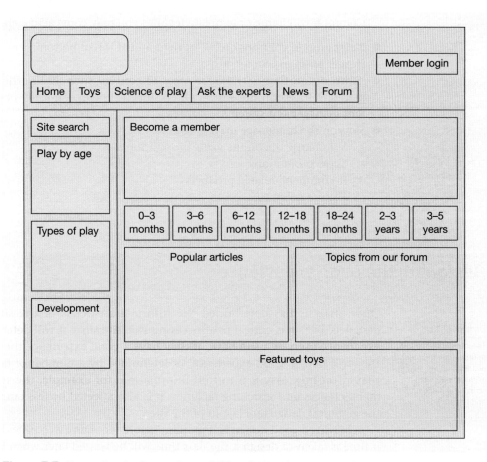

Figure 7.7 Example wireframe for a children's toy site

Blueprints illustrate how the content of a web site is related and navigated while a wireframe focuses on individual pages; with a wireframe the navigation focus becomes where it will be placed on the page. Wireframes are useful for agencies and clients to discuss the way a web site will be laid out without getting distracted by colour, style or messaging issues which should be covered separately as a creative planning activity.

Storyboarding
The use of static drawings or screenshots of the different parts of a web site to review the design concept with user groups. It can be used to develop the structure – an overall 'map' with individual pages shown separately.

The process of reviewing wireframes is sometimes referred to as **storyboarding**, although the term is often applied to reviewing creative ideas rather than formal design alternative. Early designs are drawn on large pieces of paper, or mock-ups are produced using a drawing or paint program.

At the wireframe stage, emphasis is not placed on use of colour or graphics, which will be developed in conjunction with branding or marketing teams and graphic designers and integrated into the site after the wireframe process.

According to Chaffey and Wood (2005), the aim of a wireframe will be to:

- Integrate consistently available components on the web page (e.g. navigation, search boxes);
- Order and group key types of components together;
- Develop a design that will focus the user on to core messages and content;
- Make correct use of white space to structure the page;
- Develop a page structure that can be easily reused by other web designers.

Common wireframe or template features you may come across are:

- Navigation in columns on left or right and at top or bottom;
- Header areas and footer areas;
- 'Slots' or 'portlets' – these are areas of content such as an article or list of articles placed in boxes on the screen. Often slots will be dynamically populated from a content management system;
- Slots on the homepage may be used to:
  - Summarise the online value proposition
  - Show promotions
  - Recommend related products
  - Feature news, etc.
  - Contain ads.

Designing the user experience

Design phase

The design phase defines how the site will work in the key areas of web site structure, navigation and security.

Once analysis has determined the information needs of the site, the site can be designed. Design is critical to a successful web site since it will determine the quality of experience users of a site have; if they have a good experience they will return, if not they will not! A 'good experience' is determined by a number of factors such as those that affect how easy it is to find information: for example, the structure of the site, menu choices and searching facilities. It is also affected by less tangible factors such as the graphical design and layout of the site.

Achieving a good design is important before too many web pages are developed since, if time is taken to design a site, less time will be wasted later when the site is reworked. Large sites are usually produced by creating templates comprising the graphical and menu elements to which content is added.

As mentioned previously, design is not solely a paper-based exercise, but needs to be integrated into the prototyping process. The design should be tested by review with the client and customer to ensure it is appropriate. The design of site layout, navigation and structure can be tested in two different ways. First, early designs can be paper-based – drawn by the designer on large pieces of paper – or 'mock-ups' can be produced on screen using a drawing or paint program. This process is referred to as 'storyboarding'. Second, a working, dynamic prototype can be produced in which users can select different menu options on-screen that will take them to skeleton pages (minus content) of different parts of the site.

Since the main reason given in Table 7.6 for returning to a web site is high-quality content, it is important to determine, through analysis, that the content is correct. However, the quality of content is determined by more than the text copy. It is important to achieve high-quality content through design. To help in this it is useful to consider the factors that affect quality content. These are shown in Figure 7.8. All are determined by the quality of the information.

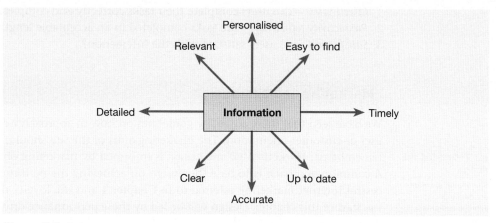

Figure 7.8 Different aspects of high-quality information content of a web site

Developing customer-oriented content

Nigel Bevan (1999a) says:

> Unless a web site meets the needs of the intended users it will not meet the needs of the organization providing the web site. Web site development should be user-centred, evaluating the evolving design against user requirements.

How can this customer-oriented or user-centred content be achieved?

User-centred design starts with understanding the nature and variation within the user groups. According to Bevan (1999a), issues to consider include:

User-centred design

Design based on optimising the user experience according to all factors, including the user interface, which affect this.

- Who are the important users?
- What is their purpose for accessing the site?
- How frequently will they visit the site?
- What experience and expertise do they have?
- What nationality are they? Can they read your language?
- What type of information are they looking for?
- How will they want to use the information: read it on the screen, print it or download it?
- What type of browsers will they use? How fast will their communication links be?
- How large a screen or window will they use, with how many colours?

Rosenfeld and Morville (2002) suggest four stages of site design that also have a user-centred basis:

1 Identify different audiences.
2 Rank importance of each to business.
3 List the three most important information needs of audience.
4 Ask representatives of each audience type to develop their own wish lists.

We noted in Chapter 2 that customer persona and scenario analysis is a powerful technique of understanding different audiences which can be used to inform and test web site design.

Evaluating designs

A test of effective design for usability is dependent on three areas according to Bevan (1999b):

1 *Effectiveness* – can users complete their tasks correctly and completely?
2 *Productivity (efficiency)* – are tasks completed in an acceptable length of time?
3 *Satisfaction* – are users satisfied with the interaction?

Marketing-led site design

We have seen that there are many guidelines on how to approach web site design from a user or customer orientation. The marketing aims of the site should, however, always be remembered. Marketing-led site design is informed by marketing objectives and tactics. A common approach is to base the design on achieving the performance drivers of successful Internet marketing referred to in Chapter 4 and the loyalty drivers referred to at the start of this chapter. Design will be led by these performance drivers as follows:

Marketing-led site design

Site design elements are developed to achieve customer acquisition, retention and communication of marketing messages.

- *Customer acquisition* – the online value proposition must be clear. Appropriate incentives for customer acquisition such as those described in Chapter 6 must be devised.
- *Customer conversion* – the site must engage first-time visitors. Call to action for customer acquisition and retention offers must be prominent with benefits clearly explained. The fulfilment of the offer or purchase must be as simple as possible to avoid attrition during this process.
- *Customer retention* – appropriate incentives and content for repeat visits and business must be available (see Chapter 6).
- *Service quality* – this has been covered in this chapter. Service quality is affected by site navigation, performance, availability and responsiveness to enquiries.
- *Branding* – the brand offer must be clearly explained and interaction with the brand must be possible.

Elements of site design

Once the requirements of the user and marketer are established we turn our attention to the design of the human–computer interface. Nielsen (2000b) structures his book on web usability according to three main areas, which can be interpreted as follows:

1 *site design and structure* – the overall structure of the site;
2 *page design* – the layout of individual pages;
3 *content design* – how the text and graphic content on each page is designed.

Site design and structure

The structures created by designers for web sites will vary greatly according to their audience and the site's purpose, but we can make some general observations about approaches to site design and structure and their influence on consumers. For example, Rosen and Purinton (2004) have assessed the design factors which influence a consumer (based on questionnaires of a group of students). They believe there are some basic factors that determine the effectiveness of an e-commerce site. They group these factors as follows:

- *Coherence* – simplicity of design, easy to read, use of categories (for browsing products or topics), absence of information overload, adequate font size, uncrowded presentation;
- *Complexity* – different categories of text;
- *Legibility* – use of 'mini home page' on every subsequent page, same menu on every page, site map.

You can see that these authors suggest that simplicity in design is important. Another example of research into web site design factors supports the importance of design. Fogg et al. (2003) asked students to review sites to assess the credibility of different suppliers based on the web site design. They considered these factors most important:

Design look	46.1%
Information design/structure	28.5%
Information focus	25.1%
Company motive	15.5%
Usefulness of information	14.8%
Accuracy of information	14.3%
Name recognition and reputation	14.1%
Advertising	13.8%
Bias of information	11.6%
Tone of the writing	9.0%
Identity of site sponsor	8.8%
Functionality of site	8.6%
Customer service	6.4%
Past experience with site	4.6%
Information clarity	3.7%
Performance on a test	3.6%
Readability	3.6%
Affiliations	3.4%

However, it should be borne in mind that such generalisations can be misleading based on the methodology used. Reported behaviour (e.g. through questionnaires or focus groups) may be quite different from actual observed behaviour. Leading e-retail sites (for example Amazon.com and eBay.com) and many media sites typically have a large amount of information and navigation choices available on-screen since the site designers know from testing alternative designs that consumers are quite capable of finding content relevant to them and that a wider choice of links means that the user can find the information they need without clicking through a hierarchy. When performing a real-life product search, in-depth information on the products and reviews of the product are important in making the product decision and are one of the benefits that online channels can give. Although design look is top of the list of factors presented by Fogg et al. (2003), you can see that many of the other factors are based on the quality of information.

In the following coverage, we will review the general factors which designers consider in designing the style, organisation and navigation schemes for the site.

Site style

An effective web site design will have a style that is communicated through use of colour, images, typography and layout. This should support the way a product is positioned or its brand.

Site personality

The style elements can be combined to develop a personality for a site.

We could describe a site's personality in the same way we can describe people, such as 'formal' or 'fun'. This personality has to be consistent with the needs of the target audience (Figure 7.9). A business audience often requires detailed information and prefers an information-intensive style such as that of the Cisco site (Figure 7.12) (www.cisco.com).

A consumer site is usually more graphically intensive. Before the designers pass on their creative designs to developers, they also need to consider the constraints on the user experience, such as screen resolution and colour depth, browser used and download speed.

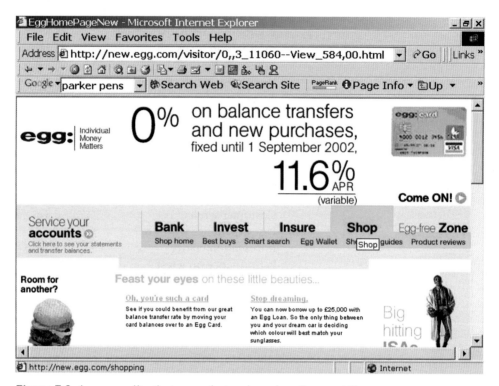

Figure 7.9 A personality that appeals to a broad audience at Egg.com

Graphic design

Graphic design of web sites represents a challenge since designers of web sites are severely constrained by a number of factors:

- *The speed of downloading graphics* – designers need to allow for home users who view sites using a slow modem across a phone line and who are unlikely to wait minutes to view a web site.
- *The screen resolutions of the computer* – designing for different screen resolutions is necessary, since some users with laptops may be operating at a low resolution such as 640 by 480 pixels, the majority at a resolution of 800 by 600 pixels, and a few at higher resolutions of 1064 by 768 pixels or greater.
- *The number of colours on screen* – some users may have monitors capable of displaying 16 million colours giving photo-realism, while other may have only 256 colours.
- *The type of web browser used* – different browsers such as Microsoft Internet Explorer and Netscape Navigator and different versions of browsers such as version 4.0 or 5.0 may display graphics or text slightly differently or may support different plug-ins (see the section in Chapter 9 on testing).

As a result of these constraints, the design of web sites is a constant compromise between what looks visually appealing and modern and what works for the older browsers, with slower connections. This is often referred to as the 'lowest common denominator problem' since this is what the designer must do – design for the old browsers, using slow links and low screen resolutions. One method for avoiding the 'lowest common denominator problem' is to offer the user a 'high-tech' or 'low-tech' choice: one for users with fast connections and high screen resolutions, and another for users who do not have these. This facility is mainly seen offered on sites produced by large companies since it requires more investment to effectively duplicate the site.

Despite these constraints, graphic design is important in determining the feel or character of a site. The graphic design can help shape the user's experience of a site and should be consistent with the brand involved.

Site organisation

Information organisation schemes
The structure chosen to group and categorise information.

In their book *Information Architecture for the World Wide Web*, Rosenfeld and Morville (2002) identify several different information organisation schemes. These can be applied for different aspects of e-commerce sites, from the whole site through to different parts of the site.

Rosenfeld and Morville (2002) identify the following information organisation schemes:

1 *Exact.* Here information can be naturally indexed. If we take the example of books, these can be alphabetical, by author or title; chronological – by date; or for travel books, for example, geographical – by place. Information on an e-commerce site may be presented alphabetically, but it is not suitable for browsing.

2 *Ambiguous.* Here the information requires classification, again taking the examples of books, the Dewey Decimal System is an ambiguous classification scheme since the librarians classify books into arbitrary categories. Such an approach is common on an e-commerce site since products and services can be classified in different ways. Other ambiguous information organisation schemes that are commonly used on web sites are where content is broken down by topic, by task or by audience. The use of metaphors is also common, a metaphor being where the web site corresponds to a familiar real-world situation. The Microsoft Windows Explorer, where information is grouped according to Folders, Files and Trash is an example of a real-world metaphor. The use of the shopping basket metaphor is widespread within e-commerce sites. It should be noted though that Nielsen (2000b) believes that metaphors can be confusing if the metaphor isn't understood immediately or is misinterpreted.

3 *Hybrid.* Here there will be a mixture of organisation schemes, both exact and ambiguous.

Rosenfeld and Morville (2002) point out that using different approaches is common on web sites, but this can lead to confusion, because the user is not clear what mental model is being followed. We can say that it is probably best to minimise the number of information organisation schemes.

Site navigation schemes

Site navigation scheme
Tools provided to the user to move between different information on a web site.

Flow
Flow describes how easy it is for users of a site to move between the different pages of content of the site.

Devising a site that is easy to use is critically dependent on the design of the site navigation scheme. Hoffman and Novak (1997) and many subsequent studies (e.g. Rettie, 2001, Smith and Sivakumar, 2004) have stressed the importance of the concept of flow in governing site usability. The concept of 'flow' was first brought to prominence by Mihaly Csikszentmihalyi, a psychology professor at the University of Chicago. In his book, *Flow: The Psychology of Optimal Experience*, he explains his theory that people are most happy when they are in a state of flow – a Zen-like state of total oneness with the activity at hand. In an online marketing context, 'Flow' essentially describes how easy it is for the users to find the information or experiences they need as they move from one page of the site to the next, but it also includes other interactions such as filling in on-screen forms. Rettie (2001) has suggested that the quality of navigation is one of the prerequisites for flow, although other factors are also important. They include: quick download time, alternative versions, auto-completion of forms, opportunities for interaction, navigation which creates choices, predictable navigation for control and segmenting content by Internet experience.

It can be suggested that there are three important aspects to a site that is easy to navigate. These are:

1 *Consistency*. The site will be easier to navigate if the user is presented with a consistent user interface when viewing the different parts of the site. For example, if the menu options in the support section of the site are on the left side of the screen, then they should also be on the left when the user moves to the 'news section' of the site.

2 *Simplicity*. Sites are easier to navigate if there are limited numbers of options. It is usually suggested that two or possibly three levels of menu are the most that are desirable. For example, there may be main menu options at the left of the screen that take the user to the different parts of the site, and at the bottom of the screen there will be specific menu options that refer to that part of the site. (Menus in this form are often referred to as 'nested'.)

3 *Context*. Context is the use of 'signposts' to indicate to users where they are located within the site – in other words to reassure users that they are not 'lost'. To help with this, the web site designer should use particular text or colour to indicate to users which part of the site they are currently using. Context can be provided by the use of JavaScript 'rollovers', where the colour of the menu option changes when the user positions the mouse over the menu option and then changes again when the menu option is selected. Many sites also have a site-map option that shows the layout and content of the whole site so the user can understand its structure. When using a well-designed site it should not be necessary to refer to such a map regularly.

Navigation

Navigation describes how easy it is to find and move between different information on a web site. It is governed by menu arrangements, site structure and the layout of individual pages.

Narrow and deep navigation

Fewer choices, more clicks to reach required content.

Broad and shallow navigation

More choices, fewer clicks to reach required content.

Deep linking

Jakob Nielsen's term for a user arriving at a site deep within its structure.

Most navigation systems are based upon a hierarchical site structure. When creating the structure, designers have to compromise between the two approaches shown in Figure 7.10. The narrow and deep approach has the benefit of fewer choices on each page, making it easier for the user to make their selection, but more clicks are required to reach a particular piece of information. The broad and shallow approach requires fewer clicks to reach the same piece of information, but the design of the screen potentially becomes cluttered. Figures 7.10(a) and 7.11 depict the narrow and deep approach and Figures 7.10(b) and 7.12 the broad and shallow approach. Note that in these cases the approaches are appropriate for both non-technical and technical audiences. A rule of thumb is that site designers should ensure it only takes three clicks to reach any piece of information on a site. This implies the use of a broad and shallow approach on most large sites. Lynch and Horton (1999) recommend a broad and shallow approach and note that designers should not conceive of a single home page where customers arrive on the site, but of different home pages according to different audience types. Each of the pages in the second row of Figure 7.10(b) could be thought of as an example of a home page which the visitors can bookmark if the page appeals to them. Nielsen (2000b) points out that many users will not arrive on the home page, but may be referred from another site or according to a print or TV advert to a particular page such as **www.b2b.com/jancomp**. He calls this process 'deep linking' and site designers should ensure that navigation and context are appropriate for users arriving on these pages.

As well as compromises on depth of links within a site it is also necessary to compromise on the amount of space devoted to menus. Nielsen (1999) points out that some sites devote so much space to navigation bars that the space available for content is

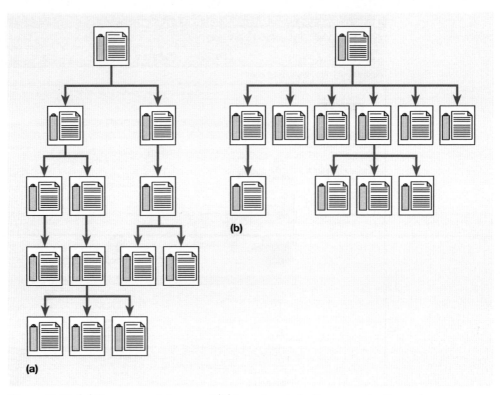

Figure 7.10 (a) Narrow and deep and (b) broad and shallow organisation schemes

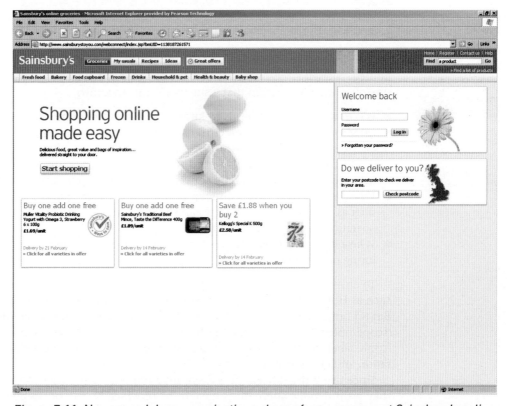

Figure 7.11 Narrow and deep organisation scheme for consumers at Sainsbury's online groceries site (http://www.sainsburystoyou.com/webconnect/index.jsp)

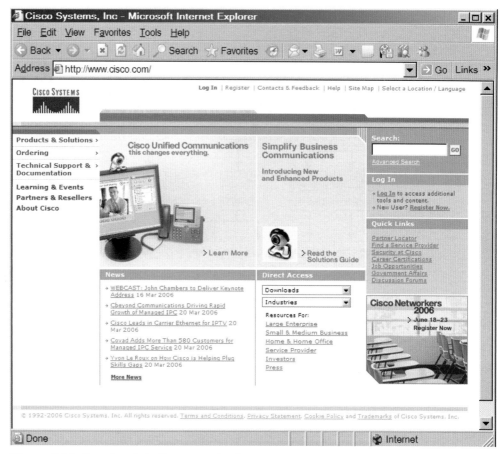

Figure 7.12 Broad and shallow organisation scheme and professional style at Cisco.com

limited. Nielsen (1999) suggests that the designer of navigation systems should consider the following information that a site user wants to know:

● *Where am I?* The user needs to know where they are on the site and this can be indicated by highlighting the current location and clear titling of pages. This can be considered as *context. Consistency* of menu locations on different pages is also required to aid cognition. Users also need to know where they are on the web. This can be indicated by a logo, which by convention is at the top or top left of a site.
● *Where have I been?* This is difficult to indicate on a site, but for task-oriented activities such as purchasing a product it can show the user that they are at the *n*th stage of an operation such as making a purchase.
● *Where do I want to go?* This is the main navigation system which gives options for future operations.

To answer these questions, clear succinct labelling is required. Widely used standards such as Home, Main page, Search, Find, Browse, FAQ, Help and About Us are preferable. But for other particular labels it is useful to have what Rosenfeld and Morville (2002) call 'scope notes' – an additional explanation. These authors also argue against the use of iconic labels or pictures without corresponding text since they are open to misinterpretation and take longer to process.

Since using the navigation system may not enable the user to find the information they want rapidly, alternatives have to be provided by the site designers. These alternatives include search, advanced search, browse and site map facilities. Whatis.com (**www.whatis.com**) illustrates these features well.

Menu options

Designing and creating the menus to support navigation present several options, and these are briefly described here. The main options are the following.

1 Text menus, buttons or images

The site user can select menus by clicking on different objects. They can click on a basic text hyperlink, underlined in blue, by default. It should be noted that these will be of different sizes according to the size the user has selected to display the text. The use of text menus only may make a site look primitive and reduce its graphic appeal. Rectangular or oval buttons can be used to highlight menu options more distinctly. Images can also be used to show menu options. For instance, customer service could be denoted by a picture of a helpdesk. Whilst these are graphically appealing it may not be obvious that they are menu options until the user positions the mouse over them. A combination of text menu options and either buttons or images is usually the best compromise. This way users have the visual appeal of buttons or images, but also the faster option of text – they can select these menus if they are waiting for graphical elements to load, or if the images are turned off in the web browser. However, icons should have the advantage that their understanding is not language-dependent.

2 Rollovers

'Rollover' is the term used to describe colour changes – where the colour of the menu option changes when the user positions the mouse over the menu option and then changes again when the menu option is selected. Rollovers are useful in that they help achieve the context referred to in the previous section, by highlighting the area of the site the user is in.

3 Positioning

Menus can be positioned at any of the edges of the screen, with left, bottom or top being conventional for Western cultures. The main design aim is to keep the position consistent between different parts of the site.

4 Frames

Frames are a feature of HTML which enable menus to be positioned at one side of the screen in a small area (frame) while the content of the page is displayed in the main frame. Frames have their advocates and detractors, but they are still used on some sites (e.g. **www.tesco.com**) which require particular functionality. Detractors point to poor display speed, difficulties in indexing content in search engines and inflexibility on positioning.

5 Number of levels

In a hierarchical structure there could be as many as ten different levels, but for simplicity it is normal to try and achieve a site structure with a nesting level of four or fewer. Even in an electronic commerce shopping site with 20,000 products it should be possible to select a product at four menu levels. For example:

- level 1 – drink;
- level 2 – spirits;
- level 3 – whisky;
- level 4 – brand x.

6 Number of options

Psychologists recommend having a limited number of choices within each menu. If a menu has more than seven, it is probably necessary to add another level to the hierarchy to accommodate the extra choices.

Page design

The page design involves creating an appropriate layout for each page. The main elements of a particular page layout are the title, navigation and content. Standard content such as copyright information may be added to every page as a footer. Issues in page design include:

- *Page elements*. We have to consider the proportion of page devoted to content compared to all other material such as headers, footers and navigation elements. The location of these elements also needs to be considered. It is conventional for the main menu to be at the top or on the left. The use of a menu system at the top of the browser window allows more space for content below.
- *The use of frames*. This is generally discouraged since it makes search engine registration more difficult and makes printing and bookmarking more difficult for visitors.
- *Resizing*. A good page layout design should allow for the user to change the size of text or work with different monitor resolutions.
- *Consistency*. Page layout should be similar for all areas of the site unless more space is required, for example for a discussion forum or product demonstration. Standards of colour and typography can be enforced through cascading style sheets.
- *Printing*. Layout should allow for printing or provide an alternative printing format.

Content design

The home page is particularly important in achieving marketing actions – if the customers do not understand or do not buy into the proposition of the site, then they will leave. Gleisser (2001) states that it is important to clarify what he refers to as 'the essentials' of: who we are, what we offer, what is inside and how to contact us.

A study of the advertising impact of web site content design has been conducted by Pak (1999). She reviewed the techniques on web sites used to communicate the message to the customer in terms of existing advertising theory. The study considered the creative strategy used, in terms of the rational and emotional appeals contained within the visuals and the text. As would be expected intuitively, the appeal of the graphics was more emotional than that for the text; the latter used a more rational appeal. The study also considered the information content of the advertisements using classification schemes such as that of Resnik and Stern (1977). The information cues are still relevant to modern web site design. Some of the main information cues, in order of frequency of use, were:

- performance (what does the product do?);
- components/content (what is the product made up of?);
- price/value;
- implicit comparison;
- availability;
- quality;
- special offers;
- explicit comparisons.

Aaker and Norris (1982) devised a framework in which the strategy for creative appeal is based on emotion and feeling, and that for rational and cognitive appeal is based on facts and logic.

Copywriting for the web is an evolving art form, but many of the rules for good copywriting are as for any media. Common errors we see on web sites are:

- too much knowledge assumed of the visitor about the company, its products and services;
- using internal jargon about products, services or departments – using undecipherable acronyms.

Web copywriters also need to take account of the user reading the content on-screen. Approaches to dealing with the limitations imposed by the customer using a monitor include:

- writing more concisely than in brochures;
- chunking, or breaking text into units of 5–6 lines at most, which allows users to scan rather than read information on web pages;
- use of lists with headline text in larger font;
- never including too much on a single page, except when presenting lengthy information such as a report which may be easier to read on a single page;
- using hyperlinks to decrease page sizes or help achieve flow within copy, either by linking to sections further down a page or linking to another page.

Smith and Chaffey (2005) summarise the essentials of good copywriting for the web under the mnemonic 'CRABS', which stands for chunking, relevance, accuracy, brevity and scannability.

Hofacker (2000) describes five stages of human information processing when a web site is being used. These can be applied to both page design and content design to improve usability and help companies get their message across to consumers. Each of the five stages summarised in Table 7.5 acts as a hurdle, since if the site design or content is too difficult to process, the customer cannot progress to the next stage. It is useful to consider the stages in order to minimise these difficulties.

Table 7.5 A summary of the characteristics of the five stages of information processing described by Hofacker (2000)

Stage	Description	Applications
1 Exposure	Content must be present for long enough to be processed	Content on banner ads may not be on screen long enough for processing and cognition
2 Attention	User s eyes will be drawn towards headings and content, not graphics and moving items on a web page (Nielsen, 2000b)	Emphasis and accurate labelling of headings is vital to gain a user's attention. Evidence suggests that users do not notice banner adverts, suffering from 'banner blindness'
3 Comprehension and perception	The user's interpretation of content	Designs that use common standards and metaphors and are kept simple will be more readily comprehended
4 Yielding and acceptance	Is information (copy) presented accepted by customers?	Copy should refer to credible sources and present counter-arguments as necessary
5 Retention	As for traditional advertising, this describes the extent to which the information is remembered	An unusual style or high degree of interaction leading to flow and user satisfaction is more likely to be recalled

Gleisser (2001) surveyed web site designers to identify consensus on what were success factors in web site design. The results of this research are used to summarise this section:

- *The home page essentials.* Segmentation, targeting and positioning play a key role in informing design. The essentials are: who we are, what we offer, what is inside and how to contact us.
- *Cater for the needs of anticipated users.* Web sites should be quick to download and easy to navigate. The users may not be able to incorporate the latest technical capabilities, such as plug-ins, so these should be used with care.
- *Update the web site frequently.* This is to encourage repeat visitors and keep customers informed of new products and offers.
- *Gathering customer information.* The web site should be used as part of a 'push' marketing strategy which includes gathering customer information and better targeting of direct marketing using a range of media.

Development and testing of content

It is not practical to provide details of the methods of developing content – for two reasons. First, to describe all the facilities available in web browsers for laying out and formatting text, and for developing interactivity, would require several books! Second, the programming standards and tools used are constantly evolving, so material is soon out-of-date.

Testing content

Development phase

'Development' is the term used to describe the creation of a web site by programmers. It involves writing the HTML content, creating graphics, and writing any necessary software code such as JavaScript or ActiveX (programming).

Testing phase

Testing involves different aspects of the content such as spelling, validity of links, formatting on different web browsers and dynamic features such as form filling or database queries.

Marketing managers responsible for web sites need to have a basic awareness of web site development and testing. We have already discussed the importance of usability testing with typical users of the system. In brief, other necessary testing steps include:

- test content displays correctly on different types and versions of web browsers;
- test plug-ins;
- test all interactive facilities and integration with company databases;
- test spelling and grammar;
- test adherence to corporate image standards;
- test to ensure all links to external sites are valid.

Testing often occurs on a separate test web server (or directory) or *test environment*, with access to the test or prototype version being restricted to the development team. When complete the web site is released or published to the main web server or *live environment*.

Tools for web site development and testing

A variety of software programs are available to help developers of web sites. Some of these tools are listed below to illustrate the range of skills a web site designer will need; an advanced web site may be built using tools from each of these categories since even the most advanced tools may not have the flexibility of the basic tools.

Basic text editors

Text editors are used to edit HTML tags. For example, '<B>Products</B>' will make the enclosed text display bold within the web browser. Such tools are often available at low cost or free – including the Notepad editor included with Windows. They are very flexible, and all web site developers will need to use them at some stage in developing content since more automated tools may not provide this flexibility and may not support the latest standard commands. Entire sites can be built using these tools, but it is more efficient to use the more advanced tools described below, and use the editors for 'tweaking' content.

Specialised HTML and graphics editors

Specialised HTML and graphics editing tools provide facilities for adding HTML tags automatically. For example, adding the Bold text tag <B> </B> to the HTML document will happen when the user clicks the bold tag. Some of these editors are WYSIWYG. Examples of standard tools include Microsoft FrontPage Express (**www.microsoft.com**) and the more sophisticated and widely used tool Dreamweaver (**www.macromedia.com**).

More advanced tools include *content management systems* which are today essential for any site which is frequently updated to support marketing. This topic is discussed further in Chapter 9. They provide advanced content editing facilities, but also provide tools to help manage and test the site, including graphic layouts of the structure of the site – making it easy to find, modify and re-publish the page. Style templates can be applied to produce a consistent 'look and feel' across the site. Tools are also available to create and manage menu options.

Examples of graphics tools include:

- Adobe Photoshop (extensively used by graphic designers, **www.adobe.com**);
- Macromedia Flash and Director-Shockwave (used for graphical animations, **www.macromedia.com**).

Promote site

Promotion of a site is a significant topic that will be part of the strategy of developing a web site. It will follow the initial development of a site and is described in detail in Chapter 8.

Service quality

Delivering service quality in e-commerce can be assessed through reviewing existing marketing frameworks for determining levels of service quality. Those most frequently used are based on the concept of a 'service-quality gap' that exists between the customer's expected level of service (from previous experience and word-of-mouth communication) and their perception of the actual level of service delivery. We can apply the elements of service quality on which Parasuraman et al. (1985) suggest that consumers judge companies. Note that there has been heated dispute about the validity of this SERVQUAL instrument framework in determining service quality, see for example Cronin and Taylor

(1992). Despite this it is still instructive to apply these dimensions of service quality to customer service on the web (see for example Chaffey and Edgar (2000), Kolesar and Galbraith (2000), Zeithaml et al. (2002) and Trocchia and Janda (2003)):

- *tangibles* – the physical appearance of facilities and communications;
- *reliability* – the ability to perform the service dependably and accurately;
- *responsiveness* – a willingness to help customers and provide prompt service;
- *assurance* – the knowledge and courtesy of employees and their ability to convey trust and confidence;
- *empathy* – providing caring, individualised attention.

Online marketers should assess what customers' expectations are in each of these areas, and identify where there is an online service-quality gap between the customer expectations and what is currently delivered.

Research across industry sectors suggests that the quality of service is a key determinant of loyalty. Feinberg et al. (2000) report that when reasons why customers leave a company are considered, over 68% leave because of 'poor service experience', with other factors such as price (10%) and product issues (17%) less significant. Poor service experience was subdivided as follows:

- poor access to the right person (41%);
- unaccommodating (26%);
- rude employees (20%);
- slow to respond (13%).

This survey was conducted for traditional business contacts, but it is instructive since these reasons given for poor customer service have their equivalents online through e-mail communications and delivery of services on-site.

We will now examine how the five determinants of online service quality apply online.

Online service-quality gap

The mismatch between what is expected and delivered by an online presence.

Tangibles

It can be suggested that the tangibles dimension is influenced by ease of use and visual appeal based on the structural and graphic design of the site. Design factors that influence this variable are described later in this chapter. The importance customers attach to these different aspects of service quality is indicated by the compilation in Table 7.6 which considers the reasons why customers return to a site.

Table 7.6 Ten key reasons for returning to site

Reason to return	Percentage of respondents
1 High-quality content	75
2 Ease of use	66
3 Quick to download	58
4 Updated frequently	54
5 Coupons and incentives	14
6 Favourite brands	13
7 Cutting-edge technology	12
8 Games	12
9 Purchasing capabilities	11
10 Customisable content	10

Source: Forrester Research poll of 8600 online households, 1998

Reliability

The reliability dimension is dependent on the availability of the web site or, in other words, how easy it is to connect to the web site as a user. Many companies fail to achieve 100% availability and potential customers may be lost for ever, if they attempt to use the site when it is unavailable.

Reliability of e-mail response is also a key issue, Chaffey and Edgar (2000) reported on a survey of 361 UK web sites across different sectors. Of those in the sample, 331 (or 92 per cent) were accessible at the time of the survey and, of these, 299 provided an e-mail contact point. E-mail enquiries were sent to all of these 299 web sites; of these, 9 undeliverable mail messages were received. It can be seen that at the time of the survey, service availability was certainly not universal. Surprisingly, more recent surveys suggest some improvement, but still indicate a poor quality of service overall. Transversal (2005), the provider of the MetaFAQ software to answer customers' responses online found the following reliability of response:

- *Average number of questions answered*:
  - Travel 1.2 out of 10
  - Telecoms 1 out of 10
  - Average all companies 2.1 out of 10
- *Percentage of companies that responded to e-mail*:
  - Travel 40 per cent
  - Telecoms 70 per cent
  - Average 56 per cent
- *Average e-mail response time*:
  - Travel 42 hours
  - Telecoms 32 hours
  - Average 33 hours.

Responsiveness

The same survey showed that responsiveness was poor overall: of the 290 successfully delivered e-mails, a 62 per cent response rate occurred within a 28-day period. For over a third of companies there was zero response!

Of the companies that did respond, there was a difference in responsiveness (excluding immediately delivered automated responses) from 8 minutes to over 19 working days! Whilst the mean overall was 2 working days, 5 hours and 11 minutes, the median across all sectors (on the basis of the fastest 50 per cent of responses received) was 1 working day and 34 minutes. The median result suggests that response within one working day represents best practice and could form the basis for consumer expectations.

Responsiveness is also indicated by the performance of the web site: the time it takes for a page request to be delivered to the user's browser as a page impression. Data from monitoring services such as Keynote (**www.keynote.com**) indicate that there is a wide variability in the delivery of information and hence service quality from web servers hosted at ISPs, and companies should be careful to monitor this and specify levels of quality with suppliers in service-level agreements (SLAs). Table 7.2 shows the standard set by the best-performing sites and the difference from the worst-performing sites.

Assurance

In an e-mail context, assurance can best be considered as the quality of response. In the survey reported by Chaffey and Edgar (2000), of 180 responses received, 91 per cent delivered a personalised human response, with 9 per cent delivering an automated response which did not address the individual enquiry; 40 per cent of responses answered or referred to all three questions, with 10 per cent answering two questions and 22 per cent one. Overall, 38 per cent did not answer any of the specific questions posed!

A further assurance concern of e-commerce web sites is the privacy and security of customer information (see Chapter 3). A company that adheres to the UK Internet Shopping Is Safe (ISIS) (**www.imrg.org/isis**) or TRUSTe principles (**www.truste.org**) will provide better assurance than one that does not. Smith and Chaffey (2005) suggest that the following actions can be used to achieve assurance in an e-commerce site:

1 provide clear and effective privacy statements;
2 follow privacy and consumer protection guidelines in all local markets;
3 make security of customer data a priority;
4 use independent certification bodies;
5 emphasise the excellence of service quality in all communications.

Empathy

Although it might be considered that empathy requires personal human contact, it can still be achieved, to an extent, through e-mail. Chaffey and Edgar (2000) report that of the responses received, 91 per cent delivered a personalised human response, with 29 per cent passing on the enquiry within their organisation. Of these 53, 23 further responses were received within the 28-day period; 30 (or 57 per cent) of passed-on queries were not responded to further.

Provision of personalisation facilities is also an indication of the empathy provided by the web site, but more research is needed as to customers' perception of the value of web pages that are dynamically created to meet a customer's information needs.

An alternative framework for considering how service quality can be delivered through e-commerce is to consider how the site provides customer service at the different stages of the buying decision discussed in Chapter 2 in the section on online buyer behaviour. Thus, quality service is not only dependent on how well the purchase itself is facilitated, but also on how easy it is for customers to select products, and on after-sales service, including fulfilment quality. The Epson UK site (**www.epson.co.uk**) illustrates how the site can be used to help in all stages of the buying process. Interactive tools are available to help users select a particular printer, and diagnose and solve faults, and technical brochures can be downloaded. Feedback is solicited on how well these services meet customers' needs.

It can be suggested that for managers wishing to apply a framework such as SERVQUAL in an e-commerce context there are three stages appropriate to managing the process:

1 *Understanding expectations.* Customer expectations for the e-commerce environment in a particular market sector must be understood. The SERVQUAL framework can be used with market research and benchmarking of other sites to understand requirements such as responsiveness and empathy. Scenarios can also be used to identify the customer expectations of using services on a site.

2 *Setting and communicating the service promise.* Once expectations are understood, marketing communications can be used to inform the customers of the level of service. This can be achieved through customer service guarantees or promises. It is better to under-promise than over-promise. A book retailer that delivers the book in 2 days when 3 days were promised will earn the customer's loyalty better than the retailer that promises 1 day, but delivers in 2! The enlightened company may also explain what it will do if it doesn't meet its promises – will the customer be recompensed? The service promise must also be communicated internally and combined with training to ensure that the service is delivered.

3 *Delivering the service promise.* Finally, commitments must be delivered through on-site service, support from employees and physical fulfilment. Otherwise, online credibility is destroyed and a customer may never return.

Tables 7.7 and 7.8 summarise the main concerns of online consumers for each of the elements of service quality. Table 7.7 summarises the main factors in the context of SERVQUAL and Table 7.8 presents the requirements from an e-commerce site that must be met for excellent customer service.

Table 7.7 Online elements of service quality

Tangibles	Reliability	Responsiveness	Assurance and empathy
Ease of use	Availability	Download speed	Contacts with call centre
Content quality	Reliability	E-mail response	Personalisation
Price	E-mail replies	Callback	Privacy
		Fulfilment	Security

Table 7.8 Summary of requirements for online service quality

E-mail response requirements	Web site requirements
• Defined response times and named individual responsible for replies • Use of autoresponders to confirm query is being processed • Personalised e-mail where appropriate • Accurate response to inbound e-mail by *customer-preferred channel*: outbound e-mail or phone callback • Opt-in and opt-out options must be provided for promotional e-mail with a suitable offer in exchange for a customer's provision of information • Clear layout, named individual and privacy statements in e-mail	• Support for customer-preferred channel of communication in response to enquiries (e-mail, phone, postal mail or in person) • Clearly indicated contact points for enquiries via e-mail mailto: and forms • Company internal targets for site availability and performance • Testing of site usability and efficiency of links, HTML, plug-ins and browsers to maximise availability • Appropriate graphic and structural site design to achieve ease of use and relevant content with visual appeal • Personalisation option for customers • Specific tools to help a user answer specific queries such as interactive support databases and frequently asked questions (FAQ)

Source: Chaffey and Edgar (2000)

The relationship between service quality, customer satisfaction and loyalty

Figure 6.16 highlights the importance of online service quality. If customer expectations are not met, customer satisfaction will be poor and repeat site visits will not occur, which makes it difficult to build online relationships. Note, however, that online service quality is also dependent on other aspects of the service experience including the offline component of the service such as fulfilment and the core and extended product offer including pricing. If the customer experience is satisfactory, it can be suggested that customer loyalty will develop.

Reichheld and Schefter (2000) suggest that it is key for organisations to understand, not only what determines service quality and customer satisfaction, but loyalty or repeat purchases. From their research, they suggest five 'primary determinants of loyalty' online:

1 quality customer support;
2 on-time delivery;
3 compelling product presentations;
4 convenient and reasonably priced shipping and handling;
5 clear trustworthy privacy policies.

Figure 7.13 shows a more recent compilation of consumers' opinions of the importance of these loyalty drivers in the online context. It can be seen that it is the after-sales support and service which are considered to be most important – the ease of use and navigation are relatively unimportant.

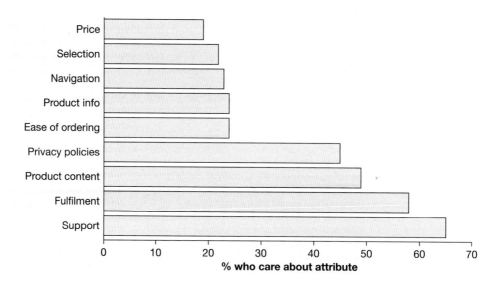

Figure 7.13 Customer ratings of importance of attributes of online experience
Source: J.P. Morgan report on e-tailing 2000

Of course, the precise nature of the loyalty drivers will differ between companies. Reichheld and Schefter (2000) reported that Dell Computer has created a customer experience council that has researched key loyalty drivers, identified measures to track these and put in place an action plan to improve loyalty. The loyalty drivers and their summary metrics were:

1 Driver: *order fulfilment*. Metrics: ship to target – percentage that ship on time exactly as the customer specified.
2 Driver: *product performance*. Metrics: initial field incident rate – the frequency of problems experienced by customers.

3 Driver: *post-sale service and support*. Metrics: on-time, first-time fix – the percentage of problems fixed on the first visit by a service representative who arrives at the time promised.

Rigby et al. (2000) assessed repeat-purchase drivers in grocery, clothing and consumer electronics e-tail. It was found that key loyalty drivers were similar to those of Dell, including correct delivery of order, but other factors such as price, ease of use and customer support were more important.

To summarise this section and in order to more fully understand the online expectations of service quality, complete Activity 7.3.

Activity 7.3 **An example of factors determining online service quality**

visit the w.w.w.

Purpose

To understand the elements of online service quality.

Activity

Think back to your experience of purchasing a book or CD online. Alternatively, visit a site and go through the different stages. Write down your expectations of service quality from when you first arrive on the web site until the product is delivered. There should be around ten different stages.

Case Study 7 **Refining the online customer experience at dabs.com**

This case study highlights the importance placed on web site design as part of the customer experience by dabs.com which is one of the UK's leading Internet retailers of IT and technology products from manufacturers such as Sony, Hewlett-Packard, Toshiba and Microsoft.

Company background and history

Dabs.com was originally created by entrepreneur David Atherton in partnership with writer Bruce Smith (the name 'dabs' comes from the combined initials of their two names). Their first venture, Dabs Press was a publisher of technology books. Although David and Bruce remain firm friends, Dabs has been 100% owned by David since 1990.

Dabs Direct was launched in 1990, as a mail-order firm which mainly promoted itself through ads in home technology magazines such as *Personal Computer World* and *Computer Shopper*.

Dabs.com was launched in 1999 at the height of the dot-com boom, but unlike many dot-com start-up businesses, dabs.com was based on an existing offline business.

In its first year, dabs.com was loss-making with £1.2 million lost in 2000–1; this was partly due to including free delivery as part of the proposition to acquire new customers.

In 2003, the company opened its first 'bricks and mortar' store at Liverpool John Lennon Airport and it has also opened an operation in France (**www.dabs.fr**). The

French site remains, but the retail strategy has now ended since margins were too low, despite a positive effect in building awareness of the brand in retail locations.

Strategy

The importance that dabs.com owners place on customer experience and usability is suggested by their mission statement, which places customer experience at its core together with choice and price. Dabs.com's mission is:

to provide customers with a quick and easy way of buying the products they want, at the most competitive prices around, delivered directly to their door.

Growth has been conservatively managed, since as a privately held company dabs.com has to grow profitably rather than take on debts. Dabs.com has reviewed the potential of other European countries for distribution and may select a country where broadband access is high such as Sweden or the Netherlands. Countries such as Italy where consumers traditionally prefer face-to-face sales would not be early candidates to target for an opening.

In terms of products, dabs.com has focused on computers and related products, but is considering expanding into new categories or even ranges. Initially these will be related to what computer users need while they are working.

Dabs.com in 2005

In 2005, dabs.com is a £200 million company with 235 staff, holding 15,000 lines for a customer base of almost 1.5 million and processing around 5000 customer orders every day. Dabs.com has 8m visits a month from around 750,000 unique users. Its catalogue contains 20,000 products with laptops, LCD monitors and external hard drives among the main sales lines.

NCC (2005) reports that dabs.com believes that what its customers require is a dynamic site that provides comprehensive information on its product ranges, delivery charges, returns policy, financing services and rewards scheme. It also provides dabs.tv, a video service that allows customers to see more complex products in greater detail.

Jonathan Wall, Dab's marketing director, sees security as important as part of the customer experience, and to protect the business, he says:

We were one of the first e-businesses to adopt Visa's 'Verified by Visa' 3D secure payment authentication system and we've also implemented MasterCard's SecureCode variant. We've always worked closely with both credit card companies and it's a concern that dates back to our mail order side. The threat of being attacked and defrauded is always in the forefront of our thoughts.

Delivery

To ensure delivery as promised, Jonathan Wall explains the importance dabs.com attach to IT:

We invest as much in our highly automated warehouse as we do in our marketing. Our systems use a sophisticated combination of dynamic bins and unique product numbering. A lot of the management team come from technical backgrounds. Our back office system was written in OpenVMS by our IT director. Our sales processing system was written in-house.

Staffing

According to NCC (2005), staff skills are viewed as important from technology staff, to product buyers. Wall says:

We pay a higher than average salary, and that means we get a higher level of staff. And we really see the effect of that in the way our buyers and merchandisers approach the market.

Dabs.com ended offline sales in September 2001, after online sales reached half of turnover. This enabled it to reduce costs. Although its consumer sales are online, dabs.com does retain a call centre for customer service and account management services for its business clients who spend £15,000 or more per year. Excellence in customer service is also seen as part of the customer experience and helps dabs.com reduce complaints to trading standards officers compared to some of its online rivals such as eBuyer.com.

Europe is the next challenge: the company launched Dabs.fr in France in 2004. But all will depend on its ability to adapt quickly to any changes in customer behaviour.

The 2003 site update

In 2003, dabs.com achieved a year-on-year profits rise from £2.5m to £5.1m and sales rise from £150m to £200m. It predicted the growth will continue, with sales reaching £350m in 2005. Dabs has about one million unique visitors monthly and adds a further 30,000 new users every month. This success has been achieved in just 4 years from the launch of its first transactional site in 1999. The site reassures each visitor, by the scale of its success. On 5 December it read:

- 1,098,412 customers
- 37,093 orders in December
- 21,289 products available for sale.

Dabs's marketing director, Jonathan Wall, talking to *IT Week* (2003) explained how the initial growth occurred, and how future growth will be sustained: 'We dominate the PC hobbyist/ IT professional sector, but our business must evolve. We want to cast our net further so that we are appealing to people who are interested in technology as a whole. New customers need a new approach. We have built a new environment and a new web site for this target audience.'

In mid-2003 dabs.com launched a site to help it achieve sales to the new audience. Research was used to help develop the new site. The usability of the existing web site was tested and the new concept was also shown to a focus group. After analysing the responses Dabs created a pilot site, which the same focus group then approved. In total, the new site took 10 months to develop and was an investment of £750,000.

The 2005 site update

NCC (2005) says Wall makes the business case for the new site as follows:

Our new site will take us right up there to the top of the field, you have to try and stay ahead. We'll have guided navigation, still quite rare on a UK site, which will help customers to find what they're looking for more intuitively. Early e-commerce customers knew that they specifically wanted a Sony Vaio laptop, for example. New customers just know that they want a laptop that's small and fast and costs less than £1,000. Guided navigation means they can search according to a product's attributes rather than specific brands and models.

Since the average selling price of laptops is going down, slim margins are decreased further. Wall says: 'Selling electronic equipment on the web has traditionally been passive but by redesigning our site we'll be able to show customers what another extra £50 spent on a laptop will buy them.'

Although the previous site was only updated 2 years ago, he describes the need to keep ahead of competitors as 'a cat and mouse thing'.

But new site advances must be combined with competitive prices, Wall says:

Online customers are price-loyal, not retailer-loyal. The customer is only as loyal as the cheapest price they can pay for a product. It means your competitors are only ever one click away. We have to do everything to keep our customers on our site. Getting them to pay that price to you, rather than your competitor, means that you'll need to exploit the constantly-evolving benefits of digital technology to make their buying experience on your site as fluent and satisfactory as possible.

On-site search capabilities

Part of the new site is improved on-site search capabilities from Endeca, which powers the search of Walmart and Circuit City sites in the US. Search is important to increasing conversion rates, and so increasing sales, since if a user is not presented with a relevant product when they search, they are likely to try another retailer. The search capability should strike a balance between delivering too many results and too few. Channel Register (2005) reports that dabs.com hopes to increase conversion rate by up to 50% by updating the site's search and navigation features. The current conversion rate is 3.5% and it is hoped this will be increased to nearer 5%.

Endeca's new search allows users to select products by attributes including price, brand and even size and weight. This method of narrowing down the search should result in the customer being left to choose from a list of 10 or 20 products rather than hundreds.

Another aspect of the business case for the new site is to ensure the customer makes the right decision since product returns are costly for dabs.com and annoying for the customer.

Dabs.com marketing director Jonathan Wall explained: 'When we launched the website in 1999 people knew what they wanted. Now we find a large tranche of customers might know the type of product they want to buy but not which model they want. The new site is about guiding them through the process.'

Accessibility

Since dabs.com has tech-savvy customers, it has to support them as they adopt new ways of browsing. Dabs.com found that by 1995 nearly a fifth of its users were using the Mozilla Firefox browser, so a further requirement for the new site was to make it accessible to users browsing with a range of browsers such as Firefox, Opera and Apple's Safari.

Marketing communications

Marketing communications approaches used by dabs.com are summarised in Chapter 8 in Mini Case Study 8.5 *'Electronic retailers cut back on their e-communications spend'*. For customer acquisition, the main communications tools that are used are:

- Search engine marketing (the main investment)
- Referrals from affiliates (this has been reduced)
- Online display advertising on third-party sites (limited)
- PR
- Sponsorship (shirt sponsorship for Premiership team Fulham).

Sources: Channel Register (2005), *IT Week* (2003), NCC (2005)

Questions

1 The management of dabs.com have invested in several major upgrades to its online presence in order to improve the online customer experience. Assess the reasons for the need to invest in site upgrades by referring to the dabs.com example. To what extent do you think major, regular site upgrades are inevitable?

2 Compare the quality of the online customer experience of dabs.com by visiting the site and those of its competitors such as **www.ebuyer.com** and **www.euroffice.com**. Explain the categories of criteria you have used to make your assessment.

Summary

1 An effective online customer experience is dependent on many factors, including the visual elements of the site design and how it has been designed for usability, accessibility and performance.

2 Careful planning and execution of web site implementation is important, in order to avoid the need for extensive reworking at a later stage if the design proves to be ineffective.

3 Implementation is not an isolated process; it should be integrated with the Internet marketing strategy. Analysis, design and implementation should occur repeatedly in an iterative, prototyping approach based on usability testing that involves the client and the users to produce an effective design.

4 A feasibility study should take place before the initiation of a major web site project. A feasibility study will assess:

- the costs and benefits of the project;
- the difficulty of achieving management and staff commitment to the project;
- the availability of domain names to support the project;
- the responsibilities and stages necessary for a successful project.

5 The choice of host for a web site should be considered carefully since this will govern the quality of service of the web site.

6 Options for analysis of users' requirements for a web site include:

- interviews with marketing staff;
- questionnaire sent to companies;
- usability and accessibility testing;
- informal interviews with key accounts;
- focus groups;
- reviewing competitors' web sites.

7 The design phase of developing a web site includes specification of:

- the information architecture or structure of the web site using techniques such as site maps, blueprints and wireframes;
- the flow, controlled by the navigation and menu options;
- the graphic design and brand identity;
- country-specific localisation;
- the service quality of online forms and e-mail messages.

Exercises

Self-assessment exercises

1 Explain the term 'prototyping' in relation to web site creation.

2 What tasks should managers undertake during initiation of a web page?

3 What is domain name registration?

4 List the factors that determine web site 'flow'.

5 Explain the structure of an HTML document and the concept of 'tags'.

6 List the options for designing web site menu options.

7 What is a hierarchical web site structure?

8 What are the factors that control the performance of a web site?

Essay and discussion questions

1 Discuss the relative effectiveness of the different methods of assessing the customers' needs for a web site.

2 Select three web sites of your choice and compare their design effectiveness. You should describe design features such as navigation, structure and graphic design.

3 Explain how strategy, analysis, design and implementation of a web site should be integrated through a prototyping approach. Describe the merits and problems of the prototyping approach.

4 When designing the interactive services of a web site such as online forms and e-mails to customers, what steps should the designer take to provide a quality service to customers?

Examination questions

1 What is web site prototyping? Give three benefits of this approach.

2 What controls on a web site project are introduced at the initiation phase of the project?

3 A company is selecting an ISP. Explain:
   (a) what an ISP is;
   (b) which factors will affect the quality of service delivered by the ISP.

4 How are focus groups used to gain understanding of customer expectations of a web site?

5 Name, and briefly explain, four characteristics of the information content of a site that will govern whether a customer is likely to return to that web site.

6 When the graphic design and page layout of a web site are being described, what different factors associated with type and set-up of a PC and its software should the designer take into account?

7 What is meant by 'opt-in'? Why should it be taken into account as part of web site design?

References

Aaker, D. and Norris, N. (1982) Characteristics of TV commercials perceived as informative, *Journal of Advertising*, 25(2), 22–34.

Bevan, N. (1999a) Usability issues in web site design. *Proceedings of the 6th Interactive Publishing Conference, November*. Available online at **www.usability.serco.com**.

Bevan, N. (1999b) Common industry format usability tests. Proceedings of UPA'98, Usability Professionals Association, Scottsdale, Arizona, 29 June – 2 July 1999. Available online at **www.usability.serco.com**.

BSI (1999) BS 13407 Human-centred design processes for interactive systems. British Standards Institute.

Chaffey, D. and Edgar, M. (2000) Measuring online service quality, *Journal of Targeting, Analysis and Measurement for Marketing*, 8(4) (May), 363–78.

Chaffey, D. and Wood, S. (2005) *Business Information Management*. Financial Times/Prentice Hall, Harlow.

Channel Register (2005) Dabs.com in £500K makeover, Channel Register, **www.channelregister.co.uk**, John Leyden, 2 September.

Cronin, J. and Taylor, S. (1992) Measuring service quality: a reexamination and extension, *Journal of Marketing*, 56, 55–63.

de Chernatony, L. (2001) Succeeding with brands on the Internet, *Journal of Brand Management*, 8(3), 186–95.

Feinberg, R., Trotter, M. and Anton, J. (2000) At any time – from anywhere – in any form. In D. Renner (ed.) *Defying the Limits, Reaching New Heights in Customer Relationship Management.* Report from Montgomery Research Inc, San Francisco, CA. http://feinberg.crmproject.com.

Fogg, B., Soohoo, C., Danielson, D., Marable, L., Stanford, J. and Tauber, E. (2003) How do people evaluate a web site's credibility? A Consumer WebWatch research report, prepared by Stanford Persuasive Technology Lab.

Gleisser, G. (2001) Building customer relationships online: the web site designer's perspective, *Journal of Consumer Marketing*, 18(6), 488–502.

Hofacker, C. (2000) *Internet Marketing.* Wiley, New York.

Hoffman, D.L. and Novak, T.P. (1997) A new marketing paradigm for electronic commerce, *The Information Society*, Special issue on electronic commerce, 13, 43–54.

IT Week (2003) E-shop adds to attractions. By David Neal, *IT Week* 12-09-2003, p. 24, www.itweek.co.uk.

Kolesar, M. and Galbraith, R. (2000) A services-marketing perspective on e-retailing, *Internet Research: Electronic Networking Applications and Policy*, 10(5), 424–38.

Lynch, P. and Horton, S. (1999) *Web Style Guide. Basic Design Principles for Creating Web Sites.* Yale University Press, New Haven, CT.

Morgan, R. (1996) An Internet marketing framework for the World Wide Web, *Journal of Marketing Management*, 12, 757–75.

NCC (2005) dabs.com benefits from innovative approach. *Principia*. NCC members magazine. Issue 37, May/June. www.nccmembership.co.uk/pooled/articles/BF_WEBART/view.asp?Q=BF_WEBART_162441.

Nielsen, J. (1999) Details in study methodology can give misleading results. Jakob Nielsen's Alertbox, 21 February. www.useit.com/alertbox/990221.html.

Nielsen, J. (2000a) Novice vs. expert users, Jakob Nielsen's Alertbox, 6 February. www.useit.com/alertbox/20000206.html.

Nielsen, J. (2000b) *Designing Web Usability.* New Riders Publishing, USA.

Ong, C. (1995) Practical aspects of marketing on the WWW, MBA Dissertation, University of Sheffield, UK.

Pak, J. (1999) Content dimensions of web advertising: a cross national comparison, *International Journal of Advertising*, 18(2), 207–31.

Parasuraman, A., Zeithaml, V. and Berry, L. (1985) A conceptual model of service quality and its implications for future research, *Journal of Marketing*, 49, Fall, 48.

The Register (2004) Wobbly shopping carts blight UK e-commerce, *The Register.Co.uk*, 4 June.

Reichheld, F. and Schefter, P. (2000) E-loyalty, your secret weapon, *Harvard Business Review*, July–August, 105–13.

Resnik, A. and Stern, A. (1977) An analysis of information content in television advertising, *Journal of Marketing*, January, 50–3.

Rettie, R., (2001), An exploration of flow during Internet use, *Internet Research*, 11(2), 103–13.

Rigby, D., Bavega, S., Rastoi, S., Zook, C. and Hancock, S. (2000) The value of customer loyalty and how you can capture it. Bain and Company/Mainspring Whitepaper, 17 March. Published at www.mainspring.com.

Robertson, J. (2003) Information design using card sorting. Step Two. Available online at www.steptwo.com.au/papers/cardsorting/index.html.

Rosen, D. and Purinton, E. (2004) Website design: viewing the web as a cognitive landscape, *Journal of Business Research*, 57(7), 787–94.

Rosenfeld, L. and Morville, P. (2002) *Information Architecture for the World Wide Web*, 2nd edn. O'Reilly, Sebastopol, CA.

SciVisum (2005) Internet Campaign Effectiveness Study, Press Release, July. www.scivisum.co.uk.

Smith, D. and Sivakumar, K. (2004) Flow and Internet shopping behavior: a conceptual model and research propositions, *Journal of Business Research*, 57(10), 1199–208.

Smith, P.R. and Chaffey, D. (2005) *E-marketing Excellence – at the Heart of E-Business*, 2nd edn. Butterworth Heinemann, Oxford.

Smith, S. and Wheeler, J. (2002) *Managing the Customer Experience.* Financial Times/Prentice Hall, London.

Sterne, J. (2001) *World Wide Web Marketing*, 3rd edn. Wiley, New York.

Transversal (2005) UK companies fail online customer service test. Transversal press release, 17 March. http://transversal.com/html/news/viewpress.php?article=42.

Trocchia, P. and Janda, S. (2003) How do consumers evaluate Internet retail service quality? *Journal of Services Marketing*, 17(3).

Wodtke, C. (2002) *Information Architecture: Blueprints for the Web*. New Riders, IN.

Zeithaml, V., Parasuraman, A., and Malhotra, A., (2002), Service quality delivery through web sites: a critical review of extant knowledge, *Academy of Marketing Science*, 30(4), 368.

Further reading

Bevan, N. (1999) Usability issues in web site design, *Proceedings of the 6th Interactive Publishing Conference, November*. Available online at **www.usability.serco.com**. Accessible lists of web-design pointers.

Noyes, J. and Baber, C. (1999) *User-centred Design of Systems*. Springer-Verlag, Berlin. Details the user-centred design approach.

Preece, J., Rogers, Y. and Sharp, H. (2002) *Interaction Design*. Wiley, New York. Clearly describes a structured approach to interaction design, including web interaction.

Web links

- **Jakob Nielsen's UseIt** (**www.useit.com**). Detailed guidelines (alertboxes) and summaries of research into usability of web media.
- **Royal National Institute for the Blind** web accessibility guidelines (**www.rnib.org.uk/accessibility**).
- **UI Access resources** on web site accessibility (**www.uiaccess.com/access_links.html**).
- **Usability News** (**www.usabilitynews.com**).
- **User Interface Engineering** (**www.uie.com**). Articles on usability which often provide a counterpoint to those of Nielsen.
- **Web Design References** (**www.d.umn.edu/itss/support/Training/Online/webdesign**). A collection from the University of Minnesota Duluth including articles and references on Accessibility, Information Architecture and Usability.
- **Worldwide Web consortium web accessibility guidelines** (see **www.w3.org/WAI**).
- **Yale University Press** (**www.webstyleguide.com**). Supporting site for Lynch, P. and Horton, S. (1999) *Web Style Guide. Basic Design Principles for Creating Web Sites*. Yale University Press, New Haven, CT. Provides a large amount of detail on design.

8

Interactive marketing communications

Chapter at a glance

Learning objectives

After reading this chapter, the reader should be able to:

● Assess the difference in communications characteristics between digital and traditional media

● Identify effective methods for online and offline promotion

● Understand the importance of integrating online and offline promotion

● Relate promotion techniques to methods of measuring site effectiveness

Questions for marketers

Key questions for marketing managers related to this chapter are:

● What are the new types of interactive marketing communications tools I can use?

● How do their characteristics differ from those of traditional media?

● What are the strengths and weaknesses of these promotional tools?

● How do I choose the best mix of online and offline communications techniques?

Links to other chapters

Related chapters are:

➤ Chapter 1 describes the 6 Is, a framework that introduces the characteristics of Internet marketing communications

➤ Chapter 2 introduces portals and search engines – one of the methods of online traffic building discussed in this chapter

➤ Chapter 3 introduces some of the legal and ethical constraints on online marketing communications

➤ Chapter 4 provides the strategic basis for Internet marketing communications

➤ Chapter 6 describes on-site communications

➤ Chapter 9 also considers the measurement of communications effectiveness

Introduction

A company that has developed a great online customer experience as discussed in Chapter 7 is only part-way to achieving successful Internet marketing outcomes. In the days of the dot-com boom a common expression was: *'If you build it, they will come'*. This famous line proved true of a baseball stadium built in the 1989 film *Field of Dreams*, but unfortunately, it doesn't apply to web sites. Berthon et al. (1998) make the analogy with a trade fair. Here, there will be many companies at different stands promoting their products and services. Effective promotion and achieving visibility of the stand is necessary to attract some of the many show visitors to that stand. Similarly, if you want to maximise quality visitors within a target audience to a web site to acquire new customers online, Internet marketers have to select the appropriate online and offline marketing communications techniques which are summarised in Figure 8.1 and form the core of this chapter. This is a major challenge since there are tens of millions of web sites with many pages, each vying to attract an audience – Google indexes over 20 billion pages.

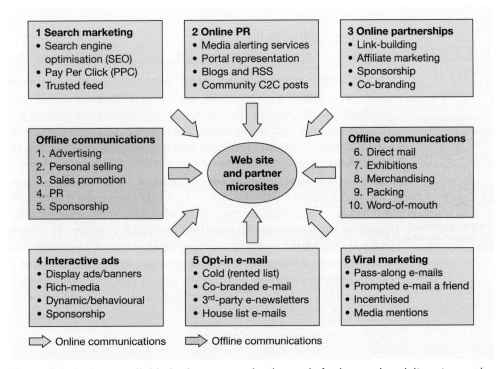

Figure 8.1 Options available in the communications mix for increasing visitors to a web site

Before reviewing the principles and success factors in deploying the communications tools shown in Figure 8.1 we start by considering the unique characteristics of digital media which we must apply for success and look at approaches for setting objectives for and tracking the success of interactive communications.

The three main objectives and tactics of developing an interactive marketing communications programme for Internet marketing are to:

Online site promotion

Internet-based techniques used to generate web site traffic.

1 use online and offline promotion to drive quality visitors or traffic to a web site;
2 use on-site communications to deliver an effective, relevant message to the visitor which helps shape customer perceptions or achieve a required marketing outcome through conversion marketing;
3 integrate all communications channels to help achieve marketing objectives by supporting mixed-mode buying.

The characteristics of interactive marketing communications

Offline site promotion

Traditional techniques such as print and TV advertising used to generate web site traffic.

Mixed-mode buying

The customer's purchase decision is influenced by a range of media such as print, TV and Internet.

Push media

Communications are broadcast from an advertiser to consumers of the message who are passive recipients.

Pull media

The consumer is proactive in selection of the message through actively seeking out a web site.

Through understanding the key interactive communications characteristics enabled through digital media we can exploit these media while guarding against their weaknesses. In this section, we will describe eight key changes in the media characteristics between traditional and new media. Note that the 6 Is in Chapter 1 provide an alternative framework that is useful for evaluating the differences between traditional media and new media.

1 From push to pull

Traditional media such as print, TV and radio are push media, one-way streets where information is mainly unidirectional, from company to customer unless direct response elements are built in. In contrast, the web is an example of pull media. This is its biggest strength and its biggest weakness. It is a strength since pull means that prospects and customers only visit a web site when it enters their head to do so, when they have a defined need – they are proactive and self-selecting. But this is a weakness since online pull means marketers have less control than in traditional communications where the message is pushed out to a defined audience. What are the e-marketing implications of the pull medium? First, we need to provide the physical stimuli to encourage visits to web sites. This may mean traditional ads, direct mail or physical reminders. Second, we need to ensure our site is optimised for search engines – it is registered and is ranked highly on relevant keyword searches. Third, e-mail is important – this is an online push medium, and it should be a priority objective of web site design to capture customers' e-mail addresses in order that opt-in e-mail can be used to push relevant and timely messages to customers. All these techniques are described further later in this chapter.

2 From monologue to dialogue

Interactivity

The medium enables a dialogue between company and customer.

Creating a dialogue through interactivity is the next important feature of the web and digital media such as mobile and interactive TV which provide the opportunity for two-way interaction with the customer. This is a key distinguishing feature of the medium according to Peters (1998), and Deighton (1996) proclaimed the interactive benefits of the Internet as a means of developing long-term relationships with customers as described in Chapter 6. For example, if a registered customer requests information, or orders a particular product, it will be possible for the supplier to contact them in future using e-mail or personalised web messages with details of new offers related to their specific interest.

But digital dialogues have a less obvious benefit also – intelligence. Interactive tools for customer self-help can help collect intelligence – clickstream analysis recorded in web analytics can help us build up valuable pictures of customer preferences.

3 From one-to-many to one-to-some and one-to-one

Mass customisation

Mass customisation is the creation of tailored marketing messages or products for individual customers or groups of customers typically using technology to retain the economies of scale and the capacity of mass marketing or production.

Personalisation

Web-based personalisation involves delivering customised content for the individual through web pages, e-mail or push technology.

Traditional push communications are one-to-many, from one company to many customers, often the same message to different segments and often poorly targeted. With digital media 'one-to-some' – reaching a niche or micro-segment becomes more practical – e-marketers can afford to tailor and target their message to different segments through providing different site content or e-mail for different audiences through mass customisation and personalisation (Chapter 6). Note that many brochureware sites do not take full advantage of the Internet and merely use the web to replicate other media channels by delivering a uniform message.

Potentially digital media provide a one-to-one communication (from company to customer) rather than the one-to-many communication (from company to customers) that is traditional in marketing using the mass media, such as newspapers or television. Figure 8.2 illustrates the interaction between an organisation (O) communicating a message (M) to customers (C) for a single-step flow of communication. It is apparent that for traditional mass marketing in (a) a single message (M_1) is communicated to all customers (C_1 to C_5).

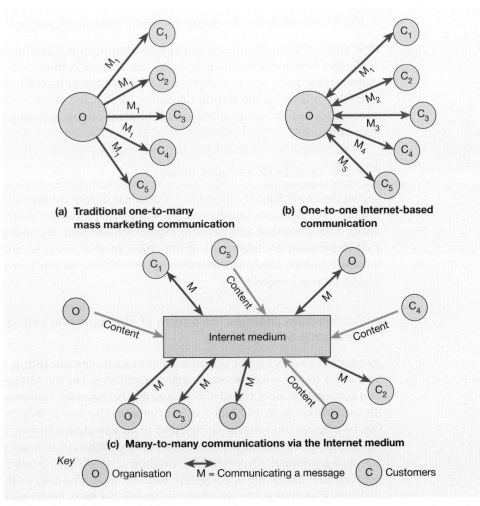

(a) **Traditional one-to-many mass marketing communication**

(b) **One-to-one Internet-based communication**

(c) **Many-to-many communications via the Internet medium**

Key
O Organisation   M = Communicating a message   C Customers

Figure 8.2 The differences between one-to-many and one-to-one communication using the Internet (organisation (O), communicating a message (M) to customers (C))

Hoffman and Novak (1997) believe that this change is significant enough to represent a new model for marketing or a new 'marketing paradigm'. They suggest that the facilities of the Internet including the web represent a computer-mediated environment in which the interactions are not between the sender and receiver of information, but with the medium itself. They say:

> consumers can interact with the medium, firms can provide content to the medium, and in the most radical departure from traditional marketing environments, consumers can provide commercially-oriented content to the media.

This situation is shown in Figure 8.2(c). This potential has not yet been fully developed since many companies are still using the Internet to provide standardised information to a general audience.

Despite the reference to a new paradigm, it is still important to apply tried and tested marketing communications concepts such as hierarchy of response and buying process to the Internet environment as described in the online customer behaviour section in Chapter 2. However, some opportunities will be missed if the Internet is merely treated as another medium similar to existing media.

4 From one-to-many to many-to-many communications

New media also enable many-to-many communications. Hoffman and Novak (1996) noted that new media are many-to-many media. Here customers can interact with other customers via a web site, in independent communities or on their personal web sites and blogs. We will see in the section on online PR that the implications of many-to-many communications are a loss of control of communications requiring monitoring of information sources.

5 From 'lean-back' to 'lean-forward'

Digital media are also intense media – they are lean-forward media in which the web site usually has the visitor's undivided attention. This intensity means that the customer wants to be in control and wants to experience flow and responsiveness to their needs. First impressions are important. If the visitor to your site does not find what they are looking for immediately, whether through poor design or slow speed, they will move on, probably never to return.

6 The medium changes the nature of standard marketing communications tools such as advertising

In addition to offering the opportunity for one-to-one marketing, the Internet can be, and still is widely, used for one-to-many advertising. On the Internet the brand essence and key concepts from the advertiser arguably becomes less important, and typically it is detailed information and independent opinions the user is seeking. The web site itself can be considered as similar in function to an advertisement (since it can inform, persuade and remind customers about the offering, although it is not paid for in the same way as a traditional advertisement). Berthon et al. (1996) consider a web site as a mix between advertising and direct selling since it can also be used to engage the visitor in a dialogue. Constraints on advertising in traditional mass media such as paying for time or space become less important. Consumers are looking for information online all the time, so advertising in search engines in short *campaign-based* bursts is inappropriate for most companies – *continuous* representation is needed.

Peters (1998) suggests that communication via the new medium is differentiated from communication using traditional media in four different ways. First, *communication style* is changed, with *immediate*, or synchronous transfer of information through online customer service being possible. Asynchronous communication, where there is a time delay between sending and receiving information as through e-mail, also occurs. Second, *social presence* or the feeling that a communications exchange is sociable, warm, personal and active may be lower if a standard web page is delivered, but can be enhanced, perhaps by personalisation. Third, the consumer has more *control of contact*, and finally the user has control of *content*, for example through personalisation facilities.

Although Hoffman and Novak (1996) point out that with the Internet the main relationships are not *directly* between sender and receiver of information, but with the web-based environment, the classic communications model of Schramm (1955) can still be used to help understand the effectiveness of marketing communication using the Internet. Figure 8.3 shows the model applied to the Internet. Four of the elements of the model that can constrain the effectiveness of Internet marketing are:

- *encoding* – this is the design and development of the site content or e-mail that aims to convey the message of the company, and is dependent on understanding of the target audience;
- *noise* – this is the external influence that affects the quality of the message; in an Internet context this can be slow download times, the use of plug-ins that the user cannot use or confusion caused by too much information on-screen;
- *decoding* – this is the process of interpreting the message, and is dependent on the cognitive ability of the receiver, which is partly influenced by the length of time they have used the Internet;
- *feedback* – this occurs through online forms and through monitoring of on-site behaviour through log files (Chapter 9).

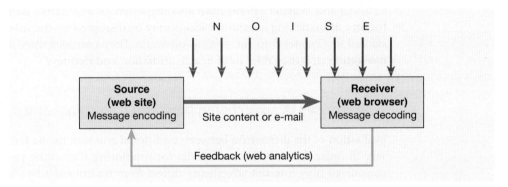

Figure 8.3 The communications model of Schramm (1955) applied to the Internet

7 Increase in communications intermediaries

If we consider advertising and PR, with traditional media, this increase occurs through a potentially large number of media owners such as TV and radio channel owners and the owners of newspaper and print publications such as magazines. In the Internet era there is a vastly increased range of media owners or publishers through which marketers can promote their services and specifically gain links to their web site. Traditional radio channels, newspapers and print titles have migrated online, but in addition there are a vast number of online-only publishers including horizontal portals (Chapter 2) such as search engines and vertical portals such as industry-specific sites. The concept of the long tail (Chapter 5) also applies to web sites in any sector. There are a handful of key sites, but many others can also be used to reach customers. The online marketer needs to select the most appropriate of this plethora of sites which customers visit to drive traffic to their web site.

8 Integration

Although new media have distinct characteristics compared to traditional media, it does not follow that we should concentrate our communications solely on digital media. Rather we should combine and integrate traditional and digital media according to their strengths. We can then achieve synergy – the sum being greater than the parts. Most of us still spend most of our time in the real world rather than the virtual world and multi-channel customers' journeys involve both media, so offline promotion of the proposition of a web site is important. It is also important to support mixed-mode buying. For example, a customer wanting to buy a computer may see a TV ad for a certain brand which raises awareness of the brand and then see a print advert that directs them across to the web site for further information. However, the customer does not want to buy online, preferring the phone, but the site allows for this by prompting with a phone number at the right time. Here all the different communications channels are mutually supporting each other.

Similarly inbound communications to a company need to be managed and are crucial to the health of a brand, as indicated by Schultz and Schultz (2004). Consider if the customer needs support for an error with their system. They may start by using the on-site diagnostics, which do not solve the problem. They then ring customer support. This process will be much more effective if support staff can access the details of the problem as previously typed in by the customer to the diagnostics package.

Evans and Wurster (1999) have also suggested an alternative framework for how the balance of marketing communications may be disrupted by the Internet which we considered in Chapter 5 in the section on Place. They consider three aspects of consumer navigation that they refer to as 'reach, affiliation and richness'.

Differences in advertising between traditional and digital media

Evaluation of the differences between traditional and new media for advertising is necessary in order to select the best media for promoting the online presence. Janal (1998) considered how Internet advertising differs from traditional advertising in a number of key areas. These are summarised in Table 8.1.

Table 8.1 Key concepts of advertising in the traditional and digital media

	Traditional media	Digital media
Space	Expensive commodity	Cheap, unlimited
Time	Expensive commodity for marketers	Expensive commodity for users
Image creation	Image most important	Information most important
	Information is secondary	Image is secondary
Communication	Push, one-way	Pull, interactive
Call to action	Incentives	Information (incentives)

We can extend this analysis by considering the effectiveness of offline media in comparison with online media. We can make the following observations:

1 *Reach of media.* We saw in Chapters 2 and 3, that access to the Internet has exceeded 50% in many developed countries. While this indicates that the Internet is now a mass medium, there are a significant minority that don't have access and cannot be reached via this medium. As we saw in Chapter 2, reach varies markedly by age and social group, so the Internet is innappropriate for reaching some groups.

2 *Media consumption.* Most customers spend more of their time in the real world than the virtual world so it follows that digital media may not be the best method to reach them. However, a counter-argument to this is that the intensity and depth of online interactions are greater and they often involve specific customer journeys related to product research or purchase.

3 *Involvement.* Use of the Internet has been described as a 'lean-forward' experience, suggesting high involvement based on the interactivity and control exerted by web users. This means that the user is receptive to content on a site. However, there is evidence that certain forms of graphic advertising such as banner adverts are filtered out when informational content is sought. A study of online newspaper readers (Poynter, 2000) found that text and captions were read first, with readers then later returning to graphics.

4 *Building awareness.* It can be argued that because of the form of their creative, some forms of offline advertising such as TV are more effective at explaining concepts and creating retention (Branthwaite et al., 2000).

We conclude this section with a review of how consumers perceive the Internet in comparison to traditional media. Refer to Mini Case Study 8.1 for the summary of the results of a qualitative survey.

| Mini Case Study 8.1 | Consumer perceptions of the Internet and different media |

Branthwaite et al. (2000) conducted a global qualitative project covering 14 countries, across North and South America, East and West Europe, Asia and Australia to investigate consumer perceptions of the Internet and other media. In order to reflect changing media habits and anticipate future trends, a young, dynamic sample were selected in the 18–35 age range, with access to the Internet, and regular users of all four media. Consumers' perceptions of the Internet, when asked to explain how they felt about the Internet in relation to different animals, were as follows:

> *The dominant sense here was of something exciting, but also inherently malevolent, dangerous and frightening in the Internet.*

The positive aspect was expressed mainly through images of a bird but also a cheetah or dolphin. These captured the spirit of freedom, opening horizons, versatility, agility, effortlessness and efficiency. Even though these impressions were relative to alternative ways of accomplishing goals, they were sometimes naive or idealistic. However, there was more scepticism about these features with substantial experience or great naivety.

Despite their idealism and enthusiasm for the Internet, these users found a prevalent and deep-rooted suspicion of the way it operated. The malevolent undertones of the Internet came through symbols of snakes or foxes predominantly, which were associated with cunning, slyness and unreliability. While these symbols embodied similar suspicions, the snake was menacing, intimidating, treacherous and evasive, while the fox was actively deceptive, predatory, surreptitious, plotting and persistent. For many

→

consumers, the Internet was felt to have a will of its own, in the form of the creators of the sites (the ghosts in the machine). A snake traps you and then tightens its grip. A fox is mischievous.

In comparison with other media, the Internet was described as follows:

The Internet seemed less like a medium of communication than the others, and more like a reservoir of information.

This distinction was based on differences in the mode of operating: other media communicated to you whereas with the Internet the user had to actively seek and extract information for themselves. In this sense, the Internet is a recessive medium that sits waiting to be interrogated, whereas other media are actively trying to target their communications to the consumer.

This meant that these users (who were not addicted or high Internet users) were usually task-orientated and focused on manipulating their way around (tunnel vision). The more inexperienced you were, the more concentration was needed, but irritation or frustration was never far away for most people.

Everywhere, regardless of experience and availability, the Internet was seen as a huge resource, with futuristic values, that indicated the way the world was going to be. It was respected for its convenience and usefulness. Through the Internet you could learn, solve problems, achieve goals, travel the world without leaving your desk, and enter otherwise inaccessible spaces. It gave choice and control, but also feelings of isolation and inadequacy. There was an onus on people wherever possible to experience this medium and use it for learning and communicating.

The most positive attitudes were in North America. Slick and well-structured web sites made a positive impression and were a valuable means of securing information through the links to other sites and to carry out e-commerce. However, even here there was frustration at slow downloading and some unco-operative sites. In other countries, there was concern at the irresponsibility of the medium, lack of seriousness and dependability. There was desire for supervisory and controlling bodies (which are common for print and TV). Banner ads were resented as contributing to the distractions and irritations. Sometimes they seemed deliberately hostile by distracting you and then getting you lost. Internet advertising had the lowest respect and status, being regarded as peripheral and trivial.

In the least economically advanced countries, the Internet was considered a divisive medium which excluded those without the resources, expertise or special knowledge.

Table 8.2 and Figure 8.4 present the final evaluation of the Internet against other media.

Table 8.2 Comparison of the properties of different media

	TV	Outdoor	Print	Internet
Intrusiveness	High	High	Low	Low
Control/selectivity of consumption	Passive	Passive	Active, selective	Active, selective
Episode attention span	Long	Short	Long	Restless, fragmented
Active processing	Low	Low	High	High
Mood	Relaxed, seeking emotional gratification	Bored, under-stimulated	Relaxed, seeking interest, stimulation	Goal-orientated Needs-related
Modality	Audio/visual	Visual	Visual	Visual (auditory increasing)
Processing	Episodic, superficial	Episodic/semantic	Semantic, deep	Semantic, deep
Context	As individual in interpersonal setting	Solitary (in public space)	Individual Personal	Alone, private

Source: Branthwaite et al. (2000)

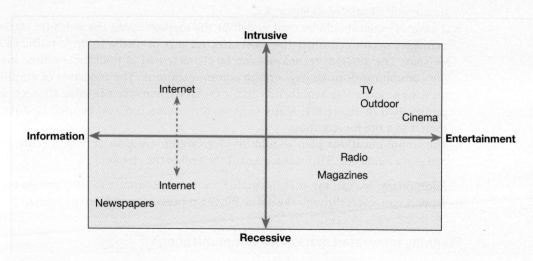

Figure 8.4 Summary of the different characteristics of media
Source: Millward Brown Qualitative

Integrated Internet marketing communications

**Integrated
marketing
communications**

The coordination of
communications
channels to deliver a
clear, consistent
message.

In common with other communications media, the Internet will be most effective when it is deployed as part of an integrated marketing communications approach. Kotler et al. (2001) describe integrated marketing communications as:

the concept under which a company carefully integrates and co-ordinates its many communications channels to deliver a clear, consistent message about the organisation and its products.

The characteristics of integrated marketing communications have been summarised by Pickton and Broderick (2001) as the 4 Cs of:

- *Coherence* – different communications are logically connected.
- *Consistency* – multiple messages support and reinforce, and are not contradictory.
- *Continuity* – communications are connected and consistent through time.
- *Complementary* – synergistic, or the sum of the parts is greater than the whole!

The 4 Cs also act as guidelines for how communications should be integrated.

Further guidelines on integrated marketing communications from Pickton and Broderick (2001) that can be usefully applied to Internet marketing are the following.

1 Communications planning is based on *clearly identified marketing communications objectives* (see later section).
2 Internet marketing involves the *full range of target audiences* (see the section on developing customer-oriented content in Chapter 7). The full range of target audiences is the customer segments plus employees, shareholders and suppliers.
3 Internet marketing should involve *management of all forms of contact*, which includes management of both outbound communications such as banner advertising or direct e-mail and inbound communications such as e-mail enquiries.

4 Internet marketing should utilise a *range of promotional tools*. These are the promotional tools illustrated in Figure 8.1.

5 *A range of media* should be used to deliver the message about the web site. Marketing managers need to consider the most effective mix of media to drive traffic to their web site. The different techniques can be characterised as traditional offline marketing communications or new online communications. The objective of employing these techniques is to acquire new traffic on an e-commerce site using the techniques summarised in Figure 8.1. Many of these techniques can also be used to drive customers to a site for retention.

6 The communications plan should involve careful selection of *most effective promotional and media mix*. This is discussed at the end of the chapter.

Additionally, we can say that integrated marketing communications should be used to support customers through the entire buying process, across different media.

Planning integrated marketing communications

The Account Planning Group (**www.apg.org.uk**), in its definition of media planning highlights the importance of the role of media planning when they say that the planner:

> *needs to understand the customer and the brand to unearth a key **insight** for the communication/solution* [Relevance].
>
> *As media channels have mushroomed and communication channels have multiplied, it has become increasingly important for communication to cut through the cynicism and **connect** with its audience* [Distinctiveness].
>
> *...the planner can provide the edge needed to ensure the solution reaches out through the clutter to its **intended audience*** [Targeted reach].
>
> *...needs to **demonstrate** how and why the communication has **performed*** [Effectiveness].

More specifically, Pickton and Broderick (2001) state that the aim of marketing communications media planning as part of integrated marketing communications should be to:

- *Reach* the target audience
- Determine the appropriate *Frequency* for messaging
- Achieve *Impact* through the creative for each media.

Media-neutral planning (MNP)

The concept of media-neutral planning (MNP) has been used to describe an approach to planning integrated marketing campaigns including online elements. Since it is a relatively new concept, it is difficult to describe absolutely. To read a review of the different interpretations see Tapp (2005) who notes that there are three different aspects of planning often encompassed with media-neutral planning:

- Channel planning, i.e. which route to market shall we take: retail, direct, sales partners, etc. (we would say this emphasis is rare);
- Communications-mix planning, i.e. how do we split our budget between advertising, direct marketing, sales promotions and PR;
- Media planning, i.e. spending money on TV, press, direct mail, and so on.

In our view, MNP is most usually applied to the second and third elements and the approach is based on reaching consumers across a range of media to maximise response. For example, Crawshaw (2004) says:

Media-neutral planning (MNP)
An approach to planning ad campaigns to maximise response across different media according to consumer usage of these media.

The simple reason we would want media-neutral communications is so that we can connect the right message with our target audience, at the right time and place to persuade them to do what we want. This will lead to powerful, effective, value for money communications that solve clients' business challenges.

A customer-centric media-planning approach is key to this process, Anthony Clifton, Planning Director at WWAV Rapp Collins Media Group is quoted by the Account Planning Group as saying (quoted in Crawshaw, 2004):

real consumer insight has to be positioned at the core of the integrated planning process and the planner must glean a complete understanding of the client's stake holders, who they are, their mindset, media consumption patterns and relationship with the business – are they 'life-time' consumers or have they purchased once, are they high value or low value customers etc. This requires lifting the bonnet of the database, segmentation and market evaluation.

Online marketers also need to remind themselves that many customers prefer to communicate via traditional media, so we should support them in this. The need for marketers to still support a range of communications channels is suggested in Mini Case Study 8.2 'Disasters Emergency Committee uses a range of media to gain donations'.

Mini Case Study 8.2	Disasters Emergency Committee uses a range of media to raise funds

There are few people who did not see the images of the human and physical devastation caused by the earthquake on the ocean floor near Sumatra, Indonesia and subsequent tsunami on 26 December 2004. These images and reports were the catalyst for unprecedented levels of individual and corporate philanthropy. From a communications perspective, it is a useful indication of channel preferences. Over £350 million was donated to the Disasters Emergency Committee (DEC) Tsunami Earthquake Appeal through a range of channels shown in Figure 8.5. While the Internet was a source of many donations, it is perhaps

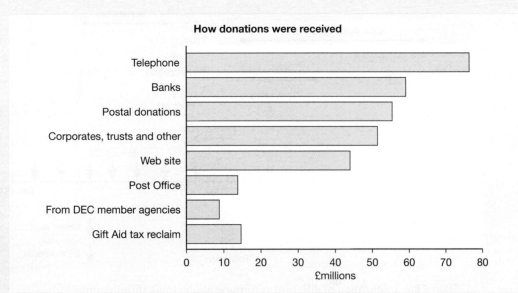

Figure 8.5 Source of donations to the 2004–5 Asian Tsunami appeal

Source: Disasters Emergency Committee (DEC) (www.dec.org.uk)

surprising that the volume of online donations is not higher and it shows the continued popularity of traditional communications channels. The popularity of the web in comparison to e-mail and SMS is also striking as indicated by these details of donations:

- *Telephone*: Over £75 million was donated through the DEC appeal telephone line. Overall the appeal received a total of 1.7 million calls via the automated system at peak times and over 100 volunteers answered 12,500 live calls.
- *Online*: On New Year's Eve, with the help of major Internet service providers, the world record for online donations was broken with over £10 million donated in 24 hours. Overall £44 million was donated online by over half a million web users.
- *Text messaging*: Major UK mobile phone operators raised £1 million by joining forces and offering a free donation mechanism – enabling people to text their gifts.
- *Interactive TV*: The Community Channel raised over £0.5 million from donors using the 'red button' on interactive TV.

Integration through time

For integrated communications to be successful, the different techniques should be successfully integrated through time as part of a campaign or campaigns.

Figure 8.6 shows how communications can be planned around a particular event. (SE denotes 'search engine'; C1 and C2 are campaigns 1 and 2.) Here we have chosen the launch of a new version of a web site, but other alternatives include a new product launch or a key seminar. This planning will help provide a continuous message to customers. It also ensures a maximum number of customers are reached using different media over the period.

In keeping with planning for other media, Pincott (2000) suggests there are two key strategies in planning integrated Internet marketing communications. First, there should be a media strategy which will mainly be determined by how to reach the target audience. This will define the online promotion techniques described in this chapter and

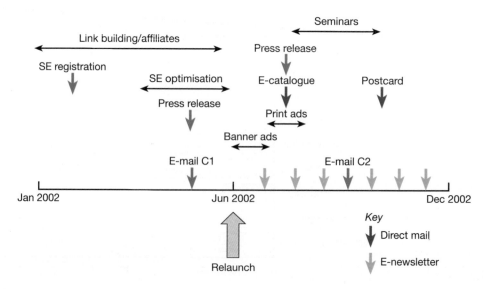

Figure 8.6 Integration of different communications tools through time

where to advertise online. Second, there is the creative strategy. Pincott says that 'the dominant online marketing paradigm is one of direct response'. However, he goes on to suggest that all site promotion will also influence perceptions of the brand.

It follows that brands do not have to drive visitors to their own site; through advertising and creating interactive microsites on third-party sites, they can potentially be more effective in reaching their audience who are more likely to spend their time on online media sites than on destination brand sites.

Mini Case Study 8.3   Which planet are you on?

Consider the options for online promotion of a fast-moving consumer goods brand (FMCG) such as coffee (e.g. Nescafe, www.nescafe.co.uk), tomato ketchup (e.g., Heinz, www.heinzketchup.com), or toiletries (e.g., Andrex, www.andrexpuppy.co.uk). The challenge is obvious – it is difficult to reach a large audience similar to using mass media such as TV, magazines or outdoor. Such destination sites will only attract a limited number of visitors, such as brand loyalists (who it is important to engage since these are often key advocates of these products) or students researching the brands! Another approach which can drive more volume is to use on-pack promotions or direct response TV and print campaigns that encourage consumers to enter competitions and engage into e-mail or text message dialogue in keeping with their profile. The 2005 Walkers Crisps (www.walkers.co.uk) 'Win With Walkers' competition is a good example of this. Walkers gave away an iPod Mini every five minutes (8,700 in total) to texters who responded to messages on 600 million packets of crisps. The campaign was supported by a £1.5 million advertising push, featuring ex-footballer Gary Lineker. In September alone, 5% of the UK population entered, which must explain why I didn't win when I texted in at four in the morning!

The final approach, which is required to achieve reach volume is to advertise on third party sites. Figure 8.7 show the options with the analogy made to the different groups of planets in the solar system and the arrows indicate which approach is selected to achieve reach or traffic building. Typically the smaller the site, the more accurate targeting is possible, but demographic targeting is possible on large portals. For example, McDonalds advertises on MSN Hotmail based on the profile of the user and Ford uses AOL to reach family-oriented purchasers.

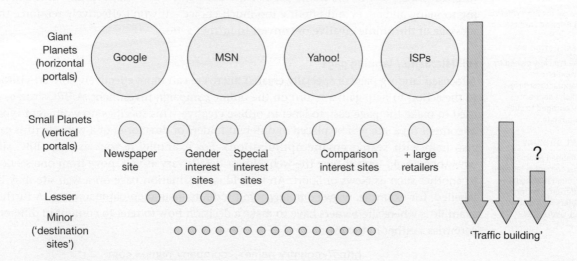

Figure 8.7 An analogy between different web sites and the planets

Campaign response mechanics

Digital media have increased the choice of response mechanisms. We will look at online and offline response mechanisms that need to be considered for both online and offline campaign media. Reviewing response mechanisms is important since too narrow may limit response, but too broad and unfocused may not give the right types of response – marketers need to emphasise the response types most favourable to the overall success of the campaign. Policies for response mechanism across campaigns should be specified by managers to ensure the right approach is used across all campaigns.

Figure 8.8 suggests the typical option of outcomes to online campaign media. From the creative such as a display ad, pay-per-click ad or rented e-mail newsletter, there are four main options.

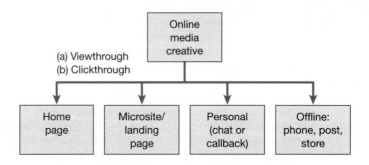

Figure 8.8 Range of response mechanisms from online media

(a) Home page

In the majority of cases, investment in online media will be wasted if visitors are driven from the media site to the home page of the destination web site. Typically it is appealing to many audiences and offering too much choice – it won't effectively reinforce the message of the online creative or convert to further action.

(b) Microsite / landing page

A focused landing page or specially created microsite can more effectively convert visitors to the action to help gain a return on the online campaign investment. A URL strategy is used to make the page easy to label in offline creative. This specifies how different types of content on a site will be placed in different folders or directories of a web site (this can also help with search engine optimisation). For example, if you visit the BBC site (**www.bbc.co.uk**) look at how the web address details vary as you move from one section to another such as News or Sport. An individual destination page on a web site may be labelled, for example, **www.company.com/products/insurance/car-insurance**. A further example is where site owners have to make a decision how to refer to content in different countries – either in the form:

http://<country-name>.<company-name>.com

or the more common

http://www.<companyname.com>.com/<country-name>

Media site

Typical location where paid-for ads are placed.

Destination web site

Site typically owned by a retailer or manufacturer brand which users are encouraged to click through to.

URL strategy

A defined approach to how content is labelled through placing it in different directories or folders with distinct web addresses.

Campaign URL or CURL
A web address specific to a particular campaign.

Campaign URLs or CURLs are commonly used today, the idea being that they will be more memorable than the standard company address and blend in with the campaign concept. For example, an insurer used the CURL **www.quotemehappy.com**, a mortgage provider **www.hateyourmortgage.com** and a phone company **www.sleeptomorrow.com**, which are memorable elements of the campaign.

(c) Personal (chat or callback)

Web callback service
A facility available on the web site for a company to contact a customer at a later time as specified by the customer.

In this case the creative or the landing page encourages campaign respondents to 'talk' directly with a human operator. It is usually referred to as a 'callback service' and integrates web and phone. Buttons or hyperlinks encourage a callback from a telephone operator or an online chat. The advantage of this approach is that it engages the customer more and will typically lead to a higher conversion-to-sale since the customer's questions and objections are more likely to be answered and the personal engagement is more likely to encourage a favourable impression.

(d) Offline: phone, post or store

Because part of a campaign is run online does not mean that offline responses should be excluded. Offline response mechanisms should not be discarded unless the cost of managing them cannot be justified, which is rarely the case. Figure 8.9 gives an example of best practice offering a range of response mechanisms.

Offline response mechanism

Web response model
The web site is used as a response mechanism for offline campaign elements such as direct mail or advertising.

We also need to include the right response mechanism for the offline media element of the campaigns such as TV ads, print ads or direct-mail pieces. The permission-based web response model (Hughes, 1999) is one that is frequently used today in direct marketing (Chapter 6). For example, this process could start with a direct mail drop or offline advert. The web site is used as the direct response mechanism, hence 'web response'. Ideally, this approach will use targeting of different segments. For example, a Netherlands bank devised a campaign targeting six different segments based on age and income. The initial letter was delivered by post and contained a PIN (personal identification number) which had to be typed in when the customer visited the site. The PIN had the dual benefit that it could be used to track responses to the campaign, while at the same time personalising the message to the consumer. When the PIN was typed in, a 'personal page' was delivered for the customer with an offer that was appropriate to their particular circumstances.

Objectives and measurement for interactive marketing communications

Traffic building
Using online and offline site promotion techniques to generate visitors to a site.

As was mentioned in the introduction to this chapter, an interactive marketing communications plan usually has three main goals:

SMART
Specific, Measurable, Actionable, Relevant and Time-related.

(1) Use online and offline communications to drive or attract visitor traffic to a web site. This process is commonly referred to as 'traffic building'.

Examples of SMART traffic building objectives:

- Generate awareness of web offering in 80% of existing customer base in one year.
- Achieve 20% 'share of search (Chapter 2)' awareness within a market.
- Achieve 100,000 new site visitors within one year.
- Convert 30% of existing customer base to regular online service users.

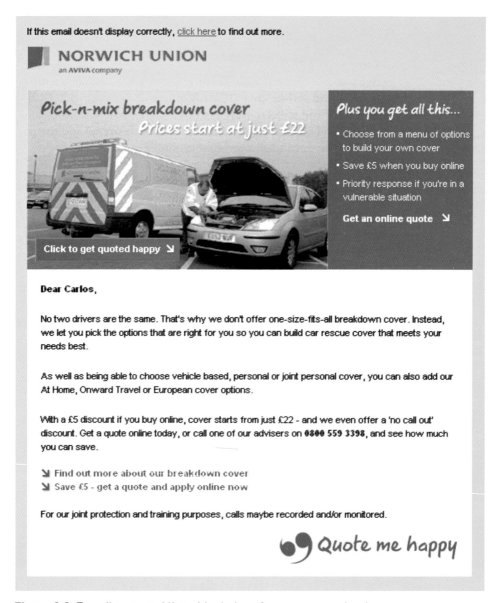

Figure 8.9 E-mail to rented list with choice of response mechanisms

Source: Norwich Union Rescue email (offers shown in this email expired March 2006), courtesy of Norwich Union Insurance

(2) Use on-site communications to deliver an effective message to the visitor which helps influence perceptions or achieves a required marketing outcome. The message delivered on-site will be based on traditional marketing communications objectives for a company's products or services. For example:

- create awareness of a product or favourability towards a brand (measured through brand research of brand awareness, brand favourability or purchase intent through using an online brand-tracking service such as Dynamic Logic, **www.dynamiclogic.com**);
- encourage trial (for example, achieve 4% conversion of new unique visitors to registration or downloads of a music service such as iTunes or Napster);
- build in-house permission-based list (grow e-mail database by 10,000 during year through data capture activities);
- encourage engagement with content (conversion of 20% of new unique visitors to product information area);
- persuade customer to purchase (conversion of 5% of unique new visitors) to purchase areas;
- encourage further purchases (conversion of 30% of first-time buyers to repeat purchasers within a 6-month period).

(3) Integrate all communications methods to help achieve marketing objectives by supporting mixed-mode buying.

Examples of mixed-mode buying objectives:

- Achieve 20% of sales achieved in the call centre as a result of web site visits.
- Achieve 20% of online sales in response to offline adverts.
- Reduce contact-centre phone enquiries by 15% by providing online customer services.

It is also worth noting that communications objectives will differ according to the stage of development of an e-commerce service. Rowley (2001) suggests that the general goals of these four stages are:

- *Contact* – promoting corporate image, publishing corporate information and offering contact information. Content.
- *Interact* – embed information exchange. Communication.
- *Transact* – online transactions and interaction with trading partners. Commerce.
- *Relate* – two-way customer relationship. Community.

Four similar levels of intensity of promotional activity are also identified by van Doren et al. (2000).

Conversion marketing objectives

Although traffic-building objectives and measures of effectiveness are often referred to in terms of traffic quantity, such as the number of visitors or page impressions, it is the traffic quality that really indicates the success of interactive marketing communications (e.g. van Doren et al., 2000; Smith and Chaffey, 2005). Traffic quality is determined by:

- whether the visitors are within the target audience for the web site;
- whether the visitors convert to on-site outcomes in line with the communications objectives.

Internet marketing objectives can also be stated in terms of conversion marketing. This technique of objective setting uses a bottom-up approach to objective setting as shown in Figure 8.10. Take, for example, the objectives of a campaign for a B2B services company such as a consultancy company, where the ultimate objective is to achieve 1000 new clients using the web site in combination with traditional media to convert leads to action. To achieve this level of new business, the marketer will need to make assumptions about the level of conversion that is needed at each stage of converting prospects to customers. This gives a core objective of 1000 new clients and different critical success factors based on the different conversion rates.

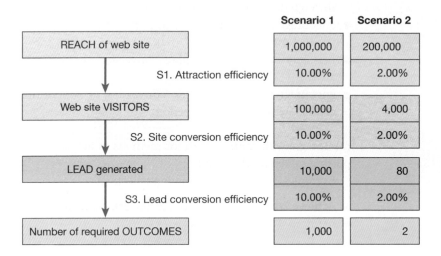

	Scenario 1	Scenario 2
REACH of web site	1,000,000	200,000
S1. Attraction efficiency	10.00%	2.00%
Web site VISITORS	100,000	4,000
S2. Site conversion efficiency	10.00%	2.00%
LEAD generated	10,000	80
S3. Lead conversion efficiency	10.00%	2.00%
Number of required OUTCOMES	1,000	2

Figure 8.10 Conversion marketing approach to objective setting for web communications

Timescales for objective setting

Smith and Chaffey (2005) refer to the relevance of timing for traffic building. They say:

Some e-marketers may consider traffic building to be a continuous process, but others may view it as a specific campaign, perhaps to launch a site or a major enhancement. Some methods tend to work best continuously; others are short term. Short-term campaigns will be for a site launch or an event such as an online trade show.

Accordingly, online marketers can develop communications objectives for different timescales:

- *Annual marketing communications objectives.* For example, achieving new site visitors or gaining qualified leads could be measured across an entire year using models like Figure 8.10 since this will be a continuous activity based on visitor building through search engines and other campaigns. Annual budgets are set to help achieve these objectives.
- *Campaign-specific communications objectives.* Internet marketing campaigns such as to support a product launch through online advertising and viral marketing. Specific objectives can be stated for each in terms of gaining new visitors, converting visitors to customers and encouraging repeat purchases. Campaign objectives should build on traditional marketing objectives, have a specific target audience and have measurable outcomes which can be attributed to the specific campaign.

Campaign cost objectives

Cost per acquisition (CPA)

The cost of acquiring a new customer. Typically limited to the communications cost and refers to cost per sale for new customers. May also refer to other outcomes such as cost per quote or enquiry.

Allowable cost per acquisition

A target maximum cost for generating leads or new customers profitably.

The final aspect of objective setting to be considered is the constraints on objectives placed by the cost of traffic building activities. A campaign will not be successful if it meets its objectives of acquiring site visitors and customers but the cost of achieving this is too high. This constraint is usually imposed simply by having a campaign budget – a necessary component of all campaigns. However, in addition it is also useful to have specific objectives for the cost of getting the visitor to the site using different communications tools such as search engine marketing combined with the cost of achieving the outcomes during their visit. This is stated as the cost per acquisition (CPA) (sometimes cost per action). Depending on context and market, CPA may refer to different outcomes. Typical cost targets include:

- cost per acquisition – of a visitor
- cost per acquisition – of a lead
- cost per acquisition – of a sale.

To control costs, it is important for managers to define a target allowable cost per acquisition such as £30 for generating a business lead or £50 for achieving sign-up to a credit card.

To summarise this section on setting objectives for interactive marketing communications and controlling costs, review Figure 8.11.

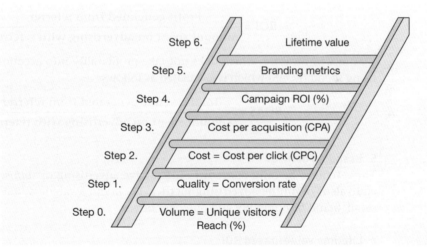

Figure 8.11 Measures used for setting campaign objectives or assessing campaign success increasing in sophistication from bottom to top

Figure 8.11 shows different measures from least sophisticated to more sophisticated as follows:

0 Volume or number of visitors

This is usually measured as thousands of unique visitors. It is preferable to using page views or hits as a measure of effectiveness, since it is opportunities to communicate with individuals. A more sophisticated measure is reach (%) or online audience share. This is only possible using panel data/audience data tools such as **www.netratings.com** or **www.hitwise.com**.

Example: An online bank has one million unique visitors per month.

1 Quality or conversion rates to action

This shows what proportion of visitors from different sources take specific marketing outcomes on the web such as lead, sale or subscription.

Example: Of these visitors 10% convert to an outcome such as logging in to their account or asking for a quote for a product.

Cost per click (CPC)

The cost of each click from a referring site to a destination site, typically from a search engine in pay-per-click search marketing.

2 Cost (cost per click)

The cost of visitor acquisition is usually measured specific to a particular online marketing tool such as pay-per-click search engine marketing since it is difficult to estimate for an entire site with many visitors referred from offline advertising.

Example: £2 CPC.

3 Cost: cost per action or acquisition (CPA)

When cost of visitor acquisition is combined with conversion to outcomes this is the cost of (customer) acquisition.

Example: £20 CPA (since only one in ten visitors take an action).

4 Return on investment (ROI)

Return on investment is used to assess the profitability of any marketing activity or indeed any investment. You will also know that there are different forms of ROI, depending on how profitability is calculated. Here we will assume it is just based on sales value or profitability based on the cost per click and conversion rate.

$$\text{ROI} = \frac{\text{Profit generated from referrer}}{\text{Amount spent on advertising with referrer}}$$

A related measure, which does not take profitability into account is return on advertising spend (ROAS) which is calculated as follows:

$$\text{ROAS} = \frac{\text{Total revenue generated from referrer}}{\text{Amount spent on advertising with referrer}}$$

5 Branding metrics

These tend to be only relevant to interactive advertising or sponsorship. They are the equivalent of offline advertising metrics, i.e. brand awareness (aided and unaided), ad recall, brand favourability and purchase intent.

6 Lifetime value-based ROI

Here the value of gaining the customer is not just based on the initial purchase, but the lifetime value (and costs) associated with the customer. This requires more sophisticated models which can be most readily developed for online retailers and online financial services providers.

Example: A bank uses a net present value model for insurance products which looks at the value over 10 years but whose main focus is on a 5-year result and takes into account:

- acquisition cost
- retention rates
- claims
- expenses.

This is valuable since it helps give them a realistic 'allowable cost per sale' which is needed to get return over 5 years. They track this in great detail, for example they will know the ROI of a Google Adwords keyphrase against an e-spotting keyphrase and will then select keyphrase and bid strategies accordingly.

Figure 8.12 shows an example of effectiveness measures for an online ad campaign for an insurance product. Here an opportunity or lead is when a quote is requested. Note that the cost of acquisition is high, but this does not take into account the synergies of online advertising with offline campaigns, i.e. those who are influenced by the ad, but do not click through immediately.

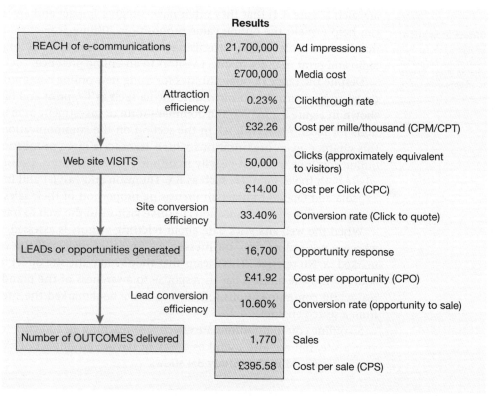

Figure 8.12 An example of effectiveness measures for an online ad campaign

Objective setting and measurement for non-transactional sites

Often, it is only the e-retailers who have data on the full range of measures in Figure 8.12 since this is essential for proving the ROI of online marketing campaigns such as display ads or pay-per-click search. If there are no products available for sale online, such as a luxury car manufacturer or a high-value B2B service offering white paper downloads, then it is less clear how to calculate ROI.

To get the most from campaigns which don't result in sale online and optimise their effectiveness, it is essential to put a value or points score on different outcomes, for example in the case of the car manufacturer, values could be assigned to brochure requests (5 points or £20), demonstration drive requests (20 points or £100) or simply visits to the site involving reviewing product features information (1 point or £1).

Through knowing the average percentage of online brochure requests or demo drive requests that convert to sales and the average order value for customers referred from the web site, then the value of these on-site outcomes can be estimated. This is only an estimate, but it can help inform campaign optimisation, by showing which referring sites, creative or PPC keywords generate desirable outcomes.

Offline promotion techniques

Online web site promotion techniques such as search engine marketing and banner advertising often take prominence when discussing methods of traffic building. But we start with using offline communications to generate site visitors since it is one of the most effective techniques to generate site traffic and the characteristics of offline media are such (Figure 8.4) that they often have a higher impact and are more creative, which can help explain the online value proposition. 'Offline promotion' refers to using communications tools such as advertising and PR delivered by traditional media such as TV, radio and print in order to direct visitors to an online presence.

Offline promotion

Using traditional media such as TV, radio and print to direct visitors to an online presence.

Despite the range of opportunities for using new online communications tools, traditional communications using offline media such as TV, print and direct mail and others shown in Figure 8.1 remain the dominant form of investment in marketing communications for most. As we will see in the section on the communications mix at the end of this chapter, even organisations which transact a large proportion of their business online continue to invest heavily in offline communications. Consider the travel sector where both travel suppliers such as BA, Thomson and easyJet and intermediaries such as Expedia and Opodo transact an increasing proportion of their sales online, but are still reliant on offline communications to drive visitors to the web to transact.

When the web analytics data about referring visitors is assessed, for most companies who are not online-only businesses, we find that over half the visitors are typically marked as 'No referrer'. This means that they visited the site direct by typing in the web address into the address bar in response to awareness of the brand generated through real-world communications (others may have bookmarked the site or clicked through from a search engine).

So offline communications are effective at reaching an audience to encourage them to visit a site, but are also useful as a way of having an impact or explaining a complex proposition as Mini Case Study 8.4 shows.

> ### Mini Case Study 8.4 Offline communications vital for finding the perfect partner at Match.com
>
> UK-based online dating company, Match.com has over 1.5 million members and in 2004 was responsible for 200,000 marriages around the world. Match.com and partner company uDate.com compete against Yahoo! Personals, Dating Direct, traditional players and a host of smaller players. Given the intense competition, Samantha Bedford, UK MD believes it is essential to invest in offline communications for continued growth. In Autumn 2005, Match.com spent over £3 million on a TV advertising campaign since they wanted to generate brand awareness given that they estimate that by 2008 the value of the online dating market will double. In addition to achieving reach and brand awareness, offline advertising is important because it enables Match.com to communicate a fairly complex message to potential customers. Focus groups showed that many singles felt they didn't need an online dating service and didn't realise how Match.com could help as part of the overall dating experience.
>
> Source: *New Media Age* (2005a)

Advantages and disadvantages of using offline communications to support e-commerce

Offline communications work since they are effective in achieving four critical things:

- Reach since newspaper, TV and postal communications are used by virtually all consumers;
- Brand awareness through using high-impact visuals;
- Emotional connection with brand again through visuals and sounds;
- Explanation of the online value proposition for a brand.

A further benefit is that for any given objective, integrated marketing communications received through different media are more effective in achieving that objective. We mentioned this cumulative reinforcement effect of integrated marketing communications when referring to the 4 Cs of coherence, consistency, continuity and complementarities earlier in the chapter. Having said this, the disadvantages of using offline communications to encourage online channel usage compared to many online communications tools are obvious. In general the disadvantages of offline communications are:

- *Higher cost*: Return on investment tends to be higher for online communications such as search engine optimisation (SEO), pay-per-click marketing or affiliate marketing.
- *Higher wastage*: The well-known expression about 'half my advertising is wasted, but I don't know which half' may be true about offline marketing, but it isn't true online if the right tracking processes are in place.
- *Poorer targeting*: Targeting by behaviour, location, time, search keyword, site and site content is readily possible online. This tends to be more targeted compared to most offline media (apart from direct marketing).
- *Poorer accountability*: It is straightforward online to track response – offline it is expensive and error-prone.
- *Less detailed information*: The detailed information to support a decision can only be cost-effectively delivered online.
- *Less personalised*: Although direct mail can be personalised, personalisation is more straightforward online.
- *Less interactive experience*: Most offline communications are one-way – interaction is possible online with the right creative.

Incidental and specific advertising of the online presence

Incidental offline advertising
Driving traffic to the web site is not a primary objective of the advert.

Specific offline advertising
Driving traffic to the web site or explaining the online proposition is a primary objective of the advert.

Two types of offline advertising can be identified: incidental and specific. Reference to the web site is incidental if the main aim of the advert is to advertise a particular product or promotion and the web site is available as an ancillary source of information if required by the viewer. Traditionally, much promotion of the web site in the offline media by traditional companies has been incidental – simply consisting of highlighting the existence of the web site by including the URL at the bottom of an advertisement. Reference to the web site is specific if it is an objective of the advert to explain the proposition of the web site in order to drive traffic to the site to achieve direct response. Here the advert will highlight the offers or services available at the web site, such as sales promotions or online customer service. Amazon commonly advertises in newspapers to achieve this. Naturally, this approach is most likely to be used by companies that only have an online presence, but existing companies can develop straplines to use which explain the web site value proposition (as Mini Case Study 4.3 'BA asks "have you clicked yet?"' in Chapter 4 illustrates well). Many state 'Visit our web site!!', but clearly, a more specific strapline can be developed which describes the overall proposition of the site ('detailed information and product guides to help you select the best product for you') or is specific to the campaign ('we will give you an instant quote online, showing how much you save with us').

Offline response mechanisms

The different response mechanics such as web response and URL strategy which we discussed earlier in the chapter have to be used to maximise response since this helps to direct potential customers to the most appropriate content on the web site. Different URLs are also useful for measuring the response of offline media campaigns since we can measure the number of visitors arriving directly at the URL by entering the domain name.

Public relations

Public relations can be an important tool for driving traffic to the web site if changes to online services or online events are significant or if a viral campaign is discussed online. The days of the launch of a web site being significant are now gone, but if a site is re-launched with significant changes to its services, this may still be worthy of mention. Many newspapers have regular features listing interesting entertainment or leisure sites or guides to specific topics such as online banking or grocery shopping. Trade magazines may also give information about relevant web sites.

Jenkins (1995) argues that one key objective for public relations is its role in transforming a negative situation into a positive achievement. The public relations transfer process he suggests is as follows:

- from ignorance to knowledge;
- from apathy to interest;
- from prejudice to acceptance;
- from hostility to sympathy.

This is a key aim of online PR which is discussed in more detail later in this chapter.

Direct marketing

Direct marketing can be an effective method of driving traffic to the web site. As mentioned earlier, a web response model can be used where the web site is the means for fulfilling the response, but a direct mail campaign is used to drive the response. Many catalogue companies will continue to use traditional direct mail to mail-out a subset of their offering, with the recipient tempted to visit the site through the fuller offering and incentives such as competitions or web-specific offers.

Other physical reminders

Since we all spend more time in the real rather than the virtual world, physical reminders explaining why customers should visit web sites are significant. What is in customers' hands and on their desk top will act as a prompt to visit a site and counter the weakness of the web as a pull medium. This is perhaps most important in the B2B context where a physical reminder in the office can be helpful. Examples, usually delivered through direct marketing, include brochures, catalogues, business cards, point-of-sale material, pens, postcards, inserts in magazines and password reminders for extranets.

Word of mouth

It is worth remembering that, in addition to the methods above, word of mouth plays an important role in promoting sites, particularly consumer sites, where the Internet is currently a novelty. Opinion Research Corporation International, ORCI, reported on a study amongst US consumers that showed that the typical Internet consumer tells 12 other people about his or her online shopping experience. This compares with the average US consumer, who tells 8.6 additional people about a favourite film and another 6.1 people about a favourite restaurant! It has been said that if the online experience is favourable a customer will tell 12 people, but if it is bad, they will tell twice as many, so word of mouth can be negative also. Parry (1998) reported that for European users, word of mouth through friends, relatives and colleagues was the most important method by which users found out about web sites, being slightly more important than search engines and directories or links from other sites.

Thus the role of opinion leaders and multi-step communications with target audiences receiving information about the Internet experience from opinion leaders, the mass media and the Internet, appear to be perhaps even more important in relation to the Internet than for other media. Dichter (1966) summarised how word-of-mouth communications work. To exploit such communications, it is necessary for marketers to use appropiate techniques to target and adapt the message for the opinion leaders when a product or service is at an early stage of diffusion (Rogers, 1983). Viral marketing (see later) will often target these opinion leaders to become advocates in initial contacts.

Online promotion techniques

Traffic-building campaign

The use of online and offline promotion techniques such as banner advertising, search engine promotion and reciprocal linking to increase the audience of a site (both new and existing customers.

In this section we will review approaches to online promotion using the different tools of Figure 8.1 from 1 to 6, including search engine marketing, online advertisements, e-mail and other methods of generating visitors to a web site. These techniques are often combined in what is known as a 'traffic-building campaign'; this is a method of increasing the audience of a site using different online (and offline) techniques. The relative importance of the online promotion techniques we will review in this section are indicated by Figure 8.13 (BrandNewWorld, 2004).

1 Search engine marketing

Search engines are vital for generating quality visitors to a web site as suggested by Figure 8.13. But being registered in the search engines is not enough. The importance of effective search engine marketing is suggested by Figure 8.14 which shows that the higher the rank of a company and products in the search engine results pages (SERPs) the more visitors will be received. It is widely thought that it is essential to be in the top

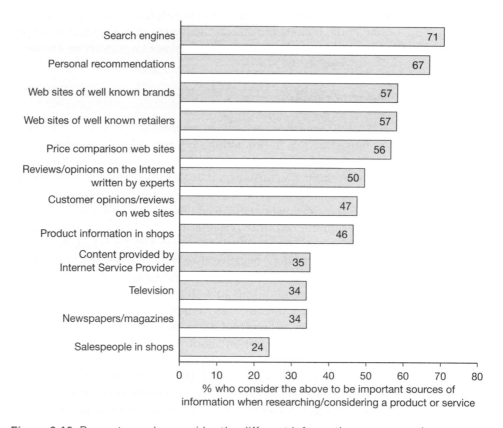

Figure 8.13 Percentage who consider the different information sources as important when researching or considering a product or service
Source: BrandNewWorld (2004)

three sites listed in the results from a search, but the figure and the box 'Understanding consumer search engine behaviour' show that some visitors can still be delivered from lower rankings.

Understanding consumer search engine behaviour

Search marketing firm iProspect conducted research on how we search; the results are instructive:

● Over half of Internet users search at least once a day.
● 81.7% will start a new search if they cannot find a relevant answer in the first 3 pages (typically 30 results). So, to some extent, it is a myth that if you are not in the top 10 you will receive no visitors – it depends on the quality and relevance of the listing also. The detailed figures were: 22.6% try another search after first few results; a further 18.6% after reviewing the first page (41.2% cumulative); 25% after checking the first two pages (67% cumulative); and 14.6% the first three pages (81.7% cumulative).
● Users tend to choose the natural search results in preference to the paid search listings; according to a sample figures for selection of natural search were 60.8% for Yahoo! and 72.3% for Google. This figure increases for experienced users. This suggests that companies that concentrate on paid listings only are limiting their visibility.
● Around half use search toolbars from one of the providers such as Google, Yahoo! or MSN (these are plug-ins for searching which are added to the browser).

Source: iProspect research, Spring 2004 (www.iprospect.com)

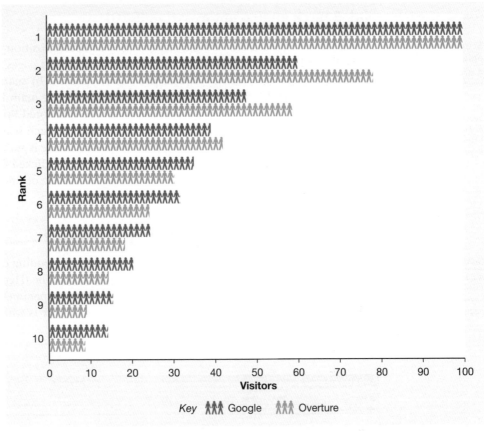

Figure 8.14 Relative traffic projections based on the ranking on search engine results pages (visitor numbers are shown relative to 100 for position 1)
Source: Atlas (2004) (http://www.atlassolutions.com/pdf/RankReport.pdf)

Remember though, that search engine marketing is only one online digital communications tool. For established brands, we commonly see from web analytics that more than half of site visitors arrive at a site, not through search engines, but directly through typing in the web address or following a bookmark (web analytics tools label these as 'no referrer'). The volume of direct visitors shows the power of branding, PR and offline communications in driving visitor traffic. In 2003, Statmarket (**www.statmarket.com**) reported that direct navigation accounted for 65% of site visits worldwide, with 21% following links and just 14% arriving by search engines. For first time visits, however, search marketing is generally found to be over 20%.

We will now review the three main search engine marketing techniques for making a company and its products visible through search engines:

(a) search engine optimisation (SEO)
(b) pay-per-click (PPC)
(c) trusted feed including paid-for inclusion.

(a) Search engine optimisation (SEO)

Search engine optimisation (SEO)

A structured approach used to increase the position of a company or its products in search engine natural or organic results listings for selected keywords or phrases.

Search engine optimisation involves achieving the highest position or ranking practical in the natural or organic listings on the search engine results pages after a specific combination of keywords (or keyphrase) has been typed in. In search engines such as Google, Yahoo! and MSN Search, the natural listings are the main listing on the left as shown in Figure 8.15(a), although there may also be sponsored links above these. The position or ranking is dependent on an algorithm used by each search engine to match relevant site page content with the keyphrase entered. There is no charge for these listings to be displayed or when a link relevant to the site is clicked upon. However, you may need to pay a search engine optimisation firm to advise or undertake optimisation work to make your web pages appear higher in the rankings.

How are the search engine results pages produced?

Spiders and robots

Automated software tools that index keywords on web pages.

Search engines compile an index of words on web sites by sending out spiders or robots to crawl around sites that are registered with that search engine (Figure 8.16). The search engine algorithm weights the index according to different parameters and then stores the index as part of a database on a web server. This index is what is searched when potential customers type in keywords.

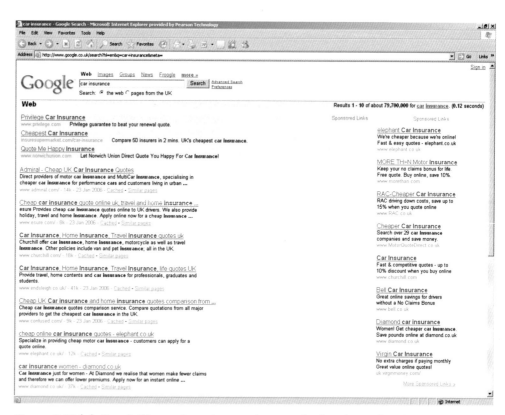

Figure 8.15 (a) Google™ search engine results page for keyphrase 'car insurance'
Source: Reprinted by permission of Google, Inc. Google™ search engine is a trademark of Google, Inc.

Search engine registration

For success in search engine marketing, the first thing that companies need to check is that they are registered with all the main search engines. While some unscrupulous search marketing companies offer to register you in the 'Top 1000 search engines', in reality, registering in the top 20 search engines of each country an organisation operates in (see compilations at SearchEngineWatch, **www.searchenginewatch.com/reports**) will probably account for more than 95% of the potential visitors. Achieving registration is now straightforward, for example, in Google there is an 'Add a URL' page (e.g. **www.google.com/addurl.html**) where you supply your home page URL and Google will then automatically index all the linked pages (it will even index your site automatically if other sites in its index link to it). If you have links from other companies that are registered with a search engine, many search engines will automatically index your site without the need to submit a URL. Companies can check that they are registered with search engines by:

1. Reviewing web analytics data which will show the frequency with which the main search robots crawl a site.
2. Using web analytics referrer information to find out which search engines a site's visitors originate from, and the pages they use.
3. Checking the number of pages that have been successfully indexed on a site. For example, in Google the search 'inurl:www.davechaffey.com' lists all the pages of Dave's site indexed by Google and gives the total number in the top right of the SERPs.

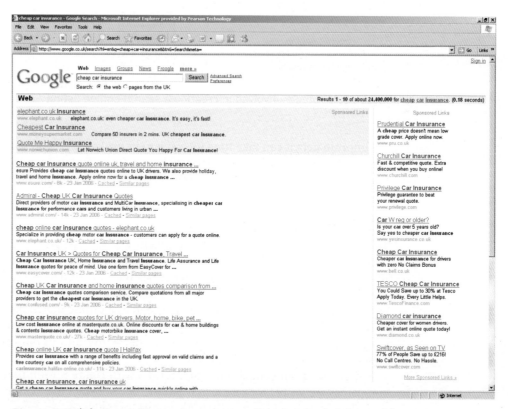

Figure 8.15 (b) Google™ search engine results page for keyphrase 'cheap car insurance'

Source: Reprinted by permission of Google, Inc. Google™ search engine is a trademark of Google, Inc.

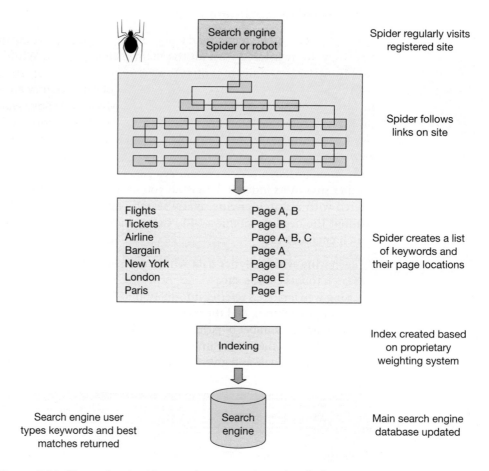

Figure 8.16 Stages involved in creating a search engine listing

Unfortunately it can take time for a site to be ranked highly in search results even if it is the index: Google reputedly places new sites in a 'sandbox' while assessing their relevance due to previous efforts to distort its index by creating interlinking sites.

Keyphrase analysis

The key to successful search engine marketing is achieving keyphrase relevance since this is what the search engines strive for – to match the combination of keywords typed into the search box to the most relevant destination content page. Notice that we say 'keyphrase' (short for 'keyword phrase') rather than 'keyword' since search engines such as Google attribute more relevance when there is a phrase match between the keywords that the user types and a phrase on a page. Despite this, many search companies and commentators talk about optimising your 'keywords' and in our opinion pay insufficient attention to keyphrase analysis.

You can see from comparing Figure 8.15(a) with Figure 8.15(b) that some well-known companies are visible for one search phrase, but not the other. Other companies which have done the appropriate analysis are visible for both.

Key sources for identifying the keyphrases your customers are likely to type when searching for your products include your market knowledge, competitors' sites, keyphrases from visitors who arrive at your site (from web analytics), the internal site search tool and the keyphrase analysis tools from vendors such as Overture (**www.overture.com**) listed at the end of the chapter. When completing keyphrase analysis we need to understand different qualifiers that users type in. For example, this list of seven different types of keyphrases with different qualifiers is taken from an Overture representative talking at Search Engine Strategies in 2004. We have added examples for 'car insurance':

1 Comparison/quality – *compare car insurance*
2 Adjective (price/product qualifiers) – *cheap car insurance, woman car insurance*
3 Intended use – *high mileage car insurance*
4 Product type – *holiday car insurance*
5 Vendor – *churchill car insurance*
6 Location – *car insurance UK*
7 Action request – *buy car insurance.*

You can see some of these types of keyphrases by using the Overture keyterm suggestion tool. For example for a single month in the UK, the most popular phrases related to car insurance were:

1 Car insurance, 1,423,350
2 Cheap car insurance, 71,979
3 Car insurance quote, 32,857
4 Woman car insurance, 21,087
5 Young driver car insurance, 17,175
6 Performance car insurance, 12,379
7 Car insurance uk, 11,719
8 aa car insurance, 7,956
9 Online car insurance quote, 7,423
10 Car insurance company, 7,186.

These data suggest the importance of ranking well for high-volume keyphrases such as 'cheap car insurance' and 'car insurance uk'.

Improving search engine ranking through SEO

Although each search engine has its own algorithm with many weighting factors and they change through time, fortunately there are common factors that influence search engine rankings. These are, in approximate order of importance:

1 Frequency of occurrence in body copy

The number of times the key phrase is repeated in the text of the web page is a key factor in determining the position for a keyphrase. Copy can be written to increase the number of times a word or phrase is used (technically, its keyphrase density) and ultimately boost position in the search engine. Note though that search engines make checks that a phrase is not repeated too many times such as 'cheap flights.. cheap flights.. cheap flights.. cheap flights.. cheap flights.. cheap flights.. cheap flights.. cheap flights..' or the keyword is hidden using the same colour text and backgound and will not list the page if this keyphrase density is too high or it believes 'search engine spamming' has occurred. Relevance is also increased by a gamut of legitimate 'tricks' such as including the keyphrase in headings (<H1>, <H2>), linking anchor text in links and using a higher density towards the start of the document.

2 Number of inbound links (Page Rank)

The more links you have from good quality sites, the better your ranking will be. Evaluation of inbound links or backlinks to determine ranking is one of the key reasons

Page Rank

A scale between 0 to 10 used by Google to assess the importance of web sites according to the number of inbound links or backlinks.

Google became popular. Page Rank helps Google deliver relevant results since it counts each link from another site as a vote. However, not all votes are equal – Google gives greater weight to links from pages which themselves have high Page Rank and where the link anchor text or adjacent text contains text relevant to the keyphrase. Google's Page Rank algorithm is what initially made it successful, but it was published by the founders and now a similar technique is used by all the main search engines. It has been refined to identify sites that are 'authority sites' for a particular type of search. For keyphrases where there is a lot of competition such as 'car insurance', the quantity and quality of inbound links may even be more important than keyphrase density in determining ranking.

Inclusion in directories such as Yahoo! or Business.com (for which a fee is payable) or the Open Directory (**www.dmoz.org**, which is currently free) is important since it can assist in boosting Page Rank.

3 Title HTML tag

The keywords in the title tag of a web page that appears at the top of a browser window are indicated in the HTML code by the <TITLE> keyword. This is significant in search engine listings since if a keyphrase appears in a title it is more likely to be listed highly than if it is only in the body text of a page. It follows that each page on a site should have a specific title giving the name of a company and the product, service or offer featured on a page. Greater weighting is given to keyphrases at the left of the title tag and those with a higher keyphrase density. The Title HTML tag is also vital in search marketing since this is typically the text underlined within the search results page which forms a hyperlink through to your web site. If the Title tag appearing on the search results page is a relevant call-to-action that demonstrates relevance you will receive more clicks which equals more visits (incidentally, Google will monitor clickthroughs to a site and will determine that your content is relevant too and boost position accordingly).

4 Meta-tags

Meta-tags

Keywords that are part of an HTML page that result in a higher search listing if they match the typed keyword.

Meta-tags are part of the HTML file, typed in by web page creators, which is read by the search engine spider or robot. They are effectively hidden from users, but are used by some search engines when robots or spiders compile their index. In the past, search engines assigned more relevance to a site containing keyphrases in its meta-tags than one that didn't. Search engine spamming of meta-tags resulted in this being an inaccurate method of assessing relevance and Google has reported that it assigns no relevance to meta-tags. However, other search engines such as 'Yahoo! Search' do assign some relevance to meta-tags, so it is best practice to incorporate these and to change them for each page with distinct content. There are two important meta-tags which are specified at the top of an HTML page using the <meta name=""> HTML keyword:

(a) The 'keywords' meta-tag highlights the key topics covered on a web page.

> *Example*: <meta name="keywords" content="book, books, shop, store, book shop, bookstore, publisher, bookshop, general, interest, departments,">

(b) The 'description' meta-tag denotes the information which will be displayed in the search results page and so is very important to describe what the web site offers to encourage searchers to click through to the site.

> Example: <meta name="description" content="The largest online book store in the world.">

Other meta-tags are used to give other information such as the type of tool used to create the web page. Remember that incorporating the names of competitors is now not only underhand, but case law in the UK has demonstrated it is illegal.

5 Alternative graphic text

A site that uses a lot of graphical material and/or plug-ins, is less likely to be listed highly. The only text on which the page will be indexed will be the <TITLE> keyword. To improve on this, graphical images can have hidden text associated with them that is not seen by the user (unless graphical images are turned off), but will be seen and indexed by the search engine. For example, text about a company name and products can be assigned to a company logo using the 'ALT' tag as follows:

> <IMG NAME= "Logo" SRC= "logo.gif" ALT="Eastern Engineering – lathes and milling machines">

Again due to search engine spamming, this factor is assigned lesser relevance than previously (unless the image is also a link), but it is best practice to use this since it is also required by accessibility law (screen-readers used by the blind and the visually impaired read-out the ALT tags).

(b) Pay-per-click (PPC) search marketing

Pay-per-click (PPC) search marketing or paid listings are similar to conventional advertising; here a relevant text ad with a link to a company page is displayed when the user of a search engine types in a specific phrase. A series of text ads usually labelled as 'sponsored links' are displayed as is shown on the right of Figure 8.15(a). Unlike conventional advertising, the advertiser doesn't pay when the ad is displayed, but only when the ad is clicked on which then leads to a visit to the advertiser's web site – hence pay per click! Most clicks result in a visit to the site, although there may be a small (usually less than 5–10%) attrition. The relative ranking of these 'paid performance placements' is typically based on the highest bidded cost-per-click value for each keyword phrase. The company which is prepared to pay the most per click gets top spot. Google also takes the relative clickthrough rates of the ads into account when ranking the sponsored links, so ads which do not appear relevant, because fewer people are clicking on them, will drop down or may even disappear off the listing.

Paid search listings, or sponsored links, are very important to achieve visibility in all search engines when an organisation is in a competitive market. If, for example, a company is promoting online insurance, gambling or retail products, there will be many companies competing using the search engine optimisation techniques described in the previous section. Often, the companies that are appearing at the top of the listing will be small companies or affiliates (see section later in chapter). Such companies are less constrained by branding guidelines and may be able to use less ethical search engine marketing techniques which are close to search engine spamming. If you look at sites near the top of the listings for any of the keyphrases above, you will find that they are often ugly pages which look bad, but that search engines like. Furthermore, smaller organisations can be more nimble, they can respond faster to changes in search engine ranking algorithms, sometimes referred to as the 'Google dance' by changing the look and feel or structure of their site. Paid listings are also available through the 'content networks' of the search engines such as Google Adsense and Yahoo! Content Match. These contextual ads are automatically displayed according to the page content (see www.davechaffey.com for examples). They can be paid for on a CPC or CPM basis.

Contextual ads
Ads relevant to page content on third party sites brokered by search ad networks.

Managing pay-per-click

To participate in PPC, clients or their agencies commonly use PPC ad networks or brokers to place and report on pay-per-click ads on different search engines. Two of the most important PPC ad networks are Yahoo! search services (formerly known as Overture, www.overture.com) and MIVA (www.miva.com). For example, in Europe, in 2004, placing an ad on Overture would enable advertisers to display the ad on Yahoo!, MSN and ISP Wanadoo/Orange Broadband. It is necessary to deal direct with Google who have their own PPC ad programme known as 'Google Adwords™' (http://adwords.google.com).

A minimum bid of 10 pence is typical, with a maximum capping on bids and amounts spent per month possible. If this sounds cheap, remember that some marketers spend millions annually on search marketing for a wide range of keyphrases. For products with a high potential value to the company such as life insurance, the cost per click can, amazingly, exceed €20!

With PPC, as for any other media, media buyers carefully evaluate the advertising costs in relation to the initial purchase value or lifetime value they feel they will achieve from the average customer. As well as considering the cost-per-click (CPC), you need to think about the conversion rate when the visitor arrives at your site. Clearly, an ad could be effective in generating clickthroughs or traffic, but not achieve the outcome required on the web site such as generating a lead or online sale. This could be because there is a poor-incentive call-to-action or the profile of the visitors is simply wrong. One implication of this is that it will often be more cost-effective if targeted microsites or landing pages are created specifically for certain keyphrases to convert users to making an enquiry or sale. These can be part of the site structure, so clicking on a 'car insurance' ad will take the visitor through to the car insurance page on a site rather than a home page.

Table 8.3 shows how cost-per-click differs between different keywords from generic to specific. It also shows the impact of different conversion rates on the overall CPA. It can be seen that niche terms that better indicate interest in a specific product such as 'woman car insurance' demand a higher fee (this may not be true for less competitive categories where niche terms can be cheaper). The table also shows the cost of PPC search in competitive categories. Advertising just on these four keywords to achieve a high ranking would cost €33,000 in a single day!

The cost per customer acquisition (CPA) can be calculated as follows:

Cost per acquisition = (100 / Conversion rate %) × Cost per click

Given the range in costs, two types of strategy can be pursued in PPC search engine advertising. If budget permits, a premium strategy can be followed to compete with the major competitors who are bidding the highest amounts on popular keywords. Such a strategy is based on being able to achieve an acceptable conversion rate once the customers are driven through to the web site. A lower-cost strategy involves bidding on lower-cost, less popular phrases. These will generate less traffic, so it will be necessary to devise a lot of these phrases to match the traffic from premium keywords.

Table 8.3 Variation in cost-per-click for different keywords in Google UK, 2004

Keywords	Clicks / Day	Avg. CPC	Cost / Day	Avg. Position	CPA @ 25% conversion	CPA @ 10% conversion
Overall	5,714	€5.9	€33,317	1.3	€23.4	€58.4
insurance	3,800	€5.4	€20,396	1.3	€21.5	€53.7
"car insurance"	1,700	€6.6	€11,119	1.2	€26.2	€65.5
"cheap car insurance"	210	€8.4	€1,757	1.1	€33.5	€83.7
"woman car insurance"	4.1	€10.5	€43	1.0	€42.2	€105.4

Source: Based on Google Adwords™ advertising programme Traffic Estimator.

Optimising pay-per-click

Each PPC keyphrase ideally needs to be managed individually in order to make sure that the bid (amount per click) remains competitive in order to show up in the top of the results. Experienced PPC marketers broaden the range of keyphrases to include lower-volume phrases. Since each advertiser will typically manage thousands of keywords to generate clickthroughs, manual bidding soon becomes impractical.

Some search engines include their own bid management tools, but if an organisation is using different pay-per-click services such as Overture, Espotting and Google, it makes sense to use a single tool to manage them all. It also makes comparison of performance easier too. Bid management software such as Atlas One Point (**www.atlasonepoint.com**) and BidBuddy (**www.bidbuddy.co.uk**) can be used across a range of PPC services to manage keyphrases across multiple PPC ad networks and optimise the costs of search engine advertising. The current CPC is regularly reviewed and your bid is reduced or increased to maintain the position you want according to different strategies and ROI limits with amounts capped such that advertisers do not pay more than the maximum they have deposited.

As more marketers have become aware of the benefits of PPC, competition has increased and this has driven up the cost-per-click (CPC) and so reduced its profitability.

Beware of the fake clicks!

Whenever the principle of PPC marketing is described to marketers, very soon a light bulb comes on and they ask, 'so we can click on competitors and bankrupt them'? Well, actually, no. The PPC ad networks detect multiple clicks from the same computer (IP address) and say they filter them out. However, there are techniques to mimic multiple clicks from different locations such as software tools to fake clicks and even services where you can pay a team of people across the world to click on these links. It is estimated that in competitive markets 1 in 5 of the clicks may be fake. While this can be factored into the conversion rates you will achieve, ultimately this could destroy PPC advertising.

(c) Trusted feed

This form of search advertising is less widely used, so we will only cover it briefly. In trusted feed, the ad or search listings content is automatically uploaded to a search engine from a catalogue or document database in a fixed format which often uses the XML data exchange standard (see **www.w3.org/XML**). This technique is mainly used by retailers that have large product catalogues for which prices and product descriptions may vary and so potentially become out-of-date in the SERPs. A related technique is paid-for inclusion (PFI). Here, PPC ads are placed within the search listings of some search engines interspersed with the organic results. In paid inclusion, the advertiser specifies pages with specific URLs for incorporation into the search engine organic listings. There is typically a fixed set-up fee and then also a PPC arrangement when the ad is clicked on. A crucial difference with other PPC types is that the position of the result in the search engine listings is not paid according to price bid, but through the normal algorithm rules of that search engine to produce the organic listings. The service most commonly used for PFI is Overture Sitematch (**www.overture.com**) which supplies search engines such as Yahoo! and MSN. Note that Google does not offer trusted feed in its main search results at the time of writing (but it does offer a free XML feed to its main Froogle shopping catalogue).

2 Online PR

The web has become very important to PR. Mike Grehan, a UK search engine marketing specialist, puts it this way:

> Both online and off, the process is much the same when using PR to increase awareness, differentiate yourself from the crowd and improve perception. Many offline PR companies now employ staff with specialist online skills. The web itself offers a plethora of news sites and services. And, of course, there are thousands and thousands of newsletters and zines covering just about every topic under the sun. Never before has there been a better opportunity to get your message to the broadest geographic and multi-demographic audience. But you need to understand the pitfalls on both sides to be able to avoid.
>
> (Grehan, 2004)

What is PR?

Let's start with an understanding of traditional PR – itself somewhat intangible. As you will know, 'PR' and 'public relations' are often used interchangeably. Unfortunately, PR is also an acronym for 'press release' or 'press relations'. Of course, the scope of PR is much wider than press releases. The UK Institute of PR (IPR, 2003) defines PR as:

> the management of reputation – the planned and sustained effort to establish and maintain goodwill and mutual understanding between an organisation and its publics.

The 'publics' referred to include the range of organisations a company interacts with and is dependent on. These include investors, customers, employees, suppliers, government organisations and non-governmental organisations such as charities.

The Public Relationships Consultants Association (PRCA, 2005) defines PR as:

> the managed process of communication between one group and another ... [it] is the method of defining messages and communicating them to target audiences in order to influence a desired response.

You can see that the PRCA definition is more action-oriented, in fact, not dissimilar to definitions for direct marketing. IPR (2003) notes that public relations involves activities such as

> media relations, corporate communications, community relations, corporate social responsibility issues and crisis management, investor relations, public affairs and internal communications.

From a marketing communications and traffic building perspective, the main activities we are interested in are media relations which are used to influence those in the marketplace. While web sites are important tools for promoting investor relations and CSR (corporate social responsibility), this is not our main focus here. The definition of PR activities above omits activities that can directly reach the consumer such as 'buzz marketing', although the media often have a role in that.

What is online PR?

Online PR or e-PR leverages the network effect of the Internet. Remember that Internet is a contraction of 'interconnected networks'! Mentions of a brand or site on other sites are powerful in shaping opinions and driving visitors to your site. The main element of online PR is maximising favourable mentions of an organisation, its brands, products or web sites on third-party web sites which are likely to be visited by its target audience. Furthermore, as we noted in the topic on search engine optimisation, the more links there are from other sites to your site, the higher your site will be ranked in the natural or organic listings of the search engines. Minimising unfavourable mentions through online reputation management is also an aspect of online PR.

Differences between online PR and traditional PR

Ranchhod et al. (2002) identify four key differences between online PR and traditional PR.

1 *The audience is connected to organisations.* Previously, there was detachment – PR people issued press releases which were distributed over the newswires, picked up by the media, and then published in their outlets. These authors say:

> the communication channel was uni-directional. The institutions communicated and the audiences consumed the information. Even when the communication was considered a two-way process, the institutions had the resources to send information to audiences through a very wide pipeline, while the audiences had only a minuscule pipeline for communicating back to the institutions.

2 *The members of the audience are connected to each other.* Through publishing their own web sites or e-newsletters or contributing to reviews or discussions on others, information can be rapidly distributed from person to person and group to group. The authors say:

> Today, a company's activity can be discussed and debated over the Internet, with or without the knowledge of that organisation. In the new environment everybody is a communicator, and the institution is just part of the network.

3 *The audience has access to other information.* Often in the past, the communicator was able to make a statement that it would be difficult for the average audience member to challenge – the Internet facilitates rapid comparison of statements. The authors say:

> It takes a matter of minutes to access multiple sources of information over the Internet. Any statement made can be dissected, analysed, discussed and challenged within hours by interested individuals. In the connected world, information does not exist in a vacuum.

4 *Audiences pull information.* This point is similar to the last one. Previously there were limited channels in terms of television and press. Today there are many sources and channels of information – this makes it more difficult for the message to be seen. The authors say:

> Until recently, television offered only a few channels. People communicated with one another by post and by phone. In these conditions, it was easy for a public relations practitioner to make a message stand out.

Online PR activities

Activities which can be considered to be online PR include:

(a) Communicating with media (journalists) online
(b) Link building
(c) Blogs, podcasting and RSS
(d) Managing how your brand is presented on third-party sites
(e) Creating a buzz – online viral marketing.

(a) Communicating with media (journalists) online

Communicating with media (journalists) online uses the Internet as a new conduit to disseminate press releases through e-mail and on-site. Options to consider for a company include: setting up a press-release area on the web site; creating e-mail alerts about news that journalists and other third parties can sign up to; submitting your news stories or releases to online news feeds. Examples include: PR Newswire: (**www.prnewswire.com**), Internetwire (**www.internetwire.com/iwire/home**), PressBox (**www.pressbox.co.uk**); PRWeb (**www.prweb.com**), Business Wire (**www.businesswire.com**). Press releases can be written for search engine optimisation (SEO).

(b) Link building

Link building
A structured activity to include good quality hyperlinks to your site from relevant sites with a good page rank.

Reciprocal links
Links which are agreed between yourself and another organisation.

Link building is a key activity for search engine optimisation. It can be considered to be an element of online PR since it is about getting your brand visible on third-party sites.

Link building needs to be a structured effort to achieve as many links into a web site as possible from referring web sites (these commonly include reciprocal links). We have also seen that your position in the search engine results pages will be higher if you have quality links into relevant content on your site (not necessarily the home page).

McGaffin (2004) provides a great introduction to implementing a structured link-building programme. The main principle of link building is as follows. McGaffin says: 'Create great content, link to great content and great content will link to you.' He describes how you should review existing links, link to competitors, set targets and then proactively enquire to suitable site owners for links.

Note on link building

You can use the syntax **link:site** in Google to see the number of quality links into a page on your site as judged by Google, e.g. **www.davechaffey.com**.

Note this also includes internal links. To exclude internal links and include pages with lower page rank or that do not have a true hyperlink, but contain the URL, search on Google for this: **www.url.com – site:www.url.com**.

For example,
www.davechaffey.com – site:www.davechaffey.com

(c) Blogs, podcasting and RSS

Web logs or 'blogs' give an easy method of regularly publishing web pages which are best described as online journals, diaries or news or events listings. They may include feedback (traceback) comments from other sites or contributors to the site. Frequency can be hourly, daily, weekly or less frequently, but daily updates are typical.

An example of a useful blog which can keep marketing professionals up-to-date about Internet marketing developments is **www.marketingvox.com** which is coupled with daily e-mail digests of stories posted. Another example, with news items and articles structured according to the chapters of a book, is Davechaffey.com (**www.daveChaffey.com**). Business blogs are created by people within an organisation. They can be useful in showing the expertise of those within the organisation, but need to be carefully controlled to avoid releasing damaging information. An example of a business blog used to showcase the expertise of its analysts is the Jupiter Research Analyst Weblogs (**http://weblogs.jupiterresearch.com**). Technology company Sun Microsystems has several hundreds of bloggers and has a policy to control them to make positive comments.

There are many free services which enable anyone to blog (for example **www.blogger.com** which was purchased by Google in 2003). Blogs were traditionally accessed through online tools (e.g. **www.bloglines.com**, **www.blogpule.com**) or software readers (**www.rssreader.com**) but were incorporated into mainstream software in 2005–6.

Podcasts are related to blogs since they can potentially be generated by individuals or organisations to voice an opinion either as audio (typically MP3) or less commonly currently as video. They have been successfully used by media organisations such as the BBC which has used them for popular programmes such as film reviews or discussions and for live recording such as the Beethoven symphonies that received over 600,000 downloads in June 2005 alone. Virgin Radio has also used podcasting, but cannot, at the time of writing, broadcast music (due to copyright restrictions) but only the presenters! A big challenge for achieving visibility for podcasts is that contents can only currently be recognised by tags and it is difficult to assess quality without listening to the start of a podcast. All the main search engines are working on techniques to make searching of voice and video content practical. In the meantime, some start-ups such as Odeo (**www.odeo.com**) and Blinkx (**www.blinkx.com**) are developing solutions.

Online communities and social networks

Companies can also potentially form or post to forums to promote their services, but it must be done in a sensitive way – it must actually contribute value to the community.

Really Simple Syndication (RSS)

Really Simple Syndication (RSS) is an extension of blogging where blog, news or any type of content is received by subscribers using the systems mentioned above. It offers a method of receiving news that uses a different broadcast method from e-mail, so is not subject to the same conflicts with spam or spam filters. Many journalists now subscribe to RSS feeds from sources such as the BBC (**http://news.bbc.co.uk/2/hi/help/3223484.stm**) which publishes RSS feed for different types of content on its site.

(d) Managing how your brand is presented on third-party sites

As part of online PR it is useful to set up monitoring services. It is also necessary to have the resources to deal with negative PR as part of online reputation management. Microsoft's PR agency reputedly has a 'rapid response' unit that can respond to online PR. Examples of alerting service include Googlealert (**www.googlealert.com**), Google Alerts (**www.google.com/alerts**) and paid services such as Market Sentinel (**www.marketsentinel.com**), Mark Monitor (**www.markmonitor.com**), Reputation Intelligence (**www.reputationintelligence.com**) and Brand Intelligence (**www.brandintelligence.com**).

(e) Creating a buzz – online viral marketing

From a functional point of view, online viral marketing often involves generating word-of-mouth and links through to a web site, so it can be considered part of online PR. However, since it takes many forms it is covered separately in a later section of this chapter.

3 Online partnerships

We showed in Chapter 5 that partnerships are an important part of today's marketing mix. The same is true online. Resources must be devoted to managing your online partners. Many large organisations have specific staff to manage these relationships. In smaller organisations partnership management is often neglected, which is a missed opportunity. There are three key types of online partnerships which need to be managed: link building (covered in the previous section, this can also be considered to be part of online PR), affiliate marketing and online sponsorship. All should involve a structured approach to managing links through to a site.

(a) Affiliate marketing

Affiliate marketing

A commission-based arrangement where an e-retailer pays sites that link to it for sales, leads (CPA-based) or less commonly visitors (CPC-based).

Affiliate marketing has become very popular with e-retailers since many achieve over 20% of their online sales through affiliates. The great thing about affiliate marketing for the e-retailer, is that they, the advertisers, do not pay until the product has been purchased or a lead generated. It is sometimes referred to as 'zero-risk advertising'. Contrast this with nearly all forms of offline promotion where there is not a direct link between the cost of promotion and the revenue gained. Affiliate marketing also contrasts with pay-per-click search engine marketing, where the retailer has to pay for the visitor irrespective of whether they purchase anything. As a result it is relatively easy to control affiliate expenditure and a company can readily ensure that spend is below the allowable cost of customer acquisition. However, affiliate marketing still has challenges in that affiliates can be potential competitors in search optimisation and pay-per-click (driving up bid prices) and they may harm your brand by association if they refer to pornography or gambling on their site, for instance. Time needs to be allocated to manage these relationships. Affiliates can be rewarded for their loyalty to encourage more referrals by tiered programmes such as that run by Amazon.

Amazon was one of the earliest adopters of affiliate marketing and it now has hundreds of thousands of affiliates that drive visitors to Amazon through links in return for commission on products sold. Internet legend records that Jeff Bezos, the creator of Amazon, was chatting to someone at a cocktail party who wanted to sell books about divorce via her web site. Subsequently, Amazon.com launched its Associates Program in July 1996 and it is still going strong. Figure 8.17 summarises the affiliate marketing process. To manage the process of finding affiliates, updating product information, tracking clicks and making payments, many companies use an affiliate network or affiliate manager such as Commission Junction (**www.cj.com**) or Trade Doubler (**www.tradedoubler.com**). Since the affiliate network takes a cut on each sale, many merchants also try to set up separate relationships with preferred affiliates often known as 'super affiliates'. Affiliate marketing is often thought to apply solely to e-retailers where the affiliate is paid if there is a purchase on the merchant site. In fact, payment can occur for any action which is recorded on the destination site, for example through a 'thank you' post-transaction page after filling a form. This could be a quote for insurance, trial of a piece of software or registration for download of a paper.

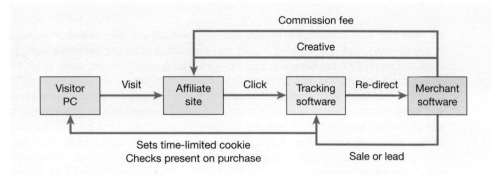

Figure 8.17 The affiliate marketing model (note that the tracking software and fee payment may be managed through an independent affiliate network manager)

Some of the issues with balancing spend between affiliate marketing and other online communications techniques and offline communications techniques are illustrated by Mini Case Study 8.5 'Electronic retailers cut back on their e-communications spend'.

Mini Case Study 8.5	Electronic retailers cut back on their e-communications spend

Technology e-retailer dabs.com (featured in Case Study 7) has traditionally used these as their main communications tools:

- Search engine marketing (the main investment)
- Referrals from affiliates (this has been reduced)
- Online display advertising on third-party sites (limited)
- PR.

Jonathan Wall, Dabs marketing director, explains how dabs.com reappraised their use of e-communications tools. He said:

We stopped all our affiliate and price-comparison marketing in February because we wanted to see what effect it had on our business and if we were getting value for money. It was proving a very expensive channel for us and we've found [stopping] it has had virtually no effect, because we're seeing that people will still go to Kelkoo to check prices and then come to our site anyway. It's like they're having a look around first and then coming to a brand they know they can trust. We're continuing with paid-for search on Google, but that's all we're doing with online marketing at the moment.

New Media Age (2005b) also reported that Empire Direct had adopted a similar approach to its communication mix, reporting that its co-founder and sales and marketing director, Manohar Showan, had revealed that the company has significantly moved from online to offline advertising. He said:

We've moved a lot more into national papers and specialist magazines, two years ago, if you'd asked me where we marketed and advertised ourselves, I would have said the majority was online. But now it's turned right round and online's the minority.

New Media Age (2005b) believes that the reason for this is not a mistrust of the very medium it's using to take sales but, instead, the result of a growing realisation that its acquisition costs were swelling online. Showan says:

→

We were very keen advocates of affiliate marketing and pay-per-click search. The trouble was we had to pay for every click and we were finding that the cost of acquiring each new customer was getting more and more. One big issue was that we were finding people would come to us through affiliates just to check information on a product they'd already bought, so we were basically paying for customers to find out how to hook up their new VCR. We still have affiliates – our main one is Kelkoo – and we still bid for clicks on Google, but not as much as we used to. One of the things we were finding with the search engines is that, with our own search optimisation and because so many people were coming to our site, we were normally very high up the list just through normal searching. In our experience, particularly with Google, if people can see what they want in the main list, they don't look to the right-hand side of the page.

(b) Online sponsorship

Online sponsorship is not straightforward. It's not just a case of mirroring existing 'real-world' sponsorship arrangements in the 'virtual world', although this is a valid option. There are many additional opportunities for sponsorship online which can be sought out, even if you don't have a big budget at your disposal.

Ryan and Whiteman (2000) define online sponsorship as:

the linking of a brand with related content or context for the purpose of creating brand awareness and strengthening brand appeal in a form that is clearly distinguishable from a banner, button, or other standardized ad unit.

For the advertiser, online sponsorship has the benefit that their name is associated with an online brand that the site visitor is already familiar with. So, for users of the ISP Wanadoo, with whom they are familiar, sponsorship builds on this existing relationship and trust. Closely related is online 'co-branding' where there is an association between two brands.

Paid-for sponsorship of another site, or part of it, especially a portal, for an extended period is another way to develop permanent links. Co-branding is a lower-cost method of sponsorship and can exploit synergies between different companies. Note that sponsorship does not have to directly drive visitors to a brand site – it may be more effective if interaction occurs on the media owner's microsite.

A great business-to-business example of online sponsorship is offered by WebTrends which sponsors the customer information channel on ClickZ.com (**www.clickz.com/experts**). They combined this sponsorship with different ads each month offering e-marketers the chance to learn about different topics such as search marketing, retention and conversion marketing through detailed white papers and 'Take 10' online video presentation by industry experts which could be downloaded by registered users. The objective of these ads was to encourage prospects to subscribe to the WebTrends WebResults e-newsletter and to assess purchase intent at sign-up enabling follow-up telemarketing by regional distributors. WebTrends reported the following results over a single year of sponsorship:

- List built to 100,000 WebResults total subscribers
- 18,000 Take 10 presentations
- 13,500 seminar attendees.

A study by Performance Research (2001) compared differences in the perception of the online audience to banner ads and sponsorships. Respondents were shown a series of web page screens; for each, one half of the respondents were shown a similar version with a banner advertisement, and the remaining half were shown a nearly identical image with web sponsorship identifications (such as 'Sponsored by', 'Powered By' and 'in association with'). The results were illuminating. Of the 500 respondents, ratings for different aspects of perception were:

- Trustworthy (28% for sponsorships to 15% for ads)
- Credible (28% to 16%)
- In tune with their interests (32% to 17%)
- Likely to enhance site experience (33% to 17%)
- More likely to consider purchasing a sponsor's product or service (41% to 23%)
- Less obtrusive (66% to 34%).

4 Interactive advertising

How positively do you view interactive advertising as a communications tool? Even today, there are relatively few advertisers who have used interactive advertising, partly because of myths promoted about interactive advertising and possibly because of bad experiences. The first 468 by 68 pixel banner ad was placed on Hotwired in 1995 and the call-to-action 'Click here!' generated a clickthrough of 25%. Since then, the clickthrough rate (CTR) has fallen dramatically with many consumers suffering from 'banner blindness' – they ignore anything on a web site that looks like an ad. The Doubleclick compilation of ad response (**www.doubleclick.com**) shows that today the average CTR is between 0.2% and 0.3%. This low response rate combined with relatively high costs of over £20 per thousand ads served has seemingly made some marketers prejudiced against interactive advertising. But we will see that there are many innovative approaches to interactive advertising which are proved to increase brand awareness and purchase intent. For example, there are now many other ad formats such as Skyscrapers and MPUs (multi-purpose advertising units) and rich-media ads with animation, audio or video or data capture and interaction. This is indicated by Figure 8.18 which uses large rectangle MPUs as well as some traditional banners which will receive lower click-through rates. Given these limitations to banner ads, most media owners, digital marketing agencies and industry bodies now refer to 'Interactive advertising' which is more suggestive of the range of options for rich-media ads, data capture ads and large-format ads such as skyscrapers.

Ad serving

The term for displaying an advertisement on a web site. Often the advertisement will be served from a web server different from the site on which it is placed.

Destination site

The site reached on clickthrough.

Microsite

A small-scale destination site reached on clickthrough which is part of the media owner's site.

Fundamentals of online advertising

Advertising on the web takes place when an advertiser pays to place advertising content on another web site. The process usually involves ad serving from a different server from that on which the page is hosted (ads can be served on destination sites in a similar way).

Advertising is possible on a range of sites in order to drive traffic to an organisation's destination site or alternately a microsite or nested ad-content on the media owner's site or on the destination site. The destination page from a banner ad will usually be designed as a specifically created direct-response page to encourage further action. For example, the nappy supplier Huggies placed an advertisement on a childcare site that led the parents clicking on this link to more detailed information on Huggies contained on the site and offering them opt-in to a loyalty programme.

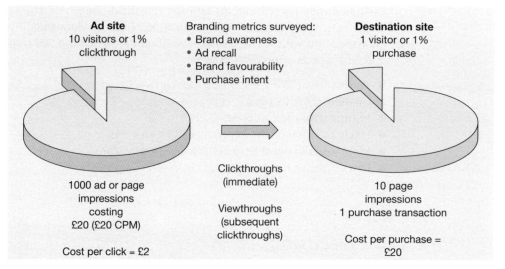

Figure 8.18 Basic model for interactive display advertising

The purpose of interactive advertising

It can be contended that each web site is in itself an advertisement since it can inform, persuade and remind customers about a company or its products and services. However, a company web site is not strictly an advertisement in the conventional sense, since money is not exchanged to place the content of the web site on a medium owned by a third party. Although Figure 8.18 implies the main aim of interactive advertising is driving traffic to a destination web site, there are other outcomes that a marketing manager may be looking to achieve through an interactive ad campaign. Cartellieri et al. (1997) identify the following objectives:

- *Delivering content.* This is the typical case where a clickthrough on a banner advertisement leads through to a destination site giving more detailed information on an offer. This is where a direct response is sought.
- *Enabling transaction.* If a clickthrough leads through to a merchant such as a travel site or an online bookstore this may lead directly to a sale. A direct response is also sought here.
- *Shaping attitudes.* An advertisement that is consistent with a company brand can help build brand awareness.
- *Soliciting response.* An advertisement may be intended to identify new leads or as a start for two-way communication. In these cases an interactive advertisement may encourage a user to type in an e-mail address or other information.
- *Encouraging retention.* The advertisement may be placed as a reminder about the company and its service and may link through to on-site sales promotions such as a prize draw.

These objectives are not mutually exclusive, and more than one can be achieved with a well-designed banner campaign. Zeff and Aronson (2001) stress the unique benefits of banner advertising as compared with those of other media. Of these, the most important are the capability to target relatively small groups of users and then to track their response. Online ads are also more responsive potentially since it is possible to place an advertisement more rapidly and make changes as required. Experienced online advertisers build in flexibility to change targeting through time. Best practice is to start wide and then narrow to a focus – allow 20% budget for high-performing ad placements (high

CTR and conversion). In an iMediaConnection interview with ING Direct VP of Marketing, Jurie Pieterse, the capability to revise creative is highlighted:

Another lesson we learned is the importance of creative. It's critical to invest in developing various creative executions to test them for best performance and constantly introduce new challengers to the top performers. We've also learned there's no single top creative unit – different creative executions and sizes perform differently from publisher to publisher.

Source: iMediaConnection (2003)

Measurement of interactive ad effectiveness

Page and ad impressions and reach
One page impression occurs when a member of the audience views a web page. One ad impression occurs when a person views an advertisement placed on the web page. Reach defines the number of unique individuals who view an advertisement.

CPM (cost per thousand)
The cost of placing an ad viewed by 1000 people.

Effective frequency
The number of exposures or ad impressions (frequency) required for an advertisement to become effective.

Clickthrough and clickthrough rate
A clickthrough (ad click) occurs each time a user clicks on a banner advertisement with the mouse to direct them to a web page that contains further information. The clickthrough rate is expressed as a percentage of total ad impressions, and refers to the proportion of users viewing an advertisement who click on it. It is calculated as the number of clickthroughs divided by the number of ad impressions.

Viewthrough
A viewthrough indicates when a user views an ad and subsequently visits a web site.

Figure 8.18 summarises the different terms used for measuring banner ad effectiveness. Each time an advertisement is viewed is referred to as an advertisement or ad impression. 'Page impressions' and 'page views' are other terms used. Since some people may view the advertisement more than one time, marketers are also interested in the reach, which is the number of unique individuals who view the advertisement. This will naturally be a smaller figure than that for ad impressions. Cost of ads is typically based on CPM or cost per thousand (*mille*) ad impressions as with other media. However, the popularity of CPC search advertising and CPA affiliate deals mean that these are options too.

There is much discussion about how many impressions of an advertisement an individual has to see for it to be effective. Novak and Hoffman (1997) note that for traditional media it is thought that fewer than three exposures will not give adequate recall. For new media, because of the greater intensity of viewing a computer screen, recall seems to be better with a smaller number of advertisements compared with old media. The technical term for adequate recall is 'effective frequency'.

When a user clicks on the advertisement, he or she will normally be directed to further information, viewing of which will result in a marketing outcome. Usually the user will be directed through to part of the corporate web site that will have been set up especially to deal with the response from the advertisement. When a user clicks on an advertisement immediately this is known as a 'clickthrough', but adserving systems (using cookies) also measure viewthrough which indicates when a user views an ad and subsequently visits a web site within a defined period such as 30 days. This increases overall response, but it should be borne in mind that users may have visited the site in response to other stimuli.

Interactive ad targeting options

Online ads can be targeted through placing ads:

1 *On a particular type of site (or part of site)* which has a specific visitor profile or type of content. So a car manufacturer can place ads on the home page of Handbag.com to appeal to a young female audience. A financial services provider can advertise in the money section of the site to target those interested in these products. To reach large mass-market audiences, advertisers can place an ad on a large portal home page such as MSN which has millions of visitors each day (sometimes known as a 'road-block' if they take all ad inventory).
2 *To target a registered user's profile.* A business software provider could advertise on the FT to target registrants' profiles such as finance directors or IT managers.
3 At a particular time of day or week.

Behavioural ad targeting

Enables an advertiser to target ads at a visitor as they move elsewhere on the site or return to the site, thus increasing the frequency or number of impressions served to an individual in the target market.

4 *To follow users' behaviour.* **Behavioural ad targeting** is all about relevance – dynamically serving relevant content, messaging or ad which matches the interests of a site visitor according to inferences about their characteristics. These inferences are made by anonymously tracking the different types of pages visited by a site user during a single visit to a site or across multiple sessions. Other aspects of the environment used by the visitor can also be determined, such as their location, browser and operating system. For example, FT.com using software from Revenue Science can identify users in eight segments: Business Education, Institutional Investor, Information Technology, Luxury and Consumer, Management, Personal Finance, Travel and Private Equity. The targeting process is shown in Figure 8.19. First the ad serving system detects whether the visitor is in the target audience (media optimisation), then creative optimisation occurs to serve the best ad for the viewer type.

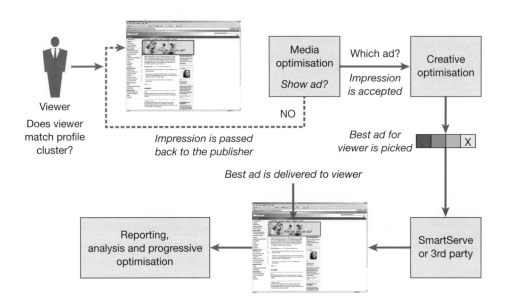

Figure 8.19 Behavioural ad targeting process
Source: Twin London (www.twinlondon.com)

Interactive ad formats

As well as the classic 468 × 60 rotating GIF banner ad which is decreasing in popularity, media owners now provide a choice of larger, richer formats which web users are more likely to notice. Research has shown that message association and awareness building are much higher for flash-based ads, rich-media ads and larger-format rectangles (multi-purpose units, MPUs) and skyscrapers. View the rich media ads at **www.eyeblaster.com** or **www.tangozebra.com** and you will agree that they definitely can't be ignored.

Interstitial ads

Ads that appear between one page and the next.

Overlay

Typically an animated ad that moves around the page and is superimposed on the web site content.

Other online ad terms you will hear include '**interstitials**' (intermediate adverts before another page appears); and the more common '**overlays**' (formerly more often known as '*superstitials*' or '*overts*') that appear above content and of course '*pop-up windows*' that are now less widely used because of their intrusion. Online advertisers face a constant battle with users who deploy pop-up blockers or less commonly ad-blocking software, but they will persist in using rich-media formats where they generate the largest response.

Making banner advertising work

As with any form of advertising, certain techniques will result in a more effective advertisement. Discussions with those who have advertised online indicate the following are important to effective advertising:

1 *Appropriate incentives are needed to achieve clickthrough.* Banner advertisements with offers such as prizes or reductions can achieve higher clickthrough rates by perhaps as much as 10 per cent.
2 *Creative design needs to be tested extensively.* Alternative designs for the advertisement need to be tested on representatives of a target audience. Anecdotal evidence suggests that the clickthrough rate can vary greatly according to the design of the advertisement, in much the same way that recall of a television advertisement will vary in line with its concept and design. Different creative designs may be needed for different sites on which advertisements are placed. Zeff and Aronson (2001) note that simply the use of the words 'click here!' or 'click now' can dramatically increase clickthrough rates because new users do not know how banners work!
3 *Placement of advertisement and timing need to be considered carefully.* The different types of placement option available have been discussed earlier in the chapter, but it should be remembered that audience volume and composition will vary through the day and the week.

Buying advertising

Banner advertising is typically paid for according to the number of web users who view the web page and the advertisement on it. These are the 'ad impressions' referred to earlier.

Web site auditors
Auditors accurately measure the usage of different sites in terms of the number of ad impressions and clickthrough rates.

- When payment is made according to the number of viewers of a site it is important that the number of viewers be measured accurately. To do this independent web site auditors are required. The main auditing body in the UK is the Audit Bureau of Circulation Electronic, ABCelectronic (**www.abce.org.uk**).

Banner advertising is purchased for a specific period. It may be purchased for the ad to be served on:

Run of site
Cost per 1000 ad impressions. CPM is usually higher for run-of-site advertisements where advertisements occur on all pages of the site.

- the run of site (the entire site);
- a section of site;
- according to keywords entered on a search engine.

Results-based payment
Advertisers pay according to the number of times the ad is clicked on.

Traditionally, the most common payment is according to the number of customers who view the page as a cost per thousand (CPM) ad or page impressions. Typical CPM is in the range £10–£50. Other options that benefit the advertiser if they can be agreed are per-clickthrough or per-action such as a purchase on the destination site. Although initially media owners were able to control charging rates and largely used a per-exposure model with the increase in unused ad inventory, there has been an increase in results-based payment methods. Organisations such as Valueclick (**www.valueclick.com**), now operate ad networks where the advertiser only pays for each response. This advertising model is similar to the affiliate method (see the earlier section 3a Affiliate marketing) except that with the affiliate method, the referring site is usually paid a commission based on the cost of the item sold.

Ad networks
Brokers who place ads for advertisers over a range of media sites using different payment models such as CPM, CPC and CPA.

Media planning – deciding on the online/offline mix for advertising

This decision is typically taken by the media planner. As we noted in the section on 'Planning integrated marketing communications', the mix between online and offline spend must reflect consumers' media consumption and the cost/response effectiveness of each medium. But, depending on the agency used, they may play it safe by putting the ad spend into what they are familiar with and what may be most rewarding in terms of commission – offline media. Many cross-media optimisation studies (XMOS) have shown that the optimal online spend for low-involvement products is surprisingly high at 10–15% of total spend. Although this is not a large amount, it compares to previous spend levels below 1% for many organisations.

XMOS research is designed to help marketers and their agencies answer the (rather involved) question 'What is the optimal mix of advertising vehicles across different media, in terms of frequency, reach and budget allocation, for a given campaign to achieve its marketing goals?'

The mix between online and offline spend is varied to maximise campaign metrics such as reach, brand awareness and purchase intent. Table 8.4 summarises the optimal mix identified for four famous brands. For example, Dove found that increasing the level of interactive advertising to 15% would have resulted in an increase in overall branding metrics of 8%. The proportion of online is small, but remember that many companies are spending less than 1% of their ad budgets online, meaning that offline frequency is too high and they may not be reaching many consumers.

Cross-media optimisation studies (XMOS)
Studies to determine the optimum spend across different media to produce the best results.

Table 8.4 Optimum media mix suggested by XMOS studies

Brand	TV	Magazine	Online
Colgate	75%	14%	11%
Kleenex	70%	20%	10%
Dove	72%	13%	15%
McDonalds	71%	16% (radio)	13%

Source: Interactive Advertising Bureau (www.iab.net/xmos)

The reasons for using and increasing the significance of online in the media mix are similar to those for using any media mix as described by Sissors and Baron (2002):

● Extend reach (adding prospects not exposed by a single medium or other media)
● Flatten frequency distribution (if audience viewing TV ads are exposed too many times, there is a law of diminishing returns and it may be better to reallocate that budget to other media)
● To reach different kinds of audiences
● To provide unique advantages in stressing different benefits based on the different characteristics of each medium
● To allow different creative executions to be implemented
● To add gross impressions if the other media is cost-efficient
● Reinforce message by using different creative stimuli.

All of these factors, and the first three in particular provide the explanation of why XMOS shows it is worthwhile to put double digit percentages into online media.

5 E-mail marketing

When devising plans for e-mail marketing communications, marketers need to plan for:

Outbound e-mail marketing

E-mails are sent to customers and prospects from an organisation.

Inbound e-mail marketing

Management of e-mails from customers by an organisation.

- **Outbound e-mail marketing**, where e-mail campaigns are used as a form of direct marketing to encourage trial and purchases and as part of a CRM dialogue;
- **Inbound e-mail marketing**, where e-mails from customers such as support enquiries are managed.

We saw in Chapter 6 that permission-based e-mail is an effective tool for building relationships with customers online. Despite the increase in spam such that the vast majority of e-mails are spam or viruses (most estimates exceed 80%), e-mail can still drive good response levels as indicated by Figure 8.20. This is particularly the case with in-house lists on which the data in Figure 8.20 are based, so e-mail communications to customers through e-newsletters or periodic e-mail blasts are today a vital communications technique for companies. Figure 8.20 shows that the key measures for e-mail marketing are:

- *Delivery rate* (here indicated by 'non-bounce rate') – e-mails will bounce if the e-mail address is no longer valid or a spam filter blocks the e-mail. So online marketers check their 'deliverability' to make sure their messages are not identified as 'false positives' by spam prevention software. Web-based e-mail providers such as Hotmail and Yahoo! Mail have introduced standard authentication techniques known as Sender ID and Domain Keys which make sure the e-mail broadcaster is who they say they are and doesn't spoof their address as many spammers do.
- *Open rate* – This is measured for HTML messages through downloaded images. It is an indication of how many customers open an e-mail, but is not accurate since some users have preview panes in their e-mail readers which load the message even if is deleted without reading and some e-mail readers such as Outlook Express now block images by default (this has resulted in a decline in open rates through time).
- *Clickthrough or click rate* – This is the number of people who click through on the e-mail of those delivered (strictly unique clicks rather than total clicks). You can see that response rates are quite high at around 10%.

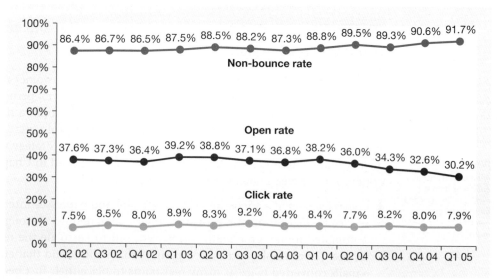

Figure 8.20 E-mail response figures
Source: Doubleclick

Opt-in e-mail options for customer acquisition

For acquiring new visitors and customers to a site, there are three main options for e-mail marketing. From the point of view of the recipient, these are:

1 *Cold e-mail campaign.* In this case, the recipient receives an opt-in e-mail from an organisation that has rented an e-mail list from a consumer e-mail list provider such as Experian (www.experian.com), Claritas (www.claritas.com) or IPT Limited (www.myoffers.co.uk) or a business e-mail list provider such as Mardev (www.mardev.com), Corpdata (www.corpdata.com) or trade publishers and event providers such as VNU. Although they have agreed to receive offers by e-mail, the e-mail is effectively cold. For example, a credit card provider could send a cold e-mail to a list member who is not currently their member. It is important to use some form of 'statement of origination', otherwise the message may be considered spam. Cold e-mails tend to have higher CPAs than other forms of online marketing, but different lists should still be evaluated.

2 *Co-branded e-mail.* Here, the recipient receives an e-mail with an offer from a company they have a reasonably strong affinity with. For example, the same credit card company could partner with a mobile service provider such as Vodafone and send out the offer to their customer (who has opted in to receive e-mails from third parties). Although this can be considered a form of cold e-mail, it is warmer since there is a stronger relationship with one of the brands and the subject line and creative will refer to both brands. Co-branded e-mails tend to be more responsive than cold e-mails to rented lists since the relationship exists and fewer offers tend to be given.

3 *Third-party e-newsletter.* In this visitor acquisition option, a company publicises itself in a third-party e-newsletter. This could be in the form of an ad, sponsorship or PR (editorial) which links through to a destination site. These placements may be set up as part of an interactive advertising ad buy since many e-newsletters also have permanent versions on the web site. Since e-newsletter recipients tend to engage with them by scanning the headlines or reading them if they have time, e-newsletter placements can be relatively cost-effective.

Viral marketing, which is discussed in the next main section, also uses e-mail as the mechanism for transferring messages.

Opt-in e-mail options for prospect conversion and customer retention (house list)

Opt-in

An individual agrees to receive e-mail communications.

House list

A list of prospect and customer names, e-mail addresses and profile information owned by an organisation.

E-mail is most widely used as a prospect conversion and customer retention tool using an opt-in house list of prospects and customers that have given permission to an organisation to contact them. For example, Lastminute.com has built a house list of over 10 million prospects and customers across Europe. Successful e-mail marketers adopt a strategic approach to e-mail and develop a contact or touch strategy which plans the frequency and content of e-mail communications as explained in Chapters 4 and 6. Some options for in-house e-mail marketing include:

● *Conversion e-mail* – someone visits a web site and expresses interest in a product or service by registering and providing their e-mail address although they do not buy. Automated follow-up e-mails can be sent out to persuade the recipient to trial the service. For example, betting company William Hill found that automated follow-up e-mails converted twice as many registrants to place their first bet compared to registrants who did not receive an e-mail.

- *Regular e-newsletter type* – options are reviewed for different frequencies such as weekly, monthly or quarterly with different content for different audiences and segments.
- *House-list campaign* – these are periodic e-mails to support different objectives such as encouraging trial of a service or newly launched product, repeat purchases or reactivation of customers who no longer use a service.
- *Event-triggered* – these tend to be less regular and are sent out perhaps every 3 or 6 months when there is news of a new product launch or an exceptional offer.
- *E-mail sequence* – software can send out a series of e-mails with the interval between e-mails determined by the marketer.

E-mail marketing success factors

Effective e-mail marketing shares much in common with effective direct e-mail copy. Chaffey (2006) uses the mnemonic CRITICAL as a checklist of questions to use to improve the response of e-mail campaigns. It stands for:

- *Creative* – This assesses the design of the e-mail including its layout, use of colour and image and the copy (see below).
- *Relevance* – Does the offer and creative of the e-mail meet the needs of the recipients?
- *Incentive* (or offer) – The WIFM factor or 'What's in it for me?' for the recipient. What benefit does the recipient gain from clicking on the hyperlink(s) in the e-mail? For example, a prize draw is a common offer for B2C brands.
- *Targeting and Timing* – Targeting is related to the relevance. Is a single message sent to all prospects or customers on the list or are e-mails with tailored creative, incentive and copy sent to the different segments on the list? Timing refers to when the e-mail is received: the time of day, day of the week, point in the month and even the year; does it relate to any particular events? There is also the relative timing – when it is received compared to other marketing communications – this depends on the integration.
- *Integration* – Are the e-mail campaigns part of your integrated marketing communications? Questions to ask include: are the creative and copy consistent with my brand? Does the message reinforce other communications? Does the timing of the e-mail campaign fit with offline communications?
- *Copy* – This is part of the creative and refers to the structure, style and explanation of the offer together with the location of hyperlinks in the e-mail.
- *Attributes (of the e-mail)* – Assess the message characteristics such as the subject line, from address, to address, date/time of receipt and format (HTML or text). Send out Multipart/MIME messages which can display HTML or text according to the capability of the e-mail reader. Offer choice of HTML or text to match users' preferences.
- *Landing page (or microsite)* – These are terms given for the page(s) reached after the recipient clicks on a link in the e-mail. Typically, on clickthrough, the recipient will be presented with an online form to profile or learn more about them. Designing the page so the form is easy to complete can effect the overall success of the campaign.

A relevant incentive, such as free information or a discount, is offered in exchange for a prospect providing their e-mail address by filling in an online form. Careful management of e-mail lists is required since, as the list ages, the addresses of customers and their profiles will change, resulting in many bounced messages and lower response rates. Data protection law also requires the facility for customers to update their details.

Managing inbound e-mail communications

For large organisations, e-mail volumes are already significant. For example, Bicknell (2002) reports that the Nationwide Bank web contact centre receives nearly 20,000 e-mails each month. According to Mark Cromack, Nationwide's senior operations manager, customer contacts by e-mail have increased fourfold between 2001 and 2002, but through choosing the right process and tools, it has only been necessary to double the number of operators. See Mini Case Study 5.3 for further information on this topic.

Successful management of inbound communications is important to service quality as perceived by customers. In order to manage these communications, organisations need to develop inbound customer contact strategies.

Inbound customer contact strategies

Approaches to managing the cost and quality of service related to management of customer enquiries.

Customer contact strategies are a compromise between delivering quality customer service with the emphasis on customer choice and minimising the cost of customer contacts. Typical operational objectives that should drive the strategies and measure their effectiveness are:

- Minimise average response time per e-mail and range of response time from slowest to fastest. This should form the basis of an advertised service quality level.
- Minimise clear-up (resolution) time – e.g. number of contacts and elapsed time to resolution.
- Maximise customer satisfaction ratings with response.
- Minimise average staff time and cost per e-mail response.

Customer contact strategies for integrating web and e-mail support into existing contact centre operations usually incorporate elements of both of the following options.

1 *Customer-preferred channel*. Here the company uses a customer-led approach where customers use their preferred channel for enquiry whether it be phone callback, e-mail or live-chat. There is little attempt made to influence the customer as to which is the preferable channel. Note that while this approach may give good customer satisfaction ratings, it is not usually the most cost-effective approach, since the cost of phone support will be higher than customer self-service on the web, or an e-mail enquiry.

2 *Company-preferred channel*. Here the company will seek to influence the customer on the medium used for contact. For example, easyJet encourages customers to use online channels rather than using voice contact to the call centre for both ordering and customer service. Customer choice is still available, but the company uses the web site to influence the choice of channel.

6 Viral marketing

Viral marketing

E-mail is used to transmit a promotional message to another potential customer.

Viral marketing harnesses the network effect of the Internet and can be effective in reaching a large number of people rapidly in the same way as a natural virus or a computer virus. It is effectively an online form of word-of-mouth communications. Although the best-known examples of viral activity are of compromising pictures or jokes being passed around offices worldwide, viral marketing is increasingly being used for commercial purposes. Smith and Chaffey (2005) say ideally, viral marketing is a clever idea, a game, a shocking idea, or a highly informative idea which makes compulsive viewing. It can be a video clip, a TV ad, a cartoon, a funny picture, a poem, song, political message, or a news item. It is so amazing, it makes people want to pass it on. A good example is shown in Figure 8.21 – the Subservient Chicken, originally launched to promote a new chicken meal by Burger King, responds to commands typed in by users. It has circulated around millions of users worldwide and is one of the most successful viral campaigns in terms of pass-along.

This is a challenge for commercial companies since to be successful, it will need to challenge convention and this may not fit well with the brand.

To make a viral campaign effective, Justin Kirby of viral marketing specialists DMC (**www.dmc.co.uk**) suggests these three things are needed (Kirby, 2003):

1 *Creative material – the 'viral agent'*. This includes the creative message or offer and how it is spread (text, image, video).
2 *Seeding*. Identifying web sites, blogs or people to send e-mail to start the virus spreading.
3 *Tracking*. To monitor the effect, to assess the return from the cost of developing the viral agent and seeding.

Godin (2001) writes about the importance of what he terms 'the ideavirus' as a marketing tool. He describes it as 'digitally augmented word-of-mouth'. What differences does the ideavirus have from word of mouth? First, transmission is more rapid, second, transmission tends to reach a larger audience, and third, it can be persistent – reference to a product on a service such as Epinions (**www.epinions.com**) remains online on a web site and can be read at a later time. Godin emphasises the importance of starting small by seeding a niche audience he describes as a 'hive' and then using advocates in spreading the virus – he refers to them as 'sneezers'. Traditionally, marketers would refer to such a grouping as 'customer advocates' or 'brand loyalists'.

Smith and Chaffey (2005) distinguish between these types of viral e-mail mechanisms:

1 *Pass-along e-mail viral*. This is where e-mail or word-of-mouth alone is used to spread the message. This is classic viral marketing such as those showcased on the Viral Bank (**www.viralbank.com**) which involves an e-mail with a link to a site such as a video or an attachment. Towards the end of a commercial e-mail it does no harm to prompt the first recipient to forward the e-mail along to interested friends or colleagues. Even if only one in 100 responds to this prompt, it is still worth it. The dramatic growth of Hotmail, reaching 10 million subscribers in just over a year, was effectively down to pass-along as people received e-mails with a signature promoting the service. Word-of-mouth helped too.

Pass-along or forwarding has worked well for video clips, either where they are attached to the e-mail or the e-mail contains a link to download the clip. If the e-mail has the 'WOW!' factor, of which more later, a lot more than one in a hundred will forward the e-mail. This mechanism is what most people consider to be viral, but there are the other mechanisms that follow too.
2 *Web-facilitated viral (E-mail prompt)*. Here, the e-mail contains a link/graphic to a web page with 'E-mail a friend' or 'E-mail a colleague'. A web form is used to collect data of the e-mail address to which the e-mail should be forwarded, sometimes with an optional message. The company then sends a separate message to the friend or colleague.
3 *Web-facilitated viral (web prompt)*. Here it is the web page such as a product catalogue or white paper which contains a link/graphic to 'E-mail a friend' or colleague. A web form is again used to collect data and an e-mail is subsequently sent.
4 *Incentivised viral*. This is distinct from the types above since the e-mail address is not freely given. This is what we need to make viral really take off. By offering some reward for providing someone else's address we can dramatically increase referrals. A common offer is to gain an additional entry for entry into a prize draw. Referring more friends gains more entries to the prize draw. With the right offer, this can more than double the response. The incentive is offered either by e-mail (option 2 above) or on a web page

(option 3). In this case, there is a risk of breaking privacy laws since the consent of the e-mail recipient may not be freely given. Usually only a single follow-up e-mail by the brand is permitted. So you should check with the lawyers if considering this.

5 *Web-link viral*. But online viral isn't just limited to e-mail. Links in discussion group postings or blogs which are from an individual are also in this category. Either way, it's important when seeding the campaign to try and get as many targeted online and offline mentions of the viral agent as you can.

Figure 8.21 Viral marketing example – Subservient Chicken (www.subservientchicken.com)

On-site promotional techniques

In addition to ensuring promotion on other sites to attract an audience to a site, communications plans should consider how to convert visitors to action and to encourage repeat visits, as we noted in the section on conversion marketing in Chapter 2. Online media sites will aim to deploy content to maximise the length of visits. Approaches for increasing conversion of customers include:

● relevant incentive or option, clearly explained;
● clear call-to-action using a prominent banner ad or text heading;
● position of call-to-action in a prime location on screen, e.g. top left or top right.

To achieve this a variety of devices can be used, both to increase the length of site visit, and to make users return. A measure of a site's ability to retain visitors has been referred to as 'site stickiness' since a 'sticky' site is difficult to drag oneself away from. Activity 8.1 is intended to highlight some of the methods that can be used to achieve the objective of repeat visits.

Activity 8.1	Methods for enhancing site stickiness and generating repeat visits

This activity is intended to highlight methods of on-site promotion which may cause people to visit a web site, stay for longer than one click and then return. For each of the following techniques, discuss:

1 how the incentives should be used;
2 why these incentives will increase the length of site visits and the likelihood of return to the site;
3 the type of company for which these techniques might work best.

Techniques

- Sponsorship of an event, team or sports personality.
- A treasure hunt on different pages of the site, with a prize.
- A screensaver.
- A site-related quiz.
- Monthly product discount on an e-commerce site.
- Regularly updated information indicated by the current date or the date new content is added.

Note that as well as 'up-front' incentives there are some simple techniques that make a site 'fresh', which can be used to generate repeat visits. These include:

- daily or weekly update of pages with a date on the web site to highlight that it is updated regularly;
- regular publication of industry- or product-specific news;
- the use of e-mails to existing customers to highlight new promotions.

Selecting the optimal communications mix

The promotion element of an Internet marketing plan requires four important decisions about investment for the online promotion or the online communications mix.

1 Investment in promotion compared to site creation and maintenance

Since there is a fixed budget for site creation, maintenance and promotion, the e-marketing plan should specify the budget for each to ensure there is a sensible balance and the promotion of the site is not underfunded. The amount spent on maintenance for each major revision of a web site is generally thought to be between a quarter and a third of the original investment. The relatively large cost of maintenance is to be expected, given the need to keep updating information in order that customers return to a web site. Figure 8.22 shows two alternatives for balancing these three variables. Figure 8.22(a) indicates a budget where traffic-building expenditure exceeds service and design. This is more typical for a dot-com company that needs to promote its brand. Figure 8.22(b) is a budget where traffic-building expenditure is less than service and design. This is more typical for a traditional bricks-and-mortar company that already has a brand recognition and an established customer base.

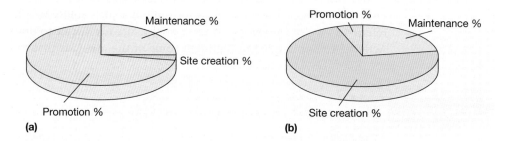

Figure 8.22 Alternatives for balance between different expenditure on Internet marketing

Analysis by Kemmler et al. (2001) of US and European e-commerce sites provided a cross-industry average of the spend on different components of Internet marketing. The top performers achieved an average operating profit of 18%. Costs were made up as follows:

- cost of goods sold (44%);
- maintenance costs (24%);
- marketing costs (14%).

2 Investment in online promotion techniques in comparison to offline promotion

A balance must be struck between these techniques. Figure 8.23 summarises the tactical options that companies have. Which do you think would be the best option for an established company as compared to a dot-com company? It seems that in both cases, offline promotion investment often exceeds that for online promotion investment. For existing companies, traditional media such as print are used to advertise the sites, while print and TV will also be widely used by dot-com companies to drive traffic to their sites.

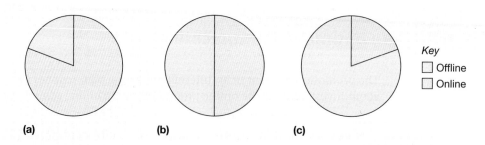

Figure 8.23 Options for the online vs offline communications mix: (a) online > offline, (b) similar online and offline, (c) offline > online

3 Investment in different online promotion techniques

Varianini and Vaturi (2000) have suggested that many online marketing failures have resulted from poor control of media spending. The communications mix should be optimised to minimise the cost of acquisition. If an online intermediary has a cost acquisition of £100 per customer while it is gaining an average commission on each sale of £5 then, clearly, the company will not be profitable unless it can achieve a large number of repeat orders from the customer.

We have reviewed a wide range of techniques that can be used to build traffic to web sites. Agrawal et al. (2001) suggest that e-commerce sites should focus on narrow segments that have demonstrated their attraction to a business model. They believe that promotion techniques such as affiliate deals with narrowly targeted sites and e-mail campaigns targeted at segments grouped by purchase histories and demographic traits are 10 to 15 times more likely than banner ads on generic portals to attract prospects who click through to purchase. Alternatively, pay-per-click ads on Google may have a higher success rate.

4 Investment in digital media and digital creative

As with traditional media, there is a tension between spend on the advertising creative and the media space purchased to run the executions. There is a danger that if spend on media is too high, then the quality of the execution and the volume of digital assets produced will be too low.

Marketing managers have to work with agencies to agree the balance and timing of all these methods. Perhaps the easiest way to start budget allocation is to look at those activities that need to take place all year. These include search engine registration, link building, affiliate campaigns and long-term sponsorships. These are often now outsourced to third-party companies because of the overhead of retaining specialist skills in-house.

Other promotional activities will follow the pattern of traditional media-buying with spending supporting specific campaigns which may be associated with new product launches or sales promotions: for example how much to pay for banner advertising as against online PR about online presence and how much to pay for search engine registration. Such investment decisions will be based on the strengths and weaknesses of the different promotion online. Table 8.5 presents a summary of the different techniques.

Deciding on the optimal expenditure on different communication techniques will be an iterative approach since past results should be analysed and adjusted accordingly. A useful analytical approach to help determine overall patterns of media buying is presented in Table 8.6. Marketers can analyse the proportion of the promotional budget that is spent on different channels and then compare this with the contribution from customers who purchase that originated using the original channel. This type of analysis, reported by Hoffman and Novak (2000), requires two different types of marketing research. First, tagging of customers can be used. We can monitor, using cookies, the numbers of customers who are referred to a web site through a particular online technique such as search engines, affiliate or banner ads, and then track the money they spend on purchases. Secondly, for other promotional techniques, tagging will not be practical. For word-of-mouth referrals, we would have to extrapolate the amount of spend for these customers through traditional market research techniques such as questionnaires. The use of tagging enables much better feedback on the effectiveness of promotional techniques than is possible in traditional media, but it requires a large investment in tracking software to achieve it.

Tagging
Tracking of origin of customers and their spending patterns.

Table 8.5 Summary of the strengths and weaknesses of different communications tools for promoting an online presence

Promotion technique	Main strengths	Main weaknesses
1a Search engine optimisation (SEO)	Highly targeted, relatively low cost cf PPC. High traffic volumes if effective	Intense competition, may compromise look of site. Changes to ranking algorithm
1b Pay-per-click (PPC) marketing	Highly targeted with controlled cost of acquisition	Relatively costly in competitive sectors and low volume compared with SEO
1c Trusted feed	Update readily to reflect changes in product lines and prices	Relatively costly, mainly relevant for e-retailers
2 Online PR	Relatively low cost and good targeting. Can control links-in	Setting up a large number of links can be time-consuming. Need to monitor comments on third-party sites
3a Affiliate marketing	Payment is by results (e.g. 10% of sale or leads goes to referring site)	Costs of payments to affiliate networks for set-up and management fees. Changes to ranking algorithm may affect volume from affiliates
3b Online sponsorship	Most effective if low-cost, long-term co-branding arrangement with synergistic site	May increase awareness, but does not necessarily lead directly to sales
4 Interactive advertising	Main intention to achieve visit, i.e. direct response model. Useful role in branding also	Response rates have declined historically because of banner blindness
5 E-mail marketing	Push medium – can't be ignored in user's inbox. Can be used for direct response link to web site	Requires opt-in for effectiveness. Better for customer retention than for acquisition? Inbox cut-through – message diluted amongst other e-mails. Limits on deliverability
6 Viral marketing	With effective creative possible to reach a large number at relatively low cost	Difficult to create powerful viral concepts and control targeting. Risks damaging brand since unsolicited messages may be received
Traditional offline advertising (TV, print, etc.)	Larger reach than most online techniques. Greater creativity possible, leading to greater impact	Targeting arguably less easy than online. Typically high cost of acquisition

Table 8.6 Relative effectiveness of different forms of marketing communications for a B2C company

Medium	Budget %	Contribution %	Effectiveness
Print (off)	20%	10%	0.5
TV (off)	25%	10%	0.25
Radio (off)	10%	5%	0.5
PR (off)	5%	15%	3
Word of mouth (off)	0%	25%	Infinite
Banners (on)	20%	20%	1
Affiliate (on)	20%	10%	0.5
Links (on)	0%	3%	Infinite
Search engine registration (on)	0%	2%	Infinite

Selecting the best promotion techniques

Suggest the best mix of promotion techniques to build traffic for the following applications:

1 well-established B2C brand with high brand awareness;
2 dot-com start-up;
3 small business aiming to export;
4 common B2C product, e.g. household insurance;
5 specialist B2B product.

5 Setting overall expenditure levels

We can use traditional approaches such as those suggested by Kotler et al. (2001). For example:

- *Affordable method* – the communications budget is set after subtracting fixed and variable costs from anticipated revenues.
- *Percentage-of-sales methods* – the communications budget is set as a percentage of forecast sales revenues.
- *Competitive parity methods* – expenditure is based on estimates of competitor expenditure. For example, e-marketing spend is typically 10–15% of the marketing budget.
- *Objective and task method* – this is a logical approach where budget is built up from all the tasks required to achieve the objectives in the communications plan.

Case Study 8 Making FMCG brands sizzle online

Context

Large fast-moving consumer goods (FMCG) organisations such as Unilever, Procter & Gamble or Masterfoods face many challenges when exploiting interactive communications. This case illustrates some of the following challenges:

- The case for interactive spend is less clear than for companies with a transactional online presence since typically no sales can be directly generated online. Instead, these companies have to assess the role of their interactive communications in generating awareness, brand favourability and purchase intent.
- Assessing the optimal amount of investment in digital media on the company web site and third-party web sites relative to offline media is difficult.
- Creative executions which work well in TV and print may work less well online. Creative variants may need to be devised to make best use of the digital media.
- Some online marketing communications tools such as search engine marketing and affiliate marketing that work well for higher-involvement products are less relevant.
- Many of the brands are marketed internationally, so some consistency of messaging across countries is required, but also with a degree of localisation.

We will look at these challenges, and some of the opportunities through looking at different examples of how varied Unilever brands have exploited digital media in different campaigns. Unilever has products in three main areas: foods, personal care and home care. In 1998 there were no digital media, but in line with the dot-com boom many sites were built over the next five years for different products. More recently, digital marketing is managed centrally, but elements are included in many campaigns as part of Unilever communications channel planning for its different brands. Response by e-mail, SMS or interactive TV is used to build the database about consumer preferences.

Birdseye develops brand positioning – 'We don't play with your food'

If you visit the Birdseye UK site (www.birdseye.co.uk), you will see that the site explains to visitors its core brand proposition through the messaging: 'We don't play with your food: Free from artificial flavours and quick frozen to keep nature's goodness locked in.'

The site also appeals to an audience who are particularly concerned about food and nutrition – the 'Health and Nutrition' section is one of the most popular on the site with content for people dieting, diabetics and vegetarians.

Interactive tools such as a 'healthy eating calculator' which calculates body mass index have proved popular. Such content is also effective at drawing visitors to the site through search engine marketing when they are searching for health and nutrition advice.

Permission marketing as Birdseye asks 'Are you a Salad Boy or a Wrap Girl?'

One example of this approach was a campaign to promote chicken fillet strips; offline print creative (100,000 leaflets) encouraged users to text in on 2 shortcode messages for the chance to win a trip to Mount Everest. Similar prizes were also offered via online partner sites and radio stations to extend the reach of the campaign further. The creative encouraged mobile phone owners to 'Text and Win' because of the immediacy and wider access to mobile phones. However, entry was also available via a web site.

Food brand Peperami has also been actively marketed online, with agency AKQA creating a 'too hot for TV' microsite that generated 20,000 orders for a trial within the first ten days and the ad was spread virally to over 100,000 online.

Lynx says: 'Spray more, get more'

Unilever-owned male bodycare brand Lynx has been an enthusiastic adopter of digital. In 2004, it won the *New Media Age* advertising effectiveness award in the online advertising category. The online Lynx Pulse campaign was created to support a TV ad, which featured a 'geeky guy' dancing in a bar with two attractive girls to the soundtrack 'Make Luv', which was later released and reached number one in the UK charts. The online creative used a series of dots to animate the dancer and featured the same music. The online creative ran as banner advertising and overlays, a 30-second screensaver on the microsite and as a viral e-mail.

The target audience for the campaign was 16–25-year-old men, and web site advertising placements included *NME*, MTV, *The Sun*, Kiss, Ministry of Sound, FHM and Student UK. The imagery was so popular that it was inserted into the end frame of the TV ad. It was also used in offline promotion activity across Europe.

The online campaign specifically aimed to raise brand awareness, offer brand interaction, promote trial and drive traffic to the Pulse microsite. It reached over 1.4m unique users online with average clickthrough rates on banners as high as 23%. According to dynamic logic figures, online advertising awareness rose by 326% after the campaign. The judges described it as 'a clever campaign with strong creative'. They also commented on the high production quality, which really stood out compared to other entrants, and said the site backed up well what the brand was doing offline.

In 2005, as part of an £11m 'Spray more, get more' marketing campaign, Lynx again created a microsite 'lynxladspad.com' with digital assets such as videos of the ads and screensavers. It also encouraged them to spray (or vote for) objects within the pad to collect 'spray points' for a chance to win prizes, including five lads' pad weekenders in Ibiza. This approach appears to be an evolution of the campaign-specific microsite which needs to be revised for each campaign. Using a more permanent site such as lynxladspad.com can be used as a holding site which is updated for each campaign. Associated microsites may still be used, for example in 2005 a viral campaign 'lynxgirlslive.com', which was a spoof adult video webcam game in which users can interact with two scantily clad females by typing in actions they want to see the girls do, such as dance, pillow fight and strip. The viral was seeded on viral and lads' sites, including Contraband.co.uk, Milkandcookies.com and various chatrooms.

Persil – making detergent fun online?

You may not have visited a detergent site recently, but Persil has shown that through developing the right proposition, this is possible. The typical target user is what Persil refers to as 'progressive mums' – busy working mothers with children aged under 10, who have Internet access both at home and work.

Persil has used interactive communications to get closer to its audience by creating an experience of interacting with the brand. Ounal Bailey, Persil brand activation manager, talking to *Revolution* (2003), explains the purpose of their on-site communications as follows: 'We wanted to create a real identity online, making persil.com a hub of information and an online brand experience. At this time, the site moved from a focus on product information to two main sections: Time-In or Product-related information and Time-Out which is about lifestyle and was divided into time for Mum such as relaxation, looking after skin and diet and time with the kids.'

One campaign which was customer-centric rather than product-centric was 'Get Creative' which encouraged the artistic tendencies of children. Persil ran a £20 million integrated campaign that included press, direct mail, radio, online and PR. The Persil 'Big Mummy' challenge saw 15,000 children submit drawings of their parents. To drive entries, Persil used expandable banners and Tangozebra's Overlayz – a dhtml format that allows highly animated creative to float across the screen. Six sites were used to place the ads, including MSN.co.uk, Yahoo! UK & Ireland and AOL UK. Expandable banners appeared on MSN.co.uk's Learning channel and Women's channel, with the Overlayz ad, featuring a 'little monster' from Persil's above-the-line work, appearing on the Women's channel. The clickthrough rate for the online ads was 8.33 per cent on MSN, though lower on other sites.

Another feature of the site which helps build relationships with consumers, is the monthly e-newsletter, then known as 'Messing About'. In 2003, there were about 75,000 subscribers. The e-mail contains content from publisher partners such as IPC's *Family Circle* magazine and a 'make and do' feature at the bottom; for example, a pair of glasses to cut out and colour in. *Revolution* (2003) reported that around 17 per cent of recipients click through to the Persil site, with figures rising as high as 24 per cent for some segments. Users who click through to the site spent 15 to 20 minutes there, although the e-mails are designed so that customers don't have to visit if they don't want to.

A branded 'Messing about' application was set up on partner sites such as Schoolsnet (**www.schoolsnet.com**) and femail.co.uk. Users could register for the e-mail and use the activity finder application. There are also 'stain solver' applications, which let users get advice on the removal of a range of stains. Bailey explains the importance of partner sites: 'We've created applications that we've distributed to places where we would expect our consumers to go, so we're not expecting them to just visit our site. We're not kidding ourselves – we are a detergent brand. The aim is for people to have the experience of Persil wherever they are. So there is a variety of places such as Tesco.com, iVillage, Schoolsnet and femail, where Persil now has a presence.'

Another approach is sampling – sub-brands, such as Persil Capsules, Persil Silk & Wool, Persil Aloe Vera have been used to gain trial and to explain more about the product. For example, when Persil Aloe Vera launched 46,000 asked for samples online – a third of the total. Bailey explains: 'Persil Aloe Vera was a big launch. People see the ad on TV and wonder what else the product does, and they can't get much information from a 30-second ad. But they can get it online.'

A final approach Persil uses to communicate with its audience is to use it to connect with the online 'directed information seekers' – for example, people look for advice on 'stain removal' via the search engines and detergent brands can gain visitors and 'time with brand' through SEO and PPC search engine marketing. Bailey says: 'Washing your clothes sounds really simple, but you'd be surprised what people don't know about getting their clothes clean and how many people use the site for that reason.'

The role of the corporate site

Although Unilever owns many brands, the corporate web site is still important. *New Media Age* (2005c) reported that Unilever is using the Internet to unify its brand worldwide, by re-launching its corporate site and 25 localised country web sites. The sites have been redesigned to reflect the company's mission statement: to meet everyday nutrition, hygiene and personal care needs through its products.

The new online image is also intended to make consumers aware that the sub-brands they buy all fall under the Unilever umbrella. The sites will present a clearer message that brands such as Dove, Knorr and Domestos originate from Unilever and will provide links to them. Unilever online communications manager, Tim Godbehere, who oversees its web strategy, explained to *New Media Age*: 'Everyone knows Hellmanns and Knorr, but not many are aware that Unilever is behind them. But only 10% of visitors to Unilever's corporate site were made up of the media and investors, even though it was designed to reach this audience. The rest were consumers. The Web sites are about getting consumers to make that connection and bringing Unilever to the forefront.'

Sources: *New Media Age* (2005c), *Revolution* (2003)

Questions

1 Summarise how Unilever and its agencies have used the marketing communications characteristics of digital media to support their brands.

2 Explain how Unilever can use specific online communications tools to reach different target audiences and achieve different objectives.

3 Select a Unilever brand not represented in the case and identify appropriate communications techniques to reach its audience.

Summary

1 Online promotion techniques include:

- *Search engine marketing* – search engine optimisation (SEO) improves position in the natural listings and pay-per-click marketing features a company in the sponsored listings.
- *Online PR* – including techniques such as link-building, blogging, RSS and reputation management.

- *Online partnerships* – including affiliate marketing (commission-based referral), co-branding and sponsorship.
- *Online advertising* – using a range of formats including banners, skyscrapers and rich media such as overlays.
- *E-mail marketing* – including rented lists, co-branded e-mails, event-triggered e-mails and ads in third-party e-newsletters for acquisition and e-newsletters and campaign e-mails to house lists.
- *Viral marketing* – developing great creative concepts which are transmitted by online word-of-mouth.

2 Offline promotion involves promoting the web site address, highlighting the value proposition of the web site and achieving web response through traditional media advertisements in print, or on television.

3 Interactive marketing communications must be developed as part of integrated marketing communications for maximum cost-effectiveness.

4 Key characteristics of interactive communications are the combination of push and pull media, user-submitted content, personalisation, flexibility and of course interactivity to create a dialogue with consumers.

5 Objectives for interactive communications include direct sales for transactional sites, but they also indirectly support brand awareness, favourability and purchase intent.

6 Important decisions in the communications mix introduced by digital media include:

- The balance between spend on media and creative for digital assets and ad executions
- The balance between spend in traditional and offline communications
- The balance between investment in continuous and campaign-based digital activity
- The balance of investment in different interactive communications tools.

Exercises

Self-assessment exercises

1 Briefly explain and give examples of online promotion and offline promotion techniques.

2 Explain the different types of payment model for banner advertising.

3 Which factors are important in governing a successful online banner advertising campaign?

4 How can a company promote itself through a search engine web site?

5 Explain the value of co-branding.

6 Explain how an online loyalty scheme may work.

7 How should web sites be promoted offline?

8 What do you think the relative importance of these Internet-based advertising techniques would be for an international chemical manufacturer?

(a) Banner advertising.
(b) Reciprocal links.
(c) E-mail.

Essay and discussion questions

1 Discuss the analogy of Berthon et al. (1998) that effective Internet promotion is similar to a company exhibiting at an industry trade show attracting visitors to its stand.

2 Discuss the merits of the different models of paying for banner advertisements on the Internet for both media owners and companies placing advertisements.

3 'Online promotion must be integrated with offline promotion.' Discuss.

4 Compare the effectiveness of different methods of online advertising including banner advertisements, e-mail inserts, site co-branding and sponsorship.

Examination questions

1 Give three examples of online promotion and briefly explain how they function.

2 Describe four different types of site on which online banner advertising for a car manufacturer's site could be placed.

3 Clickthrough is one measure of the effectiveness of banner advertising. Answer the following:

(a) What is clickthrough?
(b) Which factors are important in determining the clickthrough rate of a banner advertisement?
(c) Is clickthrough a good measure of the effectiveness of banner advertising?

4 What is meant by co-branding? Explain the significance of co-branding.

5 What are 'meta-tags'? How important are they in ensuring a web site is listed in a search engine?

6 Name three ways in which e-mail can be used for promotion of a particular web site page containing a special offer.

7 Give an example of an online loyalty scheme and briefly evaluate its strengths and weaknesses.

8 Which techniques can be used to promote a web site in offline media?

References

Agrawal, V., Arjona, V. and Lemmens, R. (2001) E-performance: the path to rational exuberance, *McKinsey Quarterly*, No. 1, 31–43.

Atlas DMT (2004) The Atlas Rank Report: How Search Engine Rank Impacts Traffic [not dated]. Atlas DMT Research (**www.atlassolutions.com**).

Berthon, P., Lane, N., Pitt, L. and Watson, R. (1998) The World Wide Web as an industrial marketing communications tool: models for the identification and assessment of opportunities, *Journal of Marketing Management*, 14, 691–704.

Berthon, P., Pitt, L. and Watson, R. (1996) Resurfing W³: research perspectives on marketing communication and buyer behaviour on the World Wide Web, *International Journal of Advertising*, 15, 287–301.

Bicknell, D. (2002) Banking on customer service, *e.Businessreview*, January, 21–2.

BrandNewWorld (2004) AOL research published at **www.aolbrandnewworld.co.uk**.

Branthwaite, A., Wood, K. and Schilling, M. (2000) The medium is part of the message – the role of media for shaping the image of a brand. *ARF/ESOMAR Conference, Rio de Janeiro, Brazil, 12–14 November*.

Cartellieri, C., Parsons, A., Rao, V. and Zeisser, M. (1997) The real impact of Internet advertising, *McKinsey Quarterly*, No. 3, 44–63.

Chaffey, D. (2006) *Total E-mail Marketing*, 2nd edn. Butterworth Heinemann, Elsevier, Oxford.

Crawshaw, P. (2004) Media neutral planning – what is it? Online article, Account Planning Group (www.apg.org.uk). No date given.

Deighton, J. (1996) The future of interactive marketing, *Harvard Business Review*, November–December, 151–62.

Dichter, E. (1966) How word-of-mouth advertising works, *Harvard Business Review*, 44 (November–December), 147–66.

Evans, P. and Wurster, T.S. (1999) Getting real about virtual commerce, *Harvard Business Review*, November, 84–94.

Godin, S. (2001) *Unleashing the Ideavirus*. Available online at: www.ideavirus.com.

Grehan, M. (2004) Increase your PR by increasing your PR. Article in E-marketing News e-newsletter, November. Source: www.e-marketing-news.co.uk/november.html#pr.

Hoffman, D.L. and Novak, T.P. (1996) Marketing in hypermedia computer-mediated environments: conceptual foundations, *Journal of Marketing*, 60 (July), 50–68.

Hoffman, D.L. and Novak, T.P. (1997) A new marketing paradigm for electronic commerce, *The Information Society*, Special issue on electronic commerce, 13 (Jan–Mar), 43–54.

Hoffman, D.L. and Novak, T.P. (2000) How to acquire customers on the web, *Harvard Business Review*, May–June, 179–88. Available online at: http://ecommerce.vanderbilt.edu/papers.html.

Hughes, A. (1999) Web Response – Modern 1:1 marketing. Database Marketing Institute article. www.dbmarketing.com/articles/Art196.htm.

iMediaConnection (2003) Interview with ING Direct VP of Marketing, Jurie Pietersie, www.mediaconnection.com/content/1333.asp.

IPR (2003) Unlocking the Potential of PR. A best practice report. *IPR and DTI*. Available from the Institute of PR (www.ipr.org.uk).

iProspect (2004) Search Behaviour Research Summary, Spring. Available at www.iprospect.com.

Janal, D. (1998) *Online Marketing Handbook: How to Promote, Advertise and Sell Your Products and Services on the Internet*. Van Nostrand Reinhold, New York.

Jenkins, F. (1995) *Public Relations Techniques*, 2nd edn. Butterworth Heinemann, Oxford.

Kemmler, T., Kubicová, M., Musslewhite, R. and Prezeau, R. (2001) E-performance II: the good, the bad and the merely average, *McKinsey Quarterly*, No. 3. Online only.

Kirby, J. (2003) Online viral marketing: next big thing or yesterday's fling? *New Media Knowledge*. Published online at www.newmediaknowledge.co.uk.

Kotler, P., Armstrong, G., Saunders, J. and Wong, V. (2001) *Principles of Marketing*, 3rd European edn. Financial Times/Prentice Hall, Harlow.

McGaffin, K. (2004) *Linking Matters. How to create an Effective Linking Strategy to Promote Your Website*. Published at www.linkingmatters.com.

New Media Age (2005a) Perfect match. By Greg Brooks, *New Media Age* 29 September. www.nma.co.uk.

New Media Age (2005b) Product placement. By Sean Hargrave, *New Media Age* 12 May.

New Media Age (2005c) Unilever unifies global brand under new sites. By Claire Armitt, *New Media Age*, October.

Novak, T. and Hoffman, D. (1997) New metrics for new media: towards the development of web measurement standards, *World Wide Web Journal*, 2(1), 213–46.

ORCI (1991) Word-of-mouth Drives E-commerce, Survey Summary, May. Opinion Research Corporation International, www.opinionresearch.com.

Parry, K. (1998) *Europe Gets Wired. A Survey of Internet Use in Great Britain, France and Germany, Research Report 1998*. KPMG Management Consulting, London.

Performance Research (2001) *Performance Research Study:'Mastering Sponsorship On-Line'*. www.performanceresearch.com/web-based-sponsorships.htm.

Peters, L. (1998) The new interactive media: one-to-one but to whom? *Marketing Intelligence and Planning*, 16(1), 22–30.

Pickton, A. and Broderick, D. (2001) *Integrated Marketing Communications*. Financial Times/Prentice Hall, Harlow.

Pincott, G. (2000) Web site promotion strategy. White paper from Millward Brown Intelliquest. Available online at www.intelliquest.com.

Poynter (2000) Eye Tracking Study (www.poynter.org/eyetrack2000).

PRCA (2005) Website definition of PR. The Public Relationships Consultants Association, **www.prca.org.uk**.

Ranchhod, A., Gurau, C. and Lace, J. (2002) On-line messages: developing an integrated communications model for biotechnology companies, *Qualitative Market Research: An International Journal*, 5(1), 6–18.

Revolution (2003) Persil Gets Playful, *Revolution*, 1 February, Casper Van Vark.

Rogers, E. (1983) *Diffusion of Innovations*, 3rd edn. Free Press, New York.

Rowley, J. (2001) Remodelling marketing communications in an Internet environment, *Internet Research: Electronic Networking Applications and Policy*, 11(3), 203–12.

Ryan, J. and Whiteman, N. (2000) Online Advertising Glossary: Sponsorships. *ClickZ Media Selling channel*. 15 May.

Schramm, W. (1955) How communication works. In *The Process and Effects of Mass Communications*, W. Schramm (ed.), pp. 3–26. University of Illinois Press, Urbana, IL.

Schultz, D. and Schultz, H. (2004). *Integrated Marketing Communications: the Next Generation*. Wiley, New York.

Sissors, J., and Baron, R. (2002) *Advertising Media Planning*, 6th edn. McGraw-Hill, Chicago.

Smith, P.R. and Chaffey, D. (2005) *E-marketing Excellence: at the Heart of E-business*, 2nd edn. Butterworth Heinemann Elsevier, Oxford.

Statmarket (2003) Statmarket press release: search engine referrals nearly double worldwide, according to WebSiteStory, 12 March. Available online at **www.statmarket.com**.

Tapp, A. (2005) Clearing up media neutral planning. *Interactive Marketing*, 6(3), 216–21.

van Doren, D., Flechner, D. and Green-Adelsberger, K. (2000) Promotional strategies on the world wide web, *Journal of Marketing Communications*, 6, 21–35.

Varianini, V. and Vaturi, D. (2000) Marketing lessons from e-failures, *McKinsey Quarterly*, No. 4, 86–97.

Zeff, R. and Aronson, B. (2001) *Advertising on the Internet*, 3rd edn. Wiley, New York.

Further reading

Fill, C. (2005) *Marketing Communications – Contexts, Contents and Strategies*, 4th edn. Financial Times/Prentice Hall, Harlow. The entire book is recommended for its integration of theory, concepts and practice.

Novak, T. and Hoffman, D. (1997) New metrics for new media: towards the development of web measurement standards, *World Wide Web Journal*, 2(1), 213–46. This paper gives detailed, clear definitions of terms associated with measuring advertising effectiveness.

Zeff, R. and Aronson, B. (2001) *Advertising on the Internet*, 3rd edn. Wiley, New York. A comprehensive coverage of online banner advertising and measurement techniques and a more limited coverage of other techniques such as e-mail-based advertising.

Web links

General Internet-marketing-related e-mail newsletters and portals

- ClickZ (**www.clickz.com**). Has columns on e-mail marketing, e-mail marketing optimisation and e-mail marketing case studies.

- DaveChaffey.com (**www.davechaffey.com**). A blog of links and articles about developments in interactive communications structured according to the chapter in this book.

- E-consultancy.com (**www.e-consultancy.com**). Best practice sections on different e-communications tools and newsletter features interviews with e-commerce practitioners.

- Marketing Sherpa (**www.marketingsherpa.com**). Articles and links on Internet marketing communications including e-mail and online advertising.

- What's New in Marketing (**www.wnim.com**). A monthly newsletter from the Chartered Institute of Marketing including many e-marketing features.

E-mail-related links

- Direct Marketing Association UK (**www.dma.org.uk**). Best practice guidelines and benchmarks of response rates.
- DoubleClick (**www.doubleclick.net**). An e-mail broadcaster and advertising network worldwide, with offices in many countries. Its site provides research of ad and e-mail marketing response rates across its clients.

Internet-advertising-related links

- Atlas (**www.atlasdmt.com**). Ad-serving and tracking provider with research about ad effectiveness.
- ClickZ (**www.clickz.com/experts**). An excellent collection of articles on online marketing communications. US-focused. Relevant sections for this chapter include: Affiliate marketing, Advertising technology, E-mail marketing, Media buying.
- eMarketer (**www.emarketer.com**). Includes reports on media spend based on compilations of other analysts.
- EyeBlaster (**www.eyeblaster.com**) is one of the main providers of rich media ad serving technologies. Its galleries have good examples.
- iMediaConnection (**www.imediaconnection.com**). Media site reporting on best practice in online advertising.
- Internet Advertising Bureau (**www.iab.net**). The widest range of studies about Internet advertising effectiveness. In UK: **www.iabuk.net**. Internet Advertising Bureau XMOS microsite (**www.iab.net/xmos**)
- Tangozebra (**www.tangozebra.co.uk**) is a UK-based provider of ad-serving technology which showcases many of the most recent ad campaigns by industry category.

Search-engine-related links

- Searchenginewatch (**www.searchenginewatch.com**). A complete resource on SEO and PPC marketing.
- Webmasterworld (**www.webmasterworld.com**). A forum, where search practitioners discuss best practice.

9

Maintaining and monitoring the online presence

Learning objectives

After reading this chapter, the reader should be able to:

● Identify the tasks necessary when managing an online presence

● Understand terms used to measure and improve site effectiveness

● Develop an appropriate process to collect measures for Internet marketing effectiveness

Questions for marketers

Key questions for marketing managers related to this chapter are:

● How much resource do I need to put into maintaining and monitoring the site?

● What processes should I use to maintain the web site?

● How do I measure the effectiveness of web marketing?

Links to other chapters

This chapter should be read in conjunction with these chapters:

➤ Chapter 4 describes the development of an Internet marketing strategy. The aim of measurement is to quantify whether the objectives of this strategy have been achieved

➤ Chapter 7 describes how to set up a web site, and should be read before this chapter to introduce the reader to concepts of web site development

➤ Chapter 8 describes methods of promoting a web site. It should be read before this chapter since one aspect of measuring the effectiveness of Internet marketing is aimed at assessing the different promotional methods

Introduction

Companies that have a successful approach to online marketing often seem to share a common characteristic. They attach great importance and devote resources to monitoring the success of their online marketing and putting in place the processes to continuously improve the performance of their digital channels. This culture of measurement is visible in the UK bank Alliance and Leicester, which in 2004 reported that they spent over 20% of their £80 million marketing communications budget on online marketing. Stephen Leonard, head of e-commerce, described their process as 'Test, Learn, Refine' (*Revolution*, 2004). Graeme Findlay, senior manager, customer acquision of e-commerce at A&L explains further:

> *Our online approach is integrated with our offline brand and creative strategy, with a focus on direct, straightforward presentation of strong value-led messages. Everything we do online, including creative, is driven by an extensive and dynamic testing process.*

Web analytics

Techniques used to assess and improve the contribution of e-marketing to a business, including reviewing traffic volume, referrals, clickstreams, online reach data, customer satisfaction surveys, leads and sales.

Seth Romanow, Director of Customer Knowledge at Hewlett-Packard, speaking at the 2004 E-metrics summit, described their process as 'Measure, Report, Analyse, Optimize'. Amazon refers to their approach as 'The Culture of Metrics' (see Case Study 9). Jim Sterne, who convenes an annual event devoted to improving online performance (**www.emetrics.org**), has summarised his view on the required approach in his book *Web Metrics* (Sterne, 2002) as 'TIMITI', which stands for Try It! Measure It! Tweak It!, i.e. online content should be reviewed and improved continuously rather than as a periodic or ad-hoc process. The importance of defining an appropriate approach to measurement and improvement is such that the term 'web analytics' has developed to describe this key Internet marketing activity. A web analytics association (**www.waa.org**) has been developed by vendors, consultants and researchers in this area. Eric Petersen, an analyst specialising in web analytics, defines it as follows:

> *Web analytics is the assessment of a variety of data, including web traffic, web-based transactions, web server performance, usability studies, user submitted information [i.e. surveys], and related sources to help create a generalised understanding of the visitor experience online.*

Petersen (2004)

You can see that in addition to what are commonly referred to as 'site statistics' about web traffic, sales transactions, usability and researching customers' views through surveys are also included. We believe, though, that the definition can be improved further – it suggests analysis for the sake of it – whereas the business purpose of analytics should be emphasised. The definition could also refer to comparison of site visitor volumes and demographics relative to competitors using panels and ISP collected data. Our definition is:

> *Web analytics is the customer-centred evaluation of the effectiveness of Internet-based marketing in order to improve the business contribution of online channels to an organisation.*

A more recent definition from the Web Analytics Association (WAA, **www.webanalyticsassociation.org**) in 2005 is:

> *Web Analytics is the objective tracking, collection, measurement, reporting and analysis of quantitative Internet data to optimize websites and web marketing initiatives.*

To succeed in a measured approach to improving results from Internet marketing we suggest that there are four main prerequisites, which are broken down as shown in Figure 9.1 into the quality of the web analytics processes including defining the right improvement measures and purchasing the right tools and the management processes such as putting in place a process where staff review results and then modify their marketing activities accordingly. In this chapter, we will review both approaches.

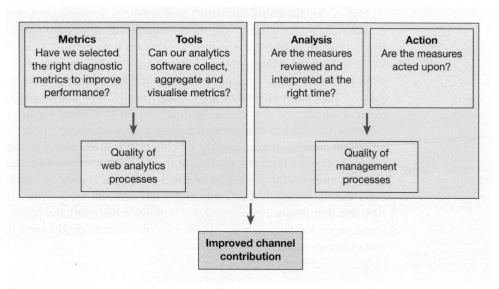

Figure 9.1 Criteria for improving performance from Internet marketing

This chapter is in two parts, the first part is about performance management, where we review the approach to improving performance through assessing appropriate measures, tools and the right process to apply them as suggested by Figure 9.1. In the second part, we review some of the issues involved with maintaining an online presence, which again involves looking at the measures, tools and process for keeping a web site up-to-date.

Performance management for Internet marketing

To improve results for any aspect of any business, performance management is vital. As Bob Napier, Chief Information Office, Hewlett-Packard was reported to have said back in the 1960s,

You can't manage what you can't measure.

The processes and systems intended to monitor and improve the performance of an organisation and specific management activities such as Internet marketing are widely known as 'performance management systems' and are based on the study of performance measurement systems.

Many organisations now have an established online presence, but there are many unanswered questions about the process by which the marketing performance of this presence is evaluated and how it is modified with a view to improving its performance. Adams et al. (2000), for example, asked managers to name their priorities for improvements to e-business performance measurement systems. Results differed for different types of organisation, reflecting the stage of evolution in their measurement. For bricks-and-mortar

Performance management system

A process used to evaluate and improve the efficiency and effectiveness of an organisation and its processes.

Performance measurement system

The process by which metrics are defined, collected, disseminated and actioned.

417

companies, developing or introducing a more comprehensive measurement system and enhancing analysis capabilities to establish what really drives business performance was most important. For clicks-and-mortar, integrating new systems with legacy systems and benchmarking against best practice were most important. Finally, dot-coms, as start-ups, were concerned with improving clickstream analysis and customer tracking and profiling and improving the entire company's performance measurement system.

Although we have stated that measurement is an important part of maintaining a web site, it is worth noting that the reality is that measurement is often neglected when a web site is first created. Measurement is often highlighted as an issue once the first version of a site has been 'up and running' for a few months, and employees start to ask questions such as 'How many customers are visiting our site, how many sales are we achieving as a result of our site and how can we improve the site to achieve a return on investment?' The consequence of this is that performance measurement is something that is often built into an online presence retrospectively. Of course, it is preferable if measurement is built into site management from the start since then a more accurate approach can be developed and it is more readily possible to apply a technique known as 'design for analysis' (DFA). Here, the site is designed so companies can better understand the types of audience and their decision points. For example, for Dell (**www.dell.com**), the primary navigation on the home page is by business type. This is a simple example of DFA since it enables Dell to estimate the proportion of different audiences to their site and, at the same time, connect them with relevant content. Other examples of DFA include:

Design for analysis (DFA)
The required measures from a site are considered during design to better understand the audience of a site and their decision points.

- Breaking up a long page or form into different parts, so you can see which parts people are interested in.
- A URL policy (see Chapter 8) used to recommend entry pages for printed material.
- Group content by audience type or buying decision and setting up content groups of related content within web analytics systems.
- Measure attrition at different points in a customer journey, e.g. exit points on a five-page buying cycle.
- A single exit page to linked sites.

Internet marketing metrics
Measures that indicate the effectiveness of Internet marketing activities in meeting customer, business and marketing objectives.

In this section, we will review approaches to performance management by examining three key elements of an Internet marketing measurement system. These are, first, the *process* for improvement, secondly, the measurement framework which specifies groups of relevant Internet marketing metrics and, finally, an assessment of the suitability of tools and techniques for collecting, analysing, disseminating and actioning results. We will review four stages of creating and implementing a performance management system.

Stage 1: Creating a performance management system

The essence of performance *management* is suggested by the definition for performance *measurement* used by Andy Neely and co-workers of Cranfield School of Management's Centre for Business Performance. They define performance measurement as

the process of quantifying the efficiency and effectiveness of past actions through acquisition, collation, sorting, analysis, interpretation and dissemination of appropriate data.

(Neely et al., 2002)

Performance management extends this definition to the process of analysis and actioning change in order to drive business performance and returns. Online marketers can apply many of the approaches of business performance management to Internet marketing. As you can see from the definition, performance is measured primarily

Effectiveness

Meeting process objectives, delivering the required outputs and outcomes. 'Doing the right thing.'

Efficiency

Minimising resources or time needed to complete a process. 'Doing the thing right.'

through information on process effectiveness and efficiency as introduced in Chapter 4 in the section on objective setting, where we noted that it is important to include both effectiveness and efficiency measures.

The need for a structured performance management process is clear if we examine the repercussions if an organisation does not have one. These include: poor linkage of measures with strategic objectives or even absence of objectives; key data not collected; data inaccuracies; data not disseminated or analysed; or no corrective action. Many of the barriers to improvement of measurement systems reported by respondents in Adams et al. (2000) also indicate the lack of an effective process. The barriers can be grouped as follows:

● *senior management myopia* – performance measurement not seen as a priority, not understood or targeted at the wrong targets – reducing costs rather than improving performance;
● *unclear responsibilities for delivering and improving the measurement system*;
● *resourcing issues* – lack of time (perhaps suggesting lack of staff motivation), the necessary technology and integrated systems;
● *data problems* – data overload or of poor quality, limited data for benchmarking.

These barriers are reinforced by the survey by Cutler and Sterne (2000) which describes the main obstacles to metrics development as lack of qualified personnel (31%), data overload (19%) and lack of technical resources (software) (19%).

To avoid these pitfalls, a coordinated, structured measurement process such as that shown in Figure 9.2 is required. Figure 9.2 indicates four key stages in a measurement process. These were defined as key aspects of annual plan control by Kotler (1997). Stage 1 is a goal-setting stage where the aims of the measurement system are defined – this will usually take the strategic Internet marketing objectives as an input to the measurement system. The aim of the measurement system will be to assess whether these goals are achieved and specify corrective marketing actions to reduce variance between target and actual key performance indicators. Stage 2, performance measurement, involves collecting data to determine the different metrics that are part of a measurement framework as discussed in the next section. Stage 3, performance diagnosis, is the analysis of results to understand the reasons for variance from objectives (the 'performance gap' of Friedman and Furey, 1999) and selection of marketing solutions to reduce variance. The purpose of stage 4, corrective action, according to Wisner and Fawcett (1991), is

> to identify competitive position, locate problem areas, assist the firm in updating strategic objectives and making tactical decisions to achieve these objectives and supply feedback after the decisions are implemented.

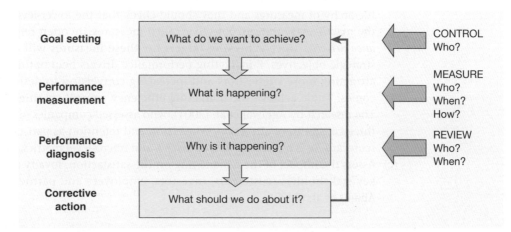

Figure 9.2 A summary of the performance measurement process

In an Internet marketing context, corrective action is the implementation of these solutions as updates to web site content, design and associated marketing communications. At this stage the continuous cycle repeats, possibly with modified goals. Bourne et al. (2000) and Plant (2000) suggest that in addition to reviewing objectives, the suitability of the metrics should also be reviewed and revised.

Measurement is not something that can occur on an ad-hoc basis because if it is left to the individual they may forget to collect the data needed. A 'measurement culture' is one in which each employee is aware of the need to collect data on how well the company is performing and on how well it is meeting its customers' needs.

Stage 2: Defining the performance metrics framework

Measurement for assessing the effectiveness of Internet marketing can be thought of as answering these questions:

1　Are corporate objectives identified in the Internet marketing strategy being met?
2　Are marketing objectives defined in the Internet marketing strategy and plan achieved?
3　Are marketing communications objectives identified in the Internet marketing plan achieved? How efficient are the different promotional techniques used to attract visitors to a site?

These measures can also be related to the different levels of marketing control specified by Kotler (1997). These include strategic control (question 1), profitability control (question 1), annual-plan control (question 2) and efficiency control (question 3).

Efficiency measures are more concerned with minimising the costs of online marketing while maximising the returns for different areas of focus such as acquiring visitors to a web site, converting visitors to outcome or achieving repeat business.

Chaffey (2000) suggests that organisations define a measurement framework which defines groupings of specific metrics used to assess Internet marketing performance. He suggests that suitable measurement frameworks will fulfil these criteria:

(a)　Include both macro-level effectiveness metrics which assess whether strategic goals are achieved and indicate to what extent e-marketing contributes to the business (revenue contribution and return on investment). This criterion covers the different levels of marketing control specified by Kotler (1997), including strategic control, profitability control and annual-plan control.

(b)　Include micro-level metrics which assess the efficiency of e-marketing tactics and implementation. Wisner and Fawcett (1991) note that typically organisations use a hierarchy of measures and they should check that the lower-level measures support the macro-level strategic objectives. Such measures are often referred to as *'performance drivers'*, since achieving targets for these measures will assist in achieving strategic objectives. E-marketing performance drivers help optimise e-marketing by attracting more site visitors and increasing conversion to desired marketing outcomes. These achieve the marketing efficiency control specified by Kotler (1997). The research by Agrawal et al. (2001), who assessed companies on metrics defined in three categories of attraction, conversion and retention as part of an e-performance scorecard, uses a combination of macro- and micro-level metrics.

(c)　Assess the impact of the e-marketing on the satisfaction, loyalty and contribution of key stakeholders (customers, investors, employees and partners) as suggested by Adams et al. (2000).

(d) The framework must be flexible enough to be applied to different forms of online presence, whether business-to-consumer, business-to-business, not-for-profit or transactional e-tail, CRM-oriented or brand-building. Much discussion of e-marketing measurement is limited to a transactional e-tail presence. Adams et al. (2000) note that a 'one-size-fits-all' framework is not desirable.

(e) Enable comparison of performance of different e-channels with other channels as suggested by Friedman and Furey (1999).

(f) The framework can be used to assess e-marketing performance against competitors' or out-of-sector best-practice.

When identifying metrics it is common practice to apply the widely used SMART mnemonic and it is also useful to consider three levels – business measures, marketing measures and specific Internet marketing measures (see objective setting section in Chapter 4).

There are a framework of measures, shown in Figure 9.3, which can be applied to a range of different companies. Metrics for the categories are generated as objectives from Internet marketing planning which then need to be monitored to assess the success of strategy and its implementation. Objectives can be devised in a top-down fashion, starting with strategic objectives for business contribution and marketing outcomes leading to tactical objectives for customer satisfaction, behaviour and site promotion. An alternative perspective is bottom-up – success in achieving objectives for site promotion, on-site customer behaviour and customer satisfaction lead sequentially to achieving objectives for marketing outcomes and business contribution.

The WebInsights™ diagnostics framework includes these key metrics:

1. **Business contribution:**
   Online revenue contribution (direct and indirect), category penetration, costs and profitability.

2. **Marketing outcomes:**
   Leads, sales, service contacts, conversion and retention efficiencies.

3. **Customer satisfaction:**
   Site usability, performance/availability, contact strategies. Opinions, attitudes and brand impact.

4. **Customer behaviour (web analytics):**
   Profiles, customer orientation (segmentation), usability, clickstreams and site actions.

5. **Site promotion:**
   Attraction efficiency. Referrer efficiency, cost of acquisition and reach. Search engine visibility and link building. E-mail marketing. Integration.

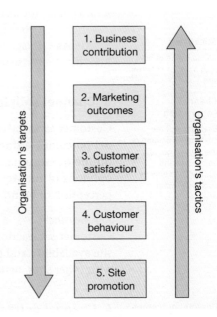

Figure 9.3 The five diagnostic categories for e-marketing measurement

Channel promotion
Measures that assess why customers visit a site – which adverts they have seen, which sites they have been referred from.

Referrer
The site that a visitor previously visited before following a link.

1 Channel promotion

These measures consider where the web site users originate – online or offline, and what are the sites or offline media that have prompted their visit. Log file analysis can be used to assess which intermediary sites customers are referred from and even which keywords they typed into search engines when trying to locate product information. Promotion is successful if traffic is generated that meets objectives of volume and quality. Quality will be determined by whether visitors are in the target market and have a propensity for the service offered (conversion rates for different referrers). Overall hits or page views are not enough – inspection of log files for companies shows that a high proportion of visitors get no further than the home page! Differences in costs of acquiring customers via different channels also need to be assessed.

Key measure:
Referral mix. For each referral source such as offline or banner ads online it should be possible to calculate:

● percentage of all referrals (or visitors);
● cost of acquisition;
● contribution to sales or other outcomes.

2 Channel buyer behaviour

Channel buyer behaviour

Describes which content is visited and the time and duration.

Once customers have been attracted to the site we can monitor content accessed, when they visit and how long they stay, and whether this interaction with content leads to satisfactory marketing outcomes such as new leads or sales. If visitors are incentivised to register on-site it is possible to build up profiles of behaviour for different segments. It is also important to recognise return visitors for whom cookies or login are used.

Key ratios are:

Bounce rates for different pages, i.e. proportion of single page visits

Stickiness

An indication of how long a visitor stays on site.

	Home page views/all page views e.g.	20% = (2358/11 612)
Stickiness	Page views/visitor sessions e.g.	6% = 11 612/2048
Repeats	Visitor sessions/visitors e.g.	2% = 2048/970

3 Channel satisfaction

Channel satisfaction

Evaluation of the customer's opinion of the service quality on the site and supporting services such as e-mail.

Customer satisfaction with the online experience is vital in achieving the desired channel outcomes, although it is difficult to set specific objectives. Online methods such as online questionnaires, focus groups and interviews can be used to assess customers' opinions of the web site content and customer service and how it has affected overall perception of brand.

Key measure:
Customer satisfaction indices. These are discussed in Chapter 7 and include ease of use, site availability and performance, and e-mail response. To compare customer satisfaction with other sites, benchmarking services can be used.

4 Channel outcomes

Channel outcomes

Record customer actions taken as a consequence of a visit to a site.

Conversion rate

Percentage of site visitors who perform a particular action such as making a purchase.

Traditional marketing objectives such as number of sales, number of leads, conversion rates and targets for customer acquisition and retention should be set and then compared to other channels. Dell Computer (**www.dell.com**) records on-site sales and also orders generated as a result of site visits, but placed by phone. This is achieved by monitoring calls to a specific phone number unique to the site.

Key measure:
Channel contribution (direct and indirect).

A widely used method of assessing channel outcomes is to review the conversion rate, which gives an indication of the percentage of site visitors who take a particular outcome. For example:

Conversion rate, visitors to purchase = 2% (10 000 visitors, of which 200 make purchases).
Conversion rate, visitors to registration = 5% (10 000 visitors, of which 500 register).

Attrition rate
Percentage of site visitors who are lost at each stage in making a purchase.

A related concept is the attrition rate which describes how many visitors are lost at each stage of visiting a site. Figure 9.4 shows that for a set time period, only a proportion of site visitors will make their way to product information, a small proportion will add an item to a basket and a smaller proportion still will actually make the purchase. A key feature of e-commerce sites is that there is a high attrition rate between a customer adding an item to a basket and subsequently making a purchase. It is surmised that this is due to fears about credit card security, and that customers are merely experimenting.

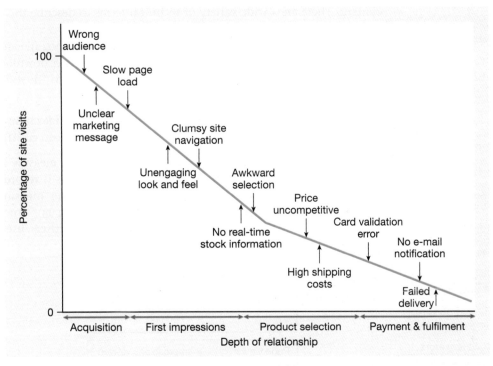

Figure 9.4 Attrition through e-commerce site activities

Channel profitability
The profitability of the web site, taking into account revenue and cost and discounted cash flow.

5 Channel profitability

A contribution to business profitability is always the ultimate aim of e-commerce. To assess this, leading companies set an Internet contribution target of achieving a certain proportion of sales via the channel. When easyJet (**www.easyjet.com**) launched its e-commerce facility in 1998, it set an Internet contribution target of 30% by 2000. They put the resources and communications plan in place to achieve this and their target was reached in 1999. Assessing contribution is more difficult for a company that cannot sell products online, but the role of the Internet in influencing purchase should be assessed. Discounted cash flow techniques are used to assess the rate of return over time.

Stage 3: Tools and techniques for collecting metrics and summarising results

Techniques to collect metrics include the collection of site-visitor activity data such as that collected from site log-files, the collection of metrics about outcomes such as online sales or e-mail enquiries and traditional marketing research techniques such as questionnaires and focus groups which collect information on the customer's experience on the web site. We start by describing methods for collecting site-visitor activity data and then review more traditional techniques of market research which assess the customer experience.

Collecting site-visitor activity data

Site-visitor activity data

Information on content and services accessed by e-commerce site visitors.

Hit

Recorded for each graphic or text file requested from a web server. It is not a reliable measure for the number of people viewing a page.

Log file analyser

A separate program such as WebTrends that is used to summarise the information on customer activity in a log file.

Page impression

A more reliable measure than a hit, denoting one person viewing one page.

Unique visitors

Individual visitors to a site measured through cookies or IP addresses on an individual computer.

Site-visitor activity data captured in web analytics systems records the number of visitors on the site and the paths or clickstreams they take through the site as they visit different content. There are a wide variety of technical terms to describe this activity data which Internet marketers need to be conversant with.

Traditionally this information has been collected using log file analysis web analytics tools. The server-based log file is added to every time a user downloads a piece of information (a hit) and is analysed using a log file analyser as illustrated by Figure 1.14. Examples of transactions within a log file are:

www.davechaffey.com – [05/Oct/2006:00:00:49 -000] 'GET /index.html HTTP/1.0' 200 33362
www.davechaffey.com – [05/Oct/2006:00:00:49 -000] 'GET /logo.gif HTTP/1.0' 200 54342

Despite their wide use in the media, hits are not a useful measure of web site effectiveness since if a page consists of 10 graphics, plus text, this is recorded as 11 hits. Page impressions or page views and unique visitors are better measures of site activity. Auditing companies such as ABC electronic (**www.abce.org.uk**), which audit sites for the purpose of proving the number of visitors to a site to advertisers, use unique visitors and page impression as the main measures.

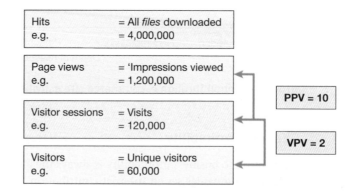

Figure 9.5 Examples of different measures of visitor volume to a web site

An example of visitor volume to a web site using different measures based on real, representative data for one month is presented in Figure 9.5. You can see how hits are much higher than page views and unique visitors and are quite misleading in terms of the 'opportunities to see' a message. We can also learn from the ratio between some of these measures – the figure indicates:

- *Pages per visit (PPV)* – the average number of pages viewed per visitor to a site (this is indicative of engagement with a site since the longer a visitor stays on a 'sticky site', the higher this value will be). PPV is a more accurate indication of stickiness than duration on a site in minutes since this figure is skewed upwards by visitors who arrive on a site and are inactive before their session times out at 30 minutes.
- *Visits per (unique) visitor (VPV)* – this suggests the frequency of site visits. Readers will realise that this value is dependent on the period that data are collected over. These data are reported for a month during which time one would not expect many returning visitors. So it is often more relevant to present these data across a quarter or a year.

Other information giving detailed knowledge of customer behaviour that can be reported by any web analytics package include:

- top pages;
- entry and exit pages;
- path or clickstream analysis showing the sequence of pages viewed;
- country of visitor origin (actually dependent on the location of their ISP);
- browser and operating system used;
- referring URL and domain (where the visitor came from).

Comparing apples to oranges?

With hundreds of different web analytics tools being used on different sites, it is important that there are standards for measuring visitor volumes. In particular, there are different techniques for measuring unique visitors which can be measured through IP addresses, but this is more accurate if it is combined with cookies and browser types. International standards bodies such as the Web Analytics Association (**www.webanalyticsassociation.org**) and UK organisations such as ABCelectronic (**www.abce.org.uk**) and JICWEB (**www.jicwebs.org**) have worked to standardise the meaning and data collection methods for different measures. See Table 9.1 or visit these sites for the latest precise definition of the terms in this section. Media buyers are particularly interested in accurate audited figures of media sites and organisations such as ABCelectronic are important for this.

Table 9.1 Terminology for key web site volume measures

Measure	Measure	Definition
1 How many? 'audience reach'	Unique users	A unique and valid identifier [for a site visitor]. Sites may use (i) IP + User – Agent, (ii) Cookie and/or (iii) Registration ID
2 How often? 'frequency metric'	Visit	A series of one or more page impressions, served to one user, which ends when there is a gap of 30 minutes or more between successive page impressions for that user
3 How busy? 'volume metric'	Page impression	A file, or combination of files, sent to a valid user as a result of that user's request being received by the server
4 What see?	Ad impressions	A file or a combination of files sent to a valid user as an individual advertisement as a result of that user's request being received by the server
5 What do?	Ad clicks	An ad impression clicked on by a valid user

Source: ABCe (www.abce.org.uk)

Collecting site outcome data

'Site outcome data' refers to a customer performing a significant action which is of value to the marketer. This is usually a transaction that is recorded. It involves more than downloading a web page, and is proactive. Key marketing outcomes include:

- registration to site or subscriptions to an e-mail newsletter;
- requests for further information such as a brochure or a request for a callback from a customer service representative;
- responding to a promotion such as an online competition;
- a sale influenced by a visit to the site;
- a sale on-site.

When reviewing the efficiency of the different e-communications tools referred to in Chapter 8, such as search engine marketing, online advertising and affiliate marketing, it is important to assess the outcomes generated. Measuring quantity of clickthroughs to a site is simplistic, it is conversion to these outcomes which should be used to assess the quality of traffic. To achieve this 'end-to-end' tracking, two main tools are used, first using cookies to identify the visitor across different sessions and secondly using tracking IDs within URLs to identify a user session.

An important aspect of measures collected offline is that the marketing outcomes may be recorded in different media according to how the customer has performed mixed-mode buying. For example, a new customer enquiry could arrive by e-mail, fax or phone. Similarly, an order could be placed online using a credit card, or by phone, fax or post. For both these cases what we are really interested in is whether the web site influenced the enquiry or sale. This is a difficult question to answer unless steps are put in place to answer it. For all contact points with customers staff need to be instructed to ask how they found out about the company, or made their decision to buy. Although this is valuable information it is often intrusive, and a customer placing an order may be annoyed to be asked such a question. To avoid alienating the customer, these questions about the role of the web site can be asked later, perhaps when the customer is filling in a registration or warranty card. Another device that can be used to identify use of the web site is to use a specific phone number on the web site, so when a customer rings to place an order, it is known that the number was obtained from the web site. This approach is used by Dell on its site.

It will be apparent that to collect some of these measures we may need to integrate different information systems. Where customers provide details such as an e-mail address and name in response to an offer, these are known as 'leads' and they may need to be passed on to a direct-sales team or recorded in a customer relationship management system. For full visibility of customer behaviour, the outcomes from these systems need to be integrated with the site-visitor activity data.

Selecting a web analytics tool

There are a bewildering range of hundreds of web analytics tools, varying from shareware packages with often primitive reporting through to complex systems which may cost hundreds of thousands of dollars a year for a popular site. Given this, it is difficult for the Internet marketer to select the best tool or tools to meet their needs. One of the first issues to consider is the different types of measures that need to be integrated within the performance management system. Figure 9.6 gives an indication of the types of data that need to be integrated; these include:

1 Operational data

Data would be ideally collected and reported within a single tool at this level, but unfortunately to obtain the best reporting it is often necessary to resort to four different types of tools/data source:

- Referrer data from acquisition campaigns such as search marketing or online advertising. Separate tools are often also required for retention e-mail marketing.
- Site-centric data about visitor volume and clickstream behaviour on the web site.
- Customer response and profile data.
- Transactional data about leads and sales which are often obtained from separate legacy systems.

2 Tactical data

These data are typically models of required response such as:

- Reach models with online audience share data for different demographic groupings from sources such as Hitwise and Netratings.
- Lifetime value models which are created to assess profitability of visitors to the site from different sources and so need to integrate with operational data.

3 Strategic data

Performance management systems for senior managers will give the big picture presented as scorecards or dashboards showing the contribution of digital channels to the organisation in terms of sales, revenue and profitability for different products. These data indicate trends and relative performance within the company and to competitors such that the Internet marketing strategy can be reviewed for effectiveness. The efficiency of the processes may be indicated, through, for example, the cost of acquisition of customers in different markets and their conversion and retention rates.

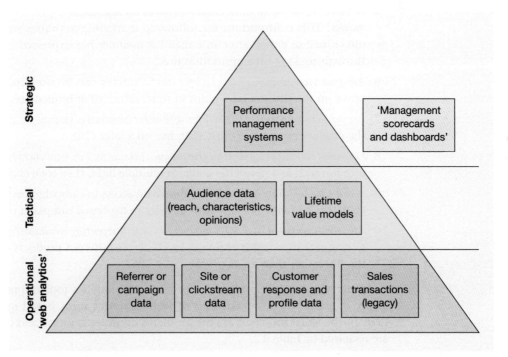

Figure 9.6 Different types of data within a performance management system for Internet marketing

So, an important requirement of a web analytics tool is that it should seek to integrate all these different data sources. The other main requirements of a web analytics tool to consider include:

● Reporting of marketing performance (many are technical tools which do not clearly report on results from a marketing perspective);
● Accuracy of technique;
● Analysis tools;
● Integration with other marketing information systems (export);
● Ease of use and configuration;
● Cost, which often varies according to site visitor volumes and number of system users;
● Suitability for reporting on e-marketing campaigns.

Many online tracking tools were originally developed to report on the performance of the site and the pages accessed rather than specifically to report on e-marketing campaigns. It is therefore important that companies have an excellent campaign reporting capability. When online marketers are reviewing the capability of tools, they should be able to answer these questions:

1 *Can the tool track through from point entry on site through to outcome?* For example, to outcomes such as registration, lead or sale? Integration with data to reflect actual leads or sales in a legacy system should also be reported.

2 *Can the tool track and compare a range of online media types?* These were explained in Chapter 8, for example, interactive (banner) ads, affiliates, e-mail marketing, natural and paid search.

3 *Can return-on-investment models be constructed?* For example, by entering costs and profitability for each product?

4 *Can reports be produced at both a detailed level and a summary level?* This enables comparison of performance for different campaigns and different parts of the business.

5 Is there *capability to track clickthroughs at an individual respondent level for e-mail campaigns?* This is important for follow-up marketing activities such as a phone call, direct mail or e-mail after an e-mail list member has expressed interest in a product through clicking on a promotion link.

6 *Are post-view responses tracked for ads?* Cookies can be used to assess visitors who arrive on the site at a later point in time, rather than immediately.

7 *Are post-click responses tracked for affiliates?* Similarly, visitors from affiliates may buy the product not on their first visit, but on a later visit.

8 *Do e-mail campaign summaries give unique clicks as well as total clicks?* If an e-mail communication such as a newsletter contains multiple links, then total clicks will be higher.

9 *Is real-time reporting available?* Is immediate access to campaign performance data available (this is usually possible with browser or tag-based campaign tracking solutions)?

10 *Are cross-campaign and cross-product or content reporting available?* Is it readily possible to compare campaigns and sales levels across different products or different parts of the site rather than an aggregate.

Accuracy is another important aspect of web analytics tool and managers need to be aware of some of the weaknesses of web analytics tools based on log file analysis. Perhaps the worst problems are the problems of undercounting and overcounting. These are reviewed in Table 9.2.

Table 9.2 Inaccuracies caused by server-based log file analysis

Sources of undercounting	Sources of overcounting
Caching in user's web browsers (when a user accesses a previously accessed file, it is loaded from the user's cache on their PC)	Frames (a user viewing a framed page with three frames will be recorded as three page impressions on a server-based system)
Caching on proxy servers (proxy servers are used within organisations or ISPs to reduce Internet traffic by storing copies of frequently used pages)	Spiders and robots (traversing of a site by spiders from different search engines is recorded as page impressions. These spiders can be excluded, but this is time-consuming)
Firewalls (these do not usually exclude page impressions, but they usually assign a single IP address for the user of the page, rather than referring to an individual's PC)	Executable files (these can also be recorded as hits or page impressions unless excluded)
Dynamically generated pages, generated 'on the fly', are difficult to assess with server-based log files	

A relatively new approach to the problems of undercounting and overcounting of server-based log file analysis described in Table 9.3 is to use a different *browser-based* or *tag-based* measurement system that records access to web pages every time a page is loaded into a user's web browser through running a short script, program or tag inserted into the web page. The key benefit of the browser-based approach is that potentially it is more accurate than server-based approaches. Figure 9.7 indicates how the browser-based approach works.

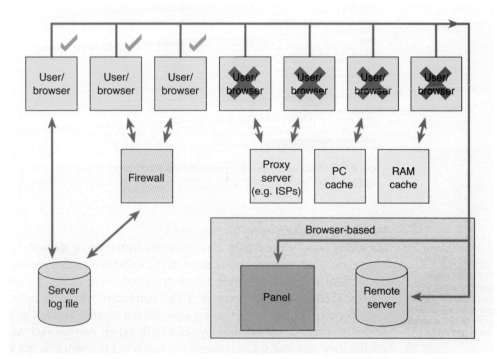

Figure 9.7 Differences between browser-based and server-based measurement systems

429

An example of the output reporting from a web analytics service is shown in Figure 9.8.

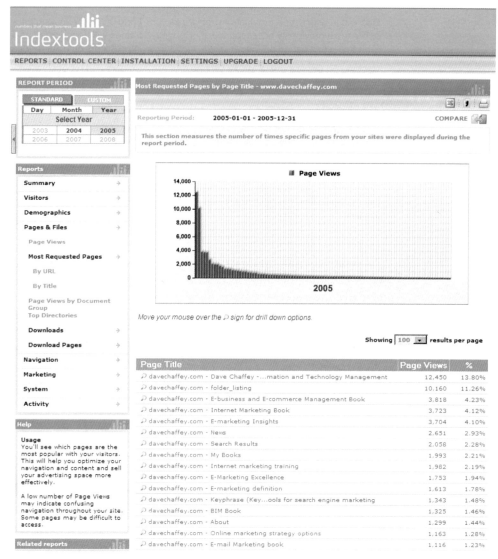

Figure 9.8 Web analytics tool Indextools used to assess page popularity in Dave Chaffey's site (www.davechaffey.com)

Marketing research using the Internet

Internet-based market research

The use of online questionnaires and focus groups to assess customer perceptions of a web site or broader marketing issues.

Marketing research will help determine the influence of the web site and related communications on customer perception of the company and its products and services. The options for conducting survey research include interviews, questionnaires and focus groups. Each of these techniques can be conducted offline or online. Offline methods are especially appropriate for companies with a smaller number of customers, who can be easily accessed, for example by sales staff. When surveys such as interviews are conducted they may not solely concern the impact of the web site, but questions about this could be part of a wider survey on customer perception of the company or its product.

Table 9.3 A comparison of different online metrics collection methods

Technique	Strengths	Weaknesses
1 Server-based log file analysis of site activity	• Directly records customer behaviour on site plus where they were referred from • Low cost	• Not based around marketing outcomes such as leads or sales • Size, even summaries may be over 50 pages long • Doesn't directly record channel satisfaction • Undercounting and overcounting • Misleading unless interpreted carefully
2 Browser-based site activity data	• Greater accuracy than server-based analysis • Counts all users, cf. panel approach	• Relatively expensive method • Similar weaknesses to server-based technique apart from accuracy • Limited demographic information
3 Panel activity and demographic data	• Provides competitor comparisons • Gives demographic profiling • Avoids undercounting and overcounting	• Depends on extrapolation from limited sample that may not be representative
4 Outcome data, e.g. enquiries, customer service e-mails	• Records marketing outcomes	• Difficulty of integrating data with other methods of data collection when collected manually or in other information systems
5 Online questionnaires. Customers are prompted randomly – every *n*th customer or after customer activity or by e-mail	• Can record customer satisfaction and profiles • Relatively cheap to create and analyse	• Difficulty of recruiting respondents who complete accurately • Sample bias – tend to be advocates or disgruntled customers who complete
6 Online focus groups. Synchronous recording	• Relatively cheap to create	• Difficult to moderate and coordinate • No visual cues, as from offline focus groups
7 Mystery shoppers. Example is customers are recruited to evaluate the site, e.g. www.emysteryshopper.com	• Structured tests give detailed feedback • Also tests integration with other channels such as e-mail and phone	• Relatively expensive • Sample must be representative

This type of measurement will use the traditional techniques of survey-based marketing research, which seek to collect primary data by gathering descriptive information about people's attitudes, preferences or buying behaviour.

The techniques that are appropriate for conducting this type of research will need to target a sample of people who actively use the web site. The best place to find these customers is on the web site! As a result, online focus groups and questionnaires administered online are becoming more common. The use of Internet-based market research is relatively new, so there is little research on what works, and what does not. However, some general comments can be made for the different survey types.

Questionnaires

Malhotra (1999) suggests that Internet surveys using questionnaires will increase in popularity since the cost is generally lower, they can be less intrusive, and they have the ability to target specific populations. Questionnaires often take the form of pop surveys. The key issues are:

431

A *Encouraging participation*. Techniques that can be used are:
- interruption on entry – a common approach where every 100th customer is prompted;
- continuous, for example click on the button to complete survey;
- on registration on site the customer can be profiled;
- after an activity such as sale or customer support the customer can be prompted for their opinion about the service;
- incentives and promotions (this can also be executed on independent sites);
- by e-mail (an e-mail prompt to visit a web site to fill in a survey or a simple e-mail survey).

B *Stages in execution*. It can be suggested that there are five stages to a successful questionnaire survey:
1 attract (button, pop-up, e-mail as above);
2 incentivise (prize or offer consistent with required sample and audience);
3 reassure (why the company is doing it – to learn, not too long and that confidentiality is protected);
4 design and execute (brevity, relevance, position);
5 follow-up (feedback).

C *Design*. Grossnickle and Raskin (2001) suggest the following approach to structuring questionnaires:
- easy, interesting questions first;
- cluster questions on same topic;
- flow topic from general to specific;
- flow topic from easier behavioural to more difficult attitudinal questions;
- easy questions last, e.g. demographics or offputting questions.

Typical questions that can be asked for determining the effectiveness of Internet marketing are:

1 *Who is visiting the site?* For example, role in buying decision? Online experience? Access location and speed? Demographics segment?
2 *Why are they visiting?* How often do they visit? Which information or service? Did they find it? Actions taken? (Can be determined through web analytics.)
3 *What do they think?* Overall opinion? Key areas of satisfaction? Specific likes or dislikes? What was missing that was expected?

Focus groups

Malhotra (1999) notes that the advantage of online focus groups is that they can be used to reach segments that are difficult to access, such as doctors, lawyers and professional people. These authors also suggest that costs are lower, they can be arranged more rapidly and can bridge the distance gap when recruiting respondents. Traditional focus groups can be conducted, where customers are brought together in a room and assess a web site; this will typically occur pre-launch as part of the prototyping activity. Testing can take the form of random use of the site, or more usefully the users will be given different scenarios to follow. It is important that focus groups use a range of familiarities (Chapter 8). Focus groups tend to be relatively expensive and time-consuming, since rather than simply viewing an advertisement, the customers need to actually interact with the web site. Conducting real-world focus groups has the benefit that the reactions of site users can be monitored; the scratch of the head and the fist hitting the desk cannot be monitored in the virtual world!

Mystery shoppers

Real-world measurement is also important since the Internet channel does not exist in isolation. It must work in unison with real-world customer service and fulfilment. Chris Russell of eMysteryShopper (**www.emysteryshopper.com**), a company that has completed online customer service surveys for major UK retailers and travel companies, says 'we also needed to make sure the bricks-and-mortar customer service support was actually supporting what the clicks-and-mortar side was promising. There is no doubt that an e-commerce site has to be a complete customer service fulfilment picture, it can't just be one bit working online that is not supported offline'. An eMysteryShopper survey involves shoppers not only commenting on site usability, but also on the service quality of e-mail and phone responses together with product fulfilment. Mystery shoppers test these areas:

- site usability;
- e-commerce fulfilment;
- e-mail and phone response (time, accuracy);
- impact on brand.

To conclude this section of the chapter, Table 9.4 summarises key offline measures of Internet marketing effectiveness.

Table 9.4 Some offline measures of Internet marketing effectiveness

Measure	Measured through
Enquiries or leads (subdivided into new customers and existing customers)	• Number of online e-mails • Phone calls mentioning web site • Faxed enquiries mentioning web site
Sales	• Online sales or sales in which customers state they found out about the product on the web site. Sales received on a phone number only publicised on a web site
Conversion rate	• Can be calculated separately for customers who are registered online and those who are not
Retention rates	• Is the 'churn' of customers using the web site lower?
Customer satisfaction	• Focus groups, questionnaires and interviews • Mystery shoppers
Brand enhancement (brand awareness, favourability and purchase intent)	• Online controlled surveys

The maintenance process

As part of the process of continuous improvement in online marketing, it is important to have a clearly defined process for making changes to the content of a web site. This process should be understood by all staff contributing content to the site, with their responsibilities clearly identified in their job descriptions. To understand the process, consider the main stages involved in publishing a page. A simple model of the work involved in maintenance is shown in Figure 9.9. It is assumed that the needs of the users and design features of the site have already been defined when the site was originally

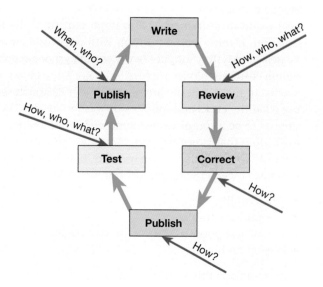

Figure 9.9 A web document review and update process

created, as described in Chapter 7. The model only applies to minor updates to copy, or perhaps updating product or company information. The different tasks involved in the maintenance process are as follows:

1 *Write*. This stage involves writing the marketing copy and, if necessary, designing the layout of copy and associated images.
2 *Review*. An independent review of the copy is necessary to check for errors before a document is published. Depending on the size of organisation, review may be necessary by one person or several people covering different aspects of content quality such as corporate image, copy-editing text to identify grammatical errors, marketing copy, branding and legality.
3 *Correct*. This stage is straightforward, and involves updates necessary as a result of stage 2.
4 *Publish (to test environment)*. The publication stage involves putting the corrected copy on a web page that can be checked further. This will be in a test environment that can only be viewed from inside a company.
5 *Test*. Before the completed web page is made available over the World Wide Web a final test will be required for technical issues such as whether the page loads successfully on different browsers.
6 *Publish (to live environment)*. Once the material has been reviewed and tested and is signed off as satisfactory it will be published to the main web site and will be accessible by customers.

How often should material be updated?

Web site content needs to be up-to-date, in line with customer expectations. The web is perceived as a dynamic medium, and customers are likely to expect new information to be posted to a site straight away. If material is inaccurate or 'stale' then the customer may not return to the site.

After a time, the information on a web page naturally becomes outdated and will need to be updated or replaced. It is important to have a mechanism defining what triggers this update process and leads to the cycle of Figure 9.9. The need for material to be updated has several facets. For the information on the site to be accurate it clearly needs to be up-to-date. Trigger procedures should be developed such that when price changes or product specifications are updated in promotional leaflets or catalogues, these changes are also reflected on the web site. Without procedures of this type, it is easy for there to be errors on the web site. This may sound obvious, but the reality is that the people contributing the updates to the site will have many other tasks to complete, and the web site could be a low priority.

A further reason for updating the site is to encourage repeat visits. For example, a customer could be encouraged to return to a business-to-business site if there is some industry news on the site. This type of content needs to be updated regularly according to the type of business, from daily, weekly to monthly. Again, a person has to be in place to collate such news and update the site frequently. Some companies such as RS Components have monthly promotions, which may encourage repeat visits to the site. It is useful to emphasise to the customer that the information is updated frequently. This is possible through simple devices such as putting the date on the home page, or perhaps just the month and year for a site that is updated less frequently.

As part of defining a web site update process, and standards, a company may want to issue guidelines that suggest how often content is updated. This may specify that content is updated as follows:

- within two days of a factual error being identified;
- a new 'news' item is added at least once a month;
- when product information has been static for two months.

Responsibilities in web site maintenance

Maintenance is easy in a small company with a single person updating the web site. That person is able to ensure that the style of the whole site remains consistent. For a slightly larger site, with perhaps two people involved with updating, the problem more than doubles since communication is required to keep things consistent. For a large organisation with many different departments and offices in different countries, site maintenance becomes very difficult, and production of a quality site is only possible when there is strong control to establish a team who all follow the same standards. Sterne (2001) suggests that the essence of successful maintenance is to have clearly identified responsibilities for different aspects of updating the web site. The questions to ask are:

- Who owns the process?
- Who owns the content?
- Who owns the format?
- Who owns the technology?

We will now consider these in more detail, reviewing the standards required to produce a good-quality web site and the different types of responsibilities involved.

Who owns the process?

One of the first areas to be defined should be the overall process for updating the site. But who agrees this process? For the large company it will be necessary to bring together all the interested parties such as those within the marketing department and the site developers – who may be an external agency or the IT department. Within these groupings there may be many people with an interest such as the marketing manager, the person with responsibility for Internet or new-media marketing, a communications manager who places above-the-line advertising, and product managers who manage the promotion of individual products and services. All of these people should have an input in deciding on the process for updating the web site. This is not simply a matter of updating the web site; there are more fundamental issues to consider, such as how communications to the customer are made consistent between the different media. Some companies such as Orange (**www.orange.co.uk**) and Ford (**www.ford.co.uk**) manage this process well, and the content of the web site is always consistent with other media campaigns in newspapers and on television. In Ford this has been achieved by breaking down the barriers between traditional-media account managers and the Internet development team, and both groups work closely together. In other organisations, a structure is adopted in which there is a person or group responsible for customer communications, and they then ensure that the message conveyed by different functions such as the web site developers and the advertisement placers is consistent. Options for structuring an organisation to integrate new and old media are given in Parsons et al. (1996).

What, then, is this process? The process will basically specify responsibilities for different aspects of site management and detail the sequence in which tasks occur for updating the site. A typical update process is outlined in Figure 9.9. If we take a specific example we can illustrate the need for a well-defined process. Imagine that a large organisation is launching a new product, promotional literature is to be distributed to customers, the media are already available, and the company wants to add information about this product to the web site. A recently recruited graduate is charged with putting the information on the site. How will this process actually occur? The following process stages need to occur:

1 Graduate reviews promotional literature and rewrites copy on a word processor and modifies graphical elements as appropriate for the web site. This is the *write* stage in Figure 9.9.
2 Product and/or marketing manager reviews the revised web-based copy. This is part of the *review* stage in Figure 9.9.
3 Corporate communications manager reviews the copy for suitability. This is also part of the *review* stage in Figure 9.9.
4 Legal adviser reviews copy. This is also part of the *review* stage in Figure 9.9.
5 Copy revised and corrected and then re-reviewed as necessary. This is the *correct* stage in Figure 9.9.
6 Copy converted to web and then published. This will be performed by a technical person such as a site developer, who will insert a new menu option to help users navigate to the new product. This person will add the HTML formatting and then upload the file using FTP to the test web site. This is the first *publish* stage in Figure 9.9.
7 The new copy on the site will be reviewed by the graduate for accuracy, and needs to be tested on different web browsers and screen resolutions if it uses a graphical design different from the standard site template. This type of technical testing will need to be carried out by the webmaster. The new version could also be reviewed on the site by the communications manager or legal adviser at this point. This is part of the *test* stage in Figure 9.9.
8 Once all interested parties agree the new copy is suitable, the pages on the test web site can be transferred to the live web site and are then available for customers to view. This is the second *publish* stage in Figure 9.9.

Note that, in this scenario, review of the copy at stages 2 to 4 happens before the copy is actually put on to the test site at stage 6. This is efficient in that it saves the technical person or webmaster having to update the page until the copy is agreed. An alternative would be for the graduate to write the copy at stage 1 and then the webmaster publishes the material before it is reviewed by the various parties. Each approach is equally valid.

It is apparent that this process is quite involved, so the process needs to be clearly understood within the company or otherwise web pages may be published that do not conform to the look and feel for the site, have not been checked for legal compliance, or may not work. The only way such a process can be detailed is if it is written down and its importance communicated to all the participants. It will also help if technology facilitates the process. In particular, a workflow system should be set up that enables each of the reviewers to comment on the copy as soon as possible and authorise it. Content management systems are now commonly used to help achieve this. The copy can be automatically e-mailed to all reviewers and then the comments received by e-mail can be collated.

The detailed standards for performing a site update will vary according to the extent of the update. For correcting a spelling mistake, for example, not so many people will need to review the change! A site re-design that involves changing the look and feel of the site will require the full range of people to be involved.

Once the process has been established, the marketing department, as the owners of the web site, will insist that the process be followed for every change that is made to the web site.

To conclude this section refer to Activity 9.1 which shows a typical web site update process and considers possible improvements.

Activity 9.1 **Optimising a content review process**

Purpose

Assess how quality control and efficiency can be balanced for revisions to web content.

Activity

The extract below and Figure 9.10 illustrate a problem of updating encountered by this company. How can they solve this problem?

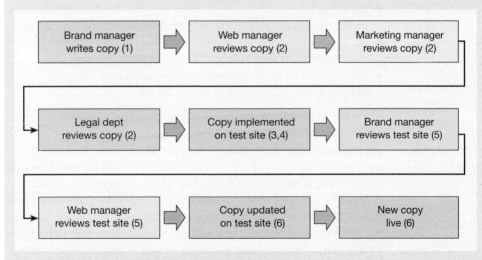

Figure 9.10 An example of a content update review process

Problem description

From when the brand manager identifies a need to update copy for their product, the update might happen as follows: brand manager writes copy (half a day), one day later the web manager reviews copy, three days later the marketing manager checks the copy, seven days later the legal department checks the copy, two days later the revised copy is implemented on the test site, two days later the brand manager reviews the test site, the next day the web manager reviews the web site, followed by updating and final review before the copy is added to the live site two days later and over a fortnight from when a relatively minor change to the site was identified!

Who owns the content?

For a medium-to-large site where the content is updated regularly, as it should be, it will soon become impossible for one person to be able to update all the content. It is logical and practical to distribute the responsibility for owning and developing different sections of the site to the people in an organisation who have the best skills and knowledge to develop that content. For example, in a large financial services company, the part of the business responsible for a certain product area should update the copy referring to their products. One person will update copy for each of savings accounts, mortgages, travel insurance, health insurance and investments. For a PC supplier, different **content developers** will be required for the product information, financing, delivery information and customer service facilities. Once the ownership of content is distributed throughout an organisation, it becomes crucial to develop guidelines and standards that help ensure that the site has a coherent 'feel' and appearance. The nature of these guidelines is described in the sections that follow.

Content developer
A person responsible for updating web pages within part of an organisation.

Who owns the format?

The format refers to different aspects of the design and layout of the site commonly referred to as its 'look and feel'. The key aim is consistency of format across the whole web site. For a large corporate site, with different staff working on different parts of the site, there is a risk that the different areas of the site will not be consistent. Defining a clear format or **site design template** for the site means that the quality of the site and customer experience will be better since:

Site design template
A standard page layout format which is applied to each page of a web site.

- *the site will be easier to use* – a customer who has become familiar with using one area of the site will be able to confidently use another part of the site;
- *the design elements of the site will be similar* – a user will feel more at home with the site if different parts look similar;
- *the corporate image and branding will be consistent with real-world branding* (if this is an objective) and similar across the entire site.

To achieve a site of this quality it is necessary for written standards to be developed. These may include different standards such as those shown in Table 9.5. The standards adopted will vary according to the size of the web site and company. Typically, larger sites, with more individual content developers, will require more detailed standards.

Note that it will be much easier to apply these quality standards across the site if the degree of scope for individual content developers to make changes to graphics or navigation is limited and they concentrate on changing text copy. To help achieve consistency, the software used to build the web site should allow templates to be designed that specify the menu structure and graphical design of the site. The content developers are then simply adding text- and graphics-based pages to specific documents and do not have to worry about the site design.

Who owns the technology?

The technology used to publish the web site is important if a company is to utilise fully the power of the Internet. Many standards such as those in Table 9.5 need to be managed in addition to the technology. The technology decision becomes more significant when a company wants to make its product catalogue available for queries or to take orders online. As these facilities are added the web site changes from an isolated system to one that must be integrated with other technologies such as the customer database, stock control and sales order processing systems. Given this integration with corporate IS, the IT department (or the company to which IT has been outsourced) will need to be involved in the development of the site and its strategy.

Table 9.5 Web site standards

Standard	Details	Applies to
Site structure	Will specify the main areas of the site, for example products, customer service, press releases, how to place content and who is responsible for each area.	Content developers
Navigation	May specify, for instance, that the main menu must always be on the left of the screen with nested (sub-) menus at the foot of the screen. The home button should be accessible from every screen at the top left corner of the screen. See Lynch and Horton (1999) for guidelines on navigation and site design.	Web site designer/webmaster usually achieves these through site templates
Copy style and page structure	General guidelines, for example reminding those writing copy that web copy needs to be briefer than its paper equivalent. Where detail is required, perhaps with product specifications, it should be broken up into chunks that are digestible on-screen. Copy and page structure should also be written for search engine optimisation to keyphrases (Chapter 8).	Individual content developers
Testing standards	Check site functions for: • different browser types and versions • plug-ins • invalid links • speed of download of graphics • spellcheck each page See text for details.	Web site designer/webmaster
Corporate branding and graphic design	Specifies the appearance of company logos and the colours and typefaces used to convey the brand message.	Web site designer/webmaster
Process	The sequence of events for publishing a new web page or updating an existing page. Who is responsible for reviewing and updating?	All
Performance	Availability and download speed figures.	Staff managing the server

As well as issues of integrating systems, there are detailed technical issues for which the technical staff in the company need to be made responsible. These include:

- availability and performance of web site server;
- checking HTML for validity and correcting broken links;
- managing different versions of web pages in the test and live environments and content management.

Content management

Content
management
·······················
Software tools for
managing additions
and amendment to web
site content.

Content management refers to when software tools (usually browser-based software running on a server) permit business users to contribute web content while an administrator keeps control of the format and style of the web site and the approval process. These tools are used to organise, manage, retrieve and archive information content throughout the life of the site.

Content management systems (CMS) provide these facilities:

- *structure authoring*: the design and maintenance of content structure (sub-components, templates, etc.), web page structure and web site structure;
- *link management*: the maintenance of internal and external links through content change and the elimination of dead links;
- *search engine visibility*: the content within the search engine must be stored and linked such that it can be indexed by search engine robots to add it to their index – this was not possible with some first-generation content management systems, but is typical of more recent content management systems;
- *input and syndication*: the loading (spidering) of externally originating content and the aggregation and dissemination of content from a variety of sources;
- *versioning*: the crucial task of controlling which edition of a page, page element or the whole site is published. Typically this will be the most recent, but previous editions should be archived and it should be possible to roll back to a previous version at the page, page element or site level;
- *security and access control*: different permissions can be assigned to different roles of users and some content may only be available through log-in details. In these cases, the CMS maintains a list of users. This facility is useful when a company needs to use the same CMS for an intranet, extranet or public Internet site which may have different levels of permission;
- *publication workflow*: content destined for a web site needs to pass through a publication process to move it from the management environment to the live delivery environment. The process may involve tasks such as format conversion (e.g. to PDF, or to WAP), rendering to HTML, editorial authorisation and the construction of composite documents in real time (personalisation and selective dissemination);
- *tracking and monitoring*: providing logs and statistical analysis of use to provide performance measures, tune the content according to demand and protect against misuse;
- *navigation and visualisation*: providing an intuitive, clear and attractive representation of the nature and location of content using colour, texture, 3D rendering or even virtual reality.

From this list of features you can see that modern CMSs are complex and many CMSs are expensive investments. Some open-source CMSs are available without the need to purchase a licence fee which have many of the features explained in this section. One example is Plone (**www.plone.org**) which is used by large organisations' web sites such as NASA. Dave Chaffey uses Plone to manage the contents for updates to this book which readers can find on his web site (**www.davechaffey.com**).

Initiatives to keep content fresh

It is often said that up-to-date content is crucial to site 'stickiness', but fresh content will not happen by accident, so companies have to consider approaches that can be used to control the quality of information. Generic approaches that we have seen which can work well are:

- Assign responsibility for particular content types of site sections;
- Make the quality of web content produced part of employee's performance appraisal;
- Produce a target schedule for publication of content;
- Identify events which trigger the publication of new content, e.g. a new product launch, price change or a press release;
- Identify stages and responsibilities in updating – who specifies, who creates, who reviews, who checks, who publishes;
- Measure the usage of content through web analytics or get feedback from site users;
- Audit and publish content to show which is up-to-date.

Case Study 9   Learning from Amazon's culture of metrics

Context

Why a case study on Amazon? Surely everyone knows about who Amazon are and what they do? Yes, well, that's maybe true, but this case goes beyond the surface to review some of the 'insider secrets' of Amazon's success.

Like eBay, Amazon.com was born in 1995. The name reflected the vision of Jeff Bezos, to produce a large-scale phenomenon like the Amazon river. This ambition has proved justified since just 8 years later, Amazon passed the $5 billion sales mark – it took Wal-Mart 20 years to achieve this.

By 2005 Amazon was a global brand with over 41 million active customers accounts and order fulfilment to more than 200 countries. Despite this volume of sales, at 31 December 2004 Amazon employed approximately 9000 full-time and part-time employees.

Vision and strategy

In their 2005 SEC filing, Amazon describe the vision of their business as to:

Relentlessly focus on customer experience by offering our customers low prices, convenience, and a wide selection of merchandise.

The vision is to offer Earth's biggest selection and to be Earth's most customer-centric company. Consider how these core marketing messages summarising the Amazon online value proposition are communicated both on-site and through offline communications.

Of course, achieving customer loyalty and repeat purchases has been key to Amazon's success. Many dot-coms failed because they succeeded in achieving awareness, but not loyalty. Amazon achieved both. In their SEC filing they stress how they seek to achieve this. They say:

We work to earn repeat purchases by providing easy-to-use functionality, fast and reliable fulfillment, timely customer service, feature rich content, and a trusted transaction environment. Key features of our websites include editorial and customer reviews; manufacturer product information; Web pages tailored to individual preferences, such as recommendations and notifications; 1-Click® technology; secure payment systems; image uploads; searching on our websites as well as the Internet; browsing; and the ability to view selected interior pages and citations, and search the entire contents of many of the books we offer with our 'Look Inside the Book' and 'Search Inside the Book' features. Our community of online customers also creates feature-rich content, including product reviews, online recommendation lists, wish lists, buying guides, and wedding and baby registries.

In practice, as is the practice for many online retailers, the lowest prices are for the most popular products, with less popular products commanding higher prices and a greater margin for Amazon. Free shipping offers are used to encourage increase in basket size since customers have to spend over a certain amount to receive free shipping. The level at which free shipping is set is critical to profitability and Amazon has changed it as competition has changed and for promotional reasons.

Amazon communicate the fulfilment promise in several ways including presentation of latest inventory availability information, delivery date estimates, and options for expedited delivery, as well as delivery shipment notifications and update facilities.

This focus on customer has translated to excellence in service with the 2004 American Customer Satisfaction Index giving Amazon.com a score of 88 which was at the time, the highest customer satisfaction score ever recorded in any service industry, online or offline.

Round (2004) notes that Amazon focuses on customer satisfaction metrics. Each site is closely monitored with standard service availability monitoring (for example, using Keynote or Mercury Interactive) site availability and download speed. Interestingly it also monitors per-minute site revenue upper/lower bounds – Round describes an alarm system rather like a power plant where if revenue on a site falls below $10,000 per minute, alarms go off! There are also internal performance service-level agreements for web services where T% of the time, different pages must return in X seconds.

Competition

In its SEC (2005) filing Amazon describes the environment for its products and services as 'intensely competitive'. It views its main current and potential competitors as: (1) physical-world retailers, catalogue retailers, publishers, vendors, distributors and manufacturers of its products, many of which possess significant brand awareness, sales volume, and customer bases, and some of which currently sell, or may sell, products or services through the Internet, mail order, or direct marketing; (2) other online e-commerce sites; (3) a number of indirect competitors, including media companies, web portals, comparison shopping web sites, and web search engines, either directly or in collaboration with other retailers; and (4) companies that provide e-commerce services, including web site development; third-party fulfilment and customer service.

Amazon believes the main competitive factors in its market segments include 'selection, price, availability, convenience, information, discovery, brand recognition, personalized services, accessibility, customer service, reliability, speed of fulfillment, ease of use, and ability to adapt to changing conditions, as well as our customers' overall experience and trust in transactions with us and facilitated by us on behalf of third-party sellers'.

For services offered to business and individual sellers, additional competitive factors include the quality of their services and tools, their ability to generate sales for third parties they serve, and the speed of performance for their services.

From auctions to marketplaces

Amazon auctions (known as 'zShops') were launched in March 1999, in large part as a response to the success of eBay. They were promoted heavily from the home page, category pages and individual product pages. Despite this, a year after its launch it had only achieved a 3.2% share of the online auction compared to 58% for eBay and it only declined from this point.

Today, competitive prices of products are available through third-party sellers in the 'Amazon Marketplace' which are integrated within the standard product listings. The strategy to offer such an auction facility was initially driven by the need to compete with eBay, but now the strategy has been adjusted such that Amazon describe it as part of the approach of low pricing.

Although it might be thought that Amazon would lose out on enabling its merchants to sell products at lower prices, in fact Amazon makes greater margin on these sales since merchants are charged a commission on each sale and it is the merchant who bears the cost of storing inventory and fulfilling the product to customers. As with eBay, Amazon is just facilitating the exchange of bits and bytes between buyers and sellers without the need to distribute physical products.

How 'the culture of metrics' started

A common theme in Amazon's development is the drive to use a measured approach to all aspects of the business, beyond the finance. Marcus (2004) describes an occasion at a corporate 'boot-camp' in January 1997 when Amazon CEO Jeff Bezos 'saw the light'. 'At Amazon, we will have a Culture of Metrics', he said while addressing his senior staff. He went on to explain how web-based business gave Amazon an 'amazing window into human behavior'. Marcus says:

> Gone were the fuzzy approximations of focus groups, the anecdotal fudging and smoke blowing from the marketing department. A company like Amazon could (and did) record every move a visitor made, every last click and twitch of the mouse. As the data piled up into virtual heaps, hummocks and mountain ranges, you could draw all sorts of conclusions about their chimerical nature, the consumer. In this sense, Amazon was not merely a store, but an immense repository of facts. All we needed were the right equations to plug into them.

James Marcus then goes on to give a fascinating insight into a breakout group discussion of how Amazon could better use measures to improve its performance. Marcus was in the Bezos group, brainstorming customer-centric metrics. Marcus (2004) summarises the dialogue, led by Bezos:

> 'First, we figure out which things we'd like to measure on the site', he said. 'For example, let's say we want a metric for customer enjoyment. How could we calculate that?'
>
> There was silence. Then somebody ventured: 'How much time each customer spends on the site?'
>
> 'Not specific enough', Jeff said.
>
> 'How about the average number of minutes each customer spends on the site per session', someone else suggested. 'If that goes up, they're having a blast.'
>
> 'But how do we factor in purchase?' I [Marcus] said feeling proud of myself. 'Is that a measure of enjoyment?'
>
> 'I think we need to consider frequency of visits, too', said a dark-haired woman I didn't recognise. 'Lot of folks are still accessing the web with those creepy-crawly modems. Four short visits from them might be just as good as one visit from a guy with a T-1. Maybe better.'

'Good point', Jeff said. 'And anyway, enjoyment is just the start. In the end, we should be measuring customer ecstasy.'

It is interesting that Amazon was having this debate about the elements of RFM analysis (described in Chapter 6) in 1997, after already having achieved $16 million of revenue in the previous year. Of course, this is a minuscule amount compared with today's billions of dollars turnover. The important point was that this was the start of a focus on metrics which can be seen through the description of Matt Round's work later in this case study.

From human to software-based recommendations

Amazon has developed internal tools to support this 'Culture of Metrics'. Marcus (2004) describes how the 'Creator Metrics' tool shows content creators how well their product listings and product copy are working. For each content editor such as Marcus, it retrieves all recently posted documents including articles, interviews, booklists and features. For each one it then gives a conversion rate to sale plus the number of page views, adds (added to basket) and repels (content requested, but the back button then used). In time, the work of editorial reviewers such as Marcus was marginalised since Amazon found that the majority of visitors used the search tools rather than read editorial and they responded to the personalised recommendations as the matching technology improved (Marcus likens early recommendations techniques to 'going shopping with the village idiot').

Experimentation and testing at Amazon

The 'Culture of Metrics' also led to a test-driven approach to improving results at Amazon. Matt Round, speaking at E-metrics 2004 when he was director of personalisation at Amazon, describes the philosophy as *'Data Trumps Intuitions'*. He explained how Amazon used to have a lot of arguments about which content and promotion should go on the all-important home page or category pages. He described how every category VP wanted top-centre and how the Friday meetings about placements for next week were getting 'too long, too loud, and lacked performance data'.

But today 'automation replaces intuitions' and real-time experimentation tests are always run to answer these questions since actual consumer behaviour is the best way to decide upon tactics.

Marcus (2004) also notes that Amazon has a culture of *experiments* of which A/B tests are key components. Examples where A/B tests are used include new home page design, moving features around the page, different algorithms for recommendations, changing search relevance rankings. These involve testing a new treatment against a previous control for a limited time of a few days

or a week. The system will randomly show one or more treatments to visitors and measure a range of parameters such as units sold and revenue by category (and total), session time, and session length. The new features will usually be launched if the desired metrics are statistically significantly better. Statistical tests are a challenge though as distributions are not normal (they have a large mass at zero for example of no purchase). There are other challenges since multiple A/B tests are running every day and A/B tests may overlap and so conflict. There are also longer-term effects where some features are 'cool' for the first two weeks and the opposite effect where changing navigation may degrade performance temporarily. Amazon also finds that as its users evolve in their online experience the way they act online has changed. This means that Amazon has to constantly test and evolve its features.

Technology

It follows that the Amazon technology infrastructure must readily support this culture of experimentation and this can be difficult to achieve with standardised content management. Amazon has achieved its competitive advantage through developing its technology internally and with a significant investment in this which may not be available to other organisations without the right focus on the online channels.

As Amazon explains in SEC (2005),

using primarily our own proprietary technologies, as well as technology licensed from third parties, we have implemented numerous features and functionality that simplify and improve the customer shopping experience, enable third parties to sell on our platform, and facilitate our fulfillment and customer service operations. Our current strategy is to focus our development efforts on continuous innovation by creating and enhancing the specialized, proprietary software that is unique to our business, and to license or acquire commercially-developed technology for other applications where available and appropriate. We continually invest in several areas of technology, including our seller platform; A9.com, our wholly-owned subsidiary focused on search technology on www.A9.com and other Amazon sites; web services; and digital initiatives.

Round (2004) describes the technology approach as 'distributed development and deployment'. Pages such as the home page have a number of content 'pods' or 'slots' which call web services for features. This makes it relatively easy to change the content in these pods and even change the location of the pods on-screen. Amazon uses a flowable or fluid page design, unlike many sites, which enables it to make the most of real-estate on-screen.

Technology also supports more standard e-retail facilities. SEC (2005) states:

→

We use a set of applications for accepting and validating customer orders, placing and tracking orders with suppliers, managing and assigning inventory to customer orders, and ensuring proper shipment of products to customers. Our transaction-processing systems handle millions of items, a number of different status inquiries, multiple shipping addresses, gift-wrapping requests, and multiple shipment methods. These systems allow the customer to choose whether to receive single or several shipments based on availability and to track the progress of each order. These applications also manage the process of accepting, authorizing, and charging customer credit cards.

Data-driven automation

Round (2004) said that 'Data is king at Amazon'. He gave many examples of data-driven automation including customer channel preferences, managing the way content is displayed to different user types such as new releases and top-sellers, merchandising and recommendation (showing related products and promotions) and also advertising through paid search (automatic ad generation and bidding).

The automated search advertising and bidding system for paid search has had a big impact at Amazon. Sponsored links were initially done by humans, but this was unsustainable due to the range of products at Amazon. The automated program generates keywords, writes ad creative, determines best landing page, manages bids, measures conversion rates, profit per converted visitor and updates bids. Again the problem of volume is there: Matt Round described how the book *How to Make Love like a Porn Star* by Jenna Jameson received tens of thousands of clicks from pornography-related searches, but few actually purchased the book. So the update cycle must be quick to avoid large losses.

There is also an automated e-mail measurement and optimisation system. The campaign calendar used to be manually managed with relatively weak measurement and it was costly to schedule and use. A new system:

- Automatically optimises content to improve customer experience;
- Avoids sending an e-mail campaign that has low click-through or high unsubscribe rate;
- Includes inbox management (avoid sending multiple e-mails/week);
- Has growing library of automated e-mail programs covering new releases and recommendations.

But there are challenges if promotions are too successful if inventory isn't available.

Your recommendations

'Customers Who Bought X … also bought Y' is Amazon's signature feature. Round (2004) describes how Amazon relies on acquiring and then crunching a massive amount of data. Every purchase, every page viewed and every search is recorded. So there are now two new versions: 'Customers who shopped for X also shopped for …', and 'Customers who searched for X also bought …'. They also have a system codenamed 'Goldbox' which is a cross-sell and awareness raising tool. Items are discounted to encourage purchases in new categories!

He also describes the challenge of techniques for sifting patterns from noise (sensitivity filtering) and clothing and toy catalogues change frequently so recommendations become out-of-date. The main challenges though are the massive data size arising from millions of customers, millions of items and recommendations made in real time.

Partnership strategy

As Amazon grew, its share price growth enabled partnership or acquisition with a range of companies in different sectors. Marcus (2004) describes how Amazon partnered with Drugstore.com (pharmacy), Living.com (furniture), Pets.com (pet supplies), Wineshopper.com (wines), HomeGrocer.com (groceries), Sothebys.com (auctions) and Kozmo.com (urban home delivery). In most cases, Amazon purchased an equity stake in these partners, so that it would share in their prosperity. It also charged them fees for placements on the Amazon site to promote and drive traffic to their sites. Similarly, Amazon charged publishers for prime position to promote books on its site which caused an initial hue-and-cry, but this abated when it was realised that paying for prominent placements was widespread in traditional booksellers and supermarkets. Many of these new online companies failed in 1999 and 2000, but Amazon had covered the potential for growth and was not pulled down by these partners, even though for some such as Pets.com it had an investment of 50%.

Analysts sometimes refer to 'Amazoning a sector', meaning that one company becomes dominant in an online sector such as book retail such that it becomes very difficult for others to achieve market share. In addition to developing, communicating and delivering a very strong proposition, Amazon has been able to consolidate its strength in different sectors through its partnership arrangements and through using technology to facilitate product promotion and distribution via these partnerships. The Amazon retail platform enables other retailers to sell products online using the Amazon user interface and infrastructure through their 'Syndicated Stores' programme. For example, in the UK, Waterstones (**www.waterstones.co.uk**)

is one of the largest traditional bookstores. It found competition with online so expensive and challenging, that eventually it entered a partnership arrangement where Amazon markets and distributes its books online in return for a commission online. Similarly, in the US, the large book retailer Borders uses the Amazon merchant platform for distributing its products. Toy retailer Toys'R'Us have a similar arrangement. Such partnerships help Amazon extend its reach into the customer-base of other suppliers, and of course, customers who buy in one category such as books can be encouraged to purchase into other areas such as clothing or electronics.

Another form of partnership referred to above is the Amazon Marketplace which enables Amazon customers and other retailers to sell their new and used books and other goods alongside the regular retail listings. A similar partnership approach is the Amazon 'Merchants@' programme which enables third-party merchants (typically larger than those who sell via the Amazon Marketplace) to sell their products via Amazon. Amazon earns fees either through fixed fees or sales commissions per unit. This arrangement can help customers who get a wider choice of products from a range of suppliers with the convenience of purchasing them through a single checkout process.

Finally, Amazon has also facilitated formation of partnerships with smaller companies through its affiliates programme. Internet legend records that Jeff Bezos, the creator of Amazon was chatting to someone at a cocktail party who wanted to sell books about divorce via her web site. Subsequently, Amazon.com launched its Associates Program in July 1996 and it is still going strong. Googling **www.google.com/search?q=www.amazon.com+-site%3Awww.amazon.com** for sites that link to the US site, shows over 4 million pages, many of which will be affiliates. Amazon does not use an affiliate network which would take commissions from sale, but thanks to the strength of its brand has developed its own affiliate programme. Amazon has created tiered performance-based incentives to encourage affiliates to sell more Amazon products.

Marketing communications

In their SEC filings Amazon states that the aims of their communications strategy are (unsurprisingly) to:

1 Increase customer traffic to our web sites
2 Create awareness of our products and services
3 Promote repeat purchases
4 Develop incremental product and service revenue opportunities
5 Strengthen and broaden the Amazon.com brand name.

Amazon also believe that their most effective marketing communications are a consequence of their focus on continuously improving the customer experience. This then creates word-of-mouth promotion which is effective in acquiring new customers and may also encourage repeat customer visits.

As well as this Marcus (2004) describes how Amazon used the personalisation enabled through technology to reach out to a difficult-to-reach market which Bezos originally called 'the hard middle'. Bezos's view was that it was easy to reach 10 people (you called them on the phone) or the ten million people who bought the most popular products (you placed a superbowl ad), but more difficult to reach those in between. The search facilities in the search engine and on the Amazon site, together with its product recommendation features meant that Amazon could connect its products with the interests of these people.

Online advertising techniques include paid search marketing, interactive ads on portals, e-mail campaigns and search engine optimisation. These are automated as far as possible, as described earlier in the case study. As previously mentioned, the affiliate programme is also important in driving visitors to Amazon and Amazon offers a wide range of methods of linking to its site to help improve conversion. For example, affiliates can use straight text links leading direct to a product page and they also offer a range of dynamic banners which feature different content such as books about Internet marketing or a search box.

Amazon also use cooperative advertising arrangements, better known as 'contra-deals' with some vendors and other third parties. For example, a print advertisement in 2005 for a particular product such as a wireless router with a free wireless laptop card promotion was to feature a specific Amazon URL in the ad. In product fulfilment packs, Amazon may include a leaflet for a non-competing online company such as Figleaves.com (lingerie) or Expedia (travel). In return, Amazon leaflets may be included in customer communications from the partner brands.

The associates programme directs customers to Amazon web sites by enabling independent web sites to make millions of products available to their audiences with fulfilment performed by Amazon or third parties. Amazon pays commissions to hundreds of thousands of participants in the associates programme when their customer referrals result in product sales.

In addition, they offer everyday free shipping options worldwide and recently announced Amazon.com Prime in the US, their first membership programme in which members receive free two-day shipping and discounted overnight shipping. Although marketing expenses do not include the costs of free shipping or promotional offers, Amazon views such offers as effective marketing tools.

→

	Year Ended December 31				
	2004	**2003**	**2002**	**2001**	**2000**
	(in thousands, except per share data)				
Net sales	$6,921,124	$5,263,699	$3,932,936	$3,122,433	$2,761,983
Income (loss) before change in accounting principle	588,451	35,282	(149,933)	(556,754)	(1,411,273)
Cumulative effect of change in accounting principle	—	—	801	(10,523)	
Net income (loss)	588,451	35,282	(149,132)	(567,277)	(1,411,273)
Basic earnings per share (1):					
Prior to cumulative effect of change in accounting principal	$ 1.45	$ 0.09	$ (0.40)	$ (1.53)	$ (4.02)
Cumulative effect of change in accounting principal	—	—	0.01	(0.03)	—
Basic earnings per share (1)	$ 1.45	$ 0.09	$ (0.39)	$ (1.56)	$ (4.02)
Diluted earnings per share (1):					
Prior to cumulative effect of change in accounting principal	$ 1.39	$ 0.08	$ (0.40)	$ (1.53)	$ (4.02)
Cumulative effect of change in accounting principal	—	—	0.01	(0.03)	—
Diluted earnings per share (1)	$ 1.39	$ 0.08	$ (0.39)	$ (1.56)	$ (4.02)
Shares used in computation of earnings (loss) per share:					
Basic	405,926	395,479	378,363	364,211	350,873
Diluted	424,757	419,352	378,363	364,211	350,873
Balance Sheet and Other Data:					
Total assets	$3,248,508	$2,162,033	$1,990,449	$1,637,547	$2,135,169
Long-term debt and other	1,855,319	1,945,439	2,277,305	2,156,133	2,127,464

Sources: Internet Retailer (2003), Marcus (2004), Round (2004), SEC (2005)

Questions

1 By referring to the case study, Amazon's web site for your country and your experience of Amazon offline communications evaluate how well Amazon communicates their core proposition and promotional offers.

2 Using the case study, characterise Amazon's approach to marketing communications.

3 Explain what distinguishes Amazon in its uses of technology for competitive advantage.

4 How does the Amazon 'culture of metrics' differ from that in other organisations from your experience.

Summary

1 A structured measurement programme is necessary to collect measures to assess a web site's effectiveness. Action can then be taken to adjust the web site strategy or promotional efforts. A measurement programme involves:

- Stage 1: Defining a measurement process.
- Stage 2: Defining a metrics framework.
- Stage 3: Selecting of tools for data collection, reporting and analysis.

2 Measures of Internet marketing effectiveness can be categorised as assessing:

- *Level 1: Business effectiveness* – these measure the impact of the web site on the whole business, and look at financial measures such as revenue and profit and promotion of corporate awareness.
- *Level 2: Marketing effectiveness* – these measure the number of leads and sales achieved via the Internet and effect of the Internet on retention rates and other aspects of the marketing mix such as branding.
- *Level 3: Internet marketing effectiveness* – these measures assess how well the site is being promoted, and do so by reviewing the popularity of the site and how good it is at delivering customer needs.

3 The measures of effectiveness referred to above are collected in two main ways – online and offline – or in combination.

4 Online measures are obtained from a web-server log file or using browser-based techniques. They indicate the number of visitors to a site, which pages they visit, and where they originated from. These also provide a breakdown of visitors through time or by country.

5 Offline measures are marketing outcomes such as enquiries or sales that are directly attributable to the web site. Other measures of the effectiveness are available through surveying customers using questionnaires, interviews and focus groups.

6 Maintaining a web site requires clear responsibilities to be identified for different roles. These include the roles of content owners and site developers, and those ensuring that the content conforms with company and legal requirements.

7 To produce a good-quality web site, standards are required to enforce uniformity in terms of:

- site look and feel;
- corporate branding;
- quality of copy.

Exercises

Self-assessment exercises

1 Why are standards necessary for controlling web site maintenance? What aspects of the site do standards seek to control?

2 Explain the difference between hits and page impressions. How are these measured?

3 Define and explain the purpose of test and live versions of a web site.

4 Why should content development be distributed through a large organisation?

5 What is the difference between online and offline metrics?

6 How can focus groups and interviews be used to assess web site effectiveness?

7 Explain how a web log file analyser works. What are its limitations?

8 Why is it useful to integrate the collection of online and offline metrics?

→

Essay and discussion questions

1 'Corporate standards for a web site's format and update process are likely to stifle the creative development of a site and reduce its value to customers.' Discuss.

2 'There is little value in the collection of online metrics recorded in a web server log file. For measurement programmes to be of value, measures based on marketing outcomes are more valuable.' Discuss.

3 You have been appointed as manager of a web site for a car manufacturer and have been asked to refine the existing metrics programme. Explain, in detail, the steps you would take to develop this programme.

4 The first version of a web site for a financial services company has been live for a year. Originally it was developed by a team of two people, and was effectively 'brochureware'. The second version of the site is intended to contain more detailed information, and will involve contributions from 10 different product areas. You have been asked to define a procedure for controlling updates to the site. Write a document detailing the update procedure, which also explains the reasons for each control.

Examination questions

1 Why are standards necessary to control the process of updating a web site? Give three examples of different aspects of a web site that need to be controlled.

2 Explain the following terms concerning measurement of web site effectiveness:
   (a) hits;
   (b) page impressions;
   (c) referring pages.

3 Measurement of web sites concerns the recording of key events involving customers using a web site. Briefly explain five different types of event.

4 Describe and briefly explain the purpose of the different stages involved in updating an existing document on a commercial web site.

5 Distinguish between a test environment and a live environment for a web site. What is the reason for having two environments?

6 Give three reasons explaining why a web site may have to integrate with existing marketing information systems and databases within a company.

7 You have been appointed as manager of a web site and have been asked to develop a metrics programme. Briefly explain the steps you would take to develop this programme.

8 If a customer can be persuaded to register his or her name and e-mail address with a web site, how can this information be used for site measurement purposes?

References

Adams, C., Kapashi, N., Neely, A. and Marr, B. (2000) Managing with measures. Measuring ebusiness performance. *Accenture white paper*. Survey conducted in conjunction with Cranfield School of Management.

Agrawal, V., Arjona, V. and Lemmens, R. (2001) E-performance: the path to rational exuberance, *McKinsey Quarterly*, No. 1, 31–43.

Bourne, M., Mills, J., Willcox, M., Neely, A. and Platts, K. (2000) Designing, implementing and updating performance measurement systems, *International Journal of Operations and Production Management*, 20(7), 754–71.

Chaffey, D. (2000) Achieving Internet marketing success, *The Marketing Review*, 1(1), 35–60.

Cutler, M. and Sterne, J. (2000) E-metrics. Business metrics for the new economy. *Netgenesis white paper*.

Friedman, L. and Furey, T. (1999) *The Channel Advantage*. Butterworth Heinemann, Oxford.

Grossnickle, J. and Raskin, O. (2001) *The Handbook of Online Marketing Research: Knowing your Customer Using the Net*. McGraw-Hill, New York.

Internet Retailer (2003) The new Wal-Mart? *Internet Retailer*, Paul Demery.

Kotler, P. (1997) *Marketing Management – Analysis, Planning, Implementation and Control*. Prentice-Hall, Englewood Cliffs, NJ.

Lynch, P. and Horton, S. (1999) *Web Style Guide. Basic Design Principles for Creating Web Sites*. Yale University Press, New Haven, CT.

Malhotra, N. (1999) *Marketing Research: An Applied Orientation*. Prentice-Hall, Upper Saddle River, NJ.

Marcus, J. (2004) *Amazonia. Five Years at the Epicentre of the Dot-com Juggernaut*. The New Press, New York.

Neely, A., Adams, C. and Kennerley, M. (2002) *The Performance Prism. The Scorecard for Measuring and Managing Business Success*. Financial Times/Prentice Hall, Harlow.

Parsons, A., Zeisser, M. and Waitman, R. (1996) Organizing for digital marketing, *McKinsey Quarterly*, No. 4, 183–92.

Petersen, E. (2004) *Web Analytics Demystified*. Self-published. Available from **www.webanalyticsdemystified.com**.

Plant, R. (2000) *eCommerce: Formulation of Strategy*. Prentice-Hall, Upper Saddle River, NJ.

Revolution (2004) Alliance and Leicester banks on e-commerce, by Philip Buxtone, *Revolution* (**www.revolutionmagazine.com**).

Round, M. (2004) Presentation to E-metrics, London, May 2005. **www.emetrics.org**.

SEC (2005) United States Securities and Exchange Commission submission Form 10-K from Amazon. For the fiscal year ended 31 December, 2004.

Sterne, J. (2001) *World Wide Web Marketing*, 3rd edn. Wiley, New York.

Sterne, J. (2002) *Web Metrics: Proven Methods for Measuring Web Site Success*. Wiley, New York.

Wisner, J. and Fawcett, S. (1991) Link firm strategy to operating decisions through performance measurement, *Production and Inventory Management Journal*, Third Quarter, 5–11.

Further reading

Berthon, P., Pitt, L. and Watson, R. (1998) The World Wide Web as an industrial marketing communication tool: models for the identification and assessment of opportunities, *Journal of Marketing Management*, 14, 691–704. This is a key paper assessing how to measure how the Internet supports purchasers through the different stages of the buying decision.

Friedman, L. and Furey, T. (1999) *The Channel Advantage*. Butterworth Heinemann, Oxford. Chapter 12 is on managing channel performance.

Sterne, J. (2001) *World Wide Web Marketing*, 3rd edn. Wiley, New York. Chapter 11 is entitled 'Measuring your success'. It mainly reviews the strengths and weaknesses of online methods.

Web links

- **ABCe** (**www.abce.org.uk**). Audited Bureau of Circulation is standard for magazines in the UK. This is the electronic auditing part. Useful for definitions and examples of traffic for UK organisations.
- **E-consultancy** (**www.e-consultancy.com**) site has a section on web analytics including buyers' guides to the tools available.

- **E-metrics** (www.emetrics.org). Jim Sterne's site has many resources for online marketing metrics.
- **Web Analytics Association** (WAA, www.webanalyticsassociation.org). The site of the trade association for web analytics has useful definitions, articles and forums on this topic.
- **Web Analytics Demystified** (www.webanalyticsdemystified.com). A site to support Eric Petersen's books with a range of content.

10

Business-to-consumer Internet marketing

Learning objectives

After reading this chapter, the reader should be able to:

● Understand the potential of online business-to-consumer markets

● Identify the key uses of the Internet within a business-to-consumer context

● Identify Internet retail formats and understand the implications of business models applied to the Internet by retail organisations

Questions for marketers

Key questions for marketing managers related to this chapter are:

● Who are the online customers?

● What are customer expectations of web-based service delivery?

● Which factors affect demand for online business-to-consumer services?

● What services can be provided online?

● What are the key considerations when developing an e-retail strategy?

Links to other chapters

This chapter builds on concepts and frameworks introduced earlier in the book. The main related chapters are as follows:

➤ Chapter 4, which introduces strategic approaches to exploiting the Internet

➤ Chapter 6, which examines customer relationship management issues

➤ Chapter 7, which provides an introduction to the characteristics of Internet consumer behaviour

➤ Chapter 8, covering issues relating to successful site development and operations

➤ Chapter 11, covering inbound retail logistics and the supply-side of operations in reseller markets

Introduction

Business-to-consumer (B2C) markets have made a significant contribution to the commercial development of the Internet. The Internet provides access to a new trading environment – a virtual marketspace, which uses digital data to facilitate market exchanges. During the last decade this marketspace has become widely accessible to consumers and in doing so has presented retail businesses with many opportunities and challenges. The success levels of Internet-based retailers has been eagerly watched and tracked by analysts around the globe as an indicator of the potential of this virtual trading environment to change fundamentally the way businesses trade with their customers. Whilst some predicted a decline in significance of Internet trading as a result of the dot-com crash, the evidence suggests the opposite as companies like Amazon, eBay and Dabs, prove to be increasingly successful. However, online success in consumer markets is not guaranteed and during the last decade retail companies have achieved varying levels of success through trading online. Those without a clear vision of how the technology can deliver added value and competitive advantage, and the corporate competencies to support their online operation (e.g. Webvan, Boo, Clickmango), have failed to realise the benefit of venturing to trade online. Perhaps as a result of a high failure rate of start up dot-coms, in the early days of commercial use of the Internet, many established high-street retailers have been slow to adopt the Internet as a sales channel. However, now they are developing successful multi-channel strategies to provide customers with choices of where to purchase their goods and services including the Internet. Some notable successes are Tesco.com, Next.com, Argos.co.uk and Figleaves.com. Furthermore, in the UK, consumer spending online is predicted to continue to grow significantly; online retailer spending is set to rise from 2.4% of the total retail spend to approximately 17% within the next four years. (Figures based on Verdict E-Retail 2005 Report, January 2005.) The importance of trading online is therefore established.

This chapter explores some of the key issues having an impact on the growth and development of online B2C markets. It begins by focusing on the consumers, examining who they are, their expectations and motivations. This discussion is followed by an investigation into what the term *e-retailing* actually means and how the Internet contributes to retailing through the virtual *retail channel*. Then, the e-retailers themselves become the focus of the chapter, with a section that explores the products and services being offered online. The chapter concludes with a brief discussion of the implications for e-retail strategy.

Key themes and concepts

This chapter addresses two key themes, which are central to understanding how businesses are utilising Internet technologies to serve consumer markets:

1 **Online customers**: this section focuses on online consumer demographics, the key factors which determine online expectations in terms of choice and service quality and the key drivers of online purchasing behaviour.
2 **E-retailing**: this section examines firstly the *online B2C trading environment* focusing on why retail businesses are going online and ways in which companies are using the Internet to serve consumer markets; and secondly, which retailers are trading online, the range of activities they are offering and the type of products and services they are selling.

Within this chapter, industry case studies are provided as illustrative examples of consumer and retailer behaviour in the online trading environment. Additionally, academic articles are introduced to support underlying theoretical issues and concepts.

Online customers

Levels of consumer demand for online shopping and services might ultimately determine the size of e-retail markets and when or if a market saturation point will be reached. Currently, influences such as, whether the consumer has access to the Internet, levels of competency in use of the technology and the perceived benefits of Internet shopping are key factors likely to impact on the success and development of e-retailing (Ballantine, 2005). Internet retailing, or e-retailing as it will be referred to for the rest of this chapter, offers the consumer an experience that is very different from shopping in the high street, for example *comparison shopping* is much easier and quicker online than in the physical world (Cude and Morganosky, 2000). An example of a business that facilitates comparison of product and prices is Kelkoo.co.uk. Indeed, in the USA, consumers use the Internet to find information about a product in the early part of the buying decision-making process as well as buying directly on the web. They are purchasing through the fixed-location store or ordering by telephone or fax less than they used to (see Mini Case Study 10.5, *The offline impact of online marketing*). Other notable differences between on- and offline shopping are: dynamic pricing, which is often linked directly to demand, *interactive promotions* and *web-stores*, which are always open.

Dynamic pricing
Prices can be updated in real time according to the type of customer or current market conditions.

As a result of the characteristics of the virtual shopping environment, the online consumer experience can become an elective and very goal-orientated activity whereby online consumers go to the Internet to seek particular information about the products and services they wish to buy. Perea et al. (2004) highlight that whilst increasingly consumers are shopping online it is not clear what drives them to shop in this way. They suggest there are various factors including ease of use, enjoyment and consumer traits, that will determine whether an individual will be an avid Internet shopper. So who are the customers who shop online?

Who are the online customers?

Many researchers have written about which sectors of society use the Internet. Hoffman and Novak (1998) focused on the impact of demographics, and highlight inequities of Internet access based on race and gender. Sorce et al. (2005) looked at age and found that 'while older shoppers search for significantly fewer products than their younger counterparts they actually purchase as much as the younger consumer'. More specifically, The National Statistics Office (UK) (2005) identified that people aged 25–44 were most likely to buy online (63%), while people aged 65 and over were least likely to buy online (41%). Mori (2005), the market research agency specialising in reporting on public opinion has maintained a consistent interest in the technology sector. Mori (2005) have been watching technology usage in general and, in particular, who is using the Internet. This data highlights important trends that can help a retailer to develop a deeper understanding of which technologies consumers might use to access the e-retailer's online offer (see Chapter 2 for further discussion).

Another variable to consider when identifying the online consumers is *where* do individuals access the Internet both in terms of the nature of the point of access and geographical location.

● *Point of access* – the nature of the location can be fixed or mobile and, say, be at home or work. According to the National Statistics Office (2005), the most common place to access the Internet was at home (88%), although 48% have accessed it at work, 29% at another person's home, 13% at a place of education and 10% at a public library. The main means of access was via a desktop computer (85%) followed by a laptop (28%) and mobile phone (22%). In Britain, in July 2005, over half of households (approximately 12.9 million) could access the Internet from home, a trend which has been increasing year on year.

● *Geographical location* – there are varying levels of Internet penetration around the globe (see Table 10.1 and Table 10.2 for various statistics). Asia now has the largest number of Internet users, followed by the European Union (EU). Interestingly the USA no longer has the highest density of users per head of population (see Table 10.2) as in Sweden over 75% of the population are connected to the Internet. The size and density of user populations vary considerably from country to country and a key reason for this is the Internet infrastructure, which has not developed to the same extent on a worldwide scale. In general, northern European countries have a higher level of Internet penetration per head of population than southern European and former Eastern bloc countries. Underdeveloped, highly populated nations tend to have a comparatively low level of Internet penetration but more rapid growth rates than compared with highly developed nations.

Table 10.1 World Internet users and population statistics (2005)

World regions	Population (2005 est.)	Population % of world	Internet usage, latest data	% Population (penetration)	Usage % of world	Usage growth 2000–2005
Africa	896,721,874	14.0 %	23,917,500	2.7 %	2.5 %	429.8 %
Asia	3,622,994,130	56.4 %	332,590,713	9.2 %	34.2 %	191.0 %
Europe	804,574,696	12.5 %	285,408,118	35.5 %	29.3 %	171.6 %
Middle East	187,258,006	2.9 %	16,163,500	8.6 %	1.7 %	392.1 %
North America	328,387,059	5.1 %	224,103,811	68.2 %	23.0 %	107.3 %
Latin America/Caribbean	546,723,509	8.5 %	72,953,597	13.3 %	7.5 %	303.8 %
Oceania / Australia	33,443,448	0.5 %	17,690,762	52.9 %	1.8 %	132.2 %
WORLD TOTAL	6,420,102,722	100.0 %	972,828,001	15.2 %	100.0 %	169.5 %

Notes: (1) Internet usage and world population statistics were updated on November 21, 2005. (2) CLICK on each world region for detailed regional information. (3) Demographic (Population) numbers are based on data contained in the world-gazetteer web site. (4) Internet usage information comes from data published by Nielsen//NetRatings, by the International Telecommunications Union, by local NICs, and by other reliable sources. (5) For definitions, disclaimer, and navigation help, see the Site Surfing Guide. (6) Information from this site may be cited, giving due credit and establishing an active link back to www.internetworldstats.com. ©Copyright 2005, Miniwatts International, Ltd. All rights reserved.

Source: www.internetworldstats.com/stats.htm

From an e-retailers perspective, digital technologies and the Internet create an opportunity to cross barriers created by time and geography. However, it should also be remembered that where people live has potential strategic and operational implications. (This issue is discussed at the end of this chapter.)

Table 10.2 Internet Usage in the EU

Country	Population (2005 est.)	Internet users, latest data	Penetration (% population)	Usage % in EU	User growth (2000–2005)
Austria	8,163,782	4,650,000	57.0 %	2.0 %	121.4 %
Belgium	10,443,012	5,100,000	48.8 %	2.2 %	155.0 %
Cyprus	950,947	298,000	31.3 %	0.1 %	148.3 %
Czech Republic	10,230,271	4,800,000	46.9 %	2.1 %	380.0 %
Denmark	5,411,596	3,762,500	69.5 %	1.7 %	92.9 %
Estonia	1,344,840	670,000	49.8 %	0.3 %	82.8 %
Finland	5,246,920	3,286,000	62.6 %	1.4 %	70.5 %
France	60,619,718	25,614,899	42.3 %	11.3 %	201.4 %
Germany	82.726,188	47,127,725	57.0 %	20.8 %	96.4 %
Greece	11,212,468	3,800,000	33.9 %	1.7 %	280.0 %
Hungary	10,083,477	3,050,000	30.2 %	1.3 %	326.6 %
Ireland	4,027,303	2,060,000	51.2 %	0.9 %	162.8 %
Italy	58,608,565	28,870,000	49.3 %	12.7 %	118.7 %
Latvia	2,306,489	810,000	35.1 %	0.4 %	440.0 %
Lithuania	3,430,836	968,000	28.2 %	0.4 %	330.2 %
Luxembourg	455,581	270,800	59.4 %	0.1 %	170.8 %
Malta	384,594	301,000	78.3 %	0.1 %	652.5 %
Netherlands	16,322,583	10,806,328	66.2 %	4.8 %	177.1 %
Poland	38,133,691	10,600,000	27.8 %	4.7 %	278.6 %
Portugal	10,463,170	6,090,000	58.2 %	2.7 %	143.6 %
Slovakia	5,379,455	2,276,000	42.3 %	1.0 %	250.2 %
Slovenia	1,956,916	950,000	48.5 %	0.4 %	216.7 %
Spain	43,435,136	16,129,731	37.1 %	7.1 %	199.4 %
Sweden	9,043,990	6,800,000	75.2 %	3.0 %	68.0 %
United Kingdom	59,889,407	37,800,000	63.1 %	16.7 %	145.5 %
European Union	460,270,935	226,890,983	49.3 %	100.0 %	143.5 %

Notes: (1) The EU Internet statistics were updated on November 21, 2005. (2) Detailed data for individual countries can be found by clicking on each country name. (3) The demographic (population) numbers are based on data contained in world-gazetteer.com. (4) The usage numbers come from various sources, mainly from data published by Nielsen//NetRatings, ITU , C-I-A, local NICs and private sources. (5) Data may be cited, giving due credit and establishing an active link to Internet World Stats. (6) For definitions, see the site surfing guide.
©Copyright 2005, Miniwatts International, Ltd. All rights reserved.

Source: www.internetworldstats.com/stats.htm © 2005, www.InternetWorldStats.com. All rights reserved

It is important for an e-retailer to recognise the differences between on- and offline target markets. Additionally, it should analyse and understand the differences in consumer behaviour between these two channels. Knowledge of who the customers are can give the e-retailer the opportunity to begin to analyse their needs (in an e-retailing context) and then to formulate a plan as to how the company might serve the online customers. Table 10.3 shows the potential impact of some consumer profile variables in online markets. As in offline markets there is a wide range of profile variables that can be used to identify and eventually segment online consumer markets.

Table 10.3 Profile variables and the potential digital impact on target markets

Profile variable	Digital impact
Age	Age can affect levels of access to technology, computer literacy, and eventually, the extent to which individuals use the Internet as part of their shopping routines. Age can also be linked to where people live and again affect the potential size of the online market; for instance if selling goods and services to China, the majority of online users are under 35.
Household size	Household size has the potential to affect the number of people involved in purchasing decisions and the direction of influence. For example, research has shown that in Europe children and teenagers can have a strong influence on purchasing based on their levels of computing competency.
Household type	Household type has the potential to affect product and service requirements; major shifts towards single person households in the UK (11% increase since 1971 to 29%) has led to a shift in purchasing patterns and times of purchasing. Online, such households can create logistical difficulties when delivering bulky and perishable goods (see Mini Case Study 10.1 for further discussion).
Income	Income affects primarily purchasing power, but also lifestyles and individual expectations of quality and levels of service will vary.
Gender	Generally, Internet populations still have a slight male bias which potentially affects the likelihood of being online and level of computing skills.
Ethnicity	Ethnicity affects access to technology and economic circumstances.
Employment status and work patterns	Employment places time constraints on online shopping behaviour, i.e. when individuals can access online shopping channels.
Mobility	Mobility affects channel access; less mobile targets may be encouraged to shop online. This also applies to macro-populations, which are poorly served by public and private transport.

In summary, online shoppers can differ from offline shoppers in terms of profiles. Online shoppers tend to be younger, wealthier, better educated, have higher 'computer literacy' and more disposable income. However, perhaps as the Internet becomes a more mainstream shopping channel the differences in consumer profiles will not be so marked as wider sectors of the world at large are able to gain access to digital channels. The next part of this section explores the expectations and motivations of online consumers (see also Activity 10.1).

Mini Case Study 10.1   The online purchasing process

Whether on- or offline, consumers are individuals who buy products or services for personal consumption.

It is important to remember, there is not a straightforward answer to who buys: for instance some purchases are based on individual impulses whilst others may involve a number of individuals who can influence the final purchase choice. Blackwell et al. (2001) suggested there are five key roles that can influence a purchase decision:

1 Initiator – starts the purchasing process
2 Influencer – tries to influence the final purchasing choice
3 Decider – has the authority to make the final choice
4 Buyer – conducts the transaction
5 User – enjoys the benefits of the purchase decision by using the product or service.

In an online purchasing situation, the initiator, decider and user roles remain similar to those in an offline purchasing situation but research has shown that the influencer and the buyer can be significantly changed (e.g. the influencer/buyer is likely to be a younger member of the household; children and teenagers who are playing an increasingly influential role in online purchasing decisions). Furthermore, they are very likely to be those persons who actually conduct the online transaction. This is important for the digital marketing managers as they need to consider how to tailor their web site content and search marketing strategy in order to communicate with this relatively new type of influencer. Increasingly, younger influencers are enjoying more power in the online purchasing situation. E-tailers (see e-retailing section) are increasingly using web sites to support the purchasing decision by providing information at the evaluation stage of the buying process and also to avert post-purchase dissonance through sophisticated after-sales support online.

Activity 10.1 'Going shopping online'

Select a product or service of your choice that you are about to or would like to be able to purchase. Visit as many web sites as required until you find a product or service that could meet your needs (see Figure 10.1, for example).

Using your online shopping experience identify:

1 The problem you were seeking to solve
2 The extent of your information searching
3 The choice criteria which informed your decision making
4 The purchase solution (your preferred product or service)
5 Evaluate the web sites you have visited in terms of how easy it was to find the information you needed to make your purchasing decision.

Online customers' expectations and motivations

In the UK, over 50% of Internet users had shopped online by the end of 2004 and this is a trend predicted to continue to grow in terms of numbers of consumers and the amount they spend (Allegra, 2005). However, it has been suggested that too many companies are failing to realise the potential of this new digital trading environment and are tending to adopt defensive strategies, taking the lead from their nearest competitors as to what the organisation should be offering online rather than capitalising on the potential provided by digital channels (Allegra, 2005). E-retailers should aim to understand how customer expectations have been raised. Key areas where customers have high expectations of online retailers are the following:

● *Logistics* – the critical link between consumer-based Internet ordering and the delivery of the product to the consumer is often referred to as the final or last mile. The last mile, including product transportation, is frequently considered the most important element of the order fulfilment process, i.e. 89% of online shoppers rate on-time delivery high in importance and 85% of buyers who receive their order on time would shop at the Internet merchant again. Thus, delivery-related issues have been shown to have a high level of importance to online shoppers (Esper et al., 2003).
● *Security and privacy of information* – customers now expect that if they are prepared to provide detailed personal and financial information it will be stored securely.

Figure 10.1 Thinking of buying a book? Examples of online book retailers

Source: www.penguin.co.uk / www.blackwell.co.uk / www.amazon.co.uk

- *Timeliness* – the speed of digital communications has raised customer expectations in terms of response times and they expect a speedy shopping experience. It is no longer acceptable to take three or four days to respond to an online customer enquiry; an online customer expects the response will be instantaneous or at least within a couple of hours. Additionally, they expect to be able to order goods and services at any time.
- *Availability* – the Internet creates a sales environment, which is not restricted by space constraints, therefore there is an increased expectation that not only will there be a wider range of goods for sale online but also the goods will be readily available for immediate delivery.
- *Convenience* – it should be easier and quicker to compare prices online; there should be easy access to a wide range of retailers without the inconvenience of having to travel to a number of different locations.
- *Customer service* – customer value is the foremost driver of competitive advantage in the Internet shopping environment and customer service can be measured by the consumer in terms of price savings, service excellence, time savings and experiential values such as entertainment, visual stimulation/reward, levels of interaction. Positive response to such factors can lead to heightened loyalty (Lee and Overby, 2004).

The increase in customer expectations can have quite wide-reaching organisational implications. The gap between customer expectations of the online offer and the actual performance can have a significant impact on online performance. Mini Case Study 10.2 explores the relationship between experiences and online success. Following your reading of this case study, you can go on to try Activity 10.2.

Mini Case Study 10.2   eTailQ

There has been a great deal of academic research looking at the relationship between quality and online success in consumer markets. Wolfinbarger and Gilly (2003) used the premise that quality is related to customer satisfaction and retention in both product and service settings as a basis for their work. In doing so they established the dimensions of etailing and developed a scale for the measurement of etail quality (eTailQ). They identified four key factors, which they found to affect levels of online customer satisfaction, and these in rank order are:

1 **Web site design:**
   (a) Easy navigation
   (b) Appropriate levels of information
   (c) Effective information search facility
   (d) Straightforward ordering
   (e) Appropriate personalisation
   (f) Appropriate product selection

2 **Fulfilment/reliability:**
   (a) Accurate display aimed at ensuring alignment between customer expectations and realisation
   (b) Delivery of the right product within promised time frame

3 **Customer service:**
   (a) Responsiveness to enquiries
   (b) Helpful
   (c) Willing service
   (d) Immediacy of response

4 **Privacy/security:**
   (a) Secure payment facilities
   (b) Secure and private personal information.

Design a web site

Design an e-retail web site for a specialist retailer serving a niche market, for example a specialist health product retailer (see Figure 10.2). Use the four key factors identified by Wolfinbarger and Gilly (2003) to guide your design. Remember to consider:

1 Who are the online customers?
2 What are the online customer expectations?
3 How can the web site deliver online customer satisfaction?

Figure 10.2 Simply Vital example of specialist company, which is using the Internet as a channel to market

Source: www.simplyvital.com

In addition to consumer expectations there are several other key concepts that have been widely cited as affecting online purchasing behaviour. These are perceived risk and trust, and loyalty.

Perceived risk and trust

Literature suggests the online trading arena is intrinsically different from any other channel to market and in essence is an unfamiliar environment (Rutter, 2001). Online consumers are buying into a trading situation that is inherently laden with uncertainty, lack of cues to reinforce trusting relationships and risk. Risk and trust are multi-dimensional constructs and have been found to improve online sales effectiveness if perceived risk is reduced and trust established.

Perceived risk conceptualised by Bauer (1960) consists of six components:

1 financial risk
2 product performance risk
3 social risk
4 psychological risk
5 physical risk
6 time/convenience loss.

Willingness to purchase is considered to be inversely affected by perceived risk. Stone and Gronhaug (1993) state that 'risk is the subjective expectation of a loss'.

Closely associated with risk is trust as it is a potential outcome of risk reduction. Trust needs to be increased and perceived risk decreased if e-retailers are to engender positive belief in the organisation's online reputation. Dimensions of trust include: service provider expertise, product performance, firm reputations, satisfaction (with past interactions) and similarity. It should be noted that some researchers have suggested that not all online customers respond in the same manner. Newholm et al. (2004) conclude that e-retailers should adopt a differential approach to building trust and raise the point that types of customers and products can significantly affect how retailers should develop approaches for handling risk and trust. Indeed 'bargain hunters' are inherently risk takers and in this case it becomes the propensity to engage in risk taking, rather than being risk averse, which drives the consumer behaviour.

The risk seeking element of online purchasing behaviour possibly begins to explain the success of the online auction platform eBay. Online auctions have seen a massive upsurge in the number of sales of second-hand goods, which are traded between unknown buyers and sellers. Each party has limited knowledge of the other's past trading performance, the levels of service quality or the condition of the goods and/or services on offer and yet millions of buyers are willing to gamble large sums of money in pursuit of goods. The high level of purchasing activity has not gone unnoticed by retailers as many now offer goods for sale within the eBay platform.

Perhaps the key question for the e-retailer to consider is what levels of trust and perceived risk are required for a selected target audience, which will actually encourage buyers to purchase in an online trading environment. Whatever the level there is perhaps an even more fundamental implication, which is how to incorporate the excitement of the unknown into the online offer.

Loyalty

Online customer loyalty has also been well researched. Srinivasan et al. (2002) identified several variables as being unique to online consumer markets (see Table 10.4). The variables are:

- *Customisation* – tailored content;
- *Contact interactivity* – dynamic nature of the buyer/seller relationship;
- *Cultivation* – relevance of online content;
- *Care* – attention retail pays to consumer buying behaviour;
- *Community* – online interaction amongst purchasing community;
- *Choice* – expectation of greater choice online;
- *Convenience* – perceived comparative advantage of online shopping;
- *Character* – web site design.

Discussion point

Suggest how each of these variables might be realised in a transactional retail web site.

This section has considered the online consumer by looking at some of the variables that can be used to identify and develop an understanding of the individuals who shop online. Moreover, it has looked at customer expectations and the key factors that are likely to affect online purchasing behaviour: risk, trust and loyalty. The next section focuses on e-retailing and looks at how companies are attempting to meet the needs of the online consumer.

Table 10.4 Loyalty variables

Loyalty variable	Web site feature
Customisation	Personally, tailored product ranges, for example lists of regular grocery purchases, favourite products, brands, etc.
Contact interactivity	Two-way communications that demonstrate the dynamic nature of the online buyer/supplier customer relationship.
Cultivation	E-mail offers relating to past purchases, informing customers when there is a discount sale on items similar to their previous purchases.
Care	Real-time stock out information/order tracking. Shoppers are looking for evidence that the retailer has paid attention to detail throughout the purchasing process.
Community	Product reviews from satisfied customers. Include a facility allowing and encouraging exchange of opinions amongst shoppers.
Choice	Online shoppers expect greater choice online. Therefore, retailer needs to offer either wide or deep (or both) product and/or service choice.
Convenience	Easy access to required information and simple transaction interface. Over-designed and cognitively complex sites tend to lose visitors before they make a purchase.
Character	Symbols, graphics, style, colours, themes can be used to reinforce brand image and convey brand personality.

Source: Based on Srinivasan et al., 2002

E-retailing

This section explores retail businesses and the activities they are offering online. It begins by discussing the development of the online trading environment, the formats being used and the types of activities retailers are offering online. This is followed by consideration of the actual products and services offered online.

Development of e-retailing

In the early 1990s commercial development of the Internet was considered by many traditional retailers to be an arcane 'geekish' environment used by computer experts and scientists. As commercial use of computer networks began to grow retail companies began to consider how the Internet might impact on trade in the future and the challenges they might face (Rowley, 1996). However, not all companies were optimistic about the retail potential of the Internet, whilst some perceived it to be an opportunity for market development and expansion (Doherty et al., 1999), others saw it as an unstable and insecure trading environment. In terms of how retailers adopted the Internet they could broadly be divided into two groups:

1 *Inactive*: companies that for various reasons perceived the Internet to be a potentially dangerous environment, with limited commercial potential: for instance, lack of security, as it gave *'crackers'* a means of entry to a company's most valuable knowledge-based assets. For such companies the approach towards Internet adoption was to watch development and do nothing (perhaps with the hope that the Internet, like citizen band

radio, would fade into obscurity) until such a time that it became clear that there would be tangible business benefits from making the investment required to develop an online presence.

2 *Active*: companies that saw the Internet as a tremendous opportunity to access and develop new markets on a global scale. For these companies the approach towards Internet adoption was more complex as they had to determine how to trade success-fully in this new virtual environment. Many companies adopted an incremental approach, testing out the feasibility of technological solutions.

> A *cracker* is a malicious meddler who tries to discover sensitive information by poking around computer networks. This term is sometimes confused with 'hacker'. According to *The New Hacker's Dictionary* (Raymond, 1996), a hacker (originally, someone who makes furniture with an axe) is a person who enjoys exploring the details of programmable systems and how to stretch their capabilities, as opposed to most users, who prefer to learn only the minimum necessary.

During the last five years the *inactive* retailers have increasingly come under pressure to accept the Internet as a durable trading environment, whereas the *active* retailers have been dealing with many difficulties associated with their early investment into e-retail-ing. Operationally, e-retailers have had to organise their companies to cope with a range of issues, for example logistics, distribution and increased financial demands, and stan-dards of online customer service. From a more strategic standpoint, retailers have spent time developing their online offer and determining how to deliver value.

A five-year study examining the extent of Internet adoption in the UK by Ellis-Chadwick et al. (2002) has found that traditional retailers are increasingly likely to have a web site and offer online trading facilities. Retailers as a whole are seen as being highly advanced in their use of computer-based technologies, so it comes as no surprise that some retail companies were quick to explore the commercial potential of the Internet. Typically, a newly established retail web site aims to cover a range of business objectives and show limited evidence of targeting of content towards specific online consumers; corporate information for investors is presented alongside details of consumer promo-tions and graduate recruitment features. However, over time the focus and strategic contribution of the online channels has changed and e-retailing is rapidly expanding. Figure 10.3 suggests how the strategic focus might change over time.

> ### Discussion point
>
> Tesco.com, has established a position of being the world's leading online grocer with an esti-mated sales turnover of £401m and profits up 37% to £21m (as at 21 September 2005). However, Iceland was the first UK retailer to offer nationwide delivery of a range of groceries ordered via the web and yet they have ceased to offer this service. Why has Tesco.com been able to establish such a dominant market position?

Destination store

A retail store in which the merchandise, selection, presentation, pricing or other unique features act as a magnet for the customer (Levy and Weitz, 1995).

From 1995 onwards, retailers continued to develop their own web presence in the form of *destination* web sites in a similar way to the development of a fixed-location destination store in the real world. Web solution companies have aimed to provide solu-tions to drive traffic to a growing number of e-retailers' online offers. However, this is not the only approach being taken; many online goods and services are sold through portals or e-malls (see Mini Case Study 10.3). Currently e-retailers are focusing on producing sus-tainable and profitable business strategies for their Internet-based operations. Established retailers using physical channels to market as well as the Internet are now demonstrating

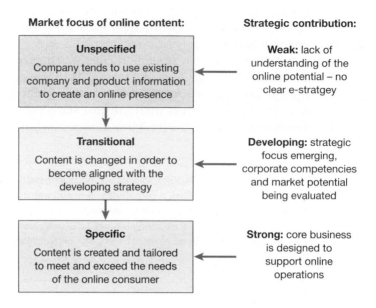

Market focus of online content:

Unspecified
Company tends to use existing company and product information to create an online presence

Transitional
Content is changed in order to become aligned with the developing strategy

Specific
Content is created and tailored to meet and exceed the needs of the online consumer

Strategic contribution:

Weak: lack of understanding of the online potential – no clear e-stratgey

Developing: strategic focus emerging, corporate competencies and market potential being evaluated

Strong: core business is designed to support online operations

Figure 10.3 E-retailing and strategic focus

that they can compete and in many instances surpass dot-com start-ups (pureplays), which only use the Internet as a route to market. According to Dennis et al. (2004) online shoppers prefer shopping at web sites operated by established high-street retailers.

As adoption of the web has expanded a number of different formats have been adopted by companies wishing to serve online consumers. According to Levy and Weitz (1995) retailers survive and prosper by satisfying customer needs more effectively than the competition, addressing customer needs through type of merchandise, variety and assortment of merchandise, and levels of customer service. Traditionally, there are two main types of established retail companies: those operating from fixed-location stores, such as department and convenience stores; and non-store-based operations such as catalogue retailing and direct selling. The fine detail of these various operating styles has gradually evolved to accommodate current customer needs. E-retailing has rapidly emerged, emulating non-store-based operations and new entrants like Amazon demonstrate how the Internet can potentially completely redefine customer needs using the Internet and the web to create a virtual retail environment with extensive global coverage. Currently there are several different formats that have been adopted by companies operating in B2C markets, including:

- *Bricks and clicks* – established retailers operating from bricks-and-mortar stores integrate the Internet into their businesses either strategically or tactically as a marketing tool or channel to market. Currently, the most successful online retailer in the world is Tesco.com, where personal shoppers select the customers' goods in local stores. This is not the only approach a business might choose to fulfil customer orders – networks of strategically placed warehouses provide another option.

- *Clicks and mortar* – virtual merchants designing their operating format to accommodate consumer demands by trading online supported by a physical distribution infrastructure. Virtual channels have distinct advantages over traditional marketing channels in that they potentially reduce barriers to entry. The location issue, considered to be the key determinant of retail patronage (Finn and Louviere, 1990), is in the physical sense reduced, along with the need for sizeable capital investment in stores. The best-known virtual merchant using this format is Amazon.com, the world's largest online bookstore.

- *Pureplays* – 'clicks-only' or virtual retailers are organisations that operate entirely online. In reality it is almost impossible for a business to operate online without a point of access to the Internet. Therefore, generally speaking, the term 'pureplay' refers to retailers that do not have fixed-location stores (e.g. **www.figleaves.com**). (The broader definition creates confusion with the term 'clicks and mortar'. Perhaps the most feasible explanation for the lack of commonly understood e-terminology is the immaturity of Internet business in general.) A variation of this category are *digital retailers* that sell products in digitised form (Dennis et al., 2004).
- *Intermediaries* – who link Internet technology and the retail supplier with the consumer. Such organisations perform the mediating task in the world of e-commerce between producers, suppliers and consumers by using consumer data, which is carefully analysed and used to target marketing campaigns. Some firms function as *infomediaries* (information intermediaries) assisting buyers and/or sellers to understand a given market. Established businesses might lack the resources, in terms of both staff and technological infrastructure, to operate their web activities internally. This creates an opportunity for the intermediary to step in and provide web solutions and they could eventually replace established retail businesses. The growth in importance of intermediaries has led to the use of the term 'reintermediation' (see Chapter 1).

  A good example of an online retail format intermediary is Respond.com (**www.respond.com**). This company uses the Internet and the web to connect buyers and sellers by e-mail. The buyer fills in an online form giving details of the product he or she wants, together with its price. This form is then sent as an e-mail to the supplier who may be able to service the enquiry. Respond.com then sends e-mails to the consumer, providing him or her with the offer.
- *Manufacturers of consumer goods* – also see the Internet as an opportunity to regain some of their power lost to the retailers in the past by the shortening of distribution channels. The process of disintermediation works by the manufacturer excluding the retailer altogether and marketing directly to the customer, thus shortening the value chain and/or the supply chain by trading electronically and shifting the balance of power closer to the end-consumer. Early examples of disintermediation originated within the banking industry, when it was noticed that information technology and industry regulation had reduced the need for retail banks as intermediaries.

Any one of these formats could become the archetypal *e-retailer* and could thus affect the future growth of the online retail market as a retail environment. Potentially, if virtual merchants (brick and clicks, pureplays, intermediaries) prove to be highly successful, established retailers operating from a fixed-location store could find themselves increasingly being replaced by new Internet-based retail formats (Van Tassel and Weitz, 1997). The implications are considerable, as Internet shopping is beginning to fundamentally alter the way that consumers shop and thus revolutionise the retail environment, transforming the local high street into a global *virtual high street*. New entrants may benefit from financial freedom to develop an organisation suited to supporting the logistical demands of the new format (thus addressing the 'last mile' problems faced by established retailers). Established retailers can create competitive advantages from brand equity and high levels of customer service – effectively preventing new entrants from establishing a foothold in highly competitive retail markets. However, if established retailers continue to dominate retail supply and develop their current integrated approach to retailing through the use of technologies such as EPOS (electronic point of sale), EFTPOS (electronic funds transfer at point of sale) and loyalty cards, bringing them closer to the customer, then the Internet could be used to support these operations. In this scenario, revolution is less likely to occur. The next section considers which retail channel and the types of activities offered by e-retailers.

Mini Case Study 10.3   E-malls

Electronic malls (e-malls) follow the format of fixed-location malls in the physical world, grouping together an assortment of retailers in one virtual destination on the Internet. However, unlike their real-world counterpart, this conventional approach to developing an online mall has had limited success as it offered few advantages to potential customers who could view the product assortment of retailers located anywhere in the world from their workstations and laptops without the need to travel, and so the advantages for the consumer of retailers being grouped together in one destination were lost. Additionally, control of the e-retailers by the management of the virtual mall is rather more complicated than in the physical world mall. The online landlord has to build trusting relationships with the e-tenants and they in return must provide reliable services (Dennis et al., 2004), a trust which is sometimes difficult to establish as individual retailers were not willing to participate in an online mall that facilitated comparison shopping.

In Europe, Blackwell's Bookshop and Victoria Wine were among the first retailers to give consumers the opportunity to buy online via the Internet. Both of these companies were the original core tenants in one of the first e-malls to serve UK online customers Barclay's electronic mall, called 'BarclaySquare,' was not particularly successful as the virtual landlord offered limited advantages to its core tenants over operating their own destination web sites. However, there are many creative ways that e-retailers are coming together in a virtual world.

Portals

These are a gateway to many web sites. There are many examples of portal sites on the web which adopt web-based solutions to the 'mall' concept and in doing so serve an array of different purposes:

- **Froogle.co.uk** – directs online customers to product information in two ways. First, it uses product information submitted electronically by merchants who take advantage of this free service. Second, as Google's spidering software crawls the Internet, Froogle automatically identifies web pages that offer products for sale. Froogle's search results are automatically generated by ranking software. Google does not accept payment for inclusion of products in these search results. Nor do they offer to place a merchant site higher in the results if they are an advertiser or offer to pay for that placement (http://froogle.google.co.uk/froogle/intl/en_uk/about.html#how).
- **EBay.co.uk** – auction site which brings together individuals around the globe who wish to trade with one another. Although not a conventional e-retailer eBay's success in the second-hand goods and collectors' markets cannot be ignored as more and more shoppers buy from within the eBay trading environment.
- **Amazon.co.uk** – a multiple category retailer which is not strictly a portal or a mall but the company has brought together, through its affiliate scheme, the product portfolios of thousands of companies in order to create a virtual shopping destination (Dennis et al., 2004), which serves the needs of millions of online shoppers.
- **Kelkoo.com** – a shopping search engine which helps online cutomers to find products and services online. A search will produce a results page which facilitates price comparison and purchasing.
- **Mysimon.com** – a comparison shopping service on the Internet for products and services. The site searches thousands of online merchants and millions of products to provide online customers with lists so they can compare selections before making a purchase.

Shopping bots

Software programs that can help online shoppers search for and compare specific products across multiple web sites; also called bots or intelligent agents.

E-malls have been a means to enable retailers to explore the potential of the web in a ready-made electronic trading environment. However, the key advantages of the real world shopping mall do not easily translate to the Internet and as a result e-malls tend to serve highly specialised markets. Notwithstanding this the core concept of a mall, bringing together goods and services from many suppliers to facilitate customer convenience, has been used creatively by some of the world's leading online companies.

Core tenants

A shopping centre or mall is usually a centrally owned managed facility. In the physical world, the management will aim to include in the mall stores that sell a different but complementary range of merchandise and include a variety of smaller and larger stores. The core tenants or 'anchor stores', as they are often called, are the dominant large-scale store operators that are expected to draw customers to the centre.

Retail channel

Retailers' use of the Internet as both a communication and a transactional channel concurrently in business-to-consumer markets.

E-retailing: the virtual channel

This section looks at how the Internet is being used as a channel to market, examining the activities retailers are engaging with online with customers. Retail channel is a term introduced by Doherty et al. (1999) to describe companies' multi-purpose adoption of the Internet, using it as both a communication and transactional channel concurrently in business-to-consumer markets. Traditionally the term *channel* describes the flow of a product from source to end-user. This definition implies a passive unidirectional system whereby the manufacturer or producer markets through a wholesaler or retailer to the consumer. Recent developments in information technology are changing this orientation by enabling retailers to focus their marketing efforts on managing customers more effectively (Mulhern, 1997). Therefore, the Internet brings the customer even closer to the retailers via a new combined marketing and distribution channel, in effect an interactive *retail channel*. This move may also suggest a shift towards a bidirectional retailer–consumer relationship, in which more power accrues to the customer (Hagel and Armstrong, 1997). As a result of the technological capacity e-retailers are becoming increasingly creative with how they are using the Internet and associated digital technologies to serve the needs of their online customers.

E-retail activities

As we have seen, businesses trading in consumer markets can choose to serve their customers via different combinations of physical and digital channels. Whatever online format a business chooses, decisions will also be taken about the actual function of any Internet- and web-based activities. These will primarily fall into one of two categories: information functions or interactive functions.

Information functions

Web sites provide retailers with an important opportunity to give customers information. Many companies see the web as a means of expanding customer services through offering their customers wider ranges of information than is possible in-store. One of the greatest advantages of the web according to UK retailers is its ability to facilitate the dispersion of low-cost information. Retailers have been proactive about providing information on their web sites, and offer a wider range of different types of information:

- *Product information* includes product descriptions and prices, promotional information and web advertisements, colour swatches and graphical images.
- *Financial information* includes company reports, annual statements and investor information. The depth of coverage can vary considerably, as can the extent of accessibility.
- *Company information* includes such items as history of the company, store location information, details of employees and company incentive schemes.
- *Press releases* appear in various forms. Some companies use press releases as part of their consumer promotions whereas others include such information in their corporate web sites aimed at enhancing the overall profile of the brand(s) (see how Ben and Jerry's are using the web, Figure 10.4).
- *Recruitment information* – companies have recruitment features providing potential applicants with job details.

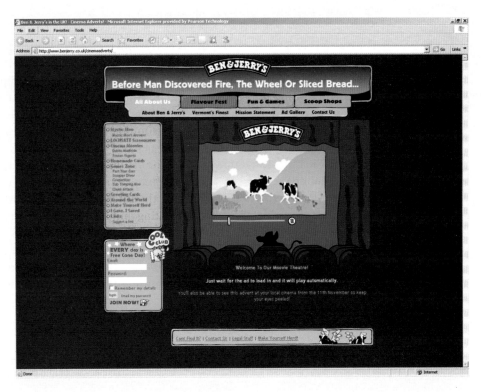

October 17, 2005 09:15 AM US Eastern Timezone

Ben & Jerry's Sows Fresh Campaign to Help Small-Scale Family Farms; New Ad Aims to Support and Raise Awareness of the Plight of Smaller Family Farms

The most immediate step consumers can take is to send a personalized letter to their representatives urging support for the Milk Income Loss Contract (MILC). This program, which helps dairy farmers survive during lean times, expired on September 30, 2005. Ben & Jerry's and the National Farmers Union have embarked on this collaborative effort to extend the MILC program and are urging both producers and consumers to help send this message to Congress.

'These ads aren't about selling ice cream,' said Walt Freese, Ben & Jerry's CEO. 'We're trying to initiate public dialogue about the fact that small and mid-size family farms are in danger of disappearing. We think Ben & Jerry's consumers care about this issue as much as we do, so we're using our marketing dollars to encourage them to tell Congress that smaller family farms are important to a diverse food supply.'

The company has launched a number of initiatives over the years to support small to mid-size family farms and sustainable practices in the dairy sector, specifically the Vermont Dairy Stewardship Alliance, the Vermont Dairy Farm Sustainability Project and the Caring Dairy Program in Europe, all of which focus on sustainable agriculture and the support of small-scale farms.

Source: Adapted from www.benjerry.com/our_company/press_center/press/

Figure 10.4 Ben and Jerry's use the web to support the cause of small and medium-sized farmers in North America.

Interactive functions

Interactive use of the Internet involves more than simply the provision of promotional information. It includes activities such as ordering of catalogues, promotional literature and 'free gifts' and encouraging customers to provide market research data as well as sales ordering and payment transactions. Interactive ways of using the Internet and the web include:

- *Marketing communications tool* – the Internet is frequently used as an advertising channel. Traditional advertising channels such as broadcasting and print media enable a one-to-many dialogue based on communications theory (Schramm, 1955) between senders and receivers. The communication process is normally constrained by time, namely the speed of response of participants, but communication can become 'conversations at electronic speeds' if conducted via interactive services such as the Internet (Fill, 1999).
- *Direct communication* – as an interactive channel for direct communication and data exchange the Internet enables focused targeting and segmentation opportunities for more closely monitoring consumer behaviour. E-mail provides a direct non-intrusive means of communication between firm and customer.
- *Online communities* – are also developing on the web and facilitating interaction between individuals and companies. Car manufactures such as Citroen and Volkswagen support many enthusiasts' sites in order to reinforce the emotional bonds between the product and the consumer via the web.
- *Marketing research tool* – the Internet's interactivity facilitates the collection of consumer data, providing the opportunity to gather personal information from online consumers while they browse through web sites, complete online questionnaires and respond to e-mails.
- *Sales channel* – the selling of goods and services online can take several different forms: the order is placed online while the delivery and payment are made through real-world channels; online ordering where the delivery of goods is required in the real world and the payment facility has options online or offline; the total process, namely the order, payment and delivery of the product occurs via the Internet.

In summary, businesses may choose to utilise the Internet and the web in a number of different ways to communicate and interact with their online consumers. The particular methods that they adopt to build an online brand may vary, from just providing information to online transactions including ordering and payment for goods and services. Issues relating to how e-retailers are using information and interactive content to build online brands is discussed in more detail in Case Study 10.

Who are the e-retailers and what are they selling?

According to Doherty et al. (1999, 2003), there are a number of characteristics of a business that are likely to determine the extent to which retailers have adopted the Internet, the online format they might choose and the products they sell. The characteristics include the following.

Size

Small and medium-sized retailers are increasingly adopting the Internet as a channel to market (see Chapter 11). The advantages include access to a wider market previously inaccessible and low-cost advertising, but the disadvantages include medium-term financial risk and scalability. Small-scale operations may be able to handle the picking and logistics due to the small numbers involved but problems will arise when expansion is considered and the need to sustain a larger operation becomes apparent. Indeed, it is *large retailers* (across Europe) that have been quick to incorporate the Internet into their retail offer. Examples are: in France, Carrefour (**www.carrefour.fr**), in Italy, Benetton (**www.benetton.com**), and in Austria, Magnet online (**www.magnet.at**). However, the web offer varies considerably – increasingly some retailers offer their entire range of goods and services via the Internet while others present selected ranges of information content only.

Activity category

The particular products and services offered to consumers can affect a business's usage of the Internet (see Mini Case Study 10.4). Products and services may be in a tangible or intangible form, each of which has associated advantages and disadvantages. Delivery is an issue for sellers of physical goods as is the Internet's inability to let customers experience the tactile qualities of a product prior to making a purchasing decision. Indeed, product category has had a profound effect on the success rate of certain online businesses. For instance, in Europe, the top product categories account for over 75% of the sales and these categories include books, music, DVD (movies), groceries, clothing games and software (Dennis et al., 2004). Whilst some of these products do not require extensive product descriptions, high-fashion items present difficulties and often there is a high return rate for clothing sold online. Digital products do not encounter the logistical difficulties associated with physical goods but encounter problems with pricing and control of copyright as a digitised product can be copied, as can music products. Ticket and online booking services (e.g. **e-bookers.com**, **expedia.com**) are enjoying comparative success online as they offer secure online transaction facilities.

Logistics

Accommodating demands for new levels of service in global electronic marketplaces could reinforce the critical significance of logistical infrastructures in determining online success (see Chapter 11). Logistical infrastructure might even determine the next generation of market leaders as its effective management provides an opportunity to create competitive advantage (Fernie and Sparks, 1998). From a retail perspective it is important to consider how the Internet is incorporated into retail activities in order to determine the importance of logistics (see Activity 10.3). If the Internet's primary role is as a promotional tool rather than a retail channel to market there is obviously less emphasis on the logistical infrastructure. Establishing a new logistical infrastructure to service the needs of Internet customers is proving to be a barrier to its immediate development as a retail channel. Established mail-order and direct marketing operators (e.g. Great Universal's **www.greatuniversal.com**) are taking advantage of the Internet channel, due to their not being store-based and having established direct distribution systems.

Outsourcing

If companies lack internal capacity they could decide to employ a third party to manage their online access, outsourcing some or all of their Internet operations (Abdel-Malek et al, 2005). From an operational perspective, fixed-location retailers might involve a third-party distribution company to bridge the gap between the customer order and delivery to the customer.

Activity 10.3 The last mile problem

Consumers are becoming increasingly aware of the Internet as a channel to market. As established brand names move part or all of their offer online, customers are regularly turning to the web to make their purchasing decisions. They are not only reviewing product information and reviews but also are now ready to buy online as a mainstream way of shopping rather than as just a novelty experience. As a result the home delivery market is growing. Paradoxically, this success is causing logistical problems, which threaten the future success of online business-to-consumer trade. The problem is how to get the goods the *last mile*. A UK government Foresight (2001) report gives estimates that by 2005 home delivery will be worth £34.5 billion. However, they also predict: 'As customer demand [for remote purchasing] increases, the likelihood of their being at home to receive their purchases decreases' (Foresight, 2001).

There have been a number of possible solutions to the delivery problem, including unattended delivery points in the form of secure purpose-built boxes or collection points at a local store where customers could collect their goods when convenient, but none have been particularly well received by the consumers. Whatever the solution at the customer end there are wider implications; at the company level they must resolve warehousing and distribution and the cost associated with providing a service which involves many deliveries of small quantities; at a societal level any increase in the number of small vans required to deliver online orders as in the case of online grocery retailer tesco.com is likely to cause further local traffic congestion.

Task

1 List five physical products that you or one of your neighbours might purchase via the Internet and require delivering to your home. Try to choose products from different categories, e.g. an item of clothing, fresh food, furniture, drink and computer equipment.
2 State the times of day you are available at home to receive delivery of these goods.
3 Describe the difficulties that an online retailer attempting to deliver the goods to you might encounter.
4 Suggest a solution for the *last mile* problem that will encourage consumers to increase the amount of goods they purchase via the Internet.

This section has discussed the choices a retailer wishing to operate online might consider and how some established characteristics of a business might affect decisions of which format to adopt for current and future online operations.

Mini Case Study 10.4   Online goods for sale in the UK

According to Verdict (2005) almost 10% of books sold in the UK are now bought over the Internet, with close to 11% of CDs and DVDs now bought online. Furthermore, white goods are becoming increasingly popular to buy online, with Internet sales now accounting for 6.6% of the market and online shopping continues to grow. UK retailers are expecting online shopping to rise by between 23% and 40% for Christmas 2005. Independent Media in Retail Group, a body that represents online stores, estimates that this will be overall 9% of retail sales at Christmas, as consumers increasingly order from home to avoid trudging around the shops. The winners in the online product categories are electrical goods. IMRG estimates that 20% of electrical goods will be sold online at Christmas compared to zero five years ago. The reason is thought to be that electrical goods are bought by brand name and model number, with little differentiation between stores other than price. Major high-street chains such as Dixons, Argos and Comet, which operate e-retail sites, are forced to keep prices low if they want to compete online with e-retail specialists such as Dabs, Empire Direct and Dell, which have no shops to support and therefore can often undercut their high-street rivals. However, online specialists, whilst developing their market share are struggling to sustain levels of profitability because although the volume of sales continues to rise, prices of new technologies such as digital cameras and flat-screen televisions are falling. At this point high-street retailers are able to fight back by offering greater levels of customer service, peace of mind through being well-known brand names and greater levels of after-sales support.

Source: Adapted from Butler (2005)

Implications for e-retail marketing strategy

The impact of an increasing number of consumers and businesses accepting the Internet and other forms of digital media as a stable channel to market is an increase in customer expectations, which creates competitive pressures and challenges for e-retailers. In part, this has been caused by new market entrants that have established their market position by, say, offering very wide and deep product choice, dynamic demand-driven pricing or instantaneous real-time purchase and delivery.

The growth in spending is amply demonstrated in Table 10.5.

Table 10.5 Growth in online buyers and their spend

	2000	2001	2002	2003	2004	2005F	2006F
Online shopping spend (£ million)	4,055	7,124	10,210	12,614	15,692	18,568	21,444
Online shopping buyers (millions)	5	8	11	14	17	20	23

Source: Allegra Strategies Forecasts/Euromonitor/APACS/ONS/IMRG

As a result, due to advances such as speed and interactivity brought about by digital technologies and the extension of trading time, customer expectations of levels of service have risen significantly. Therefore organisations are required to adopt a more dynamic and flexible approach to dealing with these raised expectations.

Allegra Strategies (2005) identified a number of performance gaps and Table 10.6 presents some of the most significant gaps and the managerial implications.

For the e-retailers it is important to identify any performance gaps and develop strategies which help to close the gaps. For example, in the case of logistics, research has found that utilising carriers (road haulage, air freight) that have higher levels of positive consumer awareness with appropriate online strategies (i.e. offering a choice of carriers) can contribute to the consumer's willingness to buy and overall satisfaction with the online buying experience. Therefore, development of strong awareness and brand image among consumers can prove to be a beneficial strategy for both the e-retailer and the carrier, since consumers have traditionally carried out the home delivery function themselves (i.e. shopping in 'brick and mortar' retail stores). Of course, this in itself raises the expectations of the care taken by the delivery agent, which has the implication of having to introduce better handling of goods as well as the speed with which the goods need to be delivered (Esper et al., 2003). A further consideration is that the retailer and the chosen carrier need to be able jointly to satisfy the consumer so that they may benefit from co-branding.

How the online consumer accesses the retailers' goods has given rise to various formats (discussed earlier in the chapter) and distribution strategies but this only forms part of the retailers e-strategy. Nicholls and Watson (2005) discuss the importance of creating e-value in order to develop profitable and long-term strategies and agree that logistics and fulfilment is a core element of online value creation but at two other important platforms: firm structure, and marketing and sales.

Firm structure can be used strategically depending on organisational capabilities and technology infrastructure. Porter (2001) described the emergence of integration and the potential impact on e-value chains. Integration can ensure faster decision making, more flexibility and attract suitable e-management specialists and capital investment (Nicholls and Watson, 2005). In the case of the UK grocery sector, larger retails have adopted different approaches towards structuring their online operations: Tesco serves 95% of the

Table 10.6 Performance gaps and managerial implications

Performance gap	Commentary	Managerial implications
The disparity between consumer expectations and web site offer	• The gap between Internet use and the lack of web site development means there is still the potential to capture browse and buy behaviour	• Companies need to develop web sites to capture this behaviour • A failure to do so will result in lost sales as consumers browse and/or buy elsewhere i.e. the effect is both 'on' and 'off' line
The disparity between brand strength offline vs online	• Retailer brand strength is frequently not reflected online. This may dilute current brand perception and leaves an opening for competitors to establish a stronger online brand presence even if they are weaker 'offline'	• The first 'dot-com' wave was concerned with establishing first mover advantage. This second wave is concerned with 'bricks and mortar' retailers establishing their brand strengths online i.e. a 'brand' wave • Any lack of investment will deliver mind share advantages to competitors even if they have a lesser brand. In this second wave it will be difficult to recover a competitive position once any brand advantage has been lost
A lack of alignment between the nature of the online competitive environment and the maturity of consumer demand	• The most advanced entrants are from overseas or national catalogue companies, the larger retailers (to a variable extent) and specialist niche companies	• The market is still at an early stage in many retail categories. There remains a potential competitive advantage for a 'bricks and mortar' retailer to 'grab this window of opportunity'
Inertia in decision-making	• There is a 'battle for budgets' within retailers i.e. retrench and invest in core business at the expense of new channels • Some retail cultures run counter to non-traditional means of 'doing business'	• Barriers to customer contact need to be removed. Budgetary constraints are misaligned where the cost of doing nothing means lost opportunity at best and and at worst lost competitive advantage • The maturing outsourcing market may unblock the cost-benefit perception

Source: Allegra Strategies (2005)

UK population by using a store-based model whereas ASDA, which offers less product lines, has based its model on the classical warehouse model. However, it is equally important to remember that the lack of a suitable infrastructure can be limiting in how the technology can be used (see Chapter 11).

Marketing and sales can be used in customer-centric value creation strategies in the form of interactive marketing communications strategies (see Chapter 4 for a detailed discussion) and revenue streams. Indeed according to Dennis et al. (2004), there are four revenue stream business models, which in turn are based on advertising, merchandising and sales, transaction fees and subscriptions.

Strategic implications for retailers wishing to be successful online are far reaching and require a retailer to develop a carefully informed strategy, which is guided by a business model that can satisfy corporate objectives through the deriving value from corporate capabilities whilst effectively meeting the expectations of the online consumer. The target market and the product category can have a significant influence on success. Now read Mini Case Study 10.5 and consider the offline impact of online marketing.

Mini Case Study 10.5　The offline impact of online marketing

Increasingly, companies are keen to understand the effect and impact of their promotional spend and particulary how different marketing communication tools perform. As with broadcast media advertising, it can be difficult to assess the impact of Internet marketing initiatives on offline sales. Traditionally, in the retail sector, it is not common practice to track the reasons why consumers arrive in a particular store to make their purchase. However according to Hewitt (2004) the Internet is 'not just a great promotion vehicle, it's also the tracking source that enables us to close the loop and see what happened after the visitor left the Web site and went shopping'. He suggests several ways in which retailers might use the Internet to follow their customers' offline purchasing behaviour. Tactics to gather information include the following.

Pre-purchase Internet surveys

Certain products and services are ideal for selling online; books, travel and entertainment tickets, and financial services whereas other products such as cars, consumer electronics and clothing are researched but not often purchased online. AOL conducted a series of surveys of 1,004 people who had purchased TVs within the last six months and 521 people who intended to buy a TV within the next six months to find the differing types of media such consumers employed to find information to inform their purchasing decision (see Figure 10.5). The surveys revealed that in-store displays (58%) and past experience/previous ownership (48%) are the most important sources of TV purchase decision making, while retailer flyers (13%) and online (12%) are ranked by TV purchasers as the most important media sources for new TV information.

This kind of survey is useful as it provides an indication of the effectiveness of online promotion. It also suggests that it is necessary to link online promotion with in-store promotion, especially if retailers are solely using the Internet as a marketing communication channel

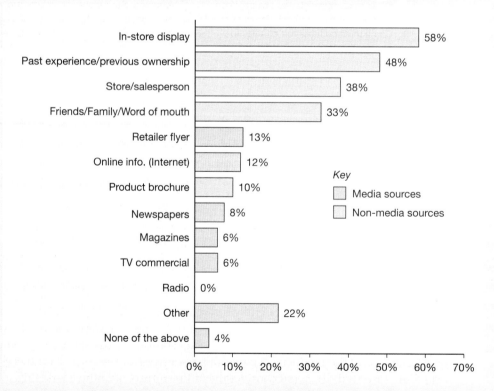

Figure 10.5 Sources of information for new TV purchases

Source: Hewitt, D. (2004) 'You CAN Tell How You're Selling Offline' from http://www.imediaconnection.com/content/2892.asp, March 01, 2004

Online coupon redemption

This technique is often used in the early adoption stages of the Internet as a marketing communication. The online advertiser incorporates/promotes a discount coupon via e-mail (or web site) and requests the customer print out a voucher and then take it to a participating store in order to redeem the discount (e.g. see Figure 10.6 concerning McArthur Glen Designer Outlets). On redemption of the printed voucher the retailer is able to analyse the impact of the online promotion on the offline purchasing behaviour and in doing so develops an understanding of their return on investment in online advertising.

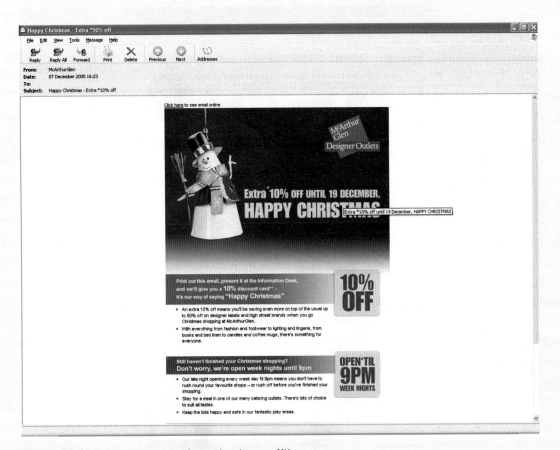

Figure 10.6 Online coupon redemption in an offline store

Share of voice

The relative advertising spend of the different competitive brands within the product category. Share of voice (SOV) is calculated by dividing a particular brand's advertising spend by the total category spend (De Pelsmacker et al., 2004).

Online rebate/gift with purchase

In this instance the retailer tracks the online customer's information through the use of cookies and offers some form of discount or gift offer with purchase. Generally, the customer will be required to register online (see Figure 10.7).

Just as consumer use of the Internet has been growing rapidly during the last decade so too has the use of the Internet as a medium to communicate a company's marketing messages. Research has shown the Internet as having an increasing share of voice when compared with other media. Furthermore, a survey conducted by PricewaterhouseCooper (2005) found that consumer advertisers are leading the online advertising spend (see Figure 10.8). The strategic implications of such findings are that retailers should be developing measurement techniques to determine the effectiveness of the online media on the offline spend.

Figure 10.7 Online rebate with online purchase: Sainsbury's online promotional offer

Question

To what extent is the Internet a ubiquitous marketing communication channel? In other words, is it possible for all types of companies operating in all sectors to communicate with all consumer target markets to an equal level of effectiveness? If not, how could retailers determine how to allocate online promotional spend?

Consumer advertiser spend surges in 2005

- Consumer advertisers represented the largest category of Internet and spending, accounting for 51 per cent of 2005 second-quarter revenues, up from 49 per cent reported for the same period in 2004.
- Computing advertisers represented the second-largest category of spending at 15 per cent of 2005 second-quarter revenues, down from the 18 per cent reported in the second quarter of 2004.
- Financial services advertisers represented the third-largest category of spending at 13 per cent of 2005 second-quarter revenues, down from the 17 per cent reported in the same period in 2004.
- Telecom companies accounted for 7 per cent of 2005 second-quarter revenues, up sharply from the 1 per cent reported in the same period in 2004, while Pharmaceutical and Healthcare accounted for 5 per cent of 2005 second-quarter revenues, consistent with the second quarter of 2004.
- Retailed the Consumer-Related categories at 48 per cent, up sharply from the 40 per cent reported for the second quarter of 2004, followed by Automotive at 22 per cent, Leisure (travel, hotel and hospitality) at 13 per cent, Entertainment (music, film and TV entertainment) at 10 per cent, and Packaged goods at 6 per cent.

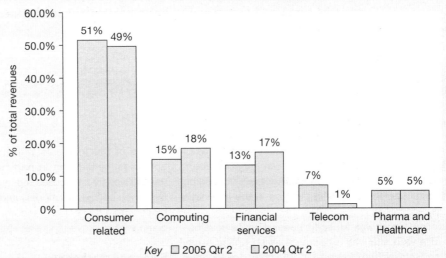

Internet ad revenues by major industry category*
2005 Q2 vs. 2004 Q2

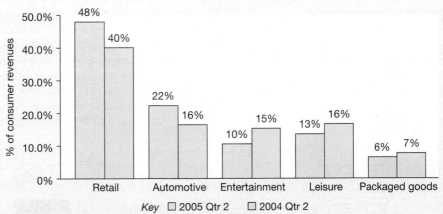

Internet ad revenues by major consumer category*
2005 Q2 vs. 2004 Q2

* Categories listed represent the top five ranked by revenue, and may not add up to 100 per cent.

Figure 10.8 Internet advertising by major industry and retail category

Source: PricewaterhouseCooper (2005)

In conclusion, it is now widely acknowledged that there is a need for a company to have a coherent e-strategy underpinned by a clear vision of how it may take advantage of the Internet. An online retailer's strategy is likely to be affected by the type of online format it adopts, the type of products and services it sells and the market segments it chooses to serve.

Retailers will defend their existing market share through consideration of strategic and competitive forces. It is the actions of retailers and their on- and offline behaviour in response to peer actions and new entrants' behaviour and success rate that are likely to shape the future of the Internet as a retail environment. Retailers need to ensure that the value created by e-retailing is additional rather than a redistribution of profitability.

It has been suggested that by removing the physical aspects of the retail offer the Internet may also provide the opportunity for increased competition (Alba et al., 1997). Pureplays can easily combine e-commerce software with scheduling and distribution to bypass traditional retail distributors. These virtual merchants could therefore threaten existing distribution channels for consumer products. The Internet is thus likely to appeal to new entrants who have not already invested in a fixed-location network. However, the boom and bust of the dot-com era has demonstrated that this opportunity must be supported with a sound business plan aimed at generating profits and not media attention *per se*.

Case Study 10 — lastminute.com: establishing and maintaining a competitive position

Retailing online renders one of the established mantras of the fixed location retailer '*location location location*' redundant. So how are the new e-retailers establishing and maintaining a competitive position in the Internet's marketspace?

lastminute.com was an early leader with its development of a web site which operated as an online travel agent and retailer (see Figure 10.9). The company founded by Martha Lane Fox and Brent Hoberman in 1998 has recently been acquired by Travelocity and Sabre Holdings.

Strategy and business model

The valuation achieved by the company at its float was seen by many at best as very unrealistic – its paper value exceeded the value of longstanding established travel agents like Thomas Cook Plc. Many dismissed lastminute.com's valuation as being an indicator of the absurdity of the dot-com phenomenon and dismissed excessive investment as irrational.

One of the problems with most of the commentary about lastminute.com in particular and e-commerce in general was that it focused too much on the front-end business idea behind the models and too little on the model's place within its sector (Panourgias, 2003). Over time the company has proved to be an established online brand.

Sales and marketing

lastminute.com built its market share by focusing on making innovative use of Internet technologies to deliver services to the end consumer that were close to the end of their shelf-life, i.e. late booking of holidays and hotel rooms. One of the core advantages is that there were few logistical issues to deal with when the purchaser takes themselves to the point of consumption (e.g. visiting the theatre, see Figure 10.10). In this way the company is able to supply both niche and increasingly mass market needs.

lastminute.com use advanced personalisation tools to deliver a highly customised online experience, sending different tailored messages to online customers who have opted in to receive online marketing, promotions and newsletters. The messages are varied according to the profile of the target customers and personalised e-mails

Figure 10.9 Lastminute.com products and services

Top 10 special offers

Forget the chart show. This is the **only top 10** that you need. From <u>smash hit musicals</u> to <u>top plays</u>, these offers are truly the best of the best.

Figure 10.10 lastminute.com theatre tickets

Source: http://www.lastminute.com/site/entertainment/theatre/product_list.html?CATID=94227

markets and accommodate the integration of a large number of businesses on the supply side into the group. An additional advantage is that having developed the expertise the team at lastminute.com is able to sell their knowledge to others thereby routing more trade and information through the portal in a similar way to other major online operators.

Competition

This has become a highly competitive sector and both online players like expedia.com, and laterooms.com, and long-established high-street brands, are competing with lastminute.com for market share. In addition, supply and demand patterns can change quickly as external events in the trading environment have an impact.

lastminute.com has become a very well-known and established online brand and has developed the technological know-how which has allowed the company to create significant competitive advantage. Furthermore, it provides its customers with a user-friendly interface, with many interactive and informative features (e.g. virtual hotel tours) that enable the customer to preview a hotel prior to booking. The company has used each of the key dimensions of e-strategy to create a very robust business model, which continues to attract both customer and suppliers.

are developed by using different blocks of text, features and promotions so that the e-mail delivers relevant content and offers (e.g. adventure holidays or cultural city breaks in European cities) to a particular type of person.

Infrastructure

Externally, lastminute.com is very effective in what it offers to its target markets; internally, its back-office systems and supply chain side of the business functions very efficiently. The key to success in this case is company-wide highly-integrated systems, which can easily be scaled up or down and deliver a high level of flexibility. As a result, the business can easily expand to meet the needs of the

Questions

1 The online travel business is growing rapidly and as a result competition is intensifying. Suggest how lastminute.com can maintain and develop its market share in the future.

2 Discuss how lastminute.com positions itself against the competition? What is the company's online value proposition?

3 Visit the web site of some of lastminute.com's leading competitors and analyse how much of a threat they pose to the company.

Summary

1   This chapter has focused on online consumers and e-retailers and in doing so has introduced some of the key issues that might eventually affect the overall success of e-retail markets.

2   Online customer expectations are being raised as they become more familiar with Internet and other digital technologies and as a result companies are being forced to adopt a more planned approach towards e-retailing. Additionally, in doing e-retail managers are considering who their customers are, how and where they access the Internet and the benefits they are seeking.

3   Web sites that do not deliver value to the online customer are unlikely to succeed. E-retailers need to develop a sound understanding of who their customers are and how best to deliver satisfaction via the Internet. Over time, retailers may begin to develop more strategically focused web sites.

4   Given current levels of growth in adoption from both consumers and retailers it is reasonable to suggest the Internet is now a well-established retail channel that provides an innovative and interactive medium for communications and transactions between e-retail businesses and online consumers.

5   The web presents opportunities for companies to adopt different retail formats to satisfy their customer needs which may include a mix of Internet and physical-world offerings. Furthermore, bricks-and-mortar retailers and pureplay retailers use the Internet in various ways and combinations including sales, ordering and payment, information provision and market research.

6   Web sites focusing on the consumer vary in their function. Some offer a whole suite of interactive services whereas others just provide information. The logistical problems associated with trading online are limiting the product assortment some retailers offer.

7   Trading via the Internet challenges e-retailers to pay close attention to the online markets they are wishing to serve and to understand there are differences between the on- and offline customer experiences.

8   The virtual environment created by the Internet and associated technologies is a growing trading platform for retailing. This arena is increasing both in terms of the number of retail businesses that are online and the extent to which the Internet is being integrated into almost every aspect of retailing. As a result retailers must choose how they can best employ the Internet in order to serve their customers rather than whether to adopt the Internet at all.

Exercises

Self-assessment exercises

1 Describe the variables that a retailer might consider when trying to identify an online target market.

2 Describe the different types of formats an online retailer might follow.

3 List the various activities a retailer might include in a customer-facing web site.

Essay and discussion questions

1 Evaluate the potential of the Internet as a 'retail channel'.

2 Discuss whether you consider that all products on sale in the high street can be sold just as easily via the Internet.

3 Australasia is home to approximately 2% of Internet users around the globe. Describe how an online retailer might choose to target a market. Illustrate your answer with examples.

4 Select three web sites that demonstrate the different ways in which a retailer might use the Internet to interact with its customers. Compare the contents of the web sites and explain what the potential benefits are for the customers of each of the sites.

Examination questions

1 It was once predicted that the Internet would replace high-street stores and that within ten years the majority of retail purchases would be made online. Discuss the extent to which you think the goods and services available via the Internet can satisfy the needs of the average consumer.

2 Compare and contrast the opportunities that a high-street e-retailer faces with those of a pureplay e-retailer.

References

Abdel-Malek, L., Kullpattaranirun, T. and Nanthavanij, S. (2005) A framework for comparing outsourcing strategies in multi-layered supply chains, *International Journal of Production Economics* 97 (3), 318.

Alba, J., Lynch, J.C., Weitz, B., Janiszewski, C., Lutz, R., Sawyer, A. and Wood, S. (1997) Interactive home shopping. Consumer, retailer and manufacturer incentives to participate in electronic marketplaces, *Journal of Marketing*, 61 (July), 38–53.

Allegra (2005) Allegra Strategies Limited, London WC2N 5BW.

Ballantine, J. (2005) Effects of interactivity and product information on consumer satisfaction in an online retail setting, *International Journal of Retail and Distribution Management*, 33(6), 461–71.

Bauer, R. (1960) Consumer behavior as risk taking, *Proceedings of the American Marketing Association*, December, 389–98.

Blackwell, R., Miniard, P. and Engel, J. (2001) *Consumer Behaviour*, Dryden, USA.

Butler, Sarah (2005) Internet stores expect a merry Christmas as online sales soar, *The Times*, 16 November. www.timesonline.co.uk/article/0,,2-1874371,00.html.

Cude, B., and Morganosky, M. (2000). Online grocery shopping: an analysis of current opportunities and future potential, *Consumer Interests Annual*, 46, 95–100.

Dennis, C., Fenech, T. and Merrilees, B. (2004) *e-retailing*. Routledge, Taylor and Francis Group, London.

De Pelsmacker, P., Geuens, M., Van den Bergh, J. (2004) *Marketing Communications: a European Perspective*, 2nd edn. Financial Times/Prentice Hall, Harlow.

Doherty, N.F., Ellis-Chadwick, F.E. and Hart, C.A. (1999) Cyber retailing in the UK: the potential of the Internet as a retail channel, *International Journal of Retail and Distribution Management*, 27(1), 22–36.

Doherty, N.F., Ellis-Chadwick, F.E. and Hart, C.A. (2003) An analysis of the factors affecting the adoption of the Internet in the UK retail sector' *Journal of Business Research*, 56 (11), 887.

Ellis-Chadwick, F.E., Doherty, N.F. and Hart, C. (2002) Signs of change? A longitudinal study of Internet adoption by UK retailers, *Journal of Retailing and Consumer Services*, 9(2).

Esper, T., Jensen, T., Turnipseed, F. and Burton, S. (2003) The last mile: an examination of effects of online retail delivery strategies on consumers, *Journal of Business Logistics*, 24 (2), 177.

Fernie, J. and Sparks, L. (1998) *Logistics and Retail Management*. Kogan Page, London.

Fill, C. (2000) *Marketing Communications – Contexts Contents and Strategies*, 3rd edn. Financial Times/Prentice Hall, Harlow.

Finn, A. and Louviere, J. (1990) Shopping centre patronage models; fashioning a consideration set segmentation solution, *Journal of Business Research*, 21, 277–88.

Foresight (2001) @ *Your Home: New Markets for Customer Service and Delivery*.

Hagel, J. III and Armstrong, A.G. (1997) *Net Gain – Expanding Markets through Virtual Communities*. Harvard Business School Press, Boston.

Hewitt, D. (2004) You can tell how you're selling offline. **www.imediaconnection.com/content/2892.asp** March.

Hoffman, D. and Novak, T. (1998) Bridging the racial divide on the Internet, *Science 280*, April 17, 390–1.

Lee, E. and Overby, J. (2004) Creating value for online shoppers: implications for satisfaction and loyalty, *Journal of Consumer Satisfaction and Loyalty*, 17, 54–68.

Levy, M. and Weitz, B.A. (1995) *Retailing Management*, 2nd edn. Irwin, Chicago.

MORI (2005) Technology Research: Technology Tracker. **www.mori.com/technology/techtracker.shtml** (accessed October, 2005).

Mulhern, F.J. (1997) Retail marketing: from distribution to integration, *International Journal of Research in Marketing*, 14, 103–24.

Newholm, T., McGoldrick, P., Keeling, K., Macaulay L. and Doherty, J. (2004), Multi-Story Trust and Online Retailer Strategies, *The International Review of Retail, Distribution and Consumer Research*, October, 14 (4), 437–56.

Nicholls, A. and Watson, A. (2005) Implementing e-value strategies in UK retailing, *International Journal of Retail and Distribution Management*, 33 (6), 426–43.

Panourgias, N. (2003) 'Lastminute.com – not just a pretty face?, **www.netimperative.com/2004/01/07/COLUMNISTS** (December, 2005).

Perea, T., Dellaret, B. and Ruyter, K. (2004) What drives consumers to shop online? A literature review, *International Journal of Service and Industry Management*, 15 (1), 102–21.

Porter, M. (2001) Strategy and the Internet, *Harvard Business Review*, March, 62–78.

PricewaterhouseCooper (2005) *Internet Advertising Revenue Report*, September 2005.

Raymond, E.S. (1996) *The New Hacker's Dictionary*, 3rd edn. MIT Press, Cambridge, MA.

Rowley, J. (1996) Retailing and shopping on the Internet, *International Journal of Retail and Distribution Management*, 24 (3), 26–37.

Rutter, J. (2001) From the sociology of trust towards a sociology of e-trust, *New Product Development and Innovation Management*, December/January, 371–85.

Schramm, W. (1955) How communication works, in W. Schramm (ed.) *The Process and Effects of Mass Communications*. University of Illinois Press, Urbana, IL.

Sorce, P., Perotti, V. and Widrick, S. (2005) Attitude and age differences in online buying, *International Journal of Retail and Distribution Management*, 33 (2), 122–32.

Srinivasan, S., Anderson, R. and Ponnavolu, K. (2002) Customer loyalty in e-commerce: an exploration of its antecedents and consequences, *Journal of Retailing*, 78, 41–50.

Stone, R. and Gronhaug, K. (1993) Perceived risk: further considerations for the marketing discipline, *European Journal of Marketing*, 27(3), 39–50.
Van Tassel, S. and Weitz, B.A. (1997) 'Interactive home shopping: all the comforts of home, *Direct Marketing*, 59(10), 40–1.
Verdict Research Limited (2005) *e-retail Report*.
Wolfinbarger, M. and Gilly, M (2003) eTailQ: dimensionalizing, measuring and predicting eTail quality, *Journal of Retailing*, 79, 183–98.

Further reading

Dennis, C., Fenech, T. and Merrilees, B. (2004) *e-retailing*. Routledge, Taylor and Francis Group, London.
Harris, L. and Dennis, C. (2002) *Marketing the e-business*. Routledge, London.
McGoldrick, P. (2002) *Retail Marketing*. McGrawHill, Maidenhead.
Mohammed, R., Fisher, R., Jaworski, B. and Addison, G. (2004) *Internet Marketing 2/e with e-commerce*. McGrawhill, Maidenhead.

Web links

- Allegra Strategies www.allegra.co.uk (November 2005).
- www.iab.net/resources/adrevenue/pdf/IAB_PwC%202005Q2.pdf (November 2005).
- National Statistics Office (2005) www.statistics.gov.uk/cci/nugget.asp?id=8 (November 2005).
- Tesco plc Interim Results 2005/6 24 Weeks ended 13 August 2005. www.tescocorporate.com/page.aspx?pointerid=9101D8A23A894B008112432E4694CEA2 (accessed 1 October 2005).
- World Internet Users and Population Statistics. www.internetworldstats.com/stats.htm (November 2005).

11

Business-to-business Internet marketing

Learning objectives

After reading this chapter, the reader should be able to:

● Identify the principal uses of the Internet in B2B markets

● Explain the meaning of the electronic market place in terms of business potential

● Understand the impact of Internet technologies on buyer–supplier processes, relationships and markets

● Discuss how companies are utilising Internet technologies as part of their marketing strategies, tactically or strategically

Questions for marketers

Key questions for marketing managers related to this chapter are:

● How are businesses using Internet technologies?

● How is the traditional sales process changed online?

● What are the applications for B2B e-commerce in our business?

● Who are our trading partners?

● What is the role of digital marketing strategies in B2B organisations?

● What is the impact of Internet technologies in B2B markets?

Links to other chapters

This chapter should be read in conjunction with these chapters:

Introduction

Many writers and researchers have generally agreed for some time that technology has the capacity to change how businesses trade, expand information processing capacity and impact on overall success. More recently, commercial usage of Internet technologies has sparked a debate focusing on the breadth and depth of the impact of these technologies. Porter (2001) strongly argued the Internet to be 'a complement to, not a cannibal of, traditional ways of competing'. However, some writers (Tapscott 1997, Gates 1999, Evans and Wurster, 2000) argue that business is completely different as a result of trading online and go as far as advocating that the Internet creates a radically different trading environment. As a result, it is suggested organisations should develop fundamentally different value propositions and new patterns of organisational behaviour in order to create sustainable business strategies for the online trading environment (Evans and Wurster, 2000). Moreover, there is some evidence to support such arguments; new market entrants have taken market share from existing companies by developing innovative market positions using seemingly unorthodox approaches, for example:

- Amazon.com established its position as the world's largest book seller using competitors' and suppliers' inventories;
- Google positioned itself as the most effective search engine by freely giving away its core service to end users;
- eBay has built its digital empire by facilitating online auctions whereby individuals rather than organisations sell their own goods to other individual customers (for further discussion of eBay trading see Case Study 10) and in doing so positioned the company as a global consumer trading arena.

Notwithstanding this debate over the impact of the Internet on business strategy, it is a fact that a critical mass (in terms of B2B usage of Internet technologies) has been arrived at and as a result it is prompting more and more businesses to have a well-developed and supported Internet presence and to trade electronically. Consequently, it is important to ensure a clear understanding of B2B Internet marketing in order for businesses to utilise available technology efficiently and effectively. This chapter focuses on business usage of Internet technologies in B2B markets and the extent to which digital technologies are re-shaping business strategies and trading environments.

Key themes and concepts

This chapter addresses four key themes which are central to understanding how businesses are utilising Internet technologies:

1 **The B2B e-context:** this section explores the circumstances in which B2B usage of the Internet occurs and highlights some features of the online trading environment which affect business involvement.
2 **Commercial exchanges in B2B markets:** this section examines: 1. the *electronic marketplace* in terms of growth, volume and global dispersion; and 2. *electronic exchanges* looking specifically at how organisations are using Internet technologies for (a) *communications*, and (b) *e-commerce* (online buying and selling).
3 **Trading relationships in B2B markets:** this section explores how trading relationships are changing as a result of online trading, the structure of the online buying group and the online supply chain.

4 **Digital marketing strategies:** this section looks at the focus of digital marketing strategies – tactical or strategic, the extent to which such strategies are integrated into an organisation's overall strategic planning; and the impact on organisational success.

Within this chapter, industry case histories are provided as illustrative examples of organisational behaviour in the online trading environment. Additionally, academic articles are introduced to support underlying theoretical issues and concepts.

B2B e-context

This section considers the features of the online trading environment that are unique and might ultimately impact on the extent to which organisations develop a web presence and trade online. *Visibility* and *transparency* are examples of unusual characteristics of the online trading environment, which can be either advantageous or not depending on an organisation's objectives. For buyers, 'marketsites' facilitate potentially lower prices and lower search and order costs, but for sellers, market share and value can become eroded over a relatively short period of time when trading in such electronic markets. From a more tactical perspective, Brynjolfsson and Kahin (2000) identified more detailed and unusual characteristics of online financial transactions (e.g. making a greater number of price adjustments), and as a result concluded online markets are (at least in part) different to off-line markets.

Regardless of the effects of trading online it is important to remember that B2B markets are different from B2C markets in a number of ways. According to Jobber (2004), in organisational markets, there are typically fewer customers that are likely to buy goods in bulk quantities and the buyer organisations tend to be larger and subsequently of great value to the supplier. What are the implications of this? First, with fewer buyers, the existence of suppliers tends to be well known. Choice criteria vary: impulse purchases, and those based on emotional motives are rare in organisational buying situations as buyers tend to be professionals who use technical and economic choice criteria to inform their decision making. This means that efforts to promote brands are different to those used for consumer brands and price setting tends to involve more negotiation between the seller and the buyer.

Marketsite
eXchange, eHub, metamediaries are terms used to refer to complex web sites that facilitate trading exchanges between companies around the globe. **MarketSite™** is a trade mark of commerceOne and considered as the leading e-marketplace operating environment.

Online environment analysis

The situation or context in which an activity takes place needs to be analysed in order to understand the full meaning of the actions which are taking place in a given trading situation. This is particularly relevant to the online trading environment. As suggested, it has unusual characteristics which can impact on the way an organisation defines its marketing strategy and the activities in which it engages online.

According to Finlay (2000) organisations operate in an environment that consists of a great many influences and a particularly important part of strategy development is being able to make sense of what is happening or likely to happen in the future in this environment (for further discussion of details of the micro- and macro-environment analysis see Chapters 2 and 3). There is much academic work focusing on various aspects of online trading situations and how characteristics of this environment potentially impact on organisational behaviour and influence strategy development. Three aspects of the trading environment are considered by focusing on academic literature in order to gain a better understanding of what is known about the B2B trading context and the online environment:

1 macro-environmental
2 micro-environmental
3 internal (organisation's operating environment).

1 Macro-environment

The *macro-environment* consists of various external factors which can affect a business's success. According to Finlay (2000), these factors may include: demographic, economic, environmental, political, legal, social and technological. Examples of how some of these analysis factors are affecting organisations operating online are as follows.

Demographic

Hoffman et al. (2000) identified the importance of demographic factors on individuals' uptake of Internet technologies and discussed in some detail the impact of how where people live will be affected by the technology infrastructure that supports their Internet access. For example, in the UK, Western Europe and North America there is a highly developed network infrastructure whereas in the Pacific Ring (excluding Japan) technological infrastructure is poor and as a result international data traffic links are very limited. Consumer demographics and the impact of inequities of Internet access have been discussed in some detail in Chapter 10. However, organisational dispersion has produced far fewer publications. The issue of dispersion of online businesses is discussed in the next key section of the chapter: Commercial exchanges in B2B markets.

Economic

Bakos (1991) examined the impact of online markets, and how internet-based electronic marketplaces affect pricing and competition. A major impact of these electronic markets is that they typically reduce the search costs buyers must pay to obtain information about the prices and product offerings available in the market. Economic theory suggests lower search costs play a key role in determining how technology can affect market efficiency and competitive behaviour. Reduced search costs deliver *direct efficiency gains* from reduced intermediation costs and *indirect* (but possibly larger) gains in allocational efficiency from better-informed buyers. Ultimately the result is increased efficiency of interorganisational transactions in the process affecting the market power of buyers and sellers.

Environmental

Do (physical) environmental issues impact on our digital marketing planning? Well for the first time many companies are developing corporate and social responsibility policies and statements. According to Dixon (2005):

> *You can have the greatest strategy in the world but if your vision of the future is wrong you just land up travelling even faster in the wrong direction. A prime example of this is the current revolution in corporate ethics and social responsibility, which is changing major board policies of many multinationals.*

Dixon (2005), an acclaimed specialist in future marketing management, suggests that corporate and social responsibilty is an insurance policy against bad news and bad news can hit any corporation and shatter market confidence, or even worse scandalise customers and cause outrage in the general public. Furthermore, the impact of Internet technology is that global media are able to stimulate great interest in exposing corporate wrongdoing, the result of which can be complete business failure. Currently, trading environments have very sensitive climates and increasingly corporations are now feeling their way through the issue of corporate and social responsibility.

Political

From a political perspective, the online environment raises many issues, for instance borderless trading: how are import duties and taxes applied and controlled and the interest of individual nations maintained when trading in an environment where there is no central control able to authorise or establish globally applicable laws? Another issue is how the Internet might affect the democratic process *per se*. Shaw (2002), considers how 'the Internet will turn political campaigns upside down'. Political debates also focus on the extent to which the accessibility of information impacts on levels of individual and organisational privacy.

Legal

The macro-environment consists of bodies of laws that affect what organisations can do and provide frameworks of rules which are enforceable. However, as far as the online environment is concerned there is no international legislation system. Even within the USA where Internet usage is advanced compared to many other parts of the world, legal controls are limited. Central issues from a B2B perspective include: intellectual property rights, taxation and data protection (see Chapter 3 for further discussion of the macro-environment and legal issues).

Social

The social environment is concerned with people's needs and wants (Finlay, 2000). From a digital marketing planning perspective, the cultural values of the society that an organisation wishes to trade with are of critical importance. Societies are constantly evolving; in economically well-developed nations, the *quality of life* has become a priority. Attitudes to work and leisure are evolving towards creating the work/life balance. Digital technology has had a wide impact on the social environment; the Internet has the potential to accentuate the differences within a single nation and between nations. There has been much discussion globally about *Information haves* and *have nots*, again primarily in B2C markets. The impact of organisational culture is generally considered within the literature as part of an internal analysis (see Internal analysis later in this section).

Technological

The major environmental influence of technology in the last decade has been the online trading arena created by the computer networks that form the Internet. This global trading environment has the impact of creating opportunities for organisations of all sizes to operate as multinational enterprises. Sambharya et al. (2005) state that innovative Internet and web-based technologies have the potential to affect the way businesses operate: 'The "new" rules include restructuring to foster a "glocal" outlook, nimbleness, empowerment of local managers / employees and the management of knowledge', thereby suggesting that technological changes not only impact at the macro-environmental level of analysis but also at the micro and internal level. For instance, trading becomes borderless, competition is intensified, procurement and production globalised, operations streamlined and made more cost effective, and lead times are reduced.

2 Micro-environmental analysis

The *micro-environment* consists of five key elements: competitors, customers, suppliers, intermediaries and other stakeholders. At this level, the organisation has much more direct control. In highly dynamic markets, competitors are constantly monitored in order to understand their next move. Relationship management with both the buy side and supply side of the exchange process is carefully controlled and managed. In addition, location of trading, virtual value chain, channel structures and trading relationships form an important part of the online trading context but are considered separately in Trading relationships in B2B markets later in this chapter (see also Chapter 2).

Arguably, *competition* is at the heart of any discussion about the micro-environmental trading environment. In 1980, Michael Porter published his classic model showing how these forces potentially shape the five main competitive forces that affect a company. In 2001, he revised this model to accommodate how the Internet influences industry structure. However, he is mindful to point out that in the dot-com boom and bust era the Internet was the cause of many distorted signals. New technologies trigger rampant experimentation that is often economically unsustainable (Porter, 2001). The value chain model has been revised to reflect experiences of how Internet and digital technologies can alter the model.

An important part of this level of analysis is to develop an understanding of customers and their behaviour in order to develop insight into how to get inside the minds of online customers and to understand the drivers and barriers which impact on how customers move through the buying process online. An important decision for digital marketing planners is which groups of customers are the most attractive targets and best match the organisation's capabilities. In business markets, purchasing decisions are almost exclusively goal-orientated. The decision-making unit (individuals involved in the purchasing decision) will vary according to the buy class, the product type and the importance of the purchase. The decision-making unit uses a range of choice criteria, mainly technical and economic, to evaluate purchasing options. Tzong-Ru and Jan-Mou (2005) argue that although the Internet has facilitated the connecting of markets across the globe it has not altered the general criteria for B2B trading. Therefore, it is perhaps reasonable to assume that choice criteria remain fairly constant whether an organisation is buying on- or offline. However, the online environment can enhance and potentially improve the efficiency of online trading by facilitating flow of logistics (leading to potential cost savings), business flow (developing and extending markets), enhanced cash flow (through streamlining and cost efficiencies in management and administration) and information flow (supporting decision making). It is important to remember that a fundamental part of the organisational buying process is customer relationship development and management. Trading via the Internet makes it possible to interact with large numbers of customers whilst still treating them as individuals due to the application of sophisticated e-CRM applications. However, it is important that such applications are supported by appropriate organisational structures (see Chapter 6 for further discussion of e-CRM).

Suppliers, intermediaries and other stakeholders are also considered as part of the macro-environmental analysis. Perhaps the most significant change to occur as a result of trading online is the nature of trading partnerships. New types of partnerships are being formed with new types of partners in electronic trading hubs (e.g. *marketsites*). Trading relationships are discussed again later in this chapter.

3 Internal analysis

Internet technologies are adopted in various ways to meet a range of business objectives. Organisations are responding differently to the opportunities and challenges created by the technology. General Electric Corporation was an early adopter of the technology and incorporated it into its transaction processing systems, which resulted in huge cost savings. Google was created through innovative use of carefully designed algorithms which enabled the company to be differentiated in the market by providing superior search services. But not all companies have been such proactive and innovative adopters of the technology. Many have taken cautious steps, say by introducing e-mail, developing a poster web site presenting company contact details and a view of the corporate headquarters, and then gradually moving towards e-commerce applications. However, increasingly, companies are looking for ways to get the best out of digital technologies: ips Intelligent Print Solutions is one such company. The company has won many industry awards for its use of digital solutions that both enhance levels of service and improve business efficiency (see Figure 11.1).

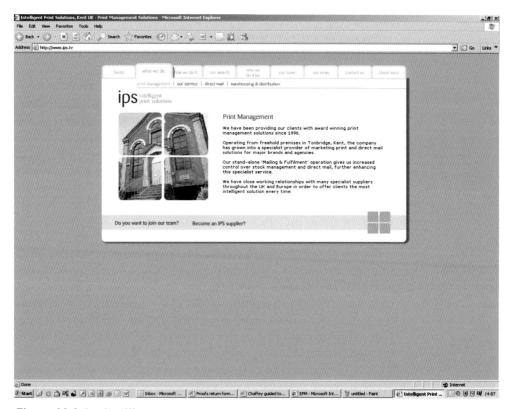

Figure 11.1 ips Intelligent
Source: www.ips/tv/

This raises the question; why are organisations adopting Internet technologies at different rates and for different purposes? An important influence on how an organisation behaves is its internal environment: the dominant culture is determined by the shared sets of values within an organisation. Some have a culture that stresses the *customer is always right* whereas others are more bureaucratic and stress the need for *doing things in an administratively correct manner.* Whatever form the dominant culture takes it will affect everything the organisation does. Two other aspects of the organisation that are likely to be important to uptake and development of Internet marketing are the *workforce* and the *technological infrastructure*.

Currently, a key problem facing the e-commerce industry is the recruitment, retention and ongoing skills development of the *workforce* responsible for the development and operation of e-commerce systems and digital marketing operations. There is a general shortage of suitably knowledgeable and skilled individuals who are innovative, strategically minded and technically qualified. The status of the employment market can have an effect on the benefits required to attract the best workers – a shortage of skilled workers can encourage companies to introduce a range of additional benefits to attract and retain suitably skilled workers. Mini Case Study 11.1 presents some examples from the Ivy League of high-tech employers.

Mini Case Study 11.1   High-tech company employee benefit schemes

Goldenberg and Tang (2005) investigated what leading technology companies have to offer now they are emerging from the dot-com bust. They found the following (see Figure 11.2a to d).

Microsoft (Redmond, Washington) offers:

- Paid leave for volunteering
- Whale watching trips
- Contemporary lunch menus
- In-house gaming
- Extensive sports facilities
- Branded coffee shops

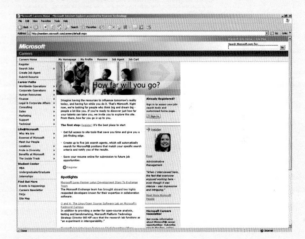

Figure 11.2a Microsoft

Souce: http://members.microsoft.com/careers/default.mspx

Electronic Arts (Redwood, California) offers:

- Paid Christmas holidays
- Onsite chiropractor
- Games coupons
- Some sports facilities
- Extra cash for working late

> Are you game? Interested in helping us shape the future of interactive entertainment? Take a moment to explore the cool opportunities across the US and the world. **Create an account** and become part of our talent community where you can create search agents to help you find your dream job at EA and you can even opt to receive notifications of jobs that may be suited for you down the road....

Figure 11.2b Electronic Arts

Source: http://jobs.ea.com/pljb/ElectronicArts/United_States applicant/index.jsp

→

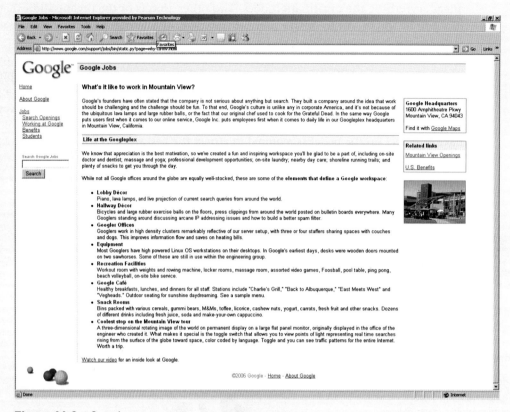

Figure 11.2c Google

Source: www.google.com/support/jobs/bin/static.py?page=why-ca-mv.html

Google (Mountain View California) offers:

- Engineers paid time for working on pet projects
- Free meals
- Communal bikes
- Running trails
- Grand piano
- Restrooms with robotic features

These examples provide some clues about the working environment of each of these companies and in doing so some insight into the dominant internal culture and expectations of the workforce. In each case there is evidence to suggest how important it is to make the working environment an enjoyable and in some cases fun place to be. Employees are provided with opportunities to engage in stimulating activities during their working hours, which potentially not only assist them to focus on their individual tasks and responsibilities but also to facilitate team building. It is likely, however, that each company has a slightly different culture and working environment.

Questions

1 What types of individuals are each of these companies trying to recruit?

2 This mini case study examines four case companies and includes online clips from the online recruitment pages (see Figures 11.2a to d). What are the key criteria you think each organsiation is conveying to its target audience when recruiting new personnel? (You will need to visit the web pages for each of these organisations and then try to determine the *value proposition* being communicated from the perspective of potential employees.)

In addition to creating the *right* culture a company needs to consider the characteristics of the working environment and ensure that *processes*, technological infrastructure and systems are effective and efficient. In the online trading environment it is often extremely difficult to achieve a long-term sustainable advantage over the competition and as a result the working environment can be very demanding. For example, in Internet marketing organisations, there are two important variables that influence customer satisfaction: the speed and accuracy of service delivery; and sustaining the technical reliability of all online systems. The significance of these variables does mean that it is important to ensure that the human resource management processes within an organisation are focused on continually investing in upgrading employee skills to ensure they are capable of fulfilling their job roles to a standard that exceeds that which is achieved by competition. It is also important to understand what causes certain employees to consistently achieve high performance standards within the organisation and then determine how effective management of these factors can contribute to sustaining a market lead over competition.

This section has considered elements of the trading environment and how these factors can be affected by the online trading environment. A key conclusion that can be drawn is that it is becoming increasingly important for businesses trading online to understand the trading context as competition intensifies and expectations of stakeholders intensify. The next aspect of B2B commerce to consider is the potential of online markets and how businesses trade electronically.

Commercial exchanges in B2B markets

The nature of the markets in which B2B e-commerce and e-marketing take place is the second major theme considered in this chapter. This section examines:

- the potential of the electronic marketplace in terms of growth, volume and global dispersion
- how organisations are using Internet technologies for communications and e-commerce.

The electronic marketplace

Rayport and Sviokla (1995) introduced the term electronic *marketspace* and suggest it is a new environment which has implications for the way in which businesses trade. The speed of development of computer, network and Internet technologies has played a key role in the rapid expansion of the *marketspace* and subsequently the commercial practice of electronic trading. It should be remembered, however, that electronic trading *per se* is not a new phenomenon; commercial exchanges have taken place using electronic data interchange (EDI) and dedicated data links between organisations for several decades. Nevertheless, what is new is Internet technologies. Communication standards and protocols create a virtual trading environment where any organisation with a computer and access to the Internet has the potential to trade in global markets. It is the aim of this section to focus on this potential and investigate growth, volume and dispersion of B2B electronic markets (the technologies and management activities taking place have been discussed in earlier chapters).

B2B markets

Traditionally, there are three main types of organisational markets in which businesses primarily trade with businesses. In the UK, the economic activities a company engages in allow it to be classified using Standard Industry Codes (SIC) that facilitate statistical analysis (at a government level) and common activity structures (for non-governmental administrational purposes). SICs were first introduced in 1948 but are regularly updated to reflect changes over time and to accommodate new products and new industries. SIC UK are integrated into European and international coding to ensure consistency in classification of organisations by activity (Central Statistical Office, 1992): for example, computer and related activities have a primary code number 72 and secondary codes for hardware (721), software (722) and data processing (723).

Industrial markets

Companies in such markets are heavily dependent on raw materials and actually producing tangible goods. SIC industrial markets include: Agriculture and hunting and forestry, Fishing, Manufacturing (fuel processing and production, chemicals and man-made fibre, metal goods, engineering and vehicles industry, printing and other manufacturing), Electricity and gas supply, and Construction. The nature of these types of industrial markets is such that some of the manufacturing sectors are dominated by a small number of very large companies. This is particularly noticeable in areas of manufacturing that require major capital funding and investment (e.g. ship building and the manufacture of chemicals). In the case of extraction industries, geography impacts on the dispersion of companies, physically bringing companies together in specific regions based on availability of and access to required raw materials. It should be noted that this does not mean all manufacturers operate on a vast scale. In the case of specialist engineering companies, they can be quite numerous, small in size and widely dispersed.

Reseller markets

Organisations in these markets buy products and services in order to resell them. Under the SIC systems these types of organisations include those engaged in: Wholesale and retail trade, Repair of motor vehicles, Motor cycles, Household and personal goods, Hotels and restaurants, Transport, storage and communications, Financial institutions, Estate agents and letting. This covers a very diverse collection of organisations and as a result company size and market-sector structures vary considerably.

Government markets

These markets consist of government agencies and bodies that buy goods and services that are required to carry out specific functions and provide particular services. Governments control vast funds of public money generated from direct and indirect taxation. In many instances, purchasing requirements exceed those of large private commercial organisations. Under the SIC system the types of organisations include: Public administration, Education, Health services, Armed forces, and Other community, social and personal services activities.

Growth, volume and dispersion of B2B electronic markets

In the first instance, questions about growth and *the rise of electronic networks and the information revolution* primarily focused on reseller markets (B2C Internet marketing is discussed in detail in Chapter 10) and questioned whether the online trading environment was 'merely another revolution in retailing formats' (Evans and Wurster, 2000). However, as commercial adoption of the Internet expanded it emerged that *information* was at the heart of value creation and competitive advantage. Evans and Wurster (2000) suggested the reason for this is that the majority of traditional principles of business strategy continued to apply in electronic markets but the *objects* of strategy such as business units, industrial supply chains, customer relationships, organisational structure, etc., were held together by a glue and this glue is *information*. They continued, stating that this glue gets dissolved by new technologies and as a result formalised and well-established business structures and supply chains are changed and begin to fragment. It soon became apparent that the online trading environment was much more than an innovative retail format and that all types of organisations would be affected to some extent by the new technologies. A recent benchmarking study by the DTI (2004) found that in the UK approximately 90% of businesses have access to the Internet (in companies with over 50 employees the percentage is approaching 100%). The report concluded that the key measure of ITC adoption is no longer about connectivity and access to the Internet, but rather the degree to which technology is being used to deliver real value for businesses. Many UK organisations are focusing on how to reduce operating costs and develop more integrated supply-side systems both internally and with partners. See Case Study 11 for further discussion of *growth*, *volume* and *dispersion* within electronic markets.

How organisations are using Internet technologies

There are many examples of how companies operating in B2B markets have utilised the Internet at different stages in the supply chain (see Figure 11.3). Typically, an organisation will begin by establishing its intention to use Internet technologies, then there will be an initial developmental period, prior to implementation. Implementation can

Figure 11.3 Solar Turbines – a Caterpillar company

Source: Screenshot from Solar Turbines web site http://mysolar.cat.com/cda/layout?m=6637&x = 7.Copyright 2005, Caterpillar Inc. All rights reserved.

involve adoption of a wide range of Internet technologies and web-based applications. Primarily, *customer-facing* web-based applications focus on a) serving a communications objective, b) serving a transactional (sales) objective, and c) pursuing both a) and b) simultaneously. *Supplier-facing* web based applications focus on a) serving a transactional (sales) objective (e.g. e-procurement) and b) managerial objectives, i.e. supplier-relationship management, supply chain management, knowledge management and application service providing.

In the case of industrial companies, web sites can be used to provide buyers with a high level of specific product information (see Figure 11.3).

Online communications

A dilemma faced by organisations operating in B2B markets is just how much information to communicate (specific principles and techniques of online communications are discussed in detail in Chapter 8). Take the example of the world's train manufacturers, where there are just five key companies. To provide potential and existing clients with information, each manufacturer will publish information about new contracts, new products and testimonials from existing customers. However, whilst this information will also be of great interest to potential customers it could also be of great value to competitors. The web provides easy access to many data sources and this has led companies to employ staff specifically to find and summarise information from competitors. Therefore it is important to strike a careful balance between disclosing too much information (for competitors) and not enough (for customers). This problem has largely been overcome by the use of password- and firewall-protected extranets (see Chapter 1 for further details).

Nevertheless, for some organisational markets being able to link customers to information is a key advantage. Take the UK government for example, which is using the Internet and the web to modernise and improve many public services by providing more web-based *customer* service information. The UK government has set a target that 100% of government services should be capable of being delivered online by 2005. The outcome is portal sites like Directgov (see Figure 11.4) that provides information about a wide range of government services and links to around 1,500 different contacts.

According to the site you can:

- 'Browse by audience groups such as 'disabled people' and 'parents' or by topics including 'money, tax and benefits', 'employment', 'education and learning' and 'motoring'. Or you can access definitive government directories or use the search engine.
- Book a driving test, tax your car, renew your passport, find out about child safety, parental leave, special educational needs and lots more.
- Link to government departments as well as relevant third parties which can offer additional trusted advice and support.

Online communications offer an opportunity to create highly tailored, fast communications that can deliver high information content at comparatively low cost (Gattiker et al., 2000). The online advertising spend has increased significantly during recent years in terms of the number of organisations advertising online and the size of the online promotional budget being spent, but recently there is a reported slow down in the growth rate of the online advertising sector. However, this slow down is not uniform as interestingly organisations are beginning to use a wider range of online promotional tools; search engine marketing is becoming particularly important in ensuring web content is visible to the chosen target market audience. Another example of a new and increasingly popular mode of online communication is online video (see Mini Case Study 11.2), which has become technologically viable as more end-users (B2B and B2C markets) have broadband Internet connections.

Figure 11.4 Directgov

Source: Directgov www.direct.gov.uk/Homepage/fs/en

Mini Case Study 11.2 Online video advertising

Jupiter Research projects that streaming media advertising spending will increase 79%, from $140 million in 2004 to $251 million in 2005. To put these numbers in context: total online advertising for 2004 was an estimated $9.3 billion or 4.6% of the $257 billion total advertising market. (Source: JupiterResearch Internet Advertising Model, July 2005 (US only))

'While online video advertising is still a small segment,' Interactive Advertising Bureau (IAB) president Greg Stuart says, 'we recognise it as a big opportunity since it gives marketers an easy way to transition their television advertising to online.' (Source: IAB).

The potential advantage of online video is cited as increased brand awareness, strong direct response and branding results and, in some cases, better results than television. Whilst at this time online video is primarily being used in B2C markets, the impact is more far reaching as it is increasing online brand equity and the value of this form of communication to organisations further *upstream* in the supply chain.

For successful use of online video it is suggested organisations should focus on customer needs and translate and integrate offline video assets into the online experience, build more effective customer facing communication strategies and ensure campaign integrity and adaptation to develop an online 'lean-in' audience, yielding decreased costs and improved response. Knowledge of end-user preferences should be used to allow users to mute or close video windows to reduce annoyance and related negative branding effects. Online video content has several potential revenue streams; premium content, users pay for content (either on a pay-per-view basis or as a subscription), advertising revenue and sponsorships. This tailored form of advertising can be implemented in multiple ways to provide online video content for specific users.

Source: Adapted from JupiterResearch's European Marketing & Advertising April 2005 report 'Online Video Advertising: Tune Content and Placements to Web Constraints'.

Online communications are not just being used at the initiation and processing stages of purchasing. Another valuable contribution being made by online communications in the later stages of the buying process is regarding *product evaluation and feedback*. The Internet offers opportunities for businesses to improve the quality of customer service and at the same time reduce costs. Quality of service can be improved by providing buyers with access to the right answer to their queries in real-time. Using customer information and diagnostic tools Dell Computers (**www.dell.com**) analyses the buyer query, diagnoses the problem and then instantly recommends possible solutions. Through providing web-based support or buyer-driven question and answer sessions Cisco has to employ fewer staff to provide the required level of after-sales support (see Mini Case Study 11.3).

Mini Case Study 11.3 Cisco excels in pre-sales and after-sales service

Cisco is a leading e-commerce business with the majority of its business online. The success has been achieved through e-commerce activities. A particularly interesting part of its online operations is its customer service provision.

In the early 1990s Cisco was a relatively small company, but was growing rapidly. This success caused a problem – a backlog in the area of after-sales support. This problem developed since Cisco's electronic components such as routers and hubs need configuration after delivery. The queries that arise are of a highly technical nature and at the time there were many customer questions. The solution was to provide online support whereby if possible customers could resolve their own problems; however, highly specialised engineers were also available to deal with particularly troublesome problems. Susan Bostrom, head of Cisco's Internet Solutions Group, said the idea was 'almost an instant success': it became a 'self-inflating balloon of knowledge'. The expansion of knowledge occurred as customers not only gleaned information from Cisco's customer query web site but also shared their experiences with Cisco and other customers. The support system has continued to be a success and today almost 80% of customer queries are answered online. Cisco's sales have increased tenfold while the number of customer support staff has only doubled.

Source: Adapted from Cisco System web site www.cisco.com

Online transactions – e-commerce

E-commerce involves the transaction of goods and services between organisations using Internet technologies and has the potential to deliver many benefits to an organisation.

According to Croom (2001) the use of Internet-based technologies will affect procurement systems by making them 'leaner'. Buyers will become more informed with increased access to product information available on the web. Changes may occur in the configuration of the buying group: the purchasing function will become more streamlined and restructuring of the supply chain will also be possible.

More informed buyers

The US-based BuyerZone.com is a leading online marketplace that brings together the premier Internet-based 'Request for Quote' service with its original award-winning purchasing guides. This research facility serves the needs of small-business owners by providing access to relevant and timely information. Additionally, BuyerZone.com provides a guided buying experience that empowers customers to evaluate easily and make quickly the right purchases for all their business needs. It is also important to be aware that a major challenge for the Internet marketers is that access to information empowers the buyer in the purchasing decision-making process, as online information becomes available to assist purchasing from all of a company's competitors. Therefore, each business needs to make an effort to provide *better* information than its competitors if it wishes to retain customers. An example of a business that uses such a tool to help assist the buying decision is Marshall Industries, which provides an on-screen tool that helps show customers the range of products available that meet their needs. Regardless of such innovations, Croom (2001) suggests that in the future, especially in 'routine purchasing' situations, companies will be more inclined to completely outsource the purchasing function and in doing so will make the quality of the information and its search facilities largely irrelevant.

Streamlining of the purchasing function

Another change to the buying process, which may occur as a result of adoption of Internet-based technology, is a change to the people involved in the buying decision. Internet solutions are in certain instances enabling organisations to streamline the purchasing function both in terms of the number of supplier contacts (electronic data interchange via the Internet facilitates access to increasing numbers of suppliers) and the empowerment of company individuals involved in the buying decision through access to consistent and coherent information. The adoption of Internet technologies can have far reaching implications for purchasing practices. Some key initiatives which B2B organisations might consider are:

- *E-procurement*: Timmers (2000) suggested that e-procurement, defined as 'tendering and procurement of goods and services', is a business model that has effectively been implemented by businesses around the globe. Kalakota and Robinson (2000) advocate that increasing an organisation's profitability through cost reduction makes online procurement an important strategic issue. For example, Marshall Industries (a large American electronic components company) was one of the first companies to recognise the advantage of information systems, computer networking, collaborative tools, intranets and the Internet. These new technologies continue to play a key role in helping Marshall differentiate its offering from that of its competitors and establish a competitive advantage in what is basically a commodities market. Marshalls demonstrate the strategic relevance of moving to online e-procurement and whilst many others have undoubtedly made significant cost savings by shifting many previously manually processed paper-based tasks to the web, it is important to consider whether this is a 'quick-fix solution' to satisfy shareholder aspirations in the light of the turbulent 'dot-com boom and bust era', showing that Internet technologies can make a real difference to profitability, or whether such models can produce long-term benefits. See Mini Case Study 11.4.

Mini Case Study 11.4 NHS Purchasing and Supply Agency

The National Health Service Purchasing Agency works with around 400 NHS trusts and health authorities and manages 3000 national purchasing contracts. The NHS spends approximately £11 billion per annum on purchasing goods and services for the health service.

The aim is for the Agency to develop and implement an e-commerce strategy that will:

- embrace and integrate all business processes from 'demand' through to payment;
- embrace all key players in the NHS supply environment;
- expect the NHS to 'act' on a once only basis in programme design and application;
- change the function of purchasing from transactional to strategic.

It is envisaged that on satisfaction of the above aims sourcing, display of products and prices and ordering of goods and transacting with suppliers will all be done electronically. Additional expectations are
that when the e-commerce strategy is fully implemented there will be systems that can offer facilities for
budgeting and planning, reporting and control, demand forecasting and more focused strategic analysis.

The scope of the e-commerce operation is to include all the NHS's primary, secondary and tertiary
suppliers into a trading network. The size of the network will be extensive but will primarily focus on B2B
trading relationships, not trading relationships with the general public (B2C).

The anticipated advantages of implementing this project are that it will:

- improve efficiency by streamlining transactional processes with suppliers. This will be achieved by
  automating manual processes, enhancing control mechanisms, optimising procurement practices,
  standardising and sharing procedures and information in a coherent and consistent manner;
- provide opportunities to obtain greater leverage over prices by aggregating demand for goods and
  services across the network;
- improve levels of transparency.

It is also anticipated that both the NHS and their suppliers will benefit from successful implementation of the e-commerce strategy.

Source: Adapted from NHS Purchasing and Supply E-Commerce Strategy for the NHS

- *Online purchasing auctions*: Real-time online purchasing auctions are used by buyers
  and suppliers globally. General Electric (GE) involves both established and non-estab-
  lished suppliers in e-auctions. The model is of a web-based electronic bidding
  mechanism that operates in a similar way to those held in traditional auction rooms
  and tendering processes. However, in the case of GE the aim is to drive costs down via
  a competitive, open bidding process. The downward movement of prices is sometimes referred to as a 'reverse auction' as opposed to a bidding situation where prices
  are driven upwards. GE purchasing managers do not always select the lowest bid as
  they will assess the potential risks associated with the supplier: say, the ability to fulfil
  the order, quality and requirements for after-sales service issues, rejection rates, quality of goods. An emergent benefit of this model is that e-auctions allow companies to
  monitor competitive pricing, which helps the organisation reduce total costs.
- *E-fulfilment*: Although not currently referred to by many as a business model, the
  delivery of goods in a timely and appropriate fashion is central to the re-engineering
  of the supply chain. According to a survey, 'fulfilment' will be an area of significant
  growth for businesses operating online. However, over 80% of organisations cannot
  fulfil international orders of tangible goods because of the complexities of shipping,
  although there are some geographical locations (e.g. parts of Europe and Asia) that are
  better served by local warehouse support networks than others. Further discussion of
  'last mile' problems can be found in Chapter 10.

Time will inevitably establish the validity of the proposition that online purchasing
practices are sustainable business models. Notwithstanding this point, there are some
key benefits associated with online purchasing which should be noted (see Table 11.1).
This table is based on Croom's (2001) investigation of the impact of web-based technology on the supply chain and the above discussions of supply-side market exchanges. The
next section examines the sell-side of organisational activities.

Table 11.1 Potential advantages of online purchasing systems

Advantage factor	Online purchasing situations
Quality of information	Ensures access to comparable information whereas incomplete knowledge can cause confusion in human-based systems as parties may not have access to the same information.
Uncertainty	Is potentially lower than for human systems. This means that in routine purchasing situations (at least) there is potential advantage in outsourcing the purchasing function. Potentially, removes some of the need for vertical integration.*
Risk	From a functional perspective risk can be reduced by improvement of buyer information. However, the risk of fraud is significantly increased when dealing with previously unknown buyers and suppliers.
Frequency	Allows better management of ordering (automated grouping of small orders is practicable).
Coordination	Rather than having networks only, coordination links existing trading partners in a tightly coupled arrangement. Such new electronic markets could conceivably include larger numbers of buyers and sellers (Malone et al., 1987). Additionally, coordination reduces the costs of searching for appropriate goods and services.

* Vertical integration refers to the practice of supply chain activities being controlled within an organisation.

Application service provision

CommerceOne, SAP Portals, Hewlett-Packard and other organisations provide open portal solutions offering fully integrated packages that provide companies with complete end-to-end solutions. In other words, their promise is to unify disparate applications, information and services. However, the availability of high-performance solutions does not necessarily equate to high levels of uptake of such solutions. Many organisations are currently taking a piecemeal approach towards the adoption of Internet technologies. There are examples where the inbound logistical and e-procurement systems are completely integrated with the outbound systems: for example, POSCO, the world's largest steel manufacturer, uses Oracle's E-Business Suite in order to reduce budgeting time (by as much as 80 days in some instances), reducing costing time and sales planning lead time, and simplifying order processing for tens of thousands of daily orders. It should be remembered that not all organisations in B2B markets have fully integrated networked systems. Indeed POSCO had many disparate systems in each application area that could no longer meet the company's growing needs. Collaboration with Oracle helped to streamline operations and foster interoperability between strategic business units throughout the company. In cases where organisational use of Internet technologies is limited, levels of involvement with the online trading process will be reduced and the organisation may be using the web to merely establish an online presence to provide customers with company information.

Trading relationships in B2B markets

This section focuses on the potential impact of the Internet on the *exchange process, buying function* and *trading partnerships*.

501

The exchange process

Traditionally, the *exchange process* would be initiated by the seller, who will attempt to satisfy the demands of the buyer either by producing goods and services that explicitly meet the buyer's needs or by aggressive sales and communications campaigns designed to persuade the buyer to purchase a particular product or service. However, in recent years, the nature of interactions between buyers and sellers, who form an important part of the exchange process, have been changing. Blenkhorn and Banting (1991) discussed the concept of reverse marketing in the mid-1980s. In the reverse marketing scenario, the buyer initiates the exchange process by making the seller aware of his purchasing requirements and in doing so changes the nature of the relationship as there is potentially more buyer involvement at earlier stages, i.e. input at product development stage. Online it is not only the direction of the motivation to purchase that is changing but also the number and type of partners engaging in the exchange process and the structure of the supply chain.

The buying function

In addition to market exchanges, the organisational *buying function* typically involves a decision-making process that is different from consumer purchasing behaviour. Organisational buying decisions are influenced by the following key factors: the power and number of individuals in the *buying group* involved in the purchasing decision, the *type and size of purchase* and *choice criteria* informing the purchase decision, and the *level of risk* involved.

- *The buying group.* Webster and Wind (1972) identified different profiles for participants involved in an organisational buying group: users, influencers, buyers, deciders and gatekeepers. The composition of the buying group varies according to a company's requirements regarding financial control and authorisation procedures.
- *The type and size of purchase.* These will vary dramatically according to the scale of the purchase. Companies such as aircraft manufacturers will have low-volume, high-value orders; others selling items such as stationery will have high-volume, low-value orders. With the low-volume, high-value purchase the Internet is not likely to be involved in the transaction itself since this will involve a special contract and financing arrangement. The high-volume, low-value orders, however, are suitable for e-commerce transactions and the Internet can offer several benefits over traditional methods of purchase such as mail and fax (e.g. speed of transfer of information, access to more detailed product information).
- *Choice criteria.* The buying decision for organisations will typically take longer and be more complicated than consumer purchasing decisions, as professional buying groups assess product specifications against their buying requirements. To assist in this evaluation, many B2B-specific portals have been created on the Internet, with the aim of uniting buyers with sellers who have the products that match their requirements. Such portals not only provide information about potential suppliers, but also enable searching of product specifications and standards and parts catalogues.
- *The level of risk.* This varies depending on the type of product. In the case of routine-purchase, low-cost goods required, say, for maintenance or repair purposes the level of risk associated with a wrong purchase is low. However, in the case of a high-cost product, for example either a capital equipment purchase or a bulk quantity of raw material used in a manufacturing process, the associated risk of making a wrong purchase is high. The Internet affords buyers and sellers the opportunity to be well

informed about a potential purchase, thereby reducing the risks associated with the functionality of a particular product or service. However, online fraud and forgery are increasing and global legal systems do not yet have laws to protect every aspect of commercial use of the Internet, especially online contracts (Sparrow, 2000). Therefore, the advantage of accessing a wide range of new trading partners across the Internet's global trading network is somewhat reduced by the threat of a previously unknown party entering into a contract fraudulently. As a result, the risk of trading with new suppliers via the Internet is potentially higher than in a face-to-face situation.

A key consideration is how Internet technologies can be used to facilitate a dialogue with the various members of the buying group. A possible approach to consider is *selective targeting*, a process involving carefully examining specific aspects of the target market and then preferentially targeting the selected market with specific online offerings. Some examples of customer segments that are commonly targeted online include:

- customers who are difficult to reach using other media – an insurance company looking to target younger drivers could use the web in this way;
- customers who are brand loyal – services to appeal to brand loyalists can be provided to support them in their role as advocates of a brand as suggested by Aaker and Joachimsthaler (2000);
- customers who are not brand loyal – conversely, incentives, promotion and a good level of service quality could be provided by the web site to try and retain such customers.

The same principles can be applied to organisational markets whereby larger customers could be offered preferential access through an extranet. Smaller companies might be offered additional services to enhance buyer–supplier relationships: online transactions, Internet-based EDI and specialist portals providing detailed information for different interests that support the buying decision.

Trading partnerships

The final consideration in this section is *trading partnerships*. Potentially, the impact of trading in the online environment is a change in the *number* of suppliers and the structure of the supply chain. In the case of Bass Breweries, adoption of an e-procurement system led to a reduction in the number of suppliers but engendered closer cooperation between the buyer and the retained suppliers.

Additionally, organisations are engaging in the exchange process with an increasingly wide range of trading partners: for example, manufacturers are directly selling to consumers, which can result in channel restructuring. There is evidence of such changes resulting from adoption of Internet technologies to buyer–supplier relationships within the financial service industry: large banking corporations supplying financial services directly to cherry picked retail customers via the Internet. Disintermediated market transactions of this kind are efficient because they remove the need to compensate agents and intermediaries in the supply chain. High-tech transactional solutions of this kind pose a serious threat to 'retail' banks that rely on a physical branch network to serve their most valuable customers (Ellis-Chadwick et al., 2002). Channel restructuring can also mean adding trading partners. A barrier for many organisations wishing to operate in digital markets is the lack of technological and logistical knowledge. Faced with this situation, a possible solution is to buy in expertise. New media intermediaries offer a wide range of services from web development and management to operational logistics. Wrigley and Lowe (2001) suggest that delivery and a company's capacity to fulfil orders is a critically important limiting factor that affects the growth of online reseller markets following the collapse of the dot-com bubble, circa 2000. Indeed, it is possible that the more an organisation is in a position to take advantage of such limiting factors the more likely will be the shift towards the online trading environment.

Other notable innovations with the potential to alter online channel relationships are:

- *Infomediation* – a related concept where middlemen hold data or information to benefit customers and suppliers.
- *Channel confluence* – occurs where distribution channels start to offer the same deal to the end-customer.
- *Peer-to-peer services* – music swapping services such as Napster and Gnutella opened up an entirely new approach to music distribution with both supplier and middleman removed completely, thus providing a great threat but also an opportunity to the music industry.
- *Affiliation* – affiliate programmes can turn customers into sales people. Many consider sales people as part of distribution. Others see them as part of the communications mix.

Restructuring of the channel to market through the use of Internet technologies can deliver significant benefits in improved efficiency and reduced costs.

This section has focused on the potential impact of the Internet on the exchange process, the buying function and trading relationships. Through the use of Internet and network technologies it is becoming possible for an organisation to build a highly streamlined sales channel online. In many organisations, there are no observable stages between inbound logistics and distribution to the final customer. There is minimum human intervention in the whole supply process, which raises the question: To what extent are trading relationships becoming 'transactional' rather than 'relational'? Perhaps this is because organisations have been developing strong links with suppliers and other stakeholders through the use of technology, which has resulted in many activities being outsourced and the creation of new and different arrangements of trading networks. Deise et al. (2000) describe value network management as 'the process of effectively deciding what to outsource in a constraint-based, real-time environment based on fluctuation'. (For discussion of customer relationship management techniques see Chapter 6.) A key point to remember is that whatever the incremental changes taking place at various stages of the trading relationship, for many organisations, trading relationships are becoming a more strategic issue. There are greater opportunities to create competitive advantage by redefining the participants of the exchange process and developing competitive differentiation by rethinking sales and service processes.

Digital marketing strategies

The final theme of this chapter is Internet marketing strategies. It should be noted that it is not the aim of this section to revisit the process of planning online marketing strategies (which has been discussed in Chapter 4), but to consider how Internet marketing strategies might be used and integrated into organisational planning activities.

So far this chapter has focused on the online trading context, the electronic marketplace and trading relationships. In essence, each of these sections forms an integral part of the online strategic planning process. According to Nicholls and Watson (2005), although e-commerce is still a relatively new business activity for many organisations there is a growing understanding within the literature of the importance of strategic thinking to the successful development of online activities. During the dot-com boom many companies were accused of a lack of strategic planning, which was ultimately said to be the cause of their business failures (Porter, 2001). E-strategy has been discussed at various levels from business re-engineering, new approaches to marketing planning to analysing and measuring specifics of web-based activities.

From a *strategic* planning perspective, Teo and Pian (2003) have found that the level of Internet adoption has a significant positive relationship with an organisation's competitive advantage, which implies that organisations should seriously consider how to engender positive support for online activities. Otherwise organisations that hesitate are likely to be superseded by existing or new competitors. Whilst in the current climate this sounds rather obvious, the business potential that can be derived from adopting Internet technologies is not always immediately clear. This situation helps to reinforce the importance of digital marketing planning as it can help to ensure organisations reduce the risk of losing their competitive edge by missing out on the benefits of new technology. On the plus side, there are increasing opportunities to benefit from innovation, growth, cost reduction, alliance, and differentiation advantages through planned adoption and development of Internet and digital technologies as more trading partners become part of the digital marketspace.

From a *tactical* planning perspective Teo and Pian (2003) suggest organisations aiming to differentiate themselves via web sites should switch their focus to internal productivity improvement and developing external partner relationships. They should look for opportunities to create productivity improvements through the use of a web site and to streamline business processes.

According to Nicholls and Watson (2005), whether businesses are adopting strategic or tactical approaches towards planning appears to be rather an *ad hoc* process. They recommend that in order to use Internet technologies effectively businesses need to analyse 'a variety of situational antecedents and then the degree to which the offline and online management infrastructure, marketing and logistics functions should be integrated can be better understood'. (See Figure 11.5 for their model of e-value creation.) The model in Figure 11.5 shows three key areas, the organisation's core strategic objectives, its business characteristics and its internal resources and competencies. Different objectives are likely to suggest a requirement for different structures and strategies. For example, the objectives of pursuing efficiency and cost reduction are likely to benefit from organisation-wide integration of Internet technologies, whereas targeting very narrow niche markets online may not require such investment. The characteristics of the organisation (e.g. size) is likely to have a significant impact on Internet strategies. Smaller organisations will have to consider carefully how to resource a fully transactional web site and handle the logistics. Furthermore, the core resources and competencies will impact on the extent to which the Internet represents an opportunity to create competitive advantage.

It is perhaps reasonable to suggest that organisations are reconsidering the e-commerce proposition in the light of the boom-and-bust dot-com era. Indeed, there is a good deal of emphasis currently being placed on the supply-side of e-commerce strategies. Streamlining of procurement systems through the use of Internet technologies can make significant cost reductions, which can produce useful financial benefits. Furthermore, organisations operating in B2B sectors are better placed to implement such systems than the B2C organisations because they are:

● familiar with the use of the similar techniques of EDI (although this is beyond the reach of many SMEs);
● under pressure to trade using e-commerce as often major customers such as supermarkets may stipulate that their suppliers must use e-commerce for reasons of efficiency and cost. Alternatively, if a company's products are not available direct on the Internet then the company may lose sales to other companies whose products are available;

505

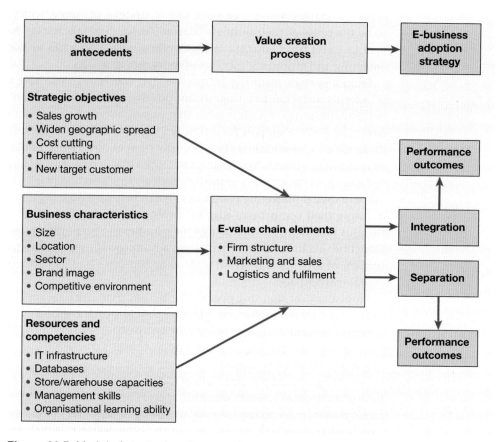

Figure 11.5 Model of strategic value creation
Source: Nicholls and Watson, 2005

- usually involved in long-term relationships, making it more worthwhile to set up links between business partners;
- more likely to be involved in a greater volume of transactions, thereby justifying the initial outlay required to develop the Internet-based systems.

Currently, it could be suggested that many organisation operating in the B2B sector are in a transitional state when planning Internet strategies. Whilst research suggests that lack of strategic foresight and strategic vision is hampering the growth and development of online business it is also likely that organisations are going through a period of learning that is equipping them with the knowledge required to develop successful Internet strategies in the future.

Case Study 11   Growth, volume and dispersion of electronic markets

Ellis-Chadwick et al. (2002) found size to be an important indicator of whether a company would a) have a web site and b) have developed a fully transactional web site. They posited, the larger the retail organisation in terms of number of outlets the more likely they are to have both a) and b) in place. They suggested this may be because those retailers with the largest network of outlets might have most to lose should they be left as observers, rather than active participants, in a vibrant Internet marketplace. Alternatively, it could be that those retailers with the largest numbers of outlets are most likely to have the investment resources, skilled personnel, scale and sophistication of logistical and technical infrastructure necessary to successfully support e-commerce.

The DTI's International benchmarking study (2004) also found size to have an effect on web site adoption, with almost 95% of large companies having active sites. It should be noted however, that in recent years, small and medium size enterprises (SMEs) have begun to take advantage of the falling costs of going online. In the UK, the rate of adoption of the Internet by SMEs is surpassing official targets and the UK government continues to invest in comprehensive programmes designed to get UK businesses online (Simpson and Docherty, 2004). Many SMEs are taking advantage of easier-to-use web applications and lower-cost outsourcing of web development and site hosting particularly to serve marketing communications objectives. Therefore, size may well continue to be a useful predictor of the level and extent of Internet adoption but as the Internet becomes more accessible a wider range of companies are looking to benefit from becoming involved with the online trading environment to serve an increasing range of business objectives.

The Department of Trade and Industry has been specifically monitoring the *dispersion* of use of ITC among UK and International Businesses and in doing so the eighth study has concluded there is a strong link between effective use of ITC and productivity. The study looked at a range of industries (see Table 11.2) in 11 different countries.

- More businesses are *discriminative*, *selective* and *focused* on the use of the technology in order to facilitate more efficient usage.
- Businesses are becoming *more responsive* to customer needs and in doing so are concentrating on the needs and expectations of the markets they serve.
- The *growth rate* of e-commerce is slowing as businesses seek to realise a wider range of benefits from technology adoption including initiatives focusing on improved efficiency, speed of access and customer communications. In the UK 19% of the total sales of businesses selling online are made through the online channel, up just 5% from 2003.

Major trends relating to the *dispersion* of Internet technologies identified by the study are:

- Significant differences in general *levels of technology adoption* across industry sectors: 96% of UK financial services businesses have a web site compared with 80% of construction businesses and 74% of UK primary businesses. This level of uptake is slightly higher than the average of the other ten nations surveyed – Australia, Canada, France, Germany, Italy, Japan, the Republic of Ireland, South Korea, Sweden and the USA – where the figures were 88%, 60% and 68% for each of the sectors respectively.
- The number of companies with *Internet access* is reaching saturation. Some 95% of all companies in countries surveyed had Internet access (see Figure 11.6.). In most countries the proportion of companies with *web sites*

Table 11.2 Industrial sector analysis

Sector	Description
Government	Public administration, education, health care
Financial services	Banking, insurance, pensions
Manufacturing	Food, drink, tobacco, textiles, clothing, motor vehicles, furniture
Transport and communication	Freight, post, telecoms
Services	Accountants, advertising, computing activities, estate agents, legal services, vehicle hiring
Primary industry	Agriculture, chemicals, mining, utilities
Retail/wholesale	Distribution, repairs, hotels, catering
Construction	Construction

Major trends potentially affecting the *growth* rate of adoption of Internet technologies identified by the study are:

- More businesses are *measuring the impact* of technology in order to determine how to deploy resources effectively.

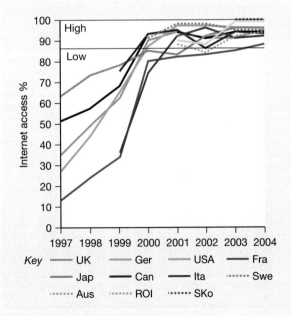

Figure 11.6 Proportion of business with Internet access

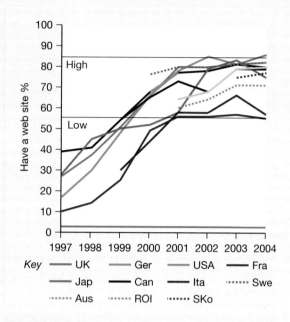

Figure 11.7 Proportion of business with a web site

online, the percentage varies across sectors from 28% to 10% (see Figure 11.8).

● Sweden, Ireland and the UK remain ahead in terms of *levels of sophistication* (see Figure 11.9).

This case has focused on the growth and dispersion of Internet adoption and e-commerce and in doing so has identified varying levels of uptake and usage of web technologies across the nations surveyed. Academic researchers (Doherty et al., 1999, Teo and Pian, 2003) have produced various models of the ways organisations use Internet technologies and how usage can be influenced by various factors, for example, levels of maturity, business integration, marketing applications and the category of the adopter.

Teo and Pian (2003) suggest that such different levels of adoption are likely to confer different degrees of competitive advantage, which they have found to be a key driver of Internet adoption (see Table 11.3) and which ultimately will affect the types of goals an organisation aims to achieve through the application of Internet technologies.

The level of adoption affects the extent to which Internet technologies impact on an organisation's practical operations. In doing so it provides a context for digital strategy formulation and ultimately the objectives pursued.

remains stable between 55% and 85% (see Figure 11.7).

● Significant variation across industries in *levels of uptake of e-commerce*. On the buy side, retail businesses are making the most significant amount of online purchases: 36% in the UK and an average of 38% across other surveyed nations. The construction sector was the lowest in terms of uptake with 17% of businesses in the UK and 21% in other nations. On the sell side, of companies that enable customers to order

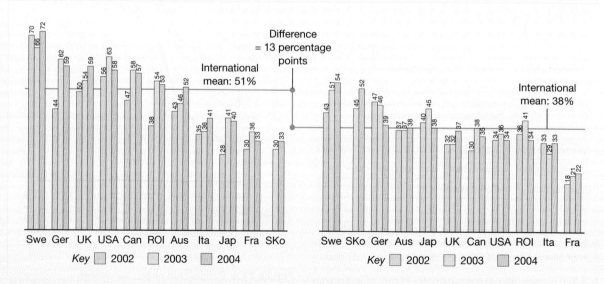

Figure 11.8 Adoption of buying and selling online

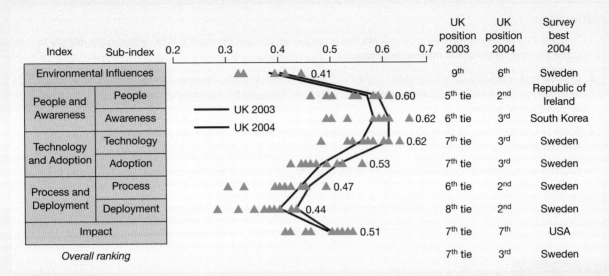

Index	Sub-index	0.2	0.3	0.4	0.5	0.6	0.7	UK position 2003	UK position 2004	Survey best 2004
Environmental Influences				0.41				9th	6th	Sweden
People and Awareness	People					0.60		5th tie	2nd	Republic of Ireland
	Awareness					0.62		6th tie	3rd	South Korea
Technology and Adoption	Technology					0.62		7th tie	3rd	Sweden
	Adoption				0.53			7th tie	3rd	Sweden
Process and Deployment	Process			0.47				6th tie	2nd	Sweden
	Deployment			0.44				8th tie	2nd	Sweden
Impact					0.51			7th tie	7th	USA
Overall ranking								7th tie	3rd	Sweden

— UK 2003
— UK 2004

Figure 11.9 Levels of sophistication of technology adoption

Source: DTI International benchmarking study 2004, www.thecma.com/accounts/CMA/documents/Nov2004/ibs2004.pdf

Table 11.3 Levels of web site development

Level of Internet adoption	Online development	Strategic contribution
Level 0 – e-mail adoption	e-mail account(s) but no web site.	Limited to **internal and intra-organisational communications**. Very limited resource implications.
Level 1 – Internet presence	Occupying a domain name or **simple web sites** providing mainly company information and brochures, therefore tending to be **static content** and **non-strategic** in nature.	Initial Internet **presence**. At this stage experimentation is taking place to build skill / knowledge base. Practically, implementation of technology is still in progress. Limited resource implications.
Level 2 – prospecting	Web sites provide customers with company information, product information (as level 1) plus news, events, **interactive content**, **personalised content**, e-mail **support**, and simple **search**.	**Prospecting.** At this point growth and development begins – providing potential customers with access to the products with minimal information-distributing cost. Growing resource implications.
Level 3 – business integration	Web sites at this level are more **complex** with added features for **interactive marketing**, **sales ordering**, **online communities** and **secure transactions**. Also includes more sophisticated versions of features found in levels 1 and 2, e.g.more comprehensive information and search facilities.	**Integration.** At this point integration begins to pull together business processes and business models. Internet strategy becomes interlinked with a firm's business strategy. Business support, as well as cross-functional links between customers and suppliers are developing.
Level 4 – business transformation	At this level the Internet-based activities are central to the organisation, transforming the overall business model throughout the organisation.	**Transformation** At this level transformation starts to take place. Internet-based operations shape the organisation's business strategies and are used to focus on building relationships and seeking new business opportunities.

Source: adapted from Teo and Pian (2003)

Questions

1 Suggest three different marketing objectives that an organisation operating in the B2B sector might identify to guide the company's use of Internet technologies.

2 Choose one of the objectives proposed in your answer to question 1 and develop an argument as to why an organisation might make this particular choice. Particularly, focus on the factors that might influence the choice of marketing objectives.

3 Apart from organisational size, suggest other factors that might influence the level and extent of Internet and web adoption.

4 Suggest ways a market-orientated B2B company operating in industrial printing markets might be using Internet technologies

Summary

1 This chapter has examined B2B use of Internet technologies from a marketing perspective. In doing so it has considered the online trading environment, online markets, trading partnerships and digital marketing strategies.

2 B2B trading is affected by the environmental trading situation. Many aspects of the online trading situation are different from the offline trading environment.

3 The trading situation needs to be analysed in order to develop understanding of the actions taking place. Online environmental analysis includes consideration of macro, micro and internal elements and how they might affect the online trading environment.

4 Commercial exchanges in B2B markets explore the potential and importance of the electronic market in terms of growth and dispersion of use of Internet technologies across different industrial sectors.

5 The growth in electronic markets has led to organisations increasingly making greater use of Internet technologies moving beyond aiming to achieve marketing communication objectives towards developing sales activities and investigating ways to develop international markets.

6 Organisational use of the Internet can lead to the development of customer-facing and supplier-facing web-based applications, which will serve different objectives and functions.

7 The sales process in B2B markets is changing and the methods of communication and the actual process of buying are changing (the buy class has a significant impact on the extent to which transactions are completely automated). Organisations are increasingly investing in e-procurement systems. Streamlining of the purchasing function is becoming more of a strategic issue as it is providing the opportunity to create differential advantage. B2B markets tend to have fewer customers placing larger orders (especially in industrial and government markets). Adoption of Internet technologies represents opportunities to streamline purchasing and sales operations and in doing so enables an organisation to make significant cost savings. Furthermore, there are also opportunities to create additional value and competitive advantage through the redesign of established offline practices.

8 Digital marketing strategies are not always integrated into a business's wider planning activities. However, this is becoming more important as organisations increasingly integrate Internet technologies into the buying and selling activities.

Exercises

Self-assessment exercises

1 Explain the significance of the online business context with specific reference to factors that are likely to affect whether a business buys and/or sells online.

2 Assess the market potential for a construction company contemplating setting up a transactional web site aiming to develop new international markets.

3 Suggest why some organisations have highly developed transactional web sites whereas others merely use the Internet for e-mail.

4 Outline the advantages and disadvantages of buying and selling online.

Essay and discussion questions

1 Discuss why a business operating in an industrial market might be cautious about putting new product specifications on the company web site.

2 Discuss to what extent trading online alters relationships between trading partners.

3 Explain how Internet technologies can contribute to the development of business strategies.

Examination question

1 Discuss the extent to which B2B e-marketplaces are fundamentally different to traditional offline markets.

References

Aaker, D. and Joachimsthaler, E. (2000) *Brand Leadership*, Free Press, New York.
Bakos, Y. (1991) A strategic analysis of electronic marketplaces, *MIS Quarterly*, 15(3), September, 295–310.
Blenkhorn, D.L. and Banting, P.M. (1991) How reverse marketing changes buyer–seller's roles, *Industrial Marketing Management*, 20(6), 185–91.
Brynjolfsson, E. and Kahin, B. (2000) *Understanding the Digital Economy*, MIT Press.
Central Statistical Office (1992) *Introduction to Standard Industrial Classification of Economic Activities* SIC(92). CSO Publications, London.
Croom, S. (2001) Restructuring supply chains through information channel innovation, *International Journal of Operations and Production Management*, 21(4), 504.
Deise, M., Nowikow, C., King, P. and Wright, A. (2000) *Executive's Guide to E-Business: From Tactics to Strategy*, Wiley, New York.

Dixon, P. (2005) *Building a Better Business*, Profile Books.

Doherty, N.F., Ellis-Chadwick, F.E. and Hart, C.A. (1999) Cyber retailing in the UK: the potential of the Internet as a retail channel, *International Journal of Retail and Distribution Management*, 27(1), 22–36.

DTI (2004) *Business in the Information Age: The International Benchmarking Study 2004*. www.thecma.com/accounts/CMA/documents/Nov2004/ibs2004.pdf.

Ellis-Chadwick, F.E., McHardy, P. and Wiesehofer, H. (2002) Online customer relationships in the European financial services sector: a cross-country investigation, *International Journal of Financial Services Marketing*, 6(4).

e-marketers (2001) UK leads European Online Ad Market (27 Aug), www.emarketer.com/estatnews.

Evans, P. and Wurster, T.S. (2000) *Blown to Bits: How the New Economics of Information Transforms Strategy*. Harvard Business School, USA.

Finlay, P. (2000) *Strategic Management: An Introduction to Business and Corporate Strategy*. Prentice Hall, Harlow, Essex.

Gates, B. (1999) Speech to students at London Business School, March.

Gattiker, U.E., Perlusz, S. and Bohmann, K. (2000) Using the Internet for B2B activities: a review and further direction for research, *Internet Research Electronic Networking Application and Policy*, 10(2), 126–40.

Goldenberg, D. and Tang, T. (2005) 'I got accepted by Google', *Wired*, February, pp. 34–5.

Hoffman, D., Novak, T. and Schlosser, E. (2000) The evolution of the digital divide: how gaps in Internet access may impact e-commerce', *Journal of Computer Mediated Communications*, 5, 3 March 2000, www.ascusc.org/jcmc/vol5/issue3/hoffman.html.

Jobber, D. (2004) *Principles of Marketing*, 4th edn. McGraw-Hill.

Jupiter Research (2005) *The Growth of Online Video Advertising*, Gainsborough House, 81 Oxford Street, Suite 206, W1D 2EU, London, UK.

Kalakota, R. and Robinson, M. (2000) *E-Business Roadmap for Success*. Addison-Wesley, Reading, MA.

Malone, T.W., Yates, J. and Benjamin, R.I. (1987) Electronic markets and electronic hierarchies, *Communications of the ACM*, 30(6), 484–96.

Nicholls, A. and Watson, A. (2005) Implementing e-value strategies in UK retailing, *International Journal of Retail and Distribution Management*, 33(6), 426–43.

Porter, M. (2001) Strategy and the Internet, *Harvard Business Review*, March, 62–78.

Rayport, J. and Sviokla, J. (1995) Exploiting the virtual value chain, *Harvard Business Review*, November – December, 75–87.

Sambharya, R., Kumaraswamy, A. and Banerjee, S. (2005) Information and the future of the Multinational Enterprise, *Journal of International Management*, 11, 143–61.

Shaw, J.T., (2002) Electronic democracy: using the Internet to transform American politics by Graeme Browning. 2nd edn, in *Serials Review*, Volume 28, Number 4, Winter 2002, pp. 351–2(2).

Simpson, M. and Docherty, A. (2004) E-commerce adoption support and advice for UK SMEs, *Journal of Small Business and Enterprise Development*, 11(3), 315–28.

Sparrow, A. (2000) *E-Commerce and the Law. The Legal Implications of Doing Business Online*. Financial Times, Prentice Hall, Harlow.

Tapscott, D. (1997) *Growing Up Digital*. McGraw-Hill, New York.

Teo, T. and Pian, Y. (2003). A contingency perspective on Internet adoption and competitive advantage, *European Journal of Information Systems*, 12(2), 78–92.

Timmers, P. (2000) *Electronic Commerce Strategies and Business to Business Trading*. Wiley, Chichester.

Tzong-Ru, L. and Jan-Mou, L. (2005) Key factors in forming an e-marketplace: an empirical analysis, *Electronic Commerce Research and Applications*.

Webster, F.E. and Wind, Y. (1972) *Organisational Buyer Behaviour*. Prentice Hall, Englewood Cliffs, NJ, 78–80.

Wrigley, N. and Lowe, M.S., editors, (2001) *Retailing, Consumption and Capital*. Addison Wesley Longman, Harlow, pp. 90–115.

Further reading

Beynon-Davis, P. (2004) *E-business*. Palgrave Macmillan, Basingstoke, Hampshire.
Jelassi, T. and Enders, A. (2005) *Strategies for E-business: Creating Value Through Electronic and Mobile Commerce*. Prentice Hall, England.
Tassabehji, R. (2003) *Applying e-commerce in Business*. Sage Publications, London.

Web links

- Brad Templeton www.templetons.com/brad/copymyths.html
- Brush Electrical Machines Limited www.fki-et.com
- CommerceOne www.commerceone.com
- Directgov www.direct.gov.uk/Homepage/fs/en
- DTI Business in the Information Age: International Benchmarking Study (2004) www.thecma.com/accounts/CMA/documents/Nov2004/ibs2004.pdf
- SIC http://qb.soc.surrey.ac.uk/resources/classification/sic92.pdf
- Solar Turbines http://esolar.cat.com/solar/main/

Glossary

A

Above the fold A term, derived from printed media, which is used to indicate whether a **banner advertisement** or other content is displayed on a web page without the need to scroll. This is likely to give higher **clickthrough**, but note that the location of the 'fold' within the web browser is dependent on the screen resolution of a user's personal computer.

Access platform A method for customers to access digital media.

Access provider A company providing services to enable a company or individual to access the **Internet**. Access providers are divided into **Internet service providers (ISPs)** and **online service providers (OSPs)**.

Accessibility An approach to site design intended to accommodate site usage using different browsers and settings particularly required by the visually impaired.

Accessibility legislation Legislation intended to assist users of web sites with disabilities including visual disability.

Acquisition *See* **Customer acquisition**.

Active Server Page (ASP) A type of **HTML** page (denoted by an .asp file name) that includes **scripts** (small programs) that are processed on a **web server** before the web page is served to the user's **web browser**. ASP is a Microsoft technology that usually runs on a **Microsoft Internet Information Server** (usually on Windows NT). The main use of such programs is to process information supplied by the user in an online **form**. A query may then be run to provide specific information to the customer such as delivery status on an order, or a personalised web page.

ActiveX A programming language standard developed by Microsoft that permits complex and graphical customer applications to be written and then accessed from a **web browser**. ActiveX components are standard controls that can be incorporated into web sites and are then automatically **downloaded** for users. Examples are graphics and animation or a calculator form for calculating interest on a loan or a control for graphing stock prices. A competitor to **Java**.

Ad creative The design and content of an ad.

Ad impression Similar in concept to a **page impression**; describes one viewing of an advertisement by a single member of its audience. The same as **ad view**, a term that is less commonly used.

Ad inventory The total number of **ad impressions** that a **web site** can sell over time (usually specified per month).

Ad rotation When advertisements are changed on a **web site** for different user sessions. This may be in response to ad **targeting** or simply displaying different advertisements from those on a list.

Ad serving The term for displaying an advertisement on a **web site**. Often the advertisement will be served from a **web server** different from the site on which it is placed. For example, the URL for displaying the advertisement is http://ad.doubleclick.net.

Ad space The area of a web page that is set aside for **banner advertising**.

Ad view Similar in concept to a **page impression**; describes one viewing of an advertisement by a single member of its audience. The same as **ad impression**, the term that is more commonly used.

Advertisement Advertisements on **web sites** are usually **banner advertisements** positioned as a masthead on the page.

Advertising broker *See* Media broker.

Advertising networks A collection of independent **web sites** of different companies and media networks, each of which has an arrangement with a single advertising broker (*see* **Media broker**) to place **banner advertisements**.

Affiliate networks A reciprocal arrangement between a company and third-party sites where traffic is directed to the company from third-party sites through **banner advertisements** and links and incentives. In return for linking to the **destination site** the third-party site will typically receive a proportion of any resulting sale.

Agents Software programs that can assist people to perform tasks such as finding particular information such as the best price for a product.

Aggregated buying A form of customer union where buyers collectively purchase a number of items at the same price and receive a volume discount.

Allowable cost per acquisition A target maximum cost for generating leads or new customers profitably.

Alt tags Alt tags appear after an image tag and contain a phrase associated with that image. For example: <img src="logo.gif" alt="Company name, company products"/>.

Analysis phase The identification of the requirements of a **web site**. Techniques to achieve this may include **focus groups**, questionnaires sent to existing customers or interviews with key accounts.

Animated banner advertisements (animated GIFs) Early **banner advertisements** featured only a single advertisement, but today they will typically involve several different images, which are displayed in sequence to help to attract attention to the banner and build up a theme, often ending with a call to action and the injunction to click on the banner. These advertisements are achieved through supplying the **ad creative** as an animated **GIF** file with different layers or frames, usually a rectangle of 468 by 60 **pixels**. Animated banner advertisements are an example of **rich-media advertisements**.

Announcements *See* **Site announcements**.

Archie A database containing information on what documents and programs are located on **FTP** servers. It would not be used in a marketing context unless one were looking for a specific piece of software or document name.

Asymmetric encryption Both parties use a related but different key to encode and decode messages.

Attrition rate Percentage of site visitors who are lost at each stage in making a purchase.

Audit (external) Consideration of the business and economic environment in which the company operates. This includes the economic, political, fiscal, legal, social, cultural and technological factors (usually referred to by the acronym **STEP** or SLEPT).

Audit (internal) A review of **web site** effectiveness.

Auditors *See* **Site auditors**.

Authentication *See* **Security methods**.

Autoresponders Software tools or **agents** running on **web servers** that automatically send a standard reply to the sender of an **e-mail** message. This may provide information for a standard request sent to, say, price_list@company_name.com, or it could simply state that the message or order has been forwarded to the relevant person and will be answered within two days. (Also known as **mailbots**.)

Availability *See* **Security methods; Site availability**.

Avatar A term used in computer-mediated environments to mean a 'virtual person'. Derived from the word's original meaning: '*n*. the descendant of a Hindu deity in a visible form; incarnation; supreme glorification of any principle'.

Backbones High-speed communications links used to enable Internet communications across a country and internationally.

Balanced scorecard A framework for setting and monitoring business performance. Metrics are structured according to customer issues, internal efficiency measures, financial measures and innovation.

Bandwidth Indicates the speed at which data are transferred using a particular network medium. It is measured in bits per second (bps).

kbps (one kilobit per second or 1000 bps; a modem operates at up to 56.6 kbps).

Mbps (one megabit per second or 1 000 000 bps; company networks operate at 10 or more Mbps).

Gbps (one gigabit per second or 1 000 000 000 bps; fibre-optic or satellite links operate at Gbps).

Banner advertisement A typically rectangular graphic displayed on a web page for purposes of brand building or driving traffic to a site. It is normally possible to perform a **clickthrough** to access further information from another **web site**. Banners may be static or animated (*see* **Animated banner advertisements**).

Behavioural loyalty Loyalty to a brand is demonstrated by repeat sales and response to marketing campaigns.

Behavioural traits of web users Web users can be broadly divided into **directed** and **undirected information seekers**.

Bid A commitment by a trader to purchase under certain conditions.

Blog Personal online diary, journal or news source compiled by one person or several people.

Bluejacking Sending a message from a mobile phone or transmitter to another mobile phone which is in close range via **Bluetooth** technology.

Blueprints Show the relationships between pages and other content components, and can be used to portray organisation, navigation and labelling systems.

Bluetooth A standard for wireless transmission of data between devices, e.g. a mobile phone and a PDA.

Brand The sum of the characteristics of a product or service perceived by a user.

Brand equity The brand assets (or liabilities) linked to a brand's name and symbol that add to (or subtract from) a service.

Brand experience The frequency and depth of interactions with a brand can be enhanced through the Internet.

Brand identity The totality of brand associations including name and symbols that must be communicated.

Branding The process of creating and evolving successful brands.

Bricks and mortar A traditional organisation with limited online presence.

Broadband technology A term referring to methods of delivering information across the **Internet** at a higher rate by increasing **bandwidth**.

Brochureware A **web site** in which a company has simply transferred ('migrated') its existing paper-based promotional literature on to the **Internet** without recognising the differences required by this medium.

Broker *See* **Media broker**.

Browser *See* **Web browser**.

Business model A summary of how a company will generate revenue, identifying its product offering, value-added services, revenue sources and target customers.

Business-to-business (B2B) Commercial transactions between an organisation and other organisations (inter-organisational marketing).

Business-to-business exchanges or marketplaces Virtual intermediaries with facilities to enable trading between buyers and sellers.

Business-to-consumer (B2C) Commercial transactions between an organisation and consumers.

Buy-side e-commerce E-commerce transactions between a purchasing organisation and its suppliers.

C

Call centre A location for **inbound** and **outbound** telemarketing.

Callback service A direct response facility available on a **web site** to enable a company to contact a customer by phone at a later time as specified by the customer.

Campaign-based e-communications E-marketing communications that are executed to support a specific marketing campaign such as a product launch, price promotion or a web site launch.

Campaign URL or CURL A web address specific to a particular campaign.

Card sorting The process of arranging a way of organising objects on the web site in a consistent manner.

Catalogue Catalogues provide a structured listing of registered **web sites** in different categories. They are similar to an electronic version of *Yellow Pages*. Yahoo! and Excite are the best known examples of catalogues. (Also known as **directories**.) The distinction between **search engines** and catalogues has become blurred since many sites now include both facilities as part of a **portal** service.

Certificate A valid copy of a **public key** of an individual or organisation together with identification information. It is issued by a **trusted third party** (TTP) or **certification authority** (CA).

Certification authority (CA) An organisation issuing and managing **certificates** or **public keys** and private keys to individuals or organisations together with identification information.

Channel buyer behaviour Describes which content is visited and the time and duration.

Channel conflicts A significant threat arising from the introduction of an **Internet** channel is that while **disintermediation** gives the opportunity for a company to sell direct and increase the profitability of products it can also threaten existing distribution arrangements with existing partners.

Channel marketing strategy Defines how a company should set specific objectives for a channel such as the Internet and vary its proposition and communications for this channel.

Channel outcomes Record customer actions taken as a consequence of a visit to a site.

Channel profitability The profitability of the web site, taking into account revenue and cost and discounted cash flow.

Channel promotion Measures that assess why customers visit a site – which adverts they have seen, which sites they have been referred from.

Channel satisfaction Evaluation of the customer's opinion of the service quality on the site and supporting services such as e-mail.

Clicks and mortar A business combining online and offline presence.

Clicks-only or Internet pureplay An organisation with principally an online presence.

Clickstream A record of the path a user takes through a **web site**. Clickstreams enable **web site** designers to assess how their site is being used.

Clickthrough A clickthrough (ad click) occurs each time a user clicks on a **banner advertisement** with the mouse to direct them to a web page that contains further information.

Clickthrough rate Expressed as a percentage of total **ad impressions**, and refers to the proportion of users viewing an advertisement who click on it. It is calculated as the number of clickthroughs divided by the number of **ad impressions**.

Click-tracking **Java** technology can be used to track movements of individual users to a **web site**.

Client–server The client–server architecture consists of client computers such as PCs sharing resources such as a database stored on a more powerful server computer.

Co-branding An arrangement between two or more companies where they agree to jointly display content and perform joint promotion using brand logos or **banner advertisements**. The aim is that the brands are strengthened if they are seen as complementary. This is a reciprocal arrangement which can occur without payment.

Cold list Data about individuals that are rented or sold by a third party.

Collaborative filtering Profiling of customer interest coupled with delivery of specific information and offers, often based on the interests of similar customers.

Commoditisation The process whereby product selection becomes more dependent on price than on differentiating features, benefits and value-added services.

Common Gateway Interface (CGI) A method of processing information on a **web server** in response to a customer's request. Typically a user will fill in a web-based **form** and the results will be processed by a CGI script (application). **Active Server Pages (ASPs)** are an alternative to a CGI script.

Competitive intelligence (CI) A process that transforms disaggregated information into relevant, accurate and usable strategic knowledge about competitors, position, performance, capabilities and intentions.

Competitor analysis Review of Internet marketing services offered by existing and new competitors and adoption by their customers.

Computer telephony integration The integration of telephony and computing to provide a platform for applications that streamline or enhance business processes.

Confidentiality *See* **Security methods**.

Consumer-to-business (C2B) Consumers approach the business with an offer.

Consumer-to-consumer (C2C) Informational or financial transactions between consumers, but usually mediated through a business site.

Contact or touch strategy Definition of the sequence and type of outbound communications required at different points in the customer lifecycle.

Content Content is the design, text and graphical information that forms a web page. Good content is the key to attracting customers to a **web site** and retaining their interest or achieving repeat visits.

Content management Software tools for managing additions and amendments to web site content.

Continuous e-communications Long-term use of e-marketing communications for customer acquisition (such as search engine and affiliate marketing) and retention (for example, e-newsletter marketing).

Convergence A trend in which different hardware devices such as televisions, computers and telephones merge and have similar functions.

Conversion marketing Using marketing communications to maximise conversion of potential customers to actual customers.

Conversion rate Proportion of visitors to a site, or viewers of an advert, who take an action.

Cookies Cookies are small text files stored on an end-user's computer to enable **web sites** to identify the user. They enable a company to identify a previous visitor to a site, and build up a profile of that visitor's behaviour. *See* **Persistent cookies, Session cookies, First-party cookies, Third-party cookies**.

Core product The fundamental features of the product that meet the user's needs.

Core tenants A shopping centre or mall is usually a centrally owned managed facility. In the physical world, the management will aim to include in the mall stores that sell a different but complementary range of merchandise and include a variety of smaller and larger stores. The core tenants or 'anchor stores' as they are often called are the dominant large-scale store operators that are expected to draw customers to the centre.

Cost models for Internet advertising These include per-exposure, per-response and per-action costs.

Cost per acquisition (CPA) The cost of acquiring a new customer. Typically limited to the communications cost and refers to cost per sale for new customers. May also refer to other outcomes such as cost per quote or enquiry.

Cost per click (CPC) The cost of each click from a referring site to a destination site, typically from a search engine in pay-per-click search marketing.

Cost per mille (CPM) Cost per 1000 **ad impressions**.

Cost per targeted mille (CPTM) Cost per targeted thousand for an advertisement. (*See also* **Targeting**.)

Countermediation Creation of a new intermediary by an established company.

Cracker A malicious meddler who tries to discover sensitive information by poking around computer networks.

Cross-selling Persuading existing customers to purchase products from other categories to their typical purchases.

Customer acquisition Strategies and techniques used to gain new customers.

Customer-centric marketing An approach to marketing based on detailed knowledge of customer behaviour within the target audience which seeks to fulfil the individual needs and wants of customers.

Customer communications channels The range of media used to communicate directly with a customer.

Customer experience *See* **Online customer experience**.

Customer extension Techniques to encourage customers to increase their involvement with an organisation.

Customer insight Knowledge about customers' needs, characteristics, preferences and behaviours based on analysis of qualitative and quantitative data. Specific insights can be used to inform marketing tactics directed at groups of customers with shared characteristics.

Customer journey A description of modern multi-channel buyer behaviour as consumers use different media to select suppliers, make purchases and gain customer support.

Customer lifecycle The stages each customer will pass through in a long-term relationship through acquisition, retention and extension.

Customer loyalty The desire on the part of the customer to continue to do business with a given supplier over time. *See* **Behavioural loyalty** and **Emotional loyalty**.

Customer orientation Providing content and services on a web site consistent with the different characteristics of the audience of the site.

Customer profiling Using the web site to find out customers' specific interests and characteristics.

Customer relationship management (CRM) A marketing-led approach to building and sustaining long-term business with customers.

Customer retention Techniques to maintain relationships with existing customers.

Customer satisfaction The extent to which a customer's expectations of product quality, service quality and price are met.

Customer scenarios (user journeys) Alternative tasks or outcomes required by a visitor to a web site. Typically accomplished in a series of stages of different tasks involving different information needs or experiences.

Customer selection Identifying key customer segments and targeting them for relationship building.

Customer touchpoints Communications channels with which companies interact directly with prospects and customers. Traditional touchpoints include face-to-face (in-store or with sales representatives), phone and mail. Digital touchpoints include web services, e-mail and potentially mobile phone.

Cybermediaries **Intermediaries** who bring together buyers and sellers or those with particular information or service needs.

Cyberspace and cybermarketing These terms were preferred by science-fiction writers and tabloid writers to indicate the futuristic nature of using the Internet, the prefix 'cyber' indicating a blurring between humans, machines and communications. The terms are not frequently used today since the terms **Internet**, **intranet** and **World Wide Web** are more specific and widely used.

Data controller Each company must have a defined person responsible for data protection.

Data fusion The combining of data from different complementary sources (usually geodemographic and lifestyle or market research and lifestyle) to 'build a picture of someone's life' (M. Evans (1998) From 1086 to 1984: direct marketing into the millennium, *Marketing Intelligence and Planning*, 16(1), 56–67).

Data subject The legal term to refer to the individual whose data are held.

Data warehousing and data mining Extracting data from legacy systems and other resources; cleaning, scrubbing and preparing data for decision support; maintaining data in appropriate data stores; accessing and analysing data using a variety of end-user tools; and mining data for significant relationships. The primary purpose of these efforts is to provide easy access to specially prepared data that can be used with decision support applications such as management reports, queries, decision support systems, executive information systems and data mining.

Database marketing The process of systematically collecting, in electronic or optical form, data about past, current and/or potential customers, maintaining the integrity of the data by continually monitoring customer purchases, by enquiring about changing status, and by using the data to formulate marketing strategy and foster personalised relationships with customers.

Decryption The process of decoding (unscrambling) a message that has been encrypted using defined mathematical rules.

Deep linking Jakob Nielsen's term for a user arriving at a site deep within its structure or where search engines index a mirrored copy of content normally inaccessible by search engine **spiders**.

Demand analysis Quantitative determination of the potential usage and business value achieved from online customers of an organisation. Qualitative analysis of perceptions of online channels is also assessed.

Demand analysis for e-commerce Assessment of the demand for e-commerce services amongst existing and potential customer segments using the ratio Access : Choose : Buy online.

Demographic characteristics Variations in attributes of the populations such as age, sex and social class.

Design for analysis (DFA) The required measures from a site are considered during design to better understand the audience of a site and their decision points.

Design phase (of site construction) The design phase defines how the site will work in the key areas of **web site** structure, **navigation** and **security**.

Destination site Frequently used to refer to the site that is visited following a **clickthrough** on a **banner advertisement**. Could also apply to any site visited following a click on a **hyperlink**.

Destination store A retail store in which the merchandise, selection, presentation, pricing or other unique features act as a magnet for the customer.

Development phase (of site construction) 'Development' is the term used to describe the creation of a **web site** by programmers. It involves writing the **HTML** content, creating graphics, and writing any necessary software code such as **Java**Script or **ActiveX** (programming).

Differential advantage A desirable attribute of a product offering that is not currently matched by competitor offerings.

Differential pricing Identical products are priced differently for different types of customers, markets or buying situations.

Digital audio broadcasting (DAB) radio Digital radio with clear sound quality with the facility to transmit text, images and video.

Digital brand A digital brand is a brand identity used for a product or company online that differs from the traditional brand. (Also known as an **online brand**.)

Digital cash An electronic version of cash in which the buyer of an item is typically anonymous to the seller. (Also referred to as **virtual** or **electronic cash** or **e-cash**.)

Digital certificates (keys) A method of ensuring **privacy** on the **Internet**. **Certificates** consist of keys made up of large numbers that are used to uniquely identify individuals. *See also* **Public key**.

Digital marketing This has a similar meaning to 'electronic marketing' – both describe the management and execution of marketing using electronic media such as the web, e-mail, interactive TV and wireless media in conjunction with digital data about customers' characteristics and behaviour.

Digital radio All types of radio broadcast as a digital signal.

Digital signatures The electronic equivalent of written signatures which are used as an online method of identifying individuals or companies using **public-key encryption**.

Digital television Information is received and displayed on a digital television using binary information (0s and 1s), giving options for better picture and sound quality and providing additional information services based on interactivity. *See also* **Interactive digital TV**.

Direct marketing Marketing to customers using one or more advertising media aimed at achieving measurable response and/or transaction.

Direct response Usually achieved in an Internet marketing context by **callback services**.

Directed information seeker Someone who knows what information he or she is looking for.

Directories Directory **web sites** provide a structured listing of registered web sites in different categories. They are similar to an electronic version of *Yellow Pages*. Yahoo! and Excite are the best known examples of directories. (Also known as **catalogues**.)

Disintermediation The removal of **intermediaries** such as distributors or brokers that formerly linked a company to its customers.

Disruptive technologies New technologies that prompt businesses to reappraise their strategic approaches.

Distribution channels The mechanism by which products are directed to customers either through intermediaries or directly.

Domain name The **web address** that identifies a **web server**. *See* **Domain name system**.

Domain name registration The process of reserving a unique **web address** that can be used to refer to the company web site.

Domain name system The domain name system (DNS) provides a method of representing Internet Protocol (IP) addresses as text-based names. These are used as **web addresses**. For example, www.microsoft.com is the representation of site 207.68.156.58. Domain names are divided into the following categories:

- Top-level domain name such as *.com* or *.co.uk*. (Also known as **Global (or generic) top-level domain names (gLTD)**.)

- Second-level domain name. This refers to the company name and is sometimes referred to as the 'enterprise name', e.g. *novell.com*.

- Third-level or sub-enterprise domain name. This may be used to refer to an individual server within an organisation, such as *support.novell.com*.

Doorway pages Specially constructed pages which feature keywords for particular product searches. These often redirect visitors to a home page.

Download The process of retrieving electronic information such as a web page or **e-mail** from another remote location such as a **web server**.

Drip irrigation Collecting information about customer needs through their lifetime.

Dynamic pricing Prices can be updated in real time according to the type of customer or current market conditions.

Dynamic web page A page that is created in real time, often with reference to a database query, in response to a user request.

Early adopters Companies or departments that invest in new marketing techniques and technologies when they first become available in an attempt to gain a competitive advantage despite the higher risk entailed than that involved in a more cautious approach.

Early (first) mover advantage An early entrant into the marketplace.

E-business *See* **Electronic business**.

E-cash *See* **Digital cash**.

E-commerce *See* **Electronic commerce**.

E-marketing *See* **Electronic marketing**.

Effective frequency The number of exposures or **ad impressions** (frequency) required for an advertisement to become effective.

Effectiveness Meeting process objectives, delivering the required outputs and outcomes. 'Doing the right thing.'

Efficiency Minimising resources or time needed to complete a process. 'Doing the thing right.'

E-government The use of Internet technologies to provide government services to citizens.

Electronic business (e-business) All electronically mediated information exchanges, both within an organisation and with external stakeholders, supporting the range of business processes.

Electronic cash *See* **Digital cash**.

Electronic commerce (e-commerce) All financial and informational electronically mediated exchanges between an organisation and its external stakeholders. (*See* **Buy-side e-commerce** and **Sell-side e-commerce**.)

Electronic commerce transactions Transactions in the trading of goods and services conducted using the Internet and other digital media.

Electronic customer relationship management Using digital communications technologies to maximise sales to existing customers and encourage continued usage of online services.

Electronic data interchange (EDI) The exchange, using digital media, of standardised business documents such as purchase orders and invoices between buyers and sellers.

Electronic mail (e-mail) Sending messages or documents, such as news about a new product or sales promotion between individuals. A primitive form of **push** channel. E-mail may be **inbound** or **outbound**.

Electronic mail advertising Advertisements contained within e-mail such as newsletters.

Electronic mall *See* **Virtual mall**.

Electronic marketing Achieving marketing objectives through use of electronic communications technology.

Electronic marketspace A virtual marketplace such as the **Internet** in which no direct contact occurs between buyers and sellers.

Electronic Shopping or ES test This test was developed by de Kare-Silver to assess the extent to which consumers are likely to purchase a particular retail product using the **Internet**.

Electronic tokens Units of digital currency that are in a standard electronic format.

E-marketing *See* **Electronic marketing**.

Emergent strategy Strategic analysis, strategic development and strategy implementation are interrelated and are developed together.

Emotional loyalty Loyalty to a brand is demonstrated by favourable perceptions, opinions and recommendations.

Encryption The scrambling of information into a form that cannot be interpreted. **Decryption** is used to make the information readable.

Enterprise application integration The middleware technology that is used to connect together different software applications and their underlying databases is now known as 'enterprise application integration (EAI)' (*Internet World*, 1999).

Entry page The page at which a visitor enters a **web site**. It is identified by a **log file analyser**. *See also* **Exit page** and **Referring site**.

Environmental scanning and analysis The process of continuously monitoring the environment and events and responding accordingly.

According to Dennis et al. (2004), the business of e-retailing is defined as the sale of goods and services via the Internet or other electronic channels for individual consumers. This definition includes all e-commerce and related activities that ultimately result in transactions.

Ethical standards Practices or behaviours which are morally acceptable to society.

Evaluating a web site *See* **Web site measurement**.

Exchange *See* **Business-to-business exchanges or marketplaces**.

Exit page The page from which a visitor exits a **web site**. It is identified by **web analytics** services.

Expert reviews An analysis of an existing site or prototype, by an experienced usability expert who will identity deficiencies and improvements to a site based on their knowledge of web design principles and best practice.

Exposure-based payment Advertisers pay according to the number of times the ad is viewed.

Extended product Additional features and benefits beyond the core product.

Extension *See* **Customer extension**.

Extranet Formed by extending the **intranet** beyond a company to customers, suppliers, collaborators or even competitors. This is password-protected to prevent access by general Internet users.

File Transfer Protocol (FTP) A standard method for moving files across the **Internet**. FTP is available as a feature of **web browsers** that is sometimes used for marketing applications such as **downloading** files such as product price lists or specifications. Standalone FTP packages such as WSFTP are commonly used to update **HTML** files on **web servers** when **uploading** revisions to the **web server**.

Firewall A specialised software application mounted on a server at the point where the company is connected to the Internet. Its purpose is to prevent unauthorised access into the company by outsiders. Firewalls are essential for all companies hosting their own **web server**.

First-party cookies Served by the site currently in use – typical for e-commerce sites.

Flow Describes a state in which users have a positive experience from readily controlling their **navigation** and interaction on a **web site**.

Focus groups Online focus groups have been conducted by w3focus.com. These follow a bulletin board or discussion group form where different members of the focus group respond to prompts from the focus group leaders.

Form A method on a web page of entering information such as order details.

Forward auctions Item purchased by highest bid made in bidding period.

4G Fourth-generation wireless, expected to deliver wireless broadband at 20–40 Mbps (about 10–20 times the current rates of ADSL broadband service).

Frame A technique used to divide a web page into different parts such as a menu and separate content.

G

General Packet Radio Services (GPRS) A standard offering mobile data transfer and WAP access approximately 5 to 10 times faster than traditional GSM access.

Global (or generic) top-level domain names (gLTD) The part of the **domain name** that refers to the category of site. The gLTD is usually the rightmost part of the domain name such as .co.uk or .com.

Globalisation The increase of international trading and shared social and cultural values.

Gopher Gopher is a directory-based structure containing information in certain categories.

Graphic design All factors that govern the physical appearance of a web page.

Graphics Interchange Format (GIF) GIF is a graphics format used to display images within web pages. An interlaced GIF is displayed gradually on the screen, building up an image in several passes.

H

Hacker Someone who enjoys exploring the details of programmable systems and how to stretch their capabilities.

Hit A hit is recorded for each graphic or page of text requested from a **web server**. It is not a reliable measure for the number of people viewing a page. A **page impression** is a more reliable measure denoting one person viewing one page.

Home page The index page of a **web site** with menu options or links to other resources on the site. Usually denoted by <web address>/index.html.

House list A list of prospect and customer names, e-mail addresses and profile information owned by an organisation.

HTML (Hypertext Markup Language) A standard format used to define the text and layout of web pages. HTML files usually have the extension .HTML or .HTM.

HTTP (Hypertext Transfer Protocol) A standard that defines the way information is transmitted across the **Internet**.

Hype cycle A graphic representation of the maturity, adoption and business application of specific technologies.

Hyperlink A method of moving between one web site page and another, indicated to the user by text highlighted by underlining and/or a different colour. Hyperlinks can also be achieved by clicking on a graphic image such as a **banner advertisement** that is linked to another **web site**.

I

Identity theft The misappropriation of the identity of another person, without their knowledge or consent.

I-Mode A mobile access platform that enables display of colour graphics and content subscription services.

Inbound customer contact strategies Approaches to managing the cost and quality of service related to management of customer enquiries.

Inbound e-mail **E-mail** arriving at a company.

Inbound Internet-based communications Customers enquire through web-based form and e-mail (*see* **Web self-service**).

Incidental offline advertising Driving traffic to the web site is not a primary objective of the advert.

Infomediary An **intermediary** business whose main source of revenue derives from capturing consumer information and developing detailed profiles of individual customers for use by third parties.

Information architecture The combination of organisation, labelling and navigation schemes constituting an information system.

Information organisation schemes The structure chosen to group and categorise information.

Initiation of web site project This phase of the project should involve a structured review of the costs and benefits of developing a **web site** (or making a major revision to an existing web site). A successful outcome to initiation will be a decision to proceed with the site **development phase**, with an agreed budget and target completion date.

Insertion order A printed order to run an advertisement campaign. It defines the campaign name, the **web site** receiving the order and the planner or buyer giving the order, the individual advertisements to be run (or who will provide them), the sizes of the advertisements, the campaign beginning and end dates, the **CPM**, the total cost, discounts to be applied, and reporting requirements and possible penalties or stipulations relative to the failure to deliver the impressions.

Integrity *See* **Security methods**.

Intellectual property rights (IPRs) Protect the intangible property created by corporations or individuals that is protected under copyright, trade secret and patent laws.

Interactive banner advertisement A **banner advertisement** that enables the user to enter information.

Interactive digital TV (iDTV) Television displayed using a digital signal delivered by a range of media – cable, satellite, terrestrial (aerial). Interactions can be provided through phone line or cable service.

Interactivity The medium enables a dialogue between company and customer.

Intermediaries Online sites that help bring together different parties such as buyers and sellers.

Internet The physical network that links computers across the globe. It consists of the infrastructure of network servers and communication links between them that are used to hold and transport the vast amount of information on the Internet.

Internet contribution An assessment of the extent to which the **Internet** contributes to sales is a key measure of the importance of the Internet to a company.

Internet EDI Use of electronic data interchange standards delivered across non-proprietary Internet protocol networks.

Internet governance Control of the operation and use of the Internet.

Internet marketing The application of the Internet and related digital technologies in conjunction with traditional communications to achieve marketing objectives.

Internet marketing metrics *See* **Metrics for Internet marketing**.

Internet marketing strategy Definition of the approach by which Internet marketing will support marketing and business objectives.

Internet pureplay An organisation with the majority of its customer-facing operations online, e.g. Egg.

Internet Relay Chat (IRC) A communications tool that allows a text-based 'chat' between different users who are logged on at the same time. Of limited use for marketing purposes except for special-interest or youth products.

Internet service provider (ISP) Company that provides home or business users with a connection to access the Internet. It can also host **web sites** or provide a link from **web servers** to allow other companies and consumers access to a corporate web site.

Interruption marketing Marketing communications that disrupt customers' activities.

Interstitial ads Ads that appear between one page and the next.

Intranet A network within a single company that enables access to company information using the familiar tools of the **Internet** such as **web browsers** and **e-mail**. Only staff within a company can access the intranet, which will be password-protected.

Java A programming language standard supported by Sun Microsystems, which permits complex and graphical customer applications to be written and then accessed from a **web browser**. An example might be a form for calculating interest on a loan. A competitor to **ActiveX**.

Joint Photographics Experts Group (JPEG) A compressed graphics standard specified by the JPEG. Used for graphic images typically requiring use of many colours, such as product photographs where some loss of quality is acceptable. The format allows for some degradation in image quality to enable more rapid download.

Key performance indicators (KPIs) Metrics used to assess the performance of a process and/or whether goals set are achieved.

Lead Details about a potential customer (prospect). (*See* **Qualified lead**.)

Lead generation offers Offered in return for customers providing their contact details and characteristics. Commonly used in B2B marketing where free information such as a report or a seminar will be offered.

Lifetime value (LTV) The total net benefit that a customer or group of customers will provide a company over their total relationship with a company.

List broker Will cource the appropriate e-mail list(s) from the list owner.

List owner Has collected e-mail addresses which are offered for sale.

Live web site Current site accessible to customers, as distinct from **test web site**.

Localisation Designing the content of the **web site** in such a way that it is appropriate to different audiences in different countries.

Log file A file stored on a **web server** that records every item **downloaded** by users.

Log file analysers **Web analytics** tools that are used to build a picture of the amount of usage of different parts of a **web site** based on the information contained in the **log file**.

Long tail concept A frequency distribution suggesting the relative variation in popularity of items selected by consumers.

Loyalty techniques Customers sign up to an incentive scheme where they receive points for repeat purchases, which can be converted into offers such as discounts, free products or cash. (Also known as **online incentive schemes**.)

Mailbots *See* **Autoresponders**.

Maintenance process The work involved in running a live **web site** such as updating pages and checking the performance of the site.

Marketing intermediaries Firms that can help a company to promote, sell and distribute its products or services.

Marketing mix The series of seven key variables – Product, Price, Place, Promotion, People, Process and Physical evidence that are varied by marketers as part of the customer offering.

Marketing planning A logical sequence and a series of activities leading to the setting of marketing objectives and the formulation of plans for achieving them.

Marketplace *See* **Business-to-business exchanges or marketplaces**.

Marketsite eXchange, eHub, metamediaries are terms used to refer to complex web sites that facilitate trading exchanges between companies around the globe. **MarketSite™** is a trade mark of commerceOne and considered as the leading e-marketplace operating environment.

Marketspace A virtual marketplace such as the Internet in which no direct contact occurs between buyers and sellers. (Also known as **electronic marketspace**.)

Markup language *See* **HTML, XML**.

Mass customisation The ability to create tailored marketing messages or products for individual customers or a group of similar customers (a bespoke service), yet retain the economies of scale and the capacity of mass marketing or production.

Mass marketing One-to-many communication between a company and potential customers, with limited tailoring of the message.

Measurement *See* **Web site measurement**.

Media broker A company that places advertisements for companies wishing to advertise by contacting the **media owners**.

Media buyer The person within a company wishing to advertise who places the advertisement, usually via a **media broker**.

Media buying The process of purchasing media to meet the media plan requirements at the lowest costs.

Media-neutral planning (MNP) An approach to planning ad campaigns to maximise response across different media according to consumer usage of these media.

Media owners The owners of **web sites** (or other media such as newspapers) that accept advertisements.

Media planning The process of selecting the best combination of media to achieve marketing campaign objectives. Answers questions such as 'How many of the audience can I reach through different media?', 'On which media (and ad vehicles) should I place ads?', 'Which frequency should I select?', 'How much money should be spent in each medium?'

Media site Typical location where paid-for ads are placed.

Metadata Literally, data about data – a format describing the structure and content of data.

Meta search engines Meta search engines submit keywords typed by users to a range of **search engines** in order to increase the number of relevant pages since different search engines may have indexed different sites. An example is the metacrawler search engine or **www.mamma.com**.

Meta-tags Text within an **HTML** file summarising the content of the site (content meta-tag) and relevant keywords (keyword meta-tag), which are matched against the keywords typed into **search engines**.

Metrics for Internet marketing Measures that indicate the effectiveness of **Internet marketing** activities in meeting customer, business and marketing objectives.

Micropayments (microtransactions) Digital cash systems that allow very small sums of money (fractions of 1p) to be transferred, but with lower security. Such small sums do not warrant a credit card payment, because processing is too costly.

Microsite Specialised content that is part of a **web site** that is not necessarily owned by the organisation. If owned by the company it may be as part of an **extranet**. (*See also* **Nested ad content**.)

Microsoft Internet Information Server (IIS) Microsoft IIS is a **web server** developed by Microsoft that runs on Windows NT.

Mixed-mode buying The process by which a customer changes between online and offline channels during the buying process.

Multi-channel marketing Customer communications and product distribution are supported by a combination of digital and traditional channels at different points in the buying cycle.

Multi-channel marketing strategy Defines how different marketing channels should integrate and support each other in terms of their proposition development and communications based on their relative merits for the customer and the company.

Navigation The method of finding and moving between different information and pages on a **web site**. It is governed by menu arrangements, site structure and the layout of individual pages.

Nested ad content This refers to the situation when the person undertaking the **clickthrough** is not redirected to a corporate or brand site, but is instead taken to a related page on the same site as that on which the advertisement is placed. (Sometimes referred to as **microsite**.)

Non-repudiability *See* **Security methods**.

Notification The process whereby companies register with the data protection register to inform about their data holdings.

O

Offer An incentive in direct marketing or a product offering.

Offline promotion *See* **Promotion (online and offline)**.

Offline web metric Offline measures are those that are collated by marketing staff recording particular marketing outcomes such as an enquiry or a sale. They are usually collated manually, but could be collated automatically.

One-to-one marketing A unique dialogue that occurs directly between a company and individual customers (or less strictly with groups of customers with similar needs). The dialogue involves a company in listening to customer needs and responding with services to meet these needs.

Online brand *See* **Digital brand**.

Online branding How online channels are used to support brands that, in essence, are the sum of the characteristics of a product or service as perceived by a user.

Online customer experience The combination of rational and emotional factors of using a company's online services that influences customers' perceptions of a brand online.

Online incentive schemes *See* **Loyalty techniques**.

Online intermediary sites Web sites that facilitate exchanges between consumer and business suppliers.

Online promotion *See* **Promotion (online and offline)**.

Online promotion contribution An assessment of the proportion of customers (new or retained) who are reached by online communications and are influenced as a result.

Online revenue contribution An assessment of the direct contribution of the Internet or other digital media to sales, usually expressed as a percentage of overall sales revenue.

Online services providers (OSPs) An OSP is sometimes used to distinguish large **Internet service providers (ISPs)** from other access providers. In the UK, AOL, Freeserve, VirginNet and LineOne can be considered OSPs since they have a large amount of specially developed content available to their subscribers. Note that this term is not used as frequently as ISP, and the distinction between ISPs and OSPs is a blurred one since all OSPs are also **ISPs** and the distinction only occurs according to the amount of premium content (only available to customers) offered as part of the service.

Online service-quality gap The mismatch between what is expected and delivered by an online presence.

Online value proposition (OVP) A statement of the benefits of e-commerce services that ideally should not be available in competitor offerings or offline offerings.

Online web metrics Online measures are those that are collected automatically on the **web server**, often in a server **log file**.

Operational effectiveness Performing similar activities better than rivals. This includes efficiency of processes.

Opt-in A customer proactively agrees to receive further information.

Opt-in e-mail The customer is only contacted when he or she has explicitly asked for information to be sent (usually when filling in an on-screen form).

Opt-out e-mail The customer is not contacted subsequently if he or she has explicitly stated that he or she does not want to be contacted in future. Opt-out or **unsubscribe** options are usually available within the e-mail itself.

Outbound e-mail E-mail sent from a company.

Outbound Internet-based communications The web site and e-mail marketing are used to send personalised communications to customers.

Outsourcing Contracting an outside company to undertake part of the **Internet marketing** activities.

Overt Typically an animated ad that moves around the page and is superimposed on the web site content.

Page impression One page impression occurs when a member of the audience views a web page. (*See also* **Ad impression** and **Reach**.)

PageRank A scale between 0 to 10 used by Google to assess the importance of web sites according to the number of inbound links or backlinks.

Page request The process of a user selecting a **hyperlink** or typing in a **uniform resource locator (URL)** to retrieve information on a specific web page. Equivalent to **page impression**.

Page view *See* **Page impression**.

Pay-per-click (PPC) search marketing Refers to when a company pays for text ads to be displayed on the search engine results pages when a specific keyphrase is entered by the search users. It is so called since the marketer pays for each time the hypertext link in the ad is clicked on.

People variable The element of the marketing mix that involves the delivery of service to customers during interactions with those customers.

Perfect market An efficient market where there are an infinite number of suppliers and buyers and complete price transparency.

Performance drivers Critical success factors that determine whether business and marketing objectives are achieved.

Performance management system A process used to evaluate and improve the efficiency and effectiveness of an organisation and its processes.

Performance measurement system The process by which metrics are defined, collected, disseminated and actioned.

Performance metrics Measures that are used to evaluate and improve the efficiency and effectiveness of business processes.

Performance of web site Performance or quality of service is dependent on its availability and speed of access.

Permission marketing Customers agree (opt-in) to be involved in an organisation's marketing activities, usually as a result of an incentive.

Persistent cookies Cookies that remain on the computer after a visitor session has ended. Used to recognise returning visitors.

Personal data Any information about an individual stored by companies concerning their customers or employees.

Personalisation Web-based personalisation involves delivering customised content for the individual through web pages, e-mail or **push technology**.

Personas A thumbnail summary of the characteristics, needs, motivations and environment of typical web site users.

Persuasion marketing Using design elements such as layout, copy and typography together with promotional messages to encourage site users to follow particular paths and specific actions rather than giving them complete choice in their navigation.

Phishing Obtaining personal details online through sites and e-mails masquerading as legitimate businesses.

Phone-me A **callback** facility available on the **web site** for a company to contact a customer by phone at a later time, as specified by the customer.

Physical evidence variable The element of the marketing mix that involves the tangible expression of a product and how it is purchased and used.

Pixel The small dots on a computer screen that are used to represent images and text. Short for 'picture element'. Used to indicate the size of **banner advertisements**.

Place The element of the marketing mix that involves distributing products to customers in line with demand and minimising cost of inventory, transport and storage.

Plug-in A program that must be **downloaded** to view particular content such as an animation.

Podcasts Individuals and organisations post online media (audio and video) which can be viewed in the appropriate players (including the iPod which first sparked the growth in this technique).

Portal A **web site** that acts as a gateway to information and services available on the Internet by providing **search engines**, **directories** and other services such as personalised news or free e-mail.

Portfolio analysis Evaluation of value of current e-commerce services or applications.

Positioning Customers' perception of the product offer relative to those of competitors.

Prescriptive strategy The three core areas of strategic analysis, strategic development and strategy implementation are linked together sequentially.

Price elasticity of demand Measure of consumer behaviour that indicates the change in demand for a product or service in response to changes in price.

Price transparency Customer knowledge about pricing increases due to increased availability of pricing information.

Price variable The element of the marketing mix that involves defining product prices and pricing models.

Pricing model Describes the form of payment such as outright purchase, auction, rental, volume purchases and credit terms.

Primary persona A representation of the typical site user.

Privacy A moral right of individuals to avoid intrusion into their personal affairs. (*See also* **Security methods**.)

Privacy and Electronic Communications Regulations Act A law intended to control the distribution of e-mail and other online communications including cookies.

Privacy statement Information on a web site explaining how and why individuals' data are collected, processed and stored.

Process variable The element of the marketing mix that involves the methods and procedures companies use to achieve all marketing functions.

Product variable The element of the marketing mix that involves researching customers' needs and developing appropriate products. (*See* **Core product** and **Extended product**.)

Profiling *See* **Customer profiling**.

Promotion (online and offline) Online promotion uses communication via the **Internet** itself to raise awareness about a site and drive traffic to it. This promotion may take the form of links from other sites, **banner advertisements** or targeted e-mail messages. Offline promotion uses traditional media such as television or newspaper advertising and word of mouth to promote a company's **web site**.

Promotion variable The element of the marketing mix that involves communication with customers and other stakeholders to inform them about the product and the organisation.

Prosumer 'Producer + consumer'. The customer is closely involved in specifying their requirements in a product.

Prototypes and prototyping A prototype is a preliminary version of part (or a framework of all) of a **web site** that can be reviewed by its target audience, or the marketing team. Prototyping is an iterative process where web site users suggest modifications before further prototypes are made and the final version of the site is developed.

Psychographic segmentation A breakdown of customers according to different characteristics.

Public key A unique identifier of a buyer or a seller that is available to other parties to enable secure e-commerce using **encryption** based on digital certificates.

Public-key encryption An asymmetric form of **encryption** in which the keys or **digital certificates** used by the sender and receiver of information are different. The two keys are related, so only the pair of keys can be used together to encrypt and decrypt information.

Public-key infrastructure (PKI) The organisations responsible for issuing and maintaining certificates for public-key security together form the PKI.

Pull media The consumer is proactive in selection of the message through actively seeking out a web site.

Push media Communications are broadcast from an advertiser to consumers of the message who are passive recipients.

Push technology The delivery of web-based content to the user's desktop without the need for the user to visit a site to **download** information. E-mail can also be considered to be a push technology. A particular type of information is a push channel.

Qualified lead Contact and profile information for a customer with an indication of the level of their interest in product categories.

R

Reach The number of unique individuals who view an advertisement.

Really Simple Syndication (RSS) Blog, news or other content is published by an XML standard and syndicated for other sites or read by users in RSS reader software services.

RealNames A service for matching company names and brands with **web addresses**.

Referrer The site that a visitor previously visited before following a link.

Referring sites A **log file** may indicate which site a user visited immediately before visiting the current site. (*See also* **Clickthrough**, **Destination site** and **Exit page**.)

Registration (individuals) The process whereby an individual subscribes to a site or requests further information by filling in contact details and his or her needs using an electronic form.

Registration (of domain name) The process of reserving a unique **web address** that can be used to refer to the company **web site**.

Reintermediation The creation of new **intermediaries** between customers and suppliers providing services such as supplier search and product evaluation.

Relationship marketing Consistent application of up-to-date knowledge of individual customers to product and service design, which is communicated interactively in order to develop a continuous, mutually beneficial and long-term relationship.

Repeat visits If an organisation can encourage customers to return to the web site then the relationship can be maintained online.

Repurposing Developing for a new access platform, such as the web, content which was previously used for a different platform.

Resource analysis Review of the technological, financial and human resources of an organisation and how they are utilised in business processes.

Results-based payment Advertisers pay according to the number of times the ad is clicked on.

Retail channel Retailers' use of the Internet as both a communication and a transactional channel concurrently in business-to-consumer markets.

Retail format This is the general nature of the retail mix in terms of range of products and services, pricing policy, promotional programmes, operating style or store design and visual merchandising; examples include mail-order retailers (non-store-based) and department-store retailers.

Retention *See* **Customer retention**.

Return on advertising spend (ROAS) This indicates amount of revenue generated from each referrer. ROAS = Total revenue generated from referrer / Amount spent on advertising with referrer.

Return on investment (ROI) This indicates the profitability of any investment, or in an advertising context, for each referring site.

ROI = Profit generated from investment / Cost of investment.

ROI = Profit generated from referrers / Amount spent on advertising with referrer.

Return path An interaction where the customer sends information to the iDTV provider using a phone line or cable.

Revenue models Describe methods of generating income for an organisation.

Reverse auctions Item purchased from lowest-bidding supplier in bidding period.

Rich-media advertisements Advertisements that are not static, but provide animation, sound or interactivity. An example of this would be a **banner advertisement** for a loan in which a customer can type in the amount of loan required, and the cost of the loan is calculated immediately.

Robot A tool, also known as a **spider**, that is employed by **search engines** to index web pages of registered sites on a regular basis.

Run of site A situation where a company pays for **banner advertisements** to promote its services across a **web site**.

S

Sales generation offers Offers that encourage product trial. A coupon redeemed against a purchase is a classic example.

Sales promotions The Internet offers tremendous potential for sales promotions of different types since it is more immediate than any other medium – it is always available for communication, and tactical variations in the details of the promotion can be made at short notice.

Satisficing behaviour Consumers do not behave entirely rationally in product or supplier selection. They will compare alternatives, but then may make their choice given imperfect information.

Saturation of the Internet Access to the **Internet** will reach saturation as home PC ownership reaches a limit, unless other access devices become popular.

Scenario-based analysis Models of the future environment are developed from different starting points.

Scenario of use A particular path or flow of events or activities performed by a visitor to a web site.

Scripts Scripts can run either on the user's browser (client-side scripts) (*see* **Web browser**) or on the **web server** (server-side scripts).

Search engine Specialised web site that uses automatic tools known as **spiders** or **robots** to index web pages of registered sites. Users can search the index by typing in keywords to specify their interest. Pages containing these keywords will be listed, and by clicking on a **hyperlink** the user will be taken to the site.

Search engine listing The list of sites and descriptions returned by a search engine after a user types in keywords.

Search engine optimisation (SEO) A structured approach used to increase the position of a company or its products in search engine natural or organic results listings for selected keywords or phrases.

Search engine ranking The position of a site on a particular search engine, e.g. 3rd.

Secure Electronic Transaction (SET) A standard for **public-key encryption** intended to enable secure **e-commerce transactions** lead-developed by Mastercard and Visa.

Secure HTTP Encrypted **HTTP**.

Secure Sockets Layer (SSL) A commonly used **encryption** technique for scrambling data such as credit card numbers as they are passed across the Internet from a **web browser** to a **web server**.

Security methods When systems for **electronic commerce** are devised, or when existing solutions are selected, the following attributes must be present:

1 *Authentication* – are parties to the transaction who they claim to be? This is achieved through the use of digital certificates.

2 *Privacy and confidentiality* – are transaction data protected? The consumer may want to make an anonymous purchase. Are all non-essential traces of a transaction removed from the public network and all intermediary records eliminated?

3 *Integrity* – checks that the message sent is complete, i.e. that it is not corrupted.

4 *Non-repudiability* – ensures sender cannot deny sending message.

5 *Availability* – how can threats to the continuity and performance of the system be eliminated?

Seeding The viral campaign is started by sending an e-mail to a targeted group that are likely to propagate the virus.

Sense and respond communications Delivering timely, relevant communications to customers as part of a contact strategy based on assessment of their position in the customer lifecycle and monitoring specific interactions with a company's web site, e-mails and staff.

Segmentation Identification of different groups within a target market in order to develop different offerings for each group.

Sell-side e-commerce E-commerce transactions between a supplier organisation and its customers.

Server log file *See* **Online web metrics**.

Service quality The level of service received on a **web site**. Dependent on reliability, responsiveness and availability of staff and the **web site** service.

Serving Used to describe the process of displaying an advertisement on a **web site** (**ad serving**) or delivering a web page to a user's **web browser**. (*See* **Web server**.)

Share of search The audience share of Internet searchers achieved by a particular audience in a particular market.

Share of voice The relative advertising spend of the different competitive brands within the product category. Share of voice (SOV) is calculated by dividing a particular brand's advertising spend by the total category spend.

Session See **Visitor session**.

Session cookie A cookie used to manage a single visitor session.

Short Message Service (SMS) The formal name for text messaging.

Site *See* **Web site**.

Site announcements Usually used to describe the dissemination of information about a new or revised **web site**.

Site auditors Auditors accurately measure the usage for different sites as the number of ad impressions and clickthrough rates. Auditors include ABC (Audit Bureau of Circulation) and BPA (Business Publication Auditor) International.

Site availability An indication of how easy it is to connect to a **web site** as a user. In theory this figure should be 100 per cent, but for technical reasons such as failures in the server hardware or upgrades to software, sometimes users cannot access the site and the figure falls below 90 per cent.

Site design template A standard page layout format which is applied to each page of a web site.

Site map A graphical or text depiction of the relationship between different groups of content on a web site.

Site measurement *See* **Web site measurement**.

Site navigation scheme Tools provided to the user to move between different information on a web site.

Site re-launch Where a **web site** is replaced with a new version with a new 'look and feel'.

Site statistics Collected by **log file analysers**, these are used to monitor the effectiveness of a **web site**.

Site 'stickiness' An indication of how long a visitor stays on a site. **Log file analysers** can be used to assess average visit times.

Site visit One site visit records one customer visiting the site. Not equivalent to **User session**.

Site-visitor activity data Information on content and services accessed by e-commerce site visitors.

Sitemapping tools These tools diagram the layout of the **web site**, which is useful for site management, and can be used to assist users.

Situation analysis Collection and review of information about an organisation's external environment and internal processes and resources in order to inform its strategies.

SMART metrics SMART metrics must be:

- Specific;
- Measurable;
- Actionable;
- Relevant;
- Timely.

Smartcards Physical cards containing a memory chip that can be inserted into a smartcard reader before items can be purchased.

Social exclusion Part of society is excluded from the facilities available to the remainder.

Soft lock-in Electronic linkages between supplier and customer increase switching costs.

Software agents *See* **Agents**.

Spam Unsolicited e-mail (usually bulk mailed and untargeted).

Spamming Bulk e-mailing of unsolicited mail.

Specific offline advertising Driving traffic to the web site or explaining the online proposition is a primary objective of the advert.

Spider A tool, also known as a **robot**, that is employed by **search engines** to index web pages of registered sites on a regular basis.

Splash page A preliminary page that precedes the normal **home page** of a **web site**. Site users can either wait to be redirected to the home page or can follow a link to do this. Splash pages are not now commonly used since they slow down the process whereby customers find the information they need.

Sponsorship Sponsorship involves a company paying money to advertise on a **web site**. The arrangement may involve more than advertising. Sponsorship is a similar arrangement to **co-branding**.

Stage models Models for the development of different levels of Internet marketing literature.

Stages in web site development The standard stages of creation of a **web site** are **initiation**, feasibility, **analysis**, **design**, **development** (**content** creation), **testing** and **maintenance**.

Static (fixed) web page A page on the web server that is invariant.

STEP A framework for assessing the macroenvironment, standing for Social, Technological, Economic and Political (including legal).

Storyboarding Using static drawings or screenshots of the different parts of a **web site** to review the design concept with customers or clients.

Strategic analysis Collection and review of information about an organisation's internal processes and resources and external marketplace factors in order to inform strategy definition.

Strategic positioning Performing different activities from rivals or performing similar activities in different ways.

Strategy formulation Generation, review and selection of strategies to achieve strategic objectives.

Strategy process model A framework for approaching strategy development.

Streaming media Sound and video that can be experienced within a web browser before the whole clip is downloaded.

Style guide A definition of site structure, page design, typography and copy defined within a company. (*See* **Graphic design**.)

Subject access request A request by a data subject to view personal data from an organisation.

Superstitials Pop-up adverts that require interaction to remove them.

Surfer An **undirected information seeker** who is often looking for an experience rather than information.

Symmetric encryption Both parties to a transaction use the same key to encode and decode messages.

Tagging Tracking of the origin of customers and their spending patterns.

Target marketing strategy Evaluation and selection of appropriate segments and the development of appropriate offers.

Targeting (through banner advertisers) Advertising **networks** such as DoubleClick offer advertisers the ability to target advertisements dynamically on the World Wide Web through their 'DART' targeting technology. This gives advertisers a means of reaching specific audiences.

Technology convergence A trend in which different hardware devices such as TVs, computers and phone merge and have similar functions.

Telemarketing using the Internet Mainly used for inbound telemarketing, including sales lines, carelines for goods and services and response handling for direct response campaigns.

Telnet A program that allows remote access to data and text-based programs on other computer systems at different locations. For example, a retailer could check to see whether an item was in stock in a warehouse using a telnet application.

Template *See* **Site design template**.

Test web site A parallel version of the site to use before the site is made available to customers as a **live web site**.

Testing content Testing should be conducted for **plug-ins**; for interactive facilities and integration with company databases; for spelling and grammar; for adherence to corporate image standards; for implementation of **HTML** in different **web browsers**; and to ensure that links to external sites are valid.

Testing phase Testing involves different aspects of the **content** such as spelling, validity of links, formatting on different **web browsers** and dynamic features such as form filling or database queries.

Third-party cookies Served by another site to the one being viewed – typical for portals where an ad network will track remotely or where the web analytics software places a cookie.

Tipping point Using the science of social epidemics explains principles that underpin the rapid spread of ideas, products and behaviours through a population.

Trademark A trademark is a unique word or phrase that distinguishes your company. The mark can be registered as plain or designed text, artwork or a combination. In theory, colours, smells and sounds can also be trademarks.

Traffic-building campaign The use of **online** and **offline promotion** techniques such as **banner advertising**, **search engine** promotion and reciprocal linking to increase the audience of a site (both new and existing customers).

Transaction log file A web server file that records all page requests.

Transfer Control Protocol/Internet Protocol (TCP/IP) The passing of data packets around the Internet occurs via TCP/IP. For a PC to be able to receive web pages or for a server to host web pages it must be configured to support this protocol.

Trusted third parties (TTPs) Companies with which an agreement has been reached to share information.

Undirected information seeker A person who does not know what information they are looking for – a **surfer**.

Uniform (universal) resource locator (URL) Text that indicates the **web address** of a site. A specific **domain name** is typed into a **web browser** window and the browser will then locate and load the **web site**. It is in the form of:
http://www.domain-name.extension/filename.html.

Unique visitors Individual visitors to a site measured through cookies or IP addresses on an individual computer.

Unsubscribe An option to **opt out** from an e-mail newsletter or discussion group.

Upload The transfer of files from a local computer to a server. Usually achieved using **FTP**. E-mail or web site pages can be uploaded to update a remote server.

Up-selling Persuading existing customers to purchase more expensive products (typically related to existing purchase categories).

URL strategy A defined approach to how content is labelled through placing it in different directories or folders with distinct web addresses.

Usability An approach to web site design intended to enable the completion of user tasks.

Usability/user testing Representative users are observed performing representative tasks using a system.

Usenet newsgroup An electronic bulletin board used to discuss a particular topic such as a sport, hobby or business area. Traditionally accessed by special newsreader software, these can now be accessed via a **web browser** from www.deja.com.

User-centred design Design based on optimising the user experience according to all factors, including the user interface, which affect this.

User journey *See* **Customer scenarios**.

User session Used to specify the frequency of visits to a **site**. Not equivalent to **site visit**.

 V

Validation Validation services test for errors in **HTML** code which may cause a web page to be displayed incorrectly or for links to other pages that do not work.

Value chain A model that considers how supply chain activities can add value to products and services delivered to the customer.

Value network The links between an organisation and its strategic and non-strategic partners that form its external value chain.

Value proposition of site The benefits or value of a **web site** that are evident to its users.

Vertical portals These are generally business-to-business sites that will host **content** to help participants in an industry to get their work done by providing industry news, details of business techniques, and product and service reviews.

View *See* **Page impression**.

Viral marketing A marketing message is communicated from one person to another, facilitated by different media, such as word of mouth, e-mail or web sites. Implies rapid transmission of messages is intended.

Viral referral An 'e-mail a friend or colleague' component to an e-mail campaign or part of web site design.

Virtual cash *See* **Digital cash**.

Virtual community An Internet-based forum for special-interest groups to communicate using a bulletin board to post messages.

Virtual mall A **web site** that brings together different electronic retailers at a single virtual (online) location. This contrasts with a fixed-location infrastructure – the traditional arrangement where retail organisations operate from retail stores situated in fixed locations such as real-world shopping malls. (Also known as **electronic mall**.)

Virtual merchants Retailers such as Amazon that only operate online – they have no fixed-location infrastructure.

Virtual organisation An organisation that uses information and communications technology to allow it to operate without clearly defined physical boundaries between different functions. It provides customised services by outsourcing production and other functions to third parties.

Virtual private network Private network created using the public network infrastructure of the Internet.

Virtualisation The process whereby a company develops more of the characteristics of a virtual organisation.

Visit *See* **Site visit**.

 W

Walled garden A limited range of e-commerce services on iDTV (compared to the Internet).

Web 2.0 concept A collection of web services that facilitate certain behaviours online such as community participation and user-generated content, rating and tagging.

Web accessibility Designing web sites so that they can be used by people with visual impairment whatever browser/access platform they use.

Web addresses (universal resource locators – URLs) Web addresses refer to particular pages on a **web server**, which is hosted by a company or organisation. The technical name for web addresses is **uniform** or **universal resource locators (URLs)**.

Web application protocol (WAP) A standard that enables mobile phones to access text from web sites.

Web analytics Techniques used to assess and improve the contribution of e-marketing to a business, including reviewing traffic volume, referrals, clickstreams, online reach data, customer satisfaction surveys, leads and sales.

Web browsers Browsers such as Mozilla Firefox and Microsoft Internet Explorer provide an easy method of accessing and viewing information stored as **HTML** web documents on different **web servers**.

Web radio Or Internet radio is when existing broadcasts are streamed via the Internet and listened to using plug-ins such as Real Media or Windows Media Player.

Web response model The web site is used as a response mechanism for offline campaign elements such as direct mail or advertising.

Web self-service Content and services provided by an organisation to replace or complement in-store or phone customer enquiries in order to reduce costs and increase customer convenience.

Web servers Web servers are used to store the web pages accessed by **web browsers**. They may also contain databases of customer or product information, which can be queried and retrieved using a browser.

Web site **Content** accessible on the **World Wide Web** that is created by a particular organisation or individual. The location and identity of a web site is indicated by its **web address (URL)** or **domain name**. It may be stored on a single server in a single location, or a cluster of servers.

Web site measurement The process whereby metrics such as **page impressions** are collected and evaluated to assess the effectiveness of **Internet marketing** activities in meeting customers, business and marketing objectives.

Webmaster The webmaster is responsible for ensuring the quality of a **web site**. This means achieving suitable availability, speed, working links between pages and connections to company databases. In small companies the webmaster may be responsible for graphic design and content development.

Wide Area Information Service (WAIS) An Internet service that has been superseded by the World Wide Web.

Wi-Fi ('wireless fidelity') A high-speed wireless local-area network enabling wireless access to the Internet for mobile, office and home users.

Wireframe Also known as 'schematics', a way of illustrating the layout of an individual web page.

Wireless Markup Language (WML) Standard for displaying mobile pages such as transferred by WAP.

World Wide Web A medium for publishing information on the Internet. It is accessed through **web browsers**, which display web pages and can now be used to run business applications. Company information is stored on **web servers**, which are usually referred to as web sites.

XML An advanced markup language giving better control than **HTML** over format for structured information on web pages.

Index